THE ENCYCLOPEDIA OF
MIDDLE EAST WARS

THE ENCYCLOPEDIA OF MIDDLE EAST WARS

The United States in the Persian Gulf, Afghanistan, and Iraq Conflicts

VOLUME IV: T–Z

Spencer C. Tucker

Editor

Priscilla Mary Roberts

Editor, Documents Volume

Dr. Paul G. Pierpaoli Jr.

Associate Editor

Colonel Jerry D. Morelock, USAR (retired)
Major General David Zabecki, USAR (retired)
Dr. Sherifa Zuhur

Assistant Editors

FOREWORD BY
General Anthony C. Zinni, USMC (retired)

ABC-CLIO

Santa Barbara, California   Denver, Colorado   Oxford, England

Library of Congress Cataloging-in-Publication Data

The encyclopedia of Middle East wars : the United States in the Persian Gulf, Afghanistan, and Iraq conflicts / Spencer C. Tucker, editor ; Priscilla Mary Roberts, editor, documents volume.
    v.   cm.
  Includes bibliographical references and index.
  ISBN 978-1-85109-947-4 (hard copy : alk. paper) — ISBN 978-1-85109-948-1 (ebook)
  1. Middle East—History, Military—20th century—Encyclopedias.   2. Middle East—History, Military—21st century—Encyclopedias.
3. Middle East—Military relations—United States—Encyclopedias.   4. United States—Military relations—Middle
East—Encyclopedias.   5. Persian Gulf War, 1991—Encyclopedias.   6. Afghan War, 2001—Encyclopedias.   7. Iraq War, 2003—
Encyclopedias.   I. Tucker, Spencer, 1937–   II. Roberts, Priscilla Mary.
  DS63.1.E453 2010
  355.00956'03—dc22

                 2010033812

13 12 11 10 9 1 2 3 4 5

This book is also available on the World Wide Web as an ebook.
Visit abc-clio.com for details.

ABC-CLIO, LLC
130 Cremona Drive, P.O. Box 1911
Santa Barbara, California 93116–1911

This book is printed on acid-free paper ∞
Manufactured in the United States of America

About the Editors

Spencer C. Tucker, PhD, graduated from the Virginia Military Institute and was a Fulbright scholar in France. He was a U.S. Army captain and intelligence analyst in the Pentagon during the Vietnam War, then taught for 30 years at Texas Christian University before returning to his alma mater for 6 years as the holder of the John Biggs Chair of Military History. He retired from teaching in 2003. He is now Senior Fellow of Military History at ABC-CLIO. Dr. Tucker has written or edited 36 books, including ABC-CLIO's award-winning *The Encyclopedia of the Cold War* and *The Encyclopedia of the Arab-Israeli Conflict* as well as the comprehensive *A Global Chronology of Conflict*.

Priscilla Mary Roberts received her PhD from Cambridge University and is an associate professor of history and an honorary director of the Centre of American Studies at the University of Hong Kong. Dr. Roberts has received numerous research awards and was the documents editor of *The Encyclopedia of the Cold War* and *The Encyclopedia of the Arab-Israeli Conflict,* published by ABC-CLIO. She spent 2003 as a visiting Fulbright scholar at the Institute for European, Russian, and Eurasian Studies at the George Washington University in Washington, D.C.

Contents

List of Entries

List of Maps

General Maps

MIDDLE EAST

TOPOGRAPHY OF THE MIDDLE EAST

COALITION AGAINST IRAQ, AUGUST 2, 1990–FEBRUARY 28, 1991

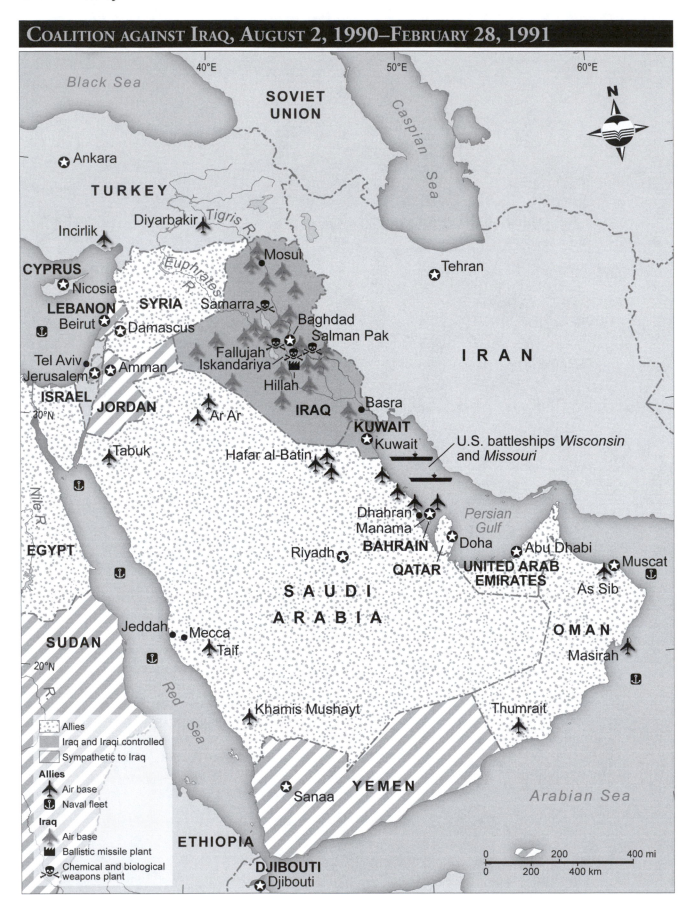

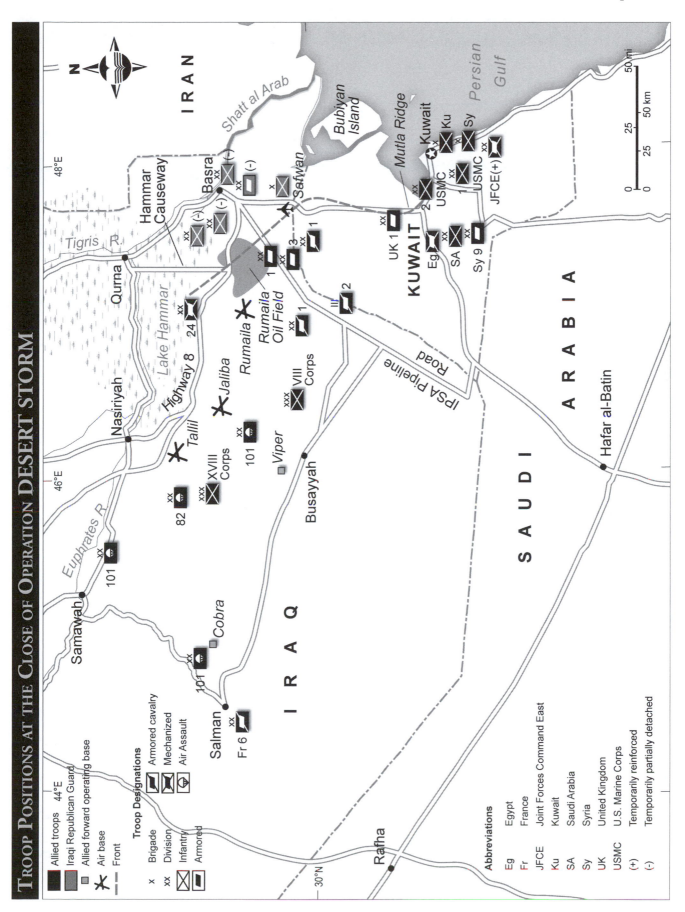

Troop Positions at the Close of Operation DESERT STORM

OPERATION ENDURING FREEDOM, 2001

from the United States

from Germany

TASHKENT

UZBEKISTAN

KYRGYZSTAN

CHINA

Samarkand

TAJIKISTAN

Dushanbe

Khorugh

TURKMENISTAN

Termiz

Mazar-e Sharif

Kunduz

Maymana

Indus R.

Kabul

Herat

Jalalabad

Peshawar

Islamabad

AFGHANISTAN

Khost

Farah

IRAN

Kandahar

Zaranj

PAKISTAN

Quetta

from Diego Garcia

INDIA

Indus R.

Amu R.

Cruise missiles launched from allied surface ships and submarines

USS *Carl Vinson*

USS *Enterprise*

△ Taliban army base
✠ Al Qaeda terrorist training camp
✶ Taliban airfield
✈ Allied airfield (staging area)
○ Probable landing zone of allied special forces units
✺ Allied attacks
▨ Area controlled by anti-Taliban Northern Alliance

0   100   200 mi
0   100   200 km

DISPOSITION OF FORCES ON THE EVE OF THE 2003 IRAQ WAR

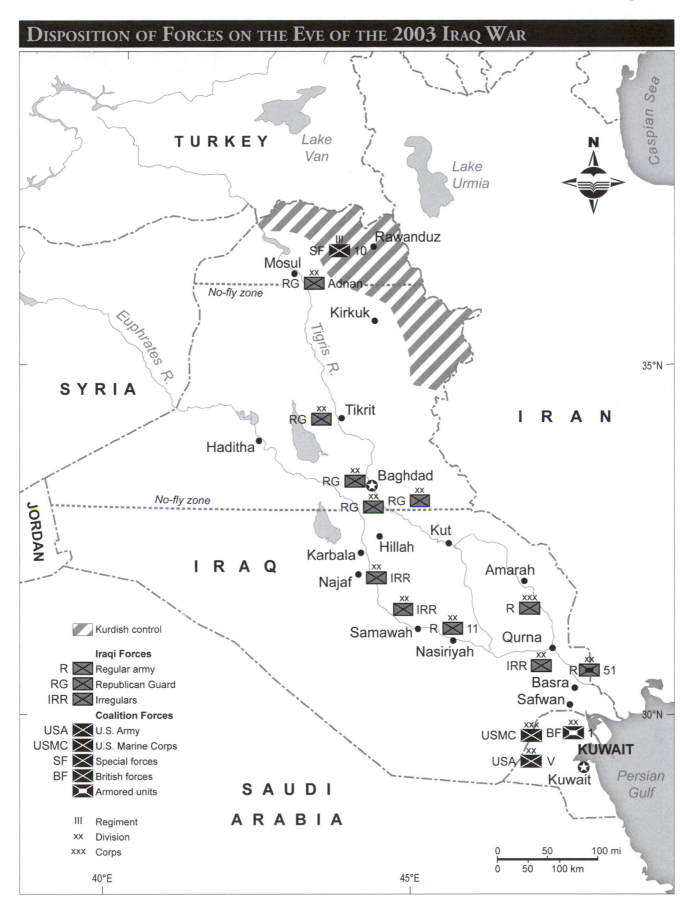

2003 IRAQ WAR

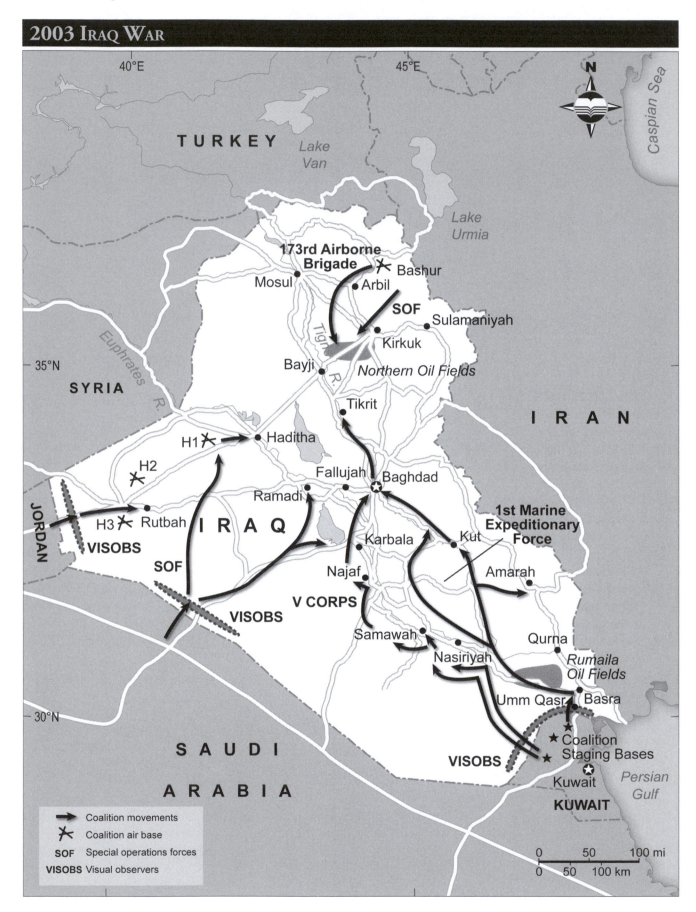

Coalition movements
Coalition air base
SOF Special operations forces
VISOBS Visual observers

T

T-54/55 Series Main Battle Tank

Soviet-designed main battle tanks (MBT). As World War II was coming to a close, Soviet tank designers were looking ahead to replace the T-34 tank. Influenced by German tank engineering and the best features of American and British vehicles supplied through the Lend-Lease program, the Soviets developed the T-44 in 1944. This tank, with a new engine and a lower hull, suffered serious problems and saw virtually no combat action. The limitations of the T-44 were largely resolved by the large-scale introduction of the T-54 in 1951.

The T-54 was powered by an upgraded engine inherited from the T-34, giving it a road speed of just over 30 miles per hour (mph). The armament was a 100-millimeter (mm) gun using fixed ammunition with a rate of fire of four rounds per minute, while armor was improved in both thickness and design. By the end of 1951 the Soviets improved on the T-54, the improved tank being designated as the T-55. The primary upgrades in the T-55 were in its improved power plant. Except for minor external changes, the tank's overall appearance and dimensions were virtually the same as the T-54. Key advantages of the T-54/55 (hereafter referred to as the T-55) series included a low silhouette, ease in learning to operate, good overall speed, and low cost. However, maintenance could be difficult and the vehicle had a short operating life span. Additionally, the crew compartment was unusually cramped and ergonomically awkward.

T-55s were sent to Egypt to see limited combat service in the 1956 Suez Crisis. They saw more extensive service in each Arab-Israeli war afterward, bearing the brunt of the tank fighting in both the 1967 Six-Day War and the 1973 Yom Kippur (Ramadan) War. They were also shipped in large numbers to Iraq, which received not only the Soviet version but also Chinese copies in the form of

the Type 59s and 69s. While the Type 59 was virtually identical to the T-55, it did have significant modifications and improvements, particularly in increased passive armor protection. This increased the weight of the tank significantly and thus reduced performance, but the added armor enhanced the protection against conventional antitank weapons. However, against the depleted uranium ammunition of the American forces in both the Persian Gulf War of 1991 and the Iraq War (2003–), the extra armor proved insufficient.

At the start of the Persian Gulf War, the Iraqi Army had approximately 4,000 T-55 tanks of all types and configurations. These formed the bulk of the MBTs in the regular army being grouped in armored brigades as part of tank or mechanized divisions. Efforts were made to employ them en masse in the early days of the coalition offensive into Kuwait, but this met with disastrous results, mostly from coalition tank and helicopter forces. On February 25 during the second day of the coalition attack, the 50th Iraqi Armored Brigade of the 12th Armored Division, still equipped with 90 Chinese Type 59 tanks and having suffered few losses during the air campaign, came under fire by M1-A1 Abrams tanks of the 2nd U.S. Squadron of the 2nd Cavalry Regiment. In a matter of minutes, the Type 59 tanks and their supporting infantry carriers were transformed into burning wreckage, with the surviving crew members quickly captured.

One tactic attempted by Iraqi T-55 tankers was to use reverse slope positions to allow for close-combat engagements to negate the better standoff capabilities of coalition Abrams and Challenger tanks. Numerous point-blank tank battles occurred in the first two days of the coalition push into Kuwait, with the Iraqi tanks suffering enormous casualties. Iraqi tactical commanders attempted to engage in combined arms counterattacks but typically in small groups at company or battalion level, and their units were thus

A Soviet T-55 main battle tank. Large numbers of these were sold to the Iraqi armed forces. (U.S. Department of Defense)

destroyed in detail. Elements of the 52nd Iraqi Armored Division were also severely mauled by advancing British Challenger tanks from the 7th Armored Brigade, successors of the famed Desert Rats from World War II. In one engagement alone, British tankers and antitank missiles knocked out more than 40 T-55s with the loss of only one soldier killed. Such lopsided engagements were the norm during the 100-hour coalition offensive to drive Iraq from Kuwait, with the total loss of T-55 tanks being around 1,500.

During the Iraq War coalition forces again encountered large numbers of T-55s, but they never saw any large-scale concerted attack from these vehicles. Instead, the Iraqi commanders tended to scatter the tanks into small platoon or company-sized groups to support their infantry in prepared positions. Only on a few occasions did the Iraqis launch tank counterattacks and even then only at the platoon or company level. One significant effort occurred on April 6, 2003, at a place called Dabagah Ridge in northern Iraq. A group of American Special Forces held a piece of terrain that they called "The Alamo" against a concerted Iraqi attack led by a platoon of T-55s, followed by two platoons of mechanized infantry in armored carriers. Supported by artillery, the Iraqi force hoped to overrun the American position but was met by the devastating fire of the new Javelin antitank missile. The tanks were easily destroyed well before they could get into range, and the Iraqi infantry was driven back with heavy losses.

American tank crews saw clearly that the T-55s were no match for depleted uranium ammunition, with the sabot rounds doing what was called a through-and-through in which the round would fly completely through the T-55. If the crew compartment is penetrated, the resulting overpressures created upon entry and released upon exit kill every living thing in that compartment. American tankers developed the tactic of first damaging the T-55 with a sabot round and then following it up with high-explosive antitank (HEAT) rounds to cause the tank to explode, thus clearly indicating that it had been killed. Estimated losses of T-55s in the Iraq War are unavailable but would have been much higher than losses of T-62s.

While an excellent tank in its day, the T-55 is today largely obsolete. But since more than 100,000 of these tanks have been produced, upgraded versions, enhanced with improved armor and fire-control systems, will continue to see service with Middle East armies well into the next decade.

Specifications for the T-55 are:

Armament: 1 100-mm D10-T2S main gun with rate of fire of 4 rounds per minute; 1 7.62-mm coaxial machine gun
Ammunition main gun: 43 rounds
Armor: Turret front, 203-mm at 0 degrees; hull front, upper, 97-mm at 58 degrees

Tank and Infantry Fighting Vehicle Specifications

	Armament	Ammunition Main Gun (rounds)	Armor	Crew/ Passengers	Weight (tons)	Length	Width	Height	Engine	Speed (mph)	Range (miles)
BMP-1 infantry fighting vehicle	1 × 73-mm 2A28 smoothbore gun with rate of fire of 7–8 rounds per minute (rpm); 1 coaxial 7.62-mm machine gun	40	23-mm maximum	3/8	13.28	22'2"	9'8"	7'1"	V-6 diesel; 300 hp at 2,000 rpm	45	340
T-55 main battle tank	1 × 100-mm D10-T2S main gun with rate of fire of 4 rpm; 1 7.62-mm coaxial machine gun	43	Turret front: 203-mm at 0°; hull front, upper: 97-mm at 58°	4	35.43	21'2"	10'9"	7'10"	V-12 diesel; 580 hp at 2,000 rpm	31	310
T-62 main battle tank	1 × 115-mm U5-TS smoothbore main gun with rate of fire of 3–5 rpm; 1 × 12.7-mm machine gun; 1 × coaxial 7.62-mm machine gun	40	Turret front: 242-mm at 0°; hull front, upper: 102-mm at 60°	4	39.37	21'9"	10'10"	7'10"	V-12 diesel; 580 hp	31	280
T-72 main battle tank	1 × 125-mm 2A46 main gun with automatic loader, rate of fire of 8 rpm; 1 × 12.7-mm NSVT machine gun; 1 × 7.62-mm coaxial machine gun	45	Turret front: 280-mm at 0°; hull front, upper: 600-mm equivalent	3	43.80	22'10"	11'9"	7'2"	V-12 multifuel; 840 hp at 2,000 rpm	37	285

Crew: 4

Weight: 35.43 tons

Length: 21 feet, 2 inches

Width: 10 feet, 9 inches

Height: 7 feet, 10 inches

Engine: V-12 diesel, 580 horsepower at 2,000 rounds per
minute

Speed: Road, 31 mph

Range: 310 miles

Russell G. Rodgers

See also

Antitank Weapons; DESERT STORM, Operation; IRAQI FREEDOM, Operation;
M1A1 and M1A2 Abrams Main Battle Tanks; T-62 Main Battle Tank;
T-72 Main Battle Tank

References

Bourque, Stephen A. *Jayhawk! The VII Corps in the Persian Gulf War.*
Washington, DC: Department of the Army, 2002.

Fontenot, Gregory, et al. *On Point: The United States Army in Iraqi
Freedom.* Annapolis, MD: Naval Institute Press, 2005.

Foss, Christopher, ed. *Jane's Armour and Artillery, 2007–2008.* Coulsdon,
Surrey, UK: Jane's Information Group, 2007.

Gordon, Michael R., and General Bernard E. Trainor. *The Generals' War:
The Inside Story of the Conflict in the Gulf.* New York: Little, Brown,
1995.

Hull, Andrew W., David R. Markov, and Steven J. Zaloga. *Soviet/Russian
Armor and Artillery Design Practices, 1945 to Present.* Darlington,
MD: Darlington Publications, 1999.

Milsom, John. *Russian Tanks, 1900–1970.* New York: Galahad Books,
1970.

Pretty, R. T., and D. H. R. Archer, eds. *Jane's Weapon Systems, 1974–75.*
London: Jane's Yearbooks, 1975.

Scales, Robert H. *Certain Victory: The U.S. Army in the Gulf War.*
Washington, DC: Brassey's, 1994.

T-62 Main Battle Tank

Soviet-designed main battle tank (MBT). The weaknesses of previous Soviet tank designs indicated that a newer vehicle with better armor and firepower was needed to defeat the latest tanks being developed in the West. Thus, the T-62 was fielded in 1961 as the replacement for the T-54/55 series tanks. In essence, it was little more than a marginal upgrade and in a number of ways was not much of an improvement over its predecessor. The primary innovation in the T-62 was in its main gun, being a smoothbore 115-millimeter (mm) capable of firing fin-stabilized sabot armor defeating and high-explosive antitank (HEAT) ammunition.

Because of the inclusion of the 115-mm gun, the ammunition became extremely bulky and difficult to handle. This caused Soviet engineers to develop a unique gunnery system for the tank. When the main gun was fired, the shell casing, instead of clattering to the floor as in most tanks of that time and thus becoming a hazard to the loader, would slide from the breech into a cradle. The gun would elevate automatically while the cradle would rock

back to mechanically eject the casing through a small port in the top rear of the turret. This created a few interesting problems. The elevating of the gun took the gunner off of his target, forcing the commander to maintain acquisition instead of searching for other targets. When the casing was ejected, the commander pressed a detent on his controls, and the gun would realign back to the original target location. Of course, this assumed that neither the T-62 nor the enemy tank had since moved. This could cause serious problems in any tank-on-tank engagement.

The T-62's most vexing problems were automotive, and these would become almost legendary. Many Middle Eastern countries were not pleased with the T-62's performance and thus continued to use the older T-55 as their MBT until a better MBT was available. The T-62's engine tended to overheat in hot climates, and in desert operations this was a serious problem. It was not uncommon to see T-62 crews operating in combat with the rear deck doors open to allow better cooling of the power plant, which of course made the engine vulnerable to small-arms fire. Moreover, when the tank was turned violently, especially in loose sand, the sprockets tended to throw the track on the inside of the turn. This was a major problem, as violent turns to disrupt the aim of enemy gunners are one means of protection during combat.

Despite its problems, the T-62 was exported to nations including Egypt, Syria, and Iraq. The T-62 saw its most extensive combat service in the October 1973 Yom Kippur (Ramadan) War, in which 300 T-62s spearheaded Syria's attempts to exploit its early success in the Golan Heights. However, the problems of the T-62, noticeable in training, became even more acute in combat service, and thus it has never lived up to its advertised potential. When the 1991 Persian Gulf War began, Iraq still possessed 1,000 T-62s in its inventory, with most of them deployed in the Republican Guard divisions. As most of those units avoided combat, the T-62 saw little action.

However, some did see action, for one regular Iraqi Army division, the 10th Armored, had some T-62s assigned to its 17th Armored Brigade. While this brigade saw limited action, a few Iraqi battalions with T-62s saw more extensive action, such as the battalion defending at Objective Minden, a bit of lonely desert just west of the Iraqi-Kuwaiti border. These tanks, along with a host of other armored vehicles, were attacked by American AH-64 Apache helicopters from the 4th Battalion, 229th Aviation Regiment, during the night of February 26, 1991, causing many of the crews to simply abandon their undamaged vehicles, which were later captured intact by coalition forces. Another T-62 battalion was probably attached to the Tawakalna Division when it was deployed to delay the coalition advance through the desert late on February 26. This force initially delayed the advance of elements of the U.S. VII Corps but was eventually overrun. The actual number of T-62s lost was probably only around 250, but precise numbers are unknown.

The next chance for the T-62 to see combat action was in the Iraq War (2003–). Unlike in the Persian Gulf War, many actions in the Iraq War have been small unit-level affairs, with Iraqi

Soldiers of the 1st Afghan National Army (ANA) Armored Battalion stand in formation with their T-62 main battle tanks (MBTs) during their graduation ceremony at Polycharky, Afghanistan, during Operation ENDURING FREEDOM in 2003. (U.S. Department of Defense)

commanders displaying significant difficulty in massing their forces for offensive action. Early in the campaign, a platoon of American M1-A1 Abrams tanks from B Company, 1–64 Armor, probing in the darkness toward Objective Liberty southwest of Nasiriyah encountered dug-in T-62s that lit up their thermal imagine sights. In a matter of two minutes the Abrams tanks had destroyed four T-62s and several other armored vehicles.

However, few T-62s were actually encountered, as American combat reports attest. For example, on April 3, 2003, the 2nd Brigade Combat Team, 3rd Infantry Division, reported destroying 33 T-72 and 19 T-55s but only 2 T-62s. Another element of the division, this time Task Force 2–69 Armor, engaged and destroyed several T-62s at Objective Custer, located at the northwest corner of Baghdad. Otherwise, few if any other T-62s were engaged or knocked out during the 40-plus days of heavy combat in Iraq. The dearth of combat service for the T-62 is indicative of the problems encountered when using this MBT. And while some Middle Eastern nations continue to deploy upgraded T-62s, their numbers are dwindling as they are being steadily replaced by the more effective T-72 or even by the older but more reliable and now upgraded T-55s. At one point in time the T-62 had a brief opportunity for enduring glory, that being during the Syrian drive into the Golan Heights in 1973. However, since then the tank has woefully underperformed.

The specification for the T-62A are:

Armament: 1 115-mm U5-TS smoothbore main gun with rate of fire of 3–5 rounds per minute, 1 12.7-mm machine gun, 1 coaxial 7.62-mm machine gun
Ammunition main gun: 40 rounds
Armor: Turret front, 242-mm at 0 degrees; hull front, upper, 102-mm at 60 degrees
Crew: 4
Weight: 39.37 tons
Length: 21 feet, 9 inches
Width: 10 feet, 10 inches
Height: 7 feet, 10 inches
Engine: V-12 diesel, 580 horsepower
Speed: Road, 31 mph
Range: 280 miles

RUSSELL G. RODGERS

See also

DESERT STORM, Operation; IRAQI FREEDOM, Operation; M1A1 and M1A2 Abrams Main Battle Tanks; T-72 Main Battle Tank

References

Bourque, Stephen A. *Jayhawk! The VII Corps in the Persian Gulf War*. Washington, DC: Department of the Army, 2002.

Fontenot, Gregory, et al. *On Point: The United States Army in Iraqi Freedom.* Annapolis, MD: Naval Institute Press, 2005.

Foss, Christopher, ed. *Jane's Armour and Artillery, 2007–2008.* Coulsdon Surrey, UK: Jane's Information Group, 2007.

Gordon, Michael R., and General Bernard E. Trainor. *The Generals' War: The Inside Story of the Conflict in the Gulf.* New York: Little, Brown, 1995.

Hull, Andrew W., David R. Markov, and Steven J. Zaloga. *Soviet/Russian Armor and Artillery Design Practices, 1945 to Present.* Darlington, MD: Darlington Publications, 1999.

Milsom, John. *Russian Tanks, 1900–1970.* New York: Galahad Books, 1970.

Scales, Robert H. *Certain Victory: The U.S. Army in the Gulf War.* Washington, DC: Brassey's, 1994.

T-72 Main Battle Tank

Soviet-designed main battle tank (MBT). Competitive designs to replace the T-55 and T-62 resulted in the development of two new tank designs by the mid-1960s. These tanks, the T-64 and T-72, caused a considerable stir in Western defense establishments. The simpler and less expensive design of the two, the T-72, became the Soviets' export tank of choice.

The T-72 took some radical departures from previous Soviet tank designs. The crew was reduced to three men, with the loader being replaced with a mechanical system. This autoloader caused considerable problems during initial testing, but those issues were soon resolved. Once developed, the autoloader delivered a rate of fire of up to 10 rounds per minute for the new 125-millimeter (mm) smoothbore main gun. Ammunition for the main gun was stowed in a revolving basket on the turret floor and included fin-stabilized sabot, high-explosive antitank (HEAT), and standard high-explosive rounds.

The T-72 was also an automotive improvement over previous Soviet tanks. And while armor protection was still somewhat conventional, the improved power plant allowed more armor to be used, with up 600-mm of armor for the hull front.

The T-72 saw its combat debut in Southern Lebanon during the Israeli offensive known as Operation PEACE FOR GALILEE, launched in June 1982. Iraq also used the T-72 to good effect during the Iran-Iraq War of the 1980s. However, it was during the 1991 Persian Gulf War and the Iraq War (2003–) that the T-72 saw some of its most extensive tank-on-tank action.

During the Persian Gulf War, Iraq had approximately 1,000 T-72s, of which about 300 were the newer T-72M with thicker armor. These were mostly grouped in the Republican Guard divisions that were placed in operational reserve in northern Kuwait. As coalition forces plunged through the Iraqi defenses, the Iraqi Army began to pull out of Kuwait, and several Republican Guard divisions were detailed to provide a screen to the west of Kuwait to delay the advancing U.S. VII Corps. The Tawakalna Mechanized Division, supplied with 280 T-72s, occupied a poorly prepared screen over a 30-mile area when it was probed by American forces on February 29, 1991.

In several successive battles, including the now-famous one at 73 Easting on February 26, most of the Tawakalna Division's T-72s were destroyed. In one particular engagement, the 1st Armored Division's 1st Battalion, 37th Armor, shot up 24 T-72s with a loss of only 4 M1-A1 tanks, damaged by friendly fire. The Tawakalna's tankers did show some ability and courage in the fight, such as keeping their engines off to reduce thermal signatures and waiting for the American tanks to move through their positions to engage them in the flank. In one instance, a T-72 was able to knock out an M1-A1 and injure two of its crew at a range of 1,000 yards with a well-placed flank shot in the turret ring. However, better training and communications, not to mention numbers (the Tawakalna was outnumbered four to one), were clearly on the side of the American forces, allowing them to better coordinate their assets in a combined-arms fight.

The second major engagement involved T-72s of the Iraqi Medina Armored Division at a place later dubbed Medina Ridge on February 27. This Iraqi division had moved into hastily prepared positions just west of the Rumaila oil fields to protect a large Iraqi logistics center there. Elements of their 2nd Brigade were preparing lunch when they were surprised by the 2nd Brigade of the U.S. 1st Armored Division. Visibility was limited to 1,500 yards, but the M1-A1s' thermal sights allowed the Americans to spot the surprised Iraqis beyond this range. Crews from Lieutenant Colonel Steve Whitcomb's 2nd Battalion, 70th Armor, and Lieutenant Colonel William Feyk's 4th Battalion, 70th Armor, began to shoot up T-72s as if they were on a gunnery range, even as the Iraqis attempted to return fire by shooting at the M1-A1s' muzzle blasts. Some T-72s were destroyed as far off as 4,200 yards. In just over one hour, the Iraqi armored brigade had been destroyed, with more than 50 hulks of burning T-72s littering the desert. In many instances, the turrets had been blown off by the detonation of the ammunition on the turret floor caused by the incendiary splash of the American depleted uranium sabot rounds, dubbed "silver bullets" by the tankers. The total number of T-72s lost during Operation DESERT STORM was probably no more than 150, but the exact number is unknown.

The next serious engagement for the T-72 occurred in the Iraq War, but this time most were used in small groups rather than in larger formations, as in the Persian Gulf War. One tank-on-tank action occurred on April 3–4, 2003, when elements of the 3rd Infantry Division's 2nd Brigade Combat Team (BCT) were hit by a counterattack of the Medina Armored Division's 10th Armored Brigade just south of Baghdad at what Americans called Objective Saints. The Iraqis led with a company of T-72s, followed by mounted infantry. When three of the tanks were destroyed, killing the Iraqi brigade commander, the remainder of the brigade withdrew only to attempt a flanking maneuver, whereby American Abrams and Bradleys bagged another 15 T-72s and a number of infantry carriers. The next day the 2nd BCT destroyed an additional 17 T-72s.

On April 3, 2003, troopers of the 3rd Squadron, 7th Cavalry, prepared to cover the flank of the 1st BCT near Objective Montgomery. What occurred later that day was probably the only large-scale T-72 counterattack mounted by the Iraqis during the war. A battalion-sized element from the Hammurabi Division was spotted by aerial reconnaissance, and the troopers moved out with their tanks to engage them. The Iraqi tankers had positioned themselves behind a berm to spring an ambush but were spotted there and were quickly engaged. In rapid succession the American tankers shot up the Iraqi T-72s, and in 15 minutes 20 hulks were burning at the top of the berm. No precise number of T-72s lost has been released, but the number destroyed during the drive to Baghdad was probably about 200.

Despite its performance in the Persian Gulf War and the Iraq War, the T-72 is overall a very good tank, but it has faired poorly when matched against combat forces with better-trained crews, more sophisticated communications, and massive logistical support.

Specifications of the T-72 M/S Shilden Export are:

Armament: 1 125-mm 2A46 main gun with automatic loader, rate of fire of 8 rounds per minute; 1 12.7-mm NSVT machine gun; 1 7.62-mm coaxial machine gun

Ammunition main gun: 45 rounds

Armor: Turret Front, 280-mm at 0 degrees; hull front, upper, 600-mm equivalent

Crew: 3

Weight: 43.8 tons

Length: 22 feet, 10 inches

Width: 11 feet, 9 inches with skirts

Height: 7 feet, 2 inches

Engine: V-12 multifuel, 840 horsepower at 2,000 rounds per minute

Speed: Road, 37 mph

Range: 285 miles; 342 miles with long-range fuel tanks

RUSSELL G. RODGERS

See also

Antitank Weapons; Baghdad, Battle for; Bradley Fighting Vehicle; DESERT STORM, Operation; Iran-Iraq War; IRAQI FREEDOM, Operation; Medina Ridge, Battle of; M1A1 and M1A2 Abrams Main Battle Tanks; 73 Easting, Battle of; T-62 Main Battle Tank

References

Bourque, Stephen A. *Jayhawk! The VII Corps in the Persian Gulf War.* Washington, DC: Department of the Army, 2002.

Fontenot, Gregory, et al. *On Point: The United States Army in Iraqi Freedom.* Annapolis, MD: Naval Institute Press, 2005.

Foss, Christopher, ed. *Jane's Armour and Artillery, 2007–2008.* Coulsdon Surrey, UK: Jane's Information Group, 2007.

Gordon, Michael R., and General Bernard E. Trainor. *The Generals' War: The Inside Story of the Conflict in the Gulf.* New York: Little, Brown, 1995.

Hull, Andrew W., David R. Markov, and Steven J. Zaloga. *Soviet/Russian Armor and Artillery Design Practices, 1945 to Present.* Darlington, MD: Darlington Publications, 1999.

Scales, Robert H. *Certain Victory: The U.S. Army in the Gulf War.* Washington, DC: Brassey's, 1994.

Zaloga, Steven. *T-72: Soviet Main Battle Tank.* Hong Kong: Concord Publications, 1989.

Tactical Air-Launched Decoys

Air-launched preprogrammed glide decoy utilized in offensive military air campaigns to weaken enemy air defenses through creating false targets for surface-based and airborne defenses. Tactical air-launched decoys (TALDs) work by confusing and saturating enemy air defenses. In the 1970s the Brunswick Corporation first developed a line of glider-style radar vehicle decoys. Israel Military Industries (IMI) then pursued the design and in 1982 developed the Samson, the predecessor of the TALD. The IMI and the U.S. Air Force had originally worked jointly on the development of the tactical air device, but lack of funding forced the U.S. Air Force to end its involvement in the project. Four years later the IMI revealed the ADM-141 TALD, a preprogrammed vehicle that can imitate aircraft and lure enemy antiaircraft fire.

A demonstration of the IMI's decoy capabilities inspired the U.S. Navy to initially order 100 of these. The Samson gliders purchased by the U.S. Navy were carefully tested and evaluated, yielding positive results. Both Samsons and TALDs are vehicles that seek to overwhelm and inundate enemy radar. The decoys have the capacity to confuse and neutralize enemy air defenses, which in turn allows the opportunity for offensive strike aircraft to complete their missions. The navy's assessment was so encouraging that just two years later a second order was placed with IMI for an additional 1,000 Samsons and 1,500 new TALDs. In 1987 the TALD officially entered U.S. Navy service.

There are two variations of TALD vehicles. The ADM-141A (RF TALD) is equipped with emitters that emulate fighter radars and electronic countermeasures (ECM). The ADM-141B (Chaff TALD) carries 80 pounds of chaff—strips of metal foil or filings released into the atmosphere to inhibit radar detection and/or misguide radar-tracking missiles—released in increments of 40. At least 20 decoys at a time, with wings folded back, can be loaded on multiple ejector racks and carried like bombs on the McDonnell Douglas (now Boeing) F/A-18 Hornet, Grumman A-6E Intruder, Ling-Temco-Vought A-7 Corsair IIs, and Lockheed S-3 Viking.

TALDs can be launched from up to 40,000 feet or as low as 2,000 feet. From the higher altitude the decoy can travel at speeds of up to Mach .09. When launched at a lower altitude, TALDs travel at a slower speed. The glide range will also vary according to the launch altitude. Higher launches will allow the decoy to travel approximately 40 miles, while lower launches allow TALDs to

A U.S. Navy Grumman F-14 Tomcat is shown conducting a separation test of the tactical air-launched decoy (TALD), 1994. (U.S. Department of Defense)

glide about 2,000 feet. No matter the launch height, the vehicle can be preprogrammed to maneuver turns similar to fighter aircraft.

The TALD is a single-use nonpowered glide vehicle. It is superior to its predecessor, Samson, in that it is constructed with a square cross-section, allowing for an improved chaff-carrying capacity. In addition, the TALD is equipped with a more powerful active emitter and a more effective chaff distributor. Its digital flight control system is also more effective, as it can be preprogrammed with changeable speed profiles and multiple maneuver options. Each variation of TALD is equipped with different payloads to accommodate various missions.

Although still fairly new to the U.S. Navy's arsenal at the outbreak of Operation DESERT STORM in 1991, the TALD was integrated into the service's tactics during the first days of the war to support more than 2,400 coalition fixed-wing aircraft.

The war in Iraq began on January 17, 1991, when U.S. Army AH-64 Apache helicopters fired Hellfire missiles against Iraqi radar sites responsible for providing early warnings to the Iraqi air and missile defenses. This was followed by strikes by U.S.

Air Force McDonnell Douglas F-15 Eagle aircraft against Iraqi Scud surface-to-surface missile positions, while allied bombers simultaneously targeted Baghdad. Other coalition objectives in the initial stages of the war included interceptor operations centers located throughout Iraq. The most urgent mission for allied invaders in the predawn hours of January 17 was to counteract Iraq's surface-to-air missiles (SAMs). Attempts to overpower the Iraqi air defense systems made up a large portion of the overall air campaign throughout DESERT STORM. Some of the most effective air equipment working to derail the lethal SAMs were the TALDs.

In the initial attacks against Iraqi forces, U.S. Navy and U.S. Marine Corps aircraft launched a series of TALDs. Within moments of their release, the Iraqis turned on their radars to track what they believed were U.S. strike aircraft. This action revealed their locations, making them vulnerable to attack. TALDs played a significant role in weakening Iraqi air defenses: the TALDs attracted heavy enemy fire, and the glider decoys released over the skies of Baghdad drew SAMs. The Iraqis believed that they were launching the SAMs against U.S. bombers but were in effect wasting and exhausting the costly weapons on disposable decoys. In the first night of attacks, Iraqi forces firing SAMs not only squandered most of their important tactical defenses but also subsequently revealed their locations to coalition forces.

More than 100 TALDs were dropped over the Iraqi skies on the first day of the DESERT STORM campaign. The coalition combination of decoys and manned aircraft proved highly successful, as there were no coalition losses to SAMs. Air superiority was achieved by the end of the first day of operations. Subsequent phases in the air campaign, flown primarily by allied bombers and fighters, prepared the way for the advance by coalition ground forces. Within only 10 days, the Iraqi Air Force was declared neutralized.

Shortly after the conclusion of the war, the Brunswick Corporation began work on developing the improved tactical air-launched decoy (ITALD). The ADM-141C ITALD is able to travel without any external propulsion. A Teledyne CAE 312 turbojet powers the vehicle. Because it is self-propelled, the ITALD is able to fly a more accurate and realistic flight pattern. When launched at just 20,000 feet, the ITALD has more than twice the range of the ADM-141A or ADM 141-B. When launched at lower altitudes, the ITALD has the capability to ascend nearly 10,000 feet from its launch altitude. The ITALD was employed briefly at the beginning of the 2003 Iraq War (IRAQI FREEDOM) with the same results as in the 1991 Persian Gulf War, although by then Iraqi air defenses were not nearly as stout as they had been in 1991.

TARA K. SIMPSON

See also

Air Defenses in Iraq, Iraq War; Air Defenses in Iraq, Persian Gulf War; Aircraft, Electronic Warfare; Aircraft, Suppression of Enemy Air Defense; Antiaircraft Missiles, Iraqi; DESERT STORM, Operation, Coalition Air Campaign; Missiles, Surface-to-Air

References

Friedman, Norman. *The Naval Institute Guide to World Naval Weapons Systems.* Annapolis, MD: Naval Institute Press, 2006.

Gray, Colin S., and Geoffrey R. Sloan, eds. *Geopolitics, Geography, and Strategy.* New York: Routledge, 1999.

Keaney, Thomas A., and Eliot A. Cohen. *Gulf War Air Power Survey. Summary Report.* Washington, DC: U.S. Government Printing Office, 1993.

Nordeen, Lon O. *Harrier II: Validating V/STOL.* Annapolis, MD: Naval Institute Press, 2006.

Taguba, Antonio Mario
Birth Date: October 31, 1950

U.S. Army officer who was the author of a highly critical 2004 internal army report regarding detainee abuse at the Abu Ghraib Prison in Iraq. Antonio Mario Taguba was born on October 31, 1950, in the Sampaloc district of Manila in the Philippines. His father was a soldier in the Philippine Scouts and a survivor of the Bataan Death March. At age 11 Taguba immigrated with his family

to the United States. After graduating from Idaho State University in 1972 and accepting an army commission through the Reserve Officers' Training Corps (ROTC), he successfully completed training at the Armor Officer Basic and Advanced Course, the Army Command and General Staff College, and the Army War College. He later earned master's degrees in international relations, public administration, and strategic studies.

Taguba held a series of command assignments in Germany and Korea until as a colonel in 1995 he assumed command of the 2nd "St. Lo" Brigade of the 2nd Armored Division at Fort Hood, Texas. When the division was reflagged, the brigade became known as the 2nd "Warhorse" Brigade, 4th Infantry Division (Mechanized). Taguba was promoted to brigadier general in 1997, becoming only the second Filipino American to achieve the rank of general. He was subsequently appointed chief of staff of the U.S. Army Reserve Command at Fort McPherson, Georgia, and became deputy commanding general (south) of the First U.S. Army at Fort Jackson, South Carolina, in October 1998.

In early 2000 Taguba was appointed assistant division commander-forward, 24th Infantry Division (Mechanized), and later that year he became head of the U.S. Army Community and Family Support Center in Alexandria, Virginia, a social services operation for army families stationed around the world. The following year he was assigned as matériel systems analyst in the Office of the Army Chief of Staff at the Pentagon.

Taguba was promoted to major general in 2003 and was assigned as deputy commanding general of Third Army and of the Coalition Forces Land Component Command in Kuwait. Here he was regarded as a forthright, highly principled, and dedicated officer who gained the respect of his peers, superiors, and subordinates alike.

When photographs of prisoner abuse at Iraq's Abu Ghraib Prison became public in 2004, Taguba was asked to lead an investigation of the facility and the incidents but to limit its scope to the military police stationed at the prison. He quickly found evidence of involvement by intelligence agencies: the 205th Military Intelligence Brigade, commanded by Colonel Thomas Pappas, and the Central Intelligence Agency (CIA). Taguba also came upon evidence that some of the generals at U.S. military headquarters in Baghdad, including Lieutenant General Ricardo Sanchez, who commanded U.S. Army forces in Iraq, had been aware of the abuses and did nothing to stop them. Taguba later stated that the military police "were being literally exploited by the military interrogators.... [T]hose kids were poorly led, not trained, and had not been given any standard operating procedures on how they should guard the detainees." He made his report to the Defense Department in May 2004, and that same month he testified to Congress about his findings.

Although Taguba's conclusions were strongly supported by enlisted soldiers and much of the American public, some high-ranking officials in the army and the George W. Bush administration took exception to General Taguba's highly critical conclusions.

Rather than leading to more detailed investigations of other cases of detainee abuse or involvement by other higher-ups, attention now turned on Taguba himself, with General John Abizaid, head of U.S. Central Command (CENTCOM), reportedly threatening Taguba by saying that Taguba himself would be investigated.

Taguba had been scheduled to rotate to Third Army headquarters at Fort McPherson, Georgia, in June 2004 but was instead ordered back to the Pentagon in a lateral assignment for a job in the Office of the Assistant Secretary of Defense for Reserve Affairs.

In January 2006 U.S. Army vice chief of staff General Richard Cody requested that Taguba retire within a year, this in apparent retaliation for his role in the investigation, which had in the meantime been leaked to the press. Taguba left the service on January 1, 2007. Since then, he has continued to press the case of purposeful malfeasance at Abu Ghraib.

In the preface to a 2008 report by Physicians for Human Rights, Taguba declared that "there is no longer any doubt as to whether the current administration has committed war crimes. The only question that remains to be answered is whether those who ordered the use of torture will be held to account." A bipartisan U.S. Senate report released in December 2008 confirmed that top administration officials, including Secretary of Defense Donald Rumsfeld, were indeed responsible for the abuse of prisoners held under U.S. control in Iraq and elsewhere.

STEPHEN ZUNES

See also

Abizaid, John Philip; Abu Ghraib; Rumsfeld, Donald Henry; Sanchez, Ricardo S.

References

Hersh, Seymour. "The General's Report: How Antonio Taguba, Who Investigated the Abu Ghraib Scandal, Became One of its Casualties." *New Yorker,* June 25, 2007, 20–26.
Taguba, Antonio. "Preface to *Broken Laws, Broken Lives.*" Physicians for Human Rights, http://brokenlives.info/?page_id=23.
United States Army. *General Officer Biographies Index.* Washington, DC: U.S. Army Center of Military History, November 2006.

Tai, Hashim Ahmad al-Jabburi al-
Birth Date: 1944

Iraqi general and minister of defense (1995–2003). Born in Mosul in northern Iraq in 1944, Sultan Hashim Ahmad al-Jabburi al-Tai entered the Iraqi Army. He graduated from the National Security Institute in Baghdad in 1975 and saw service in the 1980–1988 Iran-Iraq War. A close relative of Iraqi leader Saddam Hussein, Tai survived several purges conducted by the Iraqi dictator and commanded in succession two different brigades, three divisions, and two corps of the Iraqi Army. In 1988 he played a major role in the punitive al-Anfal Campaign against the Kurds of northern Iraq.

During the 1991 Persian Gulf War, Tai was a lieutenant general and deputy chief of staff. He and Lieutenant General Salah Abbud Mahmud signed the cease-fire agreement that ended the war in February 1991.

Considered one of the more competent generals in the Iraqi Army, Tai was appointed minister of defense by Hussein in 1995. In the period leading up to the Iraq War, Hussein reportedly placed Tai under house arrest in order to prevent a possible coup d'état. U.S. authorities ranked him 27th on the list of most wanted former Iraqi officials.

After protracted negotiations, Tai surrendered to Major General David Petraeus on September 19, 2003, some six months after the Anglo-American–led invasion of Iraq. Reportedly, Tai was promised that his name would be removed from the list of 55 most-wanted Iraqi officials, thus protecting him from possible persecution. At the time, this concession was seen as an effort to defuse the Iraqi insurgency, many members of which were former Iraqi soldiers.

On June 24, 2007, however, Tai was sentenced to death by hanging for crimes against humanity. Although his execution was to be carried out on September 11, 2007, U.S. officials refused to surrender him to the Iraqi government.

SPENCER C. TUCKER

See also

Hussein, Saddam; Iran-Iraq War; Iraq, History of, 1990–Present; Kurds; Kurds, Massacres of; Persian Gulf War, Cease-Fire Agreement; Petraeus, David Howell

References

Bennett, Brian, and Adam Zagorin. "A Saddam Aide's Aborted Execution." *Time,* October 23, 2007, 32–33.
Karsh, Efraim. *Saddam Hussein: A Political Biography.* New York: Grove/Atlantic, 2002.
Rubin, Barry, and Thomas A. Keaney, eds. *Armed Forces in the Middle East: Politics and Strategy.* Portland, OR: Frank Cass, 2002.
Schwarzkopf, H. Norman, with Peter Petre. *It Doesn't Take a Hero: General H. Norman Schwarzkopf, the Autobiography.* New York: Bantam Books, 1993.

Taif Accords

Agreement made among Lebanese leaders at Taif, Saudi Arabia, that was to bring an end to the 25-year-long Lebanese Civil War, stabilize the Lebanese political scene, and force Israeli troops out of southern Lebanon. The Taif Accords (also known as the Taif Agreements, the National Reconciliation Accord, and the Document of National Accord) were signed on October 22, 1989, at Taif and ratified on November 4, 1989. The agreement was based in part on the 1985 Damascus Agreement, which was never implemented.

The Taif Accords were designed to decrease *ta'ifiyya* (sectarianism). The accords set forth the basis of the country itself and the role and duties of key officials. The document defines itself as a "coexistence charter." Section A defines Lebanese identiy as belonging to all and opposes identification on any other basis. Sectarianism is addressed in Section G, which calls for the abolition of the practice of hiring and appointing individuals according to their religion and for an end to mention of their sect on the national identity card. The accords spell out the duties of the president, the prime minister, the Chamber of Deputies (the legislature), the ministers, the cabinet, and the courts. The agreement also decentralized the country administratively.

The Taif Accords could not be implemented right away, as fighting in Lebanon continued. The accords were also considered controversial due to the circumstances at the time they were formulated, when Lebanon was divided between two presidents, one defying Syrian influence and the other being the ally of the Syrians. Critics also claimed that the accords essentially legitimized the presence of Syrian troops in Lebanon (they would not be withdrawn until 2005) and thereby gave Damascus a considerable say in Lebanese affairs.

Not all Lebanese leaders accepted the Taif Accords, and President Michel Aoun, a Maronite Christian, rejected the agreement out of hand. He in fact called for the dissolution of the Chamber of Deputies when the agreement was being negotiated, which detractors of the accords say made it an illegal document. While Syria understandably supported the agreement, Druze leaders also criticized it, declaring it too generous to Sunni Muslims in Lebanon. In the long run the accords were never entirely implemented, and the forced withdrawal of Syrian troops in 2005 rendered it partly moot.

In the political realm, the accords addressed the imbalance of representation in the Lebanese parliament by granting equal representation (50/50) to both Christians and Muslims. This overrode the old formula, which had given Christians a much larger representative proportion than their numbers should have yielded, by a 6 to 5 ratio. In this it reflected the new demographic realities of the country. The legislature was expanded from 108 to 128 seats, and the exact proportion of representatives was specified. The cabinet also was similarly divided equally between Muslims and Christians. The agreement also required the president (who must be a Christian) to designate the prime minister in consultation with the Chamber of Deputies.

To ensure that the civil war would be brought to a close, the accords also called for the disbanding of all national and non-national militias and the return of Lebanese evacuees to their point of origin. Most militias were indeed disarmed, although Hezbollah continued to operate within Lebanon, legally from a Lebanese perspective because of the continued occupation of southern Lebanon by Israel and its proxy Lebanese force. Finally, the agreement required a two-thirds vote among the Council of Ministers to alter the new governmental setup and provides for the protection of minority rights within Lebanon.

The Taif Accords also called for a redeployment of Syrian troops within Lebanon upon consultation with the Beirut government, although the Syrians effectively dictated such policies until they were finally forced out in 2005. Between 1990 and 2005 Damascus had an advisory role, or even the last word in certain disputes with the Lebanese government, and forced upon it a number of disadvantageous agreements. Implicit in the accords was the expectation that Syrian troops would gradually be withdrawn from Lebanon. The United States was a key player in a campaign to pressure the Syrians to withdraw from Lebanon. When this failed to occur within a reasonable time period, the international community condemned the continuing Syrian occupation. In May 2004 the George W. Bush administration invoked sanctions against Syria, in part because its policies were not in keeping "with the spirit of the 1989 Ta'if Accords." Syrian troops finally departed in April 2005 after the assassination of former Lebanese prime minister Rafic al-Hariri provoked mass demonstrations in Lebanon. Many Lebanese linked Hariri's murder to a conspiracy either launched by the Syrian government or at least carried out with its knowledge, although Damascus continues to claim that it had no connection to the murder.

PAUL G. PIERPAOLI JR. AND SHERIFA ZUHUR

See also

Damascus Agreement; Fatah; Hezbollah; Lebanon; Lebanon, Armed Forces; Lebanon, Civil War in; Syria

References

Deeb, Marius. *Syria's Terrorist War on Lebanon and the Peace Process.* New York: Palgrave Macmillan, 2003.

Long, David E., and Bernard Reich. *The Government and the Politics of the Middle East and North Africa.* Boulder, CO: Westview, 2002.

Picard, Elizabeth. *Lebanon, a Shattered Country: Myths and Realities of the Wars in Lebanon.* New York: Holmes and Meier, 2002.

Taji Bunkers, Attack on
Start Date: January 17, 1991
End Date: February 27, 1991

Coalition air assault during the Persian Gulf War on Iraq's Taji bunkers that occurred between January 17, 1991, and February 27, 1991. The Taji bunkers were two specially fortified installations at the Taji airfield, located 15 miles northwest of Baghdad. They were used to shield Iraqi government communication and control facilities. Coalition air attacks on the bunkers early in the war failed to do much damage with conventional bunker-busting bombs, however. As a result, the U.S. Air Force developed a new bomb capable of penetrating the ground and reinforced concrete and destroying the bunkers, which occurred at the end of the ground offensive. The development of the weapon was one of the fastest in modern military history.

Before the Persian Gulf War began, the Iraqi government had begun to fortify sensitive facilities throughout the country. They were sheltered by steel-reinforced concrete and/or were dug deep into the earth. Special bunkers were prepared underground for Iraqi leader Saddam Hussein and his chief subordinates to protect them and to allow them to direct operations in the event of attack. Two of the most fortified Iraqi bunkers were Taji One and Taji Two. They were located 30 to 50 feet underground, with a

2-foot-thick slab of reinforced concrete. The bunkers covered approximately the same area as a U.S. football field and featured a series of hardened concrete cylindrical corridors eight feet in diameter. According to intelligence reports, a central corridor tube connected to living quarters, communications facilities, armories, and other areas necessary for living underground and controlling Iraq's armed forces. Reports indicated that the bunkers could house 1,200 Republican Guards for up to a month.

On the first night of the war, January 17, 1991, the Taji bunkers were attacked by Lockheed F-117 Nighthawk stealth aircraft with standard bunker-busting bombs. These were 2,000-pound GBU-27 precision laser-guided bombs, with a BLU-109 hardened steel warhead to break through earth and reinforced concrete. Although direct hits were made on the bunkers, the bombs were unable to penetrate them.

Air force planners had anticipated this development, however. At the end of October 1990, Lieutenant General Thomas Ferguson, commander of the Systems Command Aeronautical Systems Division, directed his team to develop alternatives that would be able to destroy reinforced bunkers deep underground. Eleven alternatives were developed, including the use of an unmanned Boeing 727 or 737 flying bomb. None were available before the air campaign began, however.

As the air campaign progressed, the engineers at the Air Force Development Test Center offered another alternative. They suggested a heavy bomb dropped from a Boeing B-52 Stratofortress from a high altitude, which would have sufficient kinetic energy to penetrate Iraqi defenses. To develop the weapon quickly, engineers would have to use many components that were already available. The idea was approved on February 1, 1991.

The first problem was finding a tube for the bomb's body that would be able to withstand the enormous forces of impact. A Lockheed engineer remembered that a number of 8-inch howitzer gun barrels had been stored by the U.S. Army when they were no longer needed. They would be capable of providing the tube for the bomb, and several of them were available at the Watervliet, New York, arsenal. Workers there immediately began to modify the barrels into bomb canisters. Engineers decided that the proposed original 6,500-pound bomb should be reduced to about 5,000 pounds so that it could be carried by General Dynamics F-111 Aardvark bombers or McDonnell Douglas/Boeing F-15 Eagle fighters. By February 11, work had begun on the first barrel. The barrels were cut down, the chrome inside the bore was removed, and machinists bored out the interior to a 10-inch diameter. One end of the tube was modified to allow the insertion of a BLU-109 warhead. On February 16 the first two modified barrels were delivered to Eglin Air Force Base in Florida to be converted into bombs.

Wind-tunnel testing on scale models had already indicated the bombs' aerodynamic characteristics, and tests that would have taken two years were either finished in a week or skipped entirely. The modified barrels were then fitted with laser-guidance packages at Eglin. One bomb was loaded with concrete, while the other was filled with 630 pounds of molten Tritonal explosive. The completed bombs weighed 4,700 pounds and were 13 feet long, with 2.25-inch-thick walls. After being carried on an F-111E to test how the bomb would handle in the air, both test bombs were flown to Tonopah Test Range in Nevada. On February 24, the first day of the ground war, the first bomb, loaded with concrete, was dropped to test the guidance system. It penetrated more than 100 feet into the ground. On February 26 the other bomb was loaded onto a rocket sled to test its penetrating power. That bomb penetrated 22 feet of steel-reinforced concrete and then traveled one-half mile beyond.

Two other bomb casings were delivered to Eglin on February 23. Engineers immediately loaded them with Tritonal and loaded them onto a Lockheed C-141 Starlifter for delivery to Iraq on February 27. The bombs were still warm from the explosives when they arrived. Within five hours of landing, the bombs had been loaded onto F-111s for delivery against the Taji bunkers. Because a cease-fire was imminent, Washington had ordered that no bombing occur after 5:00 a.m. in Iraq. But air force leaders were anxious to test the GBU-28 in combat while there was still time. They also wanted to send a message to Hussein that no refuge was safe from attack.

Original plans had called for four F-111s to deliver the two bombs against the Taji bunkers, but the force was reduced to two by February 27. The two bombers proceeded without escort to Taji in the predawn darkness. To develop sufficient kinetic energy for the GBU-28 to penetrate the bunkers, the F-111s had to turn on their afterburners. When they did this, the F-111 pilots knew the glow from the afterburners would light them up to any Iraqi air defenses in the area. They thus hoped to deliver their bombs and escape before being shot down. Each plane would use its own laser to guide its bomb onto the target. The other plane would follow and light the target with its laser if necessary.

When the F-111s arrived over Taji, the mass of structures made it difficult to find the bunkers. The first bomber was to attack Taji Two but failed to identify the correct target. Its GBU-28 fell into an open field. The aircraft then switched places and came around over Taji again to find the bunker. Captain Tom Himes was unable to find it on his radar on the first pass, and the two aircraft had to circle around again, in full view of the Iraqi defenses. Finally, Himes found Taji Two and dropped the bomb. The smoke from the explosion took nearly a minute to come to the surface because the GBU-28 had gone so deep. The two F-111s then escaped back to Saudi Arabia without damage.

According to intelligence reports, the attack on Taji Two was a complete success. The bunker was destroyed and most of those in it were killed. Some American planners had hoped that Hussein himself would have been inside, but such was not the case. The Iraqi leadership, however, understood that even the most fortified bunker was no guarantee of protection from attack.

The process of bringing the GBU-28 from planning stage to delivery in less than six weeks was unprecedented. Other GBU-28s followed, but they were not used in combat. They have been replaced in the U.S. Air Force inventory by other penetrating bombs, especially thermobaric bombs.

TIM J. WATTS

See also

Bombs, Precision-Guided; DESERT STORM, Operation, Coalition Air Campaign; Thermobaric Bomb; United States Air Force, Persian Gulf War

References

Gordon, Michael R., and General Bernard E. Trainor. *The Generals' War: The Inside Story of the Conflict in the Gulf.* New York: Little, Brown, 1995.

Murray, Williamson. *Air War in the Persian Gulf.* Baltimore: Nautical and Aviation Publishing Company of America, 1995.

Takur Ghar, Battle of
Start Date: March 3, 2002
End Date: March 4, 2002

Military engagement fought between coalition forces and Taliban and Al Qaeda fighters that occurred on Takur Ghar Mountain in Afghanistan during March 3–4, 2002. The battle was part of the much broader Operation ANACONDA, an effort early in the Afghanistan War to drive Al Qaeda and Taliban forces from the Shah-i-Kot Valley and the Arma Mountains. Takur Ghar is a high mountain (approximately 10,500 feet) located in the Arma Mountains of southeastern Afghanistan. The peak is on the eastern border of the Shah-i-Kot Valley.

It was near the summit of Takur Ghar that fierce fighting between U.S. Special Operations Forces and Al Qaeda and Taliban soldiers took place. For the Americans, the battle proved the deadliest engagement of Operation ANACONDA. It saw three helicopter landings by U.S. forces on the mountaintop, each greeted by hostile fire.

Late on the evening of March 3, Lieutenant Colonel Peter Blaber of the U.S. Army's Delta Force was notified by Brigadier General Gregory Trebon, commander of TF-11, that two SEAL teams commanded by Lieutenant Commander Vic Hyder were to arrive in Gardez for immediate insertion into the Shah-i-Kot Valley. The two teams, known as Mako 30 and Mako 21, were to establish an observation point on or near the peak of Takur Ghar, which afforded a commanding view of the valley. Because of time constraints, however, the SEALS would have to be inserted by helicopter in order to reach the peak before daybreak. While the original insertion plan had suggested an insertion at a point some 1,400 yards east of the peak, the SEALs eventually decided upon an insertion on the peak itself.

The two teams boarded Razor 03 and Razor 04, two Boeing MH-47 Chinook helicopters, at 11:23 p.m. on March 3. However, Razor 03 experienced engine problems, and so two new MH-47s were dispatched to replace the original aircraft. The delay meant that the SEALs could not be inserted into the landing zone (LZ)

east of the peak until 2:30 a.m. on March 4, which would not permit adequate time to reach the peak before dawn. Blaber was not notified that the SEALs were now planning to insert at the peak that night.

Meanwhile, a Lockheed/Boeing AC-130 Specter gunship reconnoitered the peak and saw no enemy activity prior to the landing. However, that plane was called away to support other troops before Razor 03 and Razor 04 could arrive at the LZ. At about 2:45 a.m. Razor 03 landed at the LZ and was struck by a rocket-propelled grenade (RPG). The damaged helicopter was able to lift off, but Petty Officer First Class Neil C. Roberts fell out of the open ramp. It is believed that he died from the fall, although his ultimate fate remains in question. Some reports suggested that he was taken alive by insurgents and later killed. Razor 03 subsequently attempted to return and retrieve him, but the damaged helicopter was forced to make a crash landing in the valley below, some four miles away. Razor 04 now returned to the peak to attempt to rescue Roberts, in the process inserting Mako 30. The team immediately came under small-arms fire, and U.S. Air Force combat controller Technical Sergeant John A. Chapman was killed; two SEALs were wounded. Mako 30 was forced off the peak and requested the assistance of the Ranger quick-reaction force (QRF) located at Bagram Air Base and led by Captain Nate Self.

The QRF consisted of 19 Rangers, a Tactical Air Control Party, and a 3-man U.S. Air Force special tactics team carried by two Chinooks, Razor 01 and Razor 02. Due to satellite communications difficulties, Razor 01 was mistakenly directed to the hot LZ on the peak of Takur Ghar. Because U.S. Air Force rules prohibited AC-130 aircraft from remaining in hostile airspace in daylight, the AC-130 support protecting Mako 30 had been compelled to leave before Razor 01 had reached the LZ. Further communications problems meant that the pilot of the AC-130 was unaware that Razor 01 was incoming. At approximately 6:10 a.m. on March 4, Razor 01 reached the LZ. The aircraft came under fire, and the right door minigunner, Sergeant Phillip Svitak, was killed by small-arms fire. An RPG then hit the helicopter, destroying the right engine and forcing it down. As the Rangers and special tactics team exited the aircraft, Private First Class Matt Commons (posthumously promoted to corporal), Sergeant Brad Crose, and Specialist Marc Anderson were killed.

The surviving crew and quick-reaction force took cover in a nearby hillock, and a fierce firefight began. Razor 02, which had been diverted to Gardez as Razor 01 was landing on Takur Ghar, returned with the rest of the quick-reaction force and Lieutenant Commander Hyder at 6:25 a.m. With the newly arrived men and close air support, the force was able to consolidate its position on the peak. An enemy counterattack around noon mortally wounded Senior Airman Jason D. Cunningham, a para-rescueman. The wounded were refused medevac during the daylight hours because it was unsafe to operate evacuation helicopters.

Fortunately, Australian Special Air Service soldiers had infiltrated the area undetected prior to the first helicopter crash. They remained undetected in an observation post through the firefight and proved critical in helping to coordinate coalition air strikes to prevent the Taliban and Al Qaeda fighters from overrunning the downed aircraft.

At approximately 8:00 p.m. the QRF and Mako 30 were taken from the Takur Ghar peak. U.S. and Afghan sources reported at least 200 Taliban and Al Qaeda fighters killed during the initial assault and subsequent rescue mission. Although coalition forces eventually captured Takur Ghar, 8 U.S. soldiers were killed and several dozen were wounded.

RICHARD M. EDWARDS AND PAUL G. PIERPAOLI JR.

See also

ANACONDA, Operation; ENDURING FREEDOM, Operation; ENDURING FREEDOM, Operation, Initial Ground Campaign

References

MacPherson, Malcolm. *Roberts Ridge: A Story of Courage and Sacrifice on Takur Ghar Mountain, Afghanistan.* New York: Bantam Dell, 2008.

Naylor, Sean. *Not a Good Day to Die: The Untold Story of Operation Anaconda.* New York: Berkley Trade, 2006.

Taliban

Political and religious movement begun in Afghanistan in the 1990s. The word "Taliban" means "students" and is an Arabic word used in many Muslim countries. In the mid-1990s, however, Afghan students studying in Pakistani madrasahs adopted the name for a political-religious movement that eventually established an Islamic government in much of Afghanistan.

When Soviet forces invaded Afghanistan in 1979, many young Afghan boys and other noncombatants fled the country and were lodged in refugee camps in Iran and Pakistan. During the 10-year Soviet occupation, more than 2 million refugees, mainly Pashtuns, found refuge in Pakistan's North-West Frontier Province, especially the tribal areas. The province was also home to hundreds of madrasahs run by the Deobandi sect as well as to Wahhabi-influenced schools established by wealthy Saudi donors. Tens of thousands of Afghan and Pakistani boys thus received an Islamic education in these madrasahs.

Soviet forces departed Afghanistan in 1989, and Afghan communist forces met defeat in 1992, but civil war between rival mujahideen leaders erupted soon afterward. Much of the fighting pitted Pashtuns against ethnic Tajiks, Uzbeks, and Hazaras of northern and central Afghanistan. Pakistan, which hoped to establish lucrative trade routes with Central Asia, sought a strong Pashtun-dominated government to provide stability.

By the mid-1990s many refugee children were old enough to fight, and their strict Islamic education made them ideal recruits for the Taliban. The Taliban emerged in 1994 when Mullah Mohammed Omar led a small group of fighters in liberating several villages from local warlords. In late 1994 Pakistan enlisted the Taliban's support. Omar and approximately 200 fighters overran

Spin Boldak and Kandahar and in the process captured many weapons, including tanks, artillery, and aircraft. Their success prompted thousands of Afghan and Pakistani students to join them. By early 1995 the Taliban controlled much of the Pashtun regions of the country.

Thereafter, the Taliban confronted better-organized non-Pashtun forces in northern Afghanistan. Both sides committed numerous atrocities, mainly against rival ethnic groups. Despite several defeats, the Taliban captured Herat in 1995, Kabul in 1996, Mazar-e Sharif in 1998, and Taloqan in 1999. By 2000 fighting had largely stalemated, with the non-Pashtun Northern Alliance bottled up in northeastern Afghanistan and portions of central Afghanistan, although it still controlled Afghanistan's United Nations (UN) seat. Pakistan, Saudi Arabia, and the United Arab Emirates were the only countries to recognize the Taliban government. Pakistan, Saudi Arabia, and various Arab Gulf states also provided weapons to the Taliban, while India, Iran, Russia, and the Central Asian states supported the Northern Alliance.

Taliban ambassador to Pakistan Abdul Salem Zaeef (foreground, center) gestures during a news conference in Islamabad, Pakistan, on September 21, 2001. The Taliban rulers of Afghanistan refused to hand over terrorist leader Osama bin Laden and warned that U.S. attempts to apprehend him by force could plunge the whole region into crisis. The United States went to war with the Taliban in October for its role in harboring the terrorists believed responsible for the September 11 terrorist attacks. (AP/Wide World Photos)

Ironically, the United States initially leaned toward supporting the Taliban, but that changed after the Taliban offered sanctuary to the terrorist group Al Qaeda.

Widespread human rights violations by the Taliban provoked international condemnation, but the Taliban consistently ignored outside criticism. Its version of government was perhaps the harshest ever seen in the Muslim world. Women were virtually imprisoned in their homes, medieval-like Islamic punishment became routine for criminal offenses, and international aid organizations were expelled, with no attempt to provide for millions of destitute Afghans. The Taliban even went so far as to destroy priceless historical and cultural treasures such as the Buddhas of Bamyan, which they claimed were blasphemous to Islam.

The Taliban's downfall came following the September 11, 2001, terrorist attacks against the United States, when the Americans and other allies launched major military operations in support of the Northern Alliance in October 2001. The United States sought to topple the Taliban because it had failed to turn over Al Qaeda leader Osama bin Laden after the attacks and because it continued to give refuge to terrorists. Disenchanted Pashtuns rose up as well and established the Southern Alliance. Within weeks, most of the Taliban and foreign jihadists had fled to the tribal areas, where they found sanctuary.

The regions of southern Afghanistan and western Pakistan have historically resisted British, Afghan, and Pakistani control. Fearing internal consequences, the Pakistani government did not conduct sustained counterinsurgency operations there after the September 11 attacks. Consequently, the Taliban used the area to rebuild its forces. Although weakened, the Taliban remains a potent threat in the Pashtun regions of Afghanistan, and Pakistan and coalition forces continue to do battle with its fighters in Afghanistan. Since 2007 the number of Taliban-inspired attacks in Afghanistan has risen steadily, so much so that the United States and other coalition nations have had to expend more troops and resources to counter the Taliban resurgence. In the spring of 2009, however, with Pakistani national security threatened by Taliban advances and under heavy pressure from the United States, the Pakistani military commenced major offensive operations against Taliban-controlled areas of northwestern Pakistan.

CHUCK FAHRER

See also

Afghanistan; Al Qaeda; ENDURING FREEDOM, Operation; Madrasahs; Omar, Mohammed; Pakistan; September 11 Attacks; Soviet-Afghanistan War; Taliban, Destruction of Bamiyan and Pre-Islamic Artifacts

References

Coll, Steve. *Ghost Wars: The Secret History of the CIA, Afghanistan, and bin Laden, from the Soviet Invasion to September 10, 2001*. New York: Penguin, 2004.

Goodson, Larry P. *Afghanistan's Endless War: State Failure, Regional Politics, and the Rise of the Taliban*. Seattle: University of Washington Press, 2001.

Rashid, Ahmed. *Taliban: Militant Islam, Oil, and Fundamentalism in Central Asia*. New Haven, CT: Yale University Press, 2001.

Taliban, Destruction of Bamiyan and Pre-Islamic Artifacts

The Taliban's decision to sanction the destruction of Afghanistan's cultural heritage, including the world's tallest-standing Buddhas—the Buddhas of Bamiyan—shocked and outraged many Afghans and international observers alike. The Taliban regime, which traced it origins to the early 1990s, was a right-wing Sunni Islamic fundamentalist movement that effectively ruled Afghanistan from late 1995 until late 2001. Following a campaign to crack down on un-Islamic segments of Afghan society by conservative Islamic clerics, the Supreme Court of the Islamic Emirate of Afghanistan issued a fatwa on March 1, 2001. This fatwa sanctioned the destruction of all pre-Islamic statues and idols in Afghanistan. Almost immediately, members of the Department for the Promotion of Virtue and the Prevention of Vice set about destroying much of the cultural treasures of Afghanistan's long and storied history.

Situated at the crossroads of ancient civilizations, Afghanistan experienced successive waves of migrating peoples, each leaving its religious and cultural imprint on the Afghan landscape. As trade along the Silk Road spread, Buddhist culture spread throughout Afghanistan and came to dominate political and religious life there until the 9th century. In consequence, Buddhist architecture and iconography dotted the landscape of Afghanistan. As Islam gradually displaced Buddhism in Afghanistan, Buddhist statues and paintings were ignored because Muslims are enjoined not to recognize idols or encourage idol worship. Afghanistan's cultural history remained undiscovered until the early 20th century, when archaeologists uncovered and brought to light some of the ancient cities along the Silk Road.

Bamiyan Province's giant stone Buddha. Despite international efforts to save it, the statue was destroyed on the orders of Afghanistan's Taliban government in March 2001. (UNESCO/F. Riviere)

Following its rise to power in September 1995, the Taliban sought to create a state based on its religious interpretation of Islamic governance. In accordance with its interpretation of Sharia (Islamic law), the Taliban implemented a ban on all forms of imagery, including television, music, and sports. The first steps in destroying Afghanistan's cultural heritage began with the systematic looting of archaeological sites under Taliban control. At the Greek city of Ai Khanoum in a remote area of northeastern Takhar Province, the plunderers, under financial agreements with ruling Taliban commanders, gouged out the surface with bulldozers and probed deeply through long tunnels. Beginning in 1996, attempts were also made to destroy ancient statues housed in the National Museum in Kabul as well as pre-Islamic artifacts stored in the Ministry of Information and Culture.

In 1997 a Taliban commander trying to seize the Bamiyan Valley declared that the Bamiyan Buddhas would be destroyed as soon as the valley fell into his hands. The resulting international outcry caused the Taliban leadership to prohibit the Buddhas' destruction and to promise that the cultural heritage of Afghanistan would be protected. In 1998, however, the smaller Buddha's head and part of the shoulders were blown off, and the face of the larger Buddha was blackened by burning tires.

It was not until the United Nations (UN) Security Council imposed economic sanctions on the Taliban in December 2000 that the Taliban decided to destroy the Bamiyan Buddhas altogether. In January and February 2001 the Taliban stepped up its efforts at destroying all pre-Islamic artifacts in Afghanistan. Invoking the Islamic prohibition against the depiction of living things, the Taliban destroyed more than a dozen Greco-Buddhist statues in the National Museum. On February 26, 2001, Taliban ruler Mullah Mohammed Omar announced that all pre-Islamic statues in the Taliban-controlled areas of Afghanistan were to be destroyed, and on March 9, 2001, members of the Taliban blew up the Buddhas of Bamiyan. A few months later, smaller Buddha statues in Falodi and Kakrak were also destroyed. The destruction of the Buddhas of Bamiyan especially drew international ire because of their immense size and cultural importance; also driving global outrage at the Taliban's actions was the coverage of the destruction on television that was seen across the globe.

KEITH A. LEITICH

See also

Afghanistan; Fatwa; Omar, Mohammed; Taliban

References

Marsden, Peter. *The Taliban: War and Religion in Afghanistan.* London: Zed Books, 2002.

Nojumi, Neamatollah. *The Rise of the Taliban in Afghanistan: Mass Mobilization, Civil War and the Future of the Region.* Basingstoke, UK: Palgrave, 2002.

Taliban Insurgency, Afghanistan

Military insurgency waged against coalition and Afghan government forces by the Taliban beginning in 2002. The Taliban movement emerged in the chaos of Afghanistan in the mid-1990s, led in part by young religious scholars trained in religious schools on both sides of the Afghanistan-Pakistan border. The name "Taliban" is taken from the plural of the Arab word *talib* ("student"). The Taliban leadership is drawn from the Pashtun, the largest ethnic population in Afghanistan. Taliban leaders rely on support from the large Pashtun strongholds in Pakistan, including the North-West Frontier Province (NWFP), the Federally Administered Tribal Areas (FATA), and urban areas with large Pashtun populations (Karachi, Quetta). By the late 1990s the Taliban had established political control over more than 90 percent of Afghanistan, but because of its harsh Islamist rule—which included mass public executions, bans on music, and the destruction of ancient Buddhist religious statues at Bamyan—it was recognized diplomatically only by Saudi Arabia, Pakistan, and the United Arab Emirates.

In the late 1990s the Taliban provided sanctuary and support for the Al Qaeda organization, which had aided them in their battle against the Soviets. They received in return not only financial contributions but also military leadership and trained troops. After Al Qaeda's terrorist attacks on the United States on September 11, 2001, when the Taliban leadership refused to turn over those responsible, a coalition of forces headed by the United States actively intervened in Operation ENDURING FREEDOM in December 2001 to aid the Northern Alliance in defeating the Taliban and drive it from power. By mid-2002, however, surviving Taliban leaders were regrouping and taking control in many locations and reestablishing themselves in others.

The insurgency and the revival of the Taliban as both a military and political force would not have been possible without chaos in Afghanistan and access to sanctuaries in neighboring Pakistan, particularly the vital logistics base of Quetta and the loosely governed areas of FATA. The Quetta *shura* (council) provides leadership for Taliban military and political efforts in Afghanistan. This base could not have been maintained without the support of Pakistani officials and former officials. Pakistan's military and intelligence services have been actively supporting militants in Afghanistan and Kashmir for almost 30 years and are skilled at providing assistance in ways that are difficult to link directly to official sources.

Taliban forces are composed of ethnic Pashtuns from Afghanistan and western Pakistan and include some Afghan refugees who were in Pakistan. There are also a small number of foreign volunteers. The Taliban are comprised of forces loyal both to Taliban leader Mullah Mohammed Omar and Tehrik-i Taliban-Pakistan (Pakistan Taliban, TTP). There is also a collection of allies and affiliated groups. The best-known allied forces include Al Qaeda, Hezb-i Islami (led by veteran militant Gulbuddin Hekmetyar), and the Haqqani network (led by Jalaluddin and Sirajuddin Haqqani). They have been funded largely by Afghanistan's drug

Members of the Taliban pose with AK-47 assault rifles and rocket-propelled grenades in Zabul Province, south of Kabul, Afghanistan, October 2006. (AP/Wide World Photos)

trade, particularly in Helmand Province, and contributions from the Muslim world, often collected as *zakat* (alms or charity) at mosques throughout the world.

Insurgent efforts are organized in three theaters straddling the Afghanistan-Pakistan border (the Taliban itself prefers to speak of five fronts, creating a separate Kabul region and an overall military commander). The eastern front includes portions of FATA and the NWFP on the Pakistan side and the Afghan provinces of Nuristan, Kunar, Laghman, and Nangarhar. Hezb-i Islami is active in this theater along with other allied groups including Lashkar-e Taiba, best known for the November 26, 2008, terrorist assault on Mumbai, India. The central or southeastern front extends from Bajaur in FATA down into Baluchistan on the Pakistani side and includes the Afghan provinces of Khowst, Paktia, and Paktika. The Haqqani network has been very active here, as have large numbers of foreign fighters. The southern front is primarily manned by Taliban forces and includes the Afghan provinces of Helmand, Kandahar, Oruzgan, and Zabol.

U.S. and multinational forces in Afghanistan have faced considerable difficulty operating against the Taliban and its allies, particularly when those forces are located on Pakistani soil. Pakistani military cooperation with the coalition has been most forthcoming in the FATA, where the TTP has waged operations against the Pakistani government, and much rarer in Baluchistan, where the Taliban central and southern fronts appear to enjoy considerable freedom of movement and logistic support.

The Taliban insurgency began making significant strides in 2003–2004 in traditional Taliban strongholds in southern Afghanistan, particularly in the vicinity of Kandahar and in Helmand Province. Taliban forces initially infiltrated across from bases in Pakistan but gradually developed base areas inside Afghanistan itself. The limits of the Taliban's capabilities, however, were demonstrated by its inability to disrupt the Afghan presidential elections in October 2004. Operations through the end of 2005 were governed mainly by the weather. Attacks peaked in December–January and then declined until March or April as full-time cadres retreated to Pakistan for the winter and local forces stood down. Since the winter of 2005–2006, however, winter operations have increased in number.

The Taliban's reach and influence grew sharply over the next few years. An increasing emphasis on creating parallel political structures to compete with the Afgan government became apparent by early 2006, when Taliban leadership announced the appointment of separate political leaders for all districts. By 2006 the Taliban claimed to operate local judiciaries in numerous provinces in southern and southeastern Afghanistan. The surge in Taliban confidence and capability prompted an influx of North Atlantic Treaty Organization (NATO) troop reinforcements to assist the Afghan government, although differing levels of commitment and rules of engagement handicapped the overall counterinsurgency effort. A Taliban final offensive launched in 2006 ended indecisively. The Taliban had proved that it was much stronger than most analysts had suspected, but it also proved incapable of defeating the Afghan government or its coalition partners.

Taliban efforts increasingly targeted local police forces, allowing it to establish a more permanent local presence. In 2007 alone, more than 900 Afghan police were murdered. The Taliban also stepped up suicide attacks against Afghan and coalition forces, from 21 in 2005 to more than 130 in 2006 and again in 2007. The TTP and Taliban allies unleashed powerful attacks against the Pakistani government in the last six months of 2007, and fighting continued in the FATA throughout 2008. In late 2008 U.S. political and military leaders committed substantial reinforcements to the Afghan theater, and following his November 2008 election victory, President-elect Barack Obama was reportedly briefed that the Afghanistan-Pakistan border constituted the single most important security problem for his incoming administration. Obama had already pledged to reinvigorate the coalition effort to defeat the insurgency in Afghanistan, in part by increasing U.S. troop strength there. Upon taking office in January 2009, he began to put in place a strategy to decrease U.S. troop commitments in Iraq so that troops and resources could be redirected to Afghanistan.

There are many explanations for the resurrection of the Taliban as a powerful force in Afghanistan, despite its woeful record of governance when it held power from 1996 to 2001. First, the Taliban has been able to expand because of the inability of the current Afghan regime of Hamid Karzai to govern effectively compounded by the failure to develop effective local police and security institutions in the years after the Taliban's initial defeat. Second, there has been a lack of Pashtun participation in the Afghan regime. Third, there are close connections between the current Afghan government and first the United States and more recently NATO and other international forces, which delegitimize the Afghan regime in the eyes of the Afghan population. The continued presence of international forces in Afghanistan allowed the Taliban to portray itself as fighting against foreign occupation. Fourth, there was a shift of U.S. focus from Afghanistan to Iraq for Operation IRAQI FREEDOM, launched in March 2003. Fifth, some within the Pakistani Army and the Pakistani government wished to reinstall a Taliban government in Afghanistan. This accusation is made somewhat more credible by both persistent Pakistani efforts to encourage negotiations with the Taliban and the presence of thousands of Taliban fighters in Baluchistan, the NWFP,

and the FATA. The United States and its coalition partners will have to wage a much larger struggle on a much larger front if they hope to defeat the resurgent Taliban. They will also have to engage the Pakistani government more aggressively to fight the Taliban insurgency in the border areas.

TIMOTHY D. HOYT

See also

Afghanistan; Al Qaeda; ENDURING FREEDOM, Operation; Hekmetyar, Gulbuddin al-Hurra; Karzai, Hamid; North Atlantic Treaty Organization in Afghanistan; Omar, Mohammed; Taliban

References

Guistozzi, Antonio. *Koran, Kalashnikov, and Laptop: The Neo-Taliban Insurgency in Afghanistan.* New York: Columbia University Press, 2008.

Jones, Seth G. *Counterinsurgency in Afghanistan: RAND Counterinsurgency Study No. 4.* Santa Monica, CA: RAND Corporation, 2008.

Rashid, Ahmed. *Descent into Chaos: The United States and the Failure of Nation-building in Pakistan, Afghanistan, and Central Asia.* New York: Viking, 2008.

———. *Taliban: Militant Islam, Oil, and Fundamentalism in Central Asia.* New Haven, CT: Yale University Press, 2001.

Tallil Airfield

A major Iraqi Air Force base located some 186 miles southeast of Baghdad in the Euphrates River Valley in southeastern Iraq near the city of Naziriah. Tallil was strategically placed to defend Highway 8, the main road from Baghdad to Kuwait that ran along the southern bank of the Euphrates.

Tallil Airfield was Iraq's second largest, encompassing some 9,000 acres, and served as one of the Sector Operations Centers (SOCs) for the Iraqi air defense system. Tallil was also known to have been a storage facility for chemical weapons and was a major target for the coalition's air campaign during the Persian Gulf War (Operation DESERT STORM) of January–February 1991. After the Persian Gulf War ended, the airfield was decommissioned. When Operation IRAQI FREEDOM began in March 2003, Tallil was an early objective. Soon after its capture, the airfield was placed back into operation and served as a major supply link for American and coalition forces.

Beginning in the late 1970s, Iraq constructed many airfields to serve its growing air force. The Iraqi Air Force included many modern aircraft, mostly from the Soviet Union and France. A total of 24 heavily fortified and defended airfields served as bases for the aircraft, with another 30 smaller dispersal airfields available.

Tallil was defended by surface-to-air missiles (SAM) and antiaircraft artillery (AAA), and hardened shelters were constructed to protect aircraft based there. These shelters had been designed and built by European contractors and met the standards established by the North Atlantic Treaty Organization (NATO). Tallil's facilities also included large numbers of hardened bunkers for storing different munitions to include bombs and air-to-air and air-to-ground missiles. During the 1980–1988 Iran-Iraq War, Saddam Hussein's forces had used chemical weapons to weaken their Iranian opponents. Aircraft delivering these chemicals had flown from Tallil, where the weapons were apparently stored.

Finally, Tallil was known by coalition planners to house a major piece of the Iraqi air defense system. The Kari air defense system, developed by French engineers, was a centralized system that linked more than 400 observation posts and radar reporting stations across Iraq. The information was forwarded to 17 Intercept Operational Centers (IOCs) that were located in hardened facilities to protect them from attack. In turn, these centers passed information to four regional SOCs. The SOC for southern Iraq was located at Tallil. The SOC would pass information about air raids to the National Air Defense Operations Center in Baghdad and would relay orders from the central command to SAM and AAA batteries as well as to the IOC in its region. Interceptor aircraft would also be controlled from the ground by these centers. As an SOC, Tallil would play an important role in defending Iraq and would therefore be a prime target for early coalition attacks.

Before the air campaign against Iraq began on January 17, 1991, the Iraqi government began moving much of the Kari communications equipment from the hardened shelters at Tallil. They recognized that the SOC would be a prime coalition target and hoped thereby to reduce their losses.

On the first night of the coalition air campaign, Tallil was struck by Lockheed F-117 Nighthawk stealth bombers in an effort to knock out the SOC. Conventional raids followed over the next few days, attempting to destroy the aircraft based at Tallil and to disable the runways. Hussein ordered most of his aircraft to remain in their hardened shelters, hoping to preserve them until the war ended. Coalition forces then began to systematically destroy the shelters, including the ones at Tallil.

On February 24, 1991, the ground offensive began. The coalition's main effort was from western Saudi Arabia, where American, British, and French forces crossed into Iraq. Their objectives included advancing to the Euphrates to cut off Iraqi troops in Kuwait. Coalition forces were then to turn east and destroy the trapped Iraqi divisions, especially the Republican Guard units that were considered the most effective of Iraq's forces. Tallil was a major objective because it controlled Highway 8. On February 26 the American 24th Infantry and the 101st Airborne divisions occupied positions straddling Highway 8. One American brigade was sent west to capture Tallil, which was accomplished in short order. The war ended with a cease-fire two days later.

U.S. forces destroyed most of the munitions and facilities at Tallil. Special attention was paid to an S-shaped bunker that was identical to others used to store chemical weapons. Although chemical handling equipment was found at Tallil, no evidence

The remains of an Iraqi helicopter at Tallil Airfield after an allied attack during Operation DESERT STORM in 1991. (U.S. Department of Defense)

surfaced that chemical weapons were present at the time. Postwar investigations about whether American soldiers had been exposed to chemical weapons confirmed that none had been present at Tallil during the brief U.S. occupation. United Nations (UN) weapons inspectors also found no evidence of chemical weapons at Tallil. Before American troops withdrew, U.S. Air Force engineers used approximately 80,000 pounds of explosives to cut the runways and taxiways every 2,000 feet, making Tallil unusable as an airfield. Hussein did not try to restore the airfield after the war.

In March 2003 American forces quickly captured Tallil during the invasion of Iraq. Five days after its capture, the airfield had been almost fully restored and was being used for transport aircraft bringing supplies for the fighting troops and humanitarian aid for Iraqis. It continues in use, and there is some indication that the Iraqi government might once again commission it as an official Iraqi air base.

TIM J. WATTS

See also

Air Defenses in Iraq, Persian Gulf War; Chemical Weapons and Warfare; DESERT STORM, Operation, Coalition Air Campaign; DESERT STORM, Operation, Ground Operations; Iran-Iraq War; IRAQI FREEDOM, Operation, Ground Campaign; Kari Air Defense System

References

Freedman, Lawrence, and Efraim Karsh. *The Gulf Conflict, 1990–1991: Diplomacy and War in the New World Order.* Princeton, NJ: Princeton University Press, 1993.

Gordon, Michael R., and General Bernard E. Trainor. *The Generals' War: The Inside Story of the Conflict in the Gulf.* New York: Little, Brown, 1995.

Tammuz I Reactor

Iraqi nuclear reactor destroyed by Israeli aircraft in 1981 while in the final stages of construction. The Tammuz I reactor was also known as the Osiraq reactor. For years, the Iraqi government, especially under Saddam Hussein, had sought to acquire nuclear technology. It claimed that this effort was for peaceful purposes, but many governments, most notably Israel, surmised that the ultimate Iraqi goal was the production of nuclear weapons. Iraq's first foray into the nuclear field came in 1959, when it entered into an agreement with the Soviet Union to build a small five-megawatt research reactor near Baghdad. The project was completed in 1968, but its small size and close supervision by Soviet technicians frustrated Iraq's goal of acquiring a facility capable of producing weapons-grade plutonium by-products.

In light of this, Iraq began to look to other sources, notably France and Italy, for more sophisticated nuclear technology. After the 1973–1974 Organization of the Petroleum Exporting Countries (OPEC) oil embargo, Iraq's huge energy reserves gave it a powerful bargaining chip as it negotiated an agreement with France for nuclear technology. In 1978, a French-led consortium signed a formal agreement to construct a nuclear plant with the Iraqi government. The terms of the agreement stipulated that Iraq would provide France with oil at discounted prices and agree to large purchases of French military hardware in exchange for construction of a nuclear complex centered on a 70-megawatt nuclear reactor.

The fuel for the proposed reactor was to be 93 percent enriched (weapons-grade) uranium. The project was originally named Osiraq, an Iraqi derivation of the name of a similar reactor in France. However, the name was soon changed to Tammuz to commemorate the time of year in which the ruling Iraqi Baath Party came to power.

Italian firms would provide expertise in the extraction of weapons-grade plutonium from the reactor's spent fuel. As the reactor complex neared completion in 1980, the Israeli government embarked on a public information campaign designed to alert the world to the dangers of allowing Iraq to acquire nuclear technology. There were also indications by then that Israel had conducted several covert intelligence and sabotage missions against scientists and equipment associated with the program.

In September 1980, Iraq invaded neighboring Iran, triggering the eight-year-long Iran-Iraq War. One of the first Iranian Air Force targets was the Tammuz I reactor. A September 30, 1980, raid by Iranian bombers failed to inflict serious damage on the facility, but it did precipitate an evacuation of several hundred French and Italian workers and brought construction on the site to a standstill. By the spring of 1981, however, many of the technicians had returned, and work was proceeding with a target date for completion of the complex later that year.

With the goal of destroying the Tammuz I reactor, Israeli aircraft struck the site on June 7, 1981. The mission, more than a year in planning and rehearsals, involved 14 aircraft flying a 700-mile mission at extremely low altitudes. Battle damage assessment indicated that the reactor building was struck and completely destroyed by 14 bombs.

Iraqi attempts to rebuild Tammuz I in the 1980s were slowed by a diversion of resources to the war with Iran and a breakdown in negotiations with France for the reconstruction of the reactor. The Tammuz site was again heavily bombed by coalition aircraft in 1991 during the Persian Gulf War, after which there were no significant efforts to rebuild.

ROBERT M. BROWN

See also

DESERT STORM, Operation; France, Middle East Policy; Iran-Iraq War; Iraq, History of, Pre-1990; Iraq, History of, 1990–Present; Israel; Israel, Armed Forces; Nuclear Weapons, Iraq's Potential for Building

References

Claire, Rodger William. *Raid on the Sun: Inside Israel's Secret Campaign That Denied Saddam the Bomb.* New York: Broadway Books, 2004.

Nakdimon, Shlomo. *First Strike: The Exclusive Story of How Israel Foiled Iraq's Attempt to Get the Bomb.* New York: Summit Books, 1987.

Perlmutter, Amos, Michael Handel, and Uri Bar-Joseph. *Two Minutes over Baghdad.* London: Frank Cass, 1982.

Tank Landing Ships, U.S.

Amphibious assault vessels that transport tanks and other vehicles, landing their payloads directly on beaches by partially grounding their hulls and extending ramps or pontoon causeways from the bows.

The tank landing ship (LST) in the U.S. Navy followed a lineage extending from the original joint British-American design for LST-1 in 1942, which produced more than 1,000 landing ships, to the final LSTs of the *Newport* (LST-1179) class, built between 1966 and 1972, and serving well into the 1990s before decommissioning or transferring to other navies. Unremarkable in appearance, the tank landing ship resembled a small tanker with its minimal superstructure placed at the stern but presented a relatively high freeboard because of its rather shallow draft. The LST was the largest ship type with the landing craft–like ability to beach itself: a ballasting system pumped water rearwards within the ship, reducing the draft under the bow; the hull bottom was flattened to ease its sliding onto the sand.

Cargo capacity in this beaching mode was 500 tons; 10 heavy tanks or 20 medium tanks could be carried on the enclosed tank deck, which was equipped with a ventilation system to disperse vehicle exhaust outside the ship. Two large bow doors swung open to each side, allowing tanks and other vehicles to drive over an extended 50-foot ramp to the beach. To hold the beached position, it was necessary for the ship to maintain some measure of speed ahead; to withdraw from the beach, the engines were simply reversed and powered up accordingly.

As useful and vital as the bow doors were on the many earlier LSTs, they could withstand little pounding from passage through even moderate seas. The blunt bow with its shallow draft also made for difficult maneuvering in windy conditions and a painfully low speed, topping out between 10 and 12 knots. Indeed, many crews joked that LST stood for "large, slow-moving target."

Despite these shortcomings, many hundreds of these ships delivered ashore the troops, tanks, and vehicles necessary for successful U.S. amphibious operations in multiple theaters of World War II and on both Korean coasts during the Korean War (1950–1953). Scores of these sturdy and adaptable vessels were converted to repair ships, auxiliary troop carriers, hospital ships, torpedo boat tenders, commercial cargo ships, railroad locomotive transports, and even light aircraft carriers for artillery-spotting Piper Cubs operating during the Salerno, Anzio, and southern French landings in 1943 and 1944. A surprising number of the original LSTs were still operating in various navies or in civilian applications after 50 years of service.

The design of the 15 postwar Terrebonne Parish–class (LST-1156 through LST-1170, built between 1952 and 1954) included increased length (from 328 feet to 384 feet) and full load displacement (from 4,800 to 5,800 tons) over the LST-1 type. Diesel engines were increased from two to four, delivering an improved speed from around 10 knots to 15 knots, and variable-pitch propellers ensured better performance in backing away from the beached position. During the years 1970 and 1971, these LSTs were decommissioned from the U.S. Navy; 12 went on to serve in the navies of Spain, Venezuela, Turkey, Greece, and Peru.

The follow-on DeSoto County–class (LST-1171 through LST-1178) comprised seven ships constructed between 1956 and 1959 that were larger (length 442 feet; full load displacement 8,000 tons) and slightly faster, at 17 knots. Three of these ships were transferred to Italy and Brazil in 1972 and 1973; the remainder left U.S. service by 1989.

Another 10 years passed before the U.S. Navy would begin deploying a new class of LSTs, built to a striking and innovative design. These were the 20-ship Newport-class of LST-1179 through LST-1198, built by Philadelphia Naval Shipyard and National Steel in San Diego, California, during 1966–1972. Their dimensions were: length, 562 feet (including derricks); beam, 69.5 feet; and draft, 6 feet (forward), 17.5 feet (aft). Displacement was 4,793 tons (light) and 8,450 tons (full load). Speed was 22 knots (20 knots sustained). Crew complement was 253 (15 officers and 238 enlisted). The Newport-class LSTs could carry 430 troops. They also carried 4 LCVPs (Landing Craft, Vehicles, and Personnel) on davits; 23 AAVs (Amphibious Assault Vehicle) or 41 2.5-ton cargo trucks on the tank deck; and an additional 29 2.5-ton cargo trucks on their main deck. Cargo capacity was 17,300 square feet for vehicles; 2,000 tons cargo transport; and 500 tons cargo beaching capability. Armament included four 3-inch (76-millimeter) guns and one 20-millimeter Phalanx close-in-weapons system (CIWs).

This last class of U.S. Navy LSTs represented something of the final word on this ship type's development. The prominent bow doors that defined the three earlier iterations of the tank landing ship were now replaced by a ramp paid out by a twin derrick over the split upper bow, whose sharper aspect at the waterline easily permitted a sustained speed of 20 knots. This narrowed bow section also tapered forward below the waterline to a depth of only six feet, allowing for smooth beaching and extension of the 112-foot aluminum ramp, which was able to pivot from side to side. A bow thruster assisted in holding position as well as in slow-speed maneuverability. As it turned out, the ramp more often than not delivered vehicles to a causeway constructed from the pontoon sections stored along the sides of the hull. In another departure from the traditional LST configuration, the Newport class featured a centrally placed cluster of a superstructure block, LCVP davits, twin funnels, and two 10-ton capacity cranes. Because the main deck cargo area extended from the stern nearly to the bow, a tunnel through the superstructure allowed free passage of vehicles in either direction.

Not only capable of off-loading vehicles and cargo across the bow ramp, the Newport-class LST could also discharge AAVs into the water through a stern hatch and ramp apparatus, either while stationary or under way. For all their advances over previous LSTs, the Newport-class LSTs nonetheless were not an unqualified success in service. They proved expensive to build, and their

The tank landing ship USS *San Bernardino* (LST-1189) as the ship deploys to the Middle East to take part in Operation DESERT SHIELD, January 1991. (U.S. Department of Defense)

cargo-carrying quotient was actually smaller than the previous LST class. Still, these ships could easily keep pace with a modern amphibious force, efficiently discharging a variety of vehicles, and built into their design was the valuable commodity of considerable bunkerage (200,000 gallons) for both vehicle and aviation fuels.

As part of the massive amphibious buildup and subsequent availability that characterized Operations DESERT SHIELD and DESERT STORM, 10 of the 20 Newport class were on hand: the *Manitowoc* (LST-1180), *Peoria* (LST-1183), *Frederick* (LST-1184), *Schenectady* (LST-1185), *Cayuga* (LST-1186), *Saginaw* (LST-1188), *San Bernardino* (LST-1189), *Spartanburg County* (LST-1192), *La Moure County* (LST-1194), and *Barbour County* (LST-1195). Between October 1992 and September 1995, all but two ships were decommissioned. *La Moure County,* part of Naval Reserve Force from 1995, ran aground off Chile during a naval exercise in September 2000. Damage was so massive that the ship was deemed a constructive total loss, and the ship was eventually sunk as a target in July 2001. The *Frederick* was decommissioned in 2002 and transferred to Mexico that same year. Twelve Newport-class LSTs now serve in the navies of Mexico, Brazil, Chile, Taiwan, Malaysia, Australia, Spain, and Morocco.

GORDON E. HOGG

See also

Dock Landing Ships, U.S. and Coalition; United States Marine Corps, Persian Gulf War; United States Navy, Persian Gulf War

References

"Appendix—Tank Landing Ships (LST)." In *Dictionary of American Naval Fighting Ships,* Vol. 7, edited by James L. Mooney. Washington, DC: Naval Historical Center, 1981.

Friedman, Norman. *U.S. Amphibious Ships and Craft: An Illustrated Design History.* Annapolis, MD: Naval Institute Press, 2002.

Polmar, Norman. *The Naval Institute Guide to the Ships and Aircraft of the U.S. Fleet.* 18th ed. Annapolis, MD: Naval Institute Press, 2005.

Sharpe, Richard, ed. *Jane's Fighting Ships: 1991–1992.* London: Jane's Information Group, 1991.

Tanzimat
Start Date: 1839
End Date: 1876

Period beginning in 1839 and lasting until 1876 during which the Ottoman Empire attempted to reform its political, economic, educational, and civil institutions. Tanzimat (Turkish for "reorganization") was begun during the reign of Mahmud II (1808–1839), driven by reforms from European-educated bureaucrats who occupied powerful positions within the Ottoman government. These officials were influenced by Western liberal thought, such as freedom of religion and nationalism, and they sought to implement these ideals into the decaying Ottoman system.

Following Mahmud's death in 1839 and the accession of his weak son, Abdulmecid (1839–1861), leadership of the Tanzimat passed to the grand vizier, Mustafa Rashid Pasha. On November 3, 1839, Rashid Pasha issued a royal decree in the presence of foreign dignitaries and Turkish officials. Known as the Hatt-i Sharif of Gulhane, the decree promised to all Ottoman subjects a secure life, the sanctity of private property, and honor, regardless of religion. The decree provided the reformers with a general framework in which to work. In 1856, the Hatt-i Humayan provided for universal military service, equal access to state employment, and equal educational opportunities to those living under Ottoman control. The National Law of 1869 later declared all Ottoman citizens equal, regardless of religion or ethnic background. The presence of European dignitaries at the issuing of the Hatt-i Sharif of Gulhane hinted at Europe's role in the reforms. Ottoman reformers believed that European pressure would help guide the empire through its reforms.

Mustafa Rashid Pasha spearheaded the early Tanzimat reforms through his leadership of the Council of Justice. The council worked to implement various provincial administrative and taxation reforms. These included the abolition of tax farming, uniform government collection of taxes, and state-sponsored internal improvements.

With Rashid Pasha's death in 1858, leadership of the Council of Justice passed to two of his students, Ali Pasha and Fuad Pasha. From 1869 to 1876, they oversaw the establishment of the new civil code, the Mejelle. Based on Sharia (Islamic law), the Mejelle codified Islamic law and removed individual interpretation from the process. New penal commercial codes were also introduced. To deal with disputes between Muslims and non-Muslims, a secular court known as the *nizame* was also established.

Tanzimat reformers also sought to extend educational opportunities to the people. The newly created Ministry of Education was created to oversee the establishment of secular schools. A number of schools of higher education were also founded, including the Civil Service School in 1859 and the Imperial Ottoman Lycée at Galatasaray in 1868. Graduates from these institutions helped form a class of political and administrative elite who dominated Turkish and Arab governments into the 20th century.

One of the key goals of Tanzimat was the promotion of the concept known as Ottomanism. By attempting to establish the equality of all of the state's citizens, the reformers believed that loyalty to the Ottoman state would emerge without consideration of race or religion. To encourage loyalty to the state, efforts were made to limit the power of the traditional religious groups. In the Imperial Rescript of 1856, power shifted from the Greek and Armenian Christian clergy to secular leaders. Non-Muslims were now included in military conscription, although they could pay for an exemption.

While Tanzimat reformers sought to eliminate a divided society by establishing equality, many Muslims saw their prominent social distinctions being stripped away. Out of the Tanzimat reforms emerged a group known as the Young Ottomans. Believing loyalty to the sultan and the empire was not enough to keep non-Muslim subjects from pulling away, the Young Ottomans supported the establishment of a popular constitutional government with its roots founded in Islam. The Young Ottomans' emphasis on Islam also gained the support of the Islamic *ulema.*

Throughout the Tanzimat period, however, the Ottoman Empire's financial situation steadily worsened. Reformers learned quickly that change costs money. Forced to borrow from European lenders during the Crimean War in 1854, reformers wasted the funds on weapons purchases and royal extravagances. In October 1854, the Sublime Porte declared the empire to be bankrupt. Financial collapse led to peasant rebellions, particularly in the Ottoman Empire's European territories. As the European powers attempted to solve these problems, the Tanzimat reforms sought one radical gesture to gain the support of Europe—the establishment of a constitutional monarchy. An opponent of constitutionalism, Sultan Abdulaziz was forced to abdicate on May 30, 1876. His successor, Murad V (1876), proved to be mentally unstable and reigned for only 93 days.

On August 31, 1876, Abdülhamid II (Abdul Hamid II) (1876–1909) assumed the throne and promised the establishment of a constitutional monarchy. More a statement of Ottomanism than a political document, the Constitution of 1876 established an elected chamber of deputies and an appointed senate. The equality of all Ottoman subjects was also reaffirmed. Power, however, remained concentrated in the hands of the sultan.

The Ottoman experiment in constitutional government was short lived. On April 24, 1877, Russia declared war on the Ottoman Empire. As Russian forces advanced toward Constantinople, Sultan Abdülhamid II seized the moment of crisis to turn against the Tanzimat reforms. On February 13, 1878, parliament and the constitution were suspended. They would not reconvene until July 1908. With the suspension of the Constitution of 1876, the Ottoman Empire moved back to an absolute monarchy. Although viewed at the time as a failure, the reforms of the Tanzimat period laid the foundations for future reforms that would emerge during the Turkish Revolution and the founding of the Republic of Turkey in 1920.

ROBERT W. MALICK

See also

Turkey, Role in Persian Gulf and Afghanistan Wars

References

Ahmad, Feroz. *Turkey: The Quest for Identity.* Oxford, UK: Oneworld, 2003.

Aksin, Sina. *Turkey, from Empire to Revolutionary Republic: The Emergence of the Turkish Nation from 1789 to the Present.* Translated by Dexter H. Mursaloglu. New York: New York University Press, 2007.

Cleveland, William L. *A History of the Modern Middle East.* 3rd ed. Boulder, CO: Westview, 2004.

Howard, Douglas A. *The History of Turkey.* Westport, CT: Greenwood, 2001.

Task Force Normandy

At 2:38 a.m. on January 17, 1991, a joint military force, collectively named Task Force Normandy and consisting of U.S. Army and U.S. Air Force helicopters, paved the way for the opening of the air campaign for Operation DESERT STORM, which marked the beginning of the end of the Iraqi occupation of Kuwait. Elements of the U.S. Army's 1st Battalion, 101st Aviation Regiment, 101st Airborne Division, commanded by Lieutenant Colonel Richard "Dick" Cody, and the U.S. Air Force's 20th Special Operations Squadron (SOS) of the 1st Special Operations Wing, commanded by Lieutenant Colonel Richard L. Comer, participated in the operation to simultaneously destroy two Iraqi air defense radar sites some 25 miles inside the Iraqi border. It was imperative that the two sites be destroyed simultaneously, so as not to alert Baghdad that hostilities had begun. The successful destruction of the sites allowed 100 U.S. Air Force and coalition aircraft to fly, undetected, to their targets deep inside Iraq, including the capital city of Baghdad, a mere 22 minutes after the destruction of the radar sites.

The first of six rehearsals for the mission began on October 10, 1990, and ended with the last rehearsal on January 10, 1991, one week prior to the actual combat mission. The rehearsals focused on flying without communication, black out, visual signals, formations, drop-off, and formation link up. Each training scenario replicated the actual mission. The 101st employed nine uniquely configured Hughes/McDonnell Douglas/Boeing AH-64 Apache helicopters for the conduct of the mission. The U.S. Air Force's 20th SOS deployed four Sikorsky MH-53J Pave Low helicopters to accompany the AH-64s. The MH-53J was selected not only for its unique combat search and rescue (CSAR) capabilities, but also for its advanced terrain-following and terrain-avoidance radar system, which made it the ideal platform to use for this type of operation. The plan called for four Pave Lows to escort the Apaches into Iraq; then the army helicopters would destroy the radar sites with their Hellfire missiles. Armed with a 20-pound high-explosive antitank (HEAT) warhead, each missile required no further guidance after launch and could hit its target without the launcher being in line of site of the target.

Because the Apaches were not as technologically advanced as the Pave Lows, the crews came up with a creative way for the army helicopters to update their navigational systems. The air force crews strung together chemical lights and dropped them out the back of their aircraft at certain points. When the army helicopters flew over the lights, they then updated their own navigational systems. On the day of the actual attack, the MH-53Js used their Global Positioning System (GPS) receivers and terrain-following radars to move the attack force to within nine miles of the target, undetected and with pinpoint accuracy.

Each AH-64 was armed with 8 Hellfire missiles as well as 19 2.75-inch rockets and 7 Fleschette rockets. A Fleschette warhead contained 2,200 steel nails with fins on one end, resembling tiny darts. Additionally, each AH-64 carried 1,200 rounds for the 30-millimeter (mm) M230 Chain Gun under the aircraft's nose.

The task force was divided into two teams, Red and White, with each team consisting of four Apaches and two Pave Lows. The aircraft were located at Al Jouf, Saudi Arabia, days prior to the operation and departed from that outpost on January 17. During the mission, a total of 29 Hellfire missiles were fired from the army aircraft, with 22 hits, 4 misses, and 3 duds. Additionally, approximately 100 Fleschette rockets were fired and 4,000 rounds of 30-mm ammunition were expended. With their mission accomplished, both teams headed back to Saudi Arabia, dodging at least two heat-seeking SA-7 surface-to-air missiles (SAMs) and small-arms fire in the process. All elements of the task force returned safely back to home base.

This near-perfect mission opened a 20-mile wide corridor that was used by air force and coalition aircraft to begin the air campaign against Iraq. Later, at a press conference, U.S. Central Command (CENTCOM) commander General H. Norman Schwarzkopf told the world that "Army AH-64 Apaches plucked the eyes of the Iraqi air defenses."

JOHN R. DABROWSKI

See also

DESERT STORM, Operation; DESERT STORM, Operation, Coalition Air Campaign; DESERT STORM, Operation, Coalition Air Forces; Schwarzkopf, H. Norman, Jr.

References

Hallion, Richard P. *Storm over Iraq: Air Power and the Gulf War.* Washington, DC: Smithsonian Institution Press, 1997.

Mackenzie, Richard. "Apache Attack." *Air Force Magazine* 74 (1991): 54–60.

Naylor, Sean D. "Flight of Eagles: 101st Airborne Division's Raids into Iraq." *Army Times* (1991): 8–12, 15.

Schwarzkopf, H. Norman, with Peter Petre. *It Doesn't Take a Hero: General H. Norman Schwarzkopf, the Autobiography.* New York: Bantam Books, 1993.

Task Force Phoenix

American-led coalition task force of about 6,000 personnel, composed largely of Army National Guard soldiers, whose mission is to train and mentor the Afghan National Army (ANA) and Afghan National Police (ANP). The task force was organized in early 2003. The training is to ensure that the ANA and ANP can defend Afghan independence and national sovereignty against both foreign and

Afghan National Army (ANA) military police trainees undergo training at Kabul Military Training Center under Task Force Phoenix Headquarters Security Support Command supervision on June 4, 2007. U.S. Army soldiers of Task Force Phoenix have the mission to train and mentor the ANA. (U.S. Department of Defense)

domestic enemies. Task Force Phoenix, now encompassing 13 coalition nations, falls under the command of the Combined Security Transition Command–Afghanistan.

From the beginning of Operation ENDURING FREEDOM, U.S. Special Operations Forces (SOF) and coalition forces began the task of training an Afghan army. As a result of a conference in Bonn, Germany, in December 2001, the United States became the lead nation for training the army. In December 2002, the interim president of the Afghan Transitional Authority, Hamid Karzai, authorized the creation of a 70,000-strong ANA, which he intended to be a volunteer force encompassing all of the ethnic and tribal affiliations in Afghan society. In February 2008, the ANA was enlarged to 80,000. In August 2008, the target end-strength would be expanded to 120,000, to be built during the succeeding five years.

With the onset of the Iraq War in March 2003, the SOF was stretched too thin to continue training the ANA. In May 2003, an infantry battalion from the U.S. Army 10th Mountain Division formed Task Force Phoenix I and assumed the mission of training and mentoring the Afghan Army. Each subsequent rotation has been led by Army National Guard units.

Task Force Phoenix II, headed by the 45th Enhanced Separate Brigade of the Oklahoma National Guard, built the first corps command in the Afghan Army. Task Force Phoenix III became a multinational task force. Led by the 76th Infantry Brigade of the Indiana National Guard, it included coalition troops from France, the United Kingdom, Canada, Romania, Bulgaria, New Zealand, and Mongolia. Task Force Phoenix III helped the Afghans to establish four regional commands in Gardez, Kandahar, Herat, and Mazar-e Sharif, demonstrating that the authority of the Afghan central government extended throughout the country. The units deployed without full manpower and equipment, however, so Task Force Phoenix IV, under the command of the 53rd Infantry Brigade from the Florida National Guard, assisted with bringing these units up to full strength.

Coalition troops train with and deploy with Afghan Army units in embedded training teams. Task Force Phoenix V, commanded by the 41st Brigade Combat Team from the Oregon National Guard, expanded these teams. Task Force Phoenix V also assisted with creating command structures such as the Afghan National Army Training Command, a two-star divisional command, which assumed responsibilities for ANA training and education in July 2006, although Task Force Phoenix continues its oversight and mentorship missions.

Training duties are divided among the contributing nations within Task Force Phoenix. American personnel assist with basic and advanced infantry training for enlisted recruits and operate the drill instructor school for noncommissioned officers. French Army and British Army personnel share duties training officers. Canada heads field training for enlisted personnel, noncommissioned officers, and officers. Other nations have assisted with field artillery training and other exercises.

In 2007, the mission for Task Force Phoenix expanded to include the training of the ANP. Task Force Phoenix VI, under the command of the 218th Heavy Separate Brigade from the South Carolina National Guard, assumed these new duties. Task Force Phoenix VII, led by the 27th Infantry Brigade Combat Team from the New York National Guard, continues this mission. A name change to Combined Joint Task Force Phoenix reflects the nature of the command, which includes coalition forces from 13 allied nations as well as personnel from the U.S. Army, Navy, Air Force, and Marine Corps.

Although Task Force Phoenix had trained more than 50,000 ANA troops by mid-2008, the ANA still lacked sufficient combat power and air support to operate independently, continuing to rely on the coalition for funding, equipment, and other support. In April 2008, the national police stood at 77,558 of the authorized 82,000 officers but lagged behind the ANA in its training and professionalism.

LISA M. MUNDEY

See also

Afghan National Army; Afghanistan; Combined Security Transition Command–Afghanistan; Karzai, Hamid; Office of Military Cooperation Afghanistan

References

Barno, David W. "Fighting 'The Other War': Counterinsurgency Strategy in Afghanistan, 2003–2005." *Military Review* (September–October 2007): 32–44.

Combat Studies Institute, Contemporary Operations Study Group. *A Different Kind of War: The United States Army Operation Enduring Freedom (OEF), September 2001–September 2005.* Fort Leavenworth, KS: Combat Studies Institute Press, 2009.

Jalali, Ali A. "The Future of Afghanistan." *Parameters* (Spring 2006): 4–19.

Maloney, Sean M. "Afghanistan Four Years On: An Assessment." *Parameters* (Autumn 2005): 21–32.

Task Group 323.2

Task group deployed to the Mediterranean Sea and formed by elements of the British Royal Navy on January 10, 1991, during Operation DESERT SHIELD. Task Group 323.2 was part of the United Kingdom's support for Operations DESERT SHIELD and DESERT STORM, code-named Operation GRANBY by the British. Task Group 323.2 was under the command of Commodore Christopher Craig.

Before Task Group 323.2 formed, the Royal Navy had already maintained a continued presence in the Persian Gulf but not in the Mediterranean Sea. During the 1980–1988 Iran-Iraq War, the Royal Navy launched Operation ARMILLA in order to protect British

shipping interests and to provide a British presence in the Persian Gulf region. When Iraq invaded Kuwait in 1990, the Royal Navy took on the additional task of enforcing United Nations (UN) sanctions against Iraq.

At the time of the Iraqi invasion of Kuwait in August 1990, ARMILLA consisted of the Type 42–class destroyer HMS *York* and the Broadsword-class frigate HMS *Battleaxe* and the Leander-class frigate HMS *Jupiter,* supported by the Royal Fleet Auxiliary support ship *Orangeleaf.* These ships were later augmented by another Type 42–class destroyer: *Glouster.* By April 1991, the Royal Navy alone had carried out more than 3,000 challenges and 36 boardings in the Persian Gulf.

The *Ark Royal,* one of three British aircraft carriers, was deployed to the Mediterranean on January 10, 1991, to head Task Group 323.2. The Task Group then consisted of the Broadsword-class frigate *Sheffield* and the support ships *Olmeda* and *Regent.* Later, the task group would be augmented by the Type 42–class destroyers *Exeter* and *Manchester.* In late January 1991, the *Manchester* was called to the Persian Gulf and replaced in the Mediterranean by the Leander-class frigate *Charybdis.*

Despite pressure from the Americans to move Task Force 323.2 forward to the Persian Gulf, Britain's Ministry of Defense resisted, insisting that the group would perform the secondary—but important—mission of providing support to coalition forces and allied communication lines in the Mediterranean and reassuring Egypt, Turkey, and other states, should the conflict expand beyond the confines of Kuwait and Iraq. This approach seemed vindicated when Iraqi president Saddam Hussein tried to expand the war by launching Scud missiles at Israel in hopes that Israel would retaliate and the Arab coalition partners would then side with Iraq against Israel. Keeping an eye on Libya was another essential task, as coalition forces feared that Libyan dictator Muammar Qaddafi might provide assistance to Iraq. The British hoped that the presence of Task Group 323.2 would prevent this.

British naval historian Eric Grove also points out that the British decision not to move Task Group 323.2 too far forward reflected a predilection within the Ministry of Defense not to give the Royal Navy too large a role in Operation GRANBY, as it was unsure of its strategic role in the immediate post–Cold War world. Task Group 323.2 was thus limited to patrolling and interdiction duties. It was disbanded shortly after the end of the Persian Gulf War in February 1991.

ROBERT G. PRICE

See also

DESERT STORM, Operation; DESERT STORM, Operation, Coalition Naval Forces; GRANBY, Operation; United Kingdom, Navy, Persian Gulf War

References

Atkinson, Rick. *Crusade: The Untold Story of the Persian Gulf War.* New York: Mariner Books, 1994.

Craig, Chris. *Call for Fire: Sea Combat in the Falklands and the Gulf War.* London: John Murray, 1995.

Craig, C. J. S. "Gulf War: The Maritime Campaign." *RUSI Journal* 137: 11–16.

Grove, Eric J. *The Royal Navy since 1815: A New Short History.* New York: Palgrave Macmillan, 2005.

Sharpe, Richard, ed. *Jane's Fighting Ships: 1991–1992.* London: Jane's Information Group, 1991.

Television, Middle Eastern

Television is one of the major sources of information in the modern world. Television stations in the Middle East have played a significant role through the broadcasting and transmitting of information, not just to the nations in that region but to the rest of the world.

As in the West, television stations in the Middle East are regulated by governments, but there is more extensive control of it by government under state-centrism or state socialism. Still, a wide variety of programs can be found on television, especially with the advent of cable and satellite TV. These have brought about an explosion of new stations and viewpoints.

Television has played an important role in the major wars in the Middle East: the ongoing war between the Palestinians and the Israelis; Israeli wars in Lebanon (1978, 1982, 1993, 1996, 2006); the Lebanese civil war (1975–1990); relentless civil war in Sudan; and the Iran-Iraq War of 1980–1988. Additionally, the 1991 Persian Gulf War, the 2001 war against the Taliban in Afghanistan, and the 2003 Iraq War have all unfolded before television cameras.

In recent decades, technological developments and the expansion in global communications, together with the establishment of cable/satellite television, have made television in the Middle East a transnational phenomenon. This expansion has been best associated with the outbreak of the Persian Gulf War in 1991. Since then, a wide range of local and regional channels has been available by subscription in the Middle East. A major example is the Qatar satellite television channel Al Jazeera, which was launched in 1996 with a $150 million grant from the emir of Qatar. In the late 1990s, Al Jazeera became very popular in the Arab world yet was oddly ignored in the West. Al Jazeera set out to counter the formula of state-supported television and its one-sided news reportage. It built a reputation for exciting debates and strong disagreements in interviews and panels.

After September 11, 2001, Al Jazeera earned the ire of the U.S. government, when the Al Jazeera formula of endeavoring to present all sides of an issue came under fire as supporting terrorism. This occurred when Al Jazeera reported atrocities in Iraq and broadcast video statements of Osama bin Laden and other Al Qaeda leaders.

In contrast to Al Jazeera, the Saudi TV channel al-Arabiyya was established on March 3, 2003, and based in the United Arab Emirates (UAE). Its primary focus is lighter entertainment, music, and dance videos. Its news coverage is influenced by the Western-allied UAE government. Alongside Al Jazeera and al-Arabiyya, there are several other Arab television channels that have facilitated a significant change in the media in relation to the Middle East. The most notable are: the LBCI (Lebanon), Future TV (Lebanon), Manar TV (Lebanon), Nile TV International (Egypt), Syria Satellite Channel (Syria), and Abu Dhabi TV (UAE).

There is now a wide range of Arab television stations broadcasting from the Middle East to other parts of the region and to the entire world. The importance of television is also seen in the coverage of the Middle East during wartime. Many Middle East channels compete to be among the first to broadcast from war zones and to send new and exclusive information to their audience. Moreover, continuously running news tickers became another way to broadcast the news around the clock, which allows an audience to follow news stories at any time. Beyond that, breaking news provides important supplements to a story when a war or a crisis is underway.

One of the problems of Middle Eastern television is that satellite television channels do not necessarily reach various sectarian communities equally. Viewers may choose to watch other channels or not to subscribe at all.

During the summer 2006 Israeli-Hezbollah War in Lebanon, there was another war underway between Arab satellite channels, which were essentially taking sides in their coverage of the conflict. Some Arab satellite stations have also clearly reflected their own politics, and some have shown biases both for and against the West. Al-Arabiyya has repeatedly sought to create undercurrents of bias during times of war. In this way, the Arabic television stations reflect the tendencies that Americans view on FOX television or, at the opposite extreme, on MSNBC.

Rami Siklawi

See also

Al Jazeera; Media and Operation DESERT STORM; War Correspondents

References

Sakr, Naomi. *Satellite Realms: Transnational Television, Globalization & the Middle East.* London: I. B. Tauris, 2001.

Taylor, Philip M. *War and the Media: Propaganda and Persuasion in the Gulf War.* Manchester, UK: Manchester University Press, 1992.

Weisenborn, Ray, ed. *Media in the Midst of War: Cairo Reporting to the Global Village.* Cairo: Adham Center for Television, 1992.

Tenet, George John
Birth Date: January 5, 1953

Career U.S. government employee, intelligence officer, and director of the U.S. Central Intelligence Agency (CIA) during 1997–2004. As CIA director, Tenet was heavily involved in Operation ENDURING FREEDOM and the decision to go to war with Iraq in 2003 (Operation IRAQI FREEDOM). Born on January 5, 1953, in Flushing, New York, George John Tenet was raised in Little Neck, Queens, New York, and earned a bachelor's degree in 1976 from

Director of the Central Intelligence Agency (CIA) George Tenet testifies on March 24, 2004, before the federal panel reviewing the September 11, 2001, terrorist attacks on the World Trade Center and Pentagon. Tenet resigned on July 11, 2004, shortly before the release of the 9/11 Commission report, which was critical of the CIA and its intelligence-gathering abilities. (AP/Wide World Photos)

Georgetown University in international relations. He received a master's degree from Columbia University's School of International and Public Affairs in 1978.

Tenet began work in the U.S. Senate in 1982 on various staffs, including that of Pennsylvania senator John L. Heinz III. From 1985 to 1988, he was a staff member for the Senate Select Committee on Intelligence and then served as its staff director from 1988 to 1993. That same year, Tenet was tapped to serve on newly elected President Bill Clinton's national security transition team. From 1993 to 1995 he served the Clinton White House as the National Security Council's senior director for intelligence programs. In July 1995, Tenet began serving as deputy director of the CIA, a post he held until he was nominated and confirmed as the CIA director in 1997. Although tradition has usually seen the CIA director replaced with the advent of a new presidential administration, in 2001 the incoming George W. Bush administration opted to keep Tenet in that post.

Tenet and the CIA had become aware of potential terrorist plots to attack the United States before September 11, 2001, especially by

the militant organization known as Al Qaeda and its leader, Osama bin Laden. Despite his knowledge of such threats, Tenet was unsuccessful in his attempts to have either the Clinton or Bush administrations take concrete action against such groups. Following the September 11, 2001, terrorist attacks on the United States, many observers blamed the failure to avert the attacks on the CIA.

In October 2001, an international force, led by the United States, launched Operation ENDURING FREEDOM in Afghanistan with the goal of capturing bin Laden, destroying the Al Qaeda terrorist organization responsible for the September 11 attacks, and removing the Taliban regime, a fundamentalist Muslim government in control of Afghanistan that had refused U.S. demands to move against Al Qaeda.

Tenet's CIA played a large role in the operational control of the war in Afghanistan. While largely successful in bringing down the Taliban and reducing the capabilities of Al Qaeda in Afghanistan, Tenet and the CIA were criticized for not capturing bin Laden. Tenet was also accused of authorizing torture as part of U.S. interrogation methods of captured Al Qaeda members during the conflict. Although the CIA admitted the use of harsh interrogation techniques, Tenet denied any allegations that the CIA had authorized torture. Many American law experts disagreed with the CIA, however, and stated that the techniques did amount to torture.

The Bush administration, meanwhile, became increasingly concerned about Iraq's capability to produce and deploy weapons of mass destruction (WMDs). Tenet repeatedly attempted to convince Bush of the vast means available to Iraqi dictator Saddam Hussein to attack his own people, neighboring countries, and other Iraqi enemies, such as the United States, with WMDs. In an exchange depicted in Bob Woodward's 2004 book *Plan of Attack*, Tenet persuaded Bush that he could convince the American people about the threat of WMDs. Indeed, he described the case regarding Iraq's possession of such weapons as a "slam dunk." Many observers have harshly criticized Tenet over the use of the phrase. Tenet has since stated that the term was taken out of context and that the words had "nothing to do with the president's decision to send American troops into Iraq." Tenet affirms that the decision to do so had already been made.

The apparent absence of WMDs in Iraq, which had been the initial and primary motivating factor in the invasion of Iraq, deeply embarrassed the Bush administration. As the insurgency in Iraq began by late 2003, legions of critics pointed to the glaring miscalculation of the presence of WMDs. This in turn seemed to feed the growing antiwar faction, both in Congress and among the general public. Under increasing fire, Tenet tendered his resignation as CIA director on June 3, 2004, citing "personal reasons" for his decision. He then went to work for a British defense technology company.

On December 14, 2004, President Bush awarded Tenet with the Presidential Medal of Freedom, which only stirred up more controversy. In April 2007, Tenet released his book *At the Center of the Storm: My Years at the CIA*. In it, Tenet unsurprisingly attempted to polish his image and also accused the Bush White House of having misconstrued his counsel as well as prewar intelligence. The book, however, has been sharply criticized by those inside and outside of the intelligence establishment who claim that the former CIA director misrepresented the facts. In 2008, Tenet became managing director of the boutique investment firm Allen & Company, based in New York City. He continues to sit on several corporate boards.

GREGORY W. MORGAN AND PAUL G. PIERPAOLI JR.

See also

Al Qaeda; Bin Laden, Osama; Bush, George Walker; Central Intelligence Agency; ENDURING FREEDOM, Operation; IRAQI FREEDOM, Operation; Nuclear Weapons, Iraq's Potential for Building; Taliban; Terrorism; Weapons of Mass Destruction

References

Tenet, George. *At the Center of the Storm: My Years at the CIA*. New York: HarperCollins, 2007.

Woodward, Bob. *Plan of Attack*. New York: Simon and Schuster, 2004.

Terrorism

There is no settled definition of the word "terrorism." Most scholars and defense analysts believe that terrorism is a tactic rather than a philosophy or set ideology. History has shown that groups may employ terrorism at some times and not at others. There is an active debate about whether terrorism is the appropriate term solely for violence by nonstate entities, or whether state terrorism must also be included. Some consider terrorism to be acts or threats of violence, directed against noncombatants, to shock or achieve a change in a political status quo by indirect means. However, others label some actions against military or governmental personnel to be terrorist in nature when they do not comply with international law. Still others write about terrorism as a pathology wherein violence is the motivating force and not merely a means to an end. This approach is problematic as it could apply to individual pathological acts of violence as in recent cases of school shootings in Western countries. Terrorism may be employed for a wide variety of ideological, religious, or economic reasons.

Terrorism is also a tool in asymmetric conflict and a force magnifier. The impact of a small number of individuals committing terrorist actions can be huge, and even a large paramilitary or military force may seem ineffective in combating it, particularly if success is measured by the complete eradication of such incidents.

Numerous academic and governmental experts recognize the arguments over what constitutes terrorism and thus do not employ the term. Certainly there has been reaction to the U.S. government's application of the term in the Global War on Terror. "Violent extremism" has been used for many years in place of "Islamic terrorism" in the Muslim world and has begun to be used in the West in the last few years. Here, the focus is on the use, or relinquishment, of violence, rather than the movement employing it.

Some analysts date modern terrorism to the Russian anarchist organization Narodnaya Volya (People's Will) of the 19th century, which attempted, through assassinations, to overthrow the czarist regime. Their methods were adopted by anarchists throughout the world, and the decades leading up to World War I were marked by frequent assassinations, including that of U.S. President William McKinley in 1901. The assassinations of the Austrian archduke

Prominent Terrorist Organizations in the Middle East

Name	Date Founded
al-Aqsa Martyrs Brigade	2000
Al Qaeda	1988
al-Zarqawi Network	2003
Fatah	1974
Hamas	1987
Hezbollah	1982
Kahane Chai	1994
Mahdi Army	2003
Palestine Liberation Front (PLF)	1959
Popular Front for the Liberation of Palestine (PFLP)	1967

Police forensics officers work through the remains of a bombed bus in the northern Israeli city of Haifa on March 5, 2003. A suicide bomber blew up the crowded bus, killing at least 15 people and wounding dozens of others. The attack ended a two-month lull in suicide bombings. (AP/Wide World Photos)

Franz Ferdinand and his wife, Sophie, in Sarajevo in June 1914 sparked the outbreak of World War I.

Terrorist activities occurred in the Middle East prior to World War I, but in most cases the group responsible for terrorist activities was either a state-controlled force that claimed to be acting in the interests of state security or engaged in war, or a militia or force fighting against the state or another organization. Examples include the genocide perpetrated by Turkish authorities against the Armenians and subsequent actions in recent years by Kurds against Turks in Turkey. Yet atrocities committed by Israeli forces in 1948 against Palestinians have often been excused as legitimate acts of war.

In numerous instances, colonial powers have been confronted by indigenous peoples employing asymmetric warfare tactics, and both have resorted to terrorism. For instance, in the conflict between Algerian nationalist groups and the French government and military, both sides engaged in acts of terrorism. The nationalist Front de Liberation Nationale (National Liberation Front, FLN) bombed crowded civilian locations frequented by Westerners as well as Algerians, and the French bombed residences in the Arab-inhabited *casbah* of Algiers and resorted to the torture of suspects in retaliation.

Terrorism by both Arabs and Jews against each other and by Jewish forces against the British mandate power occurred in Palestine in the 1930s. Following Israel's creation in 1948, Palestinian groups, some supported by neighboring Arab governments, began to launch military attacks against Israel. After Israel's victory in the 1967 Six-Day War and the rise of the Popular Movement in the refugee camps, Palestinian groups organized a wave of terrorist activities during 1969–1973. The political leadership of the movement then determined that these tactics brought too heavy an Israeli response and were detrimental to their cause, although they had served a purpose in focusing world attention on the plight of the Palestinians. In these same years, radical left-wing organizations in the United States such as the Weatherman and the Red Army in Europe and beyond (Japan) also engaged in acts of terrorism. Terrorism continued to be a major aspect of the Israeli-Palestinian confrontation and the inability to conclude an Arab-Israeli peace treaty but also as a response to Israeli military actions employing collective punishment against Palestinians or Palestinian communities.

Terrorist actions also appeared in Saudi Arabia. After the 1991 Persian Gulf War, extremists began preaching against U.S. military forces in Saudi Arabia, claiming that it was unconscionable for the Saudi government to allow Christian forces to determine the political responses of the Saudi government toward other Muslim governments and to operate from the peninsula where the holy cities of Mecca and Medina are located. Their objection was chiefly regarding the presence of Western military forces; however, Saudi Arabia has long been home to a large expatriate community in its oil industry, and some extremists objected to their presence on Saudi soil as well.

On November 13, 1993, the Office of the Program Manager/ Saudi Arabian National Guard (OPM/SANG) was badly damaged by a car bomb. Four Saudi nationals confessed and were executed on May 31, 1996. According to their confessions, they were veterans of jihads in Afghanistan, Bosnia, and Chechnya; they claimed that the Saudi rulers were apostates; and they were inspired by Islamic law to commit the attacks.

One month later, the Khobar Towers in Dhahran, Saudi Arabia, were destroyed by a truck bomb, killing 19 U.S. servicemen in a plot carried out by Saudi Hezbollah. In 1996 and again in 1998, Al Qaeda leader Osama bin Laden announced a fatwa declaring that Muslims should attack U.S. personnel and interests around the world, drive U.S. forces from Saudi Arabia, remove the Saudi royal family and other apostate Arab regimes from power, and liberate Palestine. Of these goals, the most vital, and yet most unattainable, for bin Ladin was the removal of the Saudi royal family, and in fact his campaign against the United States is based on his analysis of U.S. government support for the Saudi royal family's hold on power. Bin Laden moved to various locations—Pakistan, Afghanistan, the Sudan, and then back again to Afghanistan—to plan his campaign.

The current War on Terror began with Operation ENDURING FREEDOM in Afghanistan, a month after the devastating September 11 attacks on the United States carried out by Al Qaeda. Objectives of the operation included removing the Taliban from power, destroying Al Qaeda's training camps, and killing or capturing its operatives. In 2002, the Taliban was partially defeated, but many Al Qaeda and Taliban members escaped and new recruits soon appeared, drawn from Afghanistan and the religiously conservative northwest region of Pakistan. These groups continue to attack North Atlantic Treaty Organization (NATO) troops, Afghan government officials, and civilians. Suicide bombings, never before utilized in Afghanistan, became a regular occurrence. Taliban and Al Qaeda operatives (including bin Laden) operated with relative freedom in the northwest reaches of Pakistan and could easily slip back across the border into Afghanistan.

In 2003, Operation IRAQI FREEDOM spearheaded by the United States removed Saddam Hussein and his regime from power and liberated Iraq. However, more than 40 different groups of Sunni Muslims as well some Shiite militias opposed and began to fight the coalition forces. These included such groups as Al Qaeda in Mesopotamia, Ansar al-Islam, and others. They engaged in regular fighting but also used terrorist attacks, mainly suicide bombings, against U.S., coalition, and Iraqi forces and civilians in attempts to destabilize the country so that they might drive the United States and its allies from Iraq and take power.

Between 2003 and 2005, more than 500 suicide car bombings and vest attacks occurred. Targets included refineries, electrical stations, police stations, open-air markets, and even mosques. The insurgents' intent was to undermine the public's confidence that the government would ever be able to provide essential services and security. However, in 2006, Sunni sheikhs, with strong financial incentives from both Saudi Arabia and the coalition, formed alliances to fight against Al Qaeda in Mesopotamia and other violent Islamist groups. This strategy accompanied the Western insistence on a coalition troop surge that began in early 2007. Yet acts of terrorism increased in the spring of 2009 and targeted the sheikhs who had cooperated with the coalition forces. Other acts of terrorism with suicide and truck bombings continue to plague Afghanistan and now, increasingly, Pakistan as well.

DONALD R. DUNNE AND ELLIOT CHODOFF

See also

Al Qaeda; Al Qaeda in Iraq; Ansar al-Islam; Bin Laden, Osama; Counterterrorism Strategy; Democratization and the Global War on Terror; Global War on Terror; Hamas; Hezbollah; Mahdi Army; September 11 Attacks; Taliban

References

Crenshaw, Martha, ed. *Terrorism in Context.* University Park: Pennsylvania State University Press, 1995.

Dershowitz, Alan. *The Case for Israel.* New York: Wiley, 2003.

Gettleman, Marvin, and Stuart Schaar, eds. *The Middle East and Islamic World Reader.* New York: Grove, 2003.

Gunaratna, Rohan. *Inside Al Qaeda: Global Network of Terror.* New York: Berkley Publishing Group, 2003.

Harel, Amos, and Avi Issacharoff. *34 Days: Israel, Hezbollah and the War in Lebanon.* New York: Palgrave Macmillan, 2008.

Hoffman, Bruce. *Inside Terrorism.* New York: Columbia University Press, 2006.

Thani, Khalifa bin Hamad al-
Birth Date: 1932

Emir of Qatar from 1972 to 1995 and a member of the ruling family of al-Thani. Born in Doha, Qatar, in 1932 (exact date unknown), Sheikh Khalifa bin Hamad al-Thani was the fourth son of Hamad bin Ali al-Thani of the ruling al-Thani dynasty. His grandfather Ali bin Abdallah al-Thani was emir from 1913 to 1949, during Britain's rule of Qatar, and his father was heir apparent before his death in 1947. Sheikh Khalifa received a traditional Islamic education from private tutors.

In the 1950s, Sheikh Khalifa held government posts in the ministries of security and education. In 1960, he assumed the role of minister of finance and petroleum affairs and was largely responsible for planning his country's economic development and modernization process. Officially recognized as deputy ruler and heir apparent to the throne of Qatar that same year, in 1960, Sheikh Khalifa was responsible for government planning, policy, and implementation.

In 1968, three years before Qatar gained independence from Britain, Sheikh Khalifa served as the first prime minister of the

Sheikh Khalifa bin Hamad al-Thani, emir of Qatar, delivers an address to the General Assembly of the United Nations (UN) in 2008. (AP/Wide World Photos)

Provisional Federal Council, the forerunner of the United Arab Emirates (UAE). As such, he was influential in the establishment of the UAE, although Qatar became independent in September 1971.

Five months after Qatar became a sovereign nation, Sheikh Khalifa deposed his cousin Ahmad bin Ali al-Thani and assumed power on February 22, 1972. In addition to assuming the title of emir, Sheikh Khalifa retained his post as prime minister and immediately reorganized the government. In doing so, he oversaw enormous economic growth, supported by massive revenues from oil sales and other natural resources.

On April 19, 1972, Sheikh Khalifa amended the provisional constitution of Qatar and enlarged the advisory council. In addition, he cut the ruling family's allowance and increased spending on social services. After the price of oil increased dramatically beginning in 1973, Sheikh Khalifa initiated a wave of industrial development in areas such as fertilizer production, steel making, and petrochemicals. In 1976, he fully nationalized Qatar's oil industry.

Qatar fought as a part of the coalition mandated by the United Nations (UN) during the 1991 Persian Gulf War, and Qatari troops were among the first to engage Iraqi ground forces at the Battle of Khafji in order to liberate Kuwait. However, Sheikh Khalifa's involvement in the Persian Gulf War was somewhat limited; his son, Sheikh Hamad bin Khalifa, who wielded considerable power, essentially led Qatar during the war crisis. Additionally, Sheikh Hamad was behind the 1992 bilateral Defense Cooperation Agreement, which allowed the United States access to Qatari naval and air facilities. In 1995, Sheikh Hamad, who had been the de facto

ruler of Qatar for a number of years, deposed his father, Sheikh Khalifa, in a bloodless coup d'état. This ended the 23-year reign of the emir.

The United States and other Western states quickly recognized Sheikh Hamad as the new leader of Qatar. Sheikh Khalifa, meanwhile, toured Arab capitals, where locals greeted him with open arms. Yet his dreams of returning to power were short lived after his son gained a court order to freeze Sheikh Khalifa's bank accounts. Sheikh Khalifa lived in exile in France before returning to Qatar in 2004.

KIRSTY MONTGOMERY

See also

DESERT STORM, Operation; Qatar; United Arab Emirates

References

Cordesman, Anthony H. *Bahrain, Oman, Qatar, and the UAE: Challenges of Security.* Boulder, CO: Westview, 1997.

Metz, Helen Chapin. *Persian Gulf States: Country Studies.* 3rd ed. Washington, DC: Federal Research Division, Library of Congress, 1994.

Zahlan, Rosemarie Said. *The Making of the Modern Gulf States: Kuwait, Bahrain, Qatar, The United Arab Emirates, and Oman.* London: Unwin Hyman, 1989.

Thatcher, Margaret
Birth Date: October 13, 1925

British politician and prime minister (1979–1990). Born in Grantham, Lincolnshire, on October 13, 1925, Margaret Hilda Roberts attended Kesteven and Grantham High School for Girls then read chemistry at Somerville College, Oxford, becoming president of the Oxford University Conservative Association. Upon graduation in 1947, she worked as a research chemist and in 1951 was called to the bar as a lawyer. In 1951 she married Denis Thatcher, a wealthy businessman.

After two failed attempts, in 1959 Margaret Thatcher won election to Parliament as the Conservative member for Finchley. In 1961 she was parliamentary secretary at the Ministry of Pensions and in 1970 secretary of state for education and science under Edward Heath until his government lost the 1974 election to Harold Wilson's Labour Party. The following year, Thatcher became the Conservative leader, the first woman to head either major British political party. After four years, during which she broke decisively with the centrist consensus on the mixed economy and welfare state that had dominated all British governments since 1945, she led her party to electoral victory over Labour Prime Minister James Callaghan in 1979. This was the first of three successive general election triumphs for Thatcher, the others occurring in 1983 and 1987.

As British prime minister—the first woman to hold that position—Thatcher used monetarist measures to moderate the prevailing high inflation of the 1970s, cut taxes dramatically, trim

Known as the "Iron Lady," Margaret Thatcher was Britain's first woman prime minister (1979–1990). As leader of the Conservative Party, Thatcher was a strong ally of U.S. president Ronald Reagan. (Corel)

back the welfare state, privatize many nationalized industries, and drastically curtail the power of labor in bitter confrontations with major trade unions. Far more ideological than her predecessors, she accepted double-digit unemployment rates and the consequent short-term political unpopularity as the inevitable price of such policies.

Stridently anticommunist in outlook, while still in opposition in 1976 Thatcher had assailed Soviet policies for opposing genuine détente through intervention in Angola and opposed any weakening of the North Atlantic Treaty Organization (NATO). Dubbed the "Iron Lady" by the Soviet press, she accepted the sobriquet with pride and worked to strengthen British defenses and repair strained relations with the United States. She consciously modeled herself on Winston Churchill, another maverick Conservative prime minister who supported tough foreign policies. Her uncompromising rhetoric, strong principles, and forceful personality soon made her a major international figure, admired by conservatives and often reviled by liberals.

Thatcher consistently backed NATO, endorsing the controversial 1979 decision to deploy nuclear-armed intermediate-range cruise missiles in Western Europe and replace Britain's Polaris submarine fleet with modern Trident II submarines. In doing so, she ignored protests, including the revival of the Campaign for Nuclear Disarmament and the encampment of protestors for several years outside the American air base of Greenham Common, Berkshire. Splits within the Labour Party over defense and British membership in NATO contributed to Thatcher's subsequent reelection victories.

While taking a tough line on defense and rearmament, initially Thatcher concentrated on economic and domestic issues, leaving her foreign secretary, Lord Carrington, responsible for handling such thorny issues as negotiating a settlement in Zimbabwe (Rhodesia) in 1980 that replaced the state's breakaway white government with one dominated by Africans. From 1982, however, when against much advice she chose to send a military expedition to the South Atlantic to regain the British-controlled Falkland Islands after their seizure by Argentina, Thatcher became far more active in international affairs. She played a major part in negotiating the 1984 Joint Declaration whereby, against her own initial instincts, Britain agreed to return Hong Kong to the People's Republic of China (PRC) in 1997. Always somewhat suspicious of the European Community (EC), she did not withdraw Britain from membership but undertook hard bargaining to ensure that Britain's overall budgetary contributions to the EC declined substantially.

Thatcher privately considered Democratic President Jimmy Carter, in office when she first became prime minister, regrettably weak and unrealistic in his early policies of seeking détente with the Soviet Union. After the December 1979 Soviet-backed coup in Afghanistan, Carter took a much tougher anti-Soviet line, an attitude Thatcher welcomed and encouraged. Britain supported the United States in imposing economic sanctions on the Soviet Union in retaliation. Thatcher also shared Carter's concern when a fiercely anti-American Islamic government overthrew the Shah of Iran in 1979, causing oil prices to soar dramatically. After a mob sacked the U.S. embassy in Tehran in 1979 and American diplomatic personnel working there were held hostage for more than a year, Thatcher sympathized but declined a request from Carter to impose a broad array of sanctions on Iran. When Iraqi-trained terrorists took over the Iranian embassy in London in April 1980, she authorized armed SAS (Special Air Service) personnel to attack the building, an operation that successfully released captives held hostage there. In September 1980 Iraq attacked Iran, beginning eight years of a brutal, stalemated war. Thatcher, whose main concern was to protect western shipping in the Persian Gulf and prevent the conflict from spreading to other Gulf States, dispatched British naval forces to patrol the region.

From early 1981, Thatcher worked closely with U.S. president Ronald Reagan, whose political views on both domestic and international issues coincided almost exactly with her own, and the two soon developed a warm friendship. Internationally, she almost always backed the United States, even when Reagan's fiercely antiterrorist and anticommunist policies toward such countries as Libya, Nicaragua, and Chile generated considerable domestic and foreign criticism. In retaliation for Libya's backing of international terrorist attacks on Americans, in April 1986 U.S. warplanes bombed targets in Libya. Thatcher strongly supported the operation, allowing the American aircraft to launch their raids from British bases. During Reagan's second term, the Iran Contra scandal revealed that the Reagan administration had secretly sold arms to Iran and illicitly funneled the proceeds to the Nicaraguan Contra rebels. Thatcher remained the president's staunch and loyal friend, fiercely rebuffing all suggestions that this episode and the subsequent investigation had crippled Reagan's domestic and international political effectiveness.

During the early 1980s, Thatcher's relations with Soviet leaders Leonid Brezhnev, Yuri Andropov, and Konstantin Chernenko were frosty. Meeting Mikhail Gorbachev in December 1983 shortly before he became Soviet Communist Party secretary, she quickly developed a rapport with him and urged Reagan to give credence to Gorbachev's calls for major reductions in nuclear and conventional forces as well as his attempts at economic reform. Interestingly, fearing that Gorbachev political survival was precarious and that more hard-line Soviet officials might well replace him, Thatcher was more cautious than Reagan in sanctioning such reductions, including the 1987 Intermediate-Range Nuclear Forces (INF) Treaty, and urged the Western alliance to proceed relatively slowly. She was therefore somewhat uncomfortable with the sweeping agreements that Reagan and Gorbachev reached at Reykjavik in 1986, a meeting that, like several others between Gorbachev and Presidents Reagan and George H. W. Bush, she did not attend.

Doubts over the effectiveness of the Strategic Defense Initiative (SDI) system of antinuclear defenses that Reagan favored made Thatcher reluctant to dismantle both nuclear weapons and antinuclear defenses. Memories of German involvement in two world wars also led her to oppose unavailingly the unification of the German Democratic Republic (GDR, East Germany) and the Federal Republic of Germany (FRG, West Germany). In the late summer of 1990, she reportedly exhorted President George H. W. Bush to remain firm in opposition to the seizure of Kuwait by President Saddam Hussein of Iraq, pleadings that many believed contributed to Bush's decision to launch a war against Iraq the following year. Thatcher quickly dispatched British troops to the Persian Gulf as part of the international coalition that Bush put together. British troops and airplanes played a prominent part, second only to the United States, in the brief Persian Gulf War of 1991, in which coalition forces attained victory in a matter of days.

By then, however, Thatcher was no longer prime minister. In November 1990, Conservative opposition to Thatcher's domestic policies, especially the highly unpopular new poll tax, had created a rebellion within her own party that forced her from office. John Major replaced her as prime minister. Raised to the peerage as Baroness Thatcher, she then published several volumes of memoirs and speeches, made numerous public addresses, and somewhat ineffectively attempted to pressure her successors to follow her policies. She opposed any further strengthening of the European Union (EU) but strongly supported the continuation and enlargement of NATO. She also established a foundation to promote and encourage her free enterprise and antisocialist political views. In failing health by the early 21st century, in June 2004 she nonetheless insisted on attending her old friend Reagan's funeral and burial services, for which she had recorded a eulogy lauding his domestic and international achievements. Although her own country lacked the superpower status of the United States, much of her praise of Reagan's courage, determination, and political skills was equally applicable to Thatcher herself.

PRISCILLA ROBERTS

See also

Bush, George Herbert Walker; DESERT SHIELD, Operation; DESERT STORM, Operation; Gorbachev, Mikhail; Iran; Iran-Contra Affair; Iran-Iraq War; Iranian Revolution; Iraq, History of, Pre-1990; Iraq, History of, 1990–Present; Kuwait; North Atlantic Treaty Organization; Reagan, Ronald Wilson; United Kingdom, Middle East Policy

References

Campbell, John. *Margaret Thatcher,* Vol. 1, *The Grocer Daughter.* London: Jonathan Cape, 2000.

———. *Margaret Thatcher,* Vol. 2, *Iron Lady.* London: Jonathan Cape, 2003.

Cannadine, David. *In Churchill's Shadow: Confronting the Past in Modern Britain.* New York: Oxford University Press, 2003.

Evans, Brendan. *Thatcherism and British Politics, 1975–1999.* Stroud, Gloucestershire, UK: Sutton, 1999.

Evans, Eric J. *Thatcher and Thatcherism.* 2nd ed. New York: Routledge, 2004.

Sharp, Paul. *Thatcher's Diplomacy: The Revival of British Foreign Policy.* New York: St. Martin's, 1997.

Smith, Geoffrey. *Reagan and Thatcher.* New York: Norton, 1991.

Thatcher, Margaret. *Downing Street Years.* New York: HarperCollins, 1993.

———. *The Path to Power.* New York: HarperCollins, 1995.

Wapshott, Nicholas. *Ronald Reagan and Margaret Thatcher: A Political Marriage.* London: Sentinel, 2007.

Thermobaric Bomb

A bomb that uses atmospheric oxygen to multiply its explosive power. Generally, a thermobaric bomb produces an explosive cloud of vapor, which then ignites to produce a high-temperature explosive reaction. Thermobaric bombs have been in use among the world's militaries since the Vietnam War, but the methods needed to produce practical bombs have only recently been perfected. Large thermobaric devices can pack power comparable to tactical nuclear weapons. The weapons are also sometimes referred to as fuel-air explosives or vacuum bombs.

The physics behind a thermobaric bomb are relatively simple. An explosive mixture is packed inside a bomb casing. The mixture may be either liquid or solid. Early weapons used liquid fuels such as liquid oxygen or gasoline. Researchers have found that solid fuels work more efficiently and are significantly easier to store and maintain. Powdered aluminum is the most common solid fuel used today, but other elements can be used. Boron, silicon, titanium, magnesium, zirconium, carbon, and hydrocarbons are also employed. The fuel is often mixed with a small amount of an oxygen-rich compound to initiate a reaction. Ammonium perchlorate is commonly used.

When a thermobaric bomb is detonated, a small explosive charge ruptures the casing and the fuel is dispersed to form a cloud. The size and density of the cloud depend on weather conditions, such as humidity and wind. Researchers found that the cloud of fuel must be dense enough to set up a chain reaction, but not so dense that atmospheric oxygen is not present. After the cloud is created, a secondary explosive ignites it. The shock wave of the detonation ignites particles farther from the center, creating a larger shock wave, which can expand far beyond the limits of one produced by the same amount of conventional explosives. The temperature of the reaction may reach more than 5,000°F. Because the reaction consumes the oxygen in the area, a vacuum usually occurs in the center of the ignition, causing the remaining fuel particles and objects that have not been incinerated to be sucked into the reaction.

The effects of a thermobaric bomb can be enhanced in a number of ways. One is by having a mix of different sized particles in the fuel. Smaller particles ignite more rapidly, while larger ones burn more slowly and help to prolong the shock wave.

Excessive amounts of fuel in the bomb can also cause more incendiary effects.

Human rights groups, such as Human Rights Watch, have condemned the use of thermobaric bombs because of the indiscriminate and widespread damage they can cause among noncombatants. The central zone of the detonation stretches for many meters because the fuel is dispersed. Anyone in the central zone would almost certainly die immediately because of heat-related injuries or overpressure that would cause internal injuries. Those farther from the center of the explosion would suffer severe burns and would likely die from the effects soon afterward.

The shockwaves from thermobaric bombs also react differently than those of conventional explosives. Normal shockwaves would be stopped by hitting a wall, such as a bend in a cave. Thermobaric shockwaves travel through twists and turns in caves and other enclosed locations. The thermobaric detonation also consumes the oxygen in enclosed locations, causing those inside to suffocate.

The reaction that occurs in a thermobaric bomb is similar to that found in silo explosions and some industrial accidents. Silo explosions result when fine dust from grain mixes with air in the enclosed area of a silo and is ignited by heat, electrical sparks, or some other source. The resulting shock waves usually destroy the silos and surrounding structures.

The first attempt to develop a thermobaric bomb was by the Germans in World War II. A fuel mixture of 40 percent liquid oxygen was mixed with 60 percent dry brown coal powder. A test explosion of 8 kilograms destroyed trees within a 600-meter (650-yard) radius of the detonation. The war ended before the Germans were able to employ their bomb in action.

By the 1960s, both the United States and the Soviet Union had developed workable thermobaric bombs. In Vietnam, the United States used massive fuel-air munitions with great effect. The U.S. Air Force dropped massive 15,000-pound so-called Daisy Cutter bombs to create cleared areas for helicopter landing sites. The bombs used an aerosol action to create a cloud of fine droplets of liquid fuel just above the ground. When it was ignited, the resulting shock wave would flatten the trees for hundreds of yards around the ignition center. Unlike conventional bombs, the thermobaric weapons would not leave craters that would prevent helicopters from using the site. When the effects of the bombs were studied, commanders realized that they could use such bombs to destroy minefields and, in certain cases, to attack North Vietnamese cave complexes. There were many drawbacks to these weapons, however. They were never intended to work in confined areas and were so large that deployment was difficult.

The Daisy Cutter was also used in the 1991 Persian Gulf War. Uses included detonating minefields and destroying Iraqi trenches in the front-line defenses.

The Soviet Union developed smaller weapons during the 1960s, recognizing that thermobaric weapons can provide more power for the size than conventional weapons. Reportedly,

A BLU-118B thermobaric bomb ready for shipment at the Naval Surface Warfare Center, Indian Head, Maryland, on March 5, 2002. A thermobaric bomb was employed for the first time against Al Qaeda and Taliban forces in Afghanistan on March 2, 2002, during Operation ANACONDA. (AP/Wide World Photos)

the Soviets perfected artillery shells and shoulder-launched weapons that used thermobaric warheads. Rocket-propelled grenades (RPG) for individual soldiers were apparently used by Soviet forces during their border conflict with the Chinese in 1969. Reports of Soviet deployment of thermobaric weapons increased during the 1980s, when the Soviets employed them against the mujahideen rebels in Afghanistan. Russian forces also used thermobaric warheads against rebels in Chechnya. Reports from the fighting there compared the effects in an urban environment of one RPG with a thermobaric warhead to a conventional 152-millimeter artillery shell. The Russians have also developed a special weapons system capable of placing large numbers of thermobaric warheads onto a target. Known as the TOS-1 Buratino, it consists of a multiple rocket launcher on a T-72 tank chassis. The Buratino was used in Grozny during the Second Chechen War.

Other countries are known to have developed thermobaric weapons. Israel has fielded a fuel-air bomb for clearing minefields. The overpressure from the detonation either destroys or uncovers hidden mines quickly and effectively. The British are also believed to have thermobaric warheads, which can be delivered by weapons such as the Hellfire AGM-114N missile.

A new generation of thermobaric weapons was developed by the United States after the invasion of Afghanistan began in 2001. American planners quickly realized that the Taliban and Al Qaeda fighters would take cover in the many caves throughout the country. In October 2001, the U.S. Department of Defense ordered the acceleration of several projects that were being prepared as Advanced Concept Technology Demonstrations for use in the fighting there. A team of experts from all military services, the Department of Energy, and industry representatives took on the issue of dealing with hardened underground targets, including caves.

Work on the project began on October 11, 2001, and a prototype was ready on December 14, 2001. The solution developed by the team was a thermobaric bomb that could penetrate layers of rock and soil before exploding in an enclosed place. Known as BLU-118/B, the weapon consists of the same penetrating body used by the standard BLU-109 2000-pound bomb. Instead of high explosives, the weapon is filled with a newly developed thermobaric explosive mixture. A delayed action fuse permits the bomb to penetrate before exploding. The original BLU-118 was a 500-pound napalm weapon used during the Vietnam War.

The first test in which the BLU-118B bomb was dropped on a target took place on December 14, 2002, on a Nevada test range. A laser-guidance system was fitted to the bomb and it was dropped on a cave target from a McDonnell Douglas/Boeing F-15 Eagle attack aircraft. The tests were considered a complete success, and 10 weapons were immediately prepared for use in Afghanistan.

In March 2002, U.S. and Afghan forces were in action in Operation ANACONDA against Taliban and Al Qaeda forces near the Pakistani border. On March 3, one of the thermobaric weapons was dropped against a cave in which Al Qaeda fighters were hiding. The weapon struck near or at the mouth of the cave. Although military authorities refused to comment on the weapon's effectiveness in this instance, they announced that the concept had been proven. If a thermobaric weapon exploded in a cave or enclosed underground area, almost anyone within would be incinerated or die of internal injuries.

Additional thermobaric weapons were developed for use by American forces. During the invasion of Iraq in March–April 2003, U.S. Marines reportedly used shoulder-launched rockets with thermobaric warheads against some targets. Thermobaric warheads have also been developed for 40-mm grenades and for the AGM-114N Hellfire missile.

Perhaps inspired by American success in developing thermobaric weapons, the Russians exploded the largest such weapon ever made in September 2007. Nicknamed the "Father of All Bombs," it used 14,000 pounds of thermobaric fuel mixed with powdered aluminum.

Reportedly, terrorists have attempted to develop thermobaric bombs. Some weapons have used aluminum powder to enhance the conventional explosives also used. In 1983, the bomb that destroyed a barracks used by U.S. Marines in Lebanon was believed to have been enhanced by an explosive gas such as propane. The 1993 attack on the World Trade Center included three tanks of hydrogen in an attempt to create a more powerful blast. On September 21, 2008, a truck bomb that damaged the Islamabad Marriott Hotel included aluminum powder, which produced an extremely powerful explosion.

TIM J. WATTS

See also

Al Qaeda; ANACONDA, Operation; BLU-82/B Bomb; Bombs, Cluster; Taliban; World Trade Center Bombing

References

Boyne, Walter J. *Weapons of Desert Storm*. Chicago: Consumer Guide, 1991.

Naylor, Sean. *Not a Good Day to Die: The Untold Story of Operation Anaconda*. New York: Berkley Trade, 2006.

Werrell, Kenneth P. *Chasing the Silver Bullet: U.S. Air Force Weapons Development from Vietnam to Desert Storm*. Washington, DC: Smithsonian Institution Scholarly Press, 2003.

TIGER, Operation
Event Date: December 1990

Alternate plan developed by the U.S. Marine Corps Warfighting Laboratory at Quantico, Virginia, regarding the employment of marines in Operation DESERT STORM, the liberation of Kuwait. Marine Corps commandant General Alfred Gray instigated the planning as an alternate to the plan taking shape in Saudi Arabia under the direction of U.S. Central Command (CENTCOM) commander General H. Norman Schwarzkopf. Gray and a number of other senior Marine Corps officers were concerned about what they considered to be the high risks of a CENTCOM plan that would send the marines against the most fortified portion of the Iraqi defensive line.

Apprehensive about potential heavy marine casualties, Gray sent Secretary of Defense Richard Cheney a paper in which he proposed that the marines be utilized instead to open a "second front." Under this plan, urged on Gray by Lieutenant General Robert F. Milligan, commanding marine forces in the Pacific, the marines would attack Iraq from Turkey, Syria, western Jordan, or the Red Sea.

Gray's suggestion of an alternate land approach was dead on arrival. There was no likelihood of the marines being permitted to mount an attack from Turkey or Syria. Although both nations were part of the international coalition against Iraq, their military cooperation in it was strictly limited. A scenario involving Jordan was even less likely. Not a coalition member, Jordan had a large Palestinian population and was moreover one of the few nations supporting and supplying Iraq; U.S. policy was aimed at isolating Iraq in so far as was possible, and bringing Jordan into the fighting would only expand the battle front. Nothing, therefore, came of Gray's paper.

At the same time, Gray charged Marine Corps planners at Quantico, Virginia, to produce alternatives to the planned frontal assault on the Iraqi positions in southern Kuwait. Major General Matthew P. Caulfield headed this "Ad Hoc Study Team." The result of its labors was Operation TIGER, planning for which was completed at the end of December 1990.

TIGER was to be an amphibious operation. Although the opportunities for a landing from the Kuwaiti–Saudi Arabia border north to the Faw peninsula were limited, Caulfield believed that an amphibious assault would allow the marines to turn the Iraqi positions along the Kuwait border with Saudi Arabia. While the U.S. Army VII Corps turned Iraqi positions from the west, the marines would accomplish the same in the east, driving on Iraq's second largest city, Basra. Caulfield and marine planners believed that once Basra was taken, the entire Iraqi position to the south would collapse. At the time the plan was developed, Schwarzkopf had five marine divisions ashore and two afloat. Caulfield's plan would have seen these numbers reversed.

Gray had his reservations about the plan, but he allowed it to be sent to CENTCOM. Colonel Martin R. Steele, deputy director of the Warfighting Laboratory, carried the plan to the Gulf to be given to Lieutenant General Walter E. Boomer and to Vice Admiral Stanley Arthur, respectively the senior U.S. Marine Corps and U.S.

Navy officers. The plan was not to go directly to Schwarzkopf, who would not take kindly to a plan developed by Quantico less than a month before the start of the war. For the plan to have any hope of success, both Boomer and Arthur would have to endorse it and take it to Schwarzkopf.

Gray himself went to the theater at the end of December and received a briefing in which he was informed of the CENTCOM plan to send the 1st Marine Division north from eastern Saudi Arabia in a head-on attack against the most heavily fortified portion of the Iraqi defenses between the Wafra forest and where the Kuwaiti-Saudi border angles sharply to the northwest. Once a gap had been pried open, the 2nd Marine Division was to follow and engage the Iraqi mechanized forces immediately behind the fortified line. The Marine Corps had never before attempted to breach an enemy line on this scale. The Iraqis had sowed thousands of mines in the area, and little mine-clearing equipment was available, which would force one division to attack behind the other. Gray protested, calling the plan "another Tarawa" (in reference to the bloodbath experienced by the marines during their first major Pacific assault in November 1943 during World War II).

Gray then met privately with Schwarzkopf and expressed his reservations with the CENTCOM plan. He also sought to replace General Boomer. Schwarzkopf was surprised and upset that the Marine Corps commandant would want to change the battle plan and make an important personnel shift on such short notice, and he then met privately with Boomer, who pronounced his confidence in the CENTCOM plan. Schwarzkopf then rejected Gray's requests. Operation TIGER would not implemented.

As it turned out, Boomer's understanding of the realities on the ground regarding the Iraqis was correct. Although a number of marines were kept aboard ship and a naval task force was moved north in the Gulf in an apparent amphibious assault, it was only a feint designed to hold Iraqi coast defense units in place and keep them from reinforcing to the south.

SPENCER C. TUCKER

See also

Arthur, Stanley; Boomer, Walter; Cheney, Richard Bruce; Gray, Alfred M., Jr.; Schwarzkopf, H. Norman, Jr.

References

Gordon, Michael R., and General Bernard E. Trainor. *The Generals' War: The Inside Story of the Conflict in the Gulf.* New York: Little, Brown, 1995.

Schwarzkopf, H. Norman, with Peter Petre. *It Doesn't Take a Hero: General H. Norman Schwarzkopf, the Autobiography.* New York: Bantam Books, 1993.

Tigris and Euphrates Valley

An area of the Fertile Crescent largely occupied by present-day Iraq and referred to, in English, as the "cradle of civilization" because it was the birthplace of the world's earliest cultures. It is known in Arabic as *al-bilad al-rafhidhayn* ("land of the two rivers"; i.e., Mesopotamia). From the times of the Sumerians and Babylonians to the present, both the Tigris and the Euphrates rivers have been dammed to control flooding and harnessed for irrigation and hydroelectric power. For more than six millennia, they have been essential to the environmental, economic, and political makeup of the Persian Gulf region.

The Tigris River (Nahr al-Dijlah), the second largest river in Southwestern Asia, is 1,180 miles long; it arises in the Taurus Mountains of eastern Turkey, flows through Turkey and Syria, and joins the Euphrates River in southern Iraq at Qurna. The two rivers then form the Shatt al-Arab waterway, which empties into the Persian Gulf. By the time it reaches the Shatt al-Arab, 70 to 80 percent of the flow of the Tigris River has been diverted. Because the Tigris has been prone to flooding, which inundates large areas and collapses levees, both the Turkish and Iraqi governments have built dams and a diversion channel to control the problem.

The Euphrates (Nahr al-Furat), the longest river in Southwestern Asia at 1,730 miles, also has its origins in the highland regions of eastern Turkey, where its two major tributaries, the Murat and the Kara Su rivers, join. It flows through deep canyons and narrow gorges to Syria and, after joining with two more tributaries, it enters Iraq, where it joins with the Tigris. The river annually floods, caused by snow melting in the mountains of northeastern Turkey. The Euphrates, Greek for "fertilizing" or "fruitful," is one of the four rivers that Westerners believe flowed from the Garden of Eden, as detailed in the biblical book Genesis. It provided the water that led to the flowering of the Sumerian civilization in the fourth millennium BCE, and its river valley formed the heartland for the later empires of Babylonia and Assyria. For centuries, the river separated the Roman and Persian Empires. As the crossroads for trade between Egypt, India, and China, the Tigris-Euphrates River Valley has distinct geographical and political implications. The region has been subject to numerous invasions and controversies over the use of its waterways.

The valley's ecosystem of marshlands formed over thousands of years, but after Iraqi dictator Saddam Hussein's rise to power in the late 1970s, the ecology of the Tigris-Euphrates river system and salt marshes suffered greatly. It is estimated that up to 90 percent of the marshes and 60 percent of the wetlands were destroyed by Iraqi government policies. In the 1990s, Hussein's government water-control projects drained the marsh areas to gain military access to the region and to drive out the rebellious native Marsh Arabs, leaving only about 10,000 people. Dykes and dams were built that diverted the waters of the Tigris and Euphrates around the marshes, causing the vegetation and water that fed the surrounding soil and many of the native wildlife and their habitats to disappear. The drainage policy was reversed by the new Iraqi government following the 2003 Anglo-American–led invasion of Iraq, and roughly half of the marshes have now been restored, but whether they will fully recover is uncertain.

Lush, green fields in Iraq. Despite popular stereotypes of sand dunes and Bedouin tents, Iraq's geography is quite varied. The country's agricultural heart is the fertile zone between the Tigris and Euphrates rivers. (Steve Dutch, University of Wisconsin-Green Bay)

Controversy over water rights and use of the rivers remains. Since 1990, Turkey's Southeastern Anatolia Development Project has built 22 dams and 19 power plants. The Turkish government hopes that by the end of its development on the two rivers nearly 2 million hectares of land will be irrigated. Syria in 1993 completed the Tabaqah (Euphrates) Dam, to form a reservoir for irrigating cotton, but it and other dams have diverted much-needed water to Iraq. Building dams was not a priority during Hussein's regime, but Iraq now has seven dams in operation. Iraq is now concerned that construction of huge hydroelectric plants and dams along the two rivers by both Turkey and Syria will affect the social and economic stability of the region.

GARY KERLEY

See also
Marsh Arabs; Shatt al-Arab Waterway

References
Maxwell, Gavin. *People of the Reeds.* New York: Harper, 1957.
Metz, Helen Chapin, ed. *Iraq: A Country Study.* Washington, DC: Headquarters, Department of the Army, 1990.
Nicholson, Emma, and Peter Clark. *The Iraqi Marshlands: A Human and Environmental Study.* London: Politico's Publishing, 2002.
Thesiger, Wilfred. *The Marsh Arabs.* 2nd rev. ed. London: HarperCollins, 1985.

Tikrit

City in north-central Iraq, known primarily as the birthplace of Iraqi dictator Saddam Hussein and also as a center of the Iraqi resistance that began after the Anglo-American–led invasion of Iraq in 2003. The city is also the home of one of Hussein's many elaborate presidential palaces, known popularly by Iraqis as the Birthday Palace. Tikrit is located approximately 90 miles northnorthwest of Baghdad along the Tigris River. It serves as the administrative seat of Salahuddin Province. In 2002, prior to the Iraq War, it had a population of 550,000 people. Because of the war and the prolonged insurgency that has been centered in and around Tikrit, the city has lost a significant amount of its population, but the actual size of the exodus is not now known.

Tikrit is an old city; the first written references to it occurred in the early seventh century CE. In its earliest known history, it was known as Tagrit. The great 12th-century Muslim military leader Saladin (Salah-al din Yusuf ibn Ayyāb) was born in Tikrit. He fought Crusader forces under King Richard I of England to a standstill and captured Jerusalem in 1187. In September 1917, during World War I, Tikrit was overrun by British forces in the course of an offensive against the forces of the Ottoman Empire. A somewhat nondescript city, Tikrit gained great importance after Saddam Hussein's rise to power in the late 1970s, as he was born there on April 28, 1937. Hussein remained fiercely loyal to his Tikriti tribe (Al bu Nasir), centered in and around Tikrit, and many of his top advisers and government administrators came from that city. Hussein believed that he could trust only those from his own family or tribe. For the same reason, many of the commanders in Hussein's vaunted Iraqi Republican Guard also came from Tikrit.

Most coalition commanders believed that Hussein would seek refuge in Tikrit during an invasion of Iraq, so the city became the scene of great military concentration as soon as the Iraq War began in March 2003. Tikrit came under almost immediate and heavy aerial bombardment designed to flush out Hussein, his followers, and elements of the Republican Guard who might have sought a safe haven in the city. In April 2003, a contingent of several thousand U.S. marines and coalition forces descended on the city, accompanied by more than 300 armored vehicles, to secure it and search for any Hussein hold-outs. The city was taken with almost no resistance, but Hussein was nowhere to be found. Nevertheless, once Hussein had left Baghdad, presumably just before the invasion of Iraq began, he is believed to have fled to the vicinity of Tikrit, where he was sheltered and hidden by supporters and relatives. On December 13, 2003, U.S. forces found Hussein hidden in a small, underground bunker in a small town just outside Tikrit.

The Iraqi insurgency, meanwhile, has heavily involved Tikrit, located in the northern part of what has been called the Sunni Triangle. It has provided many insurgent fighters and has been the scene of numerous bombings and ambushes against coalition troops. By 2007, Tikrit had been partially pacified, and the U.S. Army, working with Iraqi officials, has begun to institute economic reforms in the area designed to improve education and increase job opportunities. A textile mill, the profits from which will help fund a vocational school, was already up and running by the end of 2007.

PAUL G. PIERPAOLI JR.

See also

Hussein, Saddam; Iraqi Insurgency; Republican Guard

References

Aburish, Said K. *Saddam Hussein: The Politics of Revenge.* New York: Bloomsbury, 2000.

Tripp, Charles. *A History of Iraq.* Cambridge: Cambridge University Press, 2007.

Tikriti, Hardan al-
Birth Date: 1925
Death Date: March 31, 1971

Prominent Baath Party leader and Iraqi Air Force general. Hardan Abd al-Ghaffar al-Tikriti was born in Tikrit in 1925, the son of a police officer. Like many other men of modest backgrounds from Tikrit, he joined the military and then the Baath Party. As a member of the Iraqi Air Force, Tikriti attended the Flight and Staff Academy in Baghdad and officially joined the Baath Party in 1961. He was an active Baath Party member and, as an officer who had reached the rank of brigadier general in the Iraqi Air Force by 1963, he was an extremely well-placed party member. After the Baath Party took control in Iraq with the 1963 coup, Tikriti assumed command of the Iraqi Air Force. He was a key member of the government, serving as a member of the National Council on the Revolutionary Command.

When Abd al-Salam Arif took over the government later that year, Tikriti and other moderate Baathists, such as Ahmed Hasan al-Bakr, sided with him, and Arif moved against other members of the Baath Party. As a reward for his support, Tikriti was given the post of minister of defense, which he held until 1964 when Arif began to ease Baathists out of his regime altogether. Tikriti's real power base had rested on the air force, but he was no longer its commander, and in March 1964 Arif felt secure enough to remove Tikriti as minister of defense.

Tikriti then became an active participant of the 1968 coup that ousted Arif. The coup proceeded without violence, and Tikriti was charged with informing Arif that he was to be relieved of power. He persuaded Arif to step down and withdraw to London, had a cup of tea with him, and personally escorted him to the airport.

After the coup, a Revolutionary Command Council headed the new regime with Ahmed Hasan al-Bakr as its chairman and the head of state. Tikriti regained his old positions as minister of defense and commander of the air force, but he also held the posts of deputy prime minister and deputy commander in chief and chief of staff. These posts effectively made Tikriti one of the most powerful men in Iraq and officially Bakr's second in command. The other prominent member of the council was Saddam Hussein, deputy chairman of the council for internal security and secretary general of the Baath party. All three men—Bakr, Hussein, and Tikriti—were from Tikrit. Bakr and Hussein, however, began to conspire against Tikriti because he had the strongest support among the military.

During the late 1960s and early 1970s, members of the Baathist government constantly jockeyed for position because they all recognized that the existing coalition would not last. Tikriti's conflicts with the minister of the interior, Salih Madhi Ammash, led to the dismissal of both men, and both were given the vice presidential posts. Ammash was backed by Saddam Hussein and the more civilian-oriented Baathists in his conflict with Tikriti, but the removal of both men opened up key ministries in the government that ultimately benefited Saddam Hussein. As both Ammash and Tikriti were military men, Hussein saw them as threats. Hussein was creating a new system of party apparatchiks attached to army commands who would report directly to him.

As Hussein's power grew, Tikriti's position became tenuous, and he received harsh criticism for his opposition to the use of an Iraqi brigade located in Jordan to support Palestinians against the Jordanian government in the Black September uprising of 1970. Tikriti's opposition was based on the relative weakness of the force and the potential danger of capture. Even so, his stance was pictured as disloyalty and served as a pretext to remove him from his government positions on October 15, 1970. This was part of a larger process that saw purges throughout the Iraqi government of men who had strong links to the military. These purges ultimately affected Bakr himself, while Hussein and the men from the security apparatus loyal to him continued to rise.

Recognizing Hussein's growing power, Tikriti chose to step down peaceably. He received the post as Iraqi minister to Algeria, but the Algerians refused to recognize his credentials as they had no interest in siding with one Iraqi faction over another. Rather than returning to Iraq, where he now had no position and no power, Tikriti went to Kuwait hoping for a change in Iraqi politics. He did not live long in Kuwait, however; he was shot and killed in Kuwait City on March 31, 1971. His demise has been attributed to Hussein.

MICHAEL K. BEAUCHAMP

See also

Arif, Abd al-Salam; Bakr, Ahmad Hassan al-; Hussein, Saddam; Iraq, History of, Pre-1990

References

Aburish, Said K. *Saddam Hussein: The Politics of Revenge.* New York: Bloomsbury, 2000.

Be'eri, Eliezer. *Army Officers in Arab Politics and Society.* New York: Praeger, 1970.

Tripp, Charles. *A History of Iraq.* Cambridge: Cambridge University Press, 2007.

Tillman, Patrick Daniel

Birth Date: November 6, 1976
Death Date: April 22, 2004

U.S. Army Ranger and professional football player. Tillman's April 2004 death in Afghanistan provoked a national controversy after it appeared that government officials had tried to hide the fact that he was a victim of friendly fire. Patrick Daniel Tillman was born in San Jose, California, on November 6, 1976. A natural-born athlete and a bright student, Tillman earned a football scholarship to Arizona State University in 1994, where he excelled as a linebacker and student, graduating in 1998 with a 3.8 grade point average. Voted the Pacific-10 Conference's Defensive Player of the Year for 1998, Tillman entered the National Football League (NFL) draft and became the 226th pick for that year. He began playing for the

Army corporal and former NFL star Pat Tillman in a 2003 military photo. Tillman's death in Afghanistan in 2004 from friendly fire was deliberately covered up by army authorities. (AP/World Wide Photos)

Arizona Cardinals that fall, playing the position of safety. In his first year, he started in 10 of the 16 games of the 1998–1999 season, an impressive feat for a rookie player. Tillman approached the game with gusto and was chosen by *Sports Illustrated* for its all-pro team for 2000.

Moved to enlist in the army after the September 11, 2001, terror attacks, Tillman completed the 2000–2001 season and joined the army in May 2002, along with his brother Kevin, a professional baseball player. In so doing, Tillman gave up a promising football career, a salary of more than $500,000 per year, and a pending contract that would have netted him $3.6 million over the succeeding three years.

Tillman and his brother wanted to become Army Rangers, and they completed the Ranger Indoctrination Program in the autumn of 2002 and were assigned to the 75th Ranger Regiment at Fort Lewis, Washington. Tillman was then deployed with his unit to Iraq, where he participated in the opening invasion of Operation IRAQI FREEDOM in March and April 2003. He returned to the United States and subsequently graduated from the U.S. Army's Infantry Center's Ranger School before deploying to Afghanistan in early 2004 with the rank of specialist.

The circumstances surrounding Tillman's death remain shrouded in controversy and mystery. While on patrol on April 22,

1242 Tomahawk BGM-109 Land Attack Missile

2004, Tillman was killed by three bullet wounds to the forehead. When family members were contacted by Department of Defense officials regarding Tillman's death, they were told that he had died from "hostile fire," meaning that he had been felled by enemy combatants. Because of Tillman's high-profile professional football career, his death generated much publicity. Indeed, he was the first professional football player to die in combat since 1970. The national media reported Tillman's death as a result of hostile fire.

However, more than a month after Tillman's death, on May 28, 2004, the Pentagon again contacted the family to say that Tillman had been the victim of friendly fire. The Tillman family, rightly outraged, believed that they had been lied to in an effort to cover up wrongdoing in the army and to protect army honor. Further, many have argued that the army's long delay in notifying the family of the true circumstances of Tillman's death was a way to take the spotlight off the death of a well-known and popular sports figure. Others have intimated that Tillman's criticism of the George W. Bush administration's handling of the war in Iraq and the War on Terror also was a factor in the botched cover-up. Complicating matters was the army's inexplicable failure to gather and hold on to crucial forensic evidence that might have shed more light on Tillman's death. The media turned the strange tale into a national phenomenon, and many Americans saw in it yet another reason to criticize Bush administration policies. Indeed, the growing insurgency in Iraq had already laid bare the shortcomings of Pentagon postinvasion planning and execution there.

Investigative reports seemed to confirm that the army knew from the beginning that Tillman's death was not the result of hostile fire. One report has alleged that some of Tillman's peers destroyed his uniform and body armor in an effort to hide evidence of a friendly fire incident. Those involved have been dismissed from the army. The cover-up also involved high-level army officials, who were accused of lying to the Tillman family and the American public.

Under great pressure, the inspector general of the Department of Defense opened an official investigation into Tillman's death in August 2005. That triggered a criminal investigation, conducted by the army, to determine if Tillman's death could be classified as negligent homicide. After an allegedly exhaustive investigation, in March 2007 the army ruled Tillman's death an "accident" due solely to friendly, not hostile, fire. Also in 2007, the U.S. House of Representatives held hearings on the matter, which compelled the Pentagon and White House to release hundreds of pages of documents. Mostly press clippings, the documents provided by the White House provided no new information, and indeed White House officials refused to release other documents, citing "confidentiality" concerns. The Tillman family remains unconvinced of the army's findings.

Promoted posthumously to the rank of corporal, Tillman was also awarded posthumously the Silver Star and the Purple Heart.

PAUL G. PIERPAOLI JR.

See also
Friendly Fire

References
Rand, Jonathan. *Fields of Honor: The Pat Tillman Story.* New York: Chamberlain Brothers, 2005.
Tillman, Mary, and Narda Zacchino. *Boots on the Ground at Dusk: My Tribute to Pat Tillman.* Old Saybrook, CT: Tantor Media, 2008.

Tomahawk BGM-109 Land Attack Missile

Long-range, all-weather, subsonic cruise missile, used by the U.S. Navy during Operation DESERT STORM, in various military operations in the 1990s, and during Operation IRAQI FREEDOM. General Dynamics began development of the long-range, all-weather, subsonic Tomahawk Land Attack Missile (TLAM), which is essentially an advanced ground-launched cruise missile (GLCM), in 1972. It was designed as a medium- to long-range missile to be fired from a submerged submarine. Production commenced in 1980. Because of corporate divestitures and acquisitions, Raytheon now makes the vast majority of the Tomahawks, although McDonnell Douglas manufactures some as well. The operational versions include the unitary conventional land attack TLAM-C, the bomblet-dispensing land attack TLAM-D, the nuclear land attack TLAM-A and TLAM-N, and the Tomahawk antiship missile.

The GLCM, an early version of the Tomahawk, could carry a tactical nuclear weapon. In the early 1980s, the United States deployed GLCMs to various bases in Western Europe to counter the numerical superiority of the Warsaw Pact. In 1987, U.S. president Ronald Reagan and Soviet general secretary Mikhail Gorbachev signed the Intermediate-Range Nuclear Forces (INF) Treaty by which both countries agreed to destroy their intermediate-range nuclear weapons and transporter-launchers. Most nuclear-capable Tomahawks were thus scrapped.

The Tomahawk, which usually carries a 1,000-pound warhead, is stored and launched from a pressurized canister that protects it during transportation. Four recommissioned Iowa-class battleships, several nuclear-powered cruisers, and the Virginia- and some Spruance-class destroyers used Armored Box Launchers (ABL) to store and protect the launch canisters. The ABL used gas pressure to eject the missile from the storage tube, and the missile's engine ignites after it exits the end of the tube. After the 1991 Persian Gulf War, the U.S. Navy decommissioned its ABL-equipped ships. Other surface ships and some submarines use the Vertical Launch System, derived from the launch tubes of submarine-launched ballistic missiles, which uses gas pressure to eject the missile from the canister. Other submarines use water impulse to eject their Tomahawks horizontally from a torpedo tube. The newer Los Angeles–class submarines use the Capsule Launch System. When the missile exits the water, a solid-fuel booster ignites for the first few seconds of airborne flight. After the missile transitions to cruise flight, its

A BGM-109 Tomahawk Land Attack Missile (TLAM) is launched toward a target in Iraq from the U.S. Navy guided-missile cruiser *Mississippi* during Operation DESERT STORM, January 1991. (U.S. Department of Defense)

wings unfold for lift, the air scoop is exposed, and a turbofan engine takes over to fly the missile to its target.

The missile, which weighs 3,200 pounds, flies at about 550 miles per hour and can maneuver like a radar-evading fighter plane while it skims 100 to 300 feet above the surface. Over water, the 18.3-foot long (20.5 feet with launcher) missile uses inertial guidance or the NAVSTAR Global Positioning System to follow a preset course. After crossing the shoreline, Terrain Contour Matching uses an on-board altimeter that measures the height from the TLAM to the ground to determine if the missile is in the right spot and makes any needed corrections if it does not match the prestored height. After the Tomahawk closes in on its target, the Digital Scene Matching Area Correlation system uses a computerized image of the flight path that is downloaded into the TLAM before launch to match against the actual image of the terrain below the missile in flight. If the pictures do not match, it will correct itself and then finish its mission, producing a claimed accuracy of about 10 meters (about 11 yards).

During Operation DESERT STORM, the U.S. Navy launched 297 Tomahawks, mostly during daylight, from the cruiser USS *San*

Jacinto in the Red Sea, attack submarines *Pittsburgh* and *Louisville,* and the battleships *Missouri* and *Wisconsin.* The Tomahawks hit 242 targets, which included surface-to-air missile sites, command and control centers, radar installations, electrical power facilities, and Iraq's presidential palace. The Tomahawks had their drawbacks, however, as they were less flexible and considerably more expensive than most conventional systems. Also, they had a smaller warhead, required a lengthy targeting process, and could not be retargeted after launch.

In the 1990s, President Bill Clinton employed Tomahawk cruise missiles as a primary military response to achieve political objectives and avoid unnecessary American military casualties. In January 1993, the United States fired 40 Tomahawks into Iraq after Iraq moved surface-to-air missile launchers into the southern no-fly zone. In June 1993, the United States launched 25 Tomahawks against the headquarters building of the Iraqi General Intelligence Service, which had been implicated in a series of car bombings and assassinations. During Operation DELIBERATE FORCE, in September 1995, the United States launched 13 missiles at Serbian positions, coercing Serbian president Slobodan Milosevic to agree to negotiations to end ethnic cleansing in Bosnia. In September 1996, 44 Tomahawks struck targets in central Iraq in retaliation for an Iraqi offensive against the Kurds. After the August 1998 car bombings of the American embassies in Kenya and Tanzania by Al Qaeda terrorists, the United States fired perhaps as many as 95 Tomahawks at Al Qaeda terrorist camps in Afghanistan and at a medical plant in Sudan (Operation INFINITE REACH). In December 1998, the United States launched over 300 Tomahawk missiles at targets in Iraq.

Although the Tomahawk attacks had mixed political and military results, they did allow Clinton to employ force without risk to American lives in preventing further ethnic cleansing in the Balkans and in countering global terrorism.

During Operation ALLIED FORCE in 1999, designed to force Serbia to cease ethnic cleansing of Kosovo, nine U.S. Navy surface ships and submarines off the Balkan coast fired Tomahawks at targets in Serbia. The cruise missiles destroyed nearly 50 percent of the fixed target list in key categories, including the Serbian Army and police headquarters. These missiles sustained the air campaign in the first couple of weeks, when aircraft with laser-guided bombs could not find targets because of bad weather.

Since March 2003 and the Anglo-American–led invasion of Iraq, the U.S. Navy has also expended many Tomahawks, essentially exhausting its stock of the weapons. A new Tactical Tomahawk will not reach the fleet in significant numbers at least until 2010. With the absence of future operational expenditures and the retirement of the remaining Tomahawk Block III missiles beginning in 2013, the U.S. Navy is under pressure to develop a new cruise missile to meet its operational requirements in the next decade.

ROBERT B. KANE

See also

Cruise Missiles, Employment of, Persian Gulf and Iraq Wars; INFINITE REACH, Operation; Missiles, Cruise

References

Keaney, Thomas A., and Eliot A. Cohen. *Gulf Air Power Survey Summary Report.* Washington, DC: Department of the Air Force, 1993.

Knights, Michael. *Cradle of Conflict: Iraq and the Birth of Modern U.S. Military.* Annapolis, MD: Naval Institute Press, 2005.

Owen, Robert C., ed. *Deliberate Force: A Case Study in Effective Air Campaigning.* Maxwell Air Force Base, AL: Air University Press, 2000.

Werrell, Kenneth P. *The Evolution of the Cruise Missile.* 2nd ed. Maxwell Air Force Base, AL: Air University Press, 1996.

Tonga

Small, constitutional monarchy located in the South Pacific that contributed a troop contingent to the Iraq War from 2004 to 2008. With a 2008 population of about 120,000 people, two-thirds of whom live on the principal island of Tongatapu, Tonga encompasses an archipelago of islands with a total land area of just 289 square miles. The island chain stretches nearly 500 miles north to south and is located south of Samoa and about one-third of the way from Hawaii to New Zealand. The only South Pacific island chain to avoid colonization by outside powers, Tonga joined the Commonwealth of Nations in 1970, chiefly as a measure to secure it defenses during the Cold War; before that, Tonga had concluded a protectorate agreement with the British for the same reason. King Taufa'ahau Tupou IV ruled until his death in 2006; he was succeeded by his son, King George Tupou II.

Tonga's monarchy is revered throughout the tiny nation, and unlike many European monarchies, it follows a strict line of lineal succession and has featured both male and female monarchs. The nation's political system is quite liberal and offers free education and health care to all citizens. There is virtually no heavy industry in Tonga; the majority of its income is derived from agricultural exports and a large number of Tongans who live abroad (mainly in New Zealand, Australia, and the United States) and remit part of their incomes to family members in Tonga. The tiny country has historically enjoyed close relations with the industrialized powers of the West, and for that reason its foreign policy has been pro-American and pro-British. The Tonga Defence Services (TDS) has military cooperation agreements with both New Zealand and Australia and a similar agreement with the U.S. military, which periodically trains its personnel. For these reasons, Tonga dispatched a 55-man troop detachment to the Iraq War in late 2004.

The TDS, which maintains a standing force of only 450 people, dispatched men from its Royal Marines unit. In Iraq, the Tongan personnel chiefly performed security and support functions for other coalition troops. On December 5, 2008, the Tongan Royal Marines left Iraq, presumably for good. The Tonga contingent suffered no casualties during its deployment.

PAUL G. PIERPAOLI JR.

See also

IRAQI FREEDOM, Operation, Coalition Ground Forces; New Zealand, Role in Persian Gulf, Afghanistan, and Iraq Wars

References

"Background Note: Tonga." U.S. Department of State, December 2009, http://www.state.gov/r/pa/ei/bgn/16092.htm.

Susman, Tina. "Tonga Troops End Iraq Mission." *Los Angeles Times,* December 5, 2008.

Topography, Afghanistan

Located in south-central Asia and studded with high mountains and foreboding steppes and plateaus, Afghanistan is strategically located at the crossroads of Asia and the Middle East. It is bordered by Turkmenistan, Uzbekistan, and Tajikistan to the north, Iran to the west, and Pakistan to the east and south. More than 50 percent of its entire border is shared with Pakistan, the majority of which is comprised of rugged mountains and highlands. These areas have been the traditional dwelling place and training locale for the terrorist group Al Qaeda, which was responsible for the September 11, 2001, terrorist attacks against the United States. The long (1,640 miles) and sometimes impenetrable border with Pakistan has often been the focal point of U.S. and coalition-led raids against Al Qaeda, Taliban fighters, and other insurgents. Despite the rugged terrain and harshness of the climate, however, the border has proven to be quite porous, much to the dismay of the United States, and tracking down terrorists, including Al Qaeda ringleader Osama bin Laden, has been difficult, if not impossible.

With an area of 252,772 square miles, Afghanistan is sparsely populated, with a total population of less than 32 million. The mountainous regions and high-altitude highlands are the least populated areas of the country. One of the most mountainous nations in the world, Afghanistan is home to the Hindu Kush mountain range, a subrange of the Himalayas, which soars above much of the Afghani-Pakistani border region. The highest peak in Afghanistan is Noshaq, which soars almost five miles above sea level at 24,557 feet. Just 12.3 percent of Afghanistan's land mass is currently used to sustain permanent agricultural pursuits. Much of the country is unsuitable for crops because of high mountains, lack of water, and poor, rocky soil. There are four major rivers in Afghanistan: the Amu, Hari, Kabul, and Helmand rivers.

In general, Afghanistan is a dry, continental climate with cold winters and hot summers. In the mountainous regions, snow cover can be year-round; in the low plains and deserts in the south and southeast, however, there is very little rainfall and summer temperatures are torrid. The Sistan Basin, located in southeastern Iran and southwestern Afghanistan, is one of the driest areas on the globe. The large plains of the north and west have the most consistently mild climate of all the nation's regions. In the south and southwest, floods and droughts are most frequent, while the

The Hindu Kush Mountains north of Bagram Air Base in Afghanistan. (Dennis5514/Dreamstime.com)

Hindu Kush Mountains and other ranges are often shrouded in deep snow and clouds and frequently have subzero temperatures at the higher elevations.

Afghanistan is located on active fault lines, so periodic and devastating earthquakes do occur. In a May 1998 earthquake centered northeast of the Hindu Kush Mountains, as many as 4,000 people were killed, and an estimated 125 villages were partly or totally destroyed. Afghanistan is resource and mineral-rich, although few of its resources have been exploited. Among the significant deposits to be found here are copper, zinc, iron ore, silver, gold, uranium, chromite, salt, and other minerals. It is believed that there are plentiful oil and natural-gas reserves in the north, although these have remained largely untapped because the nation has been under foreign occupation and/or civil war for almost 30 years.

Afghanistan's wildly varied and often harsh climates, rugged terrain, and high mountains make it a very difficult place in which to prosecute a war. The Soviets discovered this during their long and fruitless 1980–1988 occupation, and American and coalition forces have found this to be the case since 2001. Indeed, many U.S. Army Special Forces and Ranger teams have carried out missions on horseback, because some areas are virtually unreachable by any other means. As well, Afghanistan is landlocked, which means that anything going into the country must be flown in or trucked in overland.

Paul G. Pierpaoli Jr.

See also

Afghanistan; Afghanistan, Climate of; Al Qaeda; Bin Laden, Osama; Taliban

References

Ewans, Martin. *Afghanistan: A Short History of Its History and Politics.* New York: Harper Perennial, 2002.

McCauley, Martin. *Afghanistan and Central Asia: A Modern History.* London: Longman Publishing Group, 2002.

Topography, Kuwait and Iraq

Kuwait, which encompasses just 6,969 square miles (a bit smaller than the state of New Jersey), is a Middle Eastern nation that lies in the northwestern corner of the Arabian Peninsula. It borders Saudi Arabia to the south, Iraq to the west and north, and the Persian Gulf to the east. Despite its small size, it boasts a 120-mile sea

The Dokan River in Sulaimaniyah, Kurdistan, in northern Iraq. (iStockPhoto)

coast and has nine off-shore islands, including Bubiyan, the largest island, which encompasses 333.2 square miles.

Kuwait is essentially flat desert, which slopes gradually down from the extreme west of Shigaya and Salmi (the highest areas of the nation, about 950 feet above sea level), east to the Persian Gulf. Between west and east are a series of shallow valleys and very low hills, including Kura al-Maru, Liyah, Shagat al-Jleeb, and Afris. The southeastern portion of the country is entirely flat, with the notable exception of Ahmadi Hill, which is approximately 450 feet above sea level. A desert region that receives very little rainfall, Kuwait has no mountains and is the only nation in the world that does not have any natural lakes, reservoirs, or rivers. Fresh water is a precious commodity and is supplied mainly via limited underground supplies, neighboring countries, and, increasingly, by large desalinization plants along the coast. Because of Kuwait's relatively flat topography and lack of surface water or mountains, the area has traditionally been a crossroads for nomads and a gathering place in which to do business and conduct trade. That same topography, however, makes the small nation vulnerable to invasion, such as the Iraqi invasion of Kuwait in August 1990.

There are approximately 2.4 million people living in Kuwait, the vast majority of whom live in and around the coastal capital at Kuwait City. Less than 1 percent of Kuwait's landmass is used for agriculture, as the region's torrid climate and lack of rainfall render permanent agricultural pursuits very difficult. Because of lack of vegetation and a lack of rainfall, Kuwait is subject to raging sandstorms, especially in June and July, when high temperatures average 107°F to 114°F in most of the country.

Kuwait is home to the world's fifth-largest known petroleum reserve, which dominates the economy. Eighty percent of the government's revenue is derived from oil sales, which make up nearly 95 percent of the country's exports. During the 1991 Persian Gulf War, when Iraqi forces set ablaze hundreds of Kuwaiti oil wells as they retreated into Iraq, they unleashed an environmental catastrophe. Soot and huge lakes of oil rendered a sizable portion of southern and southeastern Kuwait virtually uninhabitable. Even today, more than 5 percent of Kuwait's landmass is covered by a semiliquified asphaltlike coating, rendering it virtually impossible to traverse.

With a landmass of 169,234 square miles (slightly larger than California) and a population of 29.3 million, Iraq is far more varied topographically than its neighbor Kuwait. It boasts a number of large cities, and the population is far more evenly distributed than that of Kuwait. Iraq occupies the northwestern portion of the Zagros mountain range, the eastern edge of the Syrian Desert, and the northwestern part of the Arabian Desert. It is bordered by

TOPOGRAPHY OF THE ARABIAN PENINSULA

Kuwait to the south, Saudi Arabia to the south and west, Syria to the northwest, Turkey to the north, and Iran to the east. Nearly land-locked, Iraq's only access to the Persian Gulf is in the far southeastern part of the country, near the Iranian and Kuwait border. The Shatt al-Arab Waterway, on the Iraqi-Iranian border, is also a key access point to the Persian Gulf.

Mainly a desert climatologically, Iraq nevertheless has varied weather and seasons. It has several large surface water supplies, including lakes and reservoirs. Its two main river systems are the Tigris and Euphrates, which bifurcate the country roughly in the middle and parallel each other. Between the two rivers is rich, fertile, arable land in which many of Iraq's farming activities take place. The far northern part of Iraq is quite mountainous, especially near the Turkish and Iranian borders. Steppes and highland yield to mountain ranges as high as 13,000 feet above sea level. Agriculture is possible here at the lower elevations, and rainfall tends to be highest in this region. In the south and southeast, near the delta of the Tigris and Euphrates rivers, the land is punctuated by large marshes, which Iraqi president Saddam Hussein attempted to eradicate in the late 1980s and early 1990s. The vast deserts in the south and southwest of the country are relatively flat and feature a classic desert environment, with scarce rainfall, torrid summers, and brief, cool (and sometimes rainy) winters. Located in the central part of Iraq, Baghdad, the capital, has a

population of about 7 million people and has a modified desert climate; summers are long and blisteringly hot, but the winters are cooler and wetter than those in the southern desert regions.

The most sparsely populated areas of Iraq are in the southern and southwestern deserts, where pastoral nomadic tribes chiefly reside. About 12 percent of Iraq's landmass in currently taken up by agriculture. The nation is home to the word's second-largest known oil reserves (behind only Saudi Arabia), although it is estimated that there remains a vast amount of oil in Iraq that has not been tapped. Other natural resources are notably absent in any significant amounts in Iraq. Except in the northeast, Iraq is subject to periodic, seasonal sandstorms that can reduce visibility to less than a tenth of a mile. In the planning for Operations DESERT STORM and IRAQI FREEDOM, U.S. military planners had to take into account the possibility of such storms. Both invasions were set for late winter and early spring to avoid the intense heat of Iraqi summers.

PAUL G. PIERPAOLI JR.

See also

Kuwait; Middle East, Climate of; Shatt al-Arab Waterway

References

Marr, Phebe. *The Modern History of Iraq*. 2nd ed. Boulder, CO: Westview, 2003.

Rodgers, Mary, ed. *Iraq in Pictures: Visual Geography Series*. Minneapolis: Lerner Publications, 1990.

Tora Bora

Mountainous and geographically remote region of eastern Afghanistan located directly north of the Afghan-Pakistan border and running more than 15 miles through the White Mountains. Tora Bora means "black dust." Although Tora Bora formally denotes a region of Afghanistan, it is commonly associated with the fortified cave complex used by mujahideen fighters in the war against the Soviet Union in the 1980s and Al Qaeda and the Taliban during the U.S. invasion of Afghanistan in late 2001. It was also the scene of a U.S. cruise missile raid in August 1998.

An area with a largely undocumented military history, the Tora Bora region possessed ties to unconventional military forces dating back at least to the early 1900s. The poorly developed infrastructure and complex logistical supply chains leading to the region offered guerrilla forces refuge from direct action. An area with peaks in excess of 14,000 feet that is often buffered by extreme weather, Tora Bora has a geographic suitability heightened by its immediate proximity to neighboring Pakistan.

During the Soviet occupation of Afghanistan (1979–1989), the U.S. Central Intelligence Agency (CIA) contributed substantially to the fortification and militarization of Tora Bora. Contributing war matériel, weapons, and advisory services, the CIA used Tora Bora as a training and logistics hub. The remoteness of the region enhanced the ability to train, equip, and deploy forces outside of Soviet-controlled areas. Tora Bora also served the mujahideen throughout the Soviet occupation and remained uncompromised through the Soviet withdrawal.

In the 1990s, Tora Bora again became an area of significance as the Taliban turned the military complex there into a training and housing area for jihadists. Osama bin Laden, the Saudi-born leader of the terrorist group Al Qaeda, also used Tora Bora as a training camp and base of operations. Although it was connected to many terrorist acts throughout the 1990s, Tora Bora escaped direct action until 1998. In reprisal for the August 7, 1998, U.S. embassy bombings in Tanzania and Kenya, which had been perpetrated by Al Qaeda, President Bill Clinton ordered cruise missile strikes against alleged terrorist camps in Tora Bora. These strikes were part of Operation INFINITE REACH (August 28, 1998), which witnessed the bombing of both Tora Bora and targets in Sudan. However, the operation resulted in only limited tangible impact to camp operations in Tora Bora.

These actions aside, the December 2001 pitched battle between U.S.-led coalition forces and the combined Taliban/Al Qaeda forces will likely define Tora Bora's history for the foreseeable

Afghan anti-Taliban fighters pray in front of their tank, overlooking the White Mountains of Tora Bora in northeastern Afghanistan, on December 10, 2001. (AP/Wide World Photos)

future. Following the September 11, 2001, terrorist attacks on the United States, President George W. Bush deployed military forces to Afghanistan in Operation ENDURING FREEDOM. Beginning in November 2001, coalition forces systematically destroyed Taliban and Al Qaeda units throughout Afghanistan in all but the most remote regions. As part of a final effort to avoid annihilation or surrender, Taliban and Al Qaeda forces understandably converged on the Tora Bora region for refuge.

Supported by substantial air power that relied heavily on precision-guided weapons, the U.S.-led coalition conducted military actions against the units defending Tora Bora for much of December 2001. With the assistance of Afghan troops, U.S. Special Operations Forces (SOF) led a focused and decisive campaign against the Tora Bora defenders. In less than two weeks, the coalition had secured the Al Qaeda complex and surrounding areas. Bin Laden, however, was never found and, as of this writing, remains at large.

Former CIA officer Gary Berntsen, who had charge of the CIA effort to capture or kill bin Laden, claimed in his book *Jawbreaker* (2005) that his group had pinpointed bin Laden's location in Tora Bora and that, had the military personnel Berntsen requested been committed, bin Laden would not have escaped.

The U.S. operations against Tora Bora in late 2001 represented the first effective integration of precision airpower in support of SOF in a full-scale and independent military operation. Most analysts agree that the decision to rely heavily on poorly trained and inadequately equipped Afghan allies rather than committing larger numbers of U.S. special operations forces permitted the Al Qaeda leadership to escape. This called into question the feasibility of combined operations by advanced Western military forces with Developing-World partners. Finally, questions remain about the feasibility of conducting direct action against an enemy that lacks both a geographic and political epicenter.

SCOTT BLANCHETTE

See also

Al Qaeda; Bin Laden, Osama; Bush, George Walker; Clinton, William Jefferson; ENDURING FREEDOM, Operation; INFINITE REACH, Operation; Soviet-Afghanistan War; Taliban

References

Bergen, Peter L. *Holy War, Inc.: Inside the Secret World of Osama bin Laden.* New York: Touchstone, 2002.

Berntsen, Gary, and Ralph Pezzullo. *Jawbreaker: The Attack on Bin Laden and Al-Qaeda; A Personal Account by the CIA's Key Field Commander.* New York: Crown, 2005.

Biddle, Stephen. *Afghanistan and the Future of Warfare: Implications for Army and Defense Policy.* Carlisle, PA: Strategic Studies Institute, 2002.

Torture of Prisoners

Torture is generally defined as the deliberate infliction of pain, whether physical or psychological, on a victim or a prisoner for a variety of purposes. In wartime, torture has historically been most commonly used as an interrogation technique to extract intelligence information from prisoners of war (POWs) in a rapid fashion. Otherwise, it has been used as a punishment and method of dehumanization. This has been particularly true in the various recent Middle East wars. Torture has also been routinely employed to achieve propaganda advantage, as in securing confessions or testimonials denouncing the policies of their own government.

Torture is banned by international law as a fundamental violation of human rights, whether inflicted on enemies or one's own population. It is specifically banned by the Third and Fourth Geneva Conventions (1929 and 1949), as well as the United Nations Convention against Torture (1987). Torture nonetheless remains a disturbingly common aspect of contemporary conflicts, and not only in the Middle East. Beyond wartime, the United Nations Convention against Torture regards capital punishment as well as many of the sanctioned legal punishments in Iran, Saudi Arabia, Libya, Pakistan, and under the Taliban to be torture.

Torture was long an established part of judicial procedure to extract confessions and was regularly employed, for example, during the Spanish Inquisition. Only in the past two centuries have there been concerted efforts to ban torture and establish penalties for its use.

There is an ongoing debate over what constitutes torture by nations that do not conform to international standards. Some nations have regularly employed drugs to extract information from prisoners and interrogators have routinely used sleep deprivation, enforced positions, light and sound bombardment, harassment, beatings, waterboarding, removal of teeth and fingernails, confinement in extremely small spaces, severe cold, and electric shocks to secure what they seek. In the United States, some police departments and law enforcement agencies had, even prior to September 11, 2001, assaulted detainees.

Amnesty International reported that more than 150 nations routinely employed torture in the period 1997 to 2000. Clearly, it remains a prominent human rights issue into the 21st century.

In the Middle East, a region that contains numerous totalitarian regimes as well as religious strife, torture has played a role in internal security, warfare, and in struggles between political movements. Israel has long used assault, sleep deprivation, enforced bodily positions, electric shock (more recently forbidden), and other "coercive interrogation" methods when questioning suspected Palestinian terrorists. Although the Israeli Supreme Court ruled that all torture was illegal, allegations of degrading and inhuman treatment of Palestinian detainees continue to be leveled against Israeli authorities. Likewise, the government of Saudi Arabia claims that torture is against Islamic law, but there is ample evidence that the Saudi regime continues to employ torture, particularly against domestic prisoners. In addition, the punishments of lashing, beheading, and amputation are considered torture by the United Nations (UN), but Saudi Arabia does not accept this position. Similar evidence of the routine use of torture in interrogations of suspects has been documented in Egypt, Iran, Iraq, Jordan, Lebanon, and Syria.

During the Israeli-Arab War of 1948–1949, the 1967 Six-Day War, and the 1973 Yom Kippur (Ramadan) War, each side accused the other of torturing POWs. There is strong evidence that prisoners were subjected to physical beatings and other forms of punishment to discover useful information and that many were killed. During the Iran-Iraq War (1980–1988), both belligerents were accused of torturing prisoners. Sometimes, the torture was designed to elicit information for tactical use on the battlefield; more often, however, the torture was for purely sadistic reasons, to punish an enemy.

In the 1991 Persian Gulf War (Operation DESERT STORM), captured coalition pilots were paraded before international news cameras showing signs of physical injuries. Upon their release, American pilots reported that they had been beaten by their Iraqi captors, who demanded that they renounce their religious beliefs in favor of Islam and that they sign statements admitting to war crimes.

During the U.S.-led Global War on Terror (from 2001), American military forces have been repeatedly accused of torturing suspected terrorists to obtain information about planned attacks on U.S. targets. In particular, human rights advocates have accused U.S. authorities of employing inhumane and degrading treatment against detainees at the Guantánamo Bay Naval Base in Cuba. This included severe beatings, waterboarding, sleep deprivation, and sensory deprivation. The detainees also claimed that they received threats of bodily harm and were humiliated sexually and forced to remain in uncomfortable positions for prolonged periods. Despite international condemnation, the United States has refused to release the majority of the prisoners held at Guantánamo Bay, has yet to charge them with a particular crime, and has not opened the facility to international observers or the media. After his administration took office in January 2009, President Barack Obama directed that the Guantánamo Bay facility be closed within a year. However, as of April 2010 it remains open, and its closure does not seem imminent.

In 2003, after the U.S.-led Operation IRAQI FREEDOM began, allegations of torture perpetrated by U.S. military personnel began to surface. These first concerned the infamous Abu Ghraib prison in Baghdad. Abu Ghraib had served as a major detention facility under the dictatorship of Saddam Hussein, and unspeakable offenses had been committed there against opponents of the regime and other prisoners. After U.S. forces took Baghdad in April 2003, they began using the prison to hold suspected terrorists and members of the Iraqi military. In April 2004, the prison came to the public's attention when photographs of naked prisoners, some hooded and attached to electrical wires, were published in a variety of media sources. An internal U.S. Army investigation determined that some guard personnel, led by Army Specialist Charles Graner, had instigated the mistreatment of prisoners without official sanction. A number of the individuals were charged and brought to trial. Others, such as those in authority, saw their military careers ended because of the scandal.

By mid-2005, there was mounting evidence that the United States had indeed engaged in torture in Afghanistan, Iraq, and

An Afghan detainee is escorted to a security cell at the U.S. detention facility at Guantánamo Bay, Cuba, May 9, 2003. Guantánamo has held suspected Al Qaeda members since 2001 and has been widely criticized by human rights organizations for holding the prisoners without formal charge. (U.S. Department of Defense)

Guantánamo, and rumors circulated concerning torture at the secret detention facilities believed to be in Jordan, Morocco, Eastern Europe, and elsewhere. This prompted a public outcry as well as protests from Human Rights Watch, Amnesty International, and even the UN. On December 30, 2005, President George W. Bush signed legislation passed by Congress that banned the torture of detainees, although critics pointed out that the president can still approve such tactics by using his broad powers as commander in chief. The law was enacted after an acrimonious fight between the Bush administration and many members of Congress, at the time controlled by his own Republican Party.

On June 12, 2008, the U.S. Supreme Court dealt the Bush administration a severe blow when it declared that suspected terrorist detainees at Guantánamo Bay may petition U.S. civilian courts to release them. The *Boumediene v. Bush* case essentially gave enemy combatants the right to file a writ of habeas corpus in a U.S. court. Just a few weeks later, on June 23, a Federal appeals court struck down the Bush administration's classification of detainees at

Guantánamo as "enemy combatants." Many argued for the closing of the Guantánamo detention facility, including some within the Bush administration, and the decision to do this by the Obama administration received the endorsement of the commander of the U.S. Central Command (CENTCOM), General David Petraeus. The disposition of the prisoners at Guantánamo remains the principal stumbling block. Thus, some claim that the Yemeni prisoners, who constitute a large number of those held there, should not be returned to Yemen. The concern is that an indigenous movement linked to Al Qaeda is known to be active there.

PAUL J. SPRINGER

See also
Abu Ghraib; Coercive Interrogation; DESERT STORM, Operation; Iran-Iraq War; IRAQI FREEDOM, Operation; Prisoners of War, Persian Gulf War

References
Danner, Mark. *Torture and Truth: America, Abu Ghraib, and the War on Terror.* New York: New York Review Books, 2004.
Friedman, Lori, ed. *How Should the United States Treat Prisoners in the War on Terror?* Farmington Hills, MI: Greenhaven, 2005.
Hersh, Seymour. *Chain of Command: The Road from 9/11 to Abu Ghraib.* New York: HarperCollins, 2004.
Human Rights Watch. *Behind Closed Doors: Torture and Detention in Egypt.* New York: Human Rights Watch, 1992.
———. *Torture and Ill-Treatment: Israel's Interrogation of Palestinians from the Occupied Territories.* New York: Human Rights Watch, 1994.
Meeropol, Rachel, and Reed Brody. *America's Disappeared: Secret Imprisonment, Detainees, and the "War on Terror."* New York: Seven Stories, 2005.
Sampson, William. *Confessions of an Innocent Man: Torture and Survival in a Saudi Prison.* Toronto: McClelland and Stewart, 2005.
Zabecki, David T. "Torture: Lessons From Vietnam and Past Wars." *Vietnam* (October 2008): 32–35.

Transportation Security Administration

U.S. government agency created in 2001 designed to oversee the safety of American ports, freeways, railroads, mass transit systems, buses, and airline terminals. The Transportation Security Administration (TSA) was established on November 19, 2001, by the Aviation and Transportation Security Act, which was a reaction to the September 11, 2001, terror attacks against the United States. Because the September 11 attacks were all carried out via commercial jetliners, the U.S. Congress and the George W. Bush administration acted quickly to shore up airline and airport security and also sought to secure other potential transportation venues from possible terrorist attacks.

The TSA concentrates most of its efforts on air security and employs the most workers for that purpose. The TSA has become ubiquitous in all U.S. airports, and the flying public is well versed in the standard safety procedures that all airline passengers must submit to before boarding commercial aircraft. There are currently no standardized safety steps involved for privately owned aircraft. At its peak in 2003, the TSA employed about 60,000 transportation security personnel; that number has dwindled to as low as 42,000 in recent years.

Prior to the promulgation of the TSA, airport security was a highly decentralized affair with only nominal oversight by the federal government. Before November 2001, airport security was entrusted to private security companies hired by: an individual airline; an individual terminal within a given airport; or the operator of an airport (sometimes a municipality, a county, or even an independent airport authority). Although some private security companies are still under contract to conduct airport security, they are all closely supervised by the TSA. Airport and airline security before 2001 was spotty and often depended on the initiative of individual airports or airlines. The result was a lack of overall coordination and lax and inconsistent procedures, which the September 11 terrorist hijackers were able to exploit.

The TSA has tried, with some success, to standardize security checks at the 450-plus airports around the country and to tighten restrictions on passengers and cargo/baggage to lessen the likelihood of another airborne terrorist attack. In addition to screening

Employees of the Transportation Security Administration (TSA) use wands to screen passengers as they pass through the security checkpoint in the main terminal of Denver International Airport, September 11, 2002. (AP/Wide World Photos)

passengers and conducting random background checks, the TSA is also responsible for scrutinizing all checked baggage and cargo that is loaded into the holds of commercial airplanes.

It took the TSA quite a while to attain the technology and man-power to check baggage and cargo, which elicited concerns that the agency's efforts were hollow ones, as virtually anyone could have rigged a piece of checked luggage or another piece of cargo with an explosive device. That has since been rectified. Until December 1, 2003, the TSA also administered the Federal Air Marshal Service, which places undercover but well-armed air marshals aboard random flights to discourage hijackers or other in-air troublemakers. The Air Marshal Service was transferred to the U.S. Bureau of Immigration and Customs Service on December 2, 2003. It has since been transferred back to the aegis of the TSA. Some have complained that there are far too few air marshals to detour would-be terrorists, but that is subject to debate since the exact number of them employed is classified information. The TSA also administers the Federal Flight Deck Officer Program, which empowers and trains pilots to carry firearms in the cockpit of an airplane to thwart would-be hijackers.

The TSA is also charged with administering security programs for other modes of transportation as well as securing ports, rail-roads, and highways. Its efforts in these areas are much less well known and in fact appear to take a backseat to air security. There has been much concern in recent years, for example, over the safety of America's ports, where security has heretofore been lax or nonexistent. Only fairly recently has the TSA begun implementing tougher security regulations in cargo ports, where it has begun to place radiation- and explosive-detecting devices that scrutinize all cargo coming in and out of port. It is unknown what, if anything, the TSA has done to secure rail lines and public transit systems, although the need to keep such measures classified may explain the lack of information.

The TSA began as an arm of the U.S. Department of Transportation, but on March 1, 2003, it fell under the administrative aegis of the U.S. Department of Homeland Security, a newly created, cabinet-level agency charged with preventing terrorist attacks and responding to natural and man-made disasters. The TSA's current budget is about $7.8 billion per year, the majority of which is spent on airline and airport security. Some have derided the agency for its sometimes lax and uneven security procedures, which have included the failure to detect weapons and bombs in baggage or on the person of an air traveler. At the other extreme, the specter of elderly people being subjected to body searches has angered many. Some civil rights groups have charged the TSA with Orwellian tactics that violate basic human rights, like the use of "Behavior Detection Officers," who scrutinize passengers in security lines and single out people they deem "suspicious." As one might expect, these officers often single out many passengers with Middle Eastern or Muslim names or appearances. Despite these problems, however, most Americans have accepted the TSA as the price to pay for increased security during an age of terrorism.

PAUL G. PIERPAOLI JR.

See also
September 11 Attacks; United States Department of Homeland Security

References
Shane, Peter M., John Podesta, and Richard C. Leone, eds. *A Little Knowledge: Privacy, Security, and Public Information after September 11.* New York: Century Foundation, 2004.
Talbot, Strobe, and Nayan Chanda, eds. *The Age of Terror: America and the World After September 11.* New York: Basic Books, 2002.

Troop Surge
See Surge, U.S. Troop Deployment, Iraq War

Truman, Harry S.
Birth Date: May 8, 1884
Death Date: December 26, 1972

U.S. senator (1935–1944), vice president (January–April 1945), and president (1945–1953). Born in Lamar, Missouri, on May 8, 1884, Harry S. Truman worked as a bank teller and farmer before seeing combat in World War I as an artillery captain in France. He then opened a clothing store in Kansas City, but it soon failed, leaving him with large debts. He won an election to be a county judge in 1922 with the backing of nearby Kansas City's political Pendergast Machine, and his record of efficiency and fair-mindedness earned him considerable respect. A Democrat, in 1934 he won a seat in the U.S. Senate, where colleagues appreciated his hard work, modesty, and amiability. Reelected in 1940, he earned national prominence during World War II as chair of a Senate committee investigating corporate waste, bureaucratic incompetence, contractor fraud, and labor abuse in defense industries.

Truman was the surprise choice to be the vice presidential candidate on President Franklin D. Roosevelt's successful 1944 reelection ticket. Truman had no international experience when he assumed the presidency upon Roosevelt's sudden death in April 1945. Truman closely guarded his authority and took actions that were decisive and at times impulsive. This was especially true in foreign affairs, where he immediately faced the challenge of emerging discord with the Soviet Union.

In July and August 1945 Truman and Soviet leader Joseph Stalin met at the Potsdam Conference but did not reach agreement on any major issues. While there, Truman received word that the test explosion of an atomic bomb had succeeded, although he made only an ambiguous reference about this to Stalin. Truman subsequently ordered atomic attacks on two Japanese cities in August. His justification was to save American lives, but he may have also used Hiroshima and Nagasaki to intimidate the Soviets and prevent them from occupying portions of northeast Asia. Although the Soviets did enter the war in the Pacific just before

Harry S. Truman succeeded to the presidency on the death of Franklin D. Roosevelt on April 12, 1945. Truman's presidency was marked by important foreign policy decisions, including the Truman Doctrine, U.S. recognition of Israel, the Marshall Plan, the North Atlantic Treaty Organization (NATO), and the U.S. military intervention in Korea. (Harry S. Truman Presidential Library)

Japan surrendered, Truman rejected Stalin's request to participate in the occupation of Japan.

Meanwhile, Truman struggled to end the civil war in China between the Guomindang (Nationalists) and the communists under the leadership of Mao Zedong. Late in 1945 Truman sent General George C. Marshall to negotiate a cease-fire and a political settlement, which never took hold. Marshall returned home in early 1947, became secretary of state, and advised Truman to disengage from China. By then, Truman had decided to initiate what eventually became the strategy of containment against the Soviet Union.

Truman's containment policy had implications not only for Europe and Asia but also for the Middle East. In 1946 he applied pressure via the United Nations (UN) to force the Soviets to withdraw from Iran. Clearly, the president worried about Soviet influence in the region and knew that the Middle East must remain aligned with the Western powers because of its vast oil reserves. The president's Truman Doctrine speech in March 1947 called for U.S. aid to any nation resisting communist domination. Congress then approved Truman's request for $400 million for Greece (to suppress a communist insurgency) and Turkey (to check Soviet advances). A proposal in June 1947 to help Europe avert economic collapse and keep communism at bay led to the Marshall Plan, an

ambitious and successful endeavor that helped reconstruct Western Europe's war-torn economy.

Truman broke with his predecessor's policies on the establishment of a Jewish state in Palestine. Unlike Roosevelt, Truman had been on record since 1940 as a supporter of a Jewish homeland in the Middle East. By 1947 the British were under pressure to leave Palestine as pro-Zionist attacks against their assets in the area increased. That same year the UN, acting on a British proposal that Truman favored, passed a resolution calling for the division of Palestine into two states. In the spring of 1948 British troops began to leave Palestine as neighboring Arab nations began massing troops along the border, poised to prevent the permanent establishment of a Jewish state following Britain's departure.

On May 14, 1948, the State of Israel declared its independence. Truman was under considerable pressure not to recognize Israel. Most of his advisers, including Secretary of State Marshall, believed that doing so would jeopardize U.S. interests and invite the enmity of Arab nations. Nevertheless, Truman recognized the State of Israel just 11 minutes after it had announced its statehood.

Fighting had already broken out between Arabs and Jews in Palestine in reaction to the UN partition, which the Arab world flatly rejected. The creation of Israel sparked the outbreak of a full-scale war that pitted the Israelis against Syria, Jordan, Egypt, Iraq, and Lebanon. Jewish forces managed to blunt the offensives into Israel, but the Truman administration did not intervene in the conflict. Instead, it pushed aggressively for a cease-fire through the UN. In March 1949 negotiations resulted in the declaration of a cease-fire and the drawing of temporary borders to separate the Jews from the Arabs.

Truman's decision has received much scrutiny. Some have argued that his decision was the product of crass political motives and the influence of Jewish lobbying groups that were heavily Democratic. Others have said that Truman was bought by influential lobbyists. None of these allegations pass history's litmus test, however. What moved Truman principally was humanitarian concern for hundreds of thousands of refugees. He also believed that the 1917 Balfour Declaration was valid. In the end, while Truman's decision genuinely seemed to be the product of pragmatic and humanitarian motives, it nevertheless paved the way for a new approach to U.S. policymaking in the Middle East.

Stalin's reaction to Truman's pursuit of containment greatly intensified the Cold War, beginning early in 1948 with the communist coup in Czechoslovakia. The Soviets then blockaded West Berlin to force U.S. and British abandonment of the city, but Truman ordered an airlift of food and supplies that compelled Stalin to restore access one year later. Countering the Soviet threat led to the 1949 creation of the North Atlantic Treaty Organization (NATO) and a U.S. commitment of military defense for Western Europe. Truman sent U.S. troops and huge amounts of military assistance across the Atlantic, but he refused to execute a similar policy in China. This led to charges that he had allowed disloyal American diplomats to undermine the Nationalists and lose China after the communists triumphed in October 1949. The Soviet explosion of an atomic bomb that September only increased popular anxiety in the United States. As fears of internal subversion grew, Truman appeared to be soft on communism when Senator Joseph R. McCarthy, an obscure Wisconsin Republican, charged that 205 communists worked in the U.S. State Department.

Early in 1950 Truman approved development of a hydrogen bomb, but he initially refused to approve National Security Council Paper 68 (NSC-68), which called for massive rearmament. When North Korea attacked South Korea in June, Truman, after brief hesitation, committed U.S. troops there because he believed that Stalin had ordered the invasion and that inaction would encourage more expansionist acts. Truman then ordered military protection for Jiang Jieshi's regime on Taiwan and greater support for the anticommunist efforts of the British in Malaya and the French in Indochina. Even before UN forces commander General Douglas MacArthur halted the initial invasion, Truman approved the plans for a follow-up offensive into North Korea that eventually provoked Chinese intervention. Truman's controversial decision to recall MacArthur in April 1951 for making public statements regarding policy that had not been cleared by the White House was highly unpopular and his public approval rating dropped to one of the lowest yet recorded. However, Truman's decision won acclaim from most military observers and European allies, and the president weathered the storm.

Armistice talks began in July 1951 but deadlocked in May 1952 after Truman refused to force the repatriation of communist prisoners of war (POWs). Unable to end the Korean War, he initiated steps to deter communist expansion on the other side of the world by implementing NSC-68, strengthening NATO militarily, and approving the initial steps that would lead to the rearming of West Germany. Truman left office in January 1953 and returned to Independence, Missouri, to write his memoirs and oversee the building of his presidential library. Truman died on December 26, 1972, in Kansas City, Missouri.

JAMES I. MATRAY

See also

Arab-Israeli Conflict, Overview; Balfour Declaration; Israel; United Kingdom, Middle East Policy; United States, Middle East Policy, 1945–Present

References

Cohen, Michael Joseph. *Truman and Israel*. Berkeley: University of California Press, 1990.

Donovan, Robert J. *Conflict and Crisis: The Presidency of Harry S. Truman, 1945–1948*. New York: Norton, 1977.

———. *Tumultuous Years: The Presidency of Harry S. Truman, 1949–1953*. New York: Norton, 1982.

McCullough, David. *Truman*. New York: Simon and Schuster, 1992.

Tsouli, Yunis

See Irhabi 007

Tunisia

North African nation. The Republic of Tunisia, an overwhelmingly Sunni Muslim nation, covers 63,170 square miles and had a 2008 population of 10.384 million. Tunisia borders Algeria to the west, Libya to the south, and the Mediterranean Sea to the east and north. Until the late 19th century, Tunisia had been dominated by various larger powers as well as Arab and Berber dynasties. In 1881, the French signed an agreement with the bey, the local Tunisian ruler, establishing a French protectorate. Tunisian society and culture was greatly affected by the long period of French colonial rule, which did not officially end until 1956.

Following World War II, a strong nationalist movement in Tunisia engaged in a protracted struggle against French colonial rule. On March 20, 1956, following arduous, delicate, and behind-the-scenes negotiations, an independence protocol was signed by representatives of the French and Tunisian governments. On July 25, 1957, the Tunisian Constituent Assembly ousted the bey, Muhammad VIII al-Amin, who was sympathetic to France and had long been unpopular. It also declared the formation of the Tunisian republic and elected Habib Bourguiba as president.

Bourguiba, who would rule until 1987, was decidedly pro-Western and modernist in his outlook and foreign policy. He also maintained cordial communications with Israeli officials, although this was not made public until years later. In discussions of common interests and subsequent public statements, Bourguiba made known his opinion that Arab states should accept the existence of Israel and pertinent United Nations (UN) resolutions as a condition for solving the Palestinian problem. Bourguiba also shocked his people by declaring that the fasting month of Ramadan was detrimental to national production and was shown on television with some others drinking orange juice as a demonstration that fasting was not required.

Bourguiba's efforts to transform Tunisia into a modern, democratic state had the backing of the majority of young, Westernized Tunisian intellectuals. His main political support came from the well-organized Neo-Destour Party, which he had founded in 1934 and which constituted the country's chief political force. The Bourguiba administration was very tolerant of its Jewish citizens, always distinguishing between the unpopular policies of the state of Israel and the Jewish population living in the country. Bourguiba was not without political rivals, however. Early in his presidency, he was strongly challenged by Salah ben Youssef, who leaned toward Egypt and Pan-Arabism, and who championed the continuation of Tunisia's ancient Islamic traditions. The people of Tunisia remain sharply divided in outlook between the rural and urban populations. A strongly religious outlook found expression in the Tendence Islamique (Islamic Tendency) political movement, which opposed Bourguiba.

But Tunisia has almost always aligned itself squarely with the West and has been considered a strong American ally. During the June 1967 Six-Day War, for example, Bourguiba refused to sever relations with the United States over its support of Israel, despite

President Dwight D. Eisenhower and his host, President Habib Bourguiba of Tunisia, left, during a visit by the U.S. president, at Bourguiba's palace in Tunis, December 17, 1959. (AP/Wide World Photos)

considerable pressure to do so from other Arab states. Tunisia also faced hostility from Egypt's leader, Gamal Abdel Nasser, with whom Bourguiba often found himself at odds, even going so far as to briefly sever diplomatic relations in October 1966.

In spite of his support of Western-style democracy, Bourguiba nevertheless exerted strong, centralized authority. The economy was closely controlled by the government, and as Tunisian Islamist movements strengthened, especially after the late 1970s, the administration in Tunis increasingly relied on censorship, illegal detentions, and other decidedly undemocratic schemes to smother radicalism.

Tunisia's stance on Israel has been marked by contradictory and paradoxical policies. These reflect Tunisia's shared experience of struggle against colonialism and general support by the Tunisian people for Arab nationalism and the Palestinian cause. For instance, Tunisia supported the October 1973 Egyptian-Syrian attack on Israel (sparking the Yom Kippur/Ramadan War) and sent close to 1,000 combatants to fight, despite historically urging a diplomatic solution to Arab-Israeli conflicts. Although Tunisia distanced itself from the Middle East's continued problems throughout the rest of the decade, from 1979 to 1989 Tunis served as the headquarters of the Arab League when the organization suspended Egypt's membership and

abandoned Cairo following President Anwar Sadat's peace agreement with Israel.

In 1982, Tunisia allowed the Palestinian Liberation Organization (PLO) to move its leadership and fighters from Beirut to Tunis after Israel's invasion of Lebanon. On October 1, 1985, Israel killed 68 Palestinians and injured many more in the bombing of a Palestinian compound in a Tunis suburb. The bombing was Israel's response to the murder of three of its citizens in Cyprus for which the PLO claimed responsibility. On April 16, 1988, Israeli commandos assassinated the PLO's second in command, Khalil al-Wazir (Abu Jihad), at his home in Tunis.

Bourguiba's heavy-handed rule and frail health combined to bring about his ouster on November 7, 1987. He had declared his intent to execute leaders of the Tendence Islamique, which would have made them martyrs and caused uproar in Tunisia. General Zine al-Abidine Ben Ali carried out a bloodless coup, declaring Bourguiba medically senile and succeeding him as president. Under Ben Ali's tenure, Tunisia has taken a moderate, nonaligned stance in its foreign relations.

Following the Oslo Accords, and the establishment of the Palestinian National Authority, the PLO departed from Tunis and returned to the West Bank and Gaza. Domestically, the Tunisian government has sought to diffuse rising pressures for a more open political system while at the same time dealing with increased Islamist militant or political movements and growing anti-Western sentiments. During the 1991 Persian Gulf War, Tunisia declined to support the international coalition arrayed against Saddam Hussein's Iraqi forces then occupying Kuwait. There was a considerable public outcry in many Arab countries, and not only Tunisia, against support of the coalition. Ben Ali's government viewed the conflict not as one of liberation but rather as one for the control of Middle Eastern oil. The Tunisian government chose not to override its population's sentiment, in contrast to some of its Arab neighbors, who did participate in the coalition.

In April 1996, Tunisia followed the lead of Morocco and opened a liaison office in Tel Aviv to strengthen cultural ties to Israel, especially with respect to Jewish tourism. While the rise of Israel's conservative Likud Party strained emerging Tunisian-Israeli relations over the next several years, on February 6, 2000, Tunisia's secretary of state met with the Israeli foreign minister in Tel Aviv, marking the first ever visit of such high-ranking officials. On October 20, 2001, Tunisia severed relations with Israel and closed its liaison office, claiming flagrant Israeli violations of Palestinian human rights that had sparked the Second (al-Aqsa) Intifada.

The 21st century has witnessed a cooling of relations between Israel and Tunisia. At the 2002 Arab summit in Beirut, President Ben Ali supported the peace plan that called for an independent Palestinian state with Jerusalem as its capital and the return of all occupied territories. In 2004, Ben Ali won a fourth five-year term. Meanwhile, Ben Ali strengthened his ties to the United States and the West, voicing support for the post-2001 War on Terror and likening it to his own battle to fight Islamic radicalism at home.

While Tunisia did not participate in Operations ENDURING FREEDOM and IRAQI FREEDOM, the Ben Ali regime cooperated with the George W. Bush administration's efforts to stymie international terrorism; in February 2004, Bush publicly thanked Ben Ali for his support of antiterrorism activities while the Tunisian president was on a state visit to Washington, D.C.

MARK SANDERS

See also

Arab-Israeli Conflict, Overview; Arab Nationalism; Egypt; Global War on Terror; Nasser, Gamal Abdel; Palestine Liberation Organization

References

Geyer, Georgie Anne. *Tunisia: The Story of a Country That Works.* London: Stacey International, 2002.

Perkins, Kenneth. *A History of Modern Tunisia.* New York: Cambridge University Press, 2004.

Turkey, Role in Persian Gulf and Afghanistan Wars

Turkey is a Eurasian nation covering 300,948 square miles of territory. Strategically located both in Europe and Asia Minor, European Turkey borders Greece and Bulgaria to the east and north; in Asia Minor it shares common borders with Georgia to the northwest; Armenia and Iran to the east; and Syria and Iraq to the south. Turkey's 2008 population was estimated to be 75.8 million people.

The Turkish government is a representative parliamentary democracy with a president, elected by popular vote, as head of state. Executive power is invested in the prime minister, elected by parliament. In recent years, three political parties have vied for power. The largest of these by far is the Justice and Development Party, followed in order of magnitude by the Republican People's Party and the Nationalist Movement Party.

A secular republic with no official religion since the days of its great leader Kemal Ataturk, Turkey is nonetheless 99 percent Muslim, with three-quarters of these Sunni. More than half of its Muslim population attends prayer services regularly. In recent years, the rise of religion, specifically Islam, in Turkish politics has been a matter of concern to many Turks as well as to the West. The Turkish Armed Forces number more than 1 million in five services branches. This makes it the second largest military in the North Atlantic Treaty Organization (NATO) after only the U.S. Armed Forces. The country also has compulsory military service.

Turkey has been generally pro-Western in its foreign policy orientation and has enjoyed close ties with the United States since World War II. It has been a member of NATO since 1952; it joined the European Union (EU) in 2004.

Turkey was among the 34-member international coalition that helped to expel Iraqi forces from Kuwait in the 1991 Persian Gulf War, although it provided no ground troops to the effort. It dispatched two frigates to the Persian Gulf and was heavily involved in basing coalition forces on its military bases, including air assets.

The Turkish government also allowed overflights of its air space when the air war began in January 1991.

Despite its limited participation in the Gulf War, Turkey did benefit from the crisis. Having fought an insurgency against militant Kurds in southern Turkey that had killed thousands of Turks since the mid-1980s, the Turkish government was relieved by the outcome of the war in that Iraq continued as a unitary state and did not break into separate states to include an independent Kurdish nation laying claim to Turkish territory. At the same time, Turkey suffered economically, at least in the short term. By November 1990, rigid enforcement of the economic blockade against Iraq had cost Turkey an estimated $3 billion in revenues, chiefly from shutting down an oil pipeline through the country. This was offset somewhat later by U.S. loan and aid guarantees.

In the aftermath of the war, Turks came to resent the phobia expressed by many Americans and West Europeans toward its Muslim identity and what it perceived as a lack of support for Ankara's efforts to stamp out demands for autonomy by its Kurdish minority (20 percent of the country's overall population) in southern Turkey. This was evident in Operation STEEL CURTAIN in March 1995, when Turkey sent 35,000 troops into the Kurdish zone of northern Iraq in an effort to trap several thousand guerrillas and halt cross-border raids by the Marxist Kurdish Workers' Party (PKK). The PKK had been fighting for more than a decade in southeastern Turkey to establish a separate Kurdish state. More than 15,000 people had been killed since 1984, and Turkey mounted the military campaign in an effort to wipe out the movement.

In the immediate aftermath of the September 11, 2001, terrorist attacks on the United States, Turkey voiced support of the United States and the so-called War on Terror. It offered airspace and refueling rights as the U.S.-led coalition began operations against Afghanistan's Taliban regime in October 2001. Beginning in 2002, Turkey dispatched troops to the International Security Assistance Force–Afghanistan (ISAF). The number of Turkish troops committed to Afghanistan has risen steadily since that time. At the start of 2009, the deployment numbered some 1,700 personnel. In early 2009, Turkey took command of the ISAF for the second time. Many of the Turkish troops are responsible for security in and around Kabul (Turkey also leads the Kabul command). Turkish troops are also active in the Wardak Province, in east-central Afghanistan. Since Turkey increased its presence in Afghanistan, public opinion has remained ambivalent about the nation's mission there.

The United States had counted on active Turkish cooperation in the 2003 Iraq War that ousted Iraqi dictator Saddam Hussein from power, but the Turks balked at the last minute despite strong financial incentives, in part because public opinion was strongly opposed to the war and in part because of concerns of the possible breakup of Iraq and the creation of a Kurdish state. This decision by the Turkish government denied the United States a secure northern base of operations for the U.S. Army 4th Infantry

U.S. and coalition military personnel unload two UH-60 Black Hawk helicopters from a C-17 Globemaster that had flown from Insurlik Air Base in Turkey to Kabul International Airport, Afghanistan, in support of Operation ENDURING FREEDOM. (U.S. Department of Defense)

Division and forced a recasting of the Anglo-American coalition's military plans, severely straining relations between the United States and Turkey.

In February 2008, Turkish military forces launched an incursion into northern Iraq, to again punish the PKK, which had been targeting Turks and Turkish forces in the southern part of the country. The brief punitive incursion, which lasted just eight days, had been preceded by Turkish air strikes against PKK targets beginning in December 2007. Both the Iraqi and U.S. governments voiced their displeasure with the incursion, terming it "counterproductive" to the stabilization of Iraq. The number of PKK fighters killed in the skirmish is subject to debate, but it is believed that as many as 550 died. Since February 2008, there have been numerous clashes between Turkish and Kurdish forces along the Iraqi-Turkish border. Turkey continues to cast a watchful eye on the future of Iraq and, because it is so strategically important geopolitically, much of the rest of the world continues to watch Turkey as well.

CEM KARADELI, KEITH LEITICH, PAUL G. PIERPAOLI JR., AND SPENCER C. TUCKER.

See also

DESERT STORM, Operation; International Security Assistance Force; Kurdistan Workers' Party; Kurds

References

Carkoglu, Ali, and William Hale, eds. *The Politics of Modern Turkey.* London: Taylor and Francis, 2008.

Mavkovsky, Alan, ed. *Turkey's New World: Changing Dynamics in Turkish Foreign Policy.* Washington, DC: Washington Institute for Near East Policy, 2000.

Robins, Philip. *Turkey and the Middle East.* New York: Council on Foreign Relations Press, 1991.

Turki, Battle of

Start Date: November 15, 2006
End Date: November 16, 2006

Battle on November 15–16, 2006, fought by American and Iraqi Army units against a well-organized group of Sunni militants with alleged ties to al-Qa'ida fi Bilad al-Rafhidayn (al-Qa'ida in the Land of the Two Rivers, or Al Qaeda in Iraq) insurgent organization. The fighting extended over a 40-hour period, with most of it occurring in Turki, in Diyala Province, about 25 miles south of Forward Operating Base Caldwell. U.S. soldiers involved in the battle were from the 82nd Airborne Division's 5th Squadron, 73rd Cavalry; the Iraqi soldiers were part of the 1st Brigade, Iraqi 5th

Division. The insurgent group had been using Turki as a training camp and fought back fiercely in the course of a 40-hour battle. American air strikes played a key role in the battle.

On November 12, Lieutenant Colonel Andrew Poppas, the operation's commander, spotted a potential insurgent hideout while on an aerial reconnaissance mission. He then dispatched a small unit to investigate. An ambush of coalition forces on November 15 began the battle. The insurgents were well organized and armed. Instead of the usual hit-and-run attacks, these insurgents held their ground and fought in place, apparently as a result of their training at Turki. Only when Poppas called in air strikes extending over nearly 12 hours were the coalition and Iraqi forces able to fight their way forward through a considerable network of trenches and canals that had been built or fortified by the insurgents. The intense, close-combat engagement saw at least 72 insurgents killed and 20 others captured. Two Americans were killed in the fighting.

During a subsequent sweep of the area, an insurgent weapons cache complex was uncovered containing six smaller caches, a number of them in underground bunkers. They contained more than 400,000 rounds of small-arms ammunition; 15,000 rounds of heavy machine-gun ammunition; 5 mortar bipods; 3 heavy machine guns; 3 antitank weapons; 2 recoilless rifles; and numerous mortar rounds, grenades, flares, and assorted artillery rounds.

The combined U.S.-Iraqi force also seized a quantity of materials for making improvised explosive devices (IEDs), including batteries, cellular phones, blasting caps, explosives, propaganda materials, and a large amount of American money.

RICHARD B. VERRONE

See also
Al Qaeda in Iraq; Iraqi Insurgency

References
Hashim, Ammed S. *Insurgency and Counter-insurgency in Iraq.* Ithaca, NY: Cornell University Press, 2006.

Ricks, Thomas E. *The Gamble: General David Petraeus and the American Military Adventure in Iraq, 2006–2008.* New York: Penguin, 2009.

Wong, Edard. "Some Fighters in Iraq Adopt New Tactics to Battle U.S." *New York Times,* November 24, 2006.

Tuwaitha Nuclear Facility

Iraqi nuclear site and, prior to the 1991 Persian Gulf War, the centerpiece of Iraq's nuclear ambitions. Tuwaitha was part of the Baghdad Nuclear Research Facility, located about 12 miles southeast of Baghdad. Tuwaitha was home to the Osiraq (Tammuz 1) nuclear reactor, which the Israeli air force bombed and destroyed in 1981. It is believed that the Iraqis had achieved up to 95 percent

An aerial photo of the destroyed Iraqi nuclear facility in Tuwaitha, some 30 miles southeast of Baghdad, on June 5, 2003. (AP/Wide World Photos)

uranium enrichment at Tuwaitha, higher than at any of its other nuclear sites. During Operation DESERT STORM, many facilities at Tuwaitha sustained heavy damage during coalition air strikes. Tuwaitha, which encompasses 23,000 acres and was surrounded by a 4-mile-long earthen berm nearly 160 feet high, was also home to the Iraqi Nuclear Commission.

As the most important of Iraq's nuclear facilities, Tuwaitha was a sprawling facility that contained research-grade nuclear reactors, plutonium-separation and waste-processing facilities, uranium-research and metallurgy labs, neutron-initiator development facilities, and other nuclear-related research laboratories. Significant amounts of industrial and nuclear waste were also stored in and around Tuwaitha, including a waste site containing several thousand acres. Just outside the Tuwaitha complex, the Iraqis had built a manufacturing plant where insulators and magnetic coils were produced to aid in their nuclear programs. The Iraqis had also built a biological weapons laboratory at Tuwaitha.

It is estimated that coalition bombing in 1991 destroyed only about 20 percent of Iraq's nuclear development facilities. Although damage at Tuwaitha was fairly extensive, it was largely limited to facilities run by the Iraqi Nuclear Power Commission and administrative offices. Damage to the reactors was not complete, and the main reactor, built after the Osiraq bombing, had been shut down before the war began. The Iraqis reported mild nuclear contamination after the air strikes on Tuwaitha, although it was closed for only a few days before reopening.

As part of the cease-fire agreement and United Nations (UN) Security Council Resolution 687 following DESERT STORM, Iraq was obliged to open Tuwaitha and other nuclear facilities to international inspections to be conducted by the International Atomic Energy Agency (IAEA). The IAEA conducted numerous inspections and in the process removed all known stores of highly enriched uranium and plutonium located at Tuwaitha. By 2002 the inspections had quarantined Iraq's low-grade enriched uranium and natural and depleted uranium in locked storage facilities on-site.

During Operation IRAQI FREEDOM, which began in March 2003, there was some controversy surrounding the IAEA's attempts to keep the Tuwaitha facility from contributing to further nuclear weapons development. Specifically, fault was found with the decision to store any nuclear materials there instead of shipping them out of the country to ensure that they did not fall into the wrong

hands. Tuwaitha, like many parts of Iraq, in particular the areas in and around Baghdad, was subject to widespread looting in the immediate aftermath of the coalition invasion. Unprepared for such problems, coalition forces were ill equipped to handle this situation. Apparently, looters infiltrated the Tuwaitha nuclear facilities and made off with much material, although it is not known for sure exactly what they took. In April 2003 U.S. Marines, who were attempting to secure Tuwaitha, claimed that they had discovered a secret cache of nuclear material and related facilities. The IAEA denied the claims, alleging that its inspectors had checked every inch of Tuwaitha and could not have overlooked such a thing. The media claimed that the facilities were in fact not new or previously undiscovered. Instead, it seemed probable that looters had broken seals placed on the material by the IAEA, making it appear as if the goods had never been inventoried. If this was indeed the case, then it cannot be known what potentially dangerous materials may have been carted off.

U.S. forces quickly took control of Tuwaitha after the looting and began to decontaminate it, with the assistance of U.S. civilian contractors. After extensive cleanup efforts, coalition forces turned over control of Tuwaitha to the Iraqi Ministerial Guard on October 7, 2003. It was the first change-of-command to take place in the aftermath of the invasion. By 2004 the Iraqis had outlined an ambitious plan to use the facilities at Tuwaitha for scientific—but not nuclear—purposes, including water, agriculture, and petrochemical endeavors. The rebuilding at Tuwaitha was not being funded by coalition authorities, but rather by the Development Fund for Iraq, established by the UN. The reconstruction efforts have been estimated to cost as much as $30 billion.

PAUL G. PIERPAOLI JR.

See also

International Atomic Energy Agency; Iraq, History of, Pre-1990; Iraq, History of, 1990–Present; Nuclear Weapons, Iraq's Potential for Building; United Nations Security Council Resolution 687

References

Khadduri, Imad. *Iraq's Nuclear Mirage: Memoirs and Delusions.* Toronto: Springhead, 2003.

U.S. Congress. *Iraq's Nuclear Weapons Capability and IAEA Inspections in Iraq: Joint Hearing before the Subcommittees on Europe and the Middle East and International Security, International Organizations, and Human Rights.* Committee on Foreign Affairs, U.S. House of Representatives. Washington, DC: U.S. Government Printing Office, 1993.

U

Ukraine, Role in Afghanistan and Iraq Wars

Eastern European nation and former Soviet republic. Independent since 1991, Ukraine's 2008 population was estimated to be 45.995 million people. The nation covers 233,089 square miles and is bordered by Belarus to the north; Russia to the north, northeast, and east; the Sea of Avov and the Black Sea to the south; Moldova and Romania to the southwest; and Hungary, Slovakia, and Poland to the west. Ukraine is a federated republic with a semipresidential political system. The president, who is popularly elected, is head of state; the prime minister, selected by parliament, is head of government. The principal political parties/coalitions include: Party of Regions; Yuliya Tymoshenko Bloc; Our Ukraine/People's Self Defense; and the Communist Party of Ukraine (CPU).

Ukraine emerged as a significant supporter of the U.S.-led coalitions in Afghanistan and Iraq. In 1994 Ukraine joined the North Atlantic Treaty Organization (NATO)'s Partnership for Peace Program and subsequently deployed peacekeeping troops as part of the alliance's peacekeeping missions in the Balkans. Following the September 2001 terrorist attacks on the United States, the Ukrainian government supported Operation ENDURING FREEDOM as a means to improving relations with the United States and the West, while providing a balance to Russian influence. Ukraine granted the United States and its coalition partners overflight rights during Operation ENDURING FREEDOM, but initially limited sorties to cargo and logistical aircraft, not combat missions.

Following the 2004 Orange Revolution, which brought pro-Western President Viktor Yushchenko to power, Ukraine increased its security cooperation with the United States. In May 2007 Ukraine deployed a small medical team (10 personnel) as part of the NATO-led International Security Assistance

A Ukrainian soldier with his 7.62-mm PKM light machine gun atop a BRT-80A armored personnel carrier in Kut, Iraq, during Operation IRAQI FREEDOM, August 2003. (U.S. Department of Defense)

Force– Afghanistan (ISAF). Most of the Ukrainians were stationed as part of the Lithuanian-led provincial reconstruction team in the Ghor region, but one medical officer was also deployed to Kabul. The Ukrainians provided medical support and assistance for local hospitals and clinics.

In 2003 Ukraine dispatched to Iraq 450 soldiers from a unit that specialized in nuclear, biological, and chemical warfare. The troops did not take part in combat operations. Relations between Ukraine and the United States were strained by the revelation that Kiev had supplied the Iraqi regime of Saddam Hussein with an air defense system prior to the U.S.-led invasion. In August 2003 Ukraine deployed a mechanized brigade to Iraq. The Ukrainians were deployed as part of the Polish-led Multi-National Force in the south-central region of Iraq, where they undertook general security missions and humanitarian operations. A small staff contingent was also deployed at coalition headquarters in Baghdad. The troops were sent first to Kuwait for training and to acclimatize.

Ukraine's peak strength in Iraq was 1,650 troops, making it the sixth-largest coalition troop contributor. Ukrainian forces generally served six-month rotations. Kiev also offered logistical support, including transport. In return for its support, Ukrainian companies were awarded a series of contracts to supply the Iraqi military with weapons, vehicles, and other supplies.

Although Yushchenko increased Ukraine's participation in Operation ENDURING FREEDOM, among his campaign pledges was a promise to withdraw Ukraine's troops from Iraq. Participation in the coalition was unpopular domestically, especially after Ukrainian casualties mounted. (Through 2008, 18 Ukrainian soldiers were killed in Iraq, and more than 30 were wounded or injured.) The country's troop strength was dramatically reduced in December 2005. Between 2005 and 2008, Ukraine maintained about 40–50 troops in Iraq. These troops provided training for Iraqi security forces. The government also participated in the NATO-led training mission in Iraq, beginning in March 2005. It sent 10 soldiers as part of the operation. In total, about 5,000 Ukrainian troops served in Iraq. Ukraine withdrew its remaining forces in December 2008.

TOM LANSFORD

See also

Afghanistan, Coalition Combat Operations in, 2002–Present; IRAQI FREE-DOM, Operation, Coalition Ground Forces; Multi-National Force–Iraq; North Atlantic Treaty Organization in Afghanistan

References

Cockburn, Patrick. *The Occupation: War and Resistance in Iraq.* New York: Verso, 2007.

Keegan, John. *The Iraq War: The Military Offensive, from Victory in 21 Days to the Insurgent Aftermath.* New York: Vintage, 2005.

Umm Qasr

Iraqi port city located on the Faw (Fao) peninsula in the southern part of the country. The city sits astride the Khawr Abd Allah estuary, which leads directly into the Persian Gulf. Umm Qasr is separated from Kuwait by a small inlet. Until the 1991 Persian Gulf War, when it was destroyed, a bridge spanned the inlet, linking the two nations.

Umm Qasr is strategically important because it is one of the Iraqis' few access points to deep water. Over the last half century, its importance has only increased as successive Iraqi regimes sought to invest in it as an alternative to the Shatt al-Arab waterway, which borders on Iran, Iraq's perennial adversary.

Over the centuries, Umm Qasr has mainly been a fishing enclave, but it has also served military purposes. In 325 BCE, Alexander the Great landed there when he undertook the conquest of Mesopotamia. During the World War II years, the city was used as a port in which American Lend-Lease supplies were dropped as they made their way to the Soviet Union. In early 1950 Iraqi King Faisal II invested heavily in Umm Qasr to rebuild and modernize its port facilities. After Faisal was overthrown in 1958, the new Iraqi government created a naval base at Umm Qasr; the city remained the chief headquarters for the Iraqi Navy until the 2003 invasion of Iraq.

In 1961, Iraqi leader Abd al-Karim Qasim accelerated the port city's development in an effort to end Iraqi reliance on the Shatt al-Arab waterway. By 1967 the city's new port facilities, including a new rail line that linked Umm Qasr with Baghdad and Basra, were completed. The new port had been constructed largely by a consortium of companies from Lebanon, West Germany, and Sweden.

Umm Qasr came under attack during the 1980–1988 Iran-Iraq War, but the port itself never fell into Iranian hands, even though the Faw peninsula was largely occupied in 1986. The Iranians were not dislodged until 1988. Umm Qasr was at the center of Iraqi-Kuwaiti tensions that led to war in 1990. Both nations claimed sovereignty over the inlet that provides access to the port, and disputes over control of two nearby islands also fed Iraqi and Kuwaiti mutual ill will. Umm Qasr was bombed heavily during Operation DESERT STORM in 1991, and after the conflict Kuwait gained control over the access inlet. The Iraqi government refused to recognize the change, however.

Between 1992 and 2003, Iraqi dictator Saddam Hussein further built up the port at Umm Qasr and redirected much ocean-going commerce to it. This was done to punish the port city of Basra, which had been at the epicenter of antigovernment rebellions that followed the Persian Gulf War. By early 2003 Umm Qasr had an estimated permanent population of some 40,000 people.

During the 2003 Anglo-American–led invasion of Iraq (Operation IRAQI FREEDOM), coalition forces targeted Umm Qasr as one of their first and primary targets. Between March 21 and March 25, 2003, British Royal Marines, the U.S. 15th Marine Expeditionary Unit, and Polish GROM (Operational Mobile Reaction Group) fought against an unexpectedly stout Iraqi resistance in and around Umm Qasr. The port was finally secured on March 25, and thereafter coalition forces used it as a transshipment point for vast amounts of humanitarian aid to the Iraqi people after the fall of Hussein's regime.

PAUL G. PIERPAOLI JR.

See also

Basra; DESERT STORM, Operation; Faw Peninsula; Iran-Iraq War; Iraq, History of, Pre-1990; Iraq, History of, 1990–Present; IRAQI FREEDOM, Operation; Shatt al-Arab Waterway; Umm Qasr, Battle of

References

Keegan, John. *The Iraq War: The Military Offensive, from Victory in 21 Days to the Insurgent Aftermath.* New York: Vintage, 2005.

Tripp, Charles. *A History of Iraq.* Cambridge: Cambridge University Press, 2007.

Umm Qasr, Battle of
Start Date: March 21, 2003
End Date: March 25, 2003

First military engagement of the 2003 Iraq War (Operation IRAQI FREEDOM). The Battle of Umm Qasr unfolded in and around the Iraqi port city of Umm Qasr, located in the southern part of the country on the Faw (Fao) peninsula, on March 21–25, 2003. The port at Umm Qasr, which is Iraq's only deep-water port, is very close to Kuwait; indeed, only a small inlet separates the two nations.

Taking control of Umm Qasr was one of the coalition's first military objectives during the opening days of Operation IRAQI FREEDOM. American and British commanders knew that seizing the city and port would deny the Iraqis any way of challenging the naval blockade. More importantly, they also hoped to secure the port as the base for a large humanitarian mission, whereby tons of food, medicine, clothing, and other supplies would be moved into Iraq once Iraqi president Saddam Hussein's regime had been toppled.

The Umm Qasr offensive, which involved the 15th U.S. Marine Expeditionary Unit, British Royal Marines, and integrated units from Poland's Operational Mobile Reaction Group (GROM), moved toward Umm Qasr overland from Kuwait and through the very southern edge of Iraq. The operation began on March 21, 2003. Coalition forces were confident that the port and surrounding city could be taken quickly and with little resistance. As a convoy of about 20 coalition vehicles lumbered toward Umm Qasr, the Iraqis peppered it with small-arms fire. They then opened up with mortar fire, taking the allies by surprise. The Americans called in British artillery support from northern Kuwait, not far from the border. While some shells hit Iraqi positions, others fell perilously close to U.S. Marine units, who were forced into a hasty withdrawal. After regrouping, the coalition forces called for M1-Abrams tanks, which then punched through Iraqi defensive positions.

U.S. marines fighting in Umm Qasr, Iraq, on March 23, 2003. (U.S. Department of Defense)

Many of the Iraqi defenders were members of Hussein's elite Republican Guard, who resorted to guerrilla-style tactics to keep coalition forces off balance. Some were disguised in civilian clothing and would hold up white flags. When coalition forces approached, they would scurry into foxholes and bunkers and open fire. The Iraqi resistance at Umm Qasr was unexpectedly stout, and some critics have claimed that coalition forces took the Iraqi threat too lightly and were thus ill prepared for a protracted fight there.

After more determined fighting on the part of the Iraqis, coalition forces made use of Bradley fighting vehicles and had intended on calling in Cobra attack helicopters to help root out resistance in and near the port. The Bradleys arrived, but the Cobras did not, as there had been insufficient time to organize a mission. On March 25 the port was declared free of Iraqi opposition, but sporadic and pitched fighting continued to occur in the old city of Umm Qasr.

Not until the first few days in April had all of Umm Qasr been pacified. Meanwhile, coalition minesweepers, U.S. Navy SEALS, and even trained dolphins began the laborious task of clearing the port waters and approaches of mines. Navy personnel made an unsettling discovery when they found a number of Iraqi civilian boats rigged with mines and explosive devices, making the minesweeping operation all the more difficult. The first ship to make it into port was the British RFA (Royal Fleet Auxiliary) *Sir Gallahad*.

The Battle of Umm Qasr gave pause to many coalition commanders and strategists who had believed that securing the port city would be a quick and easy affair. Fortunately, subsequent operations went more or less according to plan, but the battle proved that no operation, however well planned, can proceed successfully without proper intelligence and preparation.

PAUL G. PIERPAOLI JR.

See also

IRAQI FREEDOM, Operation; Umm Qasr

References

Gordon, Michael R., and General Bernard E. Trainor. *Cobra II: The Inside Story of the Invasion and Occupation of Iraq*. New York: Pantheon Books, 2006.

Keegan, John. *The Iraq War: The Military Offensive, from Victory in 21 Days to the Insurgent Aftermath*. New York: Vintage, 2005.

Underway Replenishment Ships

Support ships capable of transferring fuels, stores, and munitions to other vessels while under way at sea via connecting cables and hoses or by means of helicopters equipped for ship-to-ship cargo delivery.

The technique for underway replenishment (UNREP) was developed primarily by the U.S. Navy, beginning as early as World War I. The focus initially was on the transfer of fuel: heavy sacks of coal early on, then oil pumped through hoses, followed by the development of the means to transfer crates of ammunition, foodstuffs, and dry goods. For the transfer of diesel fuels, the receiving

ship sometimes took up a station astern of the oiler, which trailed a hose; however, weather permitting, the side-by-side approach soon had the most adherents.

Techniques became more established, transfer gear became standardized, and the optimum matching speeds for alongside operations were determined, as were the most effective yet safest distances to be maintained between different types and sizes of ships during connected replenishment (CONREP). Underway replenishment is a demanding and exacting process that keeps ships on station for weeks on end, and it can be carried out in all but the very worst weather conditions. The added use of the helicopter for vertical replenishment (VERTREP) extends the resupply capability to ships some miles distant from the supply ship, in addition to those alongside.

The U.S. Navy's first purpose-fitted UNREP ships were the more than 30 fleet oilers of the Cimarron (AO-22) class, built during World War II. The last of these, the *Caloosahatchee* (AO-98) and *Canisteo* (AO-99), served until 1989, followed by the similarly long-serving Mispillion (T-AO-105) and Neosho (T-AO-143)-classes. These ships were followed by a new Cimarron (AO-177) class, which led to the present-day Henry J. Kaiser (T-AO-187)-class, built in the late 1980s and 1990s and operated by the Military Sealift Command (MSC). When operating with an aircraft carrier battle group (CVBG), fleet oilers are routinely accompanied by both combat stores ships (AFS) and ammunition ships (AE) in order to supply the full range of necessary supplies to the squadron.

An outgrowth of the seagoing support network required by the carrier battle group was the development of the fast combat support ship (AOE), which combines the resources of oiler, combat stores ship, and ammunition ship in a single hull. First explored by the U.S. Navy in 1954 aboard the replenishment oiler *Conecuh* (AOR-110), a former German fleet supply ship rerigged for UNREP of fuels, stores, and munitions, this concept reached full expression in the new Sacramento (AOE-1) class, which joined the fleet in 1964. Very similar was the design of the Wichita (AOR-1) class of replenishment oilers, seven ships built between 1968 and 1976 that were smaller, less capable versions of the AOE and that ultimately were decommissioned in the late 1990s.

The T-AO-187 Henry J. Kaiser class of 16 ships (launched during 1985–1995) was similar to the earlier 7-ship Cimarron II (AO-177)-class, commissioned during 1981–1983 and decommissioned in 1998–1999. Dimensions were length, 677.5 feet; beam, 97.5 feet; draft, 36 feet; displacement, 9,500 tons (light) or 40,700 tons (full load); and cargo, 26,500 tons. Speed was 20 knots. Range was 6,000 nautical miles at 20 knots. Complement was 80 civilians and 204 enlisted.

The 7 ships of the AOR-1 Wichita class were launched during 1968–1974 and decommissioned during 1993–1996. Dimensions were length, 659 feet; beam, 96 feet; and draft, 33 feet. Displacement was 12,500 tons (light) or 41,350 tons (full load). Cargo capacity was 175,000 barrels of fuel, 600 tons of munitions, 200 tons of dry stores, and 100 tons of refrigerated stores. Speed was 20

The fast combat support ship USNS *Bridge* (T-AOE-10) conducts underway replenishment of the guided-missile cruiser USS *Cowpens* (CG-63) in the Pacific Ocean, August 29, 2009. (U.S. Department of Defense)

knots. Range was 10,000 nautical miles at 17 knots or 6,500 nautical miles at 20 knots. Complement was 461 (26 officers and 435 enlisted). Armament included one North Atlantic Treaty Organization (NATO) Sea Sparrow launcher and two 20-millimeter (mm) Phalanx CIWS.

Combat stores ships are also combined-duty auxiliaries; they each bring together the functions of a stores ship, a stores issue ship (AKS), and an aviation stores ship (AVS). They supply dry and refrigerated stores, spare parts, and a variety of cargo for UNREP to the fleet. Two classes of this dedicated type have been active in the U.S. Navy since the 1960s.

The first is the T-AFS-1 Mars class of seven ships. Launched during 1963–1969, three ships are in MSC active service, and four are in reserve. Dimensions are length, 580 feet; beam, 79 feet; and draft, 24 feet. Displacement is 9,200 tons (light) or 16,070 tons (full load). Speed is 21 knots, and range is 18,000 nautical miles at 11 knots or 10,000 nautical miles at 20 knots. Complement is 432 (28 officers and 404 enlisted); MSC, 136 civilian; or 26 navy (4 officers and 22 enlisted). The ships have two Boeing Vertol UH-46 Sea Knight helicopters.

The T-AFS-8 Sirius class of three ships, launched during 1966–1967, remains MSC active. Dimensions are length, 523.25 feet; beam, 72 feet; and draft, 25.5 feet. Displacement is 9,010 tons (light) or 16,792 tons (full load). Speed is 19 knots with a range of 27,500 nautical miles at 12 knots or 11,000 nautical miles at 19 knots. Complement is 103 civilian and 26 navy (4 officers and 22 enlisted). The ships carry two UH-46 Sea Knight helicopters.

AEs in the U.S. Navy have a ship-type lineage that extends back to the 1920s with the commissioning of the first purpose-built pair, the *Pyro* (AE-1) and *Nitro*. A far cry from the present-day UNREP standard, the early ammunition ships offloaded their cargo to stationary barges for transfer to the warships that would visit their solitary anchorage, generally at a safe distance from the rest of the task force or fleet. The UNREP of ammunition and stores was born of necessity in early 1945, during the U.S. Pacific Fleet's advance on Iwo Jima, and subsequently was refined after the war, particularly as the *Conecuh* (AOR-110) proved the viability of the new role of a replenishment oiler in Atlantic fleet operations.

By the era of Operation DESERT STORM, two classes of ammunition ships operated with the U.S. Navy: the aging Suribachi (AE-21) class from the 1950s and the newer and significantly advanced Kilauea (AE-26) class. In the mid-1980s five additional ammunition ships were planned, but by the early 1990s preference was given to the construction of the Supply (AOE-6) class of fast combat support ships. The specifications of the Suribachi and Kilauea classes follow.

The Canadian replenishment ship HMCS *Protecteur* participated in the U.S.-led coalition during the Persian Gulf War. Canada's participation in the conflict was the first offensive combat operation for that country since the Korean War. (U.S. Department of Defense)

The five ships of the AE-21 Suribachi class were launched during 1956–1959 and were decommissioned during 1993–1997. Dimensions are length, 512 feet; beam, 72 feet; and draft, 29 feet. Displacement is 10,000 tons (light) or 17,450 tons (full load). Speed is 20 knots, and range is 12,000 nautical miles at 15 knots and 10,000 nautical miles at 20 knots. Complement is 346 (21 officers and 325 enlisted). The ships are armed with four 3-inch (76-mm) guns and four .50-caliber machine guns.

The seven ships of the AE-26 Kilauea class ships were launched during 1967–1972. Six are active MSC, and one was decommissioned in 1990. Dimensions are length overall, 564 feet; beam, 81 feet; and draft, 28 feet. Speed is 22 knots with a range of 18,000 nautical miles at 11 knots and 10,000 nautical miles at 20 knots. Complement is 125 civilian and 26 navy (4 officers and 22 enlisted).

UNREP ships taking part in the U.S. naval component of DESERT SHIELD/DESERT STORM were the Sacramento-class fast combat support ships *Sacramento* (AOE-1), *Seattle* (AOE-3), and *Detroit* (AOE-4); the Wichita-class replenishment oilers *Kansas City* (AOR-3), *Savannah* (AOR-4), and *Kalamazoo* (AOR-6); the venerable Mispillion (T-AO-105)-class fleet oiler *Passumpsic* (T-AO-107); the Neosho-class fleet oilers *Neosho* (T-AO-143), *Hassayampa* (T-AO-145), and *Ponchatoula* (T-AO-148); the Cimarron-class fleet oilers *Cimarron* (AO-177) and *Platte* (AO-186); and the

Henry J. Kaiser–class fleet oilers *Joshua Humphreys* (T-AO-188), *Andrew J. Higgins* (T-AO-190), and *Walter S. Diehl* (T-AO-193). All of the combat stores ships of the Mars class were on hand: the *Mars* (AFS-1), *Sylvania* (AFS-2), *Niagara Falls* (AFS-3), *White Plains* (AFS-4), *Concord* (AFS-5), *San Diego* (AFS-6), and *San Jose* (AFS-7). Two of the three Sirius-class ships also participated: the *Sirius* (T-AFS-8) and the *Spica* (T-AFS-9).

The ammunition ships *Suribachi* (AE-21) and sister-ship *Haleakala* (AE-25) joined the operations, as did the *Kilauea* (T-AE-26), *Santa Barbara* (AE-28), *Mount Hood* (AE-29), *Flint* (AE-32), *Shasta* (AE-33), *Mount Baker* (AE-34), and *Kiska* (AE-35).

Replenishment ships from non-U.S. navies that participated in DESERT SHIELD/DESERT STORM were the Italian Navy's replenishment oiler *Stromboli* (A-5327), the Royal Navy's fleet oiler RFA *Orangeleaf* (A-110), the Royal Netherlands Navy's fast combat support ship *Zuiderkruis* (A-832), the replenishment oiler *Durance* (A-629) of the French Navy, the logistics support ship *Sao Miguel* (A-5208) of the Portuguese Navy, the Canadian Armed Forces' operational support ship HMCS *Protecteur* (AOR-509), and the Royal Australian Navy's replenishment oiler HMAS *Success*.

UNREP replenishment naval units have also been active in Operations ENDURING FREEDOM and IRAQI FREEDOM, supporting forces as the need arises. The U.S. naval component again has predominated, but the international contribution has been significant. From October 2001 to June 2002 and again from late 2002 on, the logistical needs of up to five CVBGs in the region were met by a leaner naval support network; many of the replenishment ships available a decade earlier had left service, challenging the new combat support ships of the Supply (AOE-6) class as they supplemented their siblings of the Sacramento class and proving the U.S. Navy's wisdom in developing flexible multirole replenishment ships in the 1990s and beyond. During the early phase of ENDURING FREEDOM, the Henry J. Kaiser–class fleet oiler *John Ericsson* (T-AO-194) and Mars-class combat stores ship *Niagara Falls* (T-AFS-3) joined the veteran combat support ships *Sacramento* (AOE-1), *Camden* (AOE-2), *Seattle* (AOE-3), and *Detroit* (AOE-4) as well as the *Supply* (AOE-6), *Arctic* (AOE-8), and *Bridge* (AOE-10) of the follow-on Supply-class ships in supporting the U.S. CVBGs. The Canadian support ship HMCS *Protecteur* was again on hand for replenishment duty, as were the French replenishment oiler *Marne* (A-630) and the Italian Navy's replenishment ship *Etna* (A-5326). Japan in 2001 dispatched a rotating group of its destroyers to the Indian Ocean in support of ENDURING FREEDOM's counterterrorism activities, accompanied in turn by the fast combat support ships *Towada* (A-422), *Tokiwa* (A-423), and *Mashuu* (A-425), but this naval presence was withdrawn in 2007.

Stationed in the region as Operation IRAQI FREEDOM got under way along with the CVBGs present were the U.S. combat stores ships *Sirius* (T-AFS-8) and *Spica* (T-AFS-9), the ammunition ship *Mount Baker* (T-AE-34), and the fleet oilers *Henry J. Kaiser* (T-AO-187), *Walter S. Diehl* (T-AO-193), and *Kanawha* (T-AO-196). The fast combat support ships *Camden* (AOE-2), *Rainier* (T-AOE-7), and *Arctic* (T-AOE-8) were also in theater along with units from other navies, including the sizable Royal Navy's Task Group 2003, among whose components were the combat store ships RFA *Fort Rosalie* (A-385) and RFA *Fort Austin* (A-386) and the fleet oiler RFA *Orangeleaf* (A-110), operating in rotation with other coalition and U.S. Navy support ships as both ENDURING FREEDOM and IRAQI FREEDOM continue to move forward.

The unique naval aspects of Operations DESERT STORM, ENDURING FREEDOM, and IRAQI FREEDOM are illustrative of the importance of UNREP to the accomplishment and sustained viability of such large-scale military undertakings. Battle groups gathered around aircraft carriers, battleships, or amphibious command or assault ships would lose both focus and momentum without the flexibility and independence afforded them by forward-deployed UNREP.

GORDON E. HOGG

See also

DESERT STORM, Operation, Coalition Naval Forces; ENDURING FREEDOM, Operation, Coalition Naval Forces; Fast Combat Support Ships; IRAQI FREEDOM, Operation, Coalition Naval Forces; Military Sealift Command; Support and Supply Ships, Strategic; United States Navy, Iraq War; United States Navy, Persian Gulf War

References

Marolda, Edward, and Robert Schneller. *Shield and Sword: The United States Navy and the Persian Gulf War.* Annapolis, MD: U.S. Naval Institute Press, 2001.

Polmar, Norman. *The Naval Institute Guide to the Ships and Aircraft of the U.S. Fleet.* 18th ed. Annapolis, MD: Naval Institute Press, 2005.

Saunders, Stephen, ed. *Jane's Fighting Ships, 2002–2003.* Coulsdon, Surrey, UK, and Alexandria, VA: Jane's Information Group, 2002.

Sharpe, Richard, ed. *Jane's Fighting Ships: 1991–1992.* London: Jane's Information Group, 1991.

Wildenberg, Thomas. *Gray Steel and Black Oil: Fast Tankers and Replenishment at Sea in the U.S. Navy, 1912–1995.* Annapolis, MD: Naval Institute Press, 1996.

United Arab Emirates

Middle Eastern federated state located in Southwest Asia along the southeastern Arabian Peninsula and bordered by the Persian Gulf to the east, Oman to the south, and Saudi Arabia to the west. Previously known as the Trucial States until 1971, the United Arab Emirates (UAE) is a federation of seven emirates: Abu Dhabi, Ajman, Fujayrah, Sharjah, Dubai, Ras Khaymah, and Umm Qaiwain. The UAE is 32,278 square miles in area, or just slightly larger than the U.S. state of South Carolina, and has an altitude ranging from sea level to 3,200 feet and a tropical and subtropical desert climate. The primary UAE commodity and export is oil. The current population is estimated at 4.6 million people, about 50 percent of whom are South Asian (including many Pakistanis, Indians, and Sri Lankans), 42 percent of whom are Amirati Arab and Iranian, and 8 percent others. Islam is practiced by 96 percent of the population; the remaining practice Hinduism, Buddhism, and varying denominations of Christianity. Owing to perpetually abundant oil revenues, the UAE is a prosperous and relatively wealthy nation with a per capita income of about $37,000 per year, making it a significant draw for foreigners from other parts of the region.

Beginning in 1853, Great Britain forced the separate emirates of the area to sign truce treaties to prevent conflicts between the emirates, reduce piracy in the Persian Gulf, and eliminate their participation in the slave trade. From the British perspective, keeping the peace among the emirates was crucial to controlling their colonial empire on the subcontinent. In 1892 the British and the emirates negotiated another treaty that tightened the bonds between the two. The sheikhs agreed not to cede territory to any other nation or enter into commercial arrangements or other venues of exchange with foreign governments without London's consent. In return, the British pledged to protect the emirates from outside aggression. In 1968 Great Britain announced its intent to allow the former treaties with the emirates to lapse. On December 2, 1971, the emirates created their own federation, the UAE. Politics in the UAE are tightly controlled by the ruling sheikhs, and there are no political parties. The presidency and the post of prime minister are both hereditary positions, and members of the

The skyline of Dubai, United Arab Emirates (UAE). (Monkey Business Images/Dreamstime.com)

Supreme Council and the Council of Ministers are all chosen by the leaders of the seven emirates.

During the Iran-Iraq War of 1980–1988 the UAE staked out a studiously ambivalent position toward the conflict. This was partly because its government sought to eschew entanglements with foreign powers, but it was also because the nation profited handsomely from the war. UAE oil revenues rose dramatically as those of Iran and Iraq flagged. In late July 1991, however, when Iraqi forces were threatening to move against Kuwait, the UAE was among the first nations to recommend joint military action to deter Iraqi aggression. Indeed, the week prior to the August 2, 1990, Iraqi invasion of Iraq, the U.S. and UAE air forces engaged in a joint air-refueling exercise meant as a warning to Iraqi dictator Saddam Hussein.

When Operation DESERT STORM, the coalition effort against Iraq, commenced in January 1991, the UAE contributed several hundred troops to the fight. The UAE also provided air support and permitted U.S. military aircraft to bomb Iraqi positions from its air fields. By mid-1991 the UAE had given or pledged as much as $6 billion to foreign nations that had waged the war against Iraq. Six UAE soldiers died during the Persian Gulf War.

The UAE has traditionally eyed Iran with trepidation since the 1979 revolution there that brought a fundamentalist Islamic republic to power. Relations between the two nations have remained tense, and disputes over control of several islands in the Persian Gulf have only added to the atmosphere of mistrust. Since its formation in 1971, the UAE has maintained generally good relations with the West and, in particular, with the United States. After the September 11, 2001, terrorist attacks against the United States, the UAE sharply condemned such violence and has been a steady and reliable partner in the Global War on Terror. In the immediate aftermath of the attacks, the UAE government promptly severed diplomatic ties with the ruling Taliban government in Afghanistan.

In terms of the Iraq War that began in March 2003 (Operation IRAQI FREEDOM), the UAE initially allowed U.S. and coalition troops access to its military facilities to prosecute the war. The UAE also contributed troops (as many as 20,000) to protect Kuwait in the event that Hussein moved against that country at the beginning of hostilities. However, as the war in Iraq dragged on, the UAE's support for it waned. The UAE joined a growing number of nations that condemned the ongoing conflict. In June 2008, the UAE's foreign minister visited Iraq, the first such visit by a high-level official from a Persian Gulf nation since 2003. There he announced that the UAE would soon be sending an in-residence ambassador to Baghdad.

WYNDHAM WHYNOT

See also

Afghanistan; DESERT STORM, Operation; ENDURING FREEDOM, Operation; Iran; Iran-Iraq War; IRAQI FREEDOM, Operation; September 11 Attacks, International Reactions to; Taliban

References

Congressional Quarterly. *The Middle East.* 10th ed. Washington, DC: CQ Press, 2005.

Davidson, Christopher M. *The United Arab Emirates: A Study in Survival.* Boulder, CO: Lynne Rienner, 2005.

Ochsenwald, William, and Sydney Nettleton Fisher. *The Middle East: A History.* 6th ed. New York: McGraw-Hill, 2004.

United Arab Republic

Political union between Egypt and Syria that commenced on February 1, 1958, and ended on September 28, 1961. By late 1957 there was considerable interest in Arab unity. In the case of Syria and Egypt, the motivation was chiefly ideological—with ruling elites in both countries dedicated to Arab unity, social revolution, and Third Worldism in foreign affairs—and secondarily political. Egyptian president Gamal Abdel Nasser had always supported Arab unity and Arabism. He made references to these in many addresses, and such pronouncements only grew with the 1956 Suez War. Nasser stressed pride in Arab origin, political cooperation, and unity when he declared that "the Arab nation is one nation."

On November 18, 1957, in Damascus, the Syrian parliament, dominated by the Baath Party, met jointly with a visiting Egyptian delegation and called for a Syrian-Egyptian federation. The Syrian prounion Baathists were apparently prompted by the growing influence of a different political faction within their own party in Syria. These leaders believed that Syria would benefit from the union, which would also destabilize their enemies within the military and competing political leaders in Syria.

Nasser was at first reluctant for a variety of reasons, including the sharp contrast in the two countries and their political and social configurations. Egypt's authoritarian military government differed sharply with Syria's multiparty parliamentary system. Nasser responded to the Syrian overture by insisting that any union would have to be a unitary rather than a federal state and that Syria would have to dissolve its political parties. The ruling group of Baathists accepted Nasser's conditions including the elimination of all political parties, which he regarded as symbols of internal division and a potential political threat.

The union was formally approved by resolutions in both national parliaments and became official on February 1, 1958. The new unitary state was known as the United Arab Republic (UAR). In the new state, the president held the bulk of the power. He had executive authority, assisted by executive councils in the Egyptian and Syrian regions. Between these and the president there would be four vice presidents, two from each region. Legislative authority would be in the hands of an assembly appointed by the president. At least half of the assembly members were to be selected from the existing Syrian and Egyptian parliaments. At an unspecified future date a new constitution would be adopted, confirmed by a plebiscite.

On February 21, 1958, both the Egyptian and Syrian regions voted nearly unanimously for the union and for Nasser as its president. On March 5 Nasser proclaimed the provisional constitution in effect. Society would be organized along the lines of social solidarity and a planned economy according to principles of social justice. Political parties were abolished. In their place was a National Union, the principles behind which the president would define. Nasser then appointed the first UAR cabinet and the two regional executive councils.

A crowd of enthusiastic Syrians gathers to greet Gamal Abdel Nasser in Damascus following the proclamation of the United Arab Republic (UAE), February 26, 1958. Nasser was the president of the new union. (AP/Wide World Photos)

On March 8 Yemen entered into a formal arrangement with the UAR, with the new entity to be known as the United Arab States. Although there was a Supreme Council of the heads of the member states—in sharp contrast to the UAR—in the United Arab States, each state retained its own form of government and, in most cases, maintained separate diplomatic representation abroad. In effect, the United Arab States was a very loose-knit organization, with Yemen largely going its own way. No doubt prompted by these developments, only weeks after the establishment of the UAR, Iraq and Jordan announced the formation of their own federation.

In foreign affairs and in his regional radio communications, Nasser claimed that the Arab peoples supported the doctrine of Arab solidarity and that it was their governments that were preventing Arab unity. Tensions immediately developed between the UAR and a number of Arab states with which there were already strains, such as Saudi Arabia, and where the governments feared Nasserists among their own population, as in Tunisia and Lebanon. Then, in the late spring of 1958, Camille Chamoun, who was opposed to Nasser, began a political struggle in Lebanon. Chamoun's foes protested, and he complained to the United States that Nasserists were threatening to take over the country. This came on the heels of a coup attempt against Jordan's King Hussein, who had other enemies as well. This possibility was stymied by the arrival in Jordan of British paratroopers, which widened the chasm between Nasserists and pro-Westerners.

In internal developments, the UAR never worked out as Nasser had hoped. By the time of the union, Nasser had firmly consolidated his rule in Egypt. There were, however, strong elements, especially among the established political figures in Syria, that resented the union with Egypt. There was also opposition among the growing numbers of Communist Party members in Syria, as Nasser had outlawed their party both in Egypt and in Syria.

To his credit, Nasser recognized the areas of Syrian reluctance regarding the UAR and at first pursued a deliberate, slow approach. For example, Syria was allowed complete economic autonomy in the first two years of the union. After about a year, however, Nasser did begin to eliminate certain Baath Party members from positions of leadership. In place of the multiparty system, he established the same National Union that existed in Egypt.

Two years after the UAR was established, Nasser did finally move, with fateful results, in the economic sphere to bring Syria in line with Egypt as far as its economic policies were concerned. In a number of speeches he stated that the UAR meant a commitment to the goals of Arab socialism. In November 1958 he introduced agrarian reform in Syria. At the same time, those in Syria who opposed the union reasserted themselves. They gained support because of the heavy-handed actions of certain Egyptian officials in Syria and because the Syrians found themselves outnumbered by Egyptians in the new mixed government. At the same time, as Nasser sought to play an increasingly active role on the world stage, he involved the UAR in a host of matters that had no direct advantage to the people of either country.

In July 1961 Nasser met this growing Syrian discontent with a number of wide-sweeping decrees that were intended to socialize the UAR and were aimed primarily at the elements of the old regime in Egypt and non-Egyptian residents of that country. Among these were the nationalization of banks, insurance companies, and hundreds of large businesses and economic enterprises; controlling government stock interest in large corporations; new income taxes that ranged up to 90 percent for the highest incomes; and new real estate taxes. These decrees took Egyptians as well as Syrians by surprise. The crowning blows came, however, when Nasser abolished the three-cabinet system in favor of a single cabinet for the UAR, sweeping aside the last vestiges of local autonomy, and introduced a common currency for both regions.

In reaction, on September 28, 1961, the Syrian military seized power in Damascus in a coup carried out without great bloodshed. The new leaders immediately announced the separation of Syria from Egypt. Although the new government's leaders expressed their support for Arab unity, they also insisted that this be based on equality rather than the dominance of one national entity over another. They also claimed that they sought socialism.

On learning of the coup Nasser at first ordered Egyptian paratroopers into action, but within hours he countermanded this and insisted that the Egyptian military in Syria surrender. According to journalist Muhammad Haykal, Nasser's longtime friend, Nasser intuitively knew that it was pointless to force an unwanted union, as it would undermine his desire to represent popular will. However, in later public pronouncements Nasser blamed the coup on "reactionaries" and "agents of imperialism."

The breakup of the UAR was greeted with great relief not only by Syria but also by the other Arab states of the region, especially Jordan. Jordan, Turkey, and Iran immediately recognized the new Syrian government.

SPENCER C. TUCKER

See also

Arab League; Arab Nationalism; Baath Party; Egypt; Nasser, Gamal Abdel; Pan-Arabism and Pan-Arabist Thought; Syria

References

Dawisha, A. I. *Egypt in the Arab World.* New York: Wiley, 1976.
Jankowski, James P. *Nasser's Egypt, Arab Nationalism, and the United Arab Republic.* Boulder, CO: Lynne Rienner, 2001.
Lenczowski, George. *The Middle East in World Affairs.* 4th ed. Ithaca, NY: Cornell University Press, 1980.
Podeh, Elie. *The Decline of Arab Unity: The Rise and Fall of the United Arab Republic.* New York: Sussex Academic, 1999.
Waterbury, John. *The Egypt of Nasser and Sadat: Political Economy of Two Regimes.* Princeton, NJ: Princeton University Press, 1983.

United Iraqi Alliance

Iraqi Shia political coalition created in 2004 in preparation for the 2005 elections held in Iraq and led by Abd al-Aziz al-Hakim of the Supreme Islamic Iraqi Council. The United Iraqi Alliance (UIA) is

Results of the December 2005 Iraqi Legislative Election

Party	Total Votes	% of Votes	Legislative Seats Received
United Iraqi Alliance	5,021,137	41.2%	128
Democratic Patriotic Alliance of Kurdistan	2,642,172	21.7%	53
Iraqi Accord Front	1,840,216	15.1%	44
Iraqi National List	977,325	8.0%	25
Iraqi National Dialogue Front	499,963	4.1%	11
Other	1,415,818	9.9%	14

a coalition of numerous political parties and groups and is generally Islamist in outlook and agenda. Nearly all the affiliated groups are Shiite, but there are a number of independent Sunni members as well.

The two most prominent parties in the alliance are Hakim's Supreme Islamic Iraqi Council (formerly Supreme Council for the Iraqi Revolution) and the Islamic Dawa Party, represented by Nuri al-Maliki, who is currently the Iraqi prime minister. Other important parties include Ahmed Chalabi's Iraqi National Congress, which quit the coalition prior to the December 2005 elections. Numerous adherents of the militant cleric Muqtada al-Sadr are also involved in the alliance. Iraq's senior Islamic cleric, Ayatollah Sayyid Ali Husayn al-Sistani, has apparently also given his unspoken blessing to the political coalition.

The UIA enjoyed a strong showing in the January 2005 nationwide elections, capturing slightly more than 4 million votes, or about 48 percent of the total. The election gave the alliance 140 seats, a majority of the 275 seats in Iraq's National Assembly. Notably, 40 seats of the 140 won by the UIA were held by women. The election triumph was especially savored by members of the Islamic Dawa Party, many of whom had been living in exile in Syria since the Saddam Hussein regime had banned the group and persecuted its adherents beginning in 1980. Indeed, the UIA has significant ties to Iran, which has led to concerns among some Iraqis and also U.S. leaders.

In March 2005 the UIA permitted representatives of the Iraqi Turkmen Front, which represents Iraq's Turkmen minority, to join. In all, the UIA counts some 20 political parties and caucuses among its ranks, having lost several prior to the December 2005 elections, which seated a permanent 275-member National Assembly. Although the UIA won more votes than the January 2005 elections, turnout was higher, so the net gain was reduced. In that election, the UIA captured 5.021 million votes, or 42 percent of the total, giving it 128 seats. This represented a drop in UIA power within the National Assembly, although the UIA still enjoyed the distinction of being the ruling coalition. In 2006 after months of tense talks and false starts, a national unity government was formed via a power-sharing arrangement among the UIA, the Iraqi Nationalist List, the Iraqi Accord Front, and the Kurdistani Alliance. Maliki was chosen to represent the coalition as prime minister.

Paul G. Pierpaoli Jr.

See also

Chalabi, Ahmed Abd al-Hadi; Hakim, Abd al-Aziz al-; Iraq, History of, 1990–Present; Maliki, Nuri Muhammed Kamil Hasan al-; Sadr, Muqtada al-; Sistani, Sayyid Ali Husayn al-; Supreme Iraqi Islamic Council

References

Nasr, Vali. *The Shia Revival: How Conflicts within Islam Will Shape the Future.* New York: Norton, 2006.

Packer, George. *The Assassins' Gate: America in Iraq.* New York: Farrar, Straus and Giroux, 2005.

Stansfield, Gareth. *Iraq: People, History, Politics.* Cambridge, UK: Polity, 2007.

United Kingdom

Island nation located off the northwestern coast of continental Europe encompassing 94,526 square miles. Although the United Kingdom is a single state, it is composed of four entities: England, Wales, Scotland, and Northern Ireland. The United Kingdom also has numerous overseas possessions. With a 2009 population of 60.944 million people, the United Kingdom is a constitutional parliamentary monarchy. The monarch is the head of state, while the prime minister is the head of government. Queen Elizabeth II has reigned as Great Britain's monarch since 1952. The nation's two main political parties are the Labour Party (a left-center party) and the Conservative Party (a right-center party). During the 1991 Persian Gulf War the Conservatives held power and helped form a strong Anglo-American response to Iraqi aggression. During the subsequent wars in Afghanistan and Iraq the British were similarly committed to maintaining a strong military alliance with the Americans, but this time under a Labour government.

When Iraqi forces seized and occupied the emirate of Kuwait in August 1990, British prime minister Margaret Thatcher reportedly exhorted President George H. W. Bush to remain firm in opposition to this, pleadings that many believed contributed to Bush's decision to launch a war against Iraq the following year. Thatcher quickly dispatched British troops to the Persian Gulf as part of the international coalition that Bush put together. Thatcher's successor, John Major, who replaced her as premier in November 1990, made considerable efforts to win public and parliamentary support for a war that many feared would be lengthy, costly, and inconclusive. Labour and Liberal Social Democratic Party leaders supported him, and only 57 members of Parliament, mostly Labour leftists, voted against it on January 15, 1991. British ground forces, aircraft, and ships played a prominent part, second only to the United States, in the brief Persian Gulf War of early 1991 in which coalition ground forces attained victory in a matter of days after an opening aerial bombing campaign lasting several weeks. Major basked in the credit for this outcome, marred only by subsequent revelations that friendly fire from U.S. forces had been responsible for a number of British casualties during the conflict.

British prime minister Margaret Thatcher, with President George H. W. Bush looking on, speaks to reporters in Washington, D.C., on August 7, 1990, following an Oval Office meeting with the president on the situation in the Persian Gulf. (AP/Wide World Photos)

The Persian Gulf War left Saddam Hussein in power, as coalition forces refused to intercede to assist domestic uprisings against his rule by dissident Iraqi Shiites and Kurds. Throughout the 1990s, Britain joined the United States in supporting comprehensive economic sanctions against Iraq, and British and American airpower maintained a no-fly zone in northern Iraq, effectively protecting local Kurdish breakaway governments. In retaliation for assorted Iraqi noncooperation and unfriendly acts, aircraft from both powers also repeatedly bombed Iraqi targets of military value. These low-level hostilities provoked occasional parliamentary and other protests in Britain, focusing particularly upon the impact of continuing sanctions on Iraqi children and other civilians, but aroused no serious opposition. Britain also supported 1998 bombing raids by U.S. aircraft on factories and training camps in Sudan and Afghanistan associated with the radical Islamist group Al Qaeda in response to car bombings of U.S. embassies in Kenya and Tanzania.

When Al Qaeda terrorist operatives attacked the United States by hijacking four civilian jetliners on September 11, 2001, and mounting suicide attacks on the World Trade Center in New York and the Pentagon building in northern Virginia, Britain joined other North Atlantic Traty Organization (NATO) allies in supporting the United States. British troops were prominent in the war that the U.S.-led coalition launched in November 2001 against the Taliban

government and Al Qaeda forces in Afghanistan, a conflict in which apparent victory was quickly attained. Maintaining military and political control proved a far more elusive goal. In late 2008 British and U.S. troops in Afghanistan and the military forces of the new Afghan government headed by Hamid Karzai still encountered substantial opposition from revived Taliban units, many of which seemed to be operating from havens in the mountains of neighboring Pakistan, a country supposedly allied with NATO.

Many critics argued that one reason for the continuing conflict in Afghanistan was the decision, spearheaded by U.S. president George W. Bush and British prime minister Tony Blair, to invade Iraq in March 2003. This new campaign, undertaken without the sanction of the United Nations (UN) and against strong opposition from several major powers, including Russia, China, France, and Germany, diverted resources in the form of troops and matériel from the ongoing struggle in Afghanistan and also absorbed much of the attention of British and American policy makers, leaving little to spare for the earlier war.

Whereas international and popular opinion had largely supported the war in Afghanistan as a justifiable response to the September 11 attacks on the United States, the invasion of Iraq aroused far more misgivings. In early 2003 public demonstrations against the anticipated war took place in the United States itself and across Europe, including Britain.

British prime minister Tony Blair addresses the House of Commons in London on March 19, 2003. In his speech, Blair urged the members of Parliament to support the use of force in Iraq. (AP/Wide World Photos)

Blair demonstrated a strong personal commitment to overthrowing Hussein, arguing passionately that both the personal brutality of his rule and what Blair claimed were Iraq's increasingly successful moves to develop chemical, biological, and nuclear weapons of mass destruction (WMDs) made the forcible removal of Hussein essential to international security. Blair faced strong opposition from members of his own Labour Party, many of whom rejected his rationale for war including former foreign secretary Robin Cook, who resigned in protest as leader of the House of Commons. In March 2003 Blair won a parliamentary majority in favor of war, including most of the Conservative Party, while some 135 Labour members voted against him. Broader public support for the war was at best lukewarm.

As with Afghanistan, overthrowing the existing regime in Iraq proved easier than maintaining control of the country or establishing a stable new indigenous government. By the end of May 2003 Hussein had been driven from power. (He was captured late that year, put on trial, and executed in December 2006.) To the embarrassment of the British and American governments, no WMDs—the stated justification for the war—were found. Official

discomfiture in both countries was compounded by public revelations in May 2003 that Blair and his advisers, like the Bush administration, had massaged or trumped up intelligence data so as to greatly exaggerate the strategic threat from Iraq to its neighbors and others. The suicide in July 2003 of David Kelly, a scientist in the British Ministry of Defense suspected of leaking this information to the media, added to this controversy, which the January 2004 report of a public inquiry headed by Lord Hutton failed to resolve.

In the absence of WMDs, British and American leaders sought to justify the war by highlighting the numerous atrocities and abuses of human rights for which Hussein's regime had been responsible and celebrating their own intention of establishing a functioning democracy in Iraq. Yet the establishment of political order proved highly problematic, and the situation degenerated into something approaching civil war, with Shia, Sunni, and Kurdish groups each supporting their own militias and using great brutality against their opponents. The methods that the U.S. government employed to prosecute the war in Iraq and, more generally, the Global War on Terror also tarnished its public image internationally. Revelations that American troops had abused Iraqi prisoners at Abu Ghraib, the illegal rendition and detention without trial of terror suspects sometimes on what appeared to be flimsy grounds to a camp in the U.S. military base of Guantánamo in Cuba and in other locations, and the readiness of Bush administration officials to endorse the use of torture and dehumanizing tactics all undercut claims by the British and American governments that they were defending human rights and democratic values. Seeking to conciliate an ally, the United States eventually released several Britons held at Guantánamo, but the damage had been done. Within Britain and around the world, popular and elite anti-Americanism soared dramatically.

After the initial victory in Iraq in 2003, British forces occupied the area around the city of Basra until September 2007, when over U.S. military opposition Gordon Brown, who had replaced Blair as prime minister the previous June, ordered them withdrawn and their mission switched to training indigenous Iraqi forces. Until then these troops had suffered a steady toll of casualties, with 176 dead and perhaps between 2,000 and 4,000 seriously wounded between 2003 and 2008. Brown was widely believed to have been a far less enthusiastic supporter than Blair of the war in Iraq. Before becoming prime minister, Brown had suggested that "mistakes" had been made in Iraq and that at some indefinite future date these would require a full-scale public inquiry. Once he took power, Brown verbally reaffirmed his commitment to the Anglo-American alliance and to stabilizing Iraq, but he also made it clear that he gave a higher priority to maintaining control of Afghanistan, where Britain had a substantial military presence, and to combating homegrown and international terrorism. It remained unclear just how long Brown envisaged deploying British forces in Iraq and Afghanistan.

Brown's emphasis on the continuing threat from terrorism reflected Britain's own experiences since 2001. By the 21st century, some 1.5 million Britons, approximately 2.8 percent of the population, were Muslims. At least some of these were highly responsive to the appeals of Al Qaeda and other radical Islamic groups, and several British nationals were captured fighting with Al Qaeda forces in Afghanistan. On July 7, 2005, 4 young British Muslim suicide bombers detonated explosive devices in the London Underground and the bus system, killing 56 people and injuring 700. A similar set of coordinated bombings was apparently planned for later in the month but failed because of defective bombs, and police arrested the would-be perpetrators. In July 2007 shortly after Brown took office, there were several unsuccessful attempts to explode car bombs in central London. Later that month car bombers attacked Glasgow Airport, killing 1 of the attackers and injuring several bystanders. The individuals responsible were not foreign infiltrators, although some of their contacts extended abroad to Jordan, Saudi Arabia, India, and Australia. Not all of these proved to be terrorist-related incidents, however.

British responses to such developments varied. The Blair and Brown governments sought to reach out to moderate Islamic leaders while keeping close surveillance on those imams who preached radical Islamic tenets and on their congregations. Feminists disliked conservative Muslim interpretations that subordinate women and were apprehensive that allowing British courts to listen to or be influenced by explanations of Sharia (Islamic law) to adjudicate domestic issues among believers would deprive Muslim women in Britain of the protection of the law. British artists and intellectuals expressed real concern that fears of provoking protests or even physical attacks from fundamentalist Muslims inhibited playwrights, writers, filmmakers, and others from producing work that might be thought critical of Islam.

In 1989 Ayatollah Ruhollah Khomeini, Iran's spiritual and political leader, had declared a fatwa against the British author Salman Rushdie, claiming that his recent novel *The Satanic Verses* blasphemed against Islam and that Rushdie was therefore an apostate. The novelist went into hiding for several years, and at least two of his translators in other countries were attacked. Sales of Rushdie's books soared with this scandal.

As Brown faced both an international economic crisis and what was likely to be a tough reelection campaign, the outlook for Britain's future Middle Eastern policies remained murky. The British military intervention in Iraq had proved unpopular with the British public and had become a major political liability, albeit one that Brown was trying to reduce by withdrawing forces from the country. Afghanistan, although less in the news, had the potential to become a lengthy and perhaps equally intractable commitment. It was also questionable whether Western countries could prevent Iran from developing nuclear weapons unless they were willing to use military force for that purpose.

British leaders also faced the problem of dealing with a serious threat of terrorism without alienating Britain's Muslim community or compromising traditional British liberal ideals. In addition, Britain had to resolve the dilemma of what constituted the acceptable limits of multiculturalism and how far, in the cause of respecting religious or traditional values and beliefs, a society should be prepared to go in tolerating intolerance.

PRISCILLA ROBERTS

See also

Blair, Tony; Brown, James Gordon; Major, John Roy; Thatcher, Margaret

References

Cook, Robin. *The Point of Departure.* New York: Simon and Schuster, 2003.

Danner, Mark. *The Secret Way to War: The Downing Street Memo and the Iraq War Buried History.* New York: New York Review Books, 2006.

El-Solh, Raghid. *Britain: 2 Wars with Iraq, 1941–1991.* Reading, UK: Ithaca Press, 1996.

Keohane, Dan. "British Policy in the Conflict." In *International Perspectives on the Gulf Conflict, 1990–1991,* edited by Alex Danchev and Dan Keohane. London: St. Martin's, 1994.

———. "The United Kingdom." In *The Iraq War and Democratic Politics,* edied by. Alex Danchev and John Macmillan. London: Routledge, 2005.

Meyer, Christopher. *DC Confidential: The Controversial Memoirs of Britain Ambassador to the U.S. at the Time of 9/11 and the Gulf War.* London: Weidenfeld and Nicolson, 2005.

Seldon, Anthony, with Chris Ballinger, Daniel Collings, and Peter Snowdon. *Blair.* London: Free Press, 2004.

Serfaty, Simon. *Architects of Delusion: Europe, America, and the Iraq War.* Philadelphia: University of Pennsylvania Press, 2008.

Steele, Jonathan. *Defeat: Why America and Britain Lost Iraq.* Berkeley, CA: Counterpoint, 2008.

United Kingdom, Air Force, Iraq War

The United Kingdom's Royal Air Force (RAF) played a significant role during Operation TELIC (the British contribution to Operation IRAQI FREEDOM). Commanded by Air Vice Marshal Glenn Torpy, Royal Air Force composite squadrons in Iraq included elements from squadrons based at RAF Marham, RAF Leeming, RAF Leuchars, RAF Coltishall, RAF Cottesmore, RAF Waddington, RAF Benson, RAF Brize Norton, RAF Lyneham, RAF Kinloss, and RAF Odiham. These squadrons operated Panavia Tornado F3, Panavia Tornado GR4, Sepecat Jaguar, and Boeing/British Aerospace AV-8B Harrier II combat aircraft; McDonnell Douglas/Boeing C-17 Globamaster II and Lockheed C-130 Hercules transport aircraft; and Vickers-Armstrong VC-10 aerial tankers. Helicopters operated by the RAF included the Boeing CH-47 Chinook heavy transport, the Aérospatiale Puma medium-lift transport, and the Westland Lynx attack helicopter. Finally, the RAF deployed the RAF Regiment to protect its air stations in the Gulf region. In all, of the 46,000 British troops to participate in the initial stages of Operation TELIC, 8,100 served in the Royal Air Force.

In comparison to the 1991 Persian Gulf War, during which a sustained air campaign of 34 days preceded the ground offensive, the plan for Operation IRAQI FREEDOM was a simultaneous launch of ground and air attacks. Popularly known by the completely inadequate misnomer of "shock and awe," the aim of these attacks was for the American and British air forces to blitz Iraq with precision weapons from the air to destroy key leadership, command-and-control, and military targets, while ground forces raced to Baghdad to topple the government.

The campaign began just after 1:00 a.m. on March 20, 2003, when the American air commander Lieutenant General Michael "Buzz" Moseley launched a pair of Lockheed F-117 Nighthawk stealth bombers to attack a target in Baghdad's downtown area, where Iraqi president Saddam Hussein and his sons, Uday and Qusay, were purportedly meeting. Following this initial attack, throughout the day of March 20, through the night of March 20–21, and throughout the day of March 21, air efforts focused on aiding allied troops who had by this time crossed into Iraq.

On the night of March 21–22 the full fury of the allied bombing campaign was launched. In all, 1,500 British and American

A Royal Air Force GR4 Tornado of the 12th Bomber Squadron in flight over Iraq, September 3, 2008. (U.S. Department of Defense)

missions were flown that night, 700 of which were by strike aircraft, and approximately 1,000 targets were hit. This firepower was augmented by the coalition naval component; British and American vessels at sea also launched 500 cruise missiles before dawn on March 22. Yet throughout these first two days and nights of the campaign, commanders placed several restrictions on bombing targets. The bridges across the Tigris and Euphrates were not destroyed, as these would be needed by the rapid advance of American and British troops. Likewise, much of the Iraqi communications infrastructure was left untouched because allied war leaders needed Iraqi troops to receive word that their political leadership had fallen. Finally, the electricity grid sustained little damage out of fear that destroying it would make postwar stability and recovery harder to accomplish. On the night of March 22–23 British and American aircraft flew 800 strike sorties, followed by an additional 1,500–2,000 sorties over the next 48 hours. On March 25 a *shamal* blew in, causing a fierce sandstorm that lasted for three days, yet still the air attacks continued unabated, with sorties rising to 2,000 in each 24-hour period.

Over this time, the attacks shifted from preplanned targets to targets of opportunity, particularly against Iraqi ground forces deployed in the defense of Baghdad. By April 4, 85 percent of all allied air attacks were focused on Iraqi ground units. The fall of Baghdad and the end of the conventional war in Iraq followed shortly thereafter. On April 8 the Iraqi Republican Guard units defending the city dispersed into smaller units, and by April 11 all Iraqi forces within the environs of Baghdad had been eliminated. In total, from March 20 to April 12 the British and American air forces flew 36,275 sorties, of which 14,050 were strike sorties. The RAF lost no aircraft to enemy fire or suffered any casualties from Iraqi guns. Tragically, however, one RAF Tornado was shot down by an American Patriot missile in a friendly fire incident, killing both crew members. Only a small number of RAF personnel and equipment remained in Iraq after mid-June 2003.

BENJAMIN GROB-FITZGIBBON

See also
United Kingdom

References
Keegan, John. *The Iraq War: The Military Offensive, from Victory in 21 Days to the Insurgent Aftermath.* New York: Vintage, 2005.
Murray, Williamson, and Robert H. Scales Jr. *The Iraq War: A Military History.* Cambridge, MA: Belknap, 2005.

United Kingdom, Air Force, Persian Gulf War

Operation GRANBY, the British code name for the 1991 Persian Gulf War (Operations DESERT SHIELD and DESERT STORM), saw the deployment of more than 7,000 Royal Air Force (RAF) troops to the Persian Gulf region. Indeed, almost all of the 89,000 personnel serving in the RAF at the time were in some way involved with the conflict.

British aircraft included at least 100 fixed-wing aircraft and 27 support helicopters. Commanded first by Air Vice Marshal Ronald Andrew Fellowes "Sandy" Wilson and then, after November 17, 1990, by Air Vice Marshal William (Bill) Wratten, the RAF served effectively alongside the U.S. Air Force throughout the conflict.

When Iraq failed to heed the deadline of January 15, 1991, imposed by the United Nations (UN) to withdraw all Iraqi troops from Kuwait, coalition forces began final preparations for an attack against Iraq. Just before 3:00 a.m. local time on January 17, the air attacks began. The immediate task was to destroy the Iraqi air defense system, which within a few hours had been made ineffective. RAF Panavia Tornado GR1 aircraft took part in the first strikes. By dawn that same day the RAF had flown 352 sorties and attacked 158 separate targets.

Following the destruction of the Iraqi air defenses, the thrust of operations changed to the suppression of Iraqi air operations, the destruction of Iraqi air capability, and the neutralization of key Iraqi command and control centers. By January 25 this mission had also been achieved. After that date no further Iraqi aircraft got off the ground, with the exception of aircraft that fled to Iran on the day the ground operations began on February 24.

The RAF played an important role in these operations, as its Tornados carried the JP233 runway-cratering bomb, a weapon unlike anything the U.S. Air Force could deploy. On January 25 coalition air forces shifted their focus from keeping Iraqi aircraft on the ground to systematically destroying them while they sat in their shelters. All told, 375 Iraqi aircraft shelters were destroyed along with 141 aircraft inside. The following day, January 26, just nine days into the campaign, the allied commanders declared complete air supremacy and no longer considered the Iraqi Air Force a threat.

Following the attainment of coalition air superiority, the RAF's runway-destroying capability was de-emphasized. The British Tornados and other aircraft were therefore tasked with concentrating on a variety of other targets, from Iraqi radar sites and oil refineries to ammunition depots and logistical storehouses. The RAF also began to engage in other air operations, such as the flying of noncombat transports and tankers in Iraqi airspace and the carrying out of reconnaissance flights. Such operations continued for another four weeks until Sunday, February 24, when after 34 days of the air campaign the ground war began with two simultaneous invasions of Kuwait. Within 100 hours the war was over, and the forces of Iraq had surrendered. The RAF operated in a supporting role throughout the 100 hours of ground combat.

The RAF also deployed to the theater Boeing 707/320 Sentry AWACS (Airborne Warning and Control System) aircraft, Sepecat Jaguar GR3 fighters, Vickers VC10 and Lockheed L-1011 Tristar (air-to-air refueling) aircraft, Lockheed C-130 Hercules (transport) aircraft, BAE Harrier GR7 light-attack aircraft, and Aérospatiale Puma and Boeing CH-47 Chinook helicopters.

In the course of the air and ground campaigns, RAF aircraft delivered more than 3,300 tons of ordnance, including more than 100 JP233 aircraft denial weapons, some 6,000 1,000-pound bombs, more than 100 antiradar missiles, and nearly 700 air-to-ground rockets. RAF helicopters flew nearly 900 sorties, the Tanker Force offloaded more than 14,300 tons of fuel, and the Air Transport Force moved more than 55,000 tons of freight.

During the war, eight RAF crew members lost their lives, three of whom were killed in training; the remaining five were killed in action. Six aircraft, all Tornados, were also lost in combat. Of these, 2 are thought to have been inadvertently flown into the ground in darkness and poor visibility, 1 was destroyed by the premature explosion of a bomb it carried, and 3 were downed by Iraqi surface-to-air missiles. Because of their low-flying tactics, the RAF lost 1 Tornado for every 80 sorties, compared to American losses of 1 aircraft for every 750 sorties. The Persian Gulf War was a considerable success for the RAF, but the war was not without cost.

BENJAMIN GROB-FITZGIBBON

See also

DESERT STORM, Operation, Coalition Air Campaign; United States Air Force, Persian Gulf War

References

Allen, Charles. *Thunder and Lightning: The RAF in the Gulf; Personal Experiences of War.* London: Her Majesty's Stationary Office, 1991.

De la Billière, General Sir Peter. *Storm Command: A Personal Account of the Gulf War.* London: HarperCollins, 1992.

Lambeth, Benjamin S. *The Winning of Air Supremacy in Operation Desert Storm.* RAND Occasional Paper P-7837. Santa Monica, CA: RAND Corporation, 1993.

United Kingdom, Army, Iraq War

The British Army was the second-largest force contributor, behind the U.S. Army, to the anti–Saddam Hussein coalition during the 2003 Iraq War (2003–). The British military operation during the Iraq War was code-named Operation TELIC. The British Army began deploying units to the region in anticipation of the conflict in January 2003, ultimately deploying some 26,000 soldiers for the invasion of Iraq. The British ground force was centered on the 1st Armoured Division, which included the 7th Armored Brigade, the 16th Air Assault Brigade, and the 102st Logistics Brigade in addition to various infantry, artillery, medical, and support units. The division was commanded by Major General Robin Brims. Royal Air Force air marshal Brian Burridge was the British national contingent commander, and British Army major general Peter Wall was his chief of staff.

The British forces were placed under the operational control of the U.S. I Marine Expeditionary Force (I MEF). The I MEF was the eastern column of the two-prong coalition advance into Iraq. Once the ground invasion began on March 22, the main elements of the I MEF advanced toward Baghdad, while the British forces, along with most of the Australian and Polish troops, undertook operations in the southeastern portion of Iraq, including first the capture of the Faw (Fao) peninsula and the strategic port of Umm

Qasr in an operation in support of Special Air Service (SAS) units and Royal Marine commandos. The division then advanced and captured the airport outside of Basra, Iraq's second-largest city, four days after the start of the invasion.

After instituting a loose blockade, on April 6 British forces launched a three-prong attack on Basra itself and captured the city after meeting light resistance. By the end of the day British forces had secured their main objectives. In an effort to minimize looting and lawlessness, officers conducted a series of negotiations with local and tribal leaders to craft an interim security agreement for Basra.

The British then assumed command of the Multi-National Force Southeast, which included their own ground units as well as contributions from a range of other states. The force endeavored to maintain security for the region around Basra in the face of a growing insurgency. As a result of the frequency of roadside bombings and mine damage, Britain purchased and deployed new armored patrol vehicles and personnel carriers.

The British also participated in the coalition program to train Iraqi security personnel, including more than 22,000 police officers.

A member of a British Army sniper team of the 42nd Royal Highland Regiment (Black Watch), Basra, Iraq, in September 2004. (U.S. Department of Defense)

British forces served as advisers to Iraqi units through transition teams, which remained with the national troops during security operations. Meanwhile, the British Ministry of Defense began to withdraw its own forces from Iraq. By May 2003 British Army forces had been reduced to 18,000. A series of rotations replaced the British 1st Armoured Division with the British 3rd Infantry Division in July 2003. Through 2004 and 2005 the British Army maintained about 8,500 troops in Iraq but began to reduce its force presence over the next several years, so that by the end of 2008 only about 4,100 troops remained. On April 30, 2009, British prime minister Gordon Brown announced the end of British combat operations in Iraq and a phased withdrawal of the remaining British forces there. By July 28, 2009, all remaining British troops had left Iraq and been redeployed to Kuwait after the Iraqi government rejected a request to extend their mission in a training capacity.

In 2005 additional troops were deployed to provide security for Iraqi national elections. Also in 2005, the British began to transfer control over basic training for military recruits to the Iraqi National Army, and British forces began to turn over military facilities to their Iraqi counterparts. Through 2006, additional provinces were turned over to Iraqi security forces.

British forces conducted a number of exercises with Iraqi forces, including Operation SINBAD from September 2006 to March of 2007. SINBAD was designed to provide security to more than 550 infrastructure projects in Basra and to dislodge antigovernment militias in the region. British troops have also participated in operations outside of their area of responsibility, such as Operation FARDH AL QANOON in which two battalions served alongside Iraqi forces in security sweeps in Baghdad.

In 2007 British forces withdrew from their last major post within Basra, creating a security vacuum that led to renewed fighting between Shiite militias. An offensive by the Iraqi Army to displace the militias failed. Nonetheless, the transfer of control meant that all four southern provinces within the scope of operations of the British had been handed over to the Iraqis.

British participation in the Iraq War was controversial among the public, who increasingly supported the withdrawal of forces after 2003. In December 2008 British prime minister Gordon Brown announced that the majority of British troops would be withdrawn from Iraq through 2009, leaving only approximately 400 troops who would continue to participate in training missions. During Britain's involvement in Iraq, 179 military personnel had been killed, and 3,598 had been wounded or injured.

TOM LANSFORD

See also

Friendly Fire; IRAQI FREEDOM, Operation, Coalition Ground Forces; Multi-National Force–Iraq; Special Air Service, United Kingdom; Special Boat Service, United Kingdom; United Kingdom, Air Force, Iraq War; United Kingdom, Marines, Iraq War; United States

References

Cockburn, Patrick. *The Occupation: War and Resistance in Iraq.* New York: Verso, 2007.

Keegan, John. *The Iraq War: The Military Offensive, from Victory in 21 Days to the Insurgent Aftermath.* New York: Vintage, 2005.

Murray, Williamson, and Robert H. Scales Jr. *The Iraq War: A Military History.* Cambridge, MA: Belknap, 2005.

United Kingdom, Army, Persian Gulf War

The British Army was the second-largest contributor to the U.S.-led coalition that liberated Kuwait during the Persian Gulf War. When the administration of U.S. president George H. W. Bush began to assemble the anti–Saddam Hussein alliance during Operation DESERT SHIELD, the British government was one of the first nations to pledge military support. However, the British Army was still in a Cold War posture, and there had not been a significant overseas deployment since the 1982 Falkland Islands War. This created a range of logistical challenges for army officials who had centered their plans and capabilities on the European theater and the country's North Atlantic Treaty Organization's obligations.

The first unit deployed by the British Army for Operation GRANBY, the British code word for the defense of Saudi Arabia and the subsequent liberation of Kuwait, was the 7th Armoured Brigade (the "Desert Rats" of World War II fame), commanded by Brigadier Patrick Cordingley, that had been stationed in Germany. The unit numbered some 12,000 troops. It was initially attached to the U.S. Marine I Expeditionary Force (I MEF). In November 2000 the British government made the decision to increase Britain's force contributions. A new formation, the British 1st Division, was established. It included the divisional headquarters, originally based in Germany; the 4th Armoured Brigade; and elements of other units from the British Army of the Rhine. The units deployed to the Persian Gulf fielded the newest and best equipment in the British Army, including the Challenger main battle tank (MBT). In addition, the 7th Armoured Brigade was transferred from the I MEF to the British 1st Division. The British division itself was attached to the U.S. VII Corps and numbered some 28,000 troops with 15,000 vehicles, including 2,600 armored vehicles. This figure included 221 Challenger MBTs, 316 Warrior infantry fighting vehicles (IFVs), and significant quantities of artillery to include 16 new multiple-launch rocket systems. Other support and logistics units as well as special operations forces and Royal Marine commandos brought total ground forces personnel to about 43,000.

Lieutenant General Peter de la Billiére was assigned to command British ground troops and as overall commander of British forces in the region. The commander of the 1st Armoured Division was Major General Rupert Anthony Smith. The British operations during DESERT SHIELD and the later DESERT STORM were designated Operation GRANBY in honor of a military hero from the Seven Years' War (1756–1763).

The 1st Armoured Division and its support units were deployed to the west of the main coalition supply centers. Consequently, a

A British soldier carrying an L85A1 rifle on patrol with Kurdish children in Zakhu, northern Iraq, in 1991. The soldier was part of Operation PROVIDE COMFORT, a multinational effort to aid Kurdish refugees in southern Turkey and northern Iraq. (U.S. Department of Defense)

significant logistics infrastructure had to be developed to supply the considerable quantities of food, fuel, and supplies that the division consumed each day. Meanwhile, battle groups that included mechanized infantry were organized around each of the two main armored brigades. Through December 2000 and early January 2001, the units undertook a series of training exercises to improve unit cohesion and to acclimatize the soldiers and equipment to the desert conditions.

In planning for the ground invasion of Kuwait, VII Corps was tasked with making a rapid advance into Kuwait and destroying the main armored and mechanized units. VII Corps was then to veer to the east and cut off the retreat of other Iraqi units, including elite Republican Guard divisions. The British were assigned as the eastern unit of the advance, and VII Corps would pivot around the British troops once they secured their objective.

Once the attack began on February 24, 1991, the British worked to protect the flank of the advance. The division's two battle groups advanced rapidly, although they lacked close air support due to inclement weather. There had been concerns among senior commanders over the ability of the Challenger MBTs to operate in the hot, dusty environment, but British armor performed well; however, the division lost about 10 percent of its vehicles to mechanical failure.

British forces routed elements of the Iraqi VII Corps and two armored brigades in a 100-hour drive that was punctuated by a succession of engagements. British troops destroyed or captured more than 200 Iraqi MBTs and more than 500 IFVs and other vehicles. The British also took more than 7,000 Iraqi prisoners. British forces reached their objective, the principal road north through Kuwait into Iraq, on February 28, although coalition forces were unable to prevent the retreat of the Republican Guard divisions into Iraq. British ground forces suffered 19 dead and 10 wounded. Nine of those killed died during a friendly fire incident when a U.S. aircraft mistakenly attacked a convoy of Warrior IFVs on February 26.

TOM LANSFORD

See also

Cruise Missiles, Employment of, Persian Gulf and Iraq Wars; Logistics, Persian Gulf War; Special Air Service, United Kingdom; Special Boat Service, United Kingdom; United Kingdom, Air Force, Persian Gulf War; United Kingdom, Marines, Persian Gulf War; United States; Vehicles, Unarmored

References

De la Billière, General Sir Peter. *Storm Command: A Personal Account of the Gulf War.* London: HarperCollins, 1992.

Lowry, Richard. *The Gulf War Chronicles: A Military History of the First War with Iraq.* Bloomington, IN: IUniverse, 2003.

United Kingdom, Marines, Iraq War

The United Kingdom's Royal Marines played a vital role during Operation TELIC (the British contribution to Operation IRAQI FREEDOM). Royal Marine forces in Iraq included the Headquarters 3th Commando Brigade, the 40th Commando, the 42th Commando, the United Kingdom Landing Force Command Support Group, the Commando Logistic Regiment Royal Marines, the 29th Commando Regiment Royal Artillery, the 539th Assault Squadron Royal Marines, the 9th Assault Squadron Royal Marines, the 59th Independent Commando Squadron Royal Engineers, and the 131st Independent Commando Squadron Royal Engineers (Volunteers). Elements of the following units were also present in Iraq: the 45th Commando, the Headquarters Commando United Kingdom Amphibious Forces, the 20th Commando Battery Royal Artillery, the Fleet Protection Group Royal Marines, the 4th Assault Squadron Royal Marines, the Royal Marines Band Service, and the Royal Marines Reserve City of London, Scotland, Bristol, Merseyside and Tyne. Finally, the following units served as attachments with the Royal Marines during Operation TELIC: C Squadron, the Queen's Dragoon Guards; C Squadron, the Royal Scots Dragoon Guards; and 18th Squadron Royal Air Force.

British forces engaged in Operation TELIC, including Royal Navy, British Army, Royal Marines, and Royal Air Force, numbered some 46,000 troops, of whom 4,000 were Royal Marines. The British ground component, including the Royal Marines, was contained within the 1st Armoured Division, which was comprised of the 7th Armoured Brigade (the famed "Desert Rats" of the Persian Gulf War), the 16th Air Assault Brigade, and the 3rd Commando Brigade Royal Marines, the latter of which had the U.S. Marine Corps' 15th Marine Expeditionary Unit attached to it. Led by Brigadier Jim Dutton, the 3rd Commando Brigade was tasked with spearheading an amphibious assault on the Faw (Fao) peninsula in southern Iraq, securing the port of Umm Qasr, and assisting in the seizure of the Basra, Iraq's second-largest city.

The amphibious landing of the 3rd Commando Brigade on the Faw peninsula was the most ambitious operation undertaken by the Royal Marines since the 1982 Falklands War, complicated by the fact that unlike in the Falklands, the landing would be opposed. The first Royal Marines to enter Iraq, spearheaded by Bravo Company, 40th Commando, left Kuwait by helicopter on the night of March 20, 2003, landing on the Faw (Fao) peninsula less than an hour later. They were soon joined by the remaining companies of 40 Commando, and were supported by artillery fire from British and American units stationed on Kuwait's Bubiyan Island, as well as from three British frigates and one Australian frigate positioned in the Persian Gulf. In addition, the 40th Commando fired more than 5,000 mortar rounds in the initial assault to help secure its positions. The 40th Commando's immediate purpose was to secure the southern Iraqi oil fields and oil infrastructure to prevent Iraqi forces from setting them alight, as they had done in the 1991 Persian Gulf War. While the 40th Commando was engaged in this task, the 42nd Commando was airlifted to positions north of 40th Commando to form a block that would prevent any Iraqi forces from moving south to engage the 40th Commando.

Following the successful seizure of the oil fields, the 40th Commando moved to secure the Iraqi banks of the Shatt al-Arab waterway, which flows along the border with Iran. The 42nd Commando moved into the port city of Umm Qasr seized earlier by U.S. marines, which they soon opened up to vital humanitarian aid. By March 30 each of these tasks had been completed. The entirety of the 40th Commando—together with L Company, 42nd Commando; C Squadron, the Queen's Dragoon Guards; and C Squadron, the Royal Scots Dragoon Guards—then embarked on Operation JAMES, a 19-hour battle involving both Lynx attack helicopters and Challenger II main battle tanks whose purpose was to secure the town of Abu al Khasib on the approach to Basra.

From there the Royal Marines moved into Basra itself, seizing control of Iraqi dictator Saddam Hussein's summer palace. By April 6, just over two weeks after the first marines of the 40th Commando had landed on Iraqi territory, Basra had fallen. The Royal Marines had succeeded in their task, taking and holding the 60-mile coastline of the Faw peninsula and opening up the port and cities of Umm Qasr, Abu al-Khasib, and Basra. Following these operations, the 3rd Commando Brigade left Iraq in June 2003. As of December 2008, there had been 12 rotations of British forces in Iraq (Operations TELIC II through TELIC XIII). The Royal Marines, however, played no great role in these deployments, in large part having deployed to Afghanistan instead. All British troops had departed Iraq by the end of July 2009. In all, the Royal Marines suffered 11 fatalities during the period of British involvement in Iraq.

BENJAMIN GROB-FITZGIBBON

See also

Basra; Basra, Battle for; Faw Peninsula; IRAQI FREEDOM, Operation; Shatt al-Arab Waterway; Umm Qasr; Umm Qasr, Battle of

References

Fox, Robert. *Iraq Campaign, 2003: Royal Navy and Royal Marines.* London: Agenda Publishing, 2003.

Keegan, John. *The Iraq War: The Military Offensive, from Victory in 21 Days to the Insurgent Aftermath.* New York: Vintage, 2005.

Murray, Williamson, and Robert H. Scales Jr. *The Iraq War: A Military History.* Cambridge, MA: Belknap, 2005.

United Kingdom, Marines, Persian Gulf War

British Royal Marines in the Persian Gulf War did not take part in the ground war of February 1991. However, a small contingent of 24 marines from K Company, 42nd Commando, did deploy as a detachment with the Royal Navy in the Persian Gulf for raiding suspect shipping. The majority of British Royal Marines participated in Operation HAVEN, part of Operation PROVIDE COMFORT that was a coalition humanitarian operation conducted in northern Iraq from April 18 to July 15, 1991. British participation numbered nearly 5,000 Royal Marines and included the 3rd Commando Brigade led by Brigadier Andrew Keeling as well as elements from the 40th Commando and 45th Commando. The 3rd Commando Brigade was also supported by the 29th Commando Royal Artillery, the 3rd Commando Brigade Air Squadron, the 59th Independent Commando Squadron, the Royal Engineers, and the Commando Logistics Regiment. Royal Marine Commando Forces were attached to the U.S. Marine Corps 24th Marine Expeditionary Unit (Special Operations Capable) and worked alongside American Special Forces and reconnaissance groups.

After the Persian Gulf War officially ended on February 28, 1991, Iraqi president Saddam Hussein turned the remainder of his armed forces against factional uprisings in both northern and southern Iraq. After quelling the Shiite revolt in southern Iraq, Hussein turned his attention to the Kurdish people in the mountainous regions of northern Iraq. Hundreds of thousands of Kurds fled to the mountains across the border into Turkey, with Iraqi armed forces and special police in pursuit. Expansive media coverage of the starving and freezing Kurdish people led both President George H. W. Bush and the United Nations (UN) Security Council to take action. On April 5, 1991, the UN adopted Security Council Resolution 688, requesting military-conducted humanitarian and security operations in northern Iraq. A coalition force led by the United States, which included 30 other nations and numbered nearly 20,000 troops, assembled in Silopi, Turkey, to administer aid to the suffering Kurds.

On April 18, 1991, the British Royal Marine Commando Forces commanded by Major General Robin J. Ross joined Operation PROVIDE COMFORT as part of a ground contingent named Joint Task Force Bravo. Even as coalition forces and Royal Marines amassed in Silopi, Turkey, the Kurdish people refused to come down from the mountains without key towns in Iraq declared secure. U.S. lieutenant general John M. Shalikashvili, overall commander of PROVIDE COMFORT, ordered Iraqi military and special police forces in the town of Zakho, Iraq, to vacate. On April 21, 1991, Joint Task Force Bravo crossed the Iraq-Turkey border into Zakho in order to secure the area. The British 45th Commando, Royal Marines, commanded by Lieutenant Colonel Jonathon Thompson, cleared Zakho on April 25, 1991. The U.S. commanders chose the 45th Commando for this mission because of the unit's recent experience with urban combat in Northern Ireland.

A small number of Kurds reluctantly returned to Zakho, while the majority remained in the mountains of Turkey, relying on coalition provisions for their survival. The reason for the lack of movement on the part of the Kurds was a fear of Iraqi Special Police in their towns across the border. To quell this fear, on April 29, 1991, General Shalikashvili ordered the start of Operation GALLANT PROVIDER, which designated Joint Task Force Bravo to expand the security area. By May, international forces and U.S. marines secured numerous towns en route to Dohuk, Iraq, the mission objective. Leaving Zakho secure, the 45th Commando assaulted and secured Amadiyah and proceeded toward Sirensk, Iraq,

where the brigade overran and took control of an important airstrip. Moving southwest, the 3rd Commando Brigade encountered the Iraqi 36th Infantry Division, which offered little resistance and slowly departed the town of Batufa.

On May 17, 1991, the 29th Commando Regiment, Royal Artillery, prepared to lay siege to Iraqi forces in Dohuk, Iraq, as coalition forces converged on the town. Fortunately the Kurds and Iraqis came to an agreement on May 18, allowing many of the Kurds to return to their homes. For the next two months British Royal Marines maintained a presence outside the towns they had secured, including Kakho, Sirensk, Batufa, and Amadiyah. In July, brief skirmishes broke out in Amadiyah between British forces and local Kurdish rebels. General Shalikashvili calmed the situation by consulting Kurdish leaders who were concerned over rumors of the coalition departure. The rumors were true, as Operation PROVIDE COMFORT ended on July 15, 1991. Coalition forces and Royal Marines completed their mission, which had provided nearly 750,000 Kurds with humanitarian support and security in their return to their Iraqi homes.

COLIN M. COLBOURN

See also
Hussein, Saddam; Kurds; PROVIDE COMFORT, Operation; Shalikashvili, John Malchese David

References
Badsey, Steven, John Pimlott, and Members of the Department of War Studies, Royal Military Academy, Sandhurst. *The Gulf War Assessed.* London: Arms and Armour, 1992.

Brown, Ronald J. *Humanitarian Operations in Northern Iraq, 1991: With Marines in Operation Provide Comfort.* Washington, DC: History and Museums Division, Headquarters, U.S. Marine Corps, 1995.

Scales, Robert H. *Certain Victory: The U.S. Army in the Gulf War.* Washington, DC: Brassey's, 1994.

Weller, M., ed. *Iraq and Kuwait: The Hostilities and Their Aftermath.* Cambridge, UK: Grotius Publications, 1993.

United Kingdom, Middle East Policy

Until 1914 the United Kingdom was, on the whole, content to exercise only informal influence in the Middle East. Only the small Crown colonies of Aden and Cyprus (acquired in 1839 and 1878, respectively) were British in a strictly legal sense. The emirates along the southeastern coast of the Arabian Peninsula, from Qatar in the Persian Gulf to Muscat and Oman, were bound to Britain by defensive treaties. Aden, important to Britain with its port and fueling capacity, was actually under the rule of the British government of India, and Britain held protectorates over western Aden and eastern Aden. British leaders perceived the strongest area power, the moribund regime of the Ottomans, more as a dependent satellite than as an adversary and therefore enjoyed British protection from predatory neighbors such as czarist Russia.

The major exception to this hands-off approach was Egypt, occupied in 1882 in response to a nationalist coup and thereafter incorporated into the British imperial sphere under the veil of a puppet monarchy. With the opening of the Suez Canal in 1869, the old route from Europe to the Indies via the Cape of Good Hope had become obsolete, and with the majority of traffic passing through the canal being of British registry, London deemed it a vital British interest to defend the maritime artery running through the Strait of Gibraltar to Port Alexandria and from there along the Red Sea corridor to Aden and the long transoceanic voyage to India. The security of this line of communications and transportation remained one of the core components of Britain's foreign policy, and control of Egypt's Canal Zone, which was eventually to become the world's largest military base, was thought crucial to imperial defense. The British, who had originally promised only a short-term intervention to stabilize Egypt's faltering government and secure the extensive financial assets owned by European investors throughout the country, made periodic noises about leaving when conditions allowed. But with each passing year, the occupation grew more permanent.

An accident of geography made Egypt crucial to British interests, and an accident of geology would make the Middle East as a whole the geopolitical key to the 20th century. The otherwise economically worthless deserts of Arabia sat atop the world's largest reservoirs of crude petroleum, the energy resource that would eventually replace coal as the most critical strategic resource on the planet. The long-term significance of this was already becoming clear before the outbreak of World War I. In 1911 Winston Churchill, at the time First Lord of the Admiralty, took the critical step of beginning the changeover of the Royal Navy from coal to more efficient oil-burning engines. Three years later he seized the prescient opportunity of buying a government majority shareholding in the Anglo-Persian Oil Company, which was busy exploiting its newly drilled fields in what is today southwestern Iran. By 1945 the economic and military implications of the Middle East's oil reserves would come to dominate the region's political fortunes.

Britain's traditional approach to Middle Eastern affairs ended in October 1914 when the Ottoman Empire's leaders took that country into World War I on the side of the Central powers. Britain declared Egypt a formal protectorate and launched an extensive military effort across the eastern Mediterranean and the Fertile Crescent. The war there began badly for the British. An ambitious but poorly executed naval effort to force the Dardanelles followed by the landing of an expeditionary force on the Gallipoli Peninsula, both in 1915, ended in ignominious evacuation, and there was another humiliating failure in Mesopotamia the following year when an Anglo-Indian expeditionary force moving up the Tigris and Euphrates was besieged and forced to surrender at Kut. But in early 1917, following reinforcement and a change of command, the Mesopotamian advance recovered its momentum, reaching and capturing Baghdad. British troops under Lieutenant General Sir Edmund Allenby launched a successful offensive from Egypt into Palestine, breaking the stubborn Ottoman line of resistance at the Third Battle of Gaza. Allenby entered Jerusalem on December 11, 1917, the first Christian general to seize the city since the Crusades. The following year, the Ottoman Empire imploded.

Britain's victory in World War I created new regional opportunities but also problems in the Middle East. In May 1916 Foreign Office envoy Mark Sykes had drawn up with his French counterpart François Georges Picot a plan to divide the former Ottoman territories in the Middle East. Britain would directly control Mesopotamia, France would control Lebanon and much of southern Anatolia, and the rest of the region would be carved up into informal spheres of European control. This, however, contradicted a promise already made by the high commissioner in Egypt to the sharif of Mecca, Hussein ibn Ali, that if the Arab chieftains revolted against Ottoman rule, the British would sponsor an independent Arab state in the Middle East at the end of the war. To complicate things further, in 1917 Foreign Secretary Arthur Balfour had announced in his famous declaration that a postwar homeland would be established for the Jewish people in Palestine.

The final result was an untidy compromise. As a consequence of the Paris Peace Conference at the end of the war, Britain and France were awarded a number of mandate colonies under the auspices of the League of Nations. France received control over Syria and Lebanon. Britain received three mandate territories. Two of these, Iraq and Transjordan, were parceled out to the Hashemite princes Faisal and Abdullah, respectively, as consolation for the failure to create a Pan-Arab state. Palestine, the third mandate, became the responsibility of the Colonial Office in London. Kuwait, at the mouth of the Mesopotamian delta, was detached from Iraq and declared a direct British protectorate.

The propping up of this shaky inheritance proved to be one of the British Empire's most intractable security problems of the 1920s onward. Nationalist feelings, both Arab and Zionist, had been permanently stirred up across the region by the rhetoric of Wilsonianism at the Paris peace talks, and tempers were flared with the widespread belief that the colonial powers had betrayed legitimate national aspirations for their own selfish benefit. A popular revolt in Iraq during 1920–1922 was suppressed by the innovative (although later controversial) employment of military aircraft in so-called aerial policing by the Royal Air Force (RAF). In the spring of 1919, urban riots against British rule in Egypt led to a general uprising in which British troops killed hundreds of protestors. Although the protectorate was formally abandoned and a state of Egyptian independence declared in 1922—later modified by the Anglo-Egyptian Treaty of 1936—Britain retained control of key political and economic aspects of the country's life, and this transparently quasi-colonial situation continued to offend Egyptian national pride.

The situation in Palestine was, if anything, even worse. Britain was committed to the stewardship of a Jewish national homeland in the mandate, although the level of political autonomy that it would enjoy was not defined, and Britain insisted that "the civil and religious rights of existing non-Jewish communities" had to be left undisturbed, a demand that was easier to make than

Sir Herbert Samuel, Emir Abdullah ibn Hussein, and Sir Wyndham Deeds at Emir Abdullah's camp at Amman, Jordan, April 1921. During these meetings, Samuel, British high commissioner, proclaimed Emir Abdullah the ruler of Transjordan, then a British mandate. (Library of Congress)

enforce. Jewish immigration quickly became the dominant issue. More than 100,000 Jews arrived in Palestine from Europe during the 1920s, and there were large transfers of land ownership as these migrants bought property from absentee landlords, displacing the Arab tenants who had traditionally worked the fields and orchards. As the resentment of the Arab fellahin (peasants and agricultural laborers) grew, the British authorities attempted to alleviate the tension by introducing immigration quotas. This angered Jewish residents and did little to heal the growing sectarian divide across the mandate.

Sporadic armed conflict between the two communities simmered until, in August 1929, 67 Jews were murdered by rioters in Hebron. This shocking event eroded what little confidence Jewish leaders had in a binational compromise future for the region and led to the rapid expansion of the paramilitary Jewish self-defense force known as Haganah. For their part the British continued their increasingly unsuccessful policy of keeping the peace, trying to favor neither side and thereby alienating both. A British inquiry into the Arab riots, the Shaw Commission, acknowledged that previous government statements about the future of the mandate had been unhelpfully vague and contradictory, with

politicians too eager to tell each community what it wanted to hear. But the subsequent 1930 Passfield White Paper could only suggest new and ultimately ineffectual restrictions on future Jewish land purchases.

The failure of Britain's efforts at de-escalation became clear in the spring of 1936, when a full-scale Arab revolt broke out across Palestine in protest against continuing Jewish immigration and land purchase. More than 20,000 British security troops spent three years suppressing the rebellion (often in unofficial cooperation with Haganah) in a counterinsurgency that was marked by often brutal policing tactics and the suspension of civil liberties. During the revolt the remaining economic ties between the Arab and Jewish communities were mostly severed, hampering the chance of any reconciliation between the two factions. Although in 1939 the revolt petered out, its containment did nothing to resolve the fundamental tensions that still plagued the mandate's political life.

Prime Minister Neville Chamberlain's government sought an opportunity to bring a final negotiated end to the conflict. Its first proposal was an Arab-Jewish summit, the 1939 St. James Conference, but this proved a failure because Arab representatives refused to even recognize the negotiating legitimacy of their Jewish counterparts. Forced to come up with a settlement of its own, Chamberlain's administration drafted a new White Paper later that year. It promised the creation within 10 years of an independent Palestinian state, to be jointly governed by Arabs and Jews. More significant for the short term, however, it limited future Jewish immigration into the mandate to 75,000 people for the next 5 years.

The White Paper infuriated Jewish settlers while failing to satisfy Arabs, and it was only the outbreak of World War II that forestalled a more vigorous reaction to the White Paper's proposals. Given the virulent anti-Semitism of Nazi Germany, mainstream Jewish organizations in Palestine were understandably willing to freeze the dispute for the duration of the war, although more extreme terrorist cells such as Lohamei Herut Israel (also known as Lehi or the Stern Gang) refused to abandon their struggle. In 1944 Lehi would assassinate Lord Moyne, the resident minister in Cairo and one of the most senior British officials in the region.

Britain faced multiple challenges to its military power in the Middle East during the war. An Italian army invaded Egypt in the autumn of 1940, and although this assault was expelled in a spectacular counteroffensive into Libya the following year, the fortunes of the desert war would soon be dramatically reversed in favor of the Axis by the arrival of the German Afrika Korps. Behind the front line, sedition openly flourished. In May 1941 British troops returned to Iraq (which had received independence nine years earlier) when a pro-German cabinet overthrew King Faisal II's government, headed by the regent Abd al-Ilah, and this performance repeated itself in Vichy-held French Syria a few weeks later and, in cooperation with the Soviet Union, in Iran in August. In July 1942 at a particularly desperate moment in the battle against German general Erwin Rommel, Egypt's King Farouk was ordered at gunpoint to dissolve his government and appoint a premier

Arab prisoners are guarded by a British soldier in the Old City of Jerusalem in the British mandate of Palestine, October 26, 1938, during the Arab Revolt against both British rule and Jewish settlement in Palestine. (Hulton Archive/Getty Images)

more accommodating toward British interests. Not until 1943 were North Africa and the Middle East secured by the Allies.

In 1945 the incoming Labour Party prime minister Clement Attlee and his foreign secretary, Ernest Bevin, faced the paradox that while the diplomatic importance of the Middle East had never been greater and Britain's nominal control over the region never stronger, the country was far less capable of exerting imperial authority than it had been before the war. According to the map, Britain's assets were impressive. Not only did it control a swath of occupied territory from Egypt to Iran, but the clearing out of Italian dictator Benito Mussolini's African colonies had left Britain in control of former Italian Somaliland, Eritrea, Tripolitania, and Cyrenaica. Only the vast and empty Arabian Desert, ruled since 1927 by the Wahhabist House of Saud, remained—at least to some extent—outside the British orbit.

Britain's finances and manpower had, however, been exhausted by six years of war. The United States was now quite clearly the much stronger of the two powers, and it was evident to everyone—including Arab nationalists restless for greater autonomy and a fairer share of oil revenues—that the British Empire was on the decline. But Bevin refused to submit to despondency. In a

September 1945 memorandum, he laid out his plan for a revitalized imperial role in the Middle East. While recognizing that gunboat diplomacy and informal rule through pliable puppet monarchs was no longer a feasible strategy, he proposed a new and more equitable set of partnerships that were to be based on British-funded economic development and Cold War defense cooperation. Bevin saw the Middle East as the keystone of his anti-Soviet strategy, with the Suez Canal base securing oil shipments to the West and long-range bomber airfields in Palestine threatening the Soviet Union's southern flank in the event of war.

Bevin's plans were bold but ultimately unrealistic. Insofar as Palestine in particular was concerned, they ignored the fact that the war had completely changed the character of Jewish politics in Europe. The Nazi so-called Final Solution had killed an estimated 6 million Jews and left at least 250,000 survivors of Hitler's death camps stranded in refugee facilities across the continent. Many of these displaced persons (DPs) sought to immigrate to Palestine in defiance of the White Paper quotas, and although British troops succeeded in intercepting and detaining many of them, the war-weary public back in the United Kingdom had little stomach for the distasteful spectacle of its soldiers imprisoning recent survivors of the Holocaust in new prisons. World sympathy for the DPs was strong particularly in the United States, where the new president, Harry Truman, was under pressure to use the enhanced diplomatic leverage of the United States to change British policy in Palestine.

Britain's ability to maintain control of the region was also under pressure. Toward the end of the war Jewish militant groups such as Irgun Tsvai Leumi (National Military Organization) had restarted their paramilitary campaigns against mandate rule, and a vicious insurgency campaign broke out that culminated in the July 1946 bombing of the King David Hotel, the British military headquarters in Jerusalem, in which 91 people died. In a period of rapid postwar demobilization and a dire manpower shortage at home, it was difficult to justify the presence of large numbers of British personnel in a province that looked increasingly headed toward civil war.

The Labour government's main political initiative was the 1946 Anglo-American Committee of Inquiry, which proposed the creation of a single binational state and the immediate entry of 100,000 Jewish DPs into Palestine. Although Attlee's administration was much more enthusiastic about the former recommendation than the latter the administration cautiously welcomed the committee's findings, but President Truman torpedoed the delicate negotiation process when he made a blunt statement implying that the larger immigration quota was the only significant element to the report. Britain's determination to find a binational solution to Palestine came to an end the following February when, beleaguered by the mounting violence in the mandate, Attlee's government announced that it was referring the problem back to the United Nations (UN). In November 1947 the UN voted for partition, a vote on which the United Kingdom abstained. The following May, Britain abruptly withdrew its last remaining personnel from the mandate, precipitating the outbreak of the first Arab-Israeli war, the Israeli War of Independence (1948–1949). Britain expected the Arab League to win this conflict and would no doubt have welcomed the emergence of an independent Palestinian entity from the postmandate wreckage, but any chance of such a scenario was ruined by the poor military showing of the Arabs in the war.

The creation of the State of Israel in May 1948 greatly complicated Britain's subsequent Middle East policy. Recognition that the Jewish state was—however imperfectly—the region's only practicing democracy, a powerful anti-Soviet bastion, and a valued client of the United States had to be balanced against the British desire not to inflame Arab sensibilities elsewhere. Cold War Anglo-Israeli relations were characterized by periods of cooperation interspersed with diplomatic prickliness, with Tel Aviv critical of what it saw as Britain's too-cozy attitude toward the Arabs and with London frustrated by the Israeli failure to settle the Palestinian question once and for all.

The 10 years that followed the end of World War II saw Britain's gradual withdrawal from many of its formal Middle East suzerainties. Nevertheless, it sought to retain key advisory links with the successor states, particularly with regard to oil exploration and defense issues. The success of this policy was mixed. In March 1946 the Transjordanian mandate was peacefully abolished, and two years later Emir Abdullah was declared monarch of the new Kingdom of Jordan. That same year Britain negotiated the Treaty of Portsmouth, an attempt to define its ongoing security relationship with Iraq, particularly with regard to the retention of RAF bases there. The treaty failed, however, to appease Iraqi nationalists and was never ratified by Baghdad. Worse than this disappointment was the 1951 crisis in Iran, when populist prime minister Mohammad Mossadegh nationalized the assets of the Anglo-Iranian Oil Company (AIOC), which forced a tense standoff with the British government. The crisis was relieved only when Mossadegh was toppled from office through the covert actions of the U.S. Central Intelligence Agency (CIA) and Britain's Secret Intelligence Service (MI6). British Petroleum (BP), a reconstruction of the AIOC, retained a 40 percent share in Iranian oil production in the postcrisis settlement, but the net result was Iran's shift into an American rather than exclusively British sphere of influence, a pervasive theme of the postwar period.

That increasing U.S. involvement in Middle Eastern affairs might not always be in Britain's best interests was illustrated by the rise to power of Gamal Abdel Nasser in Egypt following the 1952 officers' coup that dethroned King Farouk. London initially hoped to find in Nasser a more willing partner than Farouk, conceding an October 1954 treaty with Nasser that finalized the cession of the Suez base and offering to help fund the Aswan High Dam project.

However, in 1955 when Britain organized the anti-Soviet Baghdad Pact—also known as the Central Treaty Organization (CENTO)—with Turkey, Iran, Iraq, and Pakistan, an outraged Nasser denounced the agreement as neoimperialist and sought a rearmament deal with the Soviet Union. British prime minister Anthony Eden then followed the U.S. lead in withdrawing British assistance for the Aswan High Dam project. Egypt promptly nationalized the Anglo-French Suez Canal Company as compensation. Secret negotiations followed among Israel (already involved in an undeclared sniping war with Egypt) and the aggrieved British and French, and a plan was concocted to invade Egypt and unseat Nasser. Israel would invade the Sinai peninsula, giving the European powers the excuse to intervene and seize the Canal Zone as neutral peacemakers. Because Nasser's refusal to accept this intervention was more or less guaranteed, the expeditionary force would then have a legal pretext to crush the Egyptian regime.

Israel duly attacked on October 29, 1956, and a few days later a mainly British amphibious force supported by strong airpower assaulted Port Said. Although militarily successful, the invasion was a diplomatic disaster for Britain, and when the Soviet Union threatened to intervene on Nasser's side, President Dwight D. Eisenhower's administration used its financial muscle to force the British into a cease-fire and a humiliating evacuation. The Suez Crisis was the last occasion in which Britain attempted a unilateral military solution to a Middle Eastern crisis and marked the collapse of Britain's already-tottering prestige in the region. During the crisis, CENTO proved ineffective in advancing British interests. As early as 1959, Iraq had dropped out of the organization following its republican revolution, and the pact was unable to influence the course of the Arab-Israeli conflict.

With the winding down of Britain's military presence in Jordan and the granting of independence to Kuwait in 1961, the only remaining remnants of empire were now along the Arabian shoreline. The old garrison town of Aden had, with the loss of Suez, become Britain's primary defense base in the Middle East, and although London recognized that its days as a Crown colony were numbered, it was determined that any successor state should be friendly toward British interests. In January 1963 Prime Minister Harold Macmillan's government united Aden and the old Yemeni protectorate into the Federation of South Arabia (FOSA), which was promised independence within five years. However, terrorist resistance by the Egyptian-backed National Liberation Front prevented a peaceful transition of power, and after a fruitless campaign to pacify civil unrest, British troops abandoned the territory in November 1967. The failure to retain the Aden bridgehead coupled with parlous financial problems at home (set off in part by the rise in international oil prices after the 1967 Six-Day War) necessitated a comprehensive British defense review. This resulted in the decision to withdraw all remaining British forces east of Suez by the end of 1971. The political consequence of this decision for the Middle East was the reorganization of Britain's old Persian Gulf protectorates. Thus, they transformed themselves into the United Arab Emirates (UAE), and Qatar and Bahrain (which could not agree on a unified constitution with their UAE neighbors) became independent polities.

The end of empire did not of course end Britain's relationship with the Middle East. As one of the West's principal oil importers and a major supplier of advanced technology, Great Britain inevitably continued to display a strong interest in regional affairs. Although after the Suez debacle Britain no longer sought a leading role in the Arab-Israeli conflict, its position as a permanent member of the UN Security Council gave its opinions inherent significance. In general, Britain followed the lead of the United States throughout the remainder of the Cold War. But bearing in mind Britain's historical ties with the Arabian Peninsula, Britain was less publicly emphatic in its support of Israel.

Until 1990 the story of Britain's military disengagement from the region followed a clear and consistent narrative. This was rudely reversed, however, with the Iraqi invasion of Kuwait in August 1990. Great Britain actively contributed to all of the U.S.-led multinational operations that followed it, including Operations DESERT SHIELD and DESERT STORM. Britain also took part in the various airborne policing campaigns of Iraq in the 1990s including Operation DESERT FOX, an air campaign launched in December 1998 designed to destroy suspected sites where weapons of mass destruction (WMDs) were allegedly being developed.

After the September 11, 2001, terrorist attacks on the United States, Britain stood closely with its ally across the Atlantic and

A British Army Viking amphibious combat vehicle waits to refuel, Helmand Province, Afghanistan, September 2, 2008. (U.S. Department of Defense)

fully supported the operations to rid Afghanistan of the Taliban regime. An initial force of nearly 6,000 British troops was sent to Afghanistan, with the deployment stabilizing at about 5,500 troops after 2002. In 2007 the British government increased its troop commitment to Afghanistan to nearly 9,000; by the beginning of 2009 there were about 8,300 troops, most of whom were in Helmand Province. Subsequent to the Afghanistan War, the unseating of Iraqi dictator Saddam Hussein's regime in Operation IRAQI FREEDOM (2003–)—given the more prosaic title Operation TELIC by British forces—included direct involvement of British troops. As many as 45,000 British troops were on hand for the March 2003 invasion of Iraq. In September 2007 British troops withdrew from their last base in Basra to an airport garrison on the outskirts of the city, and by the end of 2008 there were approximately 4,200 troops remaining in Iraq. All British troops were withdrawn from the country by the end of July 2009. Britain also maintained a substantial air and naval presence throughout the Persian Gulf area, an epilogue that would have seemed bizarre to those witnessing the lowering of the last Union Jacks in the region 35 years earlier.

ALAN ALLPORT

See also

Anglo-Iraqi Treaty; Arab-Israeli Conflict, Overview; Baghdad Pact; Balfour Declaration; DESERT FOX, Operation; DESERT STORM, Operation; Eisenhower, Dwight David; ENDURING FREEDOM, Operation; Faisal II, King of Iraq; France, Middle East Policy; Hussein, Saddam; IRAQI FREEDOM, Operation; Nasser, Gamal Abdel; Suez Crisis; Sykes-Picot Agreement; Truman, Harry S.; United Kingdom; United States, Middle East Policy, 1917–1945; United States, Middle East Policy, 1945–Present; World War I, Impact of; World War II, Impact of

References

Abadi, Jacob. *Britain's Withdrawal from the Middle East, 1947–1971.* Middlesex, UK: Kingston, 1983.

Balfour-Paul, Glen. *The End of Empire in the Middle East.* New York: Cambridge University Press, 1991.

Cohen, Michael J., and Martin Kolinsky, eds. *The Demise of the British Empire in the Middle East.* London: Frank Cass, 1998.

Greenwood, Sean. *Britain and the Cold War, 1945–91.* New York: Macmillan, 2000.

Louis, William Roger. *The British Empire in the Middle East, 1945–1951: Arab Nationalism, the United States, and Postwar Imperialism.* New York: Oxford University Press, 1984.

Ovendale, Ritchie. *Britain, the United States, and the Transfer of Power in the Middle East, 1945–1962.* Leicester, UK: Leicester University Press, 1996.

Peterson, Tore. *The Middle East between the Great Powers: Anglo-American Conflict and Cooperation, 1952–57.* New York: Macmillan, 2000.

United Kingdom, Navy, Persian Gulf War

Based in the United Arab Emirates (UAE), the British Royal Navy had been operating in the Persian Gulf region for 10 years prior to the invasion of Kuwait by Iraq on August 2, 1990. This posture allowed the Royal Navy to react quickly when hostilities seemed imminent. Captain Anthony McEwen was initially in command of Royal Navy forces in the Gulf from the start of the crisis until September 1990; Commodore Paul Haddocks took over from McEwen and served from September until December. Commodore Christopher Craig then took command of Royal Navy forces in the Gulf from December 1990 until March 1991, at which time Operation DESERT STORM had ended.

The British presence in Saudi Arabia also provided headquarters facilities in Riyadh, and these facilities would form the foundation of the coalition's command structure as Operation DESERT SHIELD was initiated in the late summer of 1990. British warships participating in the Persian Gulf War included the Royal Navy frigates HMS *Battleaxe, Brilliant, Brave, Brazen, Jupiter,* and *London.* The destroyers HMS *Cardiff, Gloucester,* and *York* were also deployed. In addition, the hospital ship *Argus,* the tanker *Orangeleaf,* and the submarines *Opposum* and *Otus* were deployed, as were four mine countermeasure ships. The Royal Navy deployed a total of 12,500 personnel to the Persian Gulf.

The Royal Navy had four primary missions assigned to it by the coalition. The first was maritime interception operations;

these were mandated by United Nations (UN) resolutions passed in response to Iraq's invasion of Kuwait, which stipulated that any unauthorized cargo found to be headed to or from Iraq was to be stopped and confiscated. Second, the Royal Navy participated in antisurface operations against the Iraqi Navy. Third, it engaged in antiair operations against Iraqi aircraft and missiles fired at coalition ships. Finally, the Royal Navy provided countermine vessels to sweep for and eliminate the mines in the Persian Gulf.

During the conflict, the UAE provided air fields to resupply Royal Navy units with supplies and spare parts. To prevent the buildup of magnetic fields during a long sea voyage, the engines for the mine countermeasure vessels were flown into the theater. Through February 28, 1991, 137 commercial vessels had been chartered by the British government to move 300,000 tons of cargo to the Kuwaiti theater of operations.

In the face of an almost nonexistent submarine threat from the Iraqi Navy, the Royal Navy offloaded most of its antisubmarine weapons from its ships and used the empty space to house antiaircraft countermeasures to defend against surface-to-surface missiles that the Iraqi Air Force had in its inventory.

The Royal Navy also deployed helicopters in the Gulf to provide an extended area of detection beyond the ships themselves. These Westland Sea Lynxes were armed with Sea Skua antiship missiles. The Sea Skua is a radar-guided missile with a 45-pound explosive warhead. However, as the missiles reached the Gulf, their guidance systems were modified to be able to detect smaller patrol craft. First used in the 1982 Falklands War, the Sea Skua proved to be an efficient weapon in the Persian Gulf.

The Sea Skua was first employed in combat on January 29, 1991, when a U.S. Navy Seahawk helicopter detected 17 small boats and called for Royal Navy assistance. In response, the *Brazen, Gloucester,* and *Cardiff* dispatched Sea Skua–armed Sea Lynx helicopters. Twelve of the small craft, identified as Iraqi Navy units, were damaged by the helicopters, and four of the boats were sunk by Royal Navy missile fire. Later that same day, another Iraqi vessel was sunk by helicopters from the *Cardiff.*

With the success of the air campaign against the Iraqi Air Force that commenced in January 1991, the threat from air attack was markedly reduced by the time the ground war began in February. The missile threat still remained a constant concern, however. On February 25, 1991, two Iraqi Silkworm antiship missiles were fired at the U.S. battleship *Missouri.* The *Gloucester,* providing escort for the *Missouri,* detected the in-bound missiles and fired two Sea Dart surface-to-air missiles to intercept them. The Sea Darts destroyed one of the missiles, while the other fell into the sea. In the end, the Royal Navy suffered no ships lost in the course of the action.

STEVEN F. MARIN

See also

Aircraft, Helicopters; Aircraft, Helicopters, Operations DESERT SHIELD and DESERT STORM; DESERT SHIELD, Operation; DESERT STORM, Operation; Iraq, Navy; Mines, Sea, Clearing Operations, Persian Gulf and Iraq Wars; Minesweepers and Mine Hunters; United States Navy, Persian Gulf War

References

Finlan, Alastair. *The Royal Navy in the Falklands Conflict and the Gulf War: Culture and Strategy.* New York: Frank Cass, 2004.

Harding, Richard, ed. *The Royal Navy, 1930–2000: Innovation and Defense.* New York: Frank Cass, 2005.

Rose, Lisle. *Power at Sea: A Violent Peace, 1946–2006.* Columbia: University Missouri Press, 2007.

United Kingdom Forces in Afghanistan

United Kingdom military forces were involved in Afghanistan from the very beginning of Operation ENDURING FREEDOM in October 2001, and with the exception of the United States, they provided the largest number of personnel to the coalition forces there. During the initial aerial attacks in October 2001, British Royal Navy submarines fired Tomahawk missiles against Taliban and Al Qaeda locations, and Royal Air Force aircraft provided both reconnaissance and refueling aircraft to support U.S. attack aircraft. U.S. aircraft flew missions from the British base at Diego Garcia in the Indian Ocean.

In November 2001 Royal Marine commandos helped to secure the airfield at Bagram, and a 1,700-person battle group, including marine commandos, deployed to eastern Afghanistan to disrupt Al Qaeda forces and their terrorist infrastructure. These forces,

code-named Task Force Jacana, destroyed enemy bunkers and caves and provided humanitarian aid to the civilians of the area until the forces withdrew in July 2002.

With the military rout of the Taliban and Al Qaeda, the International Security Assistance Force (ISAF) was created in December 2001 to continue to assist the Afghan Transitional Government. The British played a major role in the negotiations to create ISAF under the authority of United Nations (UN) Security Council resolutions. British major general John McColl was the first head of this group, which consisted of forces from 16 nations. Britain also provided the headquarters and many of the supporting forces for ISAF as well as the brigade headquarters and an infantry battalion. The number of British forces in ISAF reached a peak of 2,100; however, all except approximately 300 were deployed to other operations after the command of ISAF was transferred to Turkey in the summer of 2002. In August 2003 the North Atlantic Treaty Organization (NATO) took over ISAF, and Britain again became a dominant element in the command.

From the beginning, British forces engaged in training the Afghan National Security Forces (ANSF) to prepare them to take over security for their own country. Provincial Reconstruction Teams (PRTs), which used civilians and small numbers of military troops to support development programs in cooperation with Afghan authorities, were the primary element in this effort. The

A Royal Marine sniper team returns enemy fire during combat at Lakari Bazaar, Afghanistan, July 19, 2009. (U.S. Department of Defense)

first PRT was established at Mazar-e Sharif, in northern Afghanistan, in May 2003, and a smaller PRT followed at Meymaneh. Germany and the Netherlands added PRTs in the north in 2004, while Britain provided the bulk of troops for a quick reaction force (QRF), based in Mazar-e Sharif, to protect the PRTs. The Meymaneh PRT was transferred to Norway in September 2005, and the Mazar-e Sharif team was transferred to Sweden in March 2006. This allowed Britain to move its forces to southern Afghanistan to engage in a more direct combat role.

In September 2004 Britain deployed six Boeing/British Aerospace McDonnell Douglas AV-8B Harrier strike aircraft to Kandahar to support ENDURING FREEDOM operations in the southern part of the country, and British forces were involved in ISAF operations as PRTs were expanded into western Afghanistan in 2005. In May 2006 Britain established the headquarters of the Allied Rapid Reaction Corps (ARRC) in Kabul and led the ISAF as it expanded operations into the challenging areas of the south and east, where insurgency forces were strongest.

In early 2006 Britain dispatched an air assault brigade and supporting elements, an original total of 3,300 military forces, to Helmand Province in southern Afghanistan. With further deployments in 2006 and 2007 the military force totals in the area reached 7,300 personnel targeted against the increasing insurgency in southern Afghanistan. In December 2007 Prince Harry, third in succession for the British throne, was secretly deployed to Afghanistan as a frontline soldier. He served for 10 weeks until his presence was discovered and reported by the media. Fearing that his presence would subject all those serving with him to greater risk of terrorist actions, the young prince was recalled in March 2008.

In June 2008 the ISAF stood at 53,000 forces supplied by 43 nations. The British commitment to ISAF was 8,380 personnel engaged in a wide range of air, land, and training missions. By the end of 2009, 245 British military personnel had died in Afghanistan.

JOE P. DUNN

See also

Afghanistan; Diego Garcia; ENDURING FREEDOM, Operation; International Security Assistance Force; Provincial Reconstruction Teams, Afghanistan; Taliban Insurgency, Afghanistan

References

Cawthorne, Nigel. *On the Front Line: True Stories of Outstanding Bravery by British Forces in Iraq and Afghanistan.* London: John Blake, 2008.

Neville, Leigh. *Special Operations Forces in Iraq (Elite).* Oxford, UK: Osprey, 2008.

United Nations

The international organization inaugurated in 1945 at the conclusion of World War II that has played an important role in modern Middle East conflicts since 1990. The United Nations (UN) is the successor organization to the League of Nations, which was itself the product of a preceding global conflagration, World War I.

Both the League of Nations and the UN were founded upon the principles of maintaining international peace and the political and territorial sovereignty of their member nation-states. The UN Charter specifically attempted to create an organization that could eradicate war, promote the fundamental human rights, establish a means by which international law could be implemented and enforced, and improve the economic and social conditions of people around the world. To achieve these aims, the UN Charter outlined the creation of six principal bodies: the General Assembly, the Security Council, the Economic and Social Council (ECOSOC), the Trusteeship Council, the International Court of Justice (ICJ), and the Secretariat (the administrative organ).

The General Assembly presents an at-large forum for all member states to discuss and debate any issue relevant to the UN Charter. The General Assembly refers matters that require action for the preservation of international peace to the Security Council. Only in rare circumstances does the General Assembly have the authority to take concrete steps to enforce peace.

The Security Council consists of 5 permanent members—France, the People's Republic of China (PRC), the Soviet Union (Russian Federation after 1991), the United States, and the United Kingdom—and 10 nonpermanent revolving members selected to represent regions of the world and elected by the General Assembly for two-year terms. Because of its mandate to maintain international security and peace, particularly through the use of sanctions and military force, the Security Council is among the most important of UN organs. The Security Council has repeatedly exercised its authority under Chapter VII of the UN Charter to force states to comply with its demands. This was demonstrated by the numerous resolutions passed on the matter of Iraq's 1990 invasion of Kuwait and subsequent resolutions passed to force Iraq to comply with UN demands and abide by the 1991 Persian Gulf War cease-fire agreement. Most importantly, the Security Council sought to dismantle Iraq's nuclear, biological, and chemical weapons programs by means of the International Atomic Energy Agency (IAEA), the United Nations Special Commission (UNSCOM), and the United Nations Monitoring, Verification and Inspection Commission (UNMOVIC). The Security Concil also played an important role in authorizing the use of force in the 1991 Persian Gulf War via Resolution 678. It did not, however, explicitly authorize the March 2003 Anglo-American–led invasion of Iraq.

The ECOSOC is composed of 54 elected members, serving for terms of three years, is charged with the tasks of coordinating the efforts of UN agencies, overseeing the relationship between the General Assembly and nongovernmental organizations, and studying international humanitarian, economic, and social matters. One such area of ECOSOC concern in the Middle East (among many) has been the status of women in Afghanistan prior to and following the U.S.-led removal of the Taliban government from power in the autumn of 1991. Another area of concern for the body has been domestic affairs in Iraq both before and after the Persian Gulf War, including the status of Iraqi minorities such as the Kurds.

The United Nations (UN) headquarters building in New York City. (Corel)

The Trusteeship Council no longer has an active agenda, having fulfilled its directive to oversee the process of self-determination of several League of Nations and UN trust territories.

The International Court of Justice (ICJ) is supervised by 15 justices, elected by an absolute majority in the Security Council and the General Assembly to serve nine-year terms. The ICJ delivers judgments in disputes between and among states and proffers advisory opinions. Recently, for instance, the ICJ held that the Israeli security fence in the West Bank was illegal. Overall, the impact of the ICJ on world affairs is rather insignificant given the fact that it averages fewer than two decisions per year and

because it has not established a record of solving violent international conflicts. Nevertheless, disputes over territorial sovereignty have been brought before the court, such as the case between Bahrain and Qatar that concluded in 2001.

The Secretariat consists of the office of secretary-general and associated staff. The secretaries-general, of whom there have been eight since 1945 including the current leader, Ban Ki Moon, is by far the most prominent UN official. The preceding leaders of the UN during the Middle East wars were Javier Pérez de Cuéllar (1982–1991), Boutros Boutros-Ghali (1992–1996), and Kofi Annan (1997–2006). Among the many responsibilities of the office, the secretary-general serves as the chief administrative officer of the UN, with the exception of the ICJ. This authority places the administrator in an important position to affect UN policy. Given the fissure within the international community over the 2003 invasion of Iraq, Secretary-General Annan encouraged nations to unite and, if necessary, to reform the UN, noting at the same time that the Global War on Terror must be tempered with tolerance. Since the advent of the Global War on Terror and the George W. Bush administration, the United States has had a rocky and contentious relationship with the UN. Indeed, the United States has openly criticized the body as well as the secretary-general.

Among many other missions in which they have been involved worldwide, UN peacekeeping forces were engaged in a 12-year-long commitment to the United Nations Iraq-Kuwait Observation Mission (UNIKOM) in which their forces supervised a demilitarized zone between Iraq and Kuwait.

Jason R. Tatlock

See also

Annan, Kofi; Bolton, John Robert, II; Boutros-Ghali, Boutros; Pérez de Cuéllar, Javier; United Nations Iraq-Kuwait Observation Commission; United Nations Monitoring, Verification and Inspection Commission; United Nations Security Council Resolution 661; United Nations Security Council Resolution 678; United Nations Security Council Resolution 687; United Nations Security Council Resolution 1284; United Nations Security Council Resolution 1441; United Nations Security Council Resolution 1483; United Nations Special Commission; United Nations Weapons Inspectors

References

Baehr, Peter R., and Leon Gordenker. *The United Nations: Reality and Ideal.* 4th ed. New York: Palgrave Macmillan, 2005.

Fasulo, Linda. *An Insider's Guide to the UN.* New Haven, CT: Yale University Press, 2004.

United Nations Assistance Mission for Afghanistan
Start Date: March 28, 2002
End Date: Continuing

United Nations (UN) mission launched on March 28, 2002, to help in the reconstruction and economic development of Afghanistan. The United Nations Assistance Mission for Afghanistan (UNAMA) was created in response to UN Security Council Resolution 1401 and was designed to support the December 2001 Bonn Agreement. In addition to upholding the tenets of the Bonn Agreement, UNAMA was charged with supervising humanitarian relief, recovery, and reconstruction programs in Afghanistan. To support the Bonn Agreement, UNAMA is also tasked with helping the government of Afghanistan achieve a stable democratic process,

Local Afghan election officials and United Nations (UN) personnel transport ballot boxes from the recent national presidential election to a waiting helicopter, September 2004. (U.S. Department of Defense)

providing strategic and political counsel to Afghani leaders, and aiding in the elimination of illegal drug cultivation and trade.

UNAMA is housed within the UN's peacekeeping operations division and maintains approximately 1,300 personnel, of whom almost 80 percent are Afghan nationals. UNAMA is headquartered in Kabul, with more than a dozen regional offices throughout the country. Since 2002, UNAMA has been headed by four special representatives of the secretary-general: Lakhdar Brahimi (2002–2004), Jean Arnault (2004–2006), Tom Koeings (2006–2007), and Kai Eide (2008–). The secretary-general is aided by two deputies, who supervise political and economic/social development issues. As part of its mission, UNAMA played a central role in national elections in 2004 and 2005. In an attempt to ensure that the Afghani government evolves into a stable, effective governing force on its own, UNAMA has not taken an active role in policy making, instead acting as an arbiter and counselor when needed.

UNAMA has come under physical attack on several occasions by extremists who deplore a Western presence in Afghanistan. In 2003 the Kandhar office was bombed, resulting in the death of a UN worker. In 2004 three UN officials charged with supervising elections were kidnapped and held for more than a month. Sporadic violence and attempted violence against UNAMA personnel have occurred throughout the nation, and the incidents began to increase in number as the Taliban insurgency gained ground in 2007. On October 28, 2009, suicide bombers attacked a guesthouse in Kabul, killing 5 UN employees and 3 other people in a furious two-hour battle. This led to the relocation of some 600 of its 1,100 staffers in the country to safer locations and temporary withdrawal of the remaining 500 from the country.

The Afghani government took the lead in elections scheduled for 2009 and 2010, which proved controversial amid allegations of voter fraud and corruption on the part of the Hamid Karzai regime, but UNAMA monitored the process and provided the Kabul government with support upon request. On March 20, 2008, UN Security Council Resolution 1806 extended the mandate of the United Nations Assistance Mission for Afghanistan for an additional year, until March 23, 2009. The UNAMA's mission was similarly extended in March 2009 and March 2010, thereby moving forward its mandate until March 2011. It is likely that UNAMA's mission will be extended beyond that, thanks to the continuing Taliban insurgency, the U.S. troop surge that began in January 2010, and ongoing instability within the Karzai administration.

Paul G. Pierpaoli Jr.

See also

Afghanistan; Bonn Agreement; Karzai, Hamid; International Security Assistance Force; Taliban Insurgency, Afghanistan; United Nations

References

Abrams, Dennis. *Hamid Karzai.* Langhorne, PA: Chelsea House, 2007.
Rashid, Ahmed. *Descent into Chaos: The United States and the Failure of Nation-building in Pakistan, Afghanistan, and Central Asia.* New York: Viking, 2008.

United Nations Draft Resolution

United Nations (UN) Security Council draft resolution sponsored by the United States, the United Kingdom, and Spain that attempted to lay the legal foundation for an invasion of Iraq. The three governments circulated two versions of the draft resolution, on February 24 and March 7, 2003. The crucial difference between the documents can be found in the final paragraphs that relate to the proposed reactions of the Security Council relevant to Resolution 1441, which had been adopted on November 8, 2002.

The significance of Resolution 1441 lay not only in its declaration that the government of Iraq was in violation of its responsibilities to comply fully with previous Security Council resolutions, particularly Resolution 687, but also that it presented Iraq with a final chance to fulfill its obligations or be in danger of suffering "serious consequences."

Of utmost importance to the Security Council was that Iraq dismantle its nuclear, biological, and chemical weapons programs as well as limit its ballistic missile production to those with a maximum range of 100 miles or less. Contained within Resolution 1441 was the protocol that the Security Council reconvene to decide what actions would be required should Iraq fail to abide by the resolution. The U.S. government assured the Security Council at the time that Resolution 1441 did not contain any "hidden triggers" for military force in the face of noncompliance. Thus, when and if Iraq was found to be in further material breach of Resolution 1441, protocol dictated a new resolution to justify further action against Iraq. It was in this context that the Spanish-, U.S.-, and British-sponsored draft resolutions were presented in February and March 2003. They were designed to be the official follow-up to Resolution 1441.

The February 24 version of the draft resolution was concise and to the point: Iraq had not utilized the final opportunity to meet the demands of the Security Council as specified by Resolution 1441. The expanded version of March 7 stipulated that Iraq had until March 17, 2003, to conform to its obligations, at which time it would be considered in material breach. The marked transformation between the two draft resolutions can only be understood when viewed in conjunction with initiatives undertaken by some of the other permanent members of the Security Council.

On February 24, 2003, the representatives of France, Russia, and Germany submitted a memorandum to the Security Council president. They indicated that military intervention should be reserved as a final option to be used only when all peaceful measures had been exhausted. In their opinion, three issues suggested that the time for war had not yet come. First, no firm evidence had been produced to demonstrate that Iraq was still in possession of weapons of mass destruction (WMDs). Second, weapons inspections via the United Nations Monitoring, Verification and Inspection Commission (UNMOVIC) had only recently hit their stride and were then progressing well and without Iraqi hindrance. Third, Iraq had been recently cooperating, albeit reluctantly, with UN inspection teams.

On March 5 the ministers for foreign affairs of France, Germany, and Russia submitted another letter to the Security Council. In no uncertain terms, they notified the council that their representatives would veto any draft resolutions that attempted to enforce Iraqi acquiescence through military force. They raised the issue in anticipation of a forthcoming Security Council meeting on March 7, at which time delegates were to debate the necessity of using force against Iraq and the need for a second resolution to supersede Resolution 1441 and authorize war.

While the British, Spanish, and American delegates hoped for the eventual adoption of its March 7 draft giving Iraq until March 17 to comply, the People's Republic of China (PRC) became one of several nations to assert that a new resolution was unnecessary and that Resolution 1441 should be allowed to run its course. Due to lack of support, the draft resolution was withdrawn. Thereafter, the March 2003 invasion of Iraq was justified, so it was argued, by Resolution 1441. That is, Resolution 1441 found Iraq in material breach of Security Council resolutions, thereby nullifying the cease-fire of Resolution 687 (April 3, 1991), and renewing the authorization for war contained in Resolution 678, passed in November 1990. The UN openly rejected this reasoning, and Secretary-General Annan subsequently proclaimed as "illegal" the military invasion of Iraq led by the United States and the United Kingdom.

JASON R. TATLOCK

See also

United Nations Security Council Resolution 678; United Nations Security Council Resolution 687; United Nations Security Council Resolution 1441

References

McGoldrick, Dominic. *From '9–11' to the 'Iraq War 2003': International Law in an Age of Complexity.* Portland, OR: Hart Publishing, 2004.

Taft, William H., IV, and Todd F. Buchwald. "Preemption, Iraq, and International Law." *American Journal of International Law* 97(3) (2003): 557–563.

Wedgwood, Ruth. "The Fall of Saddam Hussein: Security Council Mandates and Preemptive Self-Defense." *American Journal of International Law* 97(3) (2003): 576–585.

United Nations Educational, Scientific and Cultural Organization

A specialized agency of the United Nations (UN) formally established in 1946. Comprised of 166 member nations, the United Nations Educational, Scientific and Cultural Organization (UNESCO) promotes international collaboration through the dissemination of knowledge as well as multilateral cultural, educational, and scientific exchanges. The primary goal of UNESCO is the encouragement of peace by appealing to the common welfare of all nations.

The highest governing body of UNESCO is the General Conference, which is composed of representatives of all member nations and meets every two years. The Executive Board, composed of 58 representatives of member states, prepares the program for the General Conference and convenes two or three times a year. The organization is administered by the Secretariat, which is headed by the director-general and the director of the Executive Office.

There are 5 regional UNESCO coordinators. They oversee Africa, Latin America and the Caribbean, Asia and the Pacific, the Arab states, and Europe and North America. Within these 5 regions are 14 subregional offices. There are also national commissions in most member states to help integrate UNESCO's work with the work of individual member states.

UNESCO sponsors programs to spread literacy, provide adult education, and encourage universal primary education. These services particularly emphasize support for disabled people and women as well as the role of literacy in rural development. UNESCO routinely sends experts to member nations on request to advise them on educational matters and also provides educational fellowships and grants, with priority going to rural residents of developing nations that are UNESCO members.

UNESCO operates programs at the international, regional, subregional, and national levels that emphasize the use of science and technology in aiding developing countries and also promotes collaboration between industrialized countries. International-level

Members of the provincial reconstruction team and representatives of the United Nations Educational, Scientific and Cultural Organization (UNESCO) visit the Nabu Temple in the ancient city of Kalhu, now known as Nimrud, Iraq, on November 19, 2008. Nimrud is a candidate to become a protected UNESCO World Heritage site. (U.S. Department of Defense)

programs have encouraged intergovernmental collaboration in environmental sciences and natural resources research, established cooperation between developed and underdeveloped nations in the computer sciences, and worked with the world scientific community in all the basic sciences. UNESCO also develops cooperative agendas at the regional and subregional levels. At the national level, the organization sends experts on request to advise member nations on matters involving science and technology and organizes training and research programs. In addition, UNESCO has services encouraging study and research in the social sciences.

The organization's cultural heritage program has three parts. First, UNESCO promotes the application of international conventions on the protection of cultural properties and artifacts. Second, UNESCO helps member states preserve and restore cultural monuments and sites. Third, UNESCO operates training programs for museum managers, preservationists, archivists, and archaeologists.

UNESCO also promotes the international flow of information. To this end, the organization provides advisory services and assists member nations in developing training programs in communications, public information, media services, computer technology, and the like.

In the Middle East, UNESCO maintains offices in Jordan, Lebanon, Egypt, Iraq, Ramallah (a Palestinian city in the West Bank), Morocco, and Qatar. UNESCO's programs for Israel fall under its Europe and North America region. UNESCO has worked constantly and diligently to promote peace in the region by promoting mutual cooperation and dialogue between the Israelis and Arabs. Because many of the nations in the Middle East are considered developing nations, UNESCO has played a prominent role in education and poverty-mitigation efforts. UNESCO has also worked closely with nations such as Egypt to preserve their rich cultural past. Natural resource programs meanwhile have helped to increase crop irrigation in the arid region, lessen the impact of seasonal flooding and erosion, and manage precious freshwater supplies. In 1993 the organization awarded its Félix Houphouët-Boigny Peace Prize to Israel's Yitzhak Rabin and Shimon Peres and to Yasser Arafat of the Palestine Liberation Organization (PLO) in recognition of the progress made at the 1993 Oslo Accords. In 2005 UNESCO helped to establish the Israeli-Palestinian Science Organization, a nongovernmental multilateral endeavor that brings Palestinian and Israeli researchers and scientists together.

Since the overthrow of Iraqi dictator Saddam Hussein's regime in 2003, UNESCO has kept a high profile in that nation, working with U.S. and coalition partners and the Iraqi government to rebuild the country and its cultural, social, and educational foundations. UNESCO has helped strengthen the Iraqi press, has sponsored water projects, has advised the Iraqi government on ways to build and revitalize its educational institutions, has guided its cultural heritage programs, and has consistently sought to safeguard a democratic regime in the war-torn nation.

UNESCO has also been deeply involved in post-Taliban Afghanistan. There UNESCO has sought to sponsor programs to eradicate poverty, improve health care, construct educational infrastructure, and advise the Afghani government. Because so much of Afghanistan's cultural heritage had been destroyed, especially by the Taliban regime, UNESCO has engaged in myriad projects to safeguard that nation's cultural heritage and reconstruct its past from the fragments left behind by more than two decades of unrest and civil war.

PAUL G. PIERPAOLI JR.

See also

Afghanistan; Iraq, History of, 1990–Present; United Nations

References

Janello, Amy, and Brennon Jones, eds. *A Global Affair: An Inside Look at the United Nations.* New York: Jones and Janello, 1995.

Spaulding, Seth. *Historical Dictionary of the United Nations Educational, Scientific and Cultural Organization (UNESCO).* Lanham, MD: Rowan and Littlefield, 1997.

Ziring, Lawrence, Robert E. Riggs, and Jack C. Plano. *The United Nations: International Organization and World Politics.* Chicago: Wadsworth, 1993.

United Nations Iraq-Kuwait Observation Commission

Observation and peacekeeping mission established by United Nations (UN) Security Council Resolution 689, passed on April 9, 1991, and designed to enforce the Persian Gulf War cease-fire and to ensure the peaceful coexistence of Iraq and Kuwait. The United Nations Iraq-Kuwait Observation Commission (UNIKOM) accomplished its mission by monitoring the demilitarized zone (DMZ) between Iraq and Kuwait. UNIKOM was terminated on October 6, 2003.

Initially authorized to accommodate 300 international military and civilian personnel, UNIKOM's strength was greatly increased in February 1993 to 3,645 personnel after a series of border incidents at the DMZ. Two years later, in February 1995, UNIKOM's strength was reduced to 1,187 personnel. UNIKOM's troop strength fluctuated greatly during its mandate, and in October 2003 when its mission was declared complete, it consisted of just 4 official military observers and 131 civilian support staff. During its 12-year duration, which cost the UN an estimated $600 million, UNIKOM suffered 18 casualties (8 military personnel, 5 military observers, 4 international civilian staffers, and 1 local civilian staffer).

UNIKOM, like the Persian Gulf War coalition, was a broad-based international collaborative effort. The 36 participating nations included Argentina, Austria, Bangladesh, Canada, Chile, Denmark, Fiji, Finland, France, Germany, Ghana, Greece, Hungary, India, Indonesia, Ireland, Italy, Kenya, Malaysia, Nigeria,

Norway, Pakistan, the People's Republic of China (PRC), Poland, Romania, the Russian Federation, Senegal, Singapore, Sweden, Switzerland, Thailand, Turkey, the United Kingdom, the United States, Uruguay, and Venezuela. Not all nations provided military personnel or equipment, but all contributed at least some civilian personnel or military and medical support equipment and staff. There were seven force commanders during UNIKOM's mission and four chief military observers. In the spring of 1991, to provide security while UNIKOM was being organized and ramped up, five infantry companies, under UN control, were diverted from UN peacekeeping missions in Lebanon and Cyprus to the DMZ. They were withdrawn by the end of June 1991.

The DMZ was approximately 125 miles long, and UNIKOM's operations included patrols, observation points, and inspection units. UNIKOM was aided in these operation using both ground and air assets. Much of the DMZ was uninhabited, which made patrolling it somewhat easier. Initially, UNIKOM personnel were not empowered to physically prevent confrontations in the DMZ, and the UN personnel were unarmed. After a series of incidents in the DMZ, however, UNIKOM was given limited authority to prevent small-scale violations in the DMZ on February 5, 1993; three mechanized infantry battalions were now authorized. In April 1993 an additional mechanized infantry battalion from Bangladesh was deployed to the DMZ to support UNIKOM's mandate. At the same time UNIKOM was tasked with greater observation and inspection operations, which included roadblocks, vehicle inspections, and checkpoints. UNIKOM, which was headquartered at Umm Qasr, Iraq, also patrolled the waterways in and around the Faw (Fao) peninsula. Umm Qasr was located within the DMZ.

From February 1993 to the end of UNIKOM's mandate in 2003, the DMZ remained relatively calm. The mission maintained close working relations with the governments of both Iraq and Kuwait, and made frequent reports to the UN. On March 17, 2003, in anticipation of the Anglo-American–led invasion of Iraq, the UN ordered its UNIKOM personnel to leave the DMZ. A small office was established in Kuwait City so that UNIKOM could close its operations in the region. Most UNIKOM personnel returned to their home nations, and only a small administrative staff was left in Kuwait City. UNIKOM's mandate was declared a success, and UNIKOM was disbanded on October 6, 2003. In the last months of UNIKOM's existence, it helped facilitate humanitarian aid to Iraqis after the fall of Iraqi president Saddam Hussein's regime.

PAUL G. PIERPAOLI JR.

See also

Faw Peninsula; Umm Qasr; United Nations

References

Meisler, Stanley. *The United Nations: The First Fifty Years*. New York: Atlantic Monthly Press, 1997.

Weiss, Thomas G., et al., eds. *The United Nations and Changing World Politics*. Boulder, CO: Westview, 1997.

United Nations Monitoring, Verification and Inspection Commission

United Nations (UN) weapons-inspection regime created by UN Security Council Resolution 1284, passed on December 17, 1999. The United Nations Monitoring, Verification and Inspection Commission (UNMOVIC) took up the work of the previously disbanded United Nations Special Commission (UNSCOM), which had been tasked with verifying Iraq's compliance with post–Persian Gulf War agreements mandating the destruction of all Iraqi weapons of mass destruction (WMDs). More specifically, UNMOVIC's mandate was to ensure the identification and destruction of any biological, chemical, and nuclear weapons as well as missiles with a range greater than approximately 100 miles.

UN secretary-general Kofi Annan named Swedish diplomat Hans Blix to head UNMOVIC as executive chairman. Blix, who had been chairman of International Atomic Energy Agency (IAEA) from 1981 to 1997, served with UNMOVIC from March 1, 2000, to June 30, 2002. In addition to Blix, the UN appointed 16 individuals who helped Blix conduct inspections and compile verification facts.

Unlike UNSCOM, its predecessor agency, all of UNMOVIC's inspectors and employees were UN employees. This was done to quell concerns that the inspections were politically motivated or being unduly influenced by individual nation-states. The staff included scientists, analysts, engineers, operational planners, and, of course, seasoned weapons inspectors. Headquartered in New York City, UNMOVIC was divided into four operational segments: training and technical support, information, planning and operations, and analysis and assessment. Every three months the executive chairman was obliged to present a report to the UN Security Council on UNMOVIC's findings and actions in Iraq.

As it turned out, UNMOVIC proved to be as controversial as UNSCOM. Although Blix chided Iraqi president Saddam Hussein's government for playing "cat-and-mouse" games in regard to its cooperation with UN weapons inspectors, Blix's reports to the Security Council concluded that UNMOVIC had not found any illicit WMDs in Iraq. This ran counter to the George W. Bush administration's claims, however, which asserted that Iraq did indeed have WMDs. Before long the United States concluded that UNMOVIC was ineffectual and had not revealed findings of WMDs to stave off an invasion of Iraq.

On November 8, 2002, the UN Security Council passed Resolution 1441, which essentially allowed Iraq one final opportunity to cooperate fully and unconditionally with weapons inspectors and to explain contradictions in its verification process. UNMOVIC inspectors returned to Iraq that same month but were unable to unearth any credible evidence of illicit WMDs programs in Iraq. The Bush administration dismissed UNMOVIC's reports, alleging that it had evidence of WMDs in Iraq and that UNMOVIC was being pressured by the UN and the international community not to divulge evidence of WMDs in order to avoid a showdown with the Iraqis.

A United Nations (UN) weapons inspector checks a tank, thought to contain chlorine, at the al-Rashid station for water purification in Baghdad, Iraq, February 8, 2003. (AP/Wide World Photos)

On the eve of the Anglo-American–led invasion of Iraq in March 2003 UNMOVIC evacuated the country, still claiming that Iraq had disarmed appropriately. UNMOVIC continued to operate in those areas it was able to influence thereafter, but after the invasion its actions were largely completed. UNMOVIC's mandate lapsed on June 29, 2007, per UN Security Council Resolution 1762.

Many in the UN and the international community did not support the March 2003 invasion of Iraq. They further believed that the United States and Great Britain had purposely tried to sabotage and discredit UNMOVIC to help justify the war against Iraq. Blix was absolutely furious over the contretemps, and in a February 2004 report to the Security Council he admitted that Iraq should have been more forthcoming with weapons inspectors since 1991 but also maintained that UNSCOM and UNMOVIC had accomplished the task of ridding Iraq of WMDs. That same month during a television interview in Great Britain, Blix pointedly asserted that the United States and Britain had purposely overemphasized the threat of Iraqi WMDs to justify their invasion. In the end no WMDs have been located in Iraq, even after years of searching by perhaps thousands of members of the occupation forces in Iraq.

Blix claims that the United States so mistrusted him that his home and office were bugged.

PAUL G. PIERPAOLI JR.

See also

Blix, Hans; Iraq, History of, 1990–Present; United Nations Security Council Resolution 1284; United Nations Security Council Resolution 1441; United Nations Special Commission; Weapons of Mass Destruction

References

Blix, Hans. *Disarming Iraq*. New York: Pantheon, 2004.

Butler, Richard. *The Greatest Threat: Iraq, Weapons of Mass Destruction and the Growing Crisis in Global Security*. New York: PublicAffairs, 2000.

Byman, Daniel. "After the Storm: U.S. Policy toward Iraq since 1991." *Political Science Quarterly* 115(4) (2000–2001): 493–516.

United Nations Security Council Resolution 661

Resolution adopted by the United Nations (UN) Security Council on August 6, 1990, four days after the Iraqi invasion and occupation of Kuwait, which imposed a wide array of economic sanctions against Iraq. Resolution 661 had a much more substantial impact on Iraq than the council's preceding Resolution 660, passed on August 2, which had condemned the actions of Iraqi president Saddam Hussein's government and had demanded the removal of its troops from Kuwait. Indeed, Resolution 661 set in place a series of protocols that would affect Iraqi foreign relations and domestic affairs for more than a decade. In fact, the country remains under its effects even in the wake of the Anglo-American–led invasion of Iraq and the subsequent demise of the Baathist regime in 2003.

In 1990 the UN Security Council consisted of representatives from Canada, Colombia, Côte d'Ivoire, Cuba, Ethiopia, Finland, Malaysia, Romania, Yemen, and Zaire, in addition to the five permanent members of France, the United Kingdom, the United States, the Soviet Union, and the People's Republic of China (PRC). All voted in favor of Resolution 661, with the exception of the representatives of Yemen and Cuba, who abstained. The purpose of the resolution was to impose economic sanctions on Iraq until it fully complied with Resolution 660 by removing its troops from Kuwaiti territory. But as time progressed, it became the means by which the Security Council attempted to force Iraq into abandoning its biological, chemical, and nuclear weapons programs.

The resolution specifically urged all countries to impose a rigorous trade embargo on Iraq that prohibited the importing of any products and commodities from Iraq and occupied Kuwait. It also severely limited the exportation of items to Iraq, as well as the transfer of funds unless they were for medical or humanitarian purposes.

The Security Council committee responsible for the implementation of the embargo considered Resolution 661 unprecedented in terms of its severity. These sentiments were later echoed by U.S. Representative to the UN John Bolton in an address to the U.S. Senate Foreign Relations Committee on April 11, 2005. He asserted that firmness by the United States in 1990 had helped bring about the sweeping sanctions against Iraq.

Kuwait was released from the sanctions imposed by Resolution 661 on March 2, 1991, but Iraq continued to be bound by them because of its failure to adhere to additional Security Council resolutions, especially Resolution 687, which principally demanded that the Iraqi government destroy its biological, chemical, and nuclear weapons matériel, along with its longer-range ballistic missiles. Despite Iraq's lack of compliance, even after the 1991 Gulf War, the Security Council was moved by the worsening humanitarian situation in Iraq to inaugurate in 1995 the Oil-for-Food Programme, which permitted the government to export petroleum products to generate funds for humanitarian purposes.

Both the Oil-for-Food Programme, which had generated approximately $30 billion in humanitarian aid, and the Security Council committee established by Resolution 661 were dismantled shortly after the 2003 Iraqi invasion. The Security Council Resolution 1483, which outlined these developments, marked an end to the importation and exportation restrictions established by Resolution 661, with the exception of arms sales. The importation of weapons into postwar Iraq was permitted solely for the purposes of the Iraqi Coalition Provisional Authority.

Resolution 661 continued to affect Iraqi exports long after Hussein was removed from power, and as recently as April 30, 2008, the U.S. Department of Homeland Security implemented an import restriction on any item of cultural heritage originating from Iraq unless documentation could be provided to verify that the materials were legally exported prior to August 6, 1990, the date upon which Resolution 661 was adopted.

JASON R. TATLOCK

See also

Iraq, Sanctions on; United Nations; United Nations Security Council Resolution 678; United Nations Security Council Resolution 1483

References

Greenwood, Christopher. "New World Order or Old? The Invasion of Kuwait and the Rule of Law." *Modern Law Review* 55(2) (1992): 153–178.

Warbrick, Colin. "The Invasion of Kuwait by Iraq." *International and Comparative Law Quarterly* 40(2) (1991): 482–492.

United Nations Security Council Resolution 678

Resolution adopted by the United Nations (UN) Security Council on November 29, 1990, nearly four months after the invasion and occupation of Kuwait by the military forces of Iraq. Resolution 678 presented the Iraqi government with an ultimatum, literally "a pause of goodwill," to comply wholly with the UN resolutions passed since the August 2, 1990, invasion of Kuwait or face any measures deemed appropriate, including military intervention, by the UN member states working with the Kuwaiti government. The deadline for compliance was January 15, 1991.

Of utmost importance to Resolution 678 was the demand that Iraq withdraw its troops to their August 1 positions within the internationally recognized borders of Iraq, a demand previously established by Security Council Resolution 660, passed on August 2, 1990. Resolution 678 dealt with additional matters brought forth by the various resolutions preceding Resolution 678 and enumerated therein, such as the condemnation of Iraqi efforts to modify the population demographics of Kuwait by forced emigration and the obliteration of the authentic civil records established by the Kuwaiti government (Resolutions 677 and 670), the demand that Iraq treat Kuwaiti and third-state nationals humanely in accordance with international conventions and desist from taking hostages (Resolutions 674, 667, and 666), the disapproval of Iraq's treatment of diplomatic missions and their properties in Kuwait (Resolution 667), the insistence that Iraq allow and assist third-state nationals in their departure from Iraq and Kuwait (Resolution 664), the condemnation of Iraq's exportation of petroleum (Resolution 665) in the face of a trade embargo (Resolution 661), and the stipulation that the government of Iraq repeal its official declaration of the annexation of Kuwait (Resolution 662).

In 1990 the UN Security Council was composed of the 5 permanent members—the People's Republic of China (PRC), the United States, the United Kingdom, the Soviet Union, and France—as well as 10 nonpermanent members: Canada, Colombia, Côte d'Ivoire, Cuba, Ethiopia, Finland, Malaysia, Romania, Yemen, and Zaire. Resolution 678 was passed by a vote of 12 to 2 (Yemen and Cuba were opposed), with 1 abstention (China). In the 11 previous resolutions concerning Iraq and Kuwait that precipitated Resolution 678, Yemen and Cuba were routinely the only nations to abstain or vote negatively. China's abstention was a departure from its characteristic approval of resolutions associated with the Iraqi-Kuwaiti conflict and should be scrutinized against the backdrop of Chinese foreign policy following the 1989 Tiananmen Square protests, which had significantly marred China's image on the world stage. Had China vetoed Resolution 678, it would have most likely exacerbated its already strained relations with the United States, a sponsor of the resolution. Nevertheless, an abstention allowed China to maintain its previous policy regarding foreign conflicts, which held that they should be settled principally by peaceful means and not by external military intervention.

As for Yemen, it too opposed the use of force and advocated that sufficient time be allowed for the economic sanctions passed in Resolution 661 to take effect. Indeed, the Yemeni delegate, Abdullah Saleh al-Ashtal, labeled Resolution 678 the "War resolution." The Cuban representative, Malmierca Peoli, agreed, considering it tantamount to providing a blank check to the U.S. military and allied forces.

Resolution 678 not only served as the international justification of the 1991 Persian Gulf War but also seemed to justify further military action against Iraq. It, together with Resolution 687 (April 3, 1991) and Resolution 1441 (November 8, 2002), which in a similar fashion to Resolution 678 presented Iraq with one last chance to comply with the dismantling of its alleged weapons of mass destruction (WMDs) program, served as the justification for the March 2003 Anglo-American–led invasion of Iraq. Many UN members, including permanent Security Council members, rejected the use of Resolutions 678 and 687 to justify the 2003 invasion of Iraq.

JASON R. TATLOCK

See also

DESERT STORM, Operation; IRAQI FREEDOM, Operation; United Nations; United Nations Security Council Resolution 661; United Nations Security Council Resolution 687; United Nations Security Council Resolution 1441

References

Huo, Hwei-ling. "Patterns of Behavior in China Foreign Policy: The Gulf Crisis and Beyond." *Asian Survey* 32(3) (1992): 263–276.

Shichor, Yitzhak. "China and the Middle East since Tiananmen." *Annals of the American Academy of Political and Social Science* 519 (1992): 86–100.

Weston, Burns H. "Security Council Resolution 678 and Persian Gulf Decision Making: Precarious Legitimacy." *American Journal of International Law* 85(3) (1991): 516–35.

United Nations Security Council Resolution 687

United Nations (UN) Security Council resolution passed on April 3, 1991, that formally established the conditions of the Persian Gulf cease-fire and stipulated the postwar conditions for Iraq. The measure passed with 12 votes for and 1 against (Cuba). Ecuador and Yemen abstained. In the UN Charter, the member states agreed to "refrain in their international relations from the threat or use of force against the territorial integrity or political independence of any state." Article 41 of the UN Charter, however, empowers the UN Security Council to decide when and if armed force may be employed by a member state or states. In November 1990 Security Council Resolution 678 had authorized member states to use "all necessary means" to restore international peace and security after Iraq's August 1990 invasion of Kuwait.

Security Council Resolution 687, passed after coalition forces had driven the Iraqi Army from Kuwait, welcomed the restoration of Kuwait's sovereignty and declared a formal cease-fire with certain conditions. These conditions included comprehensive economic sanctions on Iraq; respect for Iraq's boundary with Kuwait and its foreign debts; the payment of reparations by Iraq to persons, corporations, and governments injured by the war against Kuwait; and internationally supervised destruction of Iraq's chemical and biological weapons and related stocks and facilities, its facilities or materials for use in developing nuclear weapons, and its long-range missiles.

On October 31, 1998, Iraq stated that it would no longer comply with UN weapons inspectors verifying its compliance with Resolution 687. Iraq claimed that the inspection process had been infiltrated by U.S. intelligence agencies. The UN weapons inspectors later reported that this had occurred but that Iraq had been effectively disarmed by 1998 in any event. Security Council Resolution 1205 of November 5, 1998, condemned Iraq's noncooperation and reaffirmed the Security Council's commitment to enforce Resolution 687. The next month the United States and Great Britain, claiming that Iraq's noncompliance revived their authority to enforce Resolution 678, bombed Iraqi air defense installations, facilities believed to be linked to prohibited weapons, Iraqi Republican Guard bases, presidential palaces, and other regime strongholds.

On November 8, 2002, the UN Security Council unanimously adopted Security Council Resolution 1441, finding Iraq in "material breach" of its disarmament obligations under Resolution 687 but giving it a "final opportunity" to comply before facing "serious consequences" to be determined by the Security Council, which remained "seized of the matter." The United States argued in the Security Council on March 27, 2003, after the Anglo-American invasion of Iraq had begun, that Iraq's material breach of Resolution 687 had revived the authority to use force under Resolution 678. President George W. Bush informed the U.S. Congress that apart from the right of the United States to self-defense under the UN Charter, Resolution 678 authorized the use of force against Iraq, just as it had in 1998. The British representative defended the war in the Security Council as a coalition action "to enforce Security Council decisions on complete Iraqi disarmament." In a report to the British Parliament, Lord Peter Goldsmith, attorney general for England and Wales, stated that Resolution 687's cease-fire provisions suspended the authorization for the use of force conditional on Iraq eliminating its weapons of mass destruction (WMDs) but that Iraq's "material breach of Resolution 687 revive[d] the authority to use force under Resolution 678." In private advice to British prime minister Tony Blair, however, Goldsmith commented that "a reasonable case can be made" that the authorization to use force in Resolution 678 could not be revived without a further Security Council resolution.

Many UN members refused to accept that the war was supported by Security Council resolutions. The French representative characterized the 2003 intervention as lacking a UN mandate and as a violation of Resolution 687's guarantee of Iraq's sovereignty and territorial integrity. The representative of the Russian Federation argued that the war violated Security Council resolutions, threatened a humanitarian disaster, and came just as Iraq was cooperating anew with UN weapons inspectors. The Chinese representative agreed. The representative of India called the war "unjustified and avoidable." The European Union's statement stressed Iraq's "territorial integrity, sovereignty, [and] political stability" but also endorsed the "full and effective disarmament of Iraq."

After the fall of the Saddam Hussein regime in April 2003, a series of Security Council resolutions modified the economic sanctions regime imposed by Resolution 687. Most notably, Resolution 1483 called upon the United States and Great Britain to restore the security of Iraq in compliance with the Geneva Conventions and other applicable international law, abolish the economic sanctions with the exception of certain arms sales, and reaffirm Iraq's disarmament obligations under Resolution 687.

HANNIBAL TRAVIS

See also

United Nations; United Nations Security Council Resolution 678; United Nations Security Council Resolution 1441; United Nations Security Council Resolution 1483; United Nations Weapons Inspectors; Weapons of Mass Destruction

References

Goldsmith, Peter Henry, Queen's Counsel and Attorney General of England and Wales. "Iraq; Resolution 1441 (Advice to the Prime Minister)." BBC News, April 28, 2005, http://news.bbc.co.uk/2/hi/uk_news/politics/vote_2005/frontpage/4492195.stm.

UN Security Council. "The Situation between Iraq and Kuwait." New York: UN Doc. S/PV.4726 (Resumption 1), March 27, 2003.

United Nations Security Council Resolution 1284

Resolution adopted by the United Nations (UN) Security Council on December 17, 1999. Resolution 1284 established the UN Monitoring, Verification, and Inspection Commission (UNMOVIC), reaffirmed the mission of the International Atomic Energy Agency (IAEA), and charged both with overseeing Iraqi compliance with previous Security Council resolutions, most notably 687, which had gone into effect on April 3, 1991. Although not all Security Council members endorsed the final draft of Resolution 1284, the council generally recognized the need for a resolution of its kind in light of the fact that UN inspections had been

Selected United Nations Security Council Resolutions Related to Iraq, 1990–2003

Resolution Number	Date	Title	Voting Results			
			Yes	No	Abstention	Nonvoting
661	August 6, 1990	On Sanctions against Iraq	13	0	2	0
678	November 29, 1990	Authorizing Member States to Use All Necessary Means to Implement Security Council Resolution 660 and All Relevant Resolutions	12	2	1	0
687	April 3, 1991	On Restoration of the Sovereignty, Independence and Territorial Integrity of Kuwait	12	1	2	0
1284	December 17, 1999	On Establishment of the United Nations Monitoring, Verification and Inspection Commission (UNMOVIC)	11	0	4	0
1441	November 8, 2002	On Decision to Set up an Enhanced Inspection Regime to Ensure Iraq's Compliance of Its Disarmament Obligations	15	0	0	0
1483	May 22, 2003	On Lifting Economic Sanctions on Iraq Imposed by Resolution 661	14	0	0	1

inactive in Iraq for a year, after having been withdrawn because of Iraqi intransigence.

UNMOVIC, which replaced the UN Special Commission (UNSCOM) created by Resolution 687, was specifically tasked with monitoring Iraq's compliance with the restrictions enumerated in paragraphs 8–10 of that same resolution. Therein the Iraqi government was informed of the necessity to destroy, remove, or render harmless its biological and chemical weapons and related matériel, as well as any ballistic missiles capable of traveling more than 100 miles. Paragraphs 12–13 of Resolution 687 further outlined the requirements for Iraq to shut down its nuclear weapons program under observation of the IAEA; Resolution 1284 reiterated the agency's role in this regard.

At the time Resolution 1284 was approved, the Security Council was composed of delegates from Argentina, Bahrain, Brazil, Canada, Gabon, Gambia, Malaysia, Namibia, the Netherlands, Slovenia, and the five permanent member states (People's Republic of China [PRC], France, the Russian Federation, the United Kingdom, and the United States). Eleven nations voted in favor of the resolution while four abstained (France, China, the Russian Federation, and Malaysia).

The Chinese government's misgivings over the final draft of the resolution revolved around two issues. First, it believed that the resolution did not adequately provide incentives to encourage Iraqi compliance by specifying the process through which UN sanctions would be suspended. Second, it asserted that a consensus had not been reached by the council members, which might therefore undermine UNMOVIC's authority. China underscored the second matter to emphasize its disapproval of the actions of certain council members, particularly the United States and Great Britain, who had ostensibly undertaken unilateral military action in Iraq (Operation DESERT FOX in 1998) and who had imposed a no-fly zone in Iraq without council approval. Echoing similar sentiments concerning illicit unilateral maneuvers, Russia chose to abstain, rather than veto, the draft resolution. It did so because only some of its former objections had been addressed. Thus while Russia gave its limited approval, it nevertheless warned that it would not stand idly by if attempts were made to impose the resolution with force. France was concerned with the ambiguity surrounding the process by which sanctions would first be suspended and then lifted.

JASON R. TATLOCK

See also

DESERT FOX, Operation; International Atomic Energy Agency; United Nations; United Nations Monitoring, Verification and Inspection Commission; United Nations Special Commission; United Nations Weapons Inspectors

References

Bennis, Phyllis. "And They Called It Peace: U.S. Policy on Iraq." *Middle East Report* 215 (2000): 4–7.

Murphy, Sean D. "Contemporary Practice of the United States Relating to International Law." *American Journal of International Law* 94(1) (2000): 102–139.

United Nations Security Council Resolution 1441

Resolution passed by the United Nations (UN) Security Council on November 8, 2002, declaring the Iraqi government noncompliant with previous UN demands to disarm and granting it a final chance to comply or face unspecified consequences. The resolution was unanimously supported by all 15 members of the Security Council at that time: Bulgaria, Cameroon, People's Republic of China (PRC), Colombia, France, Guinea, Ireland, Mauritius, Mexico, Norway, the Russian Federation, Singapore, the Syrian Arab Republic, the United Kingdom, and the United States.

Resolution 1441 reiterated the need for the Iraqi government to comply with previous Security Council resolutions going back to 1991 by dismantling its chemical, biological, and nuclear weapons programs and long-range ballistic missiles. The resolution found Iraq to be "in material breach of its obligations," specifically because of its failure to work with UN weapons inspectors in the removal, destruction, or rendering harmless of its weapons of mass destruction and accompanying matériel as per Resolution 687 (1991). The most significant element of the new resolution was its somewhat vague ultimatum, which represented Iraq's "final opportunity" to conform to Security Council demands.

The discussion and debates that ensued following the adoption of Resolution 1441 centered on the potential use of force in bringing about Iraqi compliance. At the time, the U.S. UN ambassador John Negroponte accentuated the fact that the final version of the resolution included neither "hidden triggers" nor "automaticity" concerning military action. He indicated, furthermore, that should Iraq fail to abide by Resolution 1441, the next step would be for the Security Council to determine the appropriate course of action, as outlined in the new resolution. He also stated that should the Security Council shirk its responsibilities, the resolution did not preclude member states from taking matters into their own hands to protect themselves and the world from the threat posed by Iraq. Indeed, the United States had already laid out this scenario on September 12, 2002, when President George W. Bush addressed the UN General Assembly. British UN delegate Sir Jeremy Greenstock, whose government cosponsored Resolution 1441 with the United States, shared this position.

Several members of the council, particularly France, China, and Mexico, were pleased by the removal of any language of automaticity that had existed in an earlier draft of the resolution. They were further buoyed by the process in which additional measures against Iraq would be taken, which required the agreement of the Security Council only after ascertaining the existence of a breach of Resolution 1441. Nevertheless, the Security Council seemed well aware that war was looming on the horizon and that this was one final chance for a peaceful conclusion to the standoff.

Certainly there existed by this time a deep-seated frustration with U.S. and British military actions against Iraq. The Russian Federation, for example, condemned what it considered unilateral

Members of the United Nations (UN) Security Council vote on November 8, 2002, on the U.S.-backed resolution calling for weapons inspections in Iraq. The resolution passed unanimously, 15–0. (AFP/Getty Images)

moves by these countries in attempting to force Iraqi compliance in 1998's Operation DESERT FOX, which saw air strikes against selected Iraqi targets. Resentment over the air strikes was not limited to members of the council, however. According to a report published by the U.S. State Department in 1998, 154 antiwar protests occurred worldwide, mostly in Europe, in response to that operation.

Resolution 1441 was not intended to serve as an official pretext for war with Iraq, but it surely played a significant role in the lead-up to the Anglo-American–led invasion of Iraq in March 2003, which toppled the Iraqi regime. The United States, United Kingdom, and Spain sponsored two failed resolutions—one on February 24, 2003, and another on March 7—that would have declared Iraq in material breach and that gave it until March 17 to return to compliance or face military action. The drafts failed to garner adequate support and were withdrawn. In fact, there existed a demonstrable urgency in the 4,717th meeting of the Security Council on March 11, 2003, for Iraq to meet the requirements of Resolution 1441, at which time it was noted by the delegate from Singapore that Iraq had only a few days to comply before facing dire consequences.

Shortly thereafter, on March 19, 2003, Operation IRAQI FREEDOM began. In its wake, the British delegation argued to the Security Council on March 27, 2003, that Resolution 1441 had authorized

the use of force, in conjunction with resolutions 678 and 687. The American perspective was presented in a much more nuanced fashion. The United States asserted that authorization for war came directly from Resolution 678, which had justified the use of force in the 1991 Persian Gulf War. The cessation of those hostilities had been contingent upon Resolution 687, which demanded the dismantling of Iraq's chemical, biological, and nuclear weapons programs. Resolution 1441 found Iraq in material breach of such obligations. Thus, the 1991 cease-fire was null and void, and Resolution 678 was, by default, still in effect. From this perspective, Operation IRAQI FREEDOM was essentially a continuation of the Persian Gulf War.

JASON R. TATLOCK

See also

DESERT FOX, Operation; IRAQI FREEDOM, Operation; Negroponte, John Dimitri; United Nations; United Nations Draft Resolution; United Nations Security Council Resolution 678; United Nations Security Council Resolution 687

References

Wedgwood, Ruth. "The Fall of Saddam Hussein: Security Council Mandates and Preemptive Self-Defense." *American Journal of International Law* 97(3) (2003): 576–585.

Yoo, John. "International Law and the War in Iraq." *American Journal of International Law* 97(3) (2003): 563–576.

United Nations Security Council Resolution 1483

Resolution adopted by the United Nations (UN) Security Council on May 22, 2003, that recognized coalition forces in Iraq as the legitimate governing and peacekeeping authority of the nation, called for the establishment of a transitional Iraqi governing council, and ended the economic sanctions against Iraq. Resolution 1483 was approved some two months after the start of the Anglo-American–led invasion of Iraq. At the time, the Security Council consisted of Angola, Bulgaria, Cameroon, Chile, Germany, Guinea, Mexico, Pakistan, Spain, and the Syrian Arab Republic, as well as the permanent members (People's Republic of China [PRC], France, the Russian Federation, the United Kingdom, and the United States). All voted for the resolution with the exception of the Syrian delegation.

In a subsequent meeting of the council, the Syrian representative explained that he would have likely voted favorably on the resolution had there been more time to consider the draft resolution. Syria's tentative approval was not to be misconstrued, however, as supportive of an "illegitimate war" against, and foreign occupation of, Iraq. It is clear that Syria would have preferred that Resolution 1483 not recognize the legality of the Coalition Provisional Authority, which oversaw postwar Iraq and was chiefly under British and American control.

The primary importance of Resolution 1483 was that it ended almost 13 years of international economic sanctions against Iraq. Following the Iraqi invasion of Kuwait, UN Security Council Resolution 661, adopted on August 6, 1990, had virtually sealed off Iraq from the rest of the world, banning the exportation of Iraqi goods and the importation of foreign products into Iraq, except for those items deemed necessary for medical and humanitarian purposes. The Oil-for-Food Programme, which had begun in 1995, eased certain of these restrictions, as specified in Resolution 986. As its name implies, Iraqi petroleum products could be exported to generate funds that would alleviate worsening humanitarian conditions in Iraq. When Resolution 1483 lifted the trade embargo, the Oil-for-Food Programme was thus no longer necessary and was terminated.

The resolution further outlined the required monetary and procedural protocols that would bring an official end to the Oil-for-Food Programme. Most importantly, monies generated by the program, minus administrative costs, were to be transferred to the newly established Development Fund for Iraq, an account that would be overseen by the Coalition Provisional Authority. Subsequent petroleum and natural gas revenues were to be placed in the account as well, to be utilized not only in rebuilding Iraq and providing for its humanitarian needs, but also for its disarmament and to fulfill its obligations under Resolution 687 (1991). That resolution had demanded that Iraq compensate foreign governments, individuals, and businesses for any financial or environmental harm caused by Iraqi aggression against Kuwait.

In addition to terminating the Oil-for-Food Programme, Resolution 1483 also disbanded the UN committee established by Resolution 661 to supervise the embargo against Iraq. In keeping with the desire of Security Council members to have the UN play a pivotal role in postwar Iraq, Resolution 1483 also established the office of the Special Representative for Iraq, who was tasked with several endeavors. These included the coordination of reconstruction and humanitarian efforts between the UN and nongovernmental organizations; the promotion of the return of displaced persons and refugees; the support of the creation of a democratically elected Iraqi government at the national and local levels as well as the reinvigoration of the civilian police; the facilitation of initiatives to reform the Iraqi legal system; and the safeguarding of human rights.

On May 23, 2003, Secretary General Kofi Annan informed the Security Council that he intended to appoint Sergio Vieira de Mello as his special representative for Iraq for an initial four-month term. During his brief tenure, Vieira de Mello, who was also serving as UN High Commissioner for Human Rights, died, together with 21 other people, including 14 other UN workers, during a terrorist attack on the Baghdad headquarters of the UN on August 19, 2003. Such a large-scale, targeted attack was unprecedented in the history of UN peacekeeping missions.

JASON R. TATLOCK

See also

Annan, Kofi; Iraq, Sanctions on; United Nations; United Nations Security Council Resolution 661

References

Grant, Thomas D. "The Security Council and Iraq: An Incremental Practice." *American Journal of International Law* 97(4) (2003): 823–842.

Scheffer, David J. "Beyond Occupation Law." *American Journal of International Law* 97(4) (2003): 842–860.

United Nations Special Commission

Organization established pursuant to United Nations (UN) Security Council Resolution 687, adopted on April 3, 1991. The United Nations Special Commission (UNSCOM) was tasked with overseeing, together with the International Atomic Energy Agency (IAEA), the inspection of Iraqi weapons programs to ensure compliance with UN resolutions calling for the dismantling of that nation's weapons of mass destruction (WMDs). Although the IAEA and UNSCOM cooperated in fulfilling their individual mandates, the IAEA was specifically responsible for investigating Iraq's nuclear capabilities, while UNSCOM was responsible for biological, chemical, and long-range missile armaments. Swedish diplomat Rolf Ekéus headed UNSCOM from 1991 to 1997, while Richard Butler headed it from 1997 to 1999. UNSCOM was disbanded in 1999 and replaced by the United Nations Monitoring, Verification and Inspection Commission (UNMOVIC) under the authority of Resolution 1284, adopted on December 17, 1999.

UNMOVIC was authorized in an attempt to reinvigorate the UN monitoring program with the goal of achieving Iraq's full compliance with Security Council demands. The need for a new approach was evident, for not only were weapons inspections stalled for a year (since 1998), but UNSCOM was widely perceived as biased and ineffectual, as was made evident at the meeting in which Resolution 1284 was adopted. At that time, the Chinese delegation intimated that any entity replacing the "infamous" UNSCOM must, unlike UNSCOM, operate with objectivity, impartiality, transparency, and accountability. Indeed, for the Russian Federation, the military force used by the United Kingdom and the United States against Iraq in December 1998 (Operation DESERT FOX) was both unilaterally conceived and erroneously justified by citing an inaccurate report given by Executive Chairman Butler, which had suggested that Iraq had not fully cooperated with weapons inspectors. China, moreover, went so far as to entertain the possibility that Butler had been complicit in preparing inaccurate reports that could then be utilized in an attempt to rationalize the use of force. In rebutting such allegations of impropriety, specifically as put forth by Russia in addressing the Security Council on December 16, 1998, Butler was later to argue that his conclusions about Iraqi noncompliance in his December 15 report were inescapable.

A significant difference between UNSCOM and UNMOVIC was that the organizational structure of the new investigative unit would have greater accountability and less room for unilateral movement by the executive chairperson. Butler would find these modifications problematic, but ostensibly they made UNMOVIC less susceptible to political manipulation. Certain of the key changes stipulated that the UN secretary-general would have direct charge of the commission; the appointed chairperson would require Security Council approval before assuming the post; a college of commissioners, made up of politicians rather than weapons experts, would be consulted prior to the implementation of significant policy alterations; and all personnel would be UN employees.

To be sure, UNSCOM fell victim to political infighting and global power politics, which the Iraqis were all too eager to exploit. Charges were leveled on more than one occasion—by Iraq and other UN nations—that UNSCOM was being undermined by sabotage aimed at destroying the regime of Iraqi dictator Saddam Hussein. Hussein specifically charged that the U.S. Central Intelligence Agency (CIA) had infiltrated UNSCOM, which was his justification for denying UNSCOM personnel access to certain government facilities, including the Baath Party headquarters in Baghdad.

UNSCOM was not terribly popular inside the UN either. In December 1998 Butler declared the Iraqi regime uncooperative, which triggered Operation DESERT FOX on December 16–19, 1998, a punitive bombing raid against Iraqi military targets carried out by U.S. and British naval and air assets. UNSCOM remained virtually nonoperational until December 1999, when UNMOVIC was formed.

Despite its controversial nature, UNSCOM accomplished much in its eight-year tenure. Of note was its ability to quickly implement an unprecedented weapons inspection and disarmament program when nothing of its kind had existed before. Within two months of its inception, UNSCOM had already begun inspections and was quite successful in overseeing the destruction of much illicit weapons material and equipment. Examples of the demolition of Iraq biological, chemical, and long-range missile programs overseen by UNSCOM included the destruction of 48 missiles, together with 20 tons of illicit fuel and 56 stationary missile launch sites; the eradication of 38,537 chemical munitions and chemical weapons agents totaling 690 tons; and the dismantling of the Hakam biological weapons plant and equipment from similar facilities at Manal and Safah. Hakam especially was a significant facility where such deadly biological agents as anthrax and botulinum toxin had been produced.

Immediately following the adoption of Resolution 1284 in 1999 and the consequent conclusion of the mandate of UNSCOM, the American delegation at the Security Council highlighted the important accomplishments of executive chairmen Ekéus and Butler. The former was lauded for his work in building UNSCOM from scratch; the latter was credited with sustaining UNSCOM's mission in the face of an increasingly uncooperative Iraq. What is more, both men played a key role in uncovering previously unknown weapons programs, which included biological weapons and a program to produce VX gas.

JASON R. TATLOCK

See also

Biological Weapons and Warfare; Chemical Weapons and Warfare; DESERT FOX, Operation; International Atomic Energy Agency; United Nations; United Nations Monitoring, Verification and Inspection Commission; United Nations Security Council Resolution 687; United Nations Security Council Resolution 1284; Weapons of Mass Destruction

References

Butler, Richard. *The Greatest Threat: Iraq, Weapons of Mass Destruction and the Growing Crisis in Global Security.* New York: PublicAffairs, 2000.
Byman, Daniel. "After the Storm: U.S. Policy toward Iraq since 1991." *Political Science Quarterly* 115(4) (2000–2001): 493–516.

United Nations Weapons Inspectors

Following the Persian Gulf War of 1991, the United Nations (UN) Security Council authorized a team of weapons inspectors to rid Iraq of all its weapons of mass destruction (WMDs), which included biological and chemical weapons as well as all materials related to nuclear weapons development. As a condition for the cessation of hostilities against Iraq in the Persian Gulf War (Operation DESERT STORM) following the coalition forces' liberation of Kuwait, the UN Security Council passed Resolution 687 on April 3, 1991. This called for the creation of the United Nations Special Commission (UNSCOM) to inspect and disarm Iraq's WMDs as well as all its missiles with a range greater than 90 miles.

From 1991 to 1999 UNSCOM was charged with enforcing UN Resolution 687. In 1999 a successor to UNSCOM came into being.

Iraqi citizens demonstrate their support for President Saddam Hussein as United Nations (UN) weapons inspectors enter a technology institute in Baghdad, Iraq, February 27, 2003. (AP/Wide World Photos)

It was known as the United Nations Monitoring, Verification and Inspection Committee (UNMOVIC) and was in Iraq from December 2002 to March 2003. Although Iraq repeatedly sought to conceal the extent of its WMDs program and also resisted cooperating fully with UNSCOM by, for example, denying inspectors access to certain sites, UNSCOM nevertheless engaged in significant disarmament activities. However, the sheer size of the country of Iraq, the technically complex nature of disarmament, and repeated Iraqi deception and resistance to UNSCOM efforts make it hard to know precisely the extent of success. For its part, Iraq accused UNSCOM of spying and of being a puppet of the United States and Israel.

In late 1998 UNSCOM withdrew from Iraq in the face of renewed Iraqi resistance and imminent punitive American and British air strikes in December. For the next four years, there were no weapons inspectors operating inside Iraq. This, of course, prompted concerns that Iraqi dictator Saddam Hussein had secretly renewed his WMDs program.

Beginning in 2002, U.S. president George W. Bush demanded that Iraq comply with UN resolutions and disarm once and for all or face an invasion. On November 8, 2002, UN Security Council Resolution 1441 declared that Iraq was in violation of Resolution 687. It denounced Iraq's "omissions or false statements" with

respect to its WMDs stockpiles and offered Iraq "a final opportunity to comply with its disarmament obligations." In December 2002 in the face of an imminent American and British invasion of Iraq, Hussein agreed to allow UN weapons inspectors back into the country; however, they were withdrawn in March 2003 just before the beginning of the Iraq invasion (Operation IRAQI FREEDOM) on March 20, 2003.

The head of UNMOVIC, Hans Blix, a Swedish diplomat, reported to the UN on March 7, 2003, that Iraq had not provided sufficient documentary evidence to account for its WMDs stockpiles and missiles. He expressed doubt as to whether Iraq had fully agreed to disarm. Unlike the United States, Britain, and Spain, however, a majority of members of the Security Council, including France, China, and Russia, opposed any resolution authorizing an attack or invasion of Iraq on this basis. The Americans, supported by Britain and Spain, denied that any additional UN resolution was necessary to authorize the use of force against Iraq. Indeed, they cited UN Security Council Resolution 686 of November 29, 1990, which authorized any UN member to use "all necessary means" to "restore international peace and security to the Persian Gulf Region." The three nations also pointed out that the Iraqis had violated 16 UN resolutions and in 12 years had failed to disarm. Based on the October 11, 2002, authorization by the U.S. Congress to use force against Iraq, the United States, along with Britain, commenced Operation IRAQI FREEDOM on March 20, 2003.

In the aftermath of the invasion, the Iraqi Survey Group was unable to find any WMDs. Several reasons have been advanced for this. The most obvious explanation is that Iraq had ceased its program sometime before 2003. Indeed, one of Saddam Hussein's sons-in-law, Hussein Kamal, who had charge of Iraq's WMDs program, made this claim repeatedly and with extensive detail upon defecting to Jordan in 1995, but U.S. and British intelligence agents doubted his veracity even though he, unlike other defectors, did not make efforts to secure personal financial gain. Indeed, he returned to Iraq and was killed. Upon being captured in December 2004, Saddam Hussein apparently also told American interrogators that Iraq no longer had WMDs. U.S. officials also considered the veracity of his comments problematic.

Other explanations for the absence of WMDs rest on sheer speculation and have never been verified but remain popular in certain political circles. For example, although no evidence exists to prove this claim, some critics of Operation IRAQI FREEDOM claim that the Bush administration knew Iraq had halted its WMDs program but lied to the American people to justify the invasion and regime change. Other critics of the war, mostly Democrats but some Republicans as well (most of whom had voted for the war), have since argued that Bush was misled by faulty intelligence, which was driven by the need to provide evidence to support the war rather than by a balanced appraisal of the true situation on the ground. They have concluded that the Bush administration presented only that evidence that supported its own conclusions. The U.S. Senate Intelligence Committee issued two reports in 2004 and 2006 documenting Bush administration intelligence failures regarding Iraq.

Finally, some observers believe that Iraq hid its remaining WMDs stockpiles or shipped them to Iran and/or Syria. It is highly unlikely that Iraq would ever ship such stockpiles to Iran. Although no conclusive evidence has been put forth to support this claim, its supporters cite the fact that Russian truck convoys left Iraq for Syria and other countries as coalition forces invaded. Those who support this theory also make the claim that Russia was assisting Hussein's WMDs program development.

STEFAN M. BROOKS

See also

Blix, Hans; Bush, George Walker; DESERT STORM, Operation; Hussein, Saddam; IRAQI FREEDOM, Operation; Nuclear Weapons, Iraq's Potential for Building; United Nations; United Nations Monitoring, Verification and Inspection Commission; United Nations Security Council Resolution 687; United Nations Security Council Resolution 1441; United Nations Special Commission; Weapons of Mass Destruction

References

Blix, Hans. *Disarming Iraq*. New York: Pantheon, 2004.
Butler, Richard. *The Greatest Threat: Iraq, Weapons of Mass Destruction and the Growing Crisis in Global Security*. New York: PublicAffairs, 2000.
Pearson, Graham S. *The UNSCOM Saga: Chemical and Biological Weapons Non-Proliferation*. New York: Palgrave Macmillan, 2000.
Ritter, Scott. *Endgame: Solving the Iraqi Crisis*. New York: Simon and Schuster, 2002.
Trevan, Tim. *Saddam's Secrets: The Hunt for Iraq's Weapons*. New York: HarperCollins, 1999.
Whitney, Craig. *The WMD Mirage: Iraq's Decade of Deception and America's False Premise for War*. New York: PublicAffairs, 2005.

United Services Organization

Large privately funded nonprofit organization that provides entertainment and other nonmilitary amenities to American soldiers, sailors, marines, and air personnel. Although best known to Americans for its broadcasting of Bob Hope's United Services Organization (USO) shows for American troops in Vietnam, the USO story began with its efforts to entertain American troops during World War II.

The USO was founded early in World War II (1941) through the joint efforts of the Salvation Army, the YMCA, the YWCA, and several other groups. USO centers on military bases sponsor numerous social events for soldiers and provide a welcoming environment for individual soldiers seeking a respite from military

Comedian and actor Robin Williams greets a member of the U.S. Army 4th Infantry Division stationed at Kirkuk Air Base, Iraq, in December 2003. Williams was part of a United Services Organization (USO) tour. (U.S. Department of Defense)

duties. Certainly best known for its work during World War II, by 1944 the USO had more than 3,000 centers around the globe. During that war, the USO provided celebrity entertainment involving more than 7,000 performers in more than 420,000 performances. The entertainers most closely identified with USO "shows for the troops" were the singing group the Andrews Sisters and the comedian Hope.

With the beginning of the Korean War in 1950 a smaller and reorganized USO eventually opened 24 centers in Korea and Japan, and the USO again sponsored many entertainment events for the troops. Once more, Hope was a staple of USO shows.

During the Vietnam War the USO opened its first center in Saigon in September 1963. In 1965 the USO began to expand its services throughout the Republic of Vietnam (ROV, South Vietnam). At the height of the war, in the late 1960s, the USO was operating 18 centers in South Vietnam and 7 in Thailand. U.S. entertainers performed more than 5,000 USO shows in Vietnam during the war. With the final withdrawal of American troops in 1972, USO activities in Vietnam ceased as of June 1972.

Entertaining the troops continued to be a USO priority, and the USO was active during the 1991 Persian Gulf War as well as Operations ENDURING FREEDOM and IRAQI FREEDOM. Since 2002 the USO has opened facilities in Afghanistan, Iraq, Qatar, and Kuwait and also in the Denver International Airport to help welcome home troops returning from the front. Beginning in 2008 the not-for-profit USO began receiving donations from primary and secondary schools around the United States. In 2006 the USO organized 56 celebrity entertainment tours to 25 countries, including Iraq and Afghanistan. Well over 100 celebrities and musical groups have performed under USO auspices since 2001, including Aerosmith, Ben Affleck, Drew Carey, Cedrick the Entertainer, the Dallas Cowboys Cheerleaders, Robert De Niro, Hootie and the Blowfish, and many others. USO celebrity entertainment shows continue to be effective morale boosters and are an important part of USO efforts in Iraq and Afghanistan. Increasing use of the Internet and e-mail in the United States during the late 1990s mandated that USO centers provide e-mail access to soldiers serving in the Middle East.

Other current but less well-known USO activities continue to operate out of the approximately 130 USO centers around the world. Among these, Operation Enduring Care helps meet the recovery needs of injured service members and their families through the operation of lounge areas in hospitals and medical facilities. Enduring Care also provides support for funeral escorts, mortuary personnel, and honor guards serving fallen troops. In addition, the USO solicits contributions to provide care packages and phone cards to service personnel abroad. Newer initiatives include welcome centers for returning troops at major airports; the operation of Mobile Canteens bringing refreshments, books, and other leisure items to remote military stations in the Middle East; and the creation of a Family Support fund to aid military families suffering hardships from deployment of a service member.

GAYLE AVANT

See also

ENDURING FREEDOM, Operation; IRAQI FREEDOM, Operation

References

Bloomfield, Gary L. *Duty, Honor, Applause: America's Entertainers in World War II.* New York: Globe Pequot, 2004.
Dell, Diana J. *A Saigon Party.* New York: iUniverse, 2000.

United States

North American country encompassing 3.539 million square miles. The continental United States is bordered by Canada to the north, the Atlantic Ocean to the east, the Gulf of Mexico and Mexico to the south, and the Pacific Ocean to the west. Two of the 50 states, Alaska and Hawaii, are separated from the continental United States. Alaska is bordered by Canada to the east, the Pacific Ocean to the south, the Bering Straits and Russia to the west, and the Arctic Ocean to the north, and Hawaii is surrounded by the Pacific Ocean. The United States also has several Caribbean Sea territories, including Puerto Rico, the U.S. Virgin Islands, and several Pacific Ocean territories (the northern Mariana Islands, Guam, and American Samoa plus several uninhabited islands in the Pacific Ocean). The 2008 population of the United States was approximately 304.228 million. The nation is a representative democracy dominated by two principal political groups, the Democratic Party and the Republican Party.

In November 1988 Republican vice president George H. W. Bush defeated Democratic challenger Massachusetts governor Michael Dukakis in that year's presidential election. During his tenure as president, Bush had to deal with the end of the Cold War, the collapse of the Soviet Union and its client states, and several military conflicts, including the U.S. invasion of Panama (Operation JUST CAUSE, between December 20, 1989, and January 31, 1990) and the 1991 Persian Gulf War (Operation DESERT STORM). The former campaign was quick and successful and resulted in few U.S. casualties. Less than nine months later, the United States faced a major foreign policy and military decision regarding how to respond to the Iraqi invasion of Kuwait on August 2, 1990. Fearing that Iraqi forces would continue advancing into Saudi Arabia, the Saudi government requested U.S. military assistance, laying the groundwork for the Persian Gulf War.

Within three days, U.S. rapid deployment forces had been deployed to Saudi Arabia, and additional U.S. and coalition troops followed in what came to be known as Operation DESERT SHIELD. The operation, sanctioned by the United Nations (UN), would include a coalition of 34 nations including the United States, which provided the bulk of the military forces. By January 2001 the United States had some 543,000 troops in place in the Persian Gulf.

Many Americans, including experts on the region, opposed Bush's decision to send troops to the Middle East, and a small but persistent American antiwar movement formed. Despite receiving widespread publicity, the antiwar movement gained little support from the general public, especially after the U.S. Congress approved of military operations against Iraq on January 12, 1991. The small but vocal antiwar movement was dealt further blows by Iraqi president Saddam Hussein's unsuccessful propaganda efforts and the early military successes during the war. After an intensive bombing campaign that began on January 17, 1991, ground operations, beginning on February 24, took approximately four days before Iraq surrendered and agreed to pull out of Kuwait. American and coalition casualties were remarkably few. U.S. and select coalition forces remained in the region, however, to prevent Iraq from violating the no-fly zones in the northern and southern parts of Iraq and to ensure that it abided by UN resolutions.

Bush's foreign policy and military successes were offset by a deep downswing in the American economy. The country faced a serious recession, with the unemployment rate rising from 5.4 percent in 1989 to 7.6 in 1992, an election year. America's gross domestic product (GDP) remained flat at 3 percent per year, and the Dow Jones Industrials registered a modest growth of slightly more than 1,000 points throughout Bush's tenure.

In November 1992 Democratic candidate William J. Clinton defeated Bush's reelection bid. Clinton used Bush's inability to improve a weakening economy to overcome the Bush administration's highly successful prosecution of the Persian Gulf War. After the November 1992 election and before he left office in January 1993, Bush sent U.S. troops to Somalia to back a UN-supported operation to provide military protection to international groups providing humanitarian assistance there.

American forces arrived in Somalia on December 9, 1992, and other UN peacekeeping forces soon followed. The immediate humanitarian mission was a success. President Clinton kept U.S. forces in Somalia, however, shifting their focus toward the UN's new goal of creating a stable government in Somalia. Somali clans quickly opposed these nation-building efforts and battled U.S. and UN forces; the most well-publicized battle was the Battle of Mogadishu of October 3–4, 1993, a perceived American defeat that increased public calls to withdraw American forces. Clinton ordered a gradual but relatively quick removal of U.S. forces, and the last ones departed in March 1995.

Stung by criticism over the Somalia operation, Clinton became wary of employing U.S. military forces, especially ground troops, in areas peripheral to U.S. interests. Clinton was thus reluctant to intervene in the Rwanda genocide and initially in the Balkans, yet he did respond militarily to some terrorist acts perpetrated against

William Jefferson "Bill" Clinton, flanked by his daughter Chelsea and wife Hillary Rodham Clinton, takes the oath of office as president of the United States from Chief Justice William H. Rehnquist on the west steps of the Capitol in Washington, D.C., January 20, 1993. (AP/Wide World Photos)

the United States and used limited military force to continue to patrol Iraq's no-fly zones. The August 7, 1998, bombings of the U.S. embassies in Kenya and Tanzania resulted in retaliatory cruise missile attacks against suspected terrorist havens in Sudan and Kenya. President Clinton eventually permitted U.S. troops to operate in Bosnia in cooperation with its NATO allies. U.S. secretary of state Warren Christopher achieved a significant breakthrough with Bosnia's warring factions when he was able to get the warring parties to sign the Dayton Accords on December 15, 1995. On October 12, 2000, Al Qaeda–linked terrorists used a small boat to launch a suicide attack against the Arleigh Burke–class Aegis-equipped guided-missile destroyer USS *Cole* (DDG-67) in Yemen.

Clinton's domestic policies suffered early setbacks over a controversial promise to issue an executive order to allow homosexuals to serve openly in the military, which was not carried out, and over certain cabinet-level and administration appointments. Opposed by Republicans in Congress, Clinton was forced to make compromises to enact his legislative agenda. Despite his successful implementation of a new workfare program in an attempt to reduce the number of people on welfare and passage of the Family Medical Leave Act of 1993, his health care program failed to pass. Nevertheless, the U.S. economy improved markedly during Clinton's tenure. Unemployment declined to a low of 4 percent by 2000, and the GDP rose to a high of 4.5 percent per annum growth in 1999. Stock markets benefited greatly during the 1990s, especially tech stocks, which dramatically rose in value. During Clinton's eight years in office, the Dow Jones Industrials rose by almost 8,000 points.

Throughout his two terms, Clinton was plagued by various scandals surrounding him, his wife, and his associates. Congressional investigations and an independent Department of Justice investigation eventually resulted in the U.S. House of Representatives voting to impeach Clinton in December 1998 on charges of perjury and obstruction of justice resulting from his affair with Monica Lewinsky, a young White House intern. On a party line vote, the U.S. Senate failed to convict Clinton, however, and he remained in office.

The 2000 and 2004 presidential elections were among the closest elections in U.S. history. Republican candidate George W. Bush, governor of Texas and the son of President George H. W. Bush, narrowly defeated Democratic vice president Al Gore in the 2000 election. In the tightly contested 2004 election, Bush's victory over Massachusetts Democratic senator John Kerry came down to the state of Ohio.

The horrific events of September 11, 2001, changed America's foreign policy and many aspects of America's domestic policy as well. On February 26, 1993, terrorists attempted to destroy New York City's World Trade Center (WTC) with a truck bomb, but the attack failed. On September 11, 2001, Al Qaeda terrorists hijacked four aircraft and successfully flew two of the planes into the WTC, destroying both towers and several nearby buildings. Another jet slammed into the Pentagon; the fourth one crashed in a Pennsylvania field after passengers attempted to regain control from the hijackers. In response to the attacks, Congress passed the Patriot Act in October 2001, giving the federal government sweeping powers to monitor potential terrorist activities at home and abroad.

After determining Al Qaeda's responsibility for the attacks and after Afghanistan's Taliban regime refused to extradite certain Al Qaeda personnel and meet other requirements, Bush initiated Operation ENDURING FREEDOM on October 7, 2001. U.S. and allied forces proceeded to launch a series of offensive strikes against Taliban and Al Qaeda forces and camps. Bush received broad-based support for this effort, and his approval ratings remained high.

In 2002 NATO, other allied nations, and the United States joined forces as the UN-sanctioned International Security Assistance Force–Afghanistan (ISAF) to provide military forces for nation building, humanitarian efforts, and peacekeeping efforts. As of January 2010, both ENDURING FREEDOM and the ISAF are still operating in Afghanistan. The American-led efforts in Afghanistan came under increasing criticism, however, as a Taliban-led insurgency began to emerge in late 2005. Many critics blamed the Bush administration's decision to go to war with Iraq in 2003 for the failure to arrest the growing insurgency in Afghanistan.

In addition to ENDURING FREEDOM, Bush called for a Global War on Terror. U.S. foreign and military policy now focused on eliminating or curtailing terrorist operations throughout the world. Numerous countries have allied themselves with the United States in the Global War on Terror but with decidedly mixed results.

In late 2002 Bush persuaded Congress to support military action against Iraq, leading him to initiate Operation IRAQI FREEDOM (March 20–May 1, 2003), a ground and air invasion against Iraq. He did so, however, without UN sanction when France and Russia exercised their UN Security Council veto power. The Bush White House used questionable intelligence to make the case that Saddam Hussein had to be unseated because he had weapons of mass destruction (WMDs), which were never found. The Bush administration also alleged that Iraq had connections with Al Qaeda, an allegation never proven although thousands of Islamic extremist Al Qaeda insurgents in Iraq subsequently fought against coalition forces during the occupation. The invasion did, however, remove Saddam Hussein from power and provide the people of Iraq with a chance to establish the country as the Middle East's first Muslim country democracy.

The American antiwar movement opposed the move toward war and gained far greater traction than it had during the brief Persian Gulf War. As the Iraqi insurgency took hold and as U.S. and coalition casualties quickly mounted beginning in 2004, Bush came under harsh criticism for his decision to go to war and the way in which the war was being waged. As the increasing number of American deaths and casualties in combat operations and the increased cost of the war became clearer, approval ratings for Bush and the Republicans in general began to fall. As of the end of 2009, the total estimated cost of military operations and occupations in Afghanistan and Iraq were estimated to be $1.05 trillion. For fiscal year 2010, the U.S. government will allocate more money to the Afghanistan War than the Iraq War, the first time that has happened since the Iraq War began in 2003. The Iraq War also sharply increased anti-American sentiment in the entire Islamic world, and while there were no other terrorist attacks on the United States during Bush's presidency, the war led to heightened Islamic extremism abroad.

On domestic issues, Bush was able to get several measures passed by Congress, including temporary tax cuts; the No Child Left Behind Act of 2001; the Medicare Prescription Drug, Improvement, and Modernization Act; and the Bipartisan Campaign Reform Act of 2002. Despite these modest successes, the American economy began facing tremendous headwinds during Bush's tenure. The Bush administration's efforts to reverse the economic downturn were unsuccessful.

The U.S. unemployment rate gradually rose, and the stock market saw a drop of more than 2,000 points between July 2001 and March 2003. During this same period, GDP growth dropped below 2 percent per year, with some improvement between 2004 and 2008. Although the stock market made some significant gains after 2003, as economic weaknesses became apparent the stock market underwent significant turbulence by mid-2008. The Bush administration had also turned record budget surpluses in 2001 when it had taken office into record budget deficits by 2007.

Despite the political shift at the executive and legislative levels toward the Republican Party at least through the 2004 elections, mounting popular discontent with Bush's decision to invade Iraq in 2003 and his administration's conduct of the war led to a dramatic shift of political power back to the Democrats in the 2006 midterm elections. Democratic candidates won 232 seats in the House of Representatives and 49 seats in the Senate. Two independent candidates, who stated that they would vote with the Democratic Party, also won Senate seats, thus giving the Democrats a 51 to 49 majority. This gave control of both houses of Congress to the Democrats.

The Democrats' limited majority in Congress prevented them from meeting some of their legislative objectives, especially the removal of U.S. forces from Iraq. However, since the 2006 elections, the U.S. economy suffered significant and troubling disruptions. From its record high in October 2007, the stock market began a relatively slow decline until October 2008, when the market began to gyrate wildly, sometimes plummeting hundreds of points in a single session; the overall trajectory, however, was sharply downward. This stock market meltdown wiped out trillions of dollars of investments, which forced consumers to curtail spending and employers to shed hundreds of thousands of jobs. Making matters far worse, the 2008 financial crisis caused further uncertainty. Throughout the 1990s and early 2000s, many Americans became homeowners by agreeing to either subprime mortgages or adjustable rate mortgages. These mortgages allowed individuals with lower credit scores and with limited income to buy houses with initially low mortgage payments and with little or no money down. Eventually the mortgage rates increased as the price of homes began to fall.

Traders on the floor of the New York Stock Exchange (NYSE). The NYSE is located on Wall Street in New York City and is the oldest and largest stock exchange in the United States. (Corel)

When interest rates crept up mortgage payments were readjusted upward, and many individuals were unable to refinance or to pay the increased costs of their loans. Housing foreclosure rates increased, and financial institutions began taking huge financial losses. The government-sponsored enterprises Fannie Mae and Freddie Mac, which worked in the secondary mortgage market and provided funds for mortgage lenders, were placed into government conservatorship. Other financial institutions and investment firms also faced significant financial problems; some, such as Washington Mutual, were placed under federal receivership, while others, such as Wachovia Bank, were bought by other firms before they failed. Congress's first attempt at passing a financial bailout plan failed, but after some compromises a $770 billion dollar plan was passed in early October 2008. The act put the government in the position of owning a significant interest in several banks.

Increased discontent with America's continued military presence in Iraq and a serious reversal in the U.S. economy had a significant impact on the 2008 presidential campaign and election. Although multiple candidates ran for both the Republican Party and the Democratic Party, initial favorites Senator Hillary Clinton (D-N.Y.) and former Republican New York mayor Rudy Guiliani lost their respective party's nominations. Senators John McCain (R-Ariz.) and Senator Barack Obama (D-Ill.) became their party's presidential nominees, with McCain using his status as a former prisoner of war and a "maverick" and Obama pledging to bring change.

Ironically, although most believed that the Iraq War would be the biggest campaign issue in 2008, the worsening economy and Bush's botched attempts to forestall economic collapse trumped all other issues. Obama's campaign energized his party, and he gained significant support among younger voters and the African

American community. On November 4, 2008, Obama handily won the presidential election, and the Democratic Party increased its control in Congress.

It seems clear that the Republicans were fighting an uphill battle, with an unpopular war in Iraq, a frustrated and inconclusive war in Afghanistan, and an economy that was in a virtual free fall during the second half of 2008. Between 2001 and 2008, Bush saw his approval ratings drop steadily and then precipitously, from record highs after the September 11 attacks to record lows as he left office. In late 2008 some polls showed his approval rating at just 24 percent, almost as low as Harry Truman's 22 percent in 1952 and tying Richard Nixon's 24 percent rating when he resigned in disgrace as a result of the Watergate scandal in 1974.

The Obama administration and Democrats in Congress moved quickly to place the U.S. economy on safer footing and to stanch the hemorrhaging of the financial institutions and automobile industries by passing a massive $787 billion stimulus package, which was rejected by all but a handful of congressional Republicans. As of mid-2010, the effects of the stimulus bill remain somewhat questionable, as the unemployment rate still hovered around 9.7 percent. The economy began a tepid recovery in the last quarter of 2009, which was accompanied by a steadily rising stock market, leading some economists to believe that the economy might pick up steam in the last half of 2010. Meanwhile, the Obama administration reported record deficits at the end of 2009, the result of profligate spending by the Republicans during 2000–2008, and the same by Democrats beginning in 2009.

During the summer of 2009, an increasingly acrimonious debate enveloped the nation over pending health care reform, which had been a key part of Obama's legislative agenda. As Republicans and right-wing radio and television personalities spread disinformation about the pending reform, the American public became confused and less willing to support health care legislation. Meanwhile, the White House's initial hands-off attitude toward the issue caused the president's popularity to fall precipitously. By early 2010, many had declared the Democrats' health care reform moribund. Nevertheless, Obama and the Democratic leadership in Congress secured passage of a sweeping health care reform bill in March 2010, although not a single Republican in either house of Congress voted for it.

Internationally, the Obama administration has enjoyed moderate success to date. Efforts to engage the Iranian leadership over Iran's nuclear program brought no breakthrough, largely because of the intransigence of the Iranian government. Efforts to jumpstart the Palestinian-Israeli peace process had been similarly stymied by events largely out of America's control. Israeli-American relations reached a nadir in early 2010 after Israel announced controversial plans for building settlements in contested territory. On a positive note, Obama completed a nuclear arms reduction deal with the Russians in April 2010 and has made a major and largely successful effort to repair relations with American allies and the Islamic world, which had been severely strained under the previous administration. After a thorough review, the Obama administration also ordered a major increase of 30,000 troops in Afghanistan, part of its heightened effort there coinciding with the drawdown of U.S. forces from Iraq.

WYNDHAM WHYNOT

See also

Antiwar Movements, Persian Gulf and Iraq Wars; Bush, George Herbert Walker; Bush, George Walker; Clinton, Hillary Rodham; Clinton, William Jefferson; DESERT SHIELD, Operation; DESERT STORM, Operation; ENDURING FREEDOM, Operation; Global War on Terror; IRAQI FREEDOM, Operation; McCain, John Sidney, III; Obama, Barack Hussein, II; Terrorism; United States, Middle East Policy, 1917–1945; United States, Middle East Policy, 1945–Present

References

McMahon, Kevin J., David Rankin, and Jon Kraus. *Transformed by Crisis: The Presidency of George W. Bush and American Politics.* New York: Palgrave Macmillan, 2004.

Patterson, James T. *Restless Giant: The United States from Watergate to Bush vs. Gore.* New York: Oxford University Press, 2005.

Story, Ronald, and Bruce Laurie. *The Rise of Conservatism in America, 1945–2000: A Brief History with Documents.* New York: Bedford/St. Martin's, 2008.

Tanner, Stephen. *The Wars of the Bushes: A Father and Son as Military Leaders.* Havertown, PA: Casemate, 2004.

Unger, Irwin. *Recent America: The United States since 1945.* Upper Saddle Creek, NJ: Prentice Hall, 2002.

United States, Middle East Policy, 1917–1945

Until World War I, the interests and involvement of the United States in the Middle East were limited and small-scale. Between the world wars, American oil companies, backed by successive administrations, sought to compete against the British and French for Middle Eastern petroleum concessions. During World War II, the quest to prevent seizure of Middle Eastern strategically vital oil reserves was a major factor underlying the growing U.S. military and diplomatic presence in the region. During World War II American officials collaborated with both British and Russian forces in Iran, but once hostilities had ended, escalating tensions with the Soviet Union meant that the Near and Middle East soon became a theater for Cold War conflicts and rivalries.

Until the early 20th century, official U.S. involvement in the Middle East was patchy and sporadic. The most notable undertakings were two naval wars in the very early years of the 19th century to eradicate the threat that the Barbary privateers of the North African state Morocco and neighboring Tunis, Algiers, and Tripoli, semi-independent provinces of the Ottoman Empire, posed to American maritime commerce with the Mediterranean. Both ended in a U.S. victory.

During the 19th century, American dealings with the Near and Middle East were largely private, primarily educational or commercial. In 1866 Presbyterian missionaries established the Syrian

Protestant College, which later became the American University in Beirut. Other American universities and colleges were founded in Cairo and Istanbul. American businessmen also traded with the region. By the early 20th century, American diplomats sought to ensure that the Ottoman Empire and Morocco granted their country's nationals trading privileges as favorable as those that had been accorded to European nations through the capitulatory treaties.

Under President Theodore Roosevelt, a strong proponent of an assertive U.S. international posture, in 1906 American resentatives played a leading role at the Algeciras Conference, which mediated a dispute between France and Germany over the status of Morocco, effectively making the sultanate a French protectorate. Roosevelt's belief in the forthright defense of American interests was also demonstrated in 1904, when a wealthy Greek-American resident in Tangier, Ion Perdicaris, was kidnapped by Raisuli, a Moroccan bandit. To domestic acclaim, Roosevelt dispatched seven battleships and a force of marines to Morocco, demanding that country's government ensure the safe delivery of "Perdicaris alive or Raisuli dead." Eventually, Perdicaris was released.

World War I brought enhanced, though still limited, American interest in the Middle East. Before 1914, American oil companies showed little interest in competing with European firms for the right to develop Middle Eastern petroleum sources. The war itself created new uncertainties in the region, promoting Arab nationalism and bringing the final end of Ottoman rule over the areas then known as Mesopotamia, Palestine, and Arabia (present-day Iraq, Syria, Jordan, Israel, Saudi Arabia, and the Arab emirates, as well as the province of Armenia). In late 1914 Ottoman Turkey joined the Central Powers, allied with Germany and Austria-Hungary against Great Britain and France. The latter two powers therefore encouraged Arab revolts against Ottoman rule, making somewhat ambivalent pledges to recognize the rule of Hussein ibn Ali, the high-priest or sharif of the Islamic territory of the Hedjaz, and his three sons, Ali, Feisal, and Abdullah, over Mesopotamia and Arabia. Britain and France also made secret agreements with each other envisaging the territorial division of Mesopotamia and Palestine between their two empires. In addition, in November 1917 the British government issued the Balfour Declaration, promising Jews a national home, although not a state, in Palestine.

When the United States entered World War I in April 1917, the country initially declared war only on Germany, leaving the proclamation of a formal state of hostilities with Austria-Hungary until December 1917 and refraining entirely from any declaration of war against the Ottoman Empire. In 1918 President Woodrow Wilson, rather to the distaste of diplomats in the State Department, endorsed the Balfour Declaration in principle, but at the subsequent Paris Peace Conference he made no great effort to press for the establishment of a Jewish homeland. Wilson distrusted the major Allied powers, Britain, France, and Italy, and deplored what he perceived as their eagerness to extend their own colonial holdings by annexing former colonies and other territories that had belonged to the Central Powers before 1914. The president

particularly distrusted the secret treaties and agreements the Allies had concluded with each other regarding the disposition of territories once controlled by the enemy powers.

In an effort to pressure the Allies into accepting liberal war aims, in January 1918 Wilson publicly stated that the U.S. government would only support a peace based on the Fourteen Points, idealistic and wide-ranging diplomatic principles that envisaged a nonpunitive postwar settlement, and that included national self-determination and autonomous development for lands that had been part of the Ottoman Empire prior to 1914. Britain and France responded by stating publicly that they would establish indigenous governments in these areas, regimes that would, nonetheless, be expected to accept the tutelage and guidance of more advanced nations.

American distaste for imperialism was nonetheless responsible for the creation of the mandate system at the Paris Peace Conference, whereby former colonies of the defeated powers were essentially annexed by the victors and placed under the ultimate jurisdiction of the new League of Nations. The British mandate eventually comprised present-day Iraq, Transjordan (now Jordan and the Right Bank occupied by Israel), and Palestine (now Israel), while the French controlled what is now Syria and Lebanon.

In practice, the British and French negotiated this division of the Ottoman spoils with each other, and the League of Nations mandates simply ratified their spheres of influence arrangement. In the early 1920s, Britain established monarchies in Iraq and Jordan, each ruled by one of Hussein's sons, and during the 1930s these regimes won increasing autonomy from British supervision. In 1919 and 1920 the Allies hoped to induce the United States to join the League of Nations mandatory states and accept a comparable tutelary role over Armenia, but the American government declined the invitation.

The influence of the European powers extended far beyond the Near East and Levant. The French controlled Morocco and Tunisia and regarded Algeria as an integral part of France. The British also controlled Aden and dominated Egyptian affairs. They had a maritime presence and exerted influence over the various sheikhdoms and emirates of the Gulf region, and they exchanged the promise of military protection for an alliance with Saudi Arabia. The British and Russians each sought to influence Iran and Afghanistan in what was known as the Great Game.

Between the world wars, the U.S. government held largely aloof from developments in the Middle East, declining to take any position on the situation in Palestine, where growing Jewish immigration and determined Zionist demands for the establishment of a Jewish state met official British resistance and provoked rising Arab resentment, leading to violent riots on numerous occasions. American interests remained largely commercial, with the State and Commerce departments both eager to exert pressure to encourage and facilitate access by American oil companies to the Middle East's vast petroleum resources. By the early 1930s American oil companies were beginning to explore the possibility of developing oil concessions in the Persian Gulf area. The Turkish

Petroleum Company, later renamed the Iraq Petroleum Company, a consortium that included some American oil companies, had a monopoly on exploration in much of the region, and within this grouping only British nationals could develop oil concessions in the small Persian Gulf emirates.

In 1932 Standard Oil of California (SOCAL), a firm outside the consortium that had already broken into this closed shop on oil exploration by establishing a subsidiary—albeit one including a British member on its board—in the small sheikhdom of Bahrayn (Bahrain), a British quasi-protectorate, applied for an exploratory oil license in the neighboring independent kingdom of Saudi Arabia. Seeking to improve the terms offered him, King Abdul Aziz encouraged the Iraq Petroleum Company to compete for the concession, and SOCAL eventually outbid its rival. The American firm obtained a 60-year contract granting it exclusive oil exploration and drilling rights on 360,000 square miles of eastern Saudi Arabia and a preferential option on an adjoining region, territory whose ownership Saudi Arabia still disputed with the neighboring emirate of Kuwait. The SOCAL-Saudi agreement was the first major oil concession negotiated by U.S. business in the Middle East.

In 1936 SOCAL merged with the Texas Company (Texaco), and the two established the California Texas Oil Company (CALTEX), acquiring 50 percent interests in each other's operating subsidiaries. The discovery of large quantities of oil in Saudi territory in 1938 brought the negotiation one year later of a new agreement with Saudi Arabia, with the king obtaining higher royalties in exchange for a substantial expansion of the California Arabian Standard Oil Company (CASOC)'s exclusive concession.

With a major war by then imminent in Europe, one that would almost certainly involve the Middle East, Saudi and other Middle Eastern oil fields were seen as a vital strategic prize, an asset for which the powers and governments on both sides in the impending conflict were likely to compete. Such concerns soon led to an Allied takeover of Iran, in which the U.S. government acquiesced. During the 1930s, Shah Reza Pahlavi I of Iran, who resented the fact that the British-dominated Anglo-Iranian Oil Company controlled most of Iran's oil revenues and industry, favored Nazi Germany and staffed much of his government with German advisers. From September 1939 Germany was at war with Great Britain, and in June 1941 German dictator Adolf Hitler's forces also invaded the Soviet Union, which shared a border with Iran. Russia then became a British ally. Anglo-Russian competition for influence over Iran dated back more than a century, but for the war's duration the two nations cooperated there, as they had in the early 20th century, when they divided Iran into spheres of influence. Seeking both to deny Iran's oil reserves to Germany and to protect Soviet oil fields in the nearby Caucasus, in summer 1941 both British and Soviet officials demanded that the shah expel the 2,000 Germans then resident in Iran. When he refused, military forces of the two Allied powers jointly occupied Iran, replacing the pro-German shah with his youthful son, Shah Reza Pahlavi II. Russian forces controlled the north, and the British the south, of the country.

Iranian nationalist elements feared that the foreign occupation might easily become permanent. Seeking to alleviate such concerns, and Britain's case also impelled by anxieties that, if no agreement to the contrary were concluded, Soviet troops might well remain in place when the war was over, in January 1942 the three powers concluded a treaty of alliance against Germany. This permitted British and Soviet armed forces unrestricted use of Iranian military facilities. Although Iranian nationalists resented the alliance, which was forced on them, at their insistence this agreement included clauses whereby both Britain and the Soviet Union pledged to respect the territorial integrity, sovereignty, and political independence of Iran. In addition, it provided that both British and Russian occupying forces would leave no later than six months after hostilities had ended. The treaty went into effect on February 1, 1942.

The Franklin D. Roosevelt administration welcomed this situation and quickly dispatched a military mission to Iran. Besides seeking to deny Iran's vital oil fields to Germany and Italy, the U.S. government had strong logistical reasons for doing so. By late 1941 Soviet Russia had become a major recipient of U.S. lend-lease wartime aid, and after Pearl Harbor the two nations were formally allied in war against Germany. Large quantities of lend-lease supplies destined for Russia were delivered by sea to Iran and sent on northward by rail through the Caucasus. The first task of the U.S. military mission was to expedite such shipments, in part by liaising with the Soviet forces occupying the north of Iran. Thousands of U.S. servicemen arrived in Iran as part of the Persian Gulf Command, established for this purpose.

Within the U.S. State Department, moreover, the small and close-knit team of Middle Eastern experts began to develop more ambitious schemes for U.S. involvement in the region, viewing Iran as a potential test case for their country's ability to encourage democracy and social and economic reforms in developing nations, as envisaged under the Allied Atlantic Charter of August 1941. The United States could, they believed, promote beneficial social and political change in such nations, its ability to do so enhanced by the fact that it was free from the taint of imperialism and colonialism that made British intervention so unpopular. Such benevolent U.S. involvement in Iran would also check the expansion of communist Soviet influence in the north of the country. An expanded American role in Iran would further enable the United States to provide better protection for its existing oil interests in Saudi Arabia and possibly even help it to gain a new stake in Iran's own British-dominated oil industry.

As early as 1939 Shah Reza I had attempted to entice the United States into taking more interest in his country and acting as its patron against other great powers by offering oil concessions to American firms. For similar reasons a sizable group of Iranian politicians, including the young shah, encouraged the growing American interest in their country, which they viewed as a means of countering both British and Russian influence.

In August 1943, Secretary of State Cordell Hull recommended to President Roosevelt a policy of enhanced U.S. involvement in

An oil well in Bahrain, Arabia, in December 1940. (Bettmann/Corbis)

Iran, aimed at building up that country under American patronage, guidelines Roosevelt accepted. Toward the end of the year, at the Tehran Conference, Britain, the Soviet Union, and the United States all affirmed their commitment to maintaining Iran's postwar independence and territorial integrity. This switch to a proactive U.S. policy toward Iran marked an important long-term turning point in American involvement in the Near and Middle East. From early 1943 assorted missions, often poorly coordinated, of American experts attempted to guide and direct the wholesale reform of the Iranian military, police, and finances, together with the political and agricultural systems.

In early 1943 the U.S. government also began to demonstrate new and growing interest in the Kingdom of Saudi Arabia. In April 1942 the U.S. State Department appointed a resident vice-consul in Jeddah, a post he combined with chargé d'affaires, the first occasion on which the United States possessed a physical diplomatic presence in Saudi Arabia. Even so, during 1941 and 1942 the U.S. government turned down suggestions by CASOC that it should give the kingdom official economic aid under the lend-lease program. Within the Washington bureaucracy, however, it was not just State Department diplomats who perceived the Middle East as an area of growing significance to the United States. Wartime secretary of the Navy Frank Knox and his deputy and successor, James V. Forrestal, later to be the first secretary of defense, both considered the region's oil resources a major strategic interest that the U.S. military should be prepared to secure and defend.

Matters changed at the beginning of 1943, when the American government began to deliberate whether it might be able to buy out CASOC's Saudi concession and use it as a strategic military and naval oil reserve. In March 1943 the U.S. State Department declared that Saudi Arabia was eligible for lend-lease aid on unusually generous terms. As another indication of growing official American interest in Saudi Arabia, in April 1943 the American mission in Jeddah was upgraded to a legation with a resident minister.

Official U.S. interest in Saudi Arabia continued to expand, culminating in the negotiation by the Defense Department in early August 1945 of an agreement for the construction of an American air base at the Saudi town of Dhahran, a facility that could be used if necessary to afford military protection to American oil interests in the kingdom. The new American interest in Saudi Arabia provoked friction with the British government, whose officials perceived this as an encroachment on a previously British sphere of influence. The British could not, however, come close to matching what the United States could offer Saudi Arabia in terms of economic and military aid and so had to acquiesce in growing U.S. involvement with the kingdom. American officials themselves admitted that the generous budgetary aid for 1945 they offered the Saudi government was a major factor in the successful negotiation that summer of the Dhahran air base agreement, which was subsequently repeatedly renewed. In the early 21st century, Dhahran still functions as a major air base in the Middle East.

By early 1944, concern about future access to international oil supplies was sufficiently strong to impel the State Department to seek to formulate guidelines for American international policy on oil. These envisaged ensuring American access on equal terms to

Soviet premier Joseph Stalin, U.S. president Franklin D. Roosevelt, and British prime minister Winston Churchill meet at the Soviet Embassy during the Tehran Conference, November 28–December 1, 1943. (Library of Congress)

oil supplies; conserving the Western Hemisphere's oil resources and discouraging exports of these outside the Western Hemisphere; and facilitating U.S. access to and development of Middle Eastern oil reserves, if necessary by negotiating an understanding with Great Britain to ensure maximal exploitation of these resources. U.S. officials were anxious to prevent the transfer of any American-owned Middle Eastern oil concessions to nationals of other countries and to encourage Americans to cultivate such concessions to their full potential.

State Department officials also thought it desirable that European needs for oil be met from Middle Eastern rather than Western Hemisphere sources, effectively enabling the United States to retain its hemispheric oil supplies for its own use. The April 1944 guidelines gave striking proof that the U.S. government was fully conscious that petroleum was a valuable and essential international commodity, one that was vital to the effective functioning of their country's civilian and military economies, and that State Department officials were determined, in the interests of national

security, to encourage American business interests to obtain and develop to their own and their country's maximum advantage as large a share as possible of global petroleum reserves.

American officials' eagerness to facilitate such access to Middle Eastern oil reserves contributed to growing tensions between the United States and the Soviet Union. As it became clear that the conclusive defeat of Germany, their common enemy, could be anticipated in the near future, the most important controlling factor underlying their wartime alliance, the need to destroy Hitler's regime, became ever more irrelevant. In Iran, relations between the two countries became increasingly strained from late 1944 onward, when an Iranian offer of oil concessions in the north of the country to American companies brought Soviet protests and occupying Russian troops banned Anglo-American forces from their zone of Iran and tightened their own control over the area. The independence promised Iran under the Tehran declaration seemed increasingly in jeopardy, even more so after late 1945, when the Soviet Union backed separatist forces in establishing an independent Soviet Socialist Republic in Iran's northern province of Azerbaijan, and encouraged a similar separatist movement in Kurdistan, setting up a puppet state there in early 1946.

By the end of World War II, the U.S. government had already demonstrated its determination to acquire a long-term stake in securing Middle Eastern oil reserves, resources that American officials considered valuable from both the economic and strategic perspectives. American diplomats cherished hopes that, under their own country's aegis, a benign form of guidance and direction would replace both Russian- and British-style imperialism in much of the Middle East. By late 1945, the impact of such policies was particularly apparent in U.S. dealings with Saudi Arabia, where military commitments underpinned substantial and growing American oil concessions, and Iran, where Soviet and American interests were coming into direct conflict and the stage was already set for a major early Cold War confrontation.

PRISCILLA ROBERTS

See also

France, Middle East Policy; Middle East, History of, 1918–1945; Oil; Saudi Arabia; Soviet Union, Middle East Policy; United Kingdom, Middle East Policy; United States, Middle East Policy, 1945–Present

References

Goode, James F. *The United States and Iran: In the Shadow of Musaddiq.* New York: St. Martin's, 1997.

Hart, Parker T. *Saudi Arabia and the United States: Birth of a Security Partnership.* Bloomington: Indiana University Press, 1998.

Painter, David S. *Oil and the American Century: The Political Economy of the U.S. Foreign Oil Policy, 1941–1954.* Baltimore: Johns Hopkins University Press, 1986.

Salt, Jeremy. *The Unmaking of the Middle East: A History of Western Disorder in Arab Lands.* Berkeley: University of California Press, 2008.

Yergin, Daniel. *The Prize: The Epic Quest for Oil, Money, and Power.* New York: Simon and Schuster, 1993.

United States, Middle East Policy, 1945–Present

Before World War II, American involvement in the Middle East was limited. World War II, however, encouraged nationalist forces in the Middle East, thereby weakening the British and French imperial position there. It also brought an enhanced American economic and military presence in the region, as the United States stationed troops in Iran and in 1945 acquired long-term air base rights at Dhahran, Saudi Arabia. By the time the war ended, the American government sought continuing control of the region's strategically vital oil resources. These ambitions sometimes provoked friction and tensions between the United States and its Western allies, Britain and France, two imperial powers in decline that often resented growing American economic and military might. Even more significantly, these ambitions quickly brought the United States into conflict with the Soviet Union, and the

Middle East was soon perceived as an important theater of Cold War rivalry.

From the late 1940s onward, successive American and Soviet governments competed not just to control Middle Eastern petroleum resources but also to gain international support and ideological loyalty from the patchwork of predominantly Muslim states across the area stretching from North Africa, Arabia, and the Persian Gulf to Afghanistan and Pakistan. As a rule, relatively conservative monarchical or authoritarian regimes leaned toward the United States, while radical nationalist governments tended to align themselves with the Soviets. U.S. support for the creation of the Jewish state of Israel in 1948 and increasingly close ties between those two countries further complicated American relations with Arab states throughout the region, most of whom deeply resented the existence of Israel.

The erosion of the position of European powers in the Middle East led both American and Soviet officials to seek to expand their own influence in the region. One of the earliest Cold War crises erupted over Iran. In 1941 the British and Russians had overthrown that country's Nazi-oriented monarch, Shah Reza Pahlavi I, and jointly occupied Iran, seeking to deny its oil resources to Germany and to safeguard supply routes to the Soviet Union. Both countries pledged that their forces would leave Iran within six months of the ending of hostilities in World War II.

In autumn 1945, Soviet officials backed separatist forces in establishing an independent Soviet Socialist Republic in Iran's northern province of Azerbaijan and encouraged a similar separatist movement in Kurdistan, setting up a puppet state there in early 1946. American and British forces withdrew on schedule in early 1946, but the Soviets announced their intention of retaining at least some troops in the north of the country, precipitating one of the earliest crises of the developing Cold War. The United States used the forum of the new United Nations (UN) organization to endorse Iranian demands for complete Soviet withdrawal.

After complicated maneuverings between Iranian politicians and Soviet representatives, the Soviets withdrew their forces in exchange for promised oil concessions in northern Iran. With the backing of American advisers, in late 1946 Iranian prime minister Qavam es-Sultanah, who had in the interim successfully negotiated with the United States a substantial package of military, economic, and cultural support, reneged on this bargain, and shortly afterward Iranian forces successfully overturned the Azerbaijani and Kurdish republics.

This episode contributed to growing American distrust of Soviet designs on the Middle East. Simultaneous Soviet demands that the Turkish government accord the Soviet Union special rights over the Dardanelles Straits, which was the only passage for Russian naval and commercial vessels from the Black Sea to the Mediterranean, further confirmed such suspicions. American officials encouraged the Turkish government to refuse these Soviet demands and reinforced their stance by dispatching an American naval squadron to the Mediterranean.

In early 1947 the British government announced that economic difficulties meant that it could no longer continue to provide military or financial assistance to the governments of Greece, then fighting a communist insurgency, and Turkey, raising the specter that Soviet power might move in to fill the vacuum left by Britain's departure. This crisis became the occasion for President Harry S. Truman to announce in February 1947 what became known as the Truman Doctrine, a wide-ranging pledge that the United States would provide assistance to any state threatened by internal or external communist subversion. The geographical proximity of Greece and Turkey to shipping routes along which much Middle Eastern oil was transported alarmed policy makers in Washington and encouraged the United States to provide aid. Both Greece

and Turkey subsequently received extensive economic assistance under the Marshall Plan, announced later in 1947. In 1952 the two states simultaneously became members of the North Atlantic Treaty Organization (NATO), tying them firmly into western defensive alliances.

The American quest for reliable and stable long-term allies in the Middle East itself proved more problematic. One added complication was American support for Israel, which became heavily dependent on American aid, both governmental and private. President Truman's personal inclinations were largely responsible for American endorsement of the new state, a policy that, for strategic and diplomatic reasons, the State Department and the Defense Department both attacked. Most Arab states, whether

Turkish fishermen in the Sea of Marmara use nets made possible by Marshall Plan aid from the United States, 1951. (National Archives)

conservative or radical, fiercely opposed Israel's very existence. Israel's military success in gaining and retaining previously Arab territories in several brief but bitter and hard-fought wars, in 1948–1949, 1956, 1967, and 1973, only deepened Arab resentment. Hostility toward Israel was widespread and intense in Arab countries, Turkey, and Iran, making it difficult and even personally hazardous for Middle Eastern leaders to moderate their stance and seek compromise with Israel.

In 1981, for example, a cell of a radical Islamist group assassinated President Anwar Sadat of Egypt, who with strong encouragement from U.S. president Jimmy Carter had negotiated a peace agreement with Israel two years earlier. Repeated American and other outside efforts to broker a final and permanent peace settlement and modus vivendi between Israel and its Arab opponents, including Palestinians from territories seized by Israel in the recurrent Arab-Israeli conflicts, became almost standard fixtures of the late 20th- and early 21st-centuries international diplomatic arena but were at best only partially successful. Almost invariably, they fell victim to extremist forces on both sides. Although a Palestinian state eventually came into existence on lands Israeli forces had taken in the various wars, throughout the first decade of the 21st century several key issues still remained unresolved, provoking bitter divisions among Israelis, Palestinians, and the broader Arab community.

The two countries that became the strategic linchpins of American alliance policy in the Middle East were Saudi Arabia and Iran, which together with Iraq possessed the bulk of the region's oil reserves. Under Saudi pressure, in 1950 ARAMCO (Arabian-American Oil Company) renegotiated its royalty agreement with the Saudi government so that each party received 50 percent of the profits. In 1951, Saudi Arabia signed a mutual defense agreement with the United States, and from then on a permanent American Military Training Mission was based in the kingdom. Saudi governments upgraded their military forces and placed lucrative armaments orders with American defense companies, goods they paid for with the proceeds of oil sales. In return for loyal support from the conservative Arab kingdom, for decades U.S. governments consistently overlooked the absence of democracy and disregard for international human rights standards that characterized the Saudi regime. The strong ties that the United States developed with this and other authoritarian Middle Eastern governments meant that the Americans were often perceived as representing illiberal forces opposing change and as the successors to European imperialists.

Such views were reinforced by the close American relationship with another monarchical regime, that of Iran. In 1951, the Iranian government announced its intention of nationalizing the Anglo-Iranian Oil Company; the British, who controlled the refineries, withdrew their technicians and blockaded all exports of Iranian oil, provoking severe economic difficulties within Iran. The government headed by Prime Minister Mohammad Mossadegh stood firm, and eventually, after an abortive attempt to replace him by

the young shah, Reza Pahlavi II, declared a national emergency and took control of the Iranian military. In alliance with radical Muslims and the nationalist, leftist Tudeh Party, in 1952 Mossadegh implemented nationalist reforms, especially in agriculture, and broke diplomatic relations with the United Kingdom. Britain turned to the United States for assistance, characterizing Mossadegh as a radical who was turning toward communism and steering Iran into the Soviet orbit.

The administration of Republican president Dwight D. Eisenhower, which took office in January 1953, proved sympathetic to the British and authorized the Central Intelligence Agency (CIA) to spend up to $1 million removing Mossadegh. CIA agents in Tehran spread rumors and disinformation and in some cases acted as agents provocateurs. Economic problems intensified, and Mossadegh suspended parliament and extended his emergency powers. The CIA sought to persuade the indecisive young shah to dismiss Mossadegh, while Mossadegh urged the monarch to leave the country. Eventually, in 1953, the shah dismissed Mossadegh, but the latter refused to step down from office, and the shah took refuge in Italy. Major promonarchy and antimonarchy protests were held throughout the country, as Iranians of all political stripes assumed that before long Mossadegh would declare Iran a republic and himself head of state.

Promonarchy forces, heavily funded by the CIA, gained the upper hand, however, and Iranian tanks and troops entered Tehran and besieged the prime minister's residence until Mossadegh surrendered. He was subsequently placed under house arrest, then put on trial for treason and sentenced to three years in prison. General Fazlollah Zahedi, one of the military leaders who arrested Mossadegh, became prime minister, and the shah resumed power.

From then until the shah's overthrow in 1979, he would be a key U.S. ally in the Middle East. The shah soon reached an agreement with the British and Americans, under whose terms the foreign oil companies still made substantial profits and large amounts of Iranian oil once more flowed to world markets. These revenues, together with several billions of dollars in American military and economic assistance, enabled the shah to modernize his country and make it a strong military state. The 1953 coup also represented the first occasion when the CIA was instrumental in successfully ousting another government. The success of this undertaking subsequently emboldened CIA director Allen W. Dulles and other agency officials to try to orchestrate comparable operations against several other foreign governments U.S. leaders found unpalatable—in Guatemala, Cuba, the Dominican Republic, and Chile.

In addition to its Iranian alliance, the United States attempted to persuade other Middle Eastern states to collaborate against potential Soviet expansionism. In 1955 American diplomats encouraged the establishment of the Baghdad Pact, a grouping of Turkey, Iran, Iraq, Pakistan, and Britain, which established a military liaison with the United States. The objective was to erect a bastion of anticommunist states along the Soviet Union's

The shah of Iran, Mohammad Reza Pahlavi, the president of the United States, Richard Nixon, and his wife Pat Nixon in 1969. (National Archives)

southwestern frontier. The alliance was originally known as the Middle Eastern Treaty Organization (METO). After Iraq, the only Arab member, withdrew in 1958 in the aftermath of a revolution led by the leftist and Moscow-oriented Baath Party, the United States joined as a full member and the grouping became the Central Treaty Organization (CENTO). The organization proved largely ineffective in preventing the spread of Soviet influence in the Middle East. During the 1960s and 1970s, the Soviet Union simply bypassed the CENTO states to develop close military and economic ties with Egypt, Syria, Iraq, Yemen, Somalia, and Libya, establishing bases in Egypt, Somalia, and Yemen.

Although the United States sought to portray its own policies as representing a break with the earlier Western imperialism many Arab nationalists deeply resented, these efforts were not particularly successful. American dealings with Egypt during the 1950s demonstrated that, even when the U.S. government tried to dissociate itself from European colonialism, its policies often proved unconvincing and failed to win over skeptical opponents. In 1952 Gamal Abdel Nasser, a young military officer, became president of Egypt. He was determined to reverse decades of Western-inflicted humiliation in the Arab world and to overthrow Israel. In 1955 Nasser sought and obtained arms for this purpose from the Soviet bloc, whereupon the United States withdrew promised economic assistance for a major hydroelectric project, the Aswan

Dam. Nasser then announced his intention to nationalize the Suez Canal, then still under British and French control, and to use canal revenues to finance the dam project.

Against American advice, in October 1956 the British, French, and Israelis jointly attacked Egypt, defeating its army, whereupon Nasser blocked the canal. The British, French, and Israelis thought a major Egyptian military setback would cause the Egyptian population to rise up and overthrow President Nasser. Fearing a major oil crisis, permanent Middle Eastern instability, and the further strengthening of both radical nationalism and Soviet influence, Eisenhower demanded that the invaders withdraw their forces, threatening to cease financial support for the beleaguered British currency should they refuse to do so. The crisis left Nasser more popular than ever before not only in Egypt but also in the broader Arab world and the Third World.

During the Suez Crisis, the Soviet Union also threatened to use nuclear weapons against the invaders unless they withdrew. Fearing that this move presaged enhanced Soviet interest in the region, in January 1957 Eisenhower sought congressional authority both to increase economic and military aid to anti-Soviet Middle Eastern states and to deploy American military forces in the region if necessary to oppose overt armed aggression from any nation controlled by international communism. Arab states immediately condemned the Eisenhower Doctrine. Under its auspices the United States intervened in both Lebanon and Jordan in 1958. The negative responses by the United States to the Arabist trend in the Middle East and U.S. interventions convinced some that the United States was a conservative power wedded to the status quo. Throughout the 1960s, the military-based republican governments in the Middle East tended to turn to the Soviet Union or the Eastern bloc for assistance.

In June 1967, a swift preemptive strike by Israel destroyed the Egyptian Air Force on the ground and initiated a new Arab-Israeli War, which ended in a stunning Israeli victory. The outcome was seen as a terrible defeat by the entire Arab world, and it created a new wave of misery for the Palestinians of the West Bank and Gaza, who now passed under direct Israeli military rule. The war demonstrated conclusively to the Arab world the unshakeable U.S. support for Israel over the interests of the Palestinians.

The 1967 Arab defeat had far-reaching effects. It encouraged the growth of radical movements who were opposed to the existing Arab governments and willing to engage in acts of terrorism and airline hijackings outside the region. It also discouraged moderate support for state-led Arabism. U.S. Middle East policy makers did not appear to appreciate the profound malaise in the region over the 1967 defeat.

From the early 1970s onward, the United States was forced to respond to dramatic changes in the configuration of power in the Middle East. In October 1973, Egypt, Syria, and Iraq launched a surprise attack on Israel. By the second week, Israeli forces had largely reversed early Arab successes, leaving Israel's military supplies heavily depleted. The U.S. government resupplied Israel, a move the Arab states deeply resented. In response, Arab members of the Organization of Petroleum Exporting Countries (OPEC), led by Saudi Arabia, cut back on oil production, quickly leading oil prices to quadruple. These policies stoked gathering inflation throughout the Western world, contributing to a major economic downturn that lasted throughout the 1970s. American inability to persuade OPEC, several of whose members were U.S. clients or allies, to moderate its policies contributed to a growing sense that American power was in decline. During the 1960s and 1970s, moreover, Arab states largely obtained control of their own oil industries, either, as with Saudi Arabia, through negotiations with American and other foreign firms or, where more radical states such as Libya or Iraq were concerned, through outright seizure and nationalization.

Developments in the late 1970s greatly disturbed the stability of overall U.S. strategy in the Middle East. A key American ally lost power, the shah of Iran, while Soviet military policies in Afghanistan and the Horn of Africa seemed to herald a menacing expansion of Soviet power in the region. Although Mohammad Reza Shah Pahlavi had tried to modernize his country, his authoritarian policies, persecution of opponents, and the social disruptions caused by his reforms eventually alienated many Iranians and were among the reasons why in late 1978 and early 1979 a large-scale Islamic revolution ended his rule and changed

the entire basis of the government in Iran. In a surprising action, radical Iranian students stormed the U.S. embassy in Tehran on November 4, 1979, to protest past American support for the ousted shah, especially his admission to the United States for medical treatment. They captured 52 Americans and held them hostage. In April 1980 U.S. military forces mounted an ineffectual rescue attempt in which eight American servicemen died. The entire episode was widely regarded as a major national humiliation for the United States. The hostage crisis was not ended until the inauguration of Republican president Ronald Reagan in January 1981, when the Iranians released the hostages in return for a previously negotiated agreement that the U.S. government would unfreeze blocked Iranian economic assets.

In November 1979, another American ally was shaken when 500 armed Islamic fundamentalists seized the Grand Mosque of Mecca. They had hoped to capture King Khalid and his officials, who were supposed to have been at prayer, but instead many others were taken hostage. The incident showed that religious militancy was not confined to Iran, for the hostage takers led by Juhayman al-Utaybi refused to give up. Blood could not be shed in the Grand Mosque, but eventually a fatwa was issued that permitted the use of force. The official tally from the incident was 255 dead and another 560 injured before the Grand Mosque was secured.

In Afghanistan, meanwhile, in late December 1979 a Soviet-backed palace coup replaced one leftist president with another. Soviet ground forces and paratroopers promptly entered the

An Iranian protester sets fire to a U.S. flag, while other demonstrators give a clenched-fist salute, during an anti-American protest in Tehran on November 5, 1979, the day after students stormed the U.S. embassy in Tehran and took its personnel hostage. (AP/Wide World Photos)

country, the beginning of a decade-long war in which 15,000 Soviet troops and almost 1 million Afghans died. In addition, since 1977 many thousands of Soviet and Cuban troops had been stationed in Ethiopia, supporting that nation in a war with neighboring Somalia over the disputed Ogaden territory. Top American officials interpreted these developments as evidence of a systematic effort to enhance Soviet influence in territories bordering the Middle East and to take advantage of the regional destabilization caused by recent events in Iran. These developments, together with skyrocketing oil prices and high inflation and unemployment, contributed to a growing sense of malaise and American impotence in international affairs.

President Jimmy Carter responded by proclaiming in his January 1980 State of the Union address that "business as usual" with the Soviet Union was no longer possible and that the United States would take all measures necessary to defend the Persian Gulf. The president moved to reinstitute containment policies, demanded annual 5 percent increases in military spending, proposed that young American men be compelled to register for a potential draft, and moved to create a Persian Gulf rapid deployment force. He also called for energy policies that would make the United States less dependent on foreign oil. Carter's speech, which effectively reiterated the 1957 Eisenhower Doctrine, also marked a definite break with his earlier efforts toward Soviet-American détente and disarmament, inaugurating several years of deep ideological and strategic antagonism between the two superpowers.

Throughout the 1980s, the Carter and Reagan administrations provided substantial financial support and equipment for the Afghan mujahideen, a collection of Islamist resistance groups that conducted guerrilla warfare against occupying Soviet forces. The United States also offered neighboring Pakistan funding, logistical backing, and personnel to establish and run military training camps for the mujahideen. Pakistani special forces quietly took part in the war, and their British and American counterparts were also believed to be quietly involved. The war proved a lengthy, expensive, and ultimately unwinnable morass for the Soviet Union. In 1985 a new Soviet president, Mikhail Gorbachev, came to power. Gorbachev quickly moved to initiate new policies intended to moderate decades of Cold War hostilities and bring about rapprochement with Western powers. He removed Soviet forces from the Horn of Africa. In March 1988 he also announced that all Soviet forces would be withdrawn from Afghanistan within 12 months. Although Soviet forces left Afghanistan on schedule, bitter civil war continued in Afghanistan. In the later 1990s, the country fell under the control of the radical Islamic Taliban, which allowed it to become a haven for anti-Western Muslim terrorist groups.

Following the 1979 Islamic Revolution in Iran and ensuing U.S. embassy hostage crisis, relations between the United States and Islamic Iran remained hostile. The American government imposed an embargo on all commercial and financial dealings with Iran by U.S. citizens; air traffic was suspended; and most other contacts entirely or largely halted. In September 1980,

President Saddam Hussein of Iraq began a major war against neighboring Iran, seeking to settle long-standing border disputes between the two states and to make Iraq the regional hegemon. The war soon stalemated, and for several years the two countries were bogged down in bloody stalemate. During this conflict, the United States leaned toward Iraq, and Hussein was able to purchase military supplies from the United States and other Western powers. In 1982 the United States normalized diplomatic relations with Iraq, which had been broken ever since the 1967 Arab-Israeli War. In 1987 and 1988, American naval forces in the Persian Gulf, deployed there in an effort to protect oil tankers from attack by either belligerent, skirmished repeatedly with Iranian vessels. In July 1988 an American cruiser, the *Vincennes,* shot down an Iranian passenger jet, killing 290, an incident for which the U.S. government later paid Iran almost $132 million in compensation but never apologized.

American policy was nonetheless not entirely consistent. Officials in the Reagan administration, which had publicly stated that it would not pay any ransom to secure the return of American hostages, secretly offered to sell Iran badly needed weaponry. Any monies received were to be used to support operations by American-backed antigovernment Contra guerrillas in El Salvador, thereby evading a ban the U.S. Congress had recently imposed on the use of any American government funds for this purpose. The release of American hostages would also constitute part of the purchase price. After these dealings became public in late 1986, Reagan administration officials defended them on the grounds that their contacts and negotiations with relatively moderate Iranian officials had increased the probability that more conciliatory and less anti-American political forces would eventually come to power in Iran. The Iran-Contra scandal, as it became known, was nonetheless a major political embarrassment for the Reagan administration, casting doubt on its good faith and competence as well as its stated hard-line attitude on terrorism.

The Iran-Iraq War finally ended in 1988 with no decisive victory on either side. Both countries suffered heavy losses of manpower in a war each found economically debilitating and destructive. Believing that this step would not encounter serious opposition, in August 1990 Saddam Hussein sent his forces into, and annexed, neighboring Kuwait, a small, wealthy, and oil-rich state allied with the United States. Hussein's action alarmed other rich but militarily weak Arab states nearby, notably Saudi Arabia. This was the first major international crisis since the proclamation earlier that year of the ending of the Cold War between the Soviet Union and the United States. U.S. president George H. W. Bush was instrumental in forging an international coalition, including the NATO powers, Saudi Arabia, and Japan, committed to expelling Iraqi forces from Kuwait and in winning a UN resolution authorizing such action. Hussein attempted to win support from other Arab states by proclaiming his intention of attacking Israel should coalition forces invade, but only the Palestine Liberation Organization (PLO) supported his efforts. Launched in January

Lieutenant General Walter F. Boomer, commanding general of the 1st Marine Expeditionary Force, accompanies President George H. W. Bush following the president's arrival at the division's Combat Operations Center (COC) in Saudi Arabia, November 1990. (U.S. Department of Defense)

1991, Operation DESERT STORM ended quickly and successfully as Hussein's troops were swiftly driven from Kuwait and pushed back into Iraqi territory.

Bush and his advisers soon decided to halt the invasion of Iraq, however, as they did not wish to deal with the challenges that overthrowing Hussein was likely to bring in its train, and they therefore left the weakened dictator in power but subject to confining UN sanctions and restrictions. Although the United States directly encouraged separatist Kurds in northern Iraq and Shiite Muslims in the south to rise up against Hussein's regime, they received no support from coalition forces, and Hussein's military brutally suppressed the revolts, using poison gas against the Kurds and killing tens of thousands of rebels.

Addressing Congress shortly after the Persian Gulf War had ended, a triumphant Bush promised aid to the Middle East. He then proclaimed that the ending of the Cold War had made it possible for the UN to function as its founders had originally intended, so that there was a very real prospect of a new world order, one in which freedom and respect for human rights would find a home among all nations. Critics charged that Bush envisaged that the United States would use its unrivaled military and economic might to dominate the new world order in its own interests. During the 1990s, the principal focus of U.S. international policy was

economic, as the American government concentrated on what was termed globalization, liberalizing trade and investment practices and promoting the spread of free market norms.

President William (Bill) Clinton made energetic although only partially successful efforts to reach a permanent resolution of the Palestinian-Israeli impasse, but otherwise, the Middle East attracted only sporadic attention. Despite criticism from humanitarian organizations, throughout the 1990s UN sanctions on significant trade with Iraq remained in place, although a program whereby Iraqi oil was exchanged for food was eventually initiated. British and American warplanes bombed potential military targets and enforced no-fly zones in southern and northern Iraq, permitting the Kurds there to enjoy virtual autonomy.

With the ending of the Cold War, the overarching principle of American foreign policy could no longer, as in the past four decades, be the containment of communism. The Reagan administration saw a new enemy in radical Islam.

Harvard University political scientist Samuel P. Huntington claimed global conflict was inevitable. Basing his ideas on those of historian Bernard Lewis, he suggested that international fault lines would now correspond with differing belief and value systems, such as the Western Judeo-Christian tradition, Islam, and Confucianism, and that major clashes among these civilizations must be anticipated. Many unfamiliar with the Middle East belatedly seized on Huntington's thesis following the events of September 11, 2001.

An Islamic revival had, meanwhile, shaken the Arab world, fueled in part by the shock of the defeat at the hands of Israel in 1967 but also driven by the failure of nationalist non-Islamist movements. The Islamic Revolution in Iran in 1979 was simultaneously Islamist and nationalist. The new Iranian leader, Ayatollah Ruhollah Khomeini, was hostile to the United States because he and many other Iranians feared that the United States might intervene to reverse the revolution. Certainly the U.S. government opposed the concept of an Islamic government, characterizing it as a medieval theocracy. In Afghanistan, however, throughout the 1980s equally conservative Muslim mujahideen guerrilla forces battling the Russian occupiers received substantial American economic and military aid, which came to an end once the Soviets had left.

During the 1990s, Islamic rebels battled Russian rule in Chechnya, but partly due to the failure to reach a comprehensive Israeli-Palestinian settlement, something many Muslims believed was primarily due to American bias toward Israel, militant Islamic antagonism focused increasingly on the United States. As the Soviet-Afghanistan War wound down in the late 1980s, certain Islamic mujahideen groups involved in that conflict founded a new organization known as Al Qaeda; its objective was to continue the jihad, or holy war, on other fronts. The most prominent figure in this group, Osama bin Laden, who came from a wealthy Saudi family, used his own financial resources to support its undertakings and could also tap heavily into other Arab sources of funds.

Official Saudi support for American operations during the 1991 Persian Gulf War deeply angered bin Laden, who deployed his organization not just against the United States but also against the Saudi government and other Middle Eastern nations, including Egypt, who were close American associates. Bin Laden issued public proclamations, or fatwa, demanding the expulsion of all foreign troops from Islamic lands and the overthrow of Middle Eastern governments that acquiesced in their presence. Al Qaeda personnel, expelled from Saudi Arabia, found refuge first in Sudan and then in Afghanistan, where a radical Islamic regime, the Taliban, took power in 1996. During the 1990s Al Qaeda claimed responsibility for several terrorist assaults on prominent American targets at home and overseas, including a 1993 truck bomb attack on the World Trade Center in New York, simultaneous 1998 car bombings of U.S. embassies in Kenya, Nairobi, and Dar es Salaam, Tanzania, and a 2000 suicide attack on the American destroyer USS *Cole* in Yemen. In response, the Clinton administration declared Al Qaeda a terrorist organization, and in summer 1998 reacted to the embassy bombings with air strikes on Al Qaeda training camps in Sudan and Afghanistan.

In January 2001, President George W. Bush, eldest son of the president who had launched the first Gulf War, took office. In the areas of diplomacy and defense, Bush appointed numerous top officials associated with a predominantly Republican think tank venture, the New American Century project. Many of these individuals, including Bush's influential vice president, Richard B. Cheney, a former secretary of defense, believed that the United States had been mistaken in not overthrowing Saddam Hussein in 1991 and had publicly called on Clinton, Bush's predecessor, to drive the Iraqi president from power. They argued that Hussein, who in 1998 expelled UN inspectors charged with monitoring his weapons programs, was determined to regain regional hegemony by developing chemical, biological, and nuclear weapons of mass destruction (WMDs). Since these ambitions posed a long-term threat to U.S. strategic interests, New American Century affiliates argued that their country would be morally and legally justified in taking preemptive action to overthrow him and preclude this potential danger.

The Bush administration also sought to prevent Iran from developing nuclear weapons, an ambition clearly cherished by the Iranian government, which, though now rather more secular in character than during most of the 1980s and 1990s, was nonetheless decidedly anti-American. Initially, the Bush administration accorded combating international terrorism a much lower priority.

The events of September 11, 2001, when two dozen Arab Islamic extremists associated with Al Qaeda hijacked four American airliners and used these to launch suicide attacks on the World Trade Center towers in New York and the Pentagon in Washington, D.C., brought a dramatic change, as the president publicly declared an expansive Global War on Terror. Al Qaeda claimed responsibility for the attacks, in which almost 3,000 civilians died, giving the American public a novel sense of vulnerability to terrorist threats. Bush called on the Taliban government of Afghanistan, which had provided bases and training camps for thousands of Al Qaeda operatives, to surrender bin Laden and his top advisers, but Mullah Mohammed Omar, the Afghan leader, refused as this would violate tribal and Islamic ethics. In October 2001, the United States and Britain, in collaboration with the forces of anti-Taliban Afghan Northern Alliances warlords, began military hostilities against Afghanistan. By the end of the year they had overthrown the Taliban government and driven Al Qaeda into the rugged mountains of the Afghan-Pakistan border, although coalition forces failed to capture bin Laden.

Afghan representatives subsequently held a traditional Loya Jirga assembly, which chose a Pashtun aristocrat, Hamid Karzai, as Afghanistan's new president. The new leader publicly committed his country to democracy and sought to implement wide-ranging social and economic reforms. Militarily, his regime nonetheless remained heavily dependent on British and American troops, and its authority did not extend far beyond Kabul, the Afghan capital. In 2006 a resurgence by Taliban forces threatened to destabilize the country, a development that many observers blamed on the failure of the U.S. government to concentrate on winning complete victory in Afghanistan. As the last year of Bush's presidential term began, the situation in Afghanistan remained precarious, with many expecting further Taliban territorial gains. One plausible explanation for the diversion of American resources

Four soldiers and a sailor help carry an injured worker from the Pentagon to an ambulance after a hijacked airliner crashed into the building. Military personnel from the Pentagon and nearby Fort Myer played a vital role in rescuing and treating injured personnel. (U.S. Army)

from Afghanistan was the eagerness of the Bush administration at all costs to return to its earlier agenda and launch a second war against Iraq, which began in 2003.

Throughout 2002, Bush administration officials made the case that Iraq represented the greatest and most pressing international threat to American interests, making it vital to overthrow Saddam Hussein before he could inflict long-term strategic damage on the United States. In his January 2002 State of the Union address, the president proclaimed that the three most dangerous external enemies for the United States were Iraq, Iran, and North Korea, who, he declared, constituted an "axis of evil." With support from British prime minister Tony Blair but over strong opposition from such long-term European allies of the United States as France and Germany, and to great skepticism from Russia and China, the Bush administration pressured the UN Security Council to endorse resolutions stating that Iraqi weapons programs had equipped that country with formidable armaments whose

possession put it in breach of earlier UN demands and constituted ample justification for an outside invasion designed to topple Hussein's government. UN weapons inspectors failed to unearth any quantities of such weaponry and many foreign governments doubted whether Iraq actually held appreciable stockpiles of banned armaments. Subsequent revelations suggested that Bush and his top advisers, together with their British counterparts, doctored intelligence reports to make it appear that Iraq had acquired far more in the way of stored weapons and production capabilities than was really the case. Supporters of an invasion, notably Vice President Cheney, also claimed that close ties existed between Al Qaeda and other terrorist organizations and Hussein, alleging that the Iraqi president had in some way been involved in the September 11, 2001, attacks. No information tied the Iraqi president to these attacks and Al Qaeda links were at best tenuous.

Ignoring all internal and external protests and misgivings, the Bush administration eventually proclaimed its determination to move unilaterally against Iraq even if it proved impossible to obtain a UN resolution specifically authorizing this undertaking.

Leading American supporters of war within the administration, notably Paul Wolfowitz, deputy secretary of defense, believed in addition that an invasion of Iraq would give the United States an ideal opportunity to remake the entire Middle East. From this perspective, war against Iraq came to seem almost a magic bullet, an exercise in transformational diplomacy that would recast the whole region. They argued that, by removing Hussein and replacing him with a democratic government, one that would bring Iraq the benefits of peace, prosperity, and economic development, the United States would encourage the contagious democratization of all the remaining Middle East. The belief was that the creation of a progressive, stable, flourishing, and affluent Iraq would so impress other states in the region that they would, practically automatically, seek to establish similar governmental systems themselves, almost painlessly inaugurating a benign era of American-led peaceable economic growth and forward-looking social development throughout the Middle East.

On March 20, 2003, an American-led allied coalition force, to which the British contributed by far the second most sizable contingent, launched a full-scale invasion of Iraq. Military victory was quickly attained, as coalition forces took Baghdad and other major Iraqi cities and toppled statues of Hussein. Major looting and disorder marred the allied triumph, an early indication that coalition forces might have more trouble maintaining civil control than they did winning battles. On May 1, 2003, Bush declared an end to major combat, standing on an American aircraft carrier deck before a banner declaring, "Mission Accomplished." In December 2003, American forces finally captured Hussein, who eventually stood trial and was executed three years later.

U.S. officials soon discovered, however, that it was far easier to overthrow Hussein's government than to restore peace, order, and stability to Iraq, let alone to establish a democratic government capable of exercising authority and acceptable to all parties in Iraq. Deep ethnic, religious, and political fissures divided the country. While Hussein's regime had been largely secular in outlook, his rule had relied primarily on the country's Sunni Muslim element, while the majority of the Iraq population, who were Shia Muslims, had been largely excluded from power. In addition, the Kurds of the north sought autonomy, if not outright independence, and had no wish to be controlled by a government based in Baghdad, the Iraqi capital. In mid-2003 occupying forces disbanded the largely Sunni armed forces, so that by default much power on the ground was exercised by various militia groupings, predominantly Shiite but also Sunni organizations. For several years, large areas of Iraq were in a state of virtual civil war, characterized by suicide bombing attacks against military, civilian, and religious targets, murders, kidnappings, and torture. No foreigners, whether soldiers or civilians, could count on being personally secure, nor could any Iraqis, even in the supposedly most protected areas of Baghdad.

The toll of Iraqi dead and injured was exponentially higher than the casualty figures for the coalition forces, but even those continued to rise inexorably, belying official U.S. claims of success. Only 138 U.S. soldiers were killed in Iraq before Bush declared the end of major combat; by the end of 2009, 4,370 had died.

What was supposed to be a splendid little war, bringing maximum results at minimum costs, swiftly metamorphosed into a grim quagmire, and it became ever more unclear how the United States could extricate itself from this entanglement. A brief moment of optimism after December 2005, when elections were held in Iraq under the political constitution accepted earlier that year, quickly dissipated, as it became clear that members of most ethnic groups had voted for candidates from their own groups and Iraq remained bitterly politically divided, with no genuine consensus emerging among the competing parties. Violence escalated, and the government of Prime Minister Nuri al-Maliki was widely perceived as lacking the strength and authority to control and pacify the country.

Bush administration officials alleged that Al Qaeda units had infiltrated into Iraq and charged the Syrian and Iranian governments with supporting Shiite militia forces within Iraq in an effort to promote their own political influence in the country. As casualties continued to rise, with no convincing exit strategy in sight, popular support for the war fell dramatically among the American public and politicians, and in the November 2006 midterm elections George W. Bush's Republican Party lost control of both houses of Congress.

Media revelations, illustrated with dramatic photographs and video footage, that American soldiers had savagely abused Iraqi captives held in Abu Ghraib prison and other facilities, circulated widely around the world, discrediting the Bush administration's claims that the Iraqi intervention was designed to uphold human rights and other liberal principles. Throughout the Arab and Muslim world, distrust and antagonism toward the United States soared dramatically. More broadly, the tactics the U.S. government embraced in pursuit of the Global War on Terror inflicted enormous damage on the country's international reputation.

Massive antiwar demonstrations occurred across Europe and in much of Asia. Even states that had been allies of the United States began to reconsider their support for the war. Several nations that had initially been part of the American-led international coalition and that had intervened in Iraq withdrew or reduced their forces. In Spain, the new government that won elections in March 2004, shortly after 191 Spaniards died and almost 2,000 were injured in terrorist bombings of train stations in Madrid, quickly announced that all Spanish troops would leave Iraq. The Labour politician Gordon Brown, who replaced the strongly prowar Tony Blair as British prime minister in July 2007, likewise embarked on a program of gradual British troop withdrawals.

By then, the U.S. government had announced a new strategy in Iraq. In December 2006, an independent bipartisan commission headed by James A. Baker III, former secretary of state during the first Iraq war, issued a report urging that the United States

A protest rally against the Iraq War in Kuala Lumpur, Malaysia. The poster is a caricature of U.S. secretary of state Condoleezza Rice. (Shutterstock)

should seek to stabilize the situation in Iraq. Its recommendations included increasing temporarily American military forces in Iraq, allowing Iraqi civilian and military officials and forces to take increasing responsibility for running the country themselves, providing greater aid for training and equipment that would enhance their ability to do so, leaving occupying forces only in support roles, and working in collaboration with the UN, the European Union, and other regional governments, including those of Saudi Arabia, Iran, and Syria, to restore and maintain order in Iraq. The Baker Report also urged a renewed effort to bring about a permanent Palestinian-Israeli peace settlement, a recommendation that Bush and Secretary of State Condoleezza Rice sought to implement in late 2007 and early 2008.

The Bush administration did announce a troop surge in January 2007, and by the end of that year the military situation in Iraq had immensely improved, as moderate Shiite and Sunni forces began to gain some authority, so that full-scale civil war seemed less probable. In general, violence and suicide bombings had decreased by late 2008 but unfortunately resumed in the spring of 2009.

Close cooperation with Iran, the region's most substantial Shiite Muslim power, whose relative strength was much enhanced by the weakening of neighboring Iraq and Afghanistan, its former rivals and counterweights, proved more problematic. Ever since taking office, Bush administration officials had sought to prevent

Iran from developing nuclear weapons but had only succeeded in obtaining ambiguous commitments from Iranian president Mahmoud Ahmadinejad. In July 2007, the U.S. Congress passed resolutions condemning covert Iranian military involvement in Iraq, authorizing the use of American force against Iran if deemed necessary to halt its nuclear program. Such strained relations rather precluded close Iranian cooperation with the United States and its allies over Iraq. U.S. ambassador to Iraq Zalmay Khalilzad (2005–2007) encouraged communication between Iraq and Iran, for he believed that the two neighbors could deal productively with such issues at border disputes and pilgrim traffic to Islam's holy cities. Afghan president Hamid Karzai has also said that his government is seeking a positive relationship with Iran, and he has requested that the United States not involve Afghanistan in its anti-Iran policies.

As the American presidential elections approached ever closer in 2008, Middle Eastern policy was in flux. The situation was yet further complicated in the last days of December 2007 by the assassination of former Pakistani prime minister Benazir Bhutto, who recently returned to her country after a decade of exile to contest impending democratic elections there. In Pakistan, a military government headed by former army chief President Pervez Musharraf had held power since 1999. After September 11, 2001, the U.S. government had dropped its earlier objections to Musharraf's authoritarian regime, and Pakistan had become a leading ally in the Global War on Terror, especially with U.S. efforts to extirpate Al Qaeda and its leaders.

Militant Muslim elements nonetheless enjoyed substantial political influence in much of Pakistan and were believed to be responsible possibly with the connivance of some Pakistani security officials for Bhutto's death. Following her assassination, riots and disorder convulsed much of Pakistan, bringing fears that a major American ally and regional strategic partner was itself in serious jeopardy of destabilization. Soaring oil prices added still another twist, since a large proportion of the world's petroleum reserves were located in the Middle East. In January 2008 Bush appealed to Saudi Arabia to use its influence in OPEC to reduce the cost of oil, but the response of Saudi officials was unenthusiastic.

As top U.S. politicians competed for the Republican and Democratic presidential nominations in 2008, their preferred strategies for approaching the Middle Eastern situation and especially the still-continuing American occupation of both Iraq and Afghanistan remained somewhat vague and unspecific. Most American presidential candidates stated that they sought the withdrawal of most if not all American troops from Iraq and Afghanistan but that they would endeavor to accomplish this objective while leaving governments friendly to the United States in power in those countries, so as to safeguard American interests there.

The Barack Obama administration announced in early 2009 that it would send thousands of additional troops to Afghanistan, an indication that U.S. and NATO operations in that country would intensify in the near future. The situation in Iraq has greatly stabilized, but the Obama administration admits that even when most U.S. forces are eventually withdrawn, a residual force of several thousand will remain indefinitely.

PRISCILLA ROBERTS

See also
United States, Middle East Policy, 1917–1945

References
Brands, H. W. *Into the Labyrinth: The United States and the Middle East 1945–1993.* New York: McGraw-Hill, 1994.
Cooley, John K. *Payback: America's Long War in the Middle East.* Washington, DC: Brassey's, 1991.
Goode, James F. *The United States and Iran: In the Shadow of Musaddiq.* New York: St. Martin's, 1997.
Hart, Parker T. *Saudi Arabia and the United States: Birth of a Security Partnership.* Bloomington: Indiana University Press, 1998.
Knights, Michael. *Cradle of Conflict: Iraq and the Birth of Modern U.S. Military.* Annapolis, MD: Naval Institute Press, 2005.
Lesch, David W. *The Middle East and the United States: A Historical and Political Reassessment.* New York: Perseus Books, 2006.
Painter, David S. *Oil and the American Century: The Political Economy of the U.S. Foreign Oil Policy, 1941–1954.* Baltimore: Johns Hopkins University Press, 1986.
Salt, Jeremy. *The Unmaking of the Middle East: A History of Western Disorder in Arab Lands.* Berkeley: University of California Press, 2008.
Yergin, Daniel. *The Prize: The Epic Quest for Oil, Money, and Power.* New York: Simon and Schuster, 1993.

United States, National Elections of 2000

A highly controversial election that pitted Republican George W. Bush, the son of President George H. W. Bush, against Democrat and incumbent Vice President Albert (Al) Gore. The 2000 election, held on November 7, was one of the closest in U.S. history and was not decided until December 12. The election stalemate occurred in the state of Florida, where the result came down to a margin of fewer than 1,000 votes (out of more than 6 million cast statewide), triggering a long and arduous recount process. Without Florida, which carried 25 electoral votes, neither candidate had the requisite 270 electoral votes needed to win. The election was settled in Bush's favor when the U.S. Supreme Court ruled 5 to 4 to reverse a Florida Supreme Court ruling ordering a third recount of the state's ballots (Bush already had won the initial vote count and each of the first two recounts by slim margins).

Despite numerous problems reported concerning defective and misprinted ballots and alleged irregularities at polling stations in a few south Florida counties, Bush's 537-vote edge in Florida secured him the election victory. Gore won more of the popular vote (48.4 percent to Bush's 47.9 percent) with an overall margin of 543,000 votes. This is an unusual, but not unique occurrence in American presidential elections. In the election of 1876, for example, Democrat Samuel J. Tilden won the popular vote by more than 250,000 votes (51 percent, a clear majority of the popular vote, unlike Gore's 48.4 percent), but lost the election to Republican Rutherford B. Hayes. An even more outrageous result occurred in the 1824 presidential election, in which Democrat Andrew Jackson not only received the highest number of popular votes (41.3 percent) but also won the largest tally of electoral votes (99). However, since the popular and electoral votes were split among four presidential candidates, Jackson's 99 electoral votes were not a majority. The decision went to the House of Representatives, which elected John Quincy Adams, a vote largely engineered by Speaker of the House Henry Clay, who had also been one of the four presidential candidates in the election and Jackson's bitter opponent. Adams appointed Clay his secretary of state, a move many consider a quid pro quo for his manipulation of the House vote. The Bush-Gore election of 2000 was contentious and controversial, but hardly unprecedented in American presidential elections.

The election engendered bitter indictments by many Democrats, who claimed that Bush had "stolen" the election and was thus an "illegitimate" president. Many slammed the U.S. Supreme Court for its ruling to stop the third recount and even pointed to the fact that Florida's governor at the time was Bush's brother, Jeb. Republicans countered that it was the Supreme Court's ruling that prevented Gore from "stealing" an election he had already lost in the original vote count and two recounts, pointing to the fact that nearly all of the judges on Florida's Supreme Court that had ordered the third vote recount had been appointed by Florida's former Democratic governor, Lawton Chiles.

In the House of Representatives, the Republicans lost two seats but retained their 221–212 majority over the Democrats,

Protesters hold signs and flags in front of the U.S. Supreme Court building in Washington, D.C., December 11, 2000. The court upheld an appeal by George W. Bush to stop the recount of presidential ballots in Florida in the 2000 election. (AP/Wide World Photos)

who gained one seat. In the Senate, the elections were a wash, with the Republicans losing four seats and the Democrats gaining four. This resulted in a 50–50 tie, with the Republicans controlling only with Vice President Dick Cheney's tie-breaking vote. In late spring, the Democrats gained control of the Senate by a 51–49 seat margin when Republican senator Jim Jeffords left the Republican Party and began caucusing with the Democrats. Just 11 states held gubernatorial elections, and all except 1 state house remained with the party holding power before the elections. The only change in control came in West Virginia, where a Democrat defeated an incumbent Republican governor.

The 2000 campaign focused mostly on domestic issues and did not center on U.S. military or foreign policy. Nor did it deal in any great measure with U.S. involvement in the Middle East. The two campaigns, as well as the national media, focused on subjects such as morality, family values, tax cuts, and education. Bush and Gore disagreed over how best to use the U.S. military in the Middle East and around the world, with Bush, somewhat ironically as it turned out, eschewing what he termed the "nation-building" of the Clinton years. Furthermore, although terrorism had become a growing threat throughout the 1990s, the topic received little attention during the 2000 presidential election. Also, neither candidate spoke much about national security, as most voters were not preoccupied with the topic at the time.

During the campaign, Bush and Gore debated one another about the effects of economic sanctions against Iraq. On August 6, 1990, the United Nations (UN) Security Council had adopted Resolution 661 at the urging of the United States, which imposed economic sanctions on Iraq. U.S. leaders hoped that the sanctions would make life uncomfortable for the Iraqi people and encourage them to overthrow President Saddam Hussein. William Jefferson (Bill) Clinton, the U.S. president from 1993 to 2001, and Gore, his vice president, fully supported the economic sanctions against Iraq despite pressure from left-wing groups in America and around the world that believed that the sanctions had caused the death of hundreds of thousands of Iraqi civilians. During the presidential campaign, Gore continued to support the economic sanctions against Iraq. Bush also supported them but criticized the Clinton administration for not keeping the economic sanctions as tight as they could be.

Bush also accused the Clinton administration of allowing Iraq to break its post–Persian Gulf War agreements. During the 1990s, Iraq continued to violate UN Resolution 687, adopted following the 1991 Persian Gulf War, which declared a formal cease-fire in the war and demanded the eradication of Iraq's weapons of mass destruction (WMDs). During that time, UN weapons inspectors uncovered some discrepancies in reporting by the Iraqi government on their nuclear program. Despite the attempts of the inspectors and the Clinton administration, it was feared that Iraq was still hiding possible resources of its nuclear program. Bush condemned the Clinton administration for not being more forceful in its effort to stop the Iraqi weapons development programs. Gore insisted that the Clinton administration had indeed maintained the sanctions, but that, as president, he would go further in curtailing Iraq's development of weapons. He did not elaborate on how the United States would accomplish that.

While Gore seemed to favor stronger action against Iraq for its refusal to comply with UN and U.S. demands, Bush's rhetoric against Iraq was even more forceful. Both Bush and Gore urged increased support for leaders of the Iraqi opposition in their attempts to oust Hussein. Gore, however, did not pledge direct U.S. help to remove the Iraqi dictator. Bush also spoke out against Clinton's 1998 decision to discontinue air strikes against Iraq, which were designed to injure the country's ability to continue to produce alleged WMDs. While Gore also opposed the aborting of the air strikes, he remained subdued in his opposition and did not speak out openly against Clinton's decision. Because of Gore's equivocal stance on Clinton's policies, Bush was viewed as the candidate who was more likely to use the U.S. military when he thought necessary.

Gore and Bush also disagreed on the proper role of the U.S. military. Bush accused the Clinton administration of cutting back on military budgets and cutting personnel levels while refusing to outline clear objectives for U.S. forces that were sent overseas. During his campaign, Bush was joined by retired four-star generals H. Norman Schwarzkopf and Colin Powell and blasted the Clinton administration for "neglecting" the military. Gore countered Bush's attacks by confirming current American military strength, which was stronger than any other nation's military.

Gore and Bush also opposed one another regarding the use of U.S. troops overseas. During the first presidential debate, Bush stated that he "would be very careful about using our troops as nation builders." Gore challenged Bush's statement, saying that the United States was the sole world power and therefore, the U.S. military should not shy away from "going in anywhere." Pointing to atrocities in places such as Bosnia and Kosovo that had taken place in the 1990s, Gore contended that the U.S. military should intervene in certain situations, such as stopping genocide.

Other than these rather vague positions on foreign and military policies, neither candidate made any grand statements about the use of force against Iraq or any other nation for that matter. And the subject of terrorism was barely mentioned in 2000. The nation was at peace, the economy was in the midst of one the greatest booms it had ever known, and most Americans felt secure, both at home and abroad.

After the close election that showed a divided electorate, Bush had little in the way of a popular mandate. Although the Republicans controlled Congress, the Bush administration knew that it had to move cautiously and incrementally, choosing first to take on the much-vaunted tax cuts that Bush had promised as a candidate.

Indeed, prior to the September 11 terrorist attacks on the United States, Bush was viewed by many Americans as overly cautious and usually inarticulate. That all changed, however, after September 11. Bush's rapid and decisive decisions in the days and weeks after the disasters earned him much praise and respect, even from many Democrats, all of whom now lined up behind the president in a show of American solidarity. By March 2003, the Bush administration, which previously had shown little interest in initiating decisive action in the Middle East or addressing terrorism, had initiated two wars in the region and the Global War on Terror.

GREGORY W. MORGAN AND PAUL G. PIERPAOLI JR.

See also

Bush, George Herbert Walker; Clinton, William Jefferson; ENDURING FREEDOM, Operation; Global War on Terror; Gore, Albert Arnold, Jr.; Hussein, Saddam; Iraq, History of, Pre-1990; Iraq, History of, 1990–Present; Iraq, Sanctions on; IRAQI FREEDOM, Operation; Terrorism; United Nations Security Council Resolution 687; Weapons of Mass Destruction

References

Ceaser, James W., and Andrew E. Busch. *The Perfect Tie: The True Story of the 2000 Presidential Election.* Lanham, MD: Rowman and Littlefield, 2001.

Mallaby, Sebastian. "The Irrelevant Election." *Foreign Affairs* 120 (September 2000): 74–80.

Pomper, Gerald M., et al. *The Election of 2000: Reports and Interpretations.* New York: Seven Bridges, 2001.

United States, National Elections of 2004

The 2004 U.S. national elections selected a president and vice president as well as members of both the U.S. House of Representatives and the Senate. In large measure, the elections were seen as a litmus test for the incumbent George W. Bush administration and its handling of foreign and national security policy, particularly the Global War on Terror and the Iraq War, which had begun in March 2003. The Democratic field of potential nominees going into the 2004 primaries was unusually large. The contenders included: former Senator Carol Mosely Braun; retired General Wesley Clark; former Governor Howard Dean; Senator John Edwards; former House Minority Leader Dick Gephardt; Senator Bob Graham; Senator John Kerry; Representative Dennis Kucinich; Senator Joseph Lieberman; and the Reverend Al Sharpton. Bush was not seriously challenged for the Republican Party nomination, so he remained the presumptive nominee during the entire campaign. Bush also decided to retain sitting Vice President Dick Cheney as his running mate.

Former Vermont governor Howard Dean was an early favorite and front-runner, and his scathing denunciation of the 2003 Iraq invasion and the botched postwar occupation effort was the centerpiece of his campaign. He also ran as a populist, which gave him plenty of ammunition to attack the Bush administration's economic policies and its failure to alleviate serious problems in

Democratic presidential candidate John Kerry, left, listens to President George W. Bush during their presidential debate in Coral Gables, Florida, on September 30, 2004. Debate moderator Jim Lehrer is at center. (AP/Wide World Photos)

the American health insurance system. Dean, however, was perhaps too strident and too leftist for mainstream Democrats, and he faired poorly in the January 2004 Iowa caucus, finishing a distant third, behind Kerry (the winner) and Edwards (a close runner-up). As the primaries progressed into the late winter and early spring, the many Democratic hopefuls systematically dropped out of the race as Kerry won an impressive string of state primaries. By March, Kerry, a U.S. senator from Massachusetts, had all but sewn up his party's nomination.

In early July, Kerry chose North Carolina senator John Edwards as his vice presidential running mate. Edwards had been a challenger for the presidential nomination and was a highly photogenic politician, although his experience in politics was relatively short-lived. The Democratic Convention went off without a glitch in Boston later in the month, and the two men emerged to begin their campaign against the Bush-Cheney ticket. It would prove to be a difficult fight.

Kerry's main election platform included opposition to the Iraq War, health care concerns, an uneven economy, and the evaporation of well-paying jobs in the United States. Kerry also accused the

Bush administration of having tarnished the image of the United States abroad by its flawed rationale for war in Iraq and its prosecution of the Global War on Terror in the aftermath of the September 11, 2001, terror attacks. Bush, meanwhile, capitalized on his handling of the post–September 11 environment, arguing that his policies had kept the nation safe, the proof of which could be found in the fact that no other terrorist attacks had occurred since then. He strongly defended his decision to go to war in Iraq and claimed that getting rid of Iraqi dictator Saddam Hussein was an important component of the Global War on Terror. Both implicitly and explicitly, the Bush camp suggested that a United States under a Kerry presidency would be less safe both at home and abroad. Because the economy at that point was still relatively sound, Bush and Cheney defended their economic policies, which had included large tax cuts for wealthy Americans and soaring budget deficits.

Kerry and Edwards attempted to use the growing unpopularity of the Iraq War and Bush's sagging popularity to whip up antiwar sentiment, but they were never entirely successful. The war at that point was still supported by a majority of Americans, and the Republicans tried to turn the tables by suggesting that the nation should not change presidents in the midst of a war, especially when the alternative was portrayed as indecisive. The Bush campaign labeled Kerry as a "flip-flopper" and used the senator's own words against him, particularly Kerry's bizarre backpedal that claimed he had been "for the war before [he] was against it." The Bush campaign used character assassination and innuendo to try to convince voters that Kerry could not be trusted with issues such as national security and foreign policy. The Kerry campaign was sometimes slow to react to such attacks, and its responses were not entirely effective.

A series of damaging television ads that began running in the late summer of 2004 also hurt Kerry's campaign. Sponsored by a conservative group known as the Swift Boat Veterans for Truth, the ads were an attempt to denigrate Kerry's Vietnam War experience and cast serious doubt on his character and fitness to serve as president. The Bush campaign claimed that it had nothing to do with the ads, but it did nothing to disclaim them, either. Kerry did not respond quickly or forcefully enough to them, which made him appear weak and indecisive. By late September, the Republicans and other Kerry detractors had done a credible job of portraying him as an effete Massachusetts liberal who was not in the mainstream of U.S. politics.

Kerry scored well in the first presidential debate held on September 30, 2004. He came across as articulate, knowledgeable, likable, and decisive. Bush, on the other hand, who could never be accused of eloquence, came across as sullen, defensive, testy, and out of touch. His periodic scowls and body language did little to help his poor performance. Bush fared better in the last two debates, however.

In the end, the nation was spared a repeat of the contentious outcome of the 2000 election, when Bush eked out a close but clear win in both the popular vote and the Electoral College. Bush captured 50.7 percent of the popular vote to Kerry's 48.3 percent. The Bush-Cheney ticket garnered 286 electoral votes, while Kerry-Edwards captured 251. In the House of Representatives, the Republicans picked up three additional seats, while the Democrats lost two. In the Senate, the Republicans picked up four new seats, and the Democrats lost four.

Just two years later, in the midterm 2006 congressional elections, however, the Republicans lost control of both houses of Congress. And by 2007, President Bush's approval rating dropped into the low 30 percent range, a rating only slightly higher than the lowest approval ratings notched by presidents Harry Truman (22 percent in 1952), Richard Nixon (24 percent in 1974), and Jimmy Carter (28 percent in 1979). Clearly, support of the Iraq War and the general direction of U.S. foreign and domestic policy slipped badly in the months after the 2004 elections.

PAUL G. PIERPAOLI JR.

See also

Bush, George Walker; Cheney, Richard Bruce; Global War on Terror; Kerry, John Forbes; Swift Boat Veterans for Truth; United States,

National Elections of 2000; United States, National Elections of 2006; United States, National Elections of 2008

References

O'Connor, Karen J., and Larry J. Sabato. *Essentials of American Government: Continuity and Change, 2004 Election Update.* 6th ed. New York: Longman, 2005.

Sabato, Larry J. *Divided States of America: The Slash and Burn Politics of the 2004 Presidential Election.* New York: Longman, 2005.

Thomas, Evan. *Election 2004: How Bush Won and What You can Expect for the Future.* New York: PublicAffairs, 2005.

United States, National Elections of 2006

Important midterm congressional elections that saw the Republican Party lose control of both houses of Congress. The November 2006 U.S. elections were held amid wide—and growing—public dissatisfaction with the Iraq War and the George W. Bush administration in general. Since 2004, the Iraq insurgency had become far more widespread and pernicious, claiming the lives of a considerable number of U.S. servicemen as well as Iraqis, both civilians and soldiers. Many commentators and experts feared publicly that Iraq was quickly descending into civil war. The Bush administration had been either unwilling or incapable of reversing the Iraqi decent into chaos and refused to undertake a fundamental change in its Iraq policy, which by 2006 was under fire from both Republicans and Democrats. Even retired generals had by now gone on record as opposing the way in which the conflict was being waged. The Democrats used the 2006 elections as a litmus test for the Iraq War, promising the American people that they would force changes in the nation's Iraq policy; many hinted that they would compel the White House to agree on a timetable for the removal of U.S. troops from Iraq and would insist that the timetable be upheld, regardless of the conditions on the ground.

The war in Iraq was not the only campaign issue in 2006. Many Americans were also chagrined by the high cost of waging the war and the Bush administration's profligate spending, which had turned record budget surpluses in 2001 into the country's largest budget deficits in history by 2006. Certainly, the Republicans' unwillingness to increase taxes to pay for the war or enact spending cuts was a clear indication that they had entirely abandoned fiscal conservatism, which had been a guiding principle of Republican governance for nearly 100 years.

In 2006, Republicans in Congress appeared to the average voter to be out of touch not only when it came to fiscal policy and the war in Iraq but also in regard to growing signs that the economy was slowing down. By the autumn of the year, President Bush's approval ratings had plummeted, and his unpopularity proved to be a considerable drag on Republicans running for reelection that year.

The stakes were high for the Democrats in 2006. If they managed to wrest control of Congress from the Republicans, they would control the legislative branch completely for the first time

House Democratic leader Nancy Pelosi of California celebrates at an election-night rally on Capitol Hill in Washington, D.C., on November 7, 2006. After taking control of the House of Representatives and the Senate in the elections, Democrats unanimously selected Pelosi as the first woman Speaker of the House on November 16, 2006. (AP/Wide World Photos)

since 1994. They would also be in a position to force changes in Bush administration policies, or at least block any new initiatives with which they disagreed.

In the end, the Democrats' sweep of both the House and Senate was larger than even what many Democrats were predicting. The Democrats gained 31 seats in the House while the Republicans lost 30. This gave them a 233–202 advantage. While their majority was not large enough to block Republican initiatives entirely, it certainly made the Republicans' legislative agenda much harder to implement. As a result of the election, the House elected its first female Speaker of the House, Democrat Nancy Pelosi. The Democratic victory in the Senate was not nearly as dramatic but nonetheless gave the Democrats a razor-thin majority there, too. The Democrats picked up 5 seats while the Republicans lost 6. The Democrats ended up with a 51–49 advantage, which included two independents who caucused with the Democrats. The Democratic sweep in 2006 extended to the state level as well, as no incumbent Democratic governor was unseated by a Republican. Indeed, the Democrats gained six governorships in the contests.

PAUL G. PIERPAOLI JR.

See also

United States, National Elections of 2004; United States, National Elections of 2008; Wilson, Valerie Plame

References

Abramson, Paul R., John H. Aldrich, and David W. Rohde. *Change and Continuity in the 2004 and 2006 Elections.* Washington, DC: CQ Press, 2007.

Kernell, Samuel, and Gary C. Jacobson. *The Logic of Politics under Divided Government: The Legacy of the 2006 Elections.* Washington, DC: CQ Press, 2007.

United States, National Elections of 2008

The 2008 U.S. national elections built on the previous momentum of the Democratic Party, which had swept the off-year 2006 legislative elections by gaining control of both houses of Congress. The November 4, 2008, elections resulted in more Democratic seats gained in Congress and, more important, saw the election of Democrats Barack Obama and Joseph Biden to the presidency and vice presidency, respectively. Obama was the first African American to achieve the nation's highest office and was the first Democrat to sit in the White House since President Bill Clinton (1993–2001). The election was certainly one of the most important in U.S. political history, for not only did it shatter racial barriers but it also resoundingly repudiated the Republican Party and witnessed massive voter turnout, especially among young voters, who cast their ballots overwhelmingly for the Obama/Biden ticket. Only the passage of time would tell the true magnitude of the election, but many pundits had already begun to speak of a fundamental realignment of political power in America, akin to those seen in 1896, 1932, and 1980.

Obama won the presidency by a comfortable margin over his Republican opponent, Senator John S. McCain III. He captured 52.9 percent of the popular vote compared to McCain's 45.7 percent. Obama's margin of victory in the Electoral College was even more impressive: 365 votes to McCain's 173. Obama carried every northeastern state from Minnesota and Iowa in the west to Maine and Virginia in the east. He also carried North Carolina and Florida in the South, two states that had recently trended Republican in presidential contests. In the far west, Obama carried California, Oregon, Washington, Nevada, Colorado, and New Mexico. McCain did well in the Deep South and in the sparsely populated states of the Plains and the West.

In Congress, Democrats increased their majorities in both the House and Senate. Republicans lost 21 seats, and the Democrats

Results of the 2008 U.S. Presidential Election

Name	Party	% of Popular Vote	Electoral Votes
Barack Obama	Democratic	52.92%	365
John McCain	Republican	45.66%	173
Ralph Nader	Independent	0.56%	0
Bob Barr	Libertarian	0.40%	0
Cynthia McKinney	Green	0.12%	0
Other	—	0.34%	0

Barack Obama is sworn in as the 44th president of the United States by Chief Justice John Roberts in Washington, D.C., January 20, 2009. Obama's wife Michelle holds the Bible on which President Abraham Lincoln took his oath of office. (U.S. Department of Defense)

gained an equal number. This resulted in a total of 251 seats for the Democrats and 178 seats for the Republicans, giving the Democrats a 76-seat advantage. In the Senate, the Democrats increased their seats by 8, giving them 59 (including 2 independents who caucused with the Democrats). The Republicans lost 8 seats, holding just 41 after the elections. This gave the Democrats an 18-seat majority.

It is clear that many congressional Democrats rode into power on Obama's coattails, because public opinion polls just prior to the elections showed widespread and deep voter disapproval of Congress, which had been controlled by the Democrats since January 2007. Thus, the Democratic gains may well have had more to do with President George W. Bush's unpopularity and Obama's wide appeal than voter interest in Democratic congressional candidates per se.

Obama ran a masterful, nearly flawless campaign. It was tightly organized, almost always on message, and remarkably free of gaffes and slipups. But it was Obama's awe-inspiring money raising that made the biggest difference. His campaign managers harnessed the power of the Internet in ways that McCain never could. Most of the money raised was through small, individual, online contributions. When the election was over, Obama had heavily

outspent his opponent and had raised more money than any political candidate in U.S. history.

Most lauded Obama's choice in August 2008 of longtime Democratic senator Joe Biden to be his running mate. Biden had run for the Democratic presidential nomination but had failed to garner sufficient support and had dropped out and thrown his support to Obama. In the Senate since the 1970s, Biden had much experience in Washington, knew the ins and outs of Congress, and filled in Obama's acknowledged lack of experience in foreign and military affairs.

McCain, who had become the presumptive nominee of his party well before Obama had secured his party's nomination, was also a Senate stalwart, having served in that capacity since 1987. A naval officer and Vietnam War hero, he had spent more than seven years as a prisoner of war (POW) and had endured significant torture. Few questioned his foreign policy or military bona fides, but his consistent support of the Iraq War hurt his chances among the many Americans who opposed the war. McCain's campaign was not well managed; it could not stay focused on key topics for very long, and McCain and others in his campaign were prone to verbal and political gaffes. His choice of the mostly unknown Sarah Palin as his vice presidential running mate likely handicapped his campaign, although it did garner intense media coverage, which up until Palin's nomination was dominated by the Obama candidacy. Palin's performance in news interviews dealing with her knowledge of foreign policy was comical. She projected no solid policy message other than the far-right Republican values that alienated many Americans. Vice presidents may stay in the background, but with an older presidential candidate in John McCain, whose age and health were issues, Palin seemed more of a liability than an asset.

It is a noteworthy fact that as late as June or July 2008, both candidates had been focusing largely on the Iraq War, the Global War on Terror, the Afghan War, and other national security and foreign policy imperatives. All those subjects were seen as McCain strong suits. That began to change, quickly, in August and September. The U.S. economy began to deteriorate at a dizzying pace in the late summer and early fall, precipitated by an ongoing housing crisis, an emergent subprime mortgage fiasco, and a string of spectacular bank and investment house failures. The George W. Bush administration moved haltingly and clumsily to steady the economy but to little avail. Even a massive government stimulus package failed to stop the slide. As the stock market swooned, unemployment skyrocketed, and housing prices collapsed, many Americans were convinced that neither McCain nor the Republicans could be trusted to make things right. The economic crisis played into Obama's hands, and within weeks the campaign was focused not on the Iraq War or national security but on economic security. This helped both the Democratic Party at large and the Obama campaign in particular.

Obama's rise to power can be viewed as a combination of the novelty of his message, appeal to youth, sustained opposition to many of George W. Bush's foreign and domestic policies, obviously keen intellect and masterful speaking, and well-organized campaign, as well as the precipitous decline of the U.S. economy.

Obama had his work cut out for him, for when he assumed office in 2009, the economy continued to move steadily downward. Ironically, an orderly withdrawal of U.S. forces from Iraq and shifting of emphasis to Afghanistan, which had been one of his early pledges, seemed comparatively easy compared to the intractable economic problems facing the nation.

PAUL G. PIERPAOLI JR.

See also

Antiwar Movements, Persian Gulf and Iraq Wars; Biden, Joseph Robinette, Jr.; Bush, George Walker; McCain, John Sidney, III; United States, National Elections of 2004; United States, National Elections of 2006

References

Ifell, Gwen. *Breakthrough: Politics and Rage in the Age of Obama*. New York: Doubleday Books, 2009.

Todd, Chick, and Sledon Gawiser. *How Barack Obama Won*. New York: Vintage, 2009.

USA Today Editors. *America Speaks: The Historic 2008 Election*. Chicago: Triumph Books/Random House, 2008.

United States Agency for International Development, Afghanistan

The principal U.S. government organization that supervises and distributes American foreign aid to Afghanistan, which began in earnest after the Taliban regime was toppled during Operation ENDURING FREEDOM (2001). The genesis of the Agency for International Development (AID) can be found in the 1947 Marshall Plan and President Harry S. Truman's Point Four Program of 1949. Both of these programs systematized U.S. foreign assistance in the post–World War II era.

The actual agency was created by the 1961 Foreign Assistance Act, passed by the U.S. Congress in September of that year. The act stipulated the establishment of an umbrella organization for U.S. foreign economic assistance and led to the creation of the AID on November 3, 1963. Since then, the AID has distributed hundreds of billions of dollars around the world and has served as a unifying organization that brings together almost all U.S. financial, technical, and economic development programs under one broad banner.

The AID has weathered periodic reforms measures and much criticism that it is a bureaucratic leviathan that wastes money that could be otherwise channeled to other purposes. However, it continues on, more than 45 years after its creation, as the premier U.S. foreign assistance agency. The AID receives its guidance from the U.S. secretary of state, whose job it is to ensure that AID's aims and programs are consonant with American foreign policy goals and mandates established by the U.S. Congress.

The Agency for International Development has played a central role in economic development and reconstruction in Afghanistan. Wracked by almost a quarter-century of war, foreign occupation, and violence, Afghanistan's population was desperately poor when the Taliban regime fell in late 2001. Indeed, more than 50 percent of its population lived below the international poverty level, and its civic, economic, and governmental institutions were practically nonexistent. Working in tandem with U.S. military planners in Afghanistan, in 2001 AID was asked to create a comprehensive program to create economic growth in the country, support and encourage representative government, and help establish educational and governmental entities that would enhance Afghanistan's labor market and mitigate the influence of poverty and extremism. Clearly, AID's lofty objectives are meant not only to ameliorate Afghans' living conditions but also to make it a less attractive haven for terrorists.

Road construction has been a major AID goal. This activity has helped the Afghan economy by promoting increased trade, moving laborers to viable labor markets, and even improving the health care delivery system. To date, more than 1,000 miles of roads have been built using AID funds and technical expertise.

Providing electricity to more people has also been a concern of the AID. In 2008, no more than 15 percent of Afghanistan's population has access to electricity. Because nearly 80 percent of the Afghan population is rural (and most are engaged in agriculture),

U.S. AID-supported educational programs in Afghanistan have renovated classrooms and provided new textbooks and supplies. They have also supported the education of girls, which was opposed by the Taliban. (U.S. Agency for International Development)

the electrification of the nation is key to invigorating the economy and providing its citizens with opportunities to improve their financial lot.

The AID is involved in countless endeavors in Afghanistan, working with the rural poor, local, regional, and national business enterprises, and the national government. Provincial Reconstruction Teams (PRTs) are currently helping AID funnel resources and technical personnel into the areas that are most needy. The PRTs also help to ensure that AID funds are not mismanaged or diverted to purposes not sanctioned by the agency. Educational reforms since 2001 have witnessed the building of some 675 schools throughout the country. The AID has also helped to build or rebuild 670 medical clinics, furnished millions of dollars of badly needed medicine, and has trained or lent thousands of health care workers to Afghanistan.

In 2007, AID spent $1.008 billion in Afghanistan; that amount has remained relatively constant, with the total expenditure slated to increase slightly to $1.054 billion in 2009.

PAUL G. PIERPAOLI JR.

See also

Afghanistan; ENDURING FREEDOM, Operation; Global War on Terror; Provincial Reconstruction Teams, Afghanistan; Taliban

References

Jalali, Ali A. "The Future of Afghanistan." *Parameters* (Spring 2006): 4–19.

Maloney, Sean M. "Afghanistan Four Years On: An Assessment." *Parameters* (Autumn 2005): 21–32.

McNerney, Michael J. "Stabilization and Reconstruction in Afghanistan: Are PRTs a Model or a Muddle?" *Parameters* (Winter 2005–2006): 32–46.

Rasanayagam, Angelo. *Afghanistan: A Modern History.* London: I. B. Tauris, 2005.

Williams, Garland H. *Engineering Peace: The Military Role in Post-conflict Reconstruction.* Washington, DC: United States Institute of Peace, 2005.

United States Agency for International Development, Iraq

Principal U.S. government organization that supervises and distributes American foreign aid to Iraq, which began in 2003 shortly after Operation IRAQI FREEDOM overthrew the Saddam Hussein regime. The genesis of the Agency for International Development (AID) may be found in the 1947 Marshall Plan and President Harry

A Kurdish farmer tends his crop in northern Iraq in 2007. U.S. AID workers helped to form a farmers' association with the aim of giving farmers ownership of their land. (U.S. Agency for International Development)

S. Truman's 1949 Point Four Program. Both of those programs systematized U.S. foreign assistance in the post–World War II era.

The U.S. Congress created the Agency for International Development with the passage of the 1961 Foreign Assistance Act. The act mandated the establishment of an umbrella organization for U.S. foreign economic assistance, which led to the creation of the AID on November 3, 1963. Since then, the AID has distributed hundreds of billions of dollars of aid around the world and has served as a unifying organization that brings together almost all U.S. financial, technical, and economic development programs under one broad banner.

Over the years, the AID has weathered periodic reform initiatives and considerable criticism that it is a bureaucratic leviathan that wastes money that could be channeled to other purposes. Nevertheless, it continues on, more than 45 years after its creation, as the premier U.S. foreign assistance agency. The AID receives its guidance from the U.S. secretary of state, whose job it is to ensure that AID's aims and programs are consonant with American foreign policy goals and mandates established by the U.S. Congress.

The postwar reconstruction of Iraq, a primary mandate for the AID, represents the single largest U.S. foreign aid initiative since the Marshall Plan. Among the AID's chief missions in Iraq are economic reconstruction and growth, the reinvigoration of health care and educational systems, the support of democratic institutions, the provisioning of humanitarian aid to homeless and displaced persons, and the rebuilding and upgrading of critical infrastructure, to include sewage treatment plants, electrical generation facilities, and water treatment systems. All of these activities are meant to foster representative democracy, internal security, and economic independence. Clearly, the ongoing Iraqi insurgency has made it quite difficult for AID to achieve its goals; the continuing presence of large numbers of U.S. and coalition troops in the country has also been a challenge for AID officials.

AID workers have been working with former Iraqi government officials, retraining them and readying them to take over various governmental functions. They have also been working with provincial and municipal government officials in an attempt to ensure that basic services are met at the local and regional level. AID is also working closely with the Central Bank of Iraq and the Ministry of Finance, helping them implement effective budgetary and cost-tracking measures.

From 2003 to 2006, AID added 1,292 megawatts of electricity to Iraq's electric grid, bringing electrical service to hundreds of thousands of people. AID has also rebuilt or expanded 19 water treatment plants, bringing potable water to 3.1 million Iraqis who heretofore had no access to clean water. AID improvements to sewage treatment facilities have brought modern sewage service to at least 5.1 million Iraqis. In health care, AID has also provided many improvements. In 2005 alone, almost 98 percent of all Iraqi children were vaccinated against childhood diseases. In education, AID has built, rebuilt, or refurbished thousands of schools and has developed programs to ensure that all Iraqis have access to educational institutions, from elementary level to university. In cities and towns hard hit by fighting, AID is working in tandem with other international agencies and multinational corporations to revitalize local economies.

In 2007, AID spent $1.959 billion on all programs in Iraq; in 2009 the budget was substantially less, closer to $1.49 billion. The amount of AID funds spent in Iraq since 2003 is approaching $10 billion; the United States spent $13.5 billion (albeit in 1950 dollars) on the Marshall Plan (1947–1952), which helped reconstruct all of Western Europe. Currently, there are no plans to dismantle AID in Iraq, and so considerably more money will likely be spent in the years to come. Clearly, the continuing insurgency in Iraq has hampered AID efforts to reconstruct the country, and it is anyone's guess how much money has been wasted trying to rebuild a nation that remains at war with itself.

PAUL G. PIERPAOLI JR.

See also
Iraq, History of, 1990–Present; IRAQI FREEDOM, Operation; Iraqi Insurgency

References
Agresto, John. *Mugged by Reality: The Liberation of Iraq and the Failure of Good Intentions.* New York: Encounter Books, 2007.
Glantz, Aaron. *How America Lost Iraq.* New York: Jeremy P. Tarcher, 2005.
Stephenson, James. *Losing the Golden Hour: An Insider's View of Iraq's Reconstruction.* Dulles, VA: Potomac Books, 2007.

United States Air Force, Afghanistan War

The U.S. Air Force (USAF) has provided logistical, strategic, and tactical air support in the Afghanistan War, designated Operation ENDURING FREEDOM, since the conflict began on October 7, 2001. The air force continues to provide support, now including advisory efforts, for American and coalition forces in Afghanistan. Before Operation ENDURING FREEDOM commenced, the USAF constructed the Combined Air Operations Center (CAOC) in Saudi Arabia (moved to Qatar in 2003) as the command and control center for all air operations. The CAOC monitors all air operations, provides intelligence, and relays target information to airborne aircraft. During the first six weeks of the war, Lieutenant General Charles F. "Chuck" Wald served as commander, U.S. Central Command Air Forces (CENTAF), in charge of all air forces under U.S. Central Command (CENTCOM).

On the first day of the conflict, Lieutenant General Wald ordered USAF aircraft to destroy Al Qaeda and Taliban radar systems, command facilities, surface-to-air missile sites, armored vehicles, airfields, and any enemy personnel to ensure complete American air superiority over Afghanistan. The success of the opening bombing campaign allowed American and allied Northern Alliance ground troops to capture the cities of Kabul and Mazar-e Sharif, forcing Al Qaeda and Taliban forces into a hasty retreat toward the Afghanistan-Pakistan border. In November 2001 Lieutenant General T. Michael Moseley succeeded Lieutenant General Wald as commander of U.S. CENTAF, a position he retained until August 2003. Immediately, Moseley commanded the USAF to help seize the city of Kandahar, the last remaining Taliban stronghold. After the Taliban fled from Kandahar, USAF focus turned to the Tora Bora region, a mountainous region in eastern Afghanistan with a complex network of caves where U.S. CENTCOM officials believed Taliban and Al Qaeda leaders, including Osama bin Laden, were hiding. The USAF bombed the Tora Bora region relentlessly for three weeks beginning in late November, yet bin Laden and other priority targets managed to escape into Pakistan.

As 2002 began the USAF, along with the entire U.S. military contingent, switched to a more defensive strategy, aiming to protect Afghan civilians and the emerging American-supported government. Moreover, the air force continued to provide logistical, strategic, and tactical air support when needed. In January and February 2002, Al Qaeda operatives began to assemble in the Shah-i Kot Mountains near the Pakistan-Afghan border. As part of Operation ANACONDA, the USAF provided crucial air support for the combined U.S. Army/Special Operations Forces and indigenous Afghan contingent that successfully pushed the enemy into Pakistan.

Although U.S. forces largely succeeded in driving the enemy out of Afghanistan in late 2001 and early 2002, the following months and years witnessed the evolution of a Taliban insurgency, fueled by the political developments and progress of the new Afghan government. From 2003 to the present, reacting to the renewed Taliban insurgency, USAF and coalition aircraft annually increased the number of close air support sorties in Operation ENDURING FREEDOM. In August 2003 Lieutenant General Walter E. Buchanan III took over U.S. CENTAF duties, remaining in the position until February 2006.

U.S. ground forces have relied heavily on USAF close air support to achieve tactical objectives. As part of the counterinsurgency effort in Operation ENDURING FREEDOM, air force aircraft routinely attack enemy gun emplacements, bunkers, and any insurgents that hinder the tactical objectives of U.S. ground forces. During the spring and summer months of 2003, as the Iraq War was under way, the air force offered strategic and tactical air support to fend off thousands of Taliban insurgents in southeastern Afghanistan.

Since the spring of 2003, the Taliban insurgency has continued to hamper U.S. forces. In 2008, for the first time since the beginning of the Iraq War in 2003, the number of USAF air strikes in Operation ENDURING FREEDOM surpassed those in Iraq. Moreover, in 2008 there were more close air support sorties flown in Afghanistan than in Iraq, a testament to the increasing insurgency problem in Operation ENDURING FREEDOM.

Lieutenant General Gary L. North, U.S. CENTAF commander (changed to USAFCENT [United States Air Forces Central] in March 2008) since February 2006, has added an advisory role for

A U.S. Air Force F-15E Strike Eagle takes off from Bagram Air Base in Afghanistan on a morning patrol mission. (U.S. Air Force)

the USAF in Afghanistan. Indeed, the air force has continued and will continue to provide air support in Operation ENDURING FREEDOM, yet since late 2006 many U.S. airmen have also engaged in training the Afghan Air Corps (AAC). The USAF has begun to prepare the Afghan airmen to conduct their own future air operations in conjunction with indigenous forces. In mid-2007, the USAF's Air Education and Training Command began predeployment advisory training for advisers en route to train the AAC. This advisory effort will prove a long and arduous process, as the USAF will remain in theater until the AAC and indigenous land units receive adequate training.

Currently, the USAF has increasingly embraced the use of unmanned aircraft in intelligence, surveillance, and reconnaissance missions. Throughout 2008 and early 2009, Afghan president Hamid Karzai pleaded with U.S. officials to reduce the number of civilian casualties from air strikes, which undermine the government's ability to win support from of the Afghani people. Accordingly, the USAF has increased its use of unmanned drones, using advanced technology to locate targets and help distinguish friendly personnel from the enemy.

The air force has utilized a vast array of aircraft during Operation ENDURING FREEDOM. As of April 1, 2008, USAF had undertaken nearly 194,000 sorties in support of ENDURING FREEDOM. Figures released in early 2009 reveal that 27,558 USAF personnel were serving in Afghanistan and Iraq. From the beginning of the Global War on Terror in 2001 through the end of 2009, 347,080 USAF personnel had served in Iraq and Afghanistan, and the USAF had suffered 43 killed-in-action (KIA) casualties in Operation ENDURING FREEDOM.

JOHN SOUTHARD

See also

ANACONDA, Operation; ENDURING FREEDOM, Operation; ENDURING FREEDOM, Operation, U.S. Air Campaign; Moseley, Teed Michael; United States Central Command

References

Boyne, Walter J. *Beyond the Wild Blue: A History of the U.S. Air Force, 1947–2007*. 2nd ed. New York: Thomas Dunne Books, 2007.

Cassidy, Robert. *Counterinsurgency and the Global War on Terror: Military Culture and Irregular War*. Palo Alto, CA: Stanford University Press, 2008.

Jones, Seth G. *Counterinsurgency in Afghanistan: RAND Counterinsurgency Study No. 4*. Santa Monica, CA: RAND Corporation, 2008.

Lambeth, Benjamin S. *Air Power against Terror: America's Conduct of Operation Enduring Freedom*. Santa Monica, CA: RAND Corporation, 2005.

Thaler, David E., Theodore W. Karasik, Dalia Dassa Kaye, Jennifer D. P. Moroney, Frederic Wehrey, Obaid Younossi, Farhana Ali, and Robert A. Guffey. *Future U.S. Security Relationships with Iraq and Afghanistan: U.S. Air Force Roles*. Santa Monica, CA: RAND Corporation, 2008.

United States Air Force, Iraq War

The participation of the United States Air Force (USAF) in the Iraq War, designated Operation IRAQI FREEDOM, began on March 20, 2003. The USAF has provided logistical, strategic, and tactical air support for U.S. and coalition forces since the beginning of the conflict. The USAF utilized the Combined Air Operations Center (CAOC), which U.S. forces had established at the beginning of the Afghanistan War, dubbed Operation ENDURING FREEDOM, in 2001. The CAOC, originally stationed in Saudi Arabia and moved to Qatar in 2003, monitors and controls all air operations in Operation ENDURING FREEDOM and Operation IRAQI FREEDOM. Moreover, the CAOC provides intelligence and relays target information to airborne aircraft. During the first five months of Operation IRAQI FREEDOM, Lieutenant General T. Michael Moseley served as commander, U.S. Central Command Air Forces (CENTAF), giving him command of all air forces under the U.S. Central Command (CENTCOM).

Much of the air force's efforts on the first two days of Operation IRAQI FREEDOM focused on ground support for forces moving into Iraq from Kuwait. In addition, the USAF bombed command and control targets (communication sites, artillery, surface-to-air missile sites, air-defense command centers, air-traffic-control facilities, and airfields) throughout Iraq. From late March 21 through March 22, USAF aircraft also heavily bombed the Iraqi capital of Baghdad. The initial bombing campaign, referred to as shock and awe, was aimed at ousting Iraqi president Saddam Hussein's Baath regime from power. Yet, the Iraqi government did not submit to the initial air assault. U.S. CENTCOM and U.S. CENTAF deemed many Iraqi command and control targets off limits for fear of civilian casualties, and so air strikes had limited initial effectiveness in toppling Hussein.

By early April, USAF aircraft had begun to focus more on close air support for U.S. ground forces making their way toward Baghdad, demolishing any infantry, gun and artillery emplacements, tanks, and armored vehicles that hindered the coalition advance. Simultaneously, the USAF continued to provide strategic air support in and around Baghdad, which fell to coalition forces on April 9–10, 2003. Soon after the end of the conventional aspect of Operation IRAQI FREEDOM, which was marked by the capture of Baghdad, Iraqi insurgents quickly organized, thus hindering the coalition's ability to create and maintain security in the country. The return of sovereignty to the new Iraqi government in June 2004 prompted a shift in air force strategy toward one that emphasized counterinsurgency and security.

From August 2003 to February 2006, Lieutenant General Walter E. Buchanan III served as commander of U.S. CENTAF, thus placing him in control of the air force component of the counterinsurgency in Iraq. The USAF increased its employment of unmanned aircraft for intelligence, surveillance, and reconnaissance missions, during which the remote-controlled drones searched for insurgent activity in Iraq. Moreover, the air force increased the number of "on call" close air support missions, during which aircraft remain airborne and wait for orders to strike a target near the respective area of responsibility. The Iraqi insurgents have thrived on quick, covert tactics, and the "on call" aircraft offer a timely response to often unexpected attacks on American and coalition ground forces or Iraqi civilians.

In late 2003 U.S. CENTCOM established the Multinational Security Transition Command–Iraq (MSTC-I) to develop Iraqi security personnel. Two years after the establishment of MSTC I, the USAF assumed responsibility of training and developing the

Airmen load a CH-47D Chinook heavy-lift helicopter into the cargo bay of a C-5 Galaxy at Joint Base Balad, Iraq. (U.S. Department of Defense)

Iraqi Air Force (IAF), a task still being carried out. In early 2009 newly elected U.S. president Barack Obama announced plans to draw down American forces in Iraq, heightening the need to quickly train Iraqi military and security personnel.

In February 2006 Lieutenant General Gary L. North assumed command of U.S. CENTAF (changed to USAFCENT [U.S. Air Forces Central] in March 2008). While tasked with continuing to provide close air support for U.S. and allied forces and bolstering the IAF, U.S. airmen have seen an increase of security positions on the ground. Throughout the war, the USAF has always provided base defense, but beginning in 2006, U.S. airmen have also provided convoy protection.

As the Iraqi insurgency persisted throughout 2006, President George W. Bush announced in early 2007 that U.S. forces would see a troop surge of additional soldiers and marines to Iraq. Thus, throughout 2007 and 2008 the USAF tripled the number of airmen that performed ground support duties for the U.S. Army and Marine Corps. In addition to convoy security, USAF personnel performed explosives forensic analysis and police duties in Iraqi cities. Yet the increase in grounded airmen did not translate to a decrease in air support. The year of the surge resulted in the most close air support sorties flown since the start of the insurgency in 2003. Moreover, the USAF has persisted throughout the conflict in bombing insurgent strongholds and safe houses, bomb-making facilities, and weapons stockpiles.

U.S. CENTCOM officials reported a decrease in insurgent activity in 2008 after the surge took hold. The addition of U.S. forces pushed the insurgents into open areas, offering easier targets for USAF aircraft, which explains another reason for the increase in close air support sorties in 2007. Throughout 2008 and early 2009, Iraqi ground forces have conducted operations with help from coalition airpower, including the USAF.

The USAF has utilized a vast array of aircraft during Operation IRAQI FREEDOM. As of April 1, 2008, the Air Force had flown nearly 353,000 sorties in support of Operation IRAQI FREEDOM. As of early 2009, the USAF reported 48 deaths in Operation IRAQI FREEDOM.

In early 2009, 27,558 USAF personnel were serving in Iraq and Afghanistan. Since the beginning of the Global War on Terror in 2001, 347,080 USAF personnel have served in Iraq and Afghanistan.

JOHN SOUTHARD

See also

Bush, George Walker; Iraq, Air Force; IRAQI FREEDOM, Operation; IRAQI FREEDOM, Operation, Air Campaign; Moseley, Teed Michael; United States Air Force Air Combat Command

References

Boyne, Walter J. *Beyond the Wild Blue: A History of the U.S. Air Force, 1947–2007*. 2nd ed. New York: Thomas Dunne Books, 2007.

Cassidy, Robert. *Counterinsurgency and the Global War on Terror: Military Culture and Irregular War*. Palo Alto, CA: Stanford University Press, 2008.

Donnelly, Thomas. *Operation Iraqi Freedom: A Strategic Assessment*. Washington, DC: AEI Press, 2004.

Murray, Williamson, and Robert H. Scales Jr. *The Iraq War: A Military History*. Cambridge, MA: Belknap, 2005.

Thaler, David E., Theodore W. Karasik, Dalia Dassa Kaye, Jennifer D. P. Moroney, Frederic Wehrey, Obaid Younossi, Farhana Ali, and Robert A. Guffey. *Future U.S. Security Relationships with Iraq and Afghanistan: U.S. Air Force Roles*. Santa Monica, CA: RAND Corporation, 2008.

United States Air Force, Persian Gulf War

Perhaps the most telling comment on the organization and operation of the U.S. Air Force (USAF) in the Persian Gulf War is that it differed significantly from that of the Vietnam War, when enemy territory was divided into six "packages" and mission profiles were determined by geography as much as by enemy resistance.

This is not to say that the organization of the forces employed in the Persian Gulf War was a carefully thought-out plan. It was instead an admirable, if often ad hoc, series of arrangements to meld procedures, doctrines, and availability into a single, unified air-war plan. The key to the success of this sometimes off-the-cuff execution was the early establishment of the Joint Forces Air Component Commander (JFACC) by General H. Norman Schwarzkopf, U.S. commander in chief of Central Command (CENTCOM). Schwarzkopf reported to President George H. W. Bush through the secretary of defense and selected Lieutenant General Charles A. Horner as JFACC. Horner was commander, Ninth Air Force, and commander of U.S. Central Air Force, reporting to Schwarzkopf. Horner had also commanded U.S. CENTCOM Forward in Riyadh, Saudi Arabia, so was well positioned for his tasks. (Curiously, there was no separate JFACC staff.)

The establishment of JFACC meant that, for the first time in history, U.S. air forces were largely under a single control, a vast improvement over the administration of air assets during the Vietnam War. Horner was able to exercise close tactical control by the daily issuance of the Air Tasking Order (ATO), which coordinated the available forces, assigned targets, and established schedules, routes, and all other important aspects of warfare, including the vital element of aerial refueling.

The ATO often took as many as 40 hours to prepare and ranged from as few as 200 to more than 800 pages. Air force communications were slowed by it, and the problem was compounded because the navy and the remotely located Boeing B-52 Stratofortress wings did not have the advanced technology required. Where necessary, hard copies of the ATO were hand-carried as a substitute.

In essence, JFACC would first apportion combat effort, then allocate it. Apportionment is the determination and assignment of the total expected effort by percentage (or priority) that should be devoted to the various air operations and/or geographic areas for a given period of time. Allocation translates the apportionment into the required number of sorties by specific aircraft types. Thus a decision made to take out a certain set of radar

Two U.S. Air Force F-15C Eagle fighter aircraft of the 33rd Tactical Fighter Wing and a Royal Saudi Air Force F-5E Tiger II fighter aircraft during a mission in support of Operation DESERT STORM. The aircraft were armed with AIM-9 Sidewinder air-to-air missiles. (U.S. Department of Defense)

stations would be determined by apportionment, while allocation would determine the actual aircraft and weapons to be employed in the mission.

On an organization chart, Schwarzkopf's ultimate authority was shown with a solid line, with Horner's tactical control illustrated by a parallel dotted line. In practice, Horner's decisions went out to the six major elements: the air forces of Central Command Air Force (CENTAF), Army Central Command (ARCENT), Central Command Navy (NAVCENT), Central Command Marines (MARCENT), Central Command Special Operations (SOCCENT), the Joint Task Force Proven Air Force (JTFPF), as well as to various smaller coalition air forces. Horner, as noted, commanded CENTAF, while ARCENT was commanded by Lieutenant General John Yeosock, NAVCENT by Vice Admiral Henry H. Mauz Jr., and MARCENT by Marine Lieutenant General Walter E. Boomer. Colonel Jesse Johnson commanded SOCCENT, which was tasked with the vital combat search-and-rescue task. The JTFPF was commanded by Major General James L. Jamerson, who was also the USAFE (United States Air Forces in Europe) deputy chief of staff for operations. The JTFPF composite force had 20 General Dynamics/Grumman F-111E Ravens, 24 General Dynamics F-16C Fighting Falcons, 10 McDonnell Douglas F-15 Eagles, and 4 Boeing KC-135 Stratotankers from the Strategic Air Command (SAC).

The command relationship of the CENTAF and JFACC was again combined in their administration of the four basic divisions of aircraft types and one composite unit, the JTFPF. Fighter aircraft were assigned to the 14th Air Division (P) commanded by Brigadier General Buster Glosson. Early Warning (EW) and Command, Control, and Communications (C3) aircraft were assigned to the 15th Air Division (P), commanded by Brigadier General Glenn H. Proffitt II. Military Airlift Command (MAC) aircraft were assigned to the 16th Air Division (P), commanded by Brigadier General Edward E. Tenoso, while Strategic Air Command (SAC) aircraft were assigned to the 17th Air Division (P), commanded by Brigadier General Patrick P. Caruana. Geography and ships dictated that the navy and marine air units have an even more complex command relationship, which is beyond the scope of this entry.

The air force mustered 1,404 aircraft for the February 24, 1991, DESERT STORM assault. The navy and marine corps provided 684 aircraft, while foreign air forces contributed 731, for a grand total of 2,819. U.S. aircraft flew from 28 different locations surrounding the combat area, and would execute 117,131 sorties.

Given the overwhelming striking power of U.S. forces, it is probable that even significant changes in the exact details of its organization would have made little difference in the ultimate outcome of the war. This is true, however, only because of the

Casualties, by Branch, in the U.S. Armed Forces during Operations DESERT SHIELD and DESERT STORM

	U.S. Air Force	U.S. Army	U.S. Marine Corps	U.S. Navy	Total
Serving in theater	70,741	271,654	90,866	151,081	584,342
Killed in action	20	96	22	5	143
Died of wounds	0	2	2	0	4
Nonhostile deaths	15	126	44	50	235
Wounded in action	9	354	92	12	467
Total casualties	44	578	160	67	849

flexibility inherent in the manner in which command and control was exercised, and because of the incredible support supplied by both tanker and transport aircraft.

The command and control was orchestrated through an amazing combination of satellites, ground stations, airborne command posts, and reconnaissance planes. The already overaged and overworked tanker force proved to be the glue that held all the operational and organizational components together. Some 300 tankers (almost one-half of the USAF tanker fleet) flew 15,000 sorties, refueled 46,000 aircraft, and delivered 700 million pounds of fuel. It should be pointed out that every one of these elements—tankers, airborne command posts, giant transports, and satellite systems—had been criticized at one time or another by the media and Congress as "billion dollar boondoggles."

WALTER W. BOYNE

See also

Boomer, Walter; Bush, George Herbert Walker; DESERT STORM, Operation, Coalition Air Campaign; Horner, Charles; Mauz, Henry H., Jr.; Schwarzkopf, H. Norman, Jr.; Yeosock, John J.

References

Boyne, Walter J. *Gulf War.* New York: Signet, 1991.
———. *Weapons of Desert Storm.* Chicago: Consumer Guide, 1991.
Coyne, James P. *Airpower in the Gulf.* Arlington, VA: Air Force Association, 1992.
Hallion, Richard P. *Storm over Iraq: Air Power and the Gulf War.* Washington, DC: Smithsonian Institution Press, 1997.
Winnefeld, James A., Preston Niblack, and Dana J. Johnson. *A League of Airmen: U.S. Air Power in the Gulf War.* Santa Monica, CA: RAND Corporation, 1994.

United States Air Force Air Combat Command

U.S. Air Force command that provides combat air forces to the U.S. Air Forces Europe (USAFE), Air Forces Central Command (AFCENT), and Pacific Air Forces (PACAF). The Air Combat Command (ACC) is the Air Force component of the U.S. European, Central, and Pacific Commands. ACC also serves as the air component to U.S. Northern and Joint Forces Commands and augments forces to the Southern and Strategic Commands. The ACC organizes, trains, equips, and maintains combat-ready air forces for rapid deployment and employment outside the United States. It operates fighter, bomber, reconnaissance, battle-management, and electronic-combat aircraft; provides command, control, communications, and intelligence systems; and conducts global information operations. The command also ensures the readiness of strategic air defense forces to protect the U.S. homeland.

After the collapse of communism in Eastern Europe and the Soviet Union by the early 1990s, senior U.S. defense planners concluded that the Cold War–era U.S. military structure was not suited to the post–Cold War world. They believed that a global nuclear war seemed far less likely and that U.S. military forces would increasingly be called on to participate in smaller-scale regional contingencies and humanitarian operations.

Furthermore, the actual use of air force combat aircraft since the late 1960s had blurred the long-standing distinction between the Strategic Air Command (SAC) and Tactical Air Command (TAC), originally created in September 1947. By 1965, the term "strategic" had become linked to SAC's nuclear deterrence mission, while the term "tactical" had become associated with TAC's nonnuclear operational missions in conjunction with ground and naval forces. However, during the Vietnam War, SAC's strategic Boeing B-52 Stratofortress bombers most often performed tactical missions, such as interdiction and close air support, and its Boeing KC-135 Stratotankers regularly air refueled the tactical aircraft conducting missions over Southeast Asia. Additionally, TAC's tactical fighter aircraft carried out strategic bombing of targets in North Vietnam. Operation DESERT STORM in early 1991 further blurred the distinction between the two terms with the increasing use of precision-guided (smart) weapons, which gave tactical aircraft the ability to achieve strategic results.

After the Persian Gulf War, senior air force officials reexamined roles and missions. General Merrill A. McPeak, air force chief of staff (October 1990–October 1994), envisioned a streamlined air force that would eliminate unnecessary organizational layers. The vice chief of staff, General John M. Loh (June 1990–March 1991), thinking about the strategic-tactical distinction for some time, discussed his ideas with General McPeak and air force secretary Donald B. Rice about restructuring the major commands. After he assumed command of TAC on March 26, 1991, Loh continued to examine this issue. General George L. Butler, the commander of SAC, also supported change. These three generals led the effort to integrate the assets of SAC and TAC into a single operational command.

After reviewing numerous options, senior planners agreed to a major reorganization of the air force. The new Air Mobility Command (AMC), Scott Air Force Base, Illinois, would consolidate air force airlift and most refueling aircraft into one organization. The new Strategic Command, Offutt Air Force Base, Nebraska, would receive operational control of the air force's and navy's strategic nuclear forces to conduct the former SAC's nuclear deterrence mission.

On June 1, 1992, following the official inactivation of TAC, the air force activated the new ACC at Langley Air Force Base, Virginia, with Loh as the commander. The new command became responsible for providing combat-ready forces for deterrence and air combat operations. Upon activation, ACC assumed control of all fighter resources based in the continental United States, all bombers, reconnaissance platforms, battle management resources, and intercontinental ballistic missiles (ICBMs). Furthermore, ACC received some tankers and Lockheed C-130 Herculeses in its composite, reconnaissance, and certain other combat wings.

ACC underwent additional organizational and mission changes. On February 1, 1993, the air force realigned the Air Rescue Service to the AAC, which became the U.S. Air Force Combat Rescue School later that year on July 2. On July 1, 1993, the 58th and 325th Fighter Wings, respectively, McDonnell Douglas F-16 Eagle and F-15 training units, located at Luke Air Force Base, Arizona, and Tyndall Air Force Base, Florida, transferred to the Air Education and Training Command. On the same day, the Twentieth Air Force, six ICBM wings, one ICBM test wing, and the ICBM training wing, and F. E. Warren Air Force Base, Wyoming, transferred to the Air Force Space Command. On October 1, 1993, all AMC C-130s transferred to ACC, and all ACC KC-135 tankers except those at Mountain Home Air Force Base, Idaho, transferred to AMC.

Since its creation, ACC units and personnel have participated in numerous combat operations throughout the world. In Southwest Asia, the command provided forces for Operations NORTHERN WATCH and SOUTHERN WATCH, 1992–2003, to deter Iraqi aggression after the Persian Gulf War, and in October 1994 deployed forces to counter the buildup of Iraqi troops near the Kuwaiti border. ACC also provided trained forces for Operations ENDURING FREEDOM, which began in October 2001, and IRAQI FREEDOM, which began in March 2003. ACC also provided forces for counterdrug operations, including Airborne Warning and Control System (AWACS), reconnaissance and fighter aircraft, and radar and connectivity assets.

The command supported numerous humanitarian operations throughout the 1900s: PROVIDE PROMISE, humanitarian relief to Sarajevo, Bosnia, July 1992–March 1996; DENY FLIGHT, the no-fly zone against Serbian air attacks on Bosnian civilians, April 1993–December 1995; PROVIDE COMFORT from Incirlik Air Base, Turkey, relief to Kurdish inhabitants of northern Iraq threatened by the Iraqi government, April–July 1991; GTMO at Naval Base, Guantánamo Bay, Cuba, aid to Haitian refugees, November 1991–June 1993; SAFE HAVEN, relief for Cuban refugees, September 1994–February 1995; RESTORE HOPE, relief supplies to for famine-affected

Somalia, December 1992–May 1993; and SUPPORT HOPE, United Nations (UN) humanitarian relief for victims of the Rwandan civil war, July–August 1994.

Since 1991, sweeping changes in the military policy of the United States have imposed on ACC force structure reductions and greater flexibility. The command's forces continue to perform a variety of missions, including support to international peacekeeping operations, humanitarian needs at home and abroad, and protection of American interests around the globe.

ROBERT B. KANE

See also

United States Air Force, Afghanistan War; United States Air Force, Iraq War; United States Air Force, Persian Gulf War; United States Central Command

References

Haulman, Daniel L. *Wings of Hope: The U.S. Air Force and Humanitarian Airlift Operations.* Washington, DC: Department of the Air Force, 1994.

Jolly, Randy, and William D. Mason. *The United States Air Force's Air Combat Command: Global Power for America.* Garland, TX: Aero Graphics, 1995.

Knights, Michael. *Cradle of Conflict: Iraq and the Birth of Modern U.S. Military.* Annapolis, MD: Naval Institute Press, 2005.

Lambeth, Benjamin S. *Air Power against Terror: America's Conduct of Operation Enduring Freedom.* Santa Monica, CA: RAND Corporation, 2005.

United States Army, Afghanistan War

The U.S. Army has provided the largest portion of troops and matériel to the war in Afghanistan (Operation ENDURING FREEDOM), which was the target of U.S. and coalition forces after the September 11, 2001, terror attacks against the United States. Within months of the October 2001 invasion, the Taliban regime of Afghanistan had been ousted by the army, marines, air force, and navy units operating with allied units and local (Northern Alliance) Afghan forces. The 5th Special Forces Group was the first unit to operate inside the country with the Northern Alliance, a group of mainly Tajiks and Uzbeks who opposed the Taliban.

A public affairs unit and individual soldiers of the 82nd Airborne Division arrived in theater in October 2001. In June 2002 the division's headquarters and the 3rd Brigade arrived, with the 1st Brigade replacing the 3rd in early 2003. The 1st Brigade would also deploy in April 2005. In 2004 the 1st Battalion, 505th Parachute Infantry Regiment, deployed to Afghanistan to provide security for elections being held there. Elements of the 3rd Brigade of the reorganized division were sent to Afghanistan in early 2007, mainly for engineering and support service.

Units of the 10th Mountain Division and 101st Airborne Division conducted Operation ANACONDA (March 2002), the first major battle since Tora Bora in December 2001. The 101st Airborne was the first conventional unit to be deployed after the attacks of 9/11.

Two members of the U.S. Army's 504th Parachute Infantry, 82nd Airborne Division, search for weapons caches during a sweep of an Afghan village. (U.S. Army)

After heading to Iraq (in three separate deployments), the 101st Airborne's 4th Brigade headed back to Afghanistan in early 2008.

In March 2004 the 3rd Brigade, 25th Infantry Division, rotated to Afghanistan, the first major unit of that division to take part in the Afghanistan War (the 2nd Brigade had deployed to Iraq one month earlier). In March 2005 the 173rd Airborne Brigade (as Task Force Bayonet) was sent to four provinces in southern Afghanistan, including Kandahar. In February 2007 the 173rd Airborne Brigade returned to Afghanistan to replace the 3rd Brigade, 10th Mountain Division, this time in eastern Afghanistan. During the Battle of Wanat in July 2008, a platoon of the 173rd defeated hundreds of insurgents during a dramatic attack on the 173rd's base.

In February 2009 the 10th Mountain Division's 3rd Brigade (Task Force Spartan) moved back to eastern Afghanistan and occupied some places where coalition forces had never had a strong presence. Replacing the sparsely dispersed 101st Airborne Division, Task Force Spartan was responsible for Wardak and Logar provinces. With environmental conditions dominating these underdeveloped regions, Task Force Spartan reflected the army's newest drive for increased flexibility. For instance, several divisions had been reorganized into brigade combat teams to increase flexibility in counterinsurgency operations. By 2009 most army units had considerable experience in combat plus the necessary cultural education needed for counterinsurgency in Afghanistan, since working with the local population was key to rooting out militants. For instance, the 3rd Brigade, 1st Infantry Division, upon deploying to the Maywand district of Kandahar Province, reported a lack of dialogue with the populace. After engaging in construction projects (demonstrating a permanent presence), the population gained trust in the army, and with that the 3rd Brigade could begin to disrupt the resurgence of the Taliban, which was using the district for supplies and narcotics.

Units of the army were also engaged in training Afghan security forces, ultimately for the purpose of providing the United States with an exit strategy. Units of the 3rd Brigade, 1st Infantry Division, located in the northeast, were training locals to the point that they could train their own peers. This mission also provided for a closer connection between the army and local Afghanis for increased efficiency against militants.

As of January 24, 2009, the army had suffered 341 hostile deaths and 151 nonhostile deaths in Afghanistan, for a total of 492, about six times less than army losses in Iraq. Wounded-in-action casualties accounted for 1,880, with another 340 less seriously wounded, for a total of 2,220, about 10 times less than in Iraq. However, as the U.S. Army prepared to shift its focus from Iraq to Afghanistan in early 2009, higher battle casualties were expected in Afghanistan, especially for the army, which carries the brunt of the coalition responsibilities.

DYLAN A. CYR

See also

Afghanistan, Coalition Combat Operations in, 2002–Present; ENDURING FREEDOM, Operation; ENDURING FREEDOM, Operation, Initial Ground Campaign

References

Bahmanyar, Mir. *Shadow Warriors: A History of the US Army Rangers.* Oxford, UK: Osprey, 2006.

Naylor, Sean. *Not a Good Day to Die: The Untold Story of Operation Anaconda.* New York: Berkley Trade, 2006.

Neville, Leigh. *Special Operations Forces in Iraq (Elite).* Oxford, UK: Osprey, 2008.

Tanner, Stephen. *Afghanistan: A Military History from Alexander the Great to the Fall of the Taliban.* New York: Da Capo, 2003.

United States Army, Iraq War

In the Iraq War (2003–), the U.S. Army deployed more personnel and matériel than any of the other U.S. armed services or those of its allies within the coalition. The ground forces involved were smaller than what most military commanders recommended, however, considerably increasing the risks if the coalition encountered unexpected obstacles. Since 2001 the all-volunteer U.S. Army typically had numbered some 500,000 active-duty soldiers in 10 divisions, with another 500,000 in the Army National Guard and the U.S. Army Reserve. With decreases in army strength since the end of the Vietnam War, and particularly since the end of the Cold War in 1991, reservists and National Guardsmen had taken on a greater

U.S. Army soldiers clear an island in the Tigris River in Iraq on March 26, 2005. (U.S. Department of Defense)

role. Army ground forces were organized as follows: divisions of some 20,000 personnel each; brigades of up to 4,000 individuals each; battalions (800), companies (200), and platoons (30).

U.S. Army general Tommy Franks, commander of U.S. Central Command (CENTCOM), had overall command of U.S. and coalition forces during the invasions of both Afghanistan and Iraq. Following Franks in command of U.S. forces in Iraq have been U.S. Army generals Ricardo Sanchez (June 2003–2004), George W. Casey (2004–2007), David Petraeus (2007–2008), and Raymond Odierno (2008–).

Overall commander of the land component (U.S. Army, U.S. Marine Corps, and coalition forces) in the March–April 2003 invasion of Iraq was U.S. Army lieutenant general David McKiernan, commander of the Third U.S. Army/U.S. Army Forces Central Command. Total army strength in the invasion force was some 55,000 men formed into V Corps in Kuwait, under Lieutenant General William Scott Wallace. He controlled two divisions, part of a third, and a fourth on its way. Engineer (to include bridge-builders), supply, and other units were available to be attached to the combat forces as required. The logistics element included some 2,500 trucks that would support the units moving north into Iraq toward Baghdad.

The lead element of V Corps was the 3rd Infantry Division (Mechanized). Known as the "Rock of the Marne," the 3rd

Division was commanded by Major General Buford C. Blount III and numbered some 18,000–20,000 men. Its major offensive element consisted of some 170 Abrams tanks and 200 Bradley Fighting Vehicles, with close air support from Apache Long Bow tank-killing helicopters and Black Hawk transport helicopters. It also had a brigade-sized artillery unit. The 3rd Infantry Division led the invasion of Iraq from Kuwait. Its mission was to drive north from Kuwait to the west of the Euphrates River and the I Marine Expeditionary Force.

After the invasion started, the 3rd Infantry Division was joined by the 101st Airborne Division and a brigade of the 82nd Airborne Division, which had the mission of securing objectives short of the Iraqi capital of Baghdad. The 101st Airborne Division, known as the "Screaming Eagles," numbered about 20,000 men and was the army's only air assault division. Commanded by Major General David Petraeus and organized as light infantry, it deployed 275 helicopters.

The 2nd Brigade Combat Team of the 82nd Airborne Division, known as the "Falcon Brigade," numbered about 4,000 paratroopers commanded by Colonel Arnold Neil Gordon-Bray. Its mission and that of the 101st was to provide security to bases and supply routes on the way to Baghdad.

The 173rd Airborne Brigade, based in Vicenza, Italy, parachuted into northern Iraq on March 26. Commanded by Colonel

William C. Mayville, its mission was to tie down Iraqi troops there and prevent them from reinforcing to the south, as well as to secure the Kurdish areas there, especially Kirkuk and Mosul. To accomplish this, the 173rd conducted a combat jump (Operation NORTHERN DELAY) to secure Bashur Airfield in northern Iraq. Once this was accomplished, McDonnell Douglas C-17 Globemaster aircraft carried out history's first combat air landing of main battle tanks. Troops of the Special Operations Command, comprising the 75th Ranger Regiment, the 5th Special Forces Group, and the 160th Special Operations Aviation Regiment, were to secure key bridges and operate in the Iraqi desert to cut routes to Syria and occupy areas that might be suitable for the firing of Scud missiles.

Only as the invasion came to an end did the 4th Infantry Division, which had been scheduled to invade northern Iraq from Turkey but had failed to receive permission from the Turkish government for this plan, begin arriving in Kuwait. Commanded by Major General Raymond L. Odierno, it possessed the most up-to-date equipment. The 4th Infantry Division was the army's first digitized division, with its commanders able to track the movement of its vehicles on the battlefield. The fact that it had only begun its movement to Kuwait by March 19, 2003, probably served to mislead Iraqi leader Saddam Hussein into believing that the invasion was still some time off.

Army casualties in the fighting reflect their larger proportionality of personnel in Iraq. As of January 3, 2009, a total of 4,212 Americans had died in Operation IRAQI FREEDOM, with 3,394 of these combat related. Most of the American casualties in IRAQI FREEDOM occurred after the end of the initial invasion of Iraq and the toppling of the Hussein regime at the end of April 2003. The army accounted for 2,455 of those deaths and another 604 from nonhostile deaths, equaling 3,059 of 4,212. The army's total wounded was 21,354 out of a U.S. total of 30,934. Of the army's wounded, 7,139 required medical air transport, signifying serious wounds. In 2009 the army was preparing to refocus its efforts in Afghanistan while slowly drawing down in Iraq.

DYLAN A. CYR AND SPENCER C. TUCKER

See also

Blount, Buford, III; Franks, Tommy Ray; IRAQI FREEDOM, Operation; IRAQI FREEDOM, Operation, Ground Campaign; Iraqi Insurgency; Mayville, William; McKiernan, David Deglan; Petraeus, David Howell; Scud Missiles, U.S. Search for during the Persian Gulf War; United States Army Reserve; United States Marine Corps, Iraq War; Wallace, William Scott

References

Atkinson, Rick. *In the Company of Soldiers: A Chronicle of Combat.* New York: Henry Holt, 2005.

Gerrard, Howard. *U.S. Army Soldier: Baghdad 2003–04 (Warrior).* Oxford, UK: Osprey, 2007.

Keegan, John. *The Iraq War: The Military Offensive, from Victory in 21 Days to the Insurgent Aftermath.* New York: Vintage, 2005.

Murray, Williamson, and Robert H. Scales Jr. *The Iraq War: A Military History.* Cambridge, MA: Belknap, 2005.

Neville, Leigh. *Special Operations Forces in Iraq (Elite).* Oxford, UK: Osprey, 2008.

Zinsmeister, Karl. *Boots on the Ground: A Month with the 82nd Airborne in the Battle for Iraq.* New York: St. Martin's, 2004.

United States Army, Persian Gulf War

The Iraqi invasion on August 2, 1990, prompted the United States government to send military forces to the Persian Gulf region to thwart a potential Iraqi invasion of Saudi Arabia. The first force to arrive in the region was the 82nd Airborne Division. November 1990 brought a further increase in ground support, when on November 8 President George H. W. Bush announced that the VII Corps would be transferred from Germany to the Persian Gulf. The buildup of U.S. and coalition forces in the region was dubbed Operation DESERT SHIELD. Because the Iraqi government did not meet the demands of the United Nations (UN) to abandon Kuwait by the January 15, 1991, deadline, the aerial bombing campaign that opened Operation DESERT STORM began on January 17, 1991. The ground assault against Iraqi troops in Kuwait and Iraq began on February 24.

The command responsibilities of the coalition fell to two men: General H. Norman Schwarzkopf and Saudi Arabian lieutenant general Khalid ibn Sultan ibn Abd al-Aziz al-Saud. Khalid commanded all coalition Arab forces. Schwarzkopf, as commander in chief of U.S. Central Command (CENTCOM), had overall charge of coalition operations in the war with Iraq. Serving beneath him was Lieutenant General John J. Yeosock of the U.S. Army Forces Central Command (ARCENT), who also commanded the U.S. Third Army. Below Yeosock was Lieutenant General Frederick M. Franks Jr., who commanded the VII Corps. Lieutenant General Gary E. Luck commanded the XVIII Airborne Corps. Supporting these combat forces was a vast theater structure, including but not limited to the 22nd Support Command under Major General William Gus Pagonis.

Just prior to the commencement of the ground war, there were approximately 527,000 American soldiers in the Persian Gulf region, of whom nearly 35,000 were women. The entire personnel strength of Third Army totaled 333,565 troops. The battle strength of VII Corps alone, which included the 1st and 3rd Armored Divisions, the 1st Infantry Division, the 1st Cavalry Division, and the 2nd Cavalry Regiment, among other units, numbered 146,321 soldiers. The battle strength of the XVIII Airborne Corps, which included the 82nd and 101st Airborne Divisions, and the 24th Infantry Division (Mechanized) among other units, numbered 116,040 soldiers.

Moving the required supporting manpower and equipment to drive entrenched Iraqi forces from Kuwait proved a daunting task. Commercial airliners as well as ships were chartered to help in the logistics effort. Between August 1990 and February 1991, nearly 500,000 soldiers and 600,000 tons of supplies were flown into the theater of operations. In addition, 3.4 million tons of supplies and equipment along with 6.1 million tons of fuel were shipped to the Persian Gulf by sea. Much of the equipment in

U.S. Army UH-60A Black Hawk helicopters and one AH-64A Apache helicopter, second from right, take off during Operation DESERT SHIELD, August 1990. (U.S. Department of Defense)

Europe was transported via train, barge, and convoy to European ports of debarkation. As complicated as this may seem, moving the matériel from the ports in Saudi Arabia to the inland tactical assembly areas (TAA) was equally as, if not more, difficult. There was a single road that ran from the ports to the TAAs, in which individual tanks, strapped to tractor-trailers, traveled distances of up to 300 miles. This is not to mention the transport of other vital equipment the soldiers needed to perform their missions, let alone such necessities for life as food and water. In all, it took nearly 12 weeks to assemble all the necessary resources.

Filling the gaps in the various divisions was also a complicated undertaking. Some of this was alleviated by the use of reservists, who were mobilized between August 1990 and January 1991. Of the 227,800 mobilized reservists, 47 percent were deployed to the Persian Gulf, serving predominantly in logistics roles. To help bridge language barriers, the Kuwaiti Army recruited Kuwaiti students studying in the United States to be integrated into the numerous combat divisions. For instance, in the VII Corps there were 35 such interpreters, distributed to ensure at least one per division.

Upon the commencement of hostilities, the main objective of the Third Army was to advance from the west of Kuwait and envelop the Iraqi force positioned in Kuwait, thus avoiding the bulk of Iraqi defense positions to the east in the theater. The

XVIII Airborne Corps was to protect the western flank and rear of the advancing VII Corps, which was to bear the brunt of the assault and deliver the decisive blow to the Iraqi Army. As part of its objectives, the XVIII Airborne Corps was tasked with cutting off the main supply road between Baghdad and Kuwait, which would prevent supplies and reinforcements from reaching the Iraqi forces as well as thwart any attempt of an Iraqi retreat via that route. This task went to the 101st Airborne Division, while one brigade of the 82nd Airborne, along with the French 6th Light Armored Division, covered the flank and rear of the 101st, thus creating a screen. The 24th Infantry Division, along with the 3rd Armored Calvary Regiment, also under the command of the XVIII Airborne Corps, was designated to take the key bridge crossing the Euphrates River just west of the town of Nasiriyah.

The attack of VII Corps began by a diversionary advance up the Wadi al-Batin corridor by the 1st Calvary Division, after which the main assault was led by the 1st Armored Division and the 2nd Armored Cavalry Regiment. The first objective was the logistics center of Busayyah, which was ultimately taken by the 1st Armored Division. Near this point, approximately 60 miles into Iraq, VII Corps turned east toward Kuwait to pursue its premier objective, the Iraqi Republican Guard. General Franks's concept was to concentrate his forces to defeat the renowned soldiers. However,

Army Left Hook during the Persian Gulf War

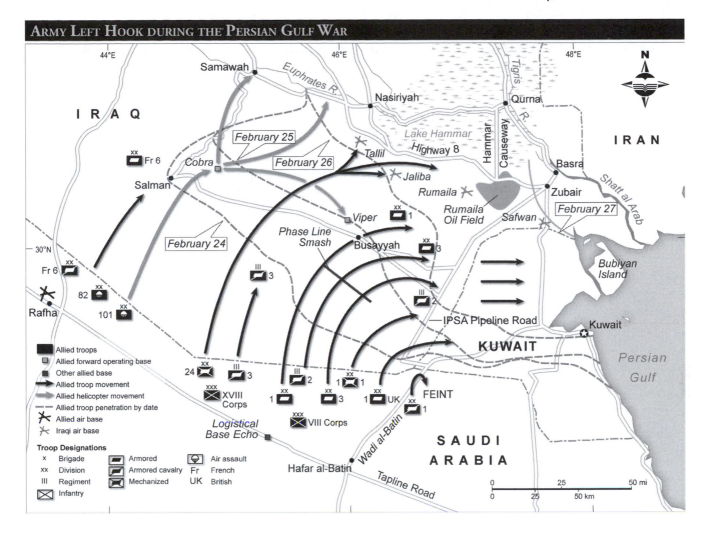

prior to this plan being executed, the Iraqi 12th Armored Division and the Republican Guards Tawakalna Division, in concert with smaller units, tried to withdraw from Kuwait. The division slammed into the 2nd Armored Cavalry, and on February 26, in the midst of a sandstorm, the two sides engaged in one of the most intense battles of the conflict. On February 27 coalition forces entered Kuwait while the 1st Armored Division battled the Iraqi Republican Guard in the Battle of Medina Ridge, in Iraq. Later that day the war was over; Kuwait was liberated, and the Iraqis had agreed to a temporary cease-fire.

As with any war, new technology influenced the way the U.S. Army fought in the Persian Gulf. This was the first major conflict utilizing the Global Positioning System (GPS), which proved invaluable. However, there were not enough GPS devices to be fixed on all of the combat vehicles. In the case of the VII Corps alone, there were only approximately 3,000 GPS devices for the 40,000-plus vehicles. As a result, the GPS devices were distributed to principal commanders and vehicles.

Another new form of technology utilized by the U.S. Army was tactical satellite telephones. These devices gave commanders in the middle of the desert the ability not only to reach their superiors in the United States or Europe, but also to communicate with other army personnel within the Persian Gulf region. Additionally, the capabilities of the personal computer and electronic mail, more commonly known as e-mail, were also put to use. This further enabled staff officers at every echelon of command to communicate with one another and their superiors.

The U.S. Army also utilized new weapons, such as the Patriot missile. Although originally intended to strike against enemy aircraft, the Patriot was modified and utilized as an antimissile system. Ultimately, this system possibly shot down as many as 70 percent of the Iraqi Scud missiles launched into Saudi Arabia and 40 percent of those launched at targets in Israel. (These figures still remain hugely controversial, however.) The Abrams M1A1 tank, equipped with a 120-mm gun, was the primary tank used by the U.S. Army in this war; however, the 2nd Brigade of the 1st Infantry Division went into battle with the older Abrams M1, equipped with a 105-mm cannon. Also used was the then-new Abrams M1A1 HA (abbreviated "HA" for heavy armor), although not on the scale of its predecessor. Despite M1A1's superiority to the Soviet-built Iraqi T-72 tank, its poor gas mileage slowed the advancing American forces.

Other new combat vehicles included the M2 Bradley Infantry Fighting Vehicle and the M3 Bradley Cavalry Fighting Vehicle.

1348 United States Army National Training Center

Other heavy combat vehicles were also used, such as the M9 Armored Combat Earthmover. The typical combat soldier was also equipped with either an M-16A1 or M-16A2 rifle.

Fortunately, actual American battlefield casualties paled in comparison to initial estimates, which had projected that nearly 1,500 soldiers would be killed in action and another 8,500 wounded. In reality, the U.S. Army and Marines combined suffered 122 battle-related deaths, of which 35 were due to friendly fire. In addition, there were 131 noncombat-related fatalities. Of this total, 15 American women in uniform lost their lives in the Persian Gulf. Approximately 450 American soldiers were officially declared wounded in combat, with 72 labeled as friendly-fire accidents. The U.S. Army turned in a stellar performance during Operation DESERT STORM, proving that the post–Cold War U.S. military establishment could defeat a stout foe with great mobility, speed, and decisiveness. The army's performance also seemed to put to rest the so-called Vietnam Syndrome.

ROB SHAFER

See also

DESERT SHIELD, Operation; DESERT STORM, Operation; DESERT STORM, Operation, Ground Operations; Franks, Frederick Melvin, Jr.; Luck, Gary Edward; Saud, Khalid ibn Sultan ibn Abd al-Aziz al-; Schwarzkopf, H. Norman, Jr.; Vietnam Syndrome; Yeosock, John J.

References

Atkinson, Rick. *Crusade: The Untold Story of the Persian Gulf War.* New York: Mariner Books, 1994.

Bourque, Stephen A. *Jayhawk! The VII Corps in the Persian Gulf War.* Washington, DC: Department of the Army, 2002.

Doughty, Robert A., and Ira D. Gruber. *Warfare in the Western World,* Vol. 2, *Military Operations since 1871.* Lexington, MA: D. C. Heath, 1996.

Freedman, Lawrence, and Efraim Karsh. *The Gulf Conflict, 1990–1991: Diplomacy and War in the New World Order.* Princeton, NJ: Princeton University Press, 1993.

Gordon, Michael R., and General Bernard E. Trainor. *The Generals' War: The Inside Story of the Conflict in the Gulf.* New York: Little, Brown, 1995.

Millett, Allan R., and Peter Maslowski. *For the Common Defense: A Military History of the United States of America.* New York: Free Press, 1994.

United States Army National Training Center

U.S. Army training installation located at Fort Irwin, California. Fort Irwin and the National Training Center (NTC) are located approximately 37 miles northeast of Barstow, California, in the High Mojave Desert, about midway between Los Angeles, California, and Las Vegas, Nevada. The NTC serves as the army's foremost combat training facility, and it is used largely to ready U.S. military personnel to wage war in harsh desert environments. Fort Irwin is a sprawling facility, covering some 1,000 square miles, and has an average daily population of 16,000–20,000 people. It is home to approximately 5,000 active-duty personnel and their dependants. In addition, some 3,500 civilians work full-time on the post, most of whom are contractors of various sorts and teachers.

Fort Irwin began its modern history as an antiaircraft range in 1941, although by 1944 it had been inactivated and placed on reserve status. In 1951, during the Korean War, Fort Irwin reopened as an armored combat training area. Its location in the desert and the sparse population of the surrounding areas made it an ideal location for this type of training. In 1971 the post was again inactivated, and for a number of years it was used as a training facility for National Guard units. In 1979, when the army decided to establish the NTC, Fort Irwin was selected, thanks to its relatively remote location and desert climate that approximates the climate of the Middle East. Once established, the NTC became—and remains—the U.S. Army's best and most prestigious training area.

The army currently bases the 11th Armored Cavalry Regiment at the NTC as the official opposing force for those units rotating through Fort Irwin for training. In the past, it has also used infantry and airborne divisions as the opposing force. Naturally, there is a focus on armored warfare doctrine and maneuvers, but thousands of infantry soldiers have also been trained here, honing their skills in desert warfare. In 1993 the army built an elaborate training facility on the post for military operations in urbanized terrain. After the September 11, 2001, terror attacks, the army has shifted the NTC's focus to counterinsurgency operations, first in reaction to the war in Afghanistan, and later to Operation IRAQI FREEDOM. Thousands of American soldiers serving in Afghanistan and Iraq have received training at the NTC.

PAUL G. PIERPAOLI JR.

See also

Counterinsurgency; United States Army, Afghanistan War; United States Army, Iraq War; United States Army, Persian Gulf War

References

Bluhm, Raymond K. *U.S. Army: A Complete History.* Westport, CT: Hugh Lauter Levin Associates, 2005.

Chapman, Anne W. *The Origins and Development of the National Training Center, 1976–1984.* Fort Monroe, VA: Office of the Command Historian, 1992.

United States Army Reserve

The U.S. Army Reserve (USAR) has its origins in U.S. Senate Bill 1424, passed on April 23, 1908, that created the Medical Reserve Corps. Four years later, the Regular United States Army Reserve was established. The National Defense Act of 1916 further established the Reserve Officer Corps, the Enlisted Reserve Corps, and the Reserve Officers' Training Corps (ROTC). The U.S. Army Reserve Command (USARC) was activated on October 1, 1992, and 95 percent of all USAR units belong to this command.

The USAR served essentially as a strategic reserve force until the dissolution of the Soviet Union in December 1991. The post–Cold War environment and the Global War on Terror, which began after the September 11, 2001, terror attacks on the United States, required that the USAR be transformed into an operational force. By the end of the 1990s, the USAR was providing almost 40 percent of the army's combat support and combat service support units. More than 92 percent of these units were assigned specific missions in the army's war plans. The validity of concentrating support missions in the USAR has been witnessed by its performance in the Middle East wars since 1990.

President George H. W. Bush, for example, obtained congressional approval to mobilize the reserve component forces of all the services for Operations DESERT STORM and DESERT SHIELD (1990–1991). On August 22, 1990, just 20 days after the Iraqi invasion of Kuwait, he authorized the secretary of defense to order reserve component units and individuals to active duty pursuant to Title 10, U.S.C. 673b. The air war began in January 1991 with 504 USAR units totaling 49,860 personnel.

Also, 20,920 individual ready reserve soldiers (IRRs), individual mobilization augmentees (IMAs), and 1,000 retirees volunteered or were also ordered to active duty during DESERT STORM. On February 24, 1991, the ground campaign began with 640 USAR units totaling 83,741 personnel. In total, more than 84,000 USAR intelligence, logistics, transportation, medical services, and construction personnel participated in the Persian Gulf War.

In the immediate aftermath of the September 11, 2001, attacks, the 77th Regional Support Command established Emergency Operations Centers to provide support requested by the New York City police and fire departments, the Federal Emergency Management Agency (FEMA), and the Federal Bureau of Investigation (FBI). The provisioning of such support by the USAR is required by Department of Defense Directive 3025.1, Military Support to Civilian Authorities. Just 72 hours after the attack, the 311th Quartermaster Company (Mortuary Affairs) from Puerto Rico began searching for human remains in the Pentagon and surrounding area. Within weeks of the attack, between 1,500 and 1,600 USAR soldiers in intelligence, military police, and logistics had been called to active duty to support Operation ENDURING FREEDOM. By March 2002 that number had risen to 8,800. At the end of 2001, 9,020 U.S. Army Reserve soldiers had been called up under the September 14, 2001, partial mobilization. Of these, 7,384 were monthly drilling reserve soldiers in 273 Troop Program Units (TPUs). The remaining 1,636 were IMAs and IRRs. There were also approximately 2,000 Active Guard Reserve (AGRs) personnel supporting missions on a daily basis.

Prior to Operation ANACONDA (March 1–18, 2002) in Afghanistan, the 911th Forward Surgical Team supported the 10th Mountain Division. USAR Public Affairs soldiers deployed with the 101st Airborne Division (Air Assault). USAR engineer soldiers improved the airport at Kandahar, and USAR medical personnel treated casualties transported to Bagram Air Base. USAR Civil Affairs soldiers repaired and built infrastructure to assist the Afghanis recover from nearly 22 years of war. The USAR's 75th Division (Training Support) assisted in training the Afghan National Army. The 345th Military Intelligence Detachment assisted the Coalition Forces Land Component Command (CFLCC) in intelligence collection and targeting of Taliban and Al Qaeda forces and individuals.

Operation IRAQI FREEDOM began on March 20, 2003, and has included many USAR forces. Most of the USAR units deployed in support were combat service support units that conducted port operations, maintenance, supply, and fuel operations. The 7th U.S. Army Reserve Command, based in Germany, mobilized and deployed 19 of its 22 units, and its commanding general was detailed as the director of the U.S. Army Europe Deployment Operations Center, responsible for planning and managing the movement of 33,000 soldiers and all their equipment from Europe to the Persian Gulf area of operations. The 459th Engineer Company built bridges across the Diyala and Euphrates rivers to support the I Marine Expeditionary Force's advance on Baghdad in April 2003. The 98th Division (Institutional Training) deployed to Iraq in late 2004 to assist the Multi-National Security Transition Command–Iraq (MNSTC-I) in training the new Iraqi Army and was the first USAR unit to do so.

By the end of 2003 the USAR had mobilized 2,322 units, and 71,587 USAR solders were serving on active duty for the Global War on Terror (Operation NOBLE EAGLE) and Operations ENDURING FREEDOM and IRAQI FREEDOM. From September 11, 2001, to October 2004, the USAR provided 36 percent of the army combat service support capability, 13 percent of the medical forces, and 27 percent of the engineer capabilities required for Operations ENDURING FREEDOM and IRAQI FREEDOM. In 2004, 1,615 units were mobilized. In 2005, 1,869 units were mobilized. Since September 11, 2001, the USAR has mobilized more than 180,000 personnel to combat terrorism around the world and to defend the U.S. homeland against terrorist attacks. More than 56,000 of them have deployed multiple times. As of December 19, 2009, there were 31,516 Army Reserve Soldiers activated for Operations NOBLE EAGLE, ENDURING FREEDOM, and IRAQI FREEDOM.

DONALD R. DUNNE

See also

DESERT STORM, Operation; DESERT SHIELD, Operation; ENDURING FREEDOM, Operation; Global War on Terror; IRAQI FREEDOM, Operation; September 11 Attacks; United States Army, Afghanistan War; United States Army, Iraq War; United States Army, Persian Gulf War; United States Marine Corps Reserve; United States Navy Reserve

References

"Army Reserve Soldiers Train Afghan National Army." *Army Reserve Magazine* 49(4) (2003): 1.

Bensburg, Robert, Michael Werner, and Christina Steiner. *The Role of the Army Reserve in the 11 September Attacks: New York City.* Fort McPherson, GA: Office of the Command Historian, Headquarters, United States Army Reserve Command, 2003.

Citizen-Soldiers of the Nation: A Brief History of the United States Army Reserve. Fort McPherson, GA: Office of the Command Historian, Headquarters, United States Army Reserve Command, 2001.

Coker, Kathryn R. *The 2004/2005 Biannual Army Reserve Historical Summary.* OCH Pub 6-4. Fort McPherson, GA: Office of the

Command Historian, Headquarters, United States Army Reserve Command, 2007.

Currie, James T., and Richard B. Crossland. *Twice the Citizen: A History of the United States Army Reserve, 1908–1995.* Department of the Army Pamphlet 140-14. Washington, DC: U.S. Government Printing Office, 1997.

Fontenot, Gregory, et al. *On Point: The United States Army in Iraqi Freedom.* Annapolis, MD: Naval Institute Press, 2005.

Musheno, Michael, and Susan Ross. *Deployed: How Reservists Bear the Burden of Iraq.* Ann Arbor: University of Michigan Press, 2008.

Woodward, Bob. *The Commanders.* New York: Simon and Schuster, 1991.

United States Central Command

One of 10 unified U.S. combatant commands responsible for U.S. military planning regarding 27 nations, stretching from the Horn of Africa through the Persian Gulf states to Central Asia. The U.S. Central Command (CENTCOM) has its primary headquarters at MacDill Air Force Base in Tampa, Florida, and a forward headquarters at Camp al Sayliyah, Qatar, to handle the demands of operations in Iraq and the Middle East.

The Ronald Reagan administration established CENTCOM on January 1, 1983, to deal with growing instability in the Middle East following the Islamic Revolution in Iran and the Soviet invasion of Afghanistan, both in 1979. Policy makers were worried that the Soviet Union or one of its client states would invade oil-producing nations and deprive the Western powers of access to this vital resource. CENTCOM was built from the assets of the Rapid Deployment Joint Task Force (RDJTF). Its first commander was General Robert C. Kingston. The original intent was that CENTCOM would not be based in the region but instead rely on political allies to provide facilities on an as-needed basis. As such, CENTCOM to this day is not assigned combat units but instead consists of five component commands that are assigned forces from their parent service as the mission requires. These include the U.S. Army Forces Central Command (ARCENT), U.S. Central Command Air Forces (USCENTAF), U.S. Marine Forces Central Command (USMARCENT), U.S. Naval Forces Central Command (USNAVCENT), and U.S. Special Operations Command Central (SOCCENT).

CENTCOM engaged in its first combat mission in August 1990 when Iraqi president Saddam Hussein ordered his armed forces to invade Kuwait. In Operation DESERT SHIELD, CENTCOM commander

CENTCOM (United States Central Command) commander General Tommy R. Franks and his deputy, Lieutenant General John P. Abizaid, listen to a briefing on the progress of Operation IRAQI FREEDOM at CENTCOM's forward headquarters in Qatar. (CENTCOM Public Affairs)

General H. Norman Schwarzkopf supervised the deployment of forces to Saudi Arabia to deter Hussein from advancing into Saudi Arabia. With a broad international consensus and the assistance of Saudi Arabia's logistics facilities, in Operation DESERT STORM, CENTCOM led the invasion of Kuwait and Iraq in February 1991 with a nine-division multinational force. The Iraqi Army was ejected from Kuwait in short order, but President George H. W. Bush decided to terminate the war without toppling the Hussein regime. For the next 12 years, CENTCOM contained Hussein's power by maintaining a permanent ground presence to the south of Iraq and enforcing no-fly zones in the north and south of the country.

Since the terror attacks of September 11, 2001, CENTCOM has become the central front in the Global War on Terror. In the late autumn of 2001, CENTCOM successfully toppled the Taliban government in Afghanistan as part of Operation ENDURING FREEDOM to destroy the Al Qaeda organization. Two years later, in March 2003, CENTCOM launched Operation IRAQI FREEDOM and ended the rule of Saddam Hussein. To support further stabilization and counterterrorism operations in these countries and the region as a whole, CENTCOM operates several joint and multinational subordinate commands: Multi-National Force–Iraq (MNF-I), Multi-National Security Transition Command–Iraq (MNSTC-I), Combined Forces Command Afghanistan, Combined Joint Task Force–Horn of Africa, and Joint Task Force Lebanon.

On February 7, 2007, the U.S. Army announced that a U.S. Africa Command (USAFRICOM) would be organized and take responsibility for CENTCOM's African portfolio, which had included Djibouti, except for Egypt. Almost all of Africa had been under European Command (EUCOM), however. EUCOM retained both Israel and Turkey.

Among CENTCOM's more notable commanders have been U.S. Army general Schwarzkopf (November 1988–August 1991), Marine Corps general Anthony Zinni (August 1997–July 2000), U.S. Army general Tommy R. Franks (July 2000–July 2003), and U.S. Army general John P. Abizaid (July 2003–March 2007). In March 2007 Admiral William Fallon assumed command, the first naval officer to hold that position. He resigned in March 2008 following public remarks that were seen as critical of the George W. Bush administration's position regarding possible hostilities with Iran. Fallon was replaced by acting commander army lieutenant general Martin Dempsey. U.S. Army general David Petraeus was confirmed by the U.S. Senate in July 2008 and assumed command that September.

JAMES E. SHIRCLIFFE JR.

See also

Al Qaeda; DESERT SHIELD, Operation; DESERT STORM, Operation; ENDURING FREEDOM, Operation; Fallon, William Joseph; Global War on Terror; IRAQI FREEDOM, Operation; Petraeus, David Howell; Schwarzkopf, H. Norman, Jr.

References

DeLong, Michael, with Noah Lukeman. *Inside CENTCOM: The Unvarnished Truth about the Wars in Afghanistan and Iraq.* Washington, DC: Regnery, 2004.
Eshel, David. *The U.S. Rapid Deployment Forces.* New York: Arco, 1985.

United States Coast Guard, Iraq War

From the very outset of Middle East operations, the U.S. Coast Guard's training and experience in these and other maritime activities played an important part in Operation IRAQI FREEDOM. Late in 2002, coast guard headquarters alerted various units in the service's Pacific Area (PACAREA) and Atlantic Area (LANTAREA) for possible deployment to the Middle East. From November 2002 through January 2003, these units began activation activities for an expected deployment in early 2003. In January, PACAREA's first major units deployed to the Persian Gulf, including the high-endurance cutter *Boutwell* (WHEC-719) and the oceangoing buoy tender *Walnut* (WLB-205). Their responsibilities included maritime interdiction operations (MIO), and the *Walnut,* in conjunction with members of the Coast Guard's National Strike Force, would lead possible oil-spill containment operations.

LANTAREA provided many units of its own, sending the high-endurance cutter *Dallas* (WHEC-716) to the Mediterranean to support and escort Military Sealift Command shipping and coalition battle groups in that theater of operations. It also sent four 110-foot patrol boats (WPBs) to Italy with support personnel and termed their base of operations Patrol Forces Mediterranean (PATFORMED) and sent a set of four WPBs to the Persian Gulf with a Bahrain-based command called Patrol Forces Southwest Asia (PATFORSWA).

The service also activated Port Security Units (PSUs) and law enforcement boarding teams (LEDETs), which had each proven successful in the 1991 Persian Gulf War. LANTAREA sent PSU 309 (Port Clinton, Ohio) to Italy to support PATFORMED while PACAREA sent PSU 311 (San Pedro, California) and PSU 313 (Tacoma, Washington) to Kuwait to protect the Kuwait Naval Base and the port of Shuaiba, respectively. LEDET personnel initially served on board the WPBs and then switched to navy patrol craft to perform MIO operations.

At 8:00 p.m. on March 19, 2003, coalition forces launched IRAQI FREEDOM. By the time hostilities commenced, all coast guard units were manned and ready. On March 20, personnel from PSU 311 and PSU 313 helped secure Iraq's offshore oil terminals. On March 21, littoral combat operations began and the 110-foot *Adak* served picket duty farther north than any other coalition unit along the Khor Abd Allah waterway. The *Adak* captured the first Iraqi maritime prisoners of the war, whose patrol boat had been destroyed upstream. On that same day, the *Adak* participated in the capture of two Iraqi tugs and a mine-laying barge.

Once initial naval operations ceased, coast guard units began securing port facilities and waterways for the shipment of humanitarian aid to Iraq. On March 24, PSU 311 personnel deployed to the Iraqi port of Umm Qasr, and four days later the 110-foot *Wrangell* led the first humanitarian aid shipment to that port facility. In addition to their primary mission of boarding vessels in the northern Persian Gulf, Coast Guard LEDET teams secured the Iraqi shoreline from caches of weapons and munitions. Buoy tender *Walnut,* the original mission of which included environmental

The U.S. Coast Guard cutter *Adak*, a 110-foot patrol boat homeported in Highlands, New Jersey, patrols the North Arabian Sea off the coast of Iraq on March 6, 2003. The *Adak* was one of four such coast guard patrol boats in the Persian Gulf in support of Operation IRAQI FREEDOM. (U.S. Coast Guard)

protection from sabotaged oil facilities, surveyed and completely restored aids to navigation markers for the shipping lanes leading to Iraq's ports.

On May 1, President George W. Bush declared an end to formal combat operations in Iraq; however, within a year the Coast Guard suffered its first and only casualty of IRAQI FREEDOM. On April 24, 2004, terrorists navigated three small vessels armed with high explosives toward Iraq's offshore oil terminals. During this attack, the navy patrol craft *Firebolt* intercepted one of the suspicious watercraft, and members of LEDET 403 and navy crewmen proceeded toward the suspicious vessel in a rigid-hull inflatable boat (RHIB). Terrorists on board the small vessel detonated their explosive cargo as the RHIB approached, overturning the boat and killing LEDET member Nathan Bruckenthal and two navy personnel. Bruckenthal was the first Coast Guardsman killed in combat since the Vietnam War, and he received full military honors in funeral services at Arlington National Cemetery.

During Operation IRAQI FREEDOM, the Coast Guard performed the same vital functions that have long represented its core missions, such as in-shore patrol, MIO operations, and port security operations. The PSUs performed their port security duties efficiently despite the fact that their units were split up between three separate port facilities and two oil terminals. The WPBs operated for many hours without maintenance in waters too shallow for any major navy assets and served as the coalition fleet's workhorses in boarding, escort, and force protection duties. The personnel of PATFORMED and PSU 309 demonstrated that Coast Guard units could serve in areas that lacked any form of Coast Guard infrastructure. PATFORSWA performed its support mission effectively even though the Coast Guard had never established such a support detachment. Fortunately, *Walnut* never had to employ its oil spill capability, but it proved indispensable for MIO operations and aids to navigation (ATON) work on the Khor Abd Allah waterway. The *Dallas* and *Boutwell* provided logistical support and force protection and MIO operations with their boarding teams.

WILLIAM H. THIESEN

See also

Military Sealift Command; United States Coast Guard, Persian Gulf War; United States Navy, Iraq War

References

Schneller, Robert J., Jr. *Anchor of Resolve: A History of U.S. Naval Forces Central Command/Fifth Fleet.* Washington, DC: Naval Historical Center, 2007.

Seeger, Eric, ed. *The United States Coast Guard: The Shield of Freedom, 2005.* Tampa, FL: Government Group Services, 2005.

Tripsas, Basil, Patrick Roth, and Renee Fye. *Coast Guard Operations during Operation Iraqi Freedom.* Alexandria, Va.: CNA Corporation, 2004.

United States Coast Guard, Persian Gulf War

Units and personnel of the U.S. Coast Guard and its predecessor services have served with distinction in every major American conflict since the founding of the United States, and the Persian Gulf War operations DESERT SHIELD and DESERT STORM proved no exception to this rule. The Coast Guard provided essential support for naval and land-based military operations that the U.S. Navy was unable to undertake. These Coast Guard activities focused on, but were not limited to, marine safety, vessel boarding, port security, and environmental protection operations.

During Operation DESERT SHIELD, which began in August 1990, Coast Guard operations served largely to ensure the safe conduct of military shipping to the Persian Gulf and enforcement of United Nations (UN) sanctions in the theater of operations. Within days of the August 2, 1990, invasion of Kuwait by Iraqi forces, President George H. W. Bush ordered the deployment of U.S. military forces to Saudi Arabia in DESERT SHIELD. By August 10, Coast Guard Marine Safety Offices (MSOs) had mobilized personnel to inspect the nearly 80 Ready Reserve Fleet (RRF) vessels activated for sea duty. MSOs throughout the nation also instituted a flexible merchant marine manning and licensing program to expedite the movement of RRF vessels. In addition, Coast Guard MSOs became responsible for port security detachments at port facilities within their respective areas of responsibility. This major effort involved overseeing security for port facilities and supervising the loading of explosives and hazardous material on board Military Sealift Command vessels bound for the Persian Gulf.

By August 16, 1990, U.S. forces initiated maritime interdiction operations consistent with UN sanctions. At the request of the Joint Chiefs of Staff, the Coast Guard committed 10 four-person law-enforcement boarding teams (LEDETs) to serve with U.S. maritime interception forces. Within two weeks of instituting maritime interdiction operations, a Coast Guard LEDET had boarded its first Iraqi-flagged vessel. In addition, the commandant of the Coast Guard designated a seven-man liaison staff to serve as Operational Command for Coast Guard forces, such as the LEDETS, that were deployed to the theater of operations.

The Persian Gulf War set many precedents for Coast Guard military operations. On August 22 President Bush authorized the call-up of reservists in support of military operations. A total of 950 Coast Guard reservists were called to active duty, and more than 500 of them were members of the Coast Guard's newly formed Port Security Units (PSUs). PSU 303 (Milwaukee, Wisconsin) became the first such unit deployed overseas when it was stationed at Dammam, Saudi Arabia. On September 22, PSU 301 (Buffalo, New York) was deployed to Jubail, Saudi Arabia, and on November 14, PSU 302 (Port Clinton, Ohio) deployed to Bahrain.

On January 16, 1991, the commencement of Operation DESERT STORM altered Coast Guard operations at home and abroad. It increased the level and tempo of the MSOs' activities as they stepped up land-based security patrols around key military and commercial waterfront facilities and enforced waterside security zones to defend against terrorist attacks. Overseas, the Coast Guard's LEDET personnel helped clear Iraqi oil platforms, securing 11 such platforms and aiding in the capture of 23 prisoners.

With the added threat of environmental warfare carried out by Iraqi forces the Coast Guard assumed yet another unprecedented mission, that of environmental protection in a war zone. On February 13, 1991, two Coast Guard Beechcraft HU-25A Falcon jets, equipped with oil-detection equipment, flew from Air Station Cape Cod to Saudi Arabia. They were joined by two Coast Guard Lockheed HC-130 Hercules cargo aircraft, which transported spare parts and support packages. The Falcons were deployed for 84 days, providing daily updated surface analysis of the location, condition, and drift projections of spilled oil to the Coast Guard–led U.S. Interagency Assessment Team.

On February 28 coalition offensive operations ceased, and on April 11 the UN declared a formal cease-fire ending the Persian Gulf War. On April 21, when coalition naval forces entered Kuwait's Mina Ash Shuwaikh Harbor, they selected a Coast Guard tactical port security boat from PSU 301 to lead the way. This event symbolized how the numerically small Coast Guard forces played an important role in military operations. The MSOs ensured a nearly 100 percent ready rate of RRF vessels, and LEDET personnel either led or supported 60 percent of the 600 boardings. A total of nearly 1,000 Coast Guard reservists were called to active duty for DESERT SHIELD and DESERT STORM, and two-thirds of them served in the first successful overseas deployment of PSUs. Coast Guard aviation units deployed in theater mapped more than 40,000 square miles of the Persian Gulf, while their aircraft maintained a readiness rate of nearly 100 percent. There were no Coast Guard fatalities during the conflict.

WILLIAM H. THIESEN

See also
DESERT SHIELD, Operation; DESERT STORM, Operation; United States Navy, Persian Gulf War

References
Marolda, Edward, and Robert Schneller. *Shield and Sword: The United States Navy and the Persian Gulf War*. Annapolis, MD: U.S. Naval Institute Press, 2001.

Matthews, James K., and Cora J. Holt. *So Many, So Much, So Far, So Fast: United States Transportation Command and Strategic Deployment for Operation Desert Shield/Desert Storm*. Washington, DC: Joint History Office, Office of the Chairman of the Joint Chiefs of Staff and Research Center, United States Transportation Command, 1996.

Pokrant, Marvin. *Desert Storm at Sea: What the Navy Really Did*. Westport, CT: Greenwood, 1999.

United States Congress and the Iraq War

In October 2002, five months prior to the March 2003 U.S. invasion of Iraq, the U.S. Congress granted President George W. Bush unprecedented war-making authority regarding Iraq. The resolution stated, incorrectly as events on the ground later showed, that Iraq possessed weapons of mass destruction (WMDs) that posed a threat to U.S. national security and that Iraq served as a base for the Al Qaeda terrorist network. With the support of the leaders of

Speaker of the House Nancy Pelosi (D-Calif.), flanked by House majority whip James E. Clyburn (D-S.C.), left, and Rep. Patrick Murphy (D-Pa.), right, meets reporters on Capitol Hill in Washington, D.C., on March 23, 2007, after a sharply divided House approved an Iraq funding bill that included a timetable for bringing U.S. troops home. (AP/Wide World Photos)

both parties, the House of Representatives adopted the resolution on October 10, 2002, by a vote of 296 to 133, and the Senate passed the resolution the following day by a vote of 77 to 23.

Critics of Operation IRAQI FREEDOM noted how experts who questioned claims that Iraq still had WMDs or ties to Al Qaeda were largely prevented from expressing their views at congressional hearings. Also silenced were those who challenged administration claims of Iraqi links to Al Qaeda or raised concerns about potential instability and armed resistance following a U.S. occupation of Iraq. It was subsequently learned that few members of Congress had actually read some of the more detailed and nuanced government intelligence reports that questioned the presence of WMDs in Iraq and that country's link to Al Qaeda. Virtually all Republicans and many Democrats were apparently convinced that authorizing the use of force was necessary to defend American interests. Some Democrats likely supported the resolution as part of a political calculation. That is, if the war were successful, they did not want to be on record as having opposed a popular war. If they voted to authorize the use of force, and the war proved to be unsuccessful or unpopular, it was assumed that voters would be more prone to blame Bush and the Republicans rather than the Democratic members of Congress who had supported him. Others claimed later that they assumed the Bush administration would use the resolution as a tool to bluff down Iraqi president Saddam Hussein, short of war.

International legal scholars, as well as Secretary General of the United Nations (UN) Kofi Annan, asserted that the U.S.-led invasion of Iraq was a violation of the UN Charter. That document prohibits war except for self-defense or when authorized by the UN Security Council. Thus, the congressional vote has been widely interpreted as a bipartisan rebuke of the post–World War II consensus against wars of aggression and an endorsement of American unilateralism.

The majority of Democrats, as well as some Republicans, later expressed regrets over their votes, although in most cases this did not take place until early 2006, when public opinion polls began showing a majority of the American public expressing opposition to the war. Exit polls in the midterm 2006 elections showed that such opposition was the single most important factor in repudiating the Republicans and electing a Democratic majority in Congress. Democratic lawmakers were then subjected to increasing pressure by their constituents to challenge the Bush administration's Iraq War policy.

In previous decades, Congress had shown a willingness to eliminate funding for unpopular overseas U.S. military operations over the objections of the executive branch, but the leadership of the new Democratic majority largely rejected that option. Instead, in 2007 there were several unsuccessful attempts to link supplemental appropriations to specific timetables for a phased withdrawal from Iraq. Democrats also called for precise benchmarks to be met by the Iraqi government, as well as other attempts to assert legislative influence over the war. Some of the more liberal legislators continued to raise moral and legal issues.

However, most of the growing number of congressional opponents emphasized concerns about whether the war was actually winnable, or whether the United States had become embroiled in a civil war among competing Iraqi factions formerly held in check by Hussein's ruthless regime, but let loose by the U.S. invasion. This thinking became increasingly apparent as a number of traditionally hawkish legislators with close ties to the military, such as Democratic representative John Murtha, began pushing for a U.S. withdrawal in late 2006. By the summer of 2007, even fairly hawkish Republicans, like Virginia senator John Warner, Indiana senator Richard Lugar, and Kentucky senator Mitch McConnell, were advocating a fundamental change of course in Iraq. While stopping short of advocating an immediate withdrawal of troops, these senators made it clear that the Bush administration had to change its policies in Iraq. The apparent success of the 2007–2008 troop surge and revised U.S. counterinsurgency strategy in Iraq, as well as the change in American administration, has tended to temper, if not eliminate, congressional criticism. In the spring of 2009 there was a rise in violence in Iraq. However, the new Barack Obama administration had already announced its intent to shift the focus of U.S. combat actions to Afghanistan, a move that many congressional critics of the Bush administration had previously called for.

STEPHEN ZUNES

See also

Al Qaeda; Annan, Kofi; Bush, George Walker; IRAQI FREEDOM, Operation; Weapons of Mass Destruction

References

Byrd, Robert C. "Preserving Constitutional War Powers." *Mediterranean Quarterly* 14(3) (Summer 2003): 1–5.

Phillips, David L. *Losing Iraq: Inside the Postwar Reconstruction Fiasco.* Boulder, CO: Westview, 2005.

Ricks, Thomas E. *Fiasco: The American Military Adventure in Iraq.* New York: Penguin, 2006.

United States Congress and the Persian Gulf War

Prior to the beginning of hostilities in Operation DESERT STORM, and during the implantation of Operation DESERT SHIELD from August 1990 to January 1991, the U.S. Congress played an active role in oversight of the growing crisis with Iraq. Iraq invaded Kuwait on August 2, 1990, and annexed that small nation. This action provided Iraqi president Saddam Hussein with major additional oil revenues and greater maritime access to the Persian Gulf. It also posed a threat to Saudi Arabia, a key U.S. ally in the region.

President George H. W. Bush responded to Hussein's action with an executive order imposing an embargo on Iraq and freezing its assets. On August 2, both the House and Senate voted unanimously to impose sanctions against Iraq. Bush also ordered the deployment of U.S. troops to Saudi Arabia to prevent an Iraqi invasion there, beginning Operation DESERT SHIELD, which eventually included an international coalition of 30 nations providing varying modes of military support. Another 18 nations provided nonmilitary support.

As passed by Congress in 1973, the War Powers Resolution requires presidents to consult with Congress before directing the military to engage in hostile activity; submit a written report to Congress within 48 hours of the introduction of U.S. forces into hostilities; and withdraw forces within 60 days (with a provision for an additional 30-day extension). Initially, the Bush administration did not report on the situation to the Congress as a whole because, technically, there were no hostilities. The only member of Congress informed of the initial deployment was Senator Sam Nunn (D-Ga.), chairman of the Senate Armed Services Committee.

President Bush was wary about seeking a vote from Congress authorizing the use of force. Part of this reluctance stemmed from political issues, for the Democrats controlled both houses of Congress. Yet beyond that there was persistent talk about the so-called Vietnam Syndrome, which allegedly had rendered the U.S. government hesitant to engage in any major confrontation out of fear that it might turn into another Vietnam War–like quagmire.

The Bush administration carried this burden quite seriously. During a White House meeting with senior Republican congressional leaders shortly after the Iraq invasion, Bush advised them of his intent. Congressman Mickey Edwards (R-Ohio), chairman of the House Republican Policy Committee, advised the president that he was constitutionally bound to secure a congressional mandate for war. Administration officials, such as Secretary of Defense Dick Cheney, later stated that the administration would have pressed forward regardless of how Congress voted.

With the congressional midterm elections approaching on November 6, 1990, the president carefully considered the best time to request a vote. Eventually, he waited until after the elections to ask for the vote requesting authority from Congress to employ force. Some suggested that Bush deferred out of respect for Congress and to avoid making the vote an election issue. Others, however, believed that he feared public opinion against the war might manifest itself in Republican election losses.

After Bush had ordered more troops to the region in November, 45 members of Congress, led by Congressman Ronald Dellums (D-Calif.), filed a lawsuit (*Dellums v. Bush*) charging that Bush had violated Article I of the Constitution and the War Powers Resolution. The judge in the case ruled against Dellums, arguing that the dispute was not ready for judicial attention.

On November 29, 1990, the United Nations (UN) approved a resolution authorizing the use of military force to expel Iraq from Kuwait, setting a deadline for January 15, 1991, for Saddam Hussein to withdraw his forces from Kuwait. This made Bush's request

Political Makeup of the U.S. Congress during the Persian Gulf and Iraq Wars

	Congress	Term	House of Representatives			Senate		
			Democratic	Republican	Other/Vacant	Democrat	Republican	Other/Vacant
Persian Gulf War	101st	January 3, 1989–January 3, 1991	261	174	0	55	45	0
	102nd	January 3, 1991–January 3, 1993	270	164	1	57	43	0
Iraq War	107th	January 3, 2001–January 3, 2003	209	222	4	50	49	1
	108th	January 3, 2003–January 3, 2005	205	229	1	48	51	1

far more palatable to the Congress. With the new Congress having been sworn in, the House and Senate set the vote on authorization of the use of military force for January 12, the first such vote taken since the Gulf of Tonkin Resolution on August 7, 1964, during the Vietnam War.

After debating for three days, the House voted 250 to 183 to authorize force if necessary. The Senate faced two measures. The first, Senate Joint Resolution 1 (S. J. Resolution 1), sponsored by Senate Majority Leader George Mitchell (D-Maine) and Senator Sam Nunn (D-Ga.), called for continuing economic sanctions against Iraq. The second, S. J. Resolution 2, was a straight yes or no vote on the use of force. Given the expected close vote, at least one senator bartered for his vote. Senator Al Gore (D-Tenn.) told the Republican leadership that he would support their position if they gave him special time to speak on the floor of the Senate. He believed that the Democrats would support the vote if they provided him with special floor time. The Republican leadership accepted his offer. Not surprisingly, S. J. Resolution 1 was defeated 46 to 53. The following vote, S. J. Resolution 2, authorizing the use of force, was approved 52 to 47 with the defection of several Democratic senators. Gore had delivered on his promise.

On January 16, 1991, coalition forces began the air attacks against Iraq in Operation DESERT STORM. Following the commencement of hostilities, a House and Senate resolution supported the president's action; there were no votes against the resolution. This was merely rhetorical window-dressing, but it did show in good faith congressional support for Bush and the war effort. The brevity of the war and its quick and unequivocal victory kept congressional meddling at bay and seemed to suggest that the Vietnam Syndrome had been laid to rest.

CLAUDE G. BERUBE

See also

Bush, George Herbert Walker; Cheney, Richard Bruce; DESERT SHIELD, Operation; DESERT STORM, Operation; Vietnam Syndrome; War Powers Act

References

Relyea, Harold, and Elaine L. Halchin. *Informing Congress: The Role of the Executive Branch in Times of War.* Hauppauge, NY: Novinka Books, 2003.

Whicker, Marcia, James Pfiffner and Raymond Moore, eds. *The Presidency and the Persian Gulf War.* Westport, CT: Praeger, 2003.

United States Coordinating and Monitoring Mission

Start Date: June 2003
End Date: January 2004

The United States Coordinating and Monitoring Mission (USCMM) was part of the peace initiative known as the Road Map to Peace in the Middle East. Established in June 2003 by the administration of President George W. Bush, the initial task of the USCMM was to test the hypothesis that both sides in the conflict were ready to take the hard steps necessary to achieve a two-state solution and a stable peace. The experience of the USCMM proved that this was an invalid assumption for both the Palestinian and Israeli sides in 2003 at the height of the Second (al-Aqsa) Intifada.

The chief of the USCMM was Ambassador John Wolf, the assistant secretary of state for nonproliferation. He assumed the USCMM mission while retaining his portfolio in the Nonproliferation Bureau. Wolf reported directly to both Secretary of State Colin Powell and National Security Advisor Condoleezza Rice. Wolf's chief of staff was Joseph Pritchard. Wolf was also assisted by a political adviser, an economic adviser, an intelligence adviser, and a police adviser. Initially there was no military representation on the USCMM. Recognizing the need for military expertise in dealing with the Israel Defense Forces (IDF) and the multitude of Palestinian security organizations, Wolf, through the State Department, requested the assignment of a general officer to serve as the senior security adviser.

The USCMM established its operating base at the U.S. consulate in West Jerusalem. The U.S. embassy in Tel Aviv was the official U.S. policy mission to the Israelis. The U.S. consulate in Jerusalem, which unlike any other American consulate in the world reported directly to the State Department and not to an embassy, was the official policy mission to the Palestinians. In 2003 the USCMM was the only official U.S. element that talked to both sides.

In early August Wolf returned to Washington for the visits by Israeli prime minister Ariel Sharon and Palestinian prime minister Mahmoud Abbas. On August 10 Major General David T. Zabecki and his executive officer, Major Kevin Mills, joined the USCMM in Jerusalem. For the first several weeks Zabecki was also assisted by Colonel Philip J. Dermer, a former foreign policy adviser to Vice President Richard Cheney. Although Zabecki worked for Wolf,

Palestinian foreign minister Nabil Shaath, right, shakes hands with U.S. Middle East envoy John Wolf during their meeting in the West Bank town of Ramallah on June 17, 2003. (AP/Wide World Photos)

he also reported directly to the Joint Staff in Washington (J-5) through the director for strategic plans and policy.

One of the major security challenges was the 11 or more Palestinian security organizations, each one its own little feudal fiefdom, reporting to different masters and competing for power with one another as well as with the various militant groups. Another challenge was the initial truce, or *hudna,* that had been called unilaterally by Hamas and Palestinian Islamic Jihad—but not the al-Aqsa Martyrs Brigades and other militant groups—for a 45-day period. Israel continually accused the Palestinians of using the relative calm of the *hudna* to regroup and rearm in preparation for future attacks. The Palestinians accused Israel of exploiting the *hudna* to expand settlements and outposts and to hunt down militant leaders. Finally, the Israelis claimed that outside actors, including Iran, Syria, and Hezbollah in Lebanon, were expending significant efforts and resources to defeat any possibility of peace and stability between the Israelis and Palestinians.

Wolf initially established a plan based on a matrix of nine spheres on which the USCMM would continually evaluate Israeli and Palestinian performance. He called these spheres "baskets." The Israeli baskets included Palestinian quality of life in the occupied territories, Israeli settlements and outposts, Palestinian prisoners, and Palestinian National Authority (PNA) revenues. The Palestinian baskets included PNA institutional reform, incitement, and security performance, which meant bringing the militant groups under control. The shared basket between the two sides was security cooperation, which focused on the phased handover of West Bank cities to Palestinian security control. Progress in resolving the issues in the baskets was used as a gauge of political will, with the idea that additional monitoring assets would be committed as the performance on both sides produced concrete results.

To support the expanded monitoring, Zabecki and Dermer developed a plan to field five monitoring teams of two monitors and one translator each to engage both sides daily in the field. At any given time two teams would work in the West Bank, one team would work in the Gaza Strip, one team would be used for rapid response to any breaking incident, and one team would be off duty but available as a reserve. The plan called for the monitors to be recruited from retired military or State Department personnel with extensive experience in the region. Until the teams could be recruited, trained, equipped, and fielded, Zabecki, Dermer, and Mills, plus Colonel Roger Bass and Lieutenant Colonel Warren Gunderman of the U.S. Military Attaché's Office in Tel Aviv, conducted numerous monitoring missions in the occupied territories to test out the monitoring procedures and to establish USCMM presence and freedom of movement.

Wolf returned to Washington briefly on August 16. At a meeting at Israeli Ministry of Defense headquarters in Tel Aviv on August 19, Major General Giora Eiland, the IDF chief of J-5, briefed Zabecki on the basic outline of a meeting he was to have with his Palestinian counterparts in the West Bank that night to negotiate the final details for the handover of several cities to Palestinian security control. That was one of the most hopeful signs of progress that the USCMM had seen so far. At about 9:30 p.m., however, as Eiland was en route to his meeting, a Palestinian suicide bomber blew up a bus in Jerusalem, killing 23 and wounding 136. Eiland turned around before reaching his destination. On August 21 an IDF helicopter strike killed Hamas leader Ismail Abu Shanab in Gaza. Shortly thereafter, Hamas and Palestinian Islamic Jihad called off the *hudna*. (Hamas reinstated a *hudna* later in 2004.)

Wolf returned to Jerusalem on August 20 and attempted to keep both sides talking to each other. On August 26 Wolf and Zabecki met with Palestinian minister for state security Muhammad Dahlan in Gaza to discuss what to do with three arms-smuggling tunnels in Rafah and a number of Qassam rockets that had been seized by Dahlan's Preventive Security Organization (PSO). Just as Wolf and Zabecki were leaving Gaza, the IDF launched an air strike into Gaza City in an attempt to kill another Hamas leader. The presence of the two senior members of the USCMM inside Gaza at the time of the strike was a blow to the mission's credibility with the Palestinians.

Wolf continued to work relentlessly on the senior political leadership on both sides, especially on issues related to the exact route of Israel's West Bank security barrier. Zabecki continued to work with the IDF and the wide range of various Palestinian security figures. On August 28 Zabecki, Bass, and Mills were conducting a reconnaissance mission inside Gaza when they received reports of a Qassam rocket firing that almost hit the main power plant at Ashkelon. Leaving the strip, the monitors proceeded to the impact site to assess the damage, which was negligible. On September 3 Zabecki met with military intelligence officers at the IDF's Southern Command headquarters in Beersheba to discuss various options to help Dahlan's PSO deal with the Rafah tunnels.

A major decline in the USCMM's prospects for any real success began on September 6 with the resignation of Abbas as Palestinian prime minister, following his long-running dispute with Yasser Arafat. No other Palestinian leader had the trust and credibility with both the Israelis and the Americans, not Abbas's successor, Ahmed Qurei, and certainly not Arafat himself, with whom the Americans and Israelis had long refused to deal. Nonetheless, the USCMM continued to push forward. On September 13 Mills and Pritchard returned to Washington to conduct initial interviews for members of the monitoring teams. On September 23 Zabecki flew to Germany to interview the lead candidate to be the operations officer of the monitoring teams.

On September 24 a USCMM convoy was fired on in Gaza in the vicinity of Beit Hanoun while police adviser John Collins was visiting Palestinian police stations. Three members of Palestinian Islamic Jihad were later arrested and charged. Wolf, meanwhile, was recalled to Washington on September 25 while the U.S. government continued to assess the developing situation with the new Qurei government.

Zabecki returned to Jerusalem on October 1. Maintaining daily phone and e-mail contact with Wolf, Zabecki continued to work the circle of security contacts on both sides and develop the plans to field the monitoring teams. On October 6 Qurei issued a statement that his government would not clamp down on the Palestinian militant groups, further decreasing the chances that Wolf would return to Jerusalem anytime soon.

On October 15 Zabecki, Mills, and Pritchard were conducting a reconnaissance mission in the West Bank's Jordan Valley when at 10:15 a.m. they received a report that a U.S. diplomatic convoy in Gaza had been hit by a roadside improvised explosive device. The convoy had been carrying personnel from the embassy in Tel Aviv to interview Fulbright Scholarship candidates in Gaza. The attack occurred at nearly the exact same point where the USCMM convoy had been attacked almost three weeks earlier. This time three American security guards, John Eric Branchizio, John Martin Linde, and Mark Thaddeus Parsons, were killed in the blast. A fourth guard, Oscar Inhosa, was seriously wounded. Upon receiving the report, the USCMM team broke off its mission and immediately returned to Jerusalem. Despite all sorts of pronouncements from various Palestinian leaders, no one was ever brought to justice for the attack. Many Palestinian newspapers immediately accused the Mossad of conducting the attack.

The USCMM mission was now all but dead. From that point on Zabecki had no more official contact with Palestinian security officials and only pro forma contacts with the IDF. On October 20 the United States informed the Israeli government that Wolf would not be returning to the region for the time being. After a final out-briefing at IDF headquarters in Tel Aviv on October 30 with Eiland and his deputy, Brigadier General Eival Gilady, Zabecki, and Mills departed Israel on November 1 and returned to their home base in Heidelberg, Germany. The remaining members of the USCMM left within days. For the next two months all the members of the USCMM remained on standby, assigned to the mission and ready to return should the situation change. As late as January 5, 2004, Secretary of State Powell told the *Washington Post* that Wolf might be sent back to the region. On January 23 the Defense Department withdrew General Zabecki from the mission.

DAVID T. ZABECKI

See also

Abbas, Mahmoud; Arafat, Yasser; Dahlan, Muhammad Yusuf; Hamas; Improvised Explosive Devices; Intifada, Second; Rice, Condoleezza; Sharon, Ariel; Wolf, John Stern

References

Leverett, Flynt, ed. *The Road Ahead: Middle East Policy in the Bush Administration's Second Term.* Washington, DC: Brookings Institution Press, 2005.

Moens, Alexander. *The Foreign Policy of George W. Bush: Values, Strategy and Loyalty.* Aldershot, Hampshire, UK: Ashgate, 2004.

United States Department of Defense

A department of the administrative branch of the U.S. federal government that coordinates and supervises all agencies and functions relating directly to national security and the U.S. military services. The headquarters of the Department of Defense is the Pentagon, constructed in 1943 in Arlington, Virginia, just across the Potomac River from Washington, D.C. The Defense Department's Pentagon staff includes political appointees (some, such as the secretary of defense, requiring congressional confirmation) who are normally replaced when presidential administrations change, career civilian civil servants who are not political appointees and therefore provide long-term continuity, and uniformed military service members assigned to serve a tour on the Defense Department staff.

The Defense Department has six major components: the Office of the Secretary of Defense and the Defense Department Staff; the Joint Chiefs of Staff (JCS) and the Joint Staff; the military service departments (departments of the army, navy, and air force); the 10 unified combatant commands; the defense agencies (including the Defense Intelligence Agency, the National Security Agency, the Missile Defense Agency, the Defense Acquisition Agency, and the Defense Threat Reduction Agency); and the Defense Department field activities (including the Department of Defense Dependent Schools, and the Defense Human Resources Activity). The Defense Department also operates several joint service schools, including the National Defense University in Washington, D.C.; the Armed Forces Staff College, in Norfolk, Virginia; and the Uniformed Services University of the Health Services.

Until the Defense Department was created in 1947, the Department of War and the Department of the Navy organized, trained, and planned the commitment of the country's land and naval forces. The U.S. Army and the U.S. Navy operated separately, and the secretary of war and secretary of the navy were equal cabinet-level positions. The U.S. Marine Corps was and remains under the Navy Department. Although it came under operational control of the Navy Department during wartime, in peacetime the U.S. Coast Guard, another uniformed, armed sea service, belonged to the Department of the Treasury (later under the Department of Transportation and, today, under the Department of Homeland Security). In 1907 the U.S. government established the first military aviation service, the Aeronautical Division of the Army's Signal Corps, which, over time, grew in size and complexity to equal that of the navy and army. Known as the Army Air Corps before World War II and, after March 1942, as the Army Air Forces, it became an independent branch as the U.S. Air Force at the Defense Department's creation in 1947.

After the Civil War, the growth of U.S. military forces and increasing U.S. global interests resulted in a growing need for greater cooperation between the army and the navy. The coordination between the two services during the 1898 Spanish-American War was dismal at best. In response, President Theodore Roosevelt established the Joint Army and Navy Board in 1903 to plan "joint" operations (i.e., military actions involving two or more different services) and resolve problems between the two services. The Joint Board, however, had little authority and limited ability to influence the secretaries of war and the navy. Interservice coordination problems and rivalries continued through World War I. Following that war, the Joint Board was reorganized and expanded, and in 1935 it was renamed the Joint Action Board of the Army and Navy; yet it still had little real authority or influence.

Immediately after the Japanese attack on Pearl Harbor, the 1941 Arcadia Conference between President Franklin D. Roosevelt and British prime minister Winston Churchill established the Combined Chiefs of Staff as the supreme military body for strategic direction of the Anglo-American war effort ("combined" operations are those involving two or more different nations). Although the British already had a well-established Chiefs of Staff Committee, the United States had no such body. As a result, the United States established the JCF in 1942, but it was an unofficial body that operated throughout the war without official legislative sanction. The functional chairman of the World War II JCS was Admiral William D. Leahy in his capacity as the chief of staff to the president. In December 1944 Leahy became the first American officer promoted to five-star rank.

The World War II JCS proved a successful concept in coordinating the actions of all U.S. military services fighting a global war. On December 19, 1945, three months after World War II ended, President Harry S. Truman proposed the creation of a unified Department of National Defense in a speech to Congress. Between July 1946 and July 1947, Congress and the White House debated the shape and authority of a unified national military establishment. Congress finally passed the National Security Act (NSA), which Truman signed on July 26, 1947, creating the National Military Establishment.

One of the most wide-ranging pieces of legislation in American history, the 1947 act also created a secretary of national defense as a cabinet-level position; established the JCS as a formal

The Pentagon in Arlington, Virginia, houses the Department of Defense. Built during World War II, it is the world's largest office building and approximately 25,000 people work there. (Library of Congress)

body; established the Department of the Air Force and the U.S. Air Force as a separate service, co-equal to the U.S. Army and U.S. Navy, under the secretary of the air force; renamed the War Department the Department of the Army; established the Central Intelligence Agency (CIA) and the National Security Council (NSC); and established the unified joint commands (today called the unified combatant commands). An amendment to the act in 1949 changed the name of the National Military Establishment to the Department of Defense; downgraded the secretaries of the army, navy, and air force to noncabinet-level positions and made them directly subordinate to the secretary of defense; and established the position of chairman of the JCS. General (promoted in 1950 to General of the Army) Omar N. Bradley was the first JCS chairman.

The new National Military Establishment began operations on September 18, 1947, with former Secretary of the Navy James V. Forrestal as the first secretary of defense. Since the 1947 and 1949 acts, Congress has passed additional laws that have given the secretary of defense more authority over the three military branches,

further defined the role of the JCS and the chairman of the JCS as military advisers, and clarified the lines of command of the president, the secretary of defense, the service secretaries, and the service chiefs of staff.

Perhaps the single biggest change introduced in 1947 was the establishment of the joint commands and the removal of the service secretaries and the service chiefs from the operational chain of command. The chain of command ran, and still runs, upward from the joint combatant commanders directly to the National Command Authority (NCA), which consists of the secretary of defense and the president. The joint combatant commands became the key link between the military and the civilian political leadership. The service secretaries and the service chiefs have support and administration roles only. The service secretaries and chiefs of staff are responsible for organizing, equipping, and training their respective services, and providing forces to the joint combatant commanders. It is the combatant commanders who fight the wars and conduct military operations. The JCS and the chair of the JCS had no direct command authority; they were advisers only.

The Goldwater-Nichols Act of 1986, signed into law by President Ronald Reagan on October 1, 1986, is the most current law that defines the command structure and organization of the Department of Defense. This act reworked the command structure of the U.S. military, introducing the most profound and sweeping changes to Defense Department since its establishment in 1947. Goldwater-Nichols reemphasized that the operational chain of command runs from the president and the secretary of defense to the combatant commanders, who command all military forces within their area of responsibility.

Goldwater-Nichols strengthened the position of the chairman of the JCS, as well as established the position of vice chief of the JCS. Previously, all primary members of the JCS, the service chiefs and the chairman, were designated equally as military advisers to the president and secretary of defense. Therefore, the unanimity this policy required among the chairman of the JCS and service chiefs often resulted in their advice on any subject being watered-down pap of dubious value, lest any single service take offense. Goldwater-Nichols, however, made the chairman the principal military adviser to the NCA, and, by law, the highest-ranking military officer in the United States. Therefore, under Goldwater-Nichols, the chairman was designated as the final arbiter for all JCS actions, essentially rectifying the previous situation in which a single service could veto an action it considered detrimental to its own parochial interests. This has eliminated many of the negative effects that interservice rivalry had exerted in the past.

Goldwater-Nichols also designated the chair of the JCS as the communications link for the passage of orders from the NCA to the combatant commanders. The chair, however, has no authority to issue orders to the commandant commands.

Goldwater-Nichols also contains provisions that have firmly embedded "jointness" within all of the military services. It provides for the routine assignment of military personnel to joint-duty positions throughout their careers, and requires their education in Defense Department joint professional development schools as part of their career development and progression. It also mandates that officers reaching general officer/flag officer rank must have served in a joint assignment (or must serve in a joint assignment immediately upon promotion to general officer/flag officer rank). Coordinated procurement procedures allow the various military services to share such technological advances as stealth and smart weapons quickly and provide other ancillary benefits—such as the interoperability of radios between services, heretofore a major operational problem. The joint implementation of new technology is also intended to facilitate the joint development of operational doctrine, although much work remains to be done more than 20 years after Goldwater-Nichols.

The first real test of Goldwater-Nichols was the 1991 Persian Gulf War (Operation DESERT STORM). The realigned organizational structure did not function exactly as intended, but it was a vast improvement over previous wars. U.S. Central Command (CENTCOM) commander General H. Norman Schwarzkopf had clearer access to the intent of the NCA, and chairman of the JCS General Colin Powell exercised greater coordination and control over the planning process than any previous chair. The coordination of all aerial assets in the theater was far from perfect, but the lessons of DESERT STORM resulted in improvements during the Iraq and Afghanistan wars.

The combatant commanders of the unified commands are the war fighters who actually conduct U.S. combat operations. The combatant commander, always a four-star general or flag officer, can come from any of the services. As of 2009 there are 10 Unified Combatant Commands, six regional and four functional. The six regional commands are the U.S. Northern Command, responsible for the defense of North America; U.S. Central Command, responsible for Egypt through the Persian Gulf region into Central Asia; U.S. European Command, responsible for Europe, Turkey, and Israel; U.S. Pacific Command, responsible for the Asia-Pacific region; U.S. Southern Command, responsible for South and Central America; and U.S. Africa Command, established in 2008, responsible for Africa excluding Egypt.

The four functional commands are the U.S. Special Operations Command, which provides special operations for all military services; U.S. Joint Forces Command, which supports other commands as a joint-force provider (for example, joint-force planning and training/education); U.S. Strategic Command, which oversees the strategic deterrent forces (the air force's nuclear-armed bombers and intercontinental ballistic missiles, and the navy's sea-launched nuclear-armed ballistic missile submarines) and coordinates the use of Defense Department's space assets; and the U.S. Transportation Command, which provides global mobility of all military assets for all regional commands.

ROBERT B. KANE AND DAVID T. ZABECKI

See also

Goldwater-Nichols Defense Reorganization Act; Joint Chiefs of Staff; United States Air Force Air Combat Command; United States Central Command; United States European Command; United States Special Operations Command; United States Transportation Command

References

Carroll, James. *House of War: The Pentagon and the Disastrous Rise of American Power.* New York: Houghton Mifflin, 2006.

Lovelace, Douglas. *Unification of the United States Armed Forces: Implementing the 1986 Department of Defense Reorganization Act.* Carlisle Barracks, PA: Strategic Studies Institute, August 6, 1996.

Locher, James R. *Victory on the Potomac: The Goldwater-Nichols Act Unifies the Pentagon.* College Station: Texas A&M University Press, 2002.

Previdi, Robert. *Civilian Control vs. Military Rule in the U.S.* New York: Hippocrene Books, 1988.

Stevenson, Charles A. *SECDEF: The Nearly Impossible Job of Secretary of Defense.* Dulles, VA: Potomac Books, 2006.

United States Department of Defense, Military Reform, Realignment, and Transformation

By the late 1980s, the approaching end of the Cold War brought with it an opportunity to reform and realign the U.S. Department of Defense. The Goldwater-Nichols Department of Defense Reorganization Act of 1986, Public Law 99–433, was the single most sweeping change to the Department of Defense since its establishment by the National Security Act of 1947. Most significantly, Goldwater-Nichols strengthened the position of the chairman of the Joint Chiefs of Staff (JCS) and eliminated ambiguities in the command structure and the chain of command; required greater coordination and interaction of the military services with the objective of improving "jointness"; restructured career management patterns for officers to require greater qualification and experience in serving on joint staffs and in joint operations; and mandated greater coordination across the services in the procurement of weapons, equipment, and technology. More than 20 years later, Goldwater-Nichols still has not quite lived up to all its initial expectations, but the resulting improvements in operational efficiency and effectiveness have nonetheless been significant.

The end of the Cold War also seemed to be ushering in an era of increased security and therefore a decreased need for defense spending, hyped by the media as the so-called peace dividend. Congress pursued that prospect in 1989 when it authorized Secretary of Defense Richard Cheney to appoint an independent Base Realignment and Closure Commission (BRACC). The commission prepared a phased plan for closing, reorganizing, or realigning military facilities and functions in the continental United States to eliminate excess capacity. In June 1990 Cheney provided Congress with a broader plan to reform the U.S. armed forces for the emerging realities of the post–Cold War era.

Cheney's plan called for a 25 percent decrease in the size of the armed forces; overseas bases would be consolidated or closed. New capabilities would allow the armed forces to deploy directly from realigned domestic bases to meet foreign crises. On August 2, 1990, President George H. W. Bush announced his support of the proposal. That very same day, Iraq launched its invasion of Kuwait.

The resulting Persian Gulf War demonstrated both the strengths and weaknesses of the Cold War U.S. military. While easily victorious, U.S. forces required months to prepare and deploy for combat (Operation DESERT SHIELD). The one-sided victory owed much to the availability of secure staging areas in Saudi Arabia and Iraq's failure to interfere with the assembling multinational force. Military planners could not count on such luck in the future.

Regional conflicts like the Persian Gulf War, peacekeeping missions, and counterterrorism operations appeared more likely than major warfare in the early 21st century, especially after the December 26, 1991, dissolution of the Soviet Union. President Bush released a new national military strategy in January 1992 that approved Cheney's concepts but amounted to only a reduction in size, rather than a major realignment, of the Department of Defense. In March 1993 the new administration of President William J. Clinton launched a review of American armed forces and strategy "from the bottom up," planning a more comprehensive series of reforms.

Secretary of Defense Leslie (Les) Aspin released the *Report on the Bottom-Up Review* in October 1993. Its contents guided American policy through 1999, moving the Defense Department further from its Cold War orientation. The review identified five basic threats to U.S. security for the foreseeable future: proliferation of weapons of mass destruction (WMDs); crises caused by the aggression of a major regional power; conflicts inspired by religious or ethnic animosity, subversion, or state-sponsored terrorism; dangers to democracy and reform in the former Warsaw Pact or elsewhere; and potential dangers from economic failure within the United States. It called for further reductions in all of the armed forces, using prepositioned supplies and improved mobility to maintain overseas capabilities despite continued declines in overseas basing.

The review assumed the existence of an ongoing change in warfare, a so-called Revolution in Military Affairs that would facilitate the planned reforms. According to this theory, advances in information technology and other recent developments introduced capabilities that could radically transform warfare. New operational and tactical concepts could exploit those capabilities. Reform of the procurement system, together with introduction of commercial practices and civilian technologies, theoretically would reduce the cost and speed the acquisition of new military hardware. Those same factors would extend the promise of these reforms into the wider administration of the Defense Department.

Some pundits even went so far as to tout what appeared to be "the changing nature of war." Many military historians and serious students of war, however, counterargued that the fundamental nature of war was not changing, and in fact never changed. Although the tools, the mechanics, the weapons, and the tactics of warfare were undoubtedly changing, and at a breathtaking pace, war itself still remained at its foundation, as Clausewitz defined it, "an act of force to compel an enemy to do our will." Despite the trappings of technology, war is and will remain an ugly, brutal business that involves killing people, or credibly threatening to do so.

The so-called Revolution in Military Affairs became a favored buzzword of politicians and uninformed journalists, but other than that has remained largely a myth. The last time there was a true revolution in military affairs was the introduction of nuclear weapons in August 1945. Everything since then has been an incremental evolution, although at times the slope of that evolution curve has been steep, indeed.

Each of the services launched its own initiatives to support the reforms ordered by the *Bottom-Up Review*. At the same time,

Cold War stockpiles and a steady decline in the size of the military allowed the services to take a procurement holiday. Very little new equipment needed to be purchased as the services expended existing matériel reserves and continued to operate equipment from the 1980s or earlier.

Future plans were coordinated through a series of Quadrennial Defense Reviews, building on the work of the *Bottom-Up Review,* and further rounds of base realignments and closures. Developing from the initial 1988 base realignment authorization, BRACC procedures sought to reduce political influence over the sensitive issue of closing bases. They did so by requiring congressional approval or disapproval of realignments proposed by the Defense Department's independent commission in a single vote, rather than on a case-by-case basis.

Service initiatives and planning for new equipment to exploit the presumed revolution in military affairs continued through the 1990s. In 1996 the JCS released *Joint Vision 2010,* describing how the individual services would continue their reform efforts and prepare for the approaching 21st century.

Army chief of staff General Eric K. Shinseki announced his intention to begin fully implementing planned reforms soon after taking office in June 1999. The Army Transformation Plan was a three-tracked process, based on the requirement to transform while at the same time maintaining the capability to operate effectively across the entire spectrum of military operations. During the initial phases of transformation the bulk of the army would be based on what was called the Legacy Force, which would still require sustainment and capitalization in future years. The Interim Force, based on newly organized Brigade Combat Teams and new weapons systems, such as the wheeled Stryker interim armored vehicle, would bridge the gap between the Legacy Force and the Objective Force, and serve as a test bed. The Objective Force was the end-state of the army transformation process. Based on the concept of the digitized battlefield, the technological component of the Objective Force was called Future Combat Systems (FCS). Introduced in 2003, FCS was the army's principal modernization program until May 2009, when Pentagon and army officials announced the cancellation of the FCS vehicle-development program.

The U.S. Air Force pursued a similar goal, reorganizing into Air Expeditionary Forces in January 2000. The U.S. Marine Corps described its intent to move beyond traditional amphibious operations into expeditionary warfare in the 2001 publication *Expeditionary Maneuver Warfare.* The U.S. Navy released *Sea Power 21,* its own vision for a future based on the revolution in military affairs, in 2002.

By the time Donald Rumsfeld became secretary of defense in January 2001, all the services had under way well-thought-out transformation programs that had been in development for years. Nonetheless, Rumsfeld immediately seized ownership of the transformation issue as if he had invented it, and dismissed as largely irrelevant all the transformation efforts in progress to that point. Rumsfeld, who had previously served as secretary of defense during the Gerald Ford administration (1975–1977), often seemed to operate as if he were unaware of the profound changes to the Department of Defense wrought by the 1986 Goldwater-Nichols Act. By any measure, the Pentagon establishment Rumsfeld took over in 2001 was a far cry from the one he had last led in 1977; yet, his apparent presumption that nothing substantial had changed in a quarter century proved immediately disruptive.

Rumsfeld especially made a point of dismissing the army's efforts, branding the service as a Cold War, obsolete, heavy tank–obsessed relic, even though the Stryker light armored vehicle was already in development and a little more than a year away from delivery.

Rumsfeld and his advisers were enamored by the prospects of all the emerging technology, despite the fact that most of it was still untested and that history clearly shows that no military technology ever works exactly as envisioned when first introduced. In the months before the terrorist attacks of September 11, 2001, Rumsfeld championed the theory that ground forces were now obsolete in modern warfare, and that future wars could be prosecuted successfully by a combination of airpower and high technology. Just days before September 11, Rumsfeld was widely expected to announce the elimination of two army divisions.

The initial quick and stunning victories in Afghanistan in 2001 and Iraq in 2003 seemed at first to vindicate Rumsfeld and his faith in the new theories. But then reality settled in, as the lingering insurgencies in both countries brought forth requirements for ground forces that grew steadily. As history has shown consistently throughout the 20th century, ground simply cannot be held and controlled solely from the air. Consequently, the U.S. Army and U.S. Marine Corps, inadequately manned for the increased global missions they were called upon to undertake, became increasingly burdened with a crushing load of personnel rotations in and out of the various combat zones. As General Shinseki warned during his retirement speech on June 11, 2003, "Beware a 12-division strategy for a 10-division army."

JEFFERY A. CHARLSTON AND DAVID T. ZABECKI

See also
Aspin, Leslie, Jr.; Cheney, Richard Bruce; DESERT STORM, Operation; Shinseki, Eric Ken; Stryker Brigades; United States Department of Defense

References
Aspin, Les. *Report on the Bottom-Up Review.* Washington, DC: Office of the Secretary of Defense, 1993.
Fontenot, Gregory, et al. *On Point: The United States Army in Iraqi Freedom.* Annapolis, MD: Naval Institute Press, 2005.
Pagonis, William G., and Jeffrey Cruikshank. *Moving Mountains: Lessons in Leadership and Logistics from the Gulf War.* Cambridge: Harvard Business School Press, 1992.
Shalikashvili, John. *Joint Vision, 2010.* Washington, DC: Joint Chiefs of Staff, 1996.

United States Department of Homeland Security

Federal cabinet-level agency established on November 25, 2002, with the passage of the Homeland Security Act of 2002. Created in the aftermath of the September 11, 2001, terrorist attacks, the Department of Homeland Security (DHS) marked the largest restructuring of the federal government since the end of World War II. The DHS commenced operations on January 24, 2003, and brought together approximately 180,000 federal employees and 22 agencies into a cabinet-level department. The DHS was created to prevent terrorist attacks within the United States, reduce the vulnerability of the United States to terrorism, and minimize the damage from, and speed the recovery after, terrorist attacks.

Homeland security within the United States was traditionally viewed as a state concern, interpreted by the Constitution as related to public health and safety. The federal government historically focused on national security while leaving local and state governments responsible for these types of domestic concerns. However, as federal power has increased in relation to the states, so has the role of the federal government in homeland security matters.

Until the war years of the 20th century, the federal government largely took a secondary role to state governments in homeland security issues. One notable exception to this trend rests with the U.S. Army Corps of Engineers. This organization was tasked with providing flood protection for the nation through such legislation as the Flood Control Act of 1936, in addition to a range of other disaster-related roles. During the Cold War, homeland security took on a truly national role with the creation of the Office of Civil and Defense Mobilization in the early 1950s. Commonly referred to as the Civil Defense Agency, this body gave the federal government a major role in preparing the domestic population for nuclear attack. Other notable federal interventions into domestic homeland security include the Office of Emergency Preparedness, established in 1961, and the Federal Emergency Management Agency (FEMA), established in 1979.

With the end of the Cold War, the federal government increasingly focused on homeland security. The rising threat of weapons of mass destruction (WMDs) and terrorism prompted the national government to take on an even greater role in homeland security. Presidential Decision Directive/National Security Council (PDD/NSC) document 39 of June 21, 1995, and PDD/NSC 63 of May 22, 1998, both reflected the increased federal focus in protecting domestic populations and resources from terrorist attacks. The National Defense Panel of 1997 called for the federal government to reform homeland security. The panel's recommendations included the need to incorporate all levels of government into managing the consequences of a WMD attack or terrorist activities. Similar findings were made by the Hart-Rudman Commission (the U.S. Commission on National Security/Twenty-First Century) in January 2001. The commission recommended a cabinet-level agency to combat terrorism.

After the September 11, 2001, terrorist attacks, the George W. Bush administration undertook significant reforms to promulgate the earlier recommendations. Bush established the Office of Homeland Security (OHS) under the direction of former Pennsylvania governor Tom Ridge on October 8, 2001, through Executive Order 13228. The goals of the OHS involved coordinating homeland security efforts among the various federal, state, and local government agencies, and the development of a comprehensive homeland security strategy. However, the new body had no real budgetary or oversight authority, and its ability to accomplish its goals was limited. The principal strategy for DHS was developed in the July 2002 National Strategy for Homeland Security White Paper and the earlier October 24, 2001, U.S. Patriot Act. Legislative authority was granted for the formation of DHS on November 25, 2002, through the Homeland Security Act.

Headquartered in Washington, D.C., DHS became the 15th cabinet department within the federal government. It was tasked to serve as the coordinating body for the 87,000 different jurisdictions within the United States. The DHS consists of four major directorates: Border and Transportation Security, Emergency Preparedness and Response, Science and Technology, and Information Analysis and Infrastructure Protection.

In the area of border and transportation security, the U.S. Custom and Border Protection agency and the U.S. Immigration and Customs Enforcement service were established. Other agencies transferred into this directorate include the Federal Protective Service, Animal and Plant Health Inspection Service, Transportation Security Administration, and the Federal Law Enforcement Training Center. The Emergency Preparedness and Response section was created when the Homeland Security Act transferred the following agencies into the DHS: FEMA; the Strategic National Stockpile, Office of Emergency Preparedness, Metropolitan Medical Response System, and the National Disaster Medical System, all transferred from the Department of Health and Human Services; Domestic Emergency Support Team, from the Department of Justice; National Domestic Preparedness Office, from the Federal Bureau of Investigation (FBI); and the Integrated Hazard Information System, from the National Oceanic and Atmospheric Administration (NOAA). In addition, the Department of Energy's Nuclear Incident Response Team can operate from DHS during emergencies. To facilitate Information Analysis and Infrastructure Protection, the act transferred to the DHS the Critical Infrastructure Assurance Office, from the Department of Commerce; Federal Computer Incident Response Center; the National Communications System, from the Department of Defense; the National Infrastructure Protection Center, from the FBI; and the National Infrastructure Simulation and Analysis Center, including the energy security and assurance program, from the Department of Energy. To deal with science and technology issues, the Homeland Security Act transferred from the Department of Energy various programs relating to the nonproliferation of chemical, biological, and nuclear weapons and research; the Environmental

The U.S. Department of Homeland Security national operations center. (U.S. Department of Homeland Security)

Measurements Laboratory; and the Lawrence Livermore National Laboratory. All functions relating to the Department of Defense's National Bio-Weapons Defense Analysis Center and the Plum Island Animal Disease Center were also transferred to the DHS.

In addition, the U.S. Coast Guard and the U.S. Secret Service were transferred into DHS. The Coast Guard is the primary agency for maritime safety and security. In addition, the Coast Guard's long history of interdiction and antismuggling operations bolstered the ability of the DHS to protect the nation's maritime boundaries. The Secret Service is the lead agency in protecting senior executive personnel and the U.S. currency and financial infrastructure. Under the DHS, the U.S. Citizenship and Immigration Services was formed to replace the Immigration and Naturalization Service. A fifth directorate, Management, is responsible for budget, facilities, and human resource issues.

In addition to the key directorates and agencies, DHS operates a number of other offices. The Office of State and Local Government Coordination serves as the primary point of contact for programs and for exchanging information between DHS and local and state agencies. The Office for Domestic Preparedness assists state and local authorities to prevent, plan for, and respond to acts of terrorism. The Office of the Private Sector facilitates communication between DHS and the business community. The Privacy Office of the U.S. Department of Homeland Security minimizes the dangers to, and safeguards, the rights to privacy of U.S. citizens in the mission of homeland security. The Office for Civil Rights and Civil Liberties provides policy and legal guidance on civil rights and civil liberties issues. These agencies were created to allay the fears and concerns of civil libertarians and ensure that the DHS does not violate the nation's civil liberties. The National Infrastructure Advisory Council provides advice to security agencies on protecting critical information systems. The Interagency Coordinating Council on Emergency Preparedness and Individuals with Disabilities ensures the consideration of disabled citizens in disaster planning.

DHS relies on other branches of government to fulfill its mission of protecting the U.S. homeland. Tasked with a largely preventive role, investigative responsibility continues to primarily rest with local, state, and federal law enforcement agencies, including the FBI. While DHS employs many of its own analysts, the majority of its intelligence-collection efforts are conducted outside of the department by other members of the intelligence community. Some called for the DHS to incorporate the FBI and the Central Intelligence Agency (CIA) into a single intelligence clearinghouse within the department. However, the two were left as autonomous entities. In order to aid states, the DHS provides funding in the form of grants and targeted expenditures to states, localities, and private bodies, including research centers.

The military also maintains a role in homeland security, chiefly through its Northern Command. The Northern Command plays a role in homeland defense as well as domestic airway security. The military currently maintains the largest capability for chemical, biological, and nuclear incident response, as well as personnel augmentation during domestic emergencies, most notably through federalization of the National Guard. One example of this type of federalization occurred with the deployment of the National Guard to bolster airport security following the September 11, 2001, terrorist attacks.

Former governor of Pennsylvania Tom Ridge was appointed the first secretary of Homeland Security and oversaw the creation of the OHS and its conversion into a cabinet-level department. By 2004 the DHS had grown to 183,000 employees with an annual budget of $36.5 billion. Ridge resigned on November 30, 2004, to pursue a career in private industry. He was replaced by Michael Chertoff on February 15, 2005. By 2008 DHS had more than 207,000 employees, and its yearly budget was approximately $45 billion. On January 21, 2009, Janet Napolitano became the third secretary of Homeland Security, assuming her duties as a cabinet member of the Barack Obama administration.

Tom Lansford

References
Daalder, Ivo H., I. M. Destler, James M. Lindsay, Paul C. Light, Robert E. Litan, Michael E. O'Hanlon, Peter R. Orszag, and James B. Steinberg. *Assessing the Department of Homeland Security.* Washington, DC: Brookings Institution Press, 2002.
Kettl, Donald F. *The Department of Homeland Security's First Year: A Report Card.* New York: Century Fund, 2004.
White, Jonathan. *Defending the Homeland: Domestic Intelligence, Law Enforcement and Security.* Belmont, CA: Wadsworth, 2003.

United States European Command

One of 10 U.S. unified combatant commands and authority offices established on August 1, 1952. Located in Stuttgart, Republic of Germany, it oversees all of the U.S. military forces in Europe. EUCOM consists of U.S. Army Europe (USAREUR), U.S. Air Forces Europe (USAFE), U.S. Naval Forces Europe (NAVEUR), U.S. Marine Forces Europe (MARFOREUR), and U.S. Special Operations Command Europe (SOCEUR). Currently EUCOM's area of responsibility covers more than 20 million square miles and more than 50 countries, including all European states as well as Iceland, Turkey, and Israel. It was the lead command for actual and potential operations during the Cold War and the conflict in Kosovo in the late 1990s. It was also the chief command for U.S. air forces flying in operations during the 1991 Persian Gulf War and the enforcement of the northern no-fly zone in Iraq (1997–2003) leading up to the U.S. invasion of Iraq in March 2003. In addition to commanding over all U.S. military forces in Europe, the commander of EUCOM also serves as the Supreme Allied Commander, Europe (SACEUR) for the North Atlantic Treaty Organization (NATO).

The combat power of EUCOM is formed around the U.S. Seventh Army, the U.S. Sixth Fleet, and the U.S. Third Air Force. Headquartered in Heidelberg, Germany, Seventh Army makes up the ground component of EUCOM. The naval component, the Sixth Fleet, patrols the Mediterranean Sea, covers Europe and NATO's southern flank, and provides protection to shipping in the Mediterranean Sea. The Third Air Force is based at Ramstein Air Base. The Southern European Task Force and its 173rd Airborne Brigade based in Vicenza, Italy, were until recently USAREUR's principal combat force south of the Alps. In December 2008 the Southern European Task Force (SETAF) became the army component of U.S. Africa Command.

EUCOM's special operations component, SOCEUR, is headquartered at Patch Barracks in Stuttgart-Vaihingen, Germany. Forces under SOCEUR include the 352nd Special Operations Group of the U.S. Air Force, based at Royal Air Force Mildenhall in the United Kingdom; the 10th Special Forces Group, a U.S. Navy SEALs unit; Naval Special Warfare Unit 2 in Germany; and other U.S. Army Special Forces elements. EUCOM also has command and control over American nuclear forces in Europe.

The first U.S. commander in chief Europe (USCINCEUR) was General Matthew B. Ridgway, former commander of the U.S. Eighth Army and the U.S. Far East Command during the Korean War (1950–1953). In 1954 EUCOM moved to a French army base (Camp des Loges) west of Paris and then to Patch Barracks, Stuttgart, Germany, in 1967, where it remains today. The troop strength of EUCOM has varied greatly over the years and has depended on the current world politico-military situation. In the 1950s and 1960s, U.S. military personnel in Europe went from 120,000 to more than 400,000 at the peak during the Cold War. Likewise, U.S. Air Forces in Europe grew from 35,000 to 136,000 personnel, and the Sixth Fleet went from 20 ships to more than 40.

The constant tension with the Soviet Union during the Cold War kept EUCOM constantly on alert and often active. Its forces participated in various American-only, joint allied, and NATO military exercises and provided military and humanitarian assistance, disaster relief, peacekeeping support, civilian evacuation, and other missions to a variety of countries throughout its theater of operations. During periods of the Cold War, EUCOM was responsible not just for Europe but also for parts of the Middle East and Africa theaters. In 1983, U.S. Central Command (CENTCOM) took over from EUCOM responsibility for the Middle East except for Israel, Syria, and Lebanon. At the same time, EUCOM was assigned responsibility for sub-Saharan Africa. In March 2004, responsibility for Syria and Lebanon was transferred to CENTCOM.

After the Cold War ended, EUCOM took its airborne command post off alert. In 1990–1991, the command began to provide forces to CENTCOM for Operation DESERT STORM. It also provided forces for operations in the Balkans as well as support against terrorist attacks in its theater after the attacks of September 11, 2001, as part of the Global War on Terror (2001–present). EUCOM has furnished forces and logistical support to the war in Afghanistan as part of Operation ENDURING FREEDOM (beginning in October 2001) and in 2003 for Operation IRAQI FREEDOM.

Since 1990, EUCOM has had eight commanders, all of whom also served as SACEUR: U.S. Army general John Galvin (1987–1992); U.S. Army general John Shalikashvili (1992–1993); U.S. Army general George Joulwan (1993–1997); U.S. Army general Wesley Clark (1997–2000); U.S. Air Force general Joseph Ralston (2000–2003); U.S. Marine Corps general James L. Jones (2003–2006); U.S. Army general Bantz J. Craddock (2006–2009); and U.S. Navy admiral James Stavridis (2009–).

RICHARD B. VERRONE

References
Bolt, Paul J., Damon V. Coletta, and Collins G. Shackelford Jr., eds. *American Defense Policy.* 8th ed. Baltimore: Johns Hopkins University Press, 2005.

Gaddis, John Lewis. *The Cold War: A New History.* New York: Penguin, 2005.

Gregory, Shaun R. *Nuclear Command and Control in NATO: Nuclear Weapons Operations and the Strategy of Flexible Response.* New York: Palgrave Macmillan, 1996.

Lindley-French, Julien. *A Chronology of European Security and Defence, 1945–2006.* New York: Oxford University Press, 2008.

United States Marine Corps, Afghanistan War

Beginning with air strikes on October 7, 2001, the U.S. and coalition invasion of Afghanistan (Operation ENDURING FREEDOM) was the military response by the United States to the terrorist attacks of September 11, 2001, after the refusal of the Taliban government of Afghanistan to hand over members of the Al Qaeda terrorist organization. On December 20, 2001, the United Nations (UN) established the International Security Assistance Force (ISAF) for internal stability and reconstruction, especially around the capital, Kabul. The ISAF was taken over by the North Atlantic Treaty Organization (NATO) in August 2003, while some U.S. forces operated independently.

For the initial invasion, coalition special forces augmented local forces (Northern Alliance) set against the Taliban, and neither army nor marine regular units were used in a significant role. Eventually, marines saw service. On November 25, 2001, marines were airlifted south of Kandahar, the first coalition stronghold. However, the Iraq War, which began in 2003, absorbed the attention of the marines until years after both invasions. Typical marine rotations in Afghanistan lasted seven months.

Throughout 2002 and early 2003, small marine units (L Company, 3rd Battalion, 6th Marine Regiment, plus a security force and a security guard battalion) were stationed in Kabul to provide security. By May 2003, most available marine units were serving in Iraq. In March 2004, the marines were back in Afghanistan operating as part of Combined Joint Task Force 76. Including the 2nd Battalion, 8th Marines and the 22nd Marine Expeditionary Unit, the marine elements (about 2,200 strong) were ordered to help provide security for the first Afghan election. Other elements of the 6th Marines and marine helicopter units also operated in Afghanistan. By mid-2004, there were about 4,200 marines and 10,000 army soldiers out of 20,000 allied personnel in the country.

Part of the marine contribution to U.S. Special Operations Command (USSOCOM), beginning in the late 1980s, included the 2nd Marine Special Operations Battalion. Totaling 2,500 marines

An Afghan child waves to a member of the 5th Marine Regiment as he patrols in the Nawa District of Helmand Province in southern Afghanistan on October 28, 2009. (U.S. Marine Corps)

and serving in Helmand Province in 2007, the 2nd Marine Special Operations Battalion focused on counterinsurgency, information warfare, and reconnaissance, as well as direct action.

Negative attention came to the Marine Corps on March 4, 2007, in the form of what came to be known as the Shinwar Massacre, a still-disputed shooting of Afghani civilians by marines firing from moving vehicles. A company of marines claimed that they were ambushed, while the Afghan Commission and even U.S. commanders concluded that excessive force had been employed. The company was pulled from Afghanistan and returned to Camp Lejeune, North Carolina.

In spring 2008, Iraq veterans of the 24th Marine Expeditionary Unit were deployed to Afghanistan. About 2,200 marines served as a mobile force in southern Afghanistan. Other units were sent to patrol the Pakistani border. Deploying concurrently with the 24th Marine Expeditionary Unit was the 2nd Battalion, 7th Marines, with the mission of training the Afghan National Security Forces. Both units served for seven months before being relieved in 2009 by the Special Purpose Marine Air-Ground Task Force–Afghanistan, consisting of about 2,200 marines drawn from across the corps, from North Carolina to Okinawa, with helicopter and logistics components. Designed to bridge the gap until the deployment of a significantly larger number of marines, it operated in Fara and Helmand provinces. Combat in Afghanistan was difficult—punctuated as it was by strong winds, sweltering temperatures, and omnipresent sand. Cleaning the sand from equipment became a constant necessity.

In early 2009, as the new Barack Obama administration prepared to shift thousands of military personnel from Iraq to Afghanistan, there was talk that a great many of these would be drawn from the Marine Corps, a course of action urged by Marine commandant General James Conway.

Unlike the Iraq War, with inconsistent casualty rates over the duration of the war and an eventual decline after the 2007 troop surge, the war in Afghanistan had witnessed a continual increase in casualties. By the end of 2009 the United States had sustained in Afghanistan a total of 936 deaths, with 137 of these being marines. U.S. wounded totaled 4,769, with the marines accounting for 856.

DYLAN A. CYR

See also

Afghanistan, Coalition Combat Operations in, 2002–Present; ENDURING FREEDOM, Operation; ENDURING FREEDOM, Operation, Initial Ground Campaign; International Security Assistance Force; United States Marine Corps Reserve

References

Rashid, Ahmed. *Descent into Chaos: The United States and the Failure of Nation-building in Pakistan, Afghanistan, and Central Asia.* New York: Viking, 2008.

———. *Jihad: The Rise of Militant Islam in Central Asia.* New York: Penguin, 2002.

Tanner, Stephen. *Afghanistan: A Military History from Alexander the Great to the Fall of the Taliban.* New York: Da Capo, 2003.

United States Marine Corps, Iraq War

U.S. Central Command (CENTCOM) commander and U.S. Army general Tommy Franks controlled all coalition forces in the invasion of Iraq. Overall command of the Combined Forces Land Component Command (U.S. Army, U.S. Marine Corps, and coalition forces) in the March 2003 invasion was vested in U.S. Army lieutenant general David McKiernan, who simultaneously commanded U.S. Third Army/U.S. Army Forces Central Command. The U.S. Army contributed the V Corps of Third Army, of which the largest single unit was the 3rd Infantry Division. As the 3rd Infantry Division drove north from Kuwait toward Baghdad west of the Euphrates River, its marine corps equivalent, the I Marine Expeditionary Force (MEF), paralleled it to the east through the Iraqi heartland. The mission of the I MEF was to cross the Tigris and support the 3rd Infantry Division by threatening Baghdad from the east.

U.S. Marine Corps structure for the Iraq War resembled that of the 1991 Persian Gulf War. The I MEF of some 60,000 men was led by Lieutenant General James Conway. It was centered on the 1st Marine Division, a veteran unit of the 1991 Gulf War now commanded by Major General James Mattis that included three infantry regiments and one artillery regiment (each similar in size to an army brigade). Each infantry regiment had three infantry battalions. The 1st Marine Division also had two battalions of Abrams tanks. In addition to the 1st Marine Division, Conway controlled the II Marine Expeditionary Force, known as Task Force Tarawa (TFT), under Brigadier General Richard Natonski. It consisted of an infantry regiment and two marine expeditionary units (MEUs). Conway also had the 3rd Marine Aircraft Wing, commanded by Major General James Amos, and the British 1st Armoured Division. In all, the U.S. Marine Corps ground-force element numbered 4 infantry regiments, 2 artillery regiments, 3 reconnaissance battalions, 2 tank battalions, a service support group, and the 3 marine aircraft groups numbering about 400 aircraft.

The marines lacked the punch of the 3rd Infantry Division. Heavy marine air support somewhat offset this in the form of Sea Knight helicopters, Sea Cobra helicopters, Super Stallion helicopters, AV-8B Harrier IIs, and F/A-18 Hornet aircraft, but the marines also would have to face the major units of the Iraqi Army, while the 3rd Infantry Division was able to skirt most of these to the west and thus advance more rapidly on Baghdad.

Waves of deserters fled following air strikes or upon learning of the approach of the coalition ground force. The first major Iraqi resistance occurred in Nasiriyah, a junction over the strategic Euphrates River, where TFT was engaged during March 23–29. TFT's success in clearing and holding open what became known as "Ambush Alley" allowed the I MEF to push north. The weather turned poor with the arrival of a *shamal,* or northerly wind, that brought on a heavy sandstorm. The 3rd Infantry Division now stalled on the west side of the Euphrates on March 26. While the I MEF could continue, thanks to air-based refueling and paved roads, it was intended to support the 3rd Infantry, not vice versa, so both divisions waited until March 30 to continue the advance.

Major Rick A. Uribe, a forward air controller assigned to the 23rd Marine Regiment, coordinates close air support as aircraft ordnance impacts in Fallujah, Iraq, November 9, 2004. (U.S. Marine Corps)

On April 5 the 3rd Infantry Division reached Baghdad, and on March 7 and 8 the marines attacked the capital from the southeast. In the advance, cooperation was excellent between marine air and ground forces. The iconic tearing down of Saddam Hussein's statute in Firdaws Square was accomplished by marines on April 9. Major combat operations were declared at an end on May 1.

The real war for coalition forces had only just begun. All three MEFs, plus the 4th Marine Division (reserves), would begin regular rotations in Iraq in the spring of 2004, beginning in Iraq's largest province, Anbar, west of Baghdad. Subsequently, the marines have served throughout Iraq, with the First Battle and Second Battle of Fallujah as their most prominent actions. The marines engaged in counterinsurgency warfare for the first time since Vietnam.

U.S. Marine Corps and marine reservist fatalities, as of January 3, 2009, totaled 1,008 (including such categories as accident, homicide, and self-inflicted). In comparison, the U.S. Army, Army Reserves, and National Guard collectively suffered 3,059 fatalities, while the U.S. Navy and Naval Reserves saw fewer than 100 deaths, making active marines the second hardest hit in terms of fatalities (marine reservists totaled fewer than 150 fatalities). Marines wounded in action by early January 2009 totaled

8,550, with many more thousands wounded due to nonhostile actions and medical issues.

DYLAN A. CYR AND SPENCER C. TUCKER

See also

"Ambush Alley"; Amos, James F.; Baghdad, Battle for; Conway, James Terry; Fallujah, First Battle of; Fallujah, Second Battle of; Fedayeen; Franks, Tommy Ray; IRAQI FREEDOM, Operation; IRAQI FREEDOM, Operation, Ground Campaign; McKiernan, David Deglan; Nasiriyah, Battle of; *Shamal*; United States Marine Corps Reserve

References

Keegan, John. *The Iraq War: The Military Offensive, from Victory in 21 Days to the Insurgent Aftermath.* New York: Vintage, 2005.

Livingston, Gary. *An Nasiriyah: The Fight for the Bridges.* North Topsail Island, NC: Caisson, 2004.

Lowry, Richard, with Howard Gerrard. *US Marines in Iraq: Operation Iraqi Freedom, 2003.* Oxford, UK: Osprey, 2006.

Murray, Williamson, and Robert H. Scales Jr. *The Iraq War: A Military History.* Cambridge, MA: Belknap, 2005.

Pritchard, Tim. *Ambush Alley: The Most Extraordinary Battle of the Iraq War.* New York: Ballantine Books, 2007.

Reynolds, Nicholas E. *Basrah, Baghdad, and Beyond: The U.S. Marine Corps in the Second Iraq War.* Annapolis, MD: Naval Institute Press, 2005.

Strebe, Amy. *Desert Dogs: The Marines of Operation Iraqi Freedom.* New York: MBI Publishing, 2004.

West, Bing, and Ray L. Smith. *The March Up: Taking Baghdad with the 1st Marine Division.* New York: Bantam, 2003.

United States Marine Corps, Persian Gulf War

The U.S. Marine Corps played a leading role in the 1991 Persian Gulf War, which saw the largest deployment of the corps since World War II. Desert warfare had been an integral part of training for most marine units, as they regularly trained at the Marine Corps Air Ground Combat Center, the world's largest marine base, at Twentynine Palms, California. Also, the Mojave Desert, near Camp Pendleton, home of the 1st Marine Division, provided regular desert training. The marine corps had sought to incorporate aviation and service support in a closer relation with combat components, in what was known as Marine Air-Ground Task Forces (MAGTF), organized into marine expeditionary units (MEUs), marine expeditionary brigades (MABs), or marine expeditionary forces (MEFs). Since the late 1980s the marine corps fielded three MEFs, commanded by a lieutenant general. Each MEF typically consists of one division, one aircraft wing, one logistics group, one expeditionary brigade, and one to three expeditionary units. An MEF, however, is a very flexible organization, and units can be attached or detached as the mission requires. The usual total strength of an MEF is about 50,000 personnel, with 18,000 being in the marine division.

Two MEFs participated in the Persian Gulf War: I MEF, containing the 1st Marine Division; and II MEF, centered on the 2nd

A marine takes aim at a target with his M249 light machine gun during Operation DESERT STORM, January 1991. (U.S. Department of Defense)

Marine Division. Receiving its deployment order on August 3, 1990, the I MEF departed for Saudi Arabia in mid-August while the II MEF deployed in December. The 1st Marine Division's 1st and 2nd Tank battalions in Saudi Arabia were the first U.S. tank units ready for operations. The 3rd Marine Air Wing and 1st Force Service Support Group also arrived early on, highlighting the marines' new focus on air, ground, and service coordination. Stationed on Okinawa and parts of Hawaii, III MEF remained ready for combat but did not deploy as a whole, although several of its units were attached to I MEF.

About 22,000 marine reservists served in support and service units, out of the total 40,000 marines available under the Selected Marine Corps Reserve, the unit-based portion of the reserves. The 4th Marine Division was the heart of Marine Reserves and provided units and individuals where needed. Originally, support units were inadequate, and the reservists made up the difference. Marines arrived piecemeal in Saudi Arabia during Operation DESERT SHIELD, their specific task being the defense of Jubail and the surrounding area.

Lieutenant General Walter Boomer, commander of Marine Forces Central Command (CENTCOM) and I Marine Expeditionary Force, had charge of the 90,000 marines in theater. Boomer was directly subordinate to CENTCOM commander U.S. Army general H. Norman Schwarzkopf, commander in chief of all coalition forces. Major General James M. "Mike" Myatt commanded the 1st Marine Division of the 1st, 3rd, 4th, and 7th Marine regiments, and the 11th Marine Artillery Regiment. Major General William Keys commanded the 2nd Marine Division of the 6th and 8th Marine regiments, and the 10th Marine Artillery Regiment, along with Colonel John Sylvester's 1st ("Tiger") Brigade of the U.S. Army's 2nd Armored Division, with M1A1 Abrams tanks. It was attached to the 2nd Marine Division to provide extra armor firepower believed necessary to deal with Iraqi T-72 tanks.

Major General Harry W. Jenkins commanded the II Marine Expeditionary Force afloat. Comprising the 4th and 5th Marine Expeditionary Brigades and the 13th Marine Expeditionary Unit, it served the important function of tying down Iraqi coast defense forces to prevent them from being sent south against the invading coalition forces moving north into Kuwait. The option of an amphibious assault remained open until it was clear that the Iraqi ground forces were rapidly collapsing. Had the assault occurred, it would not have been against the heavily defended and mined Kuwaiti coastline, but to the north, up the Shatt al-Arab waterway, against Iraq's second largest city of Basra.

In the planning for the ground campaign, Boomer anticipated that the marines would reach Kuwait within three days of the beginning of the attack. The marines planned for a breakthrough assault rather than Schwarzkopf's notion of a pinning attack that would draw in the Iraqi elite Republican Guard divisions and allow the armor-heavy U.S. Army units constituting the left hook of the offensive to block the Iraqi escape in a deep envelopment. The net effect of this action was to drive the Iraqis rapidly in the direction they needed to move if they were to escape the projected coalition trap.

Indeed, this is what occurred. In the actual ground attack, the 1st and 2nd Marine divisions and allied Arab forces who were to be accorded the honor of entering Kuwait first, broke through the Iraqi coastal defenses in a matter of a few hours, rather than being hung up for the 18–24 hours Schwarzkopf had anticipated. This forced CENTCOM to launch its left hook of VII Corps to the west of the marines somewhat early. By the fourth day of the war, marine and Arab forces had largely overrun the territory of Kuwait. Marine equipment losses in DESERT STORM were negligible. Personnel casualties totaled 23 killed and 92 wounded.

DYLAN A. CYR AND SPENCER C. TUCKER

See also

Boomer, Walter; DESERT STORM, Operation; DESERT STORM, Operation, Ground Operations; Keys, William Morgan; Myatt, James Michael; Republican Guard; Shatt al-Arab Waterway; United States Marine Corps Reserve

References

Dinackus, Thomas D. *Order of Battle: Allied Ground Forces of Operation Desert Storm*. Central Point, OR: Hellgate/PSI Research, 1999.

Finlan, Alastair. *Essential Histories: The Gulf War, 1991*. Oxford, UK: Osprey, 2003.

Head, William, and Earl H. Tilford Jr., eds. *The Eagle in the Desert: Looking Back on U.S. Involvement in the Persian Gulf War*. Westport, CT: Praeger, 1996.

Lehrack, Otto J. *America's Battalions: Marines in the First Gulf War*. Tuscaloosa: University of Alabama Press, 2005.

Nardo, Don. *American War Library—The Persian Gulf War: The War against Iraq*. Chicago: Lucent Books, 2000.

Newell, Clayton R. *The A to Z of the Persian Gulf War, 1990–1991*. Lanham, MD: Scarecrow, 2007.

———. *Historical Dictionary of the Persian Gulf War, 1990–1991*. Lanham, MD: Scarecrow, 1998.

United States Marine Corps Reserve

The U.S. Marine Corps Reserve, or Marine Forces Reserve (either MFR or MARFORRES), is the reserve element of U.S. Marine Corps, the land combat component of the U.S. Navy. The MFR's mandate is to provide unit augmentation and regular reinforcement to active, deployed Marine forces. Reservists are encouraged to be volunteers. Although the capacity of the institution could handle large numbers of drafted recruits, that has not occurred since the Vietnam War.

The MFR's main combat component is the 4th Marine Division, headquartered in New Orleans, but it has units across much of the United States. Reservists are divided into two categories: Selected Marine Corps Reserve (SMCR), which includes those assigned to reserve units; and the Individual Ready Reserve (IRR), which consists of individual reservists not assigned to units.

During the Cold War, the MFR plus the National Guard and the U.S. Army Reserve (both Army) held to their traditional roles as a force-in-reserve, meaning that, in the case of war, they would provide augmentation through combat and combat service support. Mobilization would be expected in the duration of months. Reservist marines would serve one weekend per month plus another two weeks, usually in the summer, to total the traditional 39 days of yearly service.

During the 1991 Persian Gulf War, mobilization occurred in days and weeks, instead of months, and the MFR was deployed in concurrence with active units from early on. The short duration of the war, however, limited the experience of the MFR, but its role retained its importance at the strategic level. However, the potential of the reserve in an operational capacity was now apparent. The Reserve Components of all the services proved themselves in both Operation DESERT SHIELD (defending Saudi Arabia and Kuwait in 1990) and Operation DESERT STORM (liberating Kuwait in 1991). Similarly, the MFR proved itself after the commencement of the Global War on Terror (2001–present), triggered by the attacks of September 11, 2001.

The active units of the Marine Corps and the U.S. Army became overly burdened with two separate but concurrent conflicts in the Middle East: the Afghanistan War (2001–present) and the Iraq War (2003–present). The continuance of guerrilla warfare in both Afghanistan and Iraq, despite initial coalition success in traditional warfare, continually drained active marine and army units. In response, the U.S. Department of Defense came to utilize the MFR and National Guard in a new active role in its Middle Eastern conflicts.

With this fundamental change toward an active and less traditional reserve role, the MFR had its mandate reconstituted in October 2008. The new roles of the reserve were divided into maintaining its strategic role while developing its operational expertise, plus supporting military and civilian authorities engaged in homeland defense. Underlying these roles was the conceptualization of the MFR as one component of the Total Force Policy, meaning that active and reserve forces required more integration and should be conceptualized as one, divided only by specialties of function. The reserves were considered to be "the will of the American people" in that as a part-time force the men and women were still civilians and not career soldiers.

In the mid-1970s, after the Vietnam War, then-chief of staff of the U.S. Army general Creighton Abrams believed that increased utilization of reservists would bring the American people to the fight. Many observers believe that the Abrams Doctrine has been completely vindicated by the recent experiences since 1991. For comparison, 3,000 reservists of all services were called up for duty in Vietnam while 267,300 reservists operated in Operations DESERT SHIELD and DESERT STORM. By October 2008, the Afghanistan War and the Iraq War had seen 650,000 reservists enter active duty,

Members of the Marine Corps Reserve prepare to enter and clear a house in "Combat Town" at Camp Pendleton, California, on June 19, 2008. Role players, dressed as Iraqi insurgents and armed with AK-47 rifles that fire simulated paintball rounds, add realism to the urban operations training. (U.S. Marine Corps)

making the MFR and the two reserve forces of the army essential to both wars. Their volunteer ethos reflected a direct involvement of the American people in the Global War on Terror. Furthermore, the Department of Defense believed that as civilians first, many reservists brought advanced civilian skills that complemented the active forces. For Afghanistan and Iraq, the Defense Department envisioned that each reservist would be mobilized for one year and demobilized for five years, a one-to-five "deployment-to-dwell" ratio (regular marines are expected to be on a one-to-two ratio).

U.S. conflicts in the Middle East have had the effect of drastically increasing the importance of both the U.S. Marine Corps Reserve and the U.S. Army's National Guard, philosophically supported by the need to invest the "people" into the wars. This shift was institutionally supported because, without a mandatory draft, regular active units needed more manpower.

DYLAN A. CYR

See also

United States Army Reserve; United States Navy Reserve

References

Dinackus, Thomas D. *Order of Battle: Allied Ground Forces of Operation Desert Storm*. Central Point, OR: Hellgate/PSI Research, 1999.
Lehrack, Otto J. *America's Battalions: Marines in the First Gulf War*. Tuscaloosa: University of Alabama Press, 2005.
Strebe, Amy. *Desert Dogs: The Marines of Operation Iraqi Freedom*. New York: MBI Publishing, 2004.

United States National Guard

A reserve component of the U.S. armed forces designed to augment regular forces in times of war or crisis. The National Guard, which consists of the U.S. Army National Guard and the U.S. Air Force (Air) National Guard, falls under both state and federal control. The jurisdictional distinctions are often referred to as Title 10 and Title 32, respectively. As part of a Vietnam War–era restructuring called the Total Force Policy, the National Guard has played an important and evolving role in the military operations of the United States, particularly in the Middle East. For 2008, the authorized strength of the Army National Guard was 351,300 personnel; the Air National Guard's authorized strength was 106,700 personnel. By early 2009, the Army National Guard had 366,009 personnel, or 102 percent of authorized strength. For the same period, the Air National Guard had 107,679 personnel, or a surplus of 979 personnel over the authorized strength.

After the Iraqi invasion of Kuwait on August 2, 1991, Arabic-speaking Army National Guard translators were some of the first guardsmen to volunteer for duty, as regular units such as the 82nd Airborne Division were deploying to the Middle East for Operation DESERT SHIELD. These army guardsmen became the vanguard for thousands more serving in combat, combat support, and combat service missions. Ultimately, some 37,500 Army National Guardsmen were deployed to the Persian Gulf, to join field artillery brigades that directly supported attacks by coalition forces against Iraqi forces in Kuwait when ground operations for Operation DESERT STORM began in February 1991.

The Air National Guard deployed 5,200 guardsmen to the Persian Gulf. They flew reconnaissance, supply, and combat missions. Air National Guard tanker crews also refueled thousands of aircraft during aerial refueling operations; airlifters hauled more than 100,000 tons of cargo in the combat theater, and Air National Guard Lockheed Martin F-16 Fighting Falcon fighters and McDonnell Douglas RF-4C Phantom II reconnaissance aircraft flew 4,000 sorties and dropped thousands of tons of ordnance on Iraqi positions. Significantly, neither the Army National Guard nor the Air National Guard suffered any combat casualties during the Persian Gulf War.

Following the September 11, 2001, terrorist attacks, National Guard participation in the Middle East escalated in what became the largest deployments overseas for the guard since World War II. As a result of military cutbacks during the 1990s, guard troops, particularly combat and combat support ground troops, were in high demand as active-duty planners anticipated military needs in what became the Global War on Terror, Operation ENDURING FREEDOM, and Operation IRAQI FREEDOM. Many of the changes that had made the rapid deployment of Army National Guard troops possible occurred in the 1990s. With the creation of separate enhanced brigades and brigade combat teams that could be readied for combat in 90 days, billions of dollars of modern equipment had been placed with these units in the years prior to 2001.

Thus, when Operation IRAQI FREEDOM was launched in March 2003, some 3,700 Army National Guardsmen were among coalition elements invading Iraq. Guard participation in the conflict reached a high point of 50,000 personnel in late 2005, with eight combat brigades in Iraq. In addition, National Guard units provided approximately 40 percent of the combat service and combat support units during Operation IRAQI FREEDOM, performing essential quartermaster, maintenance, water purification, ordnance disposal, and military police tasks. Almost all of the Reserve Component medical assets are in the U.S. Army Reserve (USAR). The peak number of Guardsmen serving in Afghanistan reached 11,000 by the end of 2009 as the U.S. military shifted focus from Iraq to Afghanistan.

A member of the Florida Army National Guard bids good-bye to his family before deploying in Operation DESERT SHIELD, the largest overseas deployment of Guardsmen since the Korean War. (U.S. Army)

In a significant change from the 1991 Persian Gulf War, thousands of female National Guard personnel were deployed in the Global War on Terror. By 2006, a total of 13,000 Army National Guard and 5,500 Air National Guard female personnel had been sent overseas, mostly to Iraq. Many of these women served in combat support roles and participated in direct combat actions against the enemy; several were awarded the U.S. Army's Combat Action Badge. Sergeant Leigh Ann Hester of the Kentucky Army National Guard was awarded a Silver Star when her military police unit was ambushed near Baghdad. By 2006, nine female guard soldiers had been killed in Operation IRAQI FREEDOM. Female National Guard medics served on the front lines in Afghanistan as well, earning the respect of Afghan National Army soldiers.

The National Guard also participated in nonconventional military missions associated with the Global War on Terror. Soldiers of the National Guard's 19th and 20th Special Forces Groups were some of the first guardsmen to see combat in Operation ENDURING FREEDOM and took on important tasks, such as training the Afghan Army. The Air National Guard contributed its own special operations forces to the Global War on Terror. Units included the 193rd Special Operations Wing of the Pennsylvania Air National Guard and the 280th Combat Communications Squadron of the Alabama Air National Guard.

National Guard deployments have not been without problems, as guard and regular army units continued their long-running friction. The regulars often criticized the National Guard's lack of training and intimated that guardsmen could not handle the stress of "full spectrum warfare." The army often made the situation worse by transferring guard equipment to active-duty units. Over time, these problems were resolved, however. Lengthy deployments and repeated deployments have also exacted a toll on the individual guardsmen's families and livelihood.

From 2001 to 2007, more than 250,000 guardsmen were deployed to Southwest Asia; this represented 15 percent of U.S. troops deployed to Afghanistan and 7 percent of U.S. soldiers deployed in Iraq. At the end of 2008, the National Guard Bureau reported that 432 guardsmen had been killed in action in the Afghan and Iraq wars.

Shawn Fisher

See also

Afghan National Army; DESERT SHIELD, Operation; DESERT STORM, Operation; ENDURING FREEDOM, Operation; Global War on Terror; Hester, Leigh Ann; IRAQI FREEDOM, Operation

References

Boyne, Walter J. *Beyond the Wild Blue: A History of the U.S. Air Force, 1947–2007.* 2nd ed. New York: Thomas Dunne Books, 2007.

Cordesman, Anthony H. *The Iraq War: Strategy, Tactics, and Military Lessons.* Westport, CT: Praeger, 2003.

Doubler, Michael D. *Civilian in Peace, Soldier in War: The Army National Guard, 1636–2000.* Lawrence: University Press of Kansas, 2003.

Fontenot, Gregory, et al. *On Point: The United States Army in Iraqi Freedom.* Annapolis, MD: Naval Institute Press, 2005.

Solaro, Erin. *Women in the Line of Fire: What You Should Know about Women in the Military.* Berkeley, CA: Seal, 2006.

United States Navy, Afghanistan War

The September 11, 2001, terror attacks found significant U.S. naval units within striking range of Afghanistan. On the afternoon of September 11, the aircraft carrier *Enterprise* (CVN-65) was steaming south from the Strait of Hormuz, nearing the end of a deployment to the Persian Gulf, when it received a change in orders. The ship was to reverse course and proceed to the North Arabian Sea—further orders were to follow. There the *Enterprise* joined the battle group centered on the Nimitz-class carrier *Carl Vinson* (CVN-70). The *Carl Vinson* had just reported as the forward deployed naval element of the Fifth U.S. Fleet (Vice Admiral Charles Moore, commanding) of the U.S. Central Command (CENTCOM). This multicarrier taskforce was designated CTF-50.

Half a world away in Yokosuka, Japan, meanwhile, staff officers of the U.S. Seventh Fleet were responding to classified messages from Hawaii and Washington about the feasibility of a sortie (short-notice steaming) for all or part of the Japan-based carrier *Kitty Hawk* battle group to the Indian Ocean to support contingency operations against the Taliban and the Al Qaeda terrorist

organization in Afghanistan. On October 1, 2001, the *Kitty Hawk* sailed from Yokosuka with only a stripped down contingent (about 20 aircraft) from its air wing (CVW-5). Nearly simultaneously with these events, the 26th Marine Expeditionary Unit (MEU) of the Wasp-class *Bataan* Amphibious Readiness Group (ARG) reembarked their ships. They had been conducting an exercise in Egypt when their new orders arrived calling on them to transit the Suez Canal and proceed at best speed to join the *Enterprise* and *Vinson* groups in the North Arabian Sea.

From this point, events moved quickly. Beginning on October 7, the opening day of Operation ENDURING FREEDOM, the U.S. war against the Taliban and Al Qaeda, the *Enterprise* and *Vinson* launched the first of many carrier strikes each day against targets inside Afghanistan. These included Al Qaeda training camps, mechanized forces, radar sites, and military infrastructure. The beginning of the operation also saw British and other U.S. warships launch 50 Tomahawk Land Attack Missiles (TLAMs) at similar targets. After a week-long aerial bombardment, the Taliban's command and control, air defense, and military infrastructures were largely in tatters. Clearly, the Taliban leadership had not banked on the United States being able to project power so far inland from naval and air assets.

Later in October, the *Kitty Hawk* arrived to serve as a forward operating base for special forces and their helicopter support. On October 19, special forces began to launch raids deep into Afghanistan from the *Kitty Hawk*. By this time, the *Enterprise* battle group had been relieved by the carrier *Theodore Roosevelt* battle group, which had deployed from Norfolk, Virginia, on September 19.

Not long after the arrival of the *Kitty Hawk*, the *Bataan*, 26th MEU's command ship, arrived to join the *Peleliu*, a Tarawa-class amphibious assault ship, in the Persian Gulf. The *Peleliu*'s 15th MEU had come directly from operations in the Persian Gulf after September 11. Operation ENDURING FREEDOM now settled into its decisive phase, with navy and air force close air and interdiction missions supporting special operations troops assisting the Northern Alliance and other indigenous opponents of Al Qaeda and the Taliban regime. The navy's biggest challenge during this phase, when there were no air bases yet established for U.S. forces inside or even close to Afghanistan, was the extreme distances of the missions being flown from the ships. Air force tankers helped, but often navy air crews also used their own organic tanker assets to get to the fight, in the form of the Lockheed S-3 Viking antisubmarine jet fitted with refueling packages and extra fuel tanks.

Naval air assets perhaps had their most profound success supporting the special forces team assigned to assist Hamid Karzai's anti-Taliban forces in capturing Kandahar. Guided bombs from navy planes helped blunt a Taliban counteroffensive against Karzai's forces at the Battle of Tarin Kot on November 15, 2001. By December 7, Karzai's forces had seized Kandahar, the major objective of operations in that region of Afghanistan.

Meanwhile, the follow-on forces necessary to hold Kandahar were on their way from the sea. On November 25, 2001, marine

A U.S. Navy F/A-18C Hornet is launched from the aircraft carrier *Carl Vinson* in a strike against Al Qaeda terrorist training camps and military installations in Afghanistan on October 7, 2001, as part of Operation ENDURING FREEDOM. (U.S. Department of Defense)

forces from Combined Task Force 58 (CTF-58), mostly the 15th MEU, seized an advanced operating base code-named Camp Rhino south of Kandahar that included an airstrip. They had come directly from the *Peleliu* and *Bataan* amphibious groups in the North Arabian Sea. The 15th MEU arrived at Kandahar on December 13 and took over security of the airfield.

Navy ships continued to rotate in and out of the theater as the Taliban regime collapsed and U.S. and coalition forces secured various regions of the country. On December 16, the Nimitz-class carrier *John C. Stennis* battle navy had flown more than 4,000 aircraft sorties in support of ENDURING FREEDOM. The need for naval forces was rapidly diminishing as the U.S. Army and the national contingents of other nations began to arrive in greater numbers to take over operations in-country. On January 29, 2002, the marines at Kandahar were relieved by elements of the U.S. Army's 101st Airborne Division.

Navy airpower continued to play a key role in Afghanistan into the spring of 2002, especially during Operation ANACONDA, but after this point major naval air operations drew down. Navy special forces units, or SEALs, had played a substantial role from the beginning of ENDURING FREEDOM. The SEALs were integrated into the joint special operations taking place throughout the country; however, continuing problems with command and control, among other things, played a role in the deaths of several SEALs during the hard-fought battles in the rugged mountains of the Shahikot region during Operation ANACONDA in March 2002.

Another navy element that became involved in Afghanistan relatively early and stayed on for several years consisted of the patrol and reconnaissance aircraft squadrons. These aircraft were based at a number of locations in the Indian Ocean and Persian Gulf and were among the first responders, initially providing support to the carriers in the North Arabian Sea. Once they obtained overflight clearance into Afghan airspace (flying through Pakistan), they provided critical signals intelligence and electro-optical support—especially to special forces. Later, they continued to provide both reconnaissance and base security using infrared and other electro-optic sensors.

Operation ENDURING FREEDOM could not have come at a more propitious time for the Navy. Secretary of Defense Donald Rumsfeld, prior to September 11, had reportedly looked at various proposals in his plans to transform the U.S. military. One of these included a proposal to drop the Navy's aircraft carrier strength from 12 to 8. After ENDURING FREEDOM, these plans were rejected outright because of the role played by carrier assets in the fighting. On the down side, the seemingly—and illusory—easy victory in Afghanistan with these light forward-deployed naval, marine, and special forces may have taught the George W. Bush administration the wrong lessons about how to prosecute military operations during the Global War on Terror. These may have, ironically, adversely affected force levels for the upcoming campaign in Iraq, Operation IRAQI FREEDOM, which have been roundly criticized as too scant. The war in Afghanistan, now essentially a North Atlantic Treaty Organization (NATO) conflict, continues to this day, with Navy involvement primarily coming from air support, construction battalions (SEABEEs), SEALs, and Navy personnel serving as members of Provincial Reconstruction Teams (PRTs).

JOHN T. KUEHN

See also

Bush, George Walker; ENDURING FREEDOM, Operation; Karzai, Hamid; Provincial Reconstruction Teams, Afghanistan; Rumsfeld, Donald Henry

References

Gordon, Michael R., and General Bernard E. Trainor. *Cobra II: The Inside Story of the Invasion and Occupation of Iraq*. New York: Pantheon Books, 2006.

Nathman, John B. "We Were Great." *U.S. Naval Institute Proceedings* (March 2002): 94–96.

Naylor, Sean. *Not a Good Day to Die: The Untold Story of Operation Anaconda*. New York: Berkley Trade, 2006.

Rose, Lisle. *Power at Sea: A Violent Peace, 1946–2006*. Columbia: University of Missouri Press, 2007.

Scarborough, Rowan. "Karzai, a Team Turned Tide of War." *Washington Times*, January 22, 2002, 1.

United States Navy, Iraq War

Nearly uncontested by the Iraqi Navy, U.S. sea power functioned in a variety of roles in support of the ground offensive during Operation IRAQI FREEDOM. U.S. naval operations amply demonstrated the impact of enhanced interservice coordination and technological advancements made since the 1991 Persian Gulf War.

The U.S. Navy deployed five carrier battle groups headed by the *Theodore Roosevelt* (CVN-71), *Harry S. Truman* (CVN-75), *Kitty Hawk* (CV-63), *Abraham Lincoln* (CVN-72), and *Constellation* (CV-64) and three amphibious ready groups to join coalition forces that executed Operation IRAQI FREEDOM during March–April 2003. The *Nimitz* (CVN-68) battle group was already en route for a normal deployment as the Pentagon prepared for war. In total 63,000 sailors, 83,000 marines, 84 warships, and nearly 800 navy and marine aircraft participated in the conflict under the direction of Vice Admiral Timothy Keating of the U.S. Central Command (CENTCOM).

As hostilities commenced, Navy SEALS, in conjunction with British and Polish commandoes, seized Iraq's offshore oil platforms and key pumping stations. Mine-clearing operations, including the use of trained dolphins, opened the Khor Abd Allah waterway far enough to reach the port of Umm Qasr, which would prove critical in the distribution of humanitarian aid. Iraqi forces were unable to inflict any casualties through mines, suicide boats, or antiship missiles.

On the night of March 21, 2003, in keeping with the completely misguided plans to shock and awe the enemy with U.S. firepower, surface vessels and submarines fired nearly 400 Tomahawk cruise missiles into Iraq, targeting command and communications centers principally. By the end of the following month, more than 800 Tomahawks had been fired by U.S. naval assets. Los Angeles–class attack submarines supplied one-third of those strikes, in a display of their growing versatility in the post–Cold War era. With an independent, inertially guided navigation system and a range of up to 1,500 miles, the Tomahawk was an ideal weapon, providing excellent first-strike capability against radar and command and control facilities.

During the war, naval airpower reflected a revolution in efficiency and capability as navy and marine aircraft registered more than 13,000 sorties during March–April 2003. Practically all ordnance delivered was precision-guided, which has not been the case during Operation DESERT STORM. Indeed, nearly all naval aircraft could deploy inertial- and satellite-guided all-weather bombs with 2,000-pound payloads known as Joint Direct Attack Munitions (JDAMs). As with the other services, the Navy benefited from the growing use of unmanned aerial vehicles (UAVs) to downlink real-time video surveillance for targeting data.

Operations were further enhanced by the digitization of the air tasking order (ATO), which had previously been physically delivered to carriers to specify mission assignments. The Grumman EA-6B Prowler carried augmented self-protection jamming pods to facilitate its electronic warfare mission. The newest version of the McDonnell Douglas (now Boeing) F/A-18 Super Hornet was also available for combat use. Other navy and marine aircraft in theater included the Grumman F-14 Tomcat, Sikorsky CH-53 Sea Stallion, Boeing CH-46 Sea Knight, Grumman E-2C Hawkeye, McDonnell Douglas AV-8B Harrier, Sikorsky HH-60H Seahawk, and the Lockheed S-3 Viking.

Surface warfare operations also improved, thanks to the addition of a highly versatile platform. The Arleigh Burke–class of guided missile destroyers joined the Ticonderoga-class of cruisers in featuring the Aegis weapons system to upgrade the navy's long-range strike capability and air defense network. Their phased array radars provided rapid threat prioritization and the ability to track up to 100 targets simultaneously.

Spared much of a naval threat, maritime personnel in some cases performed beyond their typical parameters. For example, navy explosive ordnance disposal teams helped clear improvised explosive devices (IEDs) from Iraqi roadsides. The P-3 Orion patrol aircraft, long a mainstay of antisubmarine operations against the former Soviet Union, performed surveillance and intelligence gathering above Iraq.

As of the end of April 2003, there were 4 navy combat and noncombat deaths and 65 marine fatalities. Although the navy performed its missions admirably, planners noted several lessons learned in anticipating future conflicts. For instance, while carriers can substitute for air bases in regions where the United States has little forward presence, future designs will have to accommodate more planes and higher sortie rates. Also, several aircraft classes,

Sailors assigned to Riverine Squadron 1 in riverine patrol boats on the Euphrates River, Iraq, in November 2007. (U.S. Navy)

including the F-14, EA-6B, E-2C, and S-3, are aging and/or have strenuous maintenance requirements. In addition, some sort of arsenal ship with long-range missile strike capability could obviate the need for slower bombers, such as the North American/Rockwell/ Boeing B-1B Lancer and Boeing B-52 Stratofortress, which could be vulnerable against an adversary with a more capable military.

JEFFREY D. BASS

See also

Iraq, Navy; United States Marine Corps, Iraq War; United States Navy, Persian Gulf War; United States Navy Reserve

References

Cordesman, Anthony H. *The Iraq War: Strategy, Tactics, and Military Lessons.* Westport, CT: Praeger, 2003.

Keegan, John. *The Iraq War: The Military Offensive, from Victory in 21 Days to the Insurgent Aftermath.* New York: Vintage, 2005.

Murray, Williamson, and Robert H. Scales Jr. *The Iraq War: A Military History.* Cambridge, MA: Belknap, 2005.

United States Navy, Persian Gulf War

The U.S. Navy provided a highly versatile instrument of war to the U.S. Central Command (CENTCOM) in the 1991 Persian Gulf War. Indeed, naval units achieved maritime supremacy, contributed to air supremacy, and carried out the deception that convinced the Iraqis that a major amphibious assault was about to occur, which ensured that Iraqi coastal defense forces did not join other Iraqi units to the south.

The U.S. Navy furnished to the coalition forces of DESERT STORM more than 100 warships and 450 aircraft, including 6 carrier battle groups. The carriers *Theodore Roosevelt* (CVN-71), *America* (CV-66), *John F. Kennedy* (CV-67), and *Saratoga* (CV-60) operated out of the Red Sea while the *Midway* (CV-41) and *Ranger* (CV-61) patrolled the Persian Gulf. A total of 300,000 naval personnel and 18,000 marines were deployed under the command of Vice Admiral Stanley Arthur. On January 17, 1991, the beginning of the air war, U.S. naval forces (including at least two Los Angeles–class attack submarines) launched more than 100 Tomahawk (TLAM) cruise missiles at Iraq, targeting primarily air defense facilities and command and control centers. Also taking part were the Iowa-class battleships *Missouri* (BB-63) and *Wisconsin* (BB-64).

By the conflict's end, the navy had launched nearly 300 Tomahawk cruise missiles as part of a battle plan that relied heavily on precision-guided munitions. Tomahawks utilized an independent, inertially guided navigation system to travel up to 1,500 miles. During the war, the *Bunker Hill* (CG-52), a Ticonderoga-class cruiser, conducted the first firing of a Tomahawk using the Vertical Launch System (VLS), designed for rapid and sustained

A diver from Detachment B, Explosive Ordnance Disposal (EOD) Mobile Unit 6, attaches an explosive charge to an Iraqi mine in the Persian Gulf on January 1, 1991. While operating with the U.S. Mine Countermeasures Group, Detachment B divers recovered or destroyed 40 Iraqi mines in the Persian Gulf and off Kuwait. (U.S. Navy)

operations against multiple targets. Each carrier battle group included Ticonderoga-class cruisers with the Aegis weapons system featuring phased array radar capable of threat prioritization and tracking up to 100 targets simultaneously. Never before had warships gone into harm's way with equipment so capable of coordinating defense against air, surface, and subsurface platforms.

Navy and Marine Corps aircraft flew nearly 30,000 sorties, some 35 percent of U.S. total, to hit targets as much as 700 miles away. The Grumman EA-6B Prowler provided electronic countermeasures for all coalition forces. Once enemy radar installations were jammed, attack aircraft, such as the Grumman A-6 Intruder, utilized high-speed, antiradiation missiles (HARM) to destroy the sites. The navy joined in the prosecution of the air war through its four stages: elimination of Iraqi strategic capabilities; neutralization of air defenses in Kuwait; isolation of the field army in Kuwait; and support of the coalition ground offensive. Although the Iraqi Air Force rapidly dispersed to avoid combat, several McDonnell Douglas (now Boeing) F/A-18 Hornets from the *Saratoga* used Sidewinder missiles to down two Soviet-made MIG-21s. Northrop Grumman E-2C Hawkeyes maintained continuous monitoring and air traffic control for the theater of battle. The conflict also saw the first employment of the Sikorsky HH-60H Seahawk rescue helicopter for a combination of medical evacuations, search and

rescue, and logistical support. The remaining Navy and Marine Corps aircraft in use were the Grumman F-14 Tomcat, McDonnell Douglas A-4 Skyhawk, and the McDonnell Douglas AV-8B Harrier.

The Persian Gulf War placed an emphasis on minesweeping not seen since World War II, as the Iraqis had been laying mines in international waters both before and during the conflict. Several Avenger-class minesweepers were transported via a floating dry dock for use in the Persian Gulf in conjunction with British and German vessels. These fiberglass-sheathed ships sported a remotely piloted mine neutralization system that included sonar, video cameras, cable cutters, and a detonating device. Paths were cleared for possible invasion routes and to facilitate naval gunfire missions. Nevertheless, the *Tripoli* (LPH-10), an Iwo Jima–class amphibious assault ship, and the Ticonderoga-class cruiser *Princeton* (CG-59) were damaged by mines and rendered temporarily out of action. By mid-March 1991, coalition forces had removed more than 200 mines from the waters near Iraq.

The small Iraqi navy of gunboats, minesweepers, and patrol craft proved inconsequential. By February 2, all Iraqi Silkworm antiship missile sites as well as vessels with missile capabilities had been eliminated.

The U.S. presence in the Persian Gulf served as a crucial diversion to mask the main assault by armored forces marshaling on

Iraq's western flank. Marines from Amphibious Readiness Group (ARG) Alfa seized the Kuwaiti island of Umm al Maradim in part to heighten the impression of a forthcoming landing. The *Wisconsin* and *Missouri* alternated positions in providing dramatic pyrotechnics with their 16-inch shells against Iraqi positions in Kuwait, sometimes with the help of unmanned aerial vehicles (UAVs). Even after the main ground attack commenced, Marine helicopters and Navy warships continued feinting seaborne attacks to tie down roughly 80,000 enemy personnel before the coalition strategy became clear. Battle-related and noncombat fatalities totaled 14 for the U.S. Navy and 50 for the Marine Corps.

JEFFREY D. BASS

See also

Arthur, Stanley; DESERT STORM, Operation; DESERT STORM, Operation, Coalition Naval Forces; United States Central Command; United States Marine Corps, Persian Gulf War; United States Navy, Persian Gulf War

References

Friedman, Norman. *Desert Victory: The War for Kuwait.* Annapolis, MD: Naval Institute Press, 1991.

Head, William, and Earl H. Tilford Jr., eds. *The Eagle in the Desert: Looking Back on U.S. Involvement in the Persian Gulf War.* Westport, CT: Praeger, 1996.

Lehrack, Otto J. *America's Battalions: Marines in the First Gulf War.* Tuscaloosa: University Alabama Press, 2005.

Marolda, Edward, and Robert Schneller. *Shield and Sword: The United States Navy and the Persian Gulf War.* Annapolis, MD: U.S. Naval Institute Press, 2001.

United States Navy Reserve

The U.S. Navy Reserve (USNR), until 2005 known as the U.S. Naval Reserve, has been used in the 1991 Persian Gulf War, the Afghanistan War, the Iraq War, and the Global War on Terror. The primary mission of the USNR, founded in 1915, is to provide mission-capable units and personnel to support the full range of naval operations during peacetime and war. In recent conflicts in the Middle East, the USNR has fulfilled this mission in a variety of capacities.

In August 1990, when Iraqi forces invaded and occupied Kuwait, the USNR numbered 123,000 personnel. These reservists fell under the broad categories of being involved in medicine, construction, aviation, cargo handling, military sealift, ship augmenters, as well as others not assigned to these principal tasks. Reservists were deployable as units or as individual augmenters to active-duty organizations.

Iraq's invasion of Kuwait triggered the largest overseas U.S. military deployment since the Vietnam War. Operation DESERT SHIELD, from August 1990 to January 1991, and Operation DESERT STORM, from January to February 1991, relied significantly on naval forces for combat power and logistics to achieve the liberation of

Kuwait. Naval reservists provided critical augmentations to the force as a whole. A total of 21,000 reservists were activated in support of DESERT SHIELD and DESERT STORM. Of this number, almost half were medical personnel. These personnel performed a number of duties, the most significant of which was "backfilling" navy medical facilities in the United States after active-duty personnel had been deployed to the Middle East on two hospital ships and several ashore treatment facilities.

The large coalition force footprint on the ground in Saudi Arabia also necessitated the construction of a significant support infrastructure. In support of this effort, more than 1,000 Navy Reserve Construction Battalion (SEABEE) personnel were deployed to the U.S. Central Command (CENTCOM) area of responsibility. Two SEABEE battalions constructed two 6,600-foot runways, a large helicopter-operating base, 12 military support routes (MSR) to facilitate marine forces deployment, and more than 900 other construction projects in support of ground forces.

Navy reservists also contributed significantly to the massive sealift effort, the largest since World War II, which enabled the

A member of the U.S. Navy Reserve conducts a security check on the underside of a vehicle near the border between Kuwait and Iraq in 2005. (U.S. Navy)

deployment of more than 4 billion pounds of cargo and 9 billion pounds of petroleum products by 215 ships over a distance of some 12,000 miles. A number of units were involved in this effort. Approximately 400 navy reservists augmented Military Sealift Command (MSC) staffs around the world in their mission of coordinating ship onloads, transits, and offloads and constituted more than 60 percent of the MSC staff. Some 645 navy reserve cargo handlers supported loading and unloading operations in the United States, Europe, and the Middle East. In the CENTCOM area of responsibility, 200 navy reservists assigned to reserve Mobile Inshore Undersea Warfare (MIUW) units provided protection to cargo offload operations with a combination of advanced electronic sensors and armed security forces.

In the decade between the end of DESERT STORM and the attacks of September 11, 2001, navy reserve personnel strength declined to approximately 80,000 people. However, during both Operations ENDURING FREEDOM and IRAQI FREEDOM, the navy reserve force provided capabilities to campaign efforts in a number of capacities. Activation of navy reserve personnel in response to the September 11 attacks began in mid-September 2001, and by early 2009, 40,000 navy reserve personnel had been called to duty for varying durations, both for ENDURING FREEDOM and IRAQI FREEDOM.

Accompanying the first U.S. Marine Corps units into Afghanistan in November 2001 were 56 USNR SEABEES, who provided critical airstrip maintenance services in the early stages of operations in that country. Subsequently, several thousand USNR SEABEES have deployed to both Afghanistan, in support of ENDURING FREEDOM, and to Iraq and Kuwait in support of IRAQI FREEDOM. SEABEE accomplishments in the initial stages of IRAQI FREEDOM in 2003 included the construction of enemy prisoner of war (POW) holding areas, repair of critical runways, maintenance of main supply routes in southern Iraq, and construction of a large pontoon bridge across the Tigris River.

Navy reserve aviation units have also contributed to ENDURING FREEDOM/IRAQI FREEDOM. U.S. Navy logistics squadrons regularly deploy detachments of one to two transport aircraft, crews, and maintainers to the CENTCOM area of responsibility to support personnel and equipment movement in support of naval operations. USNR Helicopter Combat Support Special Squadrons have also conducted several deployments supporting combat search and rescue and Naval Special Warfare operations. And in a first since the 1950–1953 Korean War, a reserve strike fighter squadron was fully integrated with an active carrier air wing, flying more than 200 combat sorties in 2003 in Iraq.

Finally, as in DESERT SHIELD and DESERT STORM, USNR provided niche capabilities typically not found in the active force but essential to smooth logistics flow into CENTCOM. Units included cargo handling battalions for ship and aircraft offload, MIUW units to conduct surface and subsurface monitoring, inshore boat units to patrol critical waterways, and customs battalions to inspect shipping.

While comprising only a small percentage of the total force deployed in support of Operations ENDURING FREEDOM and IRAQI

FREEDOM, the unique capabilities possessed by the USNR make it a potent tool in these campaigns.

ROBERT M. BROWN

See also

ENDURING FREEDOM, Operation; United States Navy, Afghanistan War; United States Navy, Iraq War; United States Navy, Persian Gulf War

References

Bruce, Allen E., and Sarah C. M. Paine. *Naval Coalition Warfare: From Napoleon to Operation Iraqi Freedom.* London: Taylor and Francis, 2007.

United States General Accounting Office. *Operation Desert Shield/Desert Storm: Use of Navy and Marine Corps Reserves.* Washington, DC: General Accounting Office, 1991.

United States Special Operations Command

Unified command responsible for the conduct of all unconventional warfare missions undertaken by the U.S. military. U.S. Special Operations Command (USSOCOM) was activated on June 1, 1987, and is headquartered at MacDill Air Force Base, Florida. It is one of the 10 unified commands in the U.S. military structure.

USSOCOM was established in response to the failure of Operation EAGLE CLAW, the 1980 attempt to free Americans taken hostage from the U.S. embassy in Tehran by Iranian revolutionaries. The preparations for and execution of EAGLE CLAW were impeded by serious problems with cross-service command and control, coordination, funding, and training. Action analysis of the failed operation led to the establishment of the Special Operations Advisory panel and the 1st Special Operations Command in 1982. In 1983, further movement to consolidate Special Operations Forces (SOF) was led by Senator Barry Goldwater (R-Ariz.). By 1984 the U.S. Congress created the Joint Special Operations Agency, but it had no operational control. Later in 1984, Senator Sam Nunn (D-Ga.), Senator William Cohen (R-Maine), and Representative Dan Daniel (D-Va.) convinced Congress to take a more active role.

Over the next two years, Congress studied the uses and funding of SOF. Senators Nunn and Cohen introduced a bill calling for a joint military operation for SOF and an office within the Department of Defense to oversee it. This organization was to be commanded by a four-star general. The Nunn-Cohen Act was signed into law in October 1986. With the dissolution of the U.S. Readiness Command, USSOCOM was created and approved for operations by President Ronald Reagan on April 13, 1987.

The first Commander in Chief Special Operations Command (USCINCSOC) was General James J. Lindsay, who served from 1987 to 1990. He was followed by General Carl W. Stiner (1990–1993), General Wayne A. Downing (1993–1996), General Henry H. Shelton (1996–1997), General Peter J. Schoomaker (1997–2000), General Charles R. Holland (2000–2003), General Bryan D. Brown (2003–2007), and Admiral Eric T. Olsen (2007–present).

USSOCOM draws its manpower from all branches of the U.S. Armed Forces. Its two original members were the U.S. Army and the U.S. Navy. Army elements include the 75th Ranger Regiment, U.S. Army Special Forces, 160th Special Operations Aviation Regiment, 4th Psychological Operations Group (Airborne), 95th Civil Affairs Battalion (Airborne), and Special Operations Support Command (Airborne). Navy elements include SEALs, Special Warfare Combatant-Craft Crewman, and Seal Delivery Vehicle Teams. The U.S. Air Force special operations units came under USSOCOM in 1990, including the 1st Special Operations Wing, the 27th Special Operations Wing, the 352nd Special Operations Group, the 353rd Special Operations Group, the 919th Special Operations Wing (U.S. Air Force Reserve), and the 193rd Special Operations Wing (Air National Guard). In 2005, the Pentagon authorized the addition of U.S. Marine Corps elements to USSOCOM, which included the Marine Special Operations Battalion, Marine Special Operations Advisory Group, and Marine Special Operations Support Group.

To handle highly classified missions requiring swift action, possible hostage rescue, and counterterrorism, USSOCOM also contains the Joint Special Operations Command consisting of 1st Special Forces Operational Detachment–Delta, Naval Special Warfare Development Group, Intelligence Support Activity, and 24th Special Tactics Squadron. Each service maintains its own command and training regime.

Since its inception, USSOCOM has played a major role in U.S. military actions. It provided forces for the safe navigation of the Persian Gulf (Operation EARNEST WILL) and the capture of Panamanian president Manuel Noriega (Operation JUST CAUSE). As world attention shifted more to the Middle East, USSOCOM again was asked to lead the way. For Operation DESERT STORM, SOF led the invasion of Iraq with strategic intelligence and by locating Scud missile sites. In the Global War on Terror, SOF and USSOCOM have won more battles, ranging from overthrowing the Taliban in Afghanistan to leading the search for Al Qaeda leader Osama bin Laden, to providing counterterrorism operations in Iraq.

SHAWN LIVINGSTON

See also

DESERT STORM, Operation; EARNEST WILL, Operation; ENDURING FREEDOM, Operation; Global War on Terror; IRAQI FREEDOM, Operation; JUST CAUSE, Operation

References

Brown, Bryan D. Dugg. "U.S. Special Operations Command: Meeting the Challenges of the 21st Century." *Joint Force Quarterly* 40 (2006): 38–43.

Clancy, Tom, Carl Stiner, and Tony Koltz. *Shadow Warriors: Inside the Special Forces.* New York: Berkley Books, 2003.

"United States Special Operations Command History: 20 (1987–2007) Proven in the Past, Vigilant Today, Prepared for the Future." MacDill Air Force Base, FL: U.S. Special Operations Command, 2007.

Zimmerman, Dwight Jon, and John Gresham. *Beyond Hell and Back: How America's Special Operations Forces Became the World's Greatest Fighting Unit.* New York: St. Martin's, 2007.

United States Transportation Command

One of 10 U.S. Department of Defense unified military commands. The United States Transportation Command (USTRANSCOM) was established in 1987. Its mission statement calls for USTRANSCOM "to provide air, land and sea transportation to the Department of Defense both in time of peace and in time of war."

USTRANSCOM grew out of the need for the U.S. military to develop a comprehensive military transportation system. This was particularly evident in the 1978 command post exercise, Operation NIFTY NUGGET. Serious deficiencies discovered in NIFTY NUGGET led to the creation the next year of the Joint Deployment Agency (JDA), with its headquarters at MacDill Air Force Base, Florida. The JDA, however, did not have authority for the integration of deployment procedures, and following authority granted under the Goldwater-Nichols Department of Defense Reorganization Act of 1986, President Ronald Reagan issued orders on April 18, 1987, for the establishment of the unified transportation command. U.S. Air Force general Duane H. Cassidy was its first commander.

USTRANSCOM headquarters is at Scott Air Force Base, Illinois. The command consists of three service components: the U.S. Air Force Air Mobility Command (AMC), the U.S. Navy Military Sealift Command (MSC), and the U.S. Army Surface Deployment and Distribution Command (SDDC). In carrying out its mission, USTRANSCOM has access both to military and commercial resources. The AMC is located at Scott Air Force Base. Its assets include the Boeing C-17 Globemaster III, Lockheed C-5 Galaxy, and Lockheed C-130 Hercules transport aircraft and the Boeing KC-135 Stratotanker and McDonnell Douglas KC-10 Extender aircraft for aerial refueling. Additional aircraft are available if required through the Civil Reserve Air Fleet, commercial aircraft that are available to transport both men and matériel in times of national crisis. The MSC is headquartered in Washington, D.C., and has access to both Fast Sealift and Ready Reserve Force ships. If necessary, the MSC can also rent space on commercial ships. The MSC has three primary roles: surge sealift, to move unit equipment to any point in the world; prepositioned sealift (this comes under USTRNASCOM once the ships are released into the common-user fleet); and sustained sealift, to maintain U.S. forces deployed overseas. The SDDC is headquartered at Scott Air Force Base, but its Operations Center is at Fort Eustis, Virginia. The SDDC has a presence in 24 ports around the world. In an average year, the SDDC supervises the movement of some 3.7 measurement tons of ocean cargo, 500,000 personal property relocations, 600,000 domestic freight shipments, 72,000 privately owned vehicles, and 518,000 passengers. Among its assets are 10,000 containers and 1,350 railroad cars.

USTRANSCOM operations run the gamut from military to humanitarian missions. During 1995, for example, USTRANSCOM supported 94 Joint Chiefs of Staff (JCS) exercises and 76 humanitarian missions. At the same time it was supporting Operations JOINT ENDEAVOR in the former Yugoslavia, PROVIDE COMFORT in Turkey, and SOUTHERN WATCH in Iraq. Over a seven-month period in

An MH-60S Seahawk helicopter from Helicopter Sea Combat Squadron (HSC) 25 flies near the U.S. Navy guided-missile destroyer *Mustin* during a vertical replenishment with the aircraft carrier *George Washington* on October 25, 2009, in the Pacific Ocean. HSC-25 was deployed aboard the Military Sealift Command dry cargo ship USNS *Alan B. Shepard*. (U.S. Department of Defense)

the run-up to the 1991 Persian Gulf War (Operation DESERT SHIELD) and during the war itself (Operation DESERT STORM), USTRANSCOM delivered to the Persian Gulf area some 504,000 personnel as well as 3.7 million tons of dry cargo and 6.12 million tons of petroleum products. In recent years USTRANSCOM has been especially busy supporting the wars in Afghanistan and Iraq (Operations ENDURING FREEDOM and IRAQI FREEDOM, respectively). Since October 2001, USTRANSCOM and its coalition partners have moved more than 2.2 million personnel and 6.12 million short tons of cargo.

SPENCER C. TUCKER

See also

IRAQI FREEDOM, Operation; Military Sealift Command; PROVIDE COMFORT, Operation; Sealift Ships; SOUTHERN WATCH, Operation; Support and Supply Ships, Strategic; United States Air Force, Afghanistan War; United States Air Force, Iraq War; United States Air Force, Persian Gulf War; United States Army, Afghanistan War; United States Army, Persian Gulf War; United States Navy, Afghanistan War; United States Navy, Persian Gulf War

References

Boyne, Walter J. *Beyond the Wild Blue: A History of the U.S. Air Force, 1947–2007.* 2nd ed. New York: Thomas Dunne Books, 2007.

Daso, Dik Alan. *The U.S. Air Force: A Complete History.* New York: Hugh Lauter Levin Associates, 2006.

Marolda, Edward, and Robert Schneller. *Shield and Sword: The United States Navy and the Persian Gulf War.* Annapolis, MD: U.S. Naval Institute Press, 2001.

Polmar, Norman. *The Naval Institute Guide to the Ships and Aircraft of the U.S. Fleet.* 18th ed. Annapolis, MD: Naval Institute Press, 2005.

Unmanned Aerial Vehicles

Unmanned aircraft flown by remote control and formerly known as remotely piloted vehicles (RPVs), unmanned aerial vehicles (UAVs) have evolved into powerful aerial reconnaissance, surveillance, and strike platforms. Although the U.S. Air Force employed AQM-34 Drones for high-risk aerial reconnaissance missions during the Vietnam War, those units were quickly retired after the conflict, and postwar funding cuts prevented any new unmanned aerial reconnaissance systems entering service. Israel subsequently pioneered RPV development, and the U.S. government became interested in using RPVs by the late 1980s. Now RPVs are an integral part of the battlefield enviornment.

The success of Israeli UAV operations over Lebanon in the early 1980s convinced the U.S. Navy to examine unmanned aircraft for artillery spotting and to provide a UAV capability for the U.S. Marine Corps. Pioneer RPVs were then acquired and embarked first aboard the Iowa-class battleship *Iowa*. Pioneer short-range UAVs saw their first operational employment during Operations DESERT SHIELD and DESERT STORM from the Iowa-class battleships and amphibious warfare ships when they flew more than 300 combat reconnaissance missions. The best-known instance of their use came when the battleship *Missouri* used its Pioneer to direct devastatingly accurate fire from its 16-inch guns against the Iraqi defenses of Faylaka Island near Kuwait City. When the battleship *Wisconsin* sent its Pioneer over the island shortly thereafter, the defenders used handkerchiefs, undershirts, and other objects to signal their surrender. DESERT STORM demonstrated the advantages of an RPV over aircraft and space-based reconnaissance systems. The foremost of these was their ability to linger over a target, providing comparatively long-term surveillance of the area. They were also cheaper than aircraft, and their loss to accident or enemy fire did not imperil a pilot and aircrew. Over the next decade, Pioneers flew some 14,000 flights and supported every major U.S. military operation.

Buoyed by the success of RPVs in Operation DESERT STORM, America's intelligence agencies and military services accelerated the development of far more capable unmanned aerial platforms.

As these entered operational testing, their greater capabilities and expense drove their sponsors to introduce the designation UAV to distinguish them from their earlier, more primitive counterparts. The primary difference was in the control system. RPVs are radio-controlled from within line of sight of the vehicle, while UAVs can be programmed to fly autonomously along a planned route, utilize satellite links that enable their operators to control them from thousands of miles away, or perform a mix of manual and autonomous operations. Stealthy and equipped to provide instantaneous and nearly continuous transmission of their collected information, UAVs have been a critical component of all major U.S. military operations since 1994 but most especially during the Global War on Terror.

All U.S. military services now operate UAVs, and their missions have expanded from reconnaissance and strike to communications relay and even tactical logistics support to units in the field. The Pioneer RPV, which entered service in 1985, has now been supplanted by a vast array of UAVs ranging from the long-range Global Hawk to the hand-launched RQ-11 Raven. The RQ-1 Predator is the best known of the UAVs in service during America's later Middle Eastern conflicts. First entering service in 1995, the Predator has a 40-hour endurance and is equipped to provide near-real reporting from a wide variety of sensor packages, including elecro-optical, infrared, and radar imaging and electronic signals (ELINT) monitoring. Flying at an operational

A Predator unmanned aerial vehicle (UAV) on a simulated aerial reconnaissance flight off the coast of southern California on December 5, 1995. (U.S. Department of Defense)

altitude above 26,000 feet, its sensors can monitor an area the size of New York City.

The Predator is most famous for its use in Hellfire missile strikes on terrorist leaders, their compounds, and entourages as part of the Global War on Terror. Developed in 2002 to ensure the rapid engagement of terrorists as opportunities arise, each strike-configured Predator carries two Hellfire air-to-surface missiles. The Predator can maintain station for 24 hours over an area 500 nautical miles from its launch point. The latest version of the Predator, the MQ-1, has a more extensive sensor suite, greater range and endurance, and higher operating ceiling. Media claims suggest that Predator strikes have killed hundreds of Taliban and Al Qaeda operatives from November 2001 into 2010 and that the number of these strikes is increasing.

Less well known but more extensively employed are the U.S. Army's FQM-151 Pointer and RQ-1 Raven short-range tactical UAVs. Weighing in at 9 and 4.5 pounds, respectively, the Pointer and RQ-1 enable special operations units and tactical ground commanders to scout the route ahead for enemy forces and improvised explosive devices (IEDs) and look behind or over buildings and blocking terrain features. The Pointer entered service with Special Forces Command in 1989 and first saw action in DESERT STORM. It has a 90-minute endurance, is hand launched, and can be controlled by an operator using a laptop. Essentially a scaled-down Pointer, the Raven has an 80-minute endurance, but microminiaturization enables it to have similar sensor capabilities. More importantly, it can be carried in a standard army backpack. Employed extensively in Iraq and Afghanistan, it is credited with saving hundreds of soldiers' lives by exposing insurgent ambushes, IEDs, and other dangers. Both UAVs cruise at 40–50 miles per hour (mph), employ autonomous and manual flight control, and link infrared or electro-optical imagery back to the operator. The Pointer's better high-altitude performance has led to its extensive use in Afghanistan.

The RQ-5 Hunter Joint Tactical UAV entered service in 1993 and conducts reconnaissance for army divisions and corps. Employed alone, it can conduct surveillance up to 120 miles (200 kilometers) from its ground-control station. That can be extended to 165 miles (300 kilometers) if a second Hunter is used to relay the link signals. It cruises at 118 mph and has a two-hour endurance at 75 miles (125 kilometers) from its launch point. The BQM-147A Dragon drone fulfills a similar function for expeditionary warfare units such as the U.S. Marine Corps Expeditionary Forces and the U.S. Army's 82nd Airborne and 101st Air Assault divisions. The 89-pound Dragon entered service in 1993 and has a 2.5-hour endurance. As with the RQ-5, it operates at an altitude of 3,000–5,000 feet and can be controlled manually, can operate autonomously, or can use autopilot with manual override.

America's longest-ranged UAV is the RQ-4 Global Hawk, which has intercontinental range, operates at altitudes above 50,000 feet, and can remain in the air for more than 42 hours. It carries electronic signal monitoring and infrared, electro-optical, and radar-imaging sensors. The Global Hawk entered service in 2002 and is operated by the U.S. Air Force's 11th and 15th Strategic Reconnaissance wings. All of its collected information can be disseminated in real time via satellite links. It can be flown manually or autonomously or via autopilot with manual override. Its operators use satellite links to maintain contact with the UAV, but it can be programmed to return to base or divert fields if it loses contact.

UAVs now constitute an integral component of all U.S. security operations from the military through to the Coast Guard and Border Patrol. The U.S. Navy is testing the use of UAVs from submarines, including those that are submerged, and aircraft carriers down to patrol craft. Microminiaturization and high-tech data links and computer systems promise to give the smallest tactical units reconnaissance capabilities beyond that imagined for major field forces 100 years ago. Future systems coming on line include the MQ-8B Fire Scout, which will enter service in 2010, and UAVs even smaller than the Raven are expected to enter service by 2012. Science fiction's reconnaissance probes have become a battlefield reality.

CARL OTIS SCHUSTER

See also
Aircraft, Reconnaissance; Al Qaeda; Antiaircraft Guns; ENDURING FREEDOM, Operation; IRAQI FREEDOM, Operation

References
Department of Defense, Office of the Under Secretary of Defense for Acquisition, Technology, and Logistics. *Unmanned Aerial Vehicles (UAVs): Roadmap, 2002–2027.* Washington, DC: Progressive Management, 2008.

Munson, Kenneth. *Jane's Unmanned Aerial Vehicles and Targets, 1995–1996.* London: Jane's, 1996.

———. *World Unmanned Aircraft.* London: Jane's, 1988.

Taylor, John William Ransom. *Jane's Pocket Book of Remotely Piloted Vehicles.* New York: Collier, 1977.

Uqair, Treaty of

Treaty signed on December 22, 1922, between Kuwait and Najd (present-day Saudi Arabia) that set a boundary between the two states and established a neutral zone of approximately 2,000 square miles to the south of Kuwait. The boundary was officially delineated in a 1969 treaty that divided the neutral zone between the two nations. Oil reserves that lie within the zone continue to be divided between the two states, both onshore and offshore.

By the early 18th century, various Arab tribesmen had settled Kuwait. Although officially ruled by the Ottoman Empire out of Basra, in reality the Kuwaitis enjoyed wide discretion over their own affairs and were ruled by local merchant tribal elites connected to the pearl industry, the most important member of which was the al-Sabah family.

Meanwhile, the British, fearful of German and Russian encroachment into the area, had created a system of alliances with states of the Persian Gulf to protect their links to India, a royal colony. Given this goal, the British were largely uninterested in matters of internal governance in the Persian Gulf, making them ideal allies for ruling families in the region.

Under Sheikh Mubarak the Great, who ruled from 1896 to 1915, the al-Sabah clan began to create its own independent power base, and it was increasingly able to raise taxes on the merchant class thanks in large part to its relationship to the British. The British soon began engaging in agreements with the al-Sabah family, giving it gunboats even though Kuwait was officially under Ottoman suzerainty. In 1899, Kuwait signed an agreement not to receive any foreign ambassadors without British permission. Thus, Kuwait came to enjoy almost de facto independence, largely pursuing its own foreign policy guided by British—and not Ottoman—interests. In 1913 the Ottoman Empire was compelled to recognize this state of affairs officially with the Anglo-Ottoman Convention, which recognized the al-Sabah family as independent Ottoman governors within their region.

With the breakup of the Ottoman Empire at the end of World War I, Kuwait continued to maintain close ties with the British and existed as a sheikhdom, albeit one under official British protection. The nebulous nature of Kuwaiti authority invited challenges to the limits of its power, however. Indeed, Kuwaiti sheikhs claimed authority well beyond their capital city, but they largely lacked the ability to enforce that authority. Kuwait nevertheless remained an important entrepôt in the region. Various tribes in the area pledged allegiance to Kuwait, and caravans routinely crossed the sheikhdom to Basra and other cities.

Kuwait was frequently subject to raids by Wahhabi Bedouins out of neighboring Nejd, operating under the authority of Abdul Aziz ibn Abdul Rahman ibn Saud. The capital city was too fortified to raid successfully, but Saudi forces chose other targets. These Bedouins made a profitable living raiding caravans and nearby Kuwaiti allied tribes, weakened Kuwaiti authority, and did serious damage to the economy. Ibn Saud argued that Kuwait had no claims beyond the city, and his control of the desert made this effectively true.

The Kuwaitis had powerful allies in the British, however. In 1920, Saud's forces defeated a Kuwaiti force in the disputed territory south of Kuwait's capitol. Later that year, in October, the Wahhabis besieged the fortified town of Jahra and in this battle the Kuwaitis defeated Saud's forces by holding out without giving in. The local merchants now convinced the al-Sabah family to call on the British, who provided support with planes, armored cars, and offshore gunboats. The Saud forces subsequently withdrew.

Given these struggles between British Arab allies and Ibn Saud, the British High Commissioner from Baghdad, Sir Percy Zacariah Cox, successfully negotiated the Treaty of Uqair, settling the land issue by establishing a neutral zone. Late in 1922, Cox traveled to the fortified town of Uqair in present-day eastern Saudi Arabia, where he met with Ibn Saud and the British political agent to Kuwait, Major John More, heard their cases, and established a neutral zone between the two powers while granting Kuwait authority well beyond the city itself. The agreement was signed on December 22. That Cox met with Saud representing himself and a fellow countryman representing Kuwait is telling, in that Kuwait was effectively operating under British suzerainty. The border between Iraq and Kuwait, however, would not be more firmly established until 1932, and it was not codified until 1969. Kuwait would retain its sheikhdom and connection to the British, not becoming fully independent until 1961.

Michael K. Beauchamp

See also

Ottoman Empire; Saudi Arabia; United Kingdom, Middle East Policy

References

Anscombe, Frederick F. *The Ottoman Gulf: The Creation of Kuwait, Saudi Arabia, and Qatar.* New York: Columbia University Press, 1997.

Fromkin, David. *A Peace to End All Peace: The Fall of the Ottoman Empire and the Creation of the Modern Middle East.* New York: Henry Holt, 1989.

Zahlan, Rosemarie Said. *The Making of the Modern Gulf States: Kuwait, Bahrain, Qatar, The United Arab Emirates, and Oman.* London: Unwin Hyman, 1989.

V

Vehicles, Unarmored

Unarmored vehicles have played a major role in the transport of troops and in other logistical functions since the introduction of the internal combustion engine in the years before the beginning of World War I. The nations involved in the 1991 Persian Gulf War, the 2001 invasion of Afghanistan, and the 2003 Iraq War employed a range of such vehicles. Many models were slightly modified versions of vehicles available on the commercial market, while others were designed and purpose-built to military specifications.

Unarmored military vehicles were divided into five broad categories. First, all countries used some form of light reconnaissance vehicle based loosely on the four-wheel drive U.S. Jeep. These scout vehicles were capable of high speed and could carry four to six soldiers or a small amount of cargo. They could also be armed with machine guns or light antitank or antiaircraft weapons. Second, there were light cargo trucks, which typically had the capacity to carry up to two-and-one-half tons cross-country or twice that load on improved roads. These were often six-wheeled and had the ability to carry either troops or cargo. Third, there were medium cargo trucks that had the ability to move up to five tons and were usually six-to-eight wheeled. Fourth, there were the heavy cargo trucks, which could handle more than seven tons, and carry tanks and other armored and tracked vehicles. Heavy trucks were typically six-to-ten wheeled. Fifth, and finally, there was a range of specialized vehicles that included ambulances, amphibious vehicles, water carriers, and communications vehicles, among others.

Like other nations in the Middle East, Iraq utilized the UAZ 69 (also commonly known as the GAZ 69), the popular Russian version of the venerable U.S. Jeep. The UAZ 69 was a four-wheel drive vehicle that came in several models, including a one-quarter-ton version for light cargo. It performed well off road and in the region's desert terrain. Iraq utilized a variety of foreign-made transport and supply trucks. Many of these were customized to adapt to the heat and harsh climate of the area. However, Iraq did not have the variety of specialized unarmored vehicles that Western countries typically possessed. When Iraqi forces overran Kuwait in August 1990, they captured a number of Kuwaiti vehicles, including the British-made Cargocat. The one-and-one-half-ton vehicle was specifically designed for the desert, and Iraqi forces confiscated scores for their use.

During the Persian Gulf War, coalition air superiority allowed the U.S.-led allies to effectively target and destroy much of Iraq's transport capability. Approximately half of Iraq's unarmored military vehicles were destroyed during the war. After the Persian Gulf War, sanctions prevented Iraq from acquiring new vehicles or parts for their existing fleet. Consequently, the military's transport arm was seriously eroded as soldiers were forced to cannibalize vehicles for replacement parts. The result was that Iraq's transport arm had limited capabilities prior to the Iraq War, and those assets were degraded quickly once combat began as trucks and other vehicles were targeted by coalition aircraft, drones, and ground units. Once the Saddam Hussein regime had fallen in April 2003, Iraqi insurgents increasingly utilized civilian vehicles, especially four-wheel drive pickup trucks, to conduct quick attacks on coalition forces. However, the vehicles proved vulnerable to ground fire and were easy to track; insurgents therefore shifted tactics by using roadside bombs and other improvised explosive devices (IEDs).

The Taliban initially used a broad assortment of unarmored vehicles, including Soviet-era trucks and civilian vehicles pressed into military service, often with improvised armaments. During Operation ENDURING FREEDOM, allied aircraft and ground units were able to effectively destroy most of the Taliban's ground limited

Members of an Egyptian ranger battalion give a demonstration for visiting dignitaries during Operation DESERT SHIELD. The soldiers standing are holding SA-7 Grail surface-to-air missiles (SAMs). (U.S. Department of Defense)

transport. Unmanned aerial drones were increasingly deployed after the fall of the Taliban in December 2001 to monitor vehicle traffic and to undertake attacks. By the 2003 winter campaigns, motorcycles had become an increasingly important vehicle for the Taliban and other insurgents concurrent with the change in tactics to increased terrorist strikes, including bombings and targeted assassinations.

The United States and its allies employed both general-purpose and highly specialized vehicles in both Iraq and Afghanistan. At the heavy end of the spectrum were vehicles such as the U.S. M-1070 Heavy Equipment Transport System (HETS). This behemoth weighed more than 41,000 tons, and with its trailer could handle a payload of 140,000 pounds, including hauling the M-1 Abrams main battle tank.

In addition to general cargo and transport trucks, the United States employed the High-Mobility Multi-Purpose Wheeled Vehicle (commonly known as the "Humvee" or "Hummer"). These four-wheel drive vehicles were much larger than the M-151 model Jeeps they replaced. They had a two-and-one-half-ton load capacity, could carry up to eight troops in addition to its two-person crew, and had a range of 300 miles. Humvees could be armed with several weapons systems, including light or heavy machine guns, antitank and antiaircraft missiles, and small howitzers. They could

also be lightly armored. Humvees had excellent climbing capabilities, and they could traverse grades of more than 25 degrees and ford water more than two feet deep. They also proved quite reliable in the desert. The United States eventually deployed more than a dozen different Humvee models. During the Persian Gulf War, the United States used approximately 20,000 Humvees, and in the Iraq War, it deployed more than 10,000 of them, making the Humvee the most widely used U.S. vehicle in both conflicts.

The British version of the Humvee was the Land Rover 90 or the 110 (later succeeded by the Defender and then the "Snatch" Land Rover, which was lightly armored). The Land Rovers came in a variety of models, and like the Humvee could be armed and configured to undertake a variety of roles. The smaller wheelbase of some of the Land Rovers made them better-suited to urban combat, especially during the Iraq War and the Iraqi insurgency (some U.S. units, including special operations forces, used the Land Rovers instead of the Humvees).

While the Humvees, Land Rovers, and other unarmored vehicles performed well in the initial phases of combat in both Iraq wars and in Afghanistan, the increasing use of IEDs revealed substantial problems with the vehicles. Insurgents in Afghanistan and Iraq quickly realized that the unarmored vehicles were vulnerable to mines, IEDs, and shoulder-fired rocket-propelled grenade

(RPG) launchers. Unarmored transport and supply vehicles were particularly vulnerable to mines and IEDs, but, because of their extensive use, Humvees and other light vehicles were the most common targets of insurgent attacks.

Through 2008, more than 1,500 Humvees had been destroyed or seriously damaged in Afghanistan and Iraq, with more than 400 U.S. service personnel killed in the attacks (almost 10 percent of total casualties). Among the British in Afghanistan and Iraq, casualties from attacks on Land Rovers accounted for one-eighth of total casualties. Land Rovers had less off-road capability than their U.S. counterparts, especially in the mountainous terrain of Afghanistan, and this forced them to remain on roads more frequently.

The U.S. and British governments were criticized for reacting too slowly to improve the armor and other protection afforded troops in light vehicles. In 2004, coalition allies in both theaters began to increase the protection in unarmored vehicles. Many troops improvised, adding ad hoc light armor to their vehicles by welding plates on the exterior or by attaching Kevlar vests to the surface areas of the Humvee. Such modifications seriously eroded the capabilities of the vehicles, as the engines and suspensions were not designed for the extra weight. The United States began reinforcing Humvees in theater with the FRAG Kit 5, which added additional armor to the door and floors of the vehicles with minimal performance sacrifices. Meanwhile, the Department of Defense dramatically increased its purchases and deployments of lightly armored versions of the Humvees, ordering an additional 2,000 of the armored models. The lightly armored Humvees weighed about 1,000 pounds more than their older counterparts and required a more powerful engine (and at $180,000 each, cost about twice as much as the unarmored versions). These vehicles could withstand a small mine or IED up to about 12 pounds and provided marginally effective protection against small-arms fire. They were still extremely vulnerable to RPGs and larger mines or IEDs. Furthermore, insurgents began to use particularly powerful bombs with shaped charges that were dubbed explosively formed penetrators (EFPs), which could easily destroy lightly armored Humvees.

Concurrent with the effort to increase armor, U.S. defense officials also increased the deployment of anti-IED devices. Most of these systems involved electronic radio-frequency jammers to prevent the detonation of IEDs. In 2007, IED use peaked, with more than 2,800 devices either detonated by insurgents or discovered by coalition forces in Iraq. The U.S. and its allies in Afghanistan and Iraq have also begun to deploy more armored vehicles with capabilities similar to those of reconnaissance and light cargo or transport vehicles. Meanwhile, the United States has plans to replace the Humvee with a new vehicle by 2012.

TOM LANSFORD

See also

Armored Warfare, Persian Gulf and Iraq Wars; High Mobility Multipurpose Wheeled Vehicle; Improvised Explosive Devices; IRAQI FREEDOM, Operation, Coalition Ground Forces; United Kingdom, Army, Iraq War; United Kingdom, Army, Persian Gulf War; United States Army,

Afghanistan War; United States Army, Iraq War; United States Marine Corps, Afghanistan War; United States Marine Corps, Iraq War; United States Marine Corps, Persian Gulf War

References

Bhatia, Michael, and Mark Sedra. *Afghanistan, Arms and Conflict: Armed Groups, Disarmament and Security in a Post-War Society.* New York: Routledge, 2008.

Cockburn, Patrick. *The Occupation: War and Resistance in Iraq.* New York: Verso, 2007.

Keegan, John. *The Iraq War: The Military Offensive, from Victory in 21 Days to the Insurgent Aftermath.* New York: Vintage, 2005.

Lacey, Jim. *Take Down: The 3rd Infantry's Twenty-one Day Assault on Baghdad.* Annapolis, MD: Naval Institute Press, 2007.

Murray, Williamson, and Robert H. Scales Jr. *The Iraq War: A Military History.* Cambridge, MA: Belknap, 2005.

Zucchino, David. *Thunder Run: The Armored Strike to Capture Baghdad.* New York: Grove, 2004.

Veterans Benefits Improvement Act of 1994

Federal legislation authorizing the secretary of veterans affairs to grant disability compensation to qualified veterans of the 1991 Persian Gulf War suffering from chronic disabilities associated with undiagnosed illnesses, including Gulf War Syndrome (GFS). The act was signed into law on November 2, 1994, by President Bill Clinton and marked the first time in U.S. history that the Department of Veterans Affairs (VA) was given permission to provide disability compensation to veterans for undiagnosed illnesses. Since the passing of the act, more than 3,700 Persian Gulf War veterans have received disability compensation under its provisions.

In addition to expanding the number of veterans able to receive disability compensation, the Veterans Benefits Improvement Act of 1994 included other requirements, such as the establishment of a standard procedure for completing medical evaluations of Persian Gulf War veterans, a requirement that the VA evaluate the medical status of all immediate family members of veterans, and the launching of a program that provides veterans with easy access to current information on available benefits. The act also added more details to the process of applying for loans through the VA.

The Veterans Benefits Improvement Act of 1994 was passed in response to the medical establishment's inability to diagnose symptoms and illnesses of thousands of veterans returning home from the Persian Gulf area during 1990–1991. Soldiers deployed to the Persian Gulf were reporting symptoms at a much higher rate than those who had not deployed there. Persian Gulf War illnesses still lack complete understanding. The existence of Gulf War Syndrome has not been positively confirmed, but recent studies have confirmed that almost 30 percent of Persian Gulf War veterans suffer from chronic multisymptom illness (CMI). After the examinations of thousands of Persian Gulf War veterans with undiagnosed illnesses, a list of common symptoms was compiled to explain medically unexplained symptoms (MUS).

Army sergeant Stephen Miller holds up a picture of his wife Bianca and son Cedrick during a hearing before the Senate Veterans Affairs Committee on Capitol Hill, August 5, 1994. The committee hears testimony from veterans and their families who believe birth defects and reproductive problems were caused by service-connected exposure to chemicals and radiation during Operation DESERT STORM. (AP/Wide World Photos)

Research continues on the mysterious illnesses suffered by Persian Gulf War veterans. In particular, researchers are studying the health effects of the many dangerous substances to which these veterans were exposed. Anthrax, Sarin nerve gas, and depleted uranium are only a few examples from the list of substances. Some of the most common symptoms of Gulf War Syndrome (or CMI) are fatigue, headaches, joint pains, muscle pains, respiratory disorders, and difficulty sleeping. Research also shows that Persian Gulf War veterans are at a greater risk for depression, anxiety, and substance abuse.

Unless dishonorably discharged or injured or made ill as a result of misconduct, all veterans injured in the line of duty during active service during wartime or peacetime are eligible for disability compensation. However, veterans have only until December 31, 2011, to file for disability compensation under the Veterans Benefits Improvement Act. The degree of disability affects how much each veteran receives. A veteran may be classified as 1 percent to 100 percent disabled. The maximum compensation that Persian Gulf veterans can receive for undiagnosed illnesses is slightly more than $2,000 a month, for complete (100 percent) disability.

Wounded soldiers are surviving at higher rates than ever before due to improvements in military medicine. So far, almost 300,000 Persian Gulf War veterans have applied for compensation and medical care. The Afghanistan War and the Iraq War have significantly increased the number of veterans needing assistance from the VA. As with those of the Persian Gulf War, many veterans of the Afghanistan and Iraq conflicts suffer from unexplained illnesses and will be covered under the Veterans Benefits Improvement Act of 1994.

Since the act will benefit the veterans of the wars in Afghanistan and Iraq, the United States government and the VA face a serious struggle in the years ahead. With the expectation of 750,000 claims, the VA must increase its budget if it hopes to provide quality care to veterans. The VA is still struggling to process claims from the Persian Gulf War and will require billions of additional dollars to provide medical care to the veterans of the later wars.

ARTHUR M. HOLST

See also

Clinton, William Jefferson; Gulf War Syndrome

References

Dyhouse, Tim. "Iraq War Vets Will Receive Benefits." *Veterans of Foreign War Magazine* 90 (2003): 12.

———. "$763 Billion Price Tag to Care for War Wounded." *Veterans of Foreign Wars Magazine* 94 (2007): 12.

Law, Randi. "Gulf War Illness: An Update." *Veterans of Foreign Wars Magazine* 94 (2007): 26–27.

Veterans Health Care Act of 1992

Comprehensive veterans health care legislation sponsored by Representative Gillespie V. "Sonny" Montgomery (D-Miss.), and passed by Congress on October 6, 1992. President George H. W. Bush signed the act into law on November 4, 1992. The Veterans Health Care Act of 1992 (Pub. L. 102–585; 106 Stat. 4943) consisted of eight titles implementing a variety of new programs within the Department of Veterans Affairs (DVA) to improve health care services for eligible American veterans of the 1991 Persian Gulf War as well as previous wars.

The Persian Gulf War sparked a flurry of legislative proposals in Congress in 1991 and 1992 to address veterans benefits. This was in large part the result of the patriotic fervor and resurgence of respect for American military personnel engendered by the conflict. In 1991 alone, close to 100 veterans bills were proposed in Congress that year. The major piece of legislation enacted in March 1991, the Persian Gulf Conflict Supplemental Authorization and Personnel Benefits Act of 1991, otherwise known as the Gulf Act, recognized the conflict as a full-fledged war. This provided opportunities for the majority of the 697,000 Persian Gulf War veterans to participate in certain existing insurance, pension, educational, medical, unemployment, and other federal benefits programs enjoyed by veterans of previous U.S. wars.

The United States military personnel involved in both phases of the war, Operation DESERT SHIELD and Operation DESERT STORM, included a comparably higher percentage of reservists and National Guard troops (17 percent) and women (7 percent) than in previous American conflicts. More than 90 percent of Persian Gulf War veterans experienced service in a combat zone for the first time. Although combat was relatively limited during the war, additional factors compounded the stress levels and health concerns of U.S. troops. These included family and employment strains precipitated by abrupt calls to active duty for reservists and National Guardsmen; environmental exposure to smoke from oil-well fires; harsh desert conditions; hazards related to various military occupational specialties; vaccinations and fears of chemical and biological warfare emissions; and the emotional impact of instantaneous television war coverage on troops and their families. All played a part in heightening the potential psychological and physical health concerns within the United States military.

In light of these issues and in addition to the Gulf Act, Congress began passing pieces of legislation upon the conclusion of Operation DESERT STORM in the spring of 1991 to address specifically veterans health issues related to posttraumatic stress disorder (PTSD) and various environmental exposures. But not until the following year did a more comprehensive health care package appear. The Veterans Health Care Act of 1992 was designed to improve and expand health care services to both Persian Gulf War veterans and other American veterans.

In recognition of the service of female Persian Gulf War veterans and a growing percentage of women serving in the military overall, Title I of the act provided for a counseling program to assist women veterans suffering from trauma associated with sexual assault and harassment while serving in the military, as well as additional women's health care and medical services. Another major provision of the act, Title VII, authorized the implementation of a Persian Gulf War Veterans Health Registry within the DVA to capture data for future research and assessments on health issues and illnesses related to service during the war. Linked to this registry within Title VII were provisions providing health examinations and consultations to veterans requesting help.

Additional titles tightened health care sharing arrangements between the DVA and the Department of Defense in order to expand services to veterans and their beneficiaries; revised nursing pay rates within the DVA to retain nurses and encourage recruitment; enacted drug-pricing reforms to reduce prescription drug costs for federal and nonprofit hospitals and clinics serving veterans; permitted federal grants to states to construct nursing home facilities for disabled and elderly veterans; expanded access of disabled veterans to medical treatment and care in non-DVA facilities; and applied federal judicial misconduct procedures to the Court of Veterans Appeals. The act served as an important foundation for subsequent legislation to improve health care benefits and resolve health-related issues for all American veterans.

MARK F. LEEP

See also
Environmental Effects of the Persian Gulf War; Gulf War Syndrome; Persian Gulf War Veterans Health Registry; Post-Traumatic Stress Disorder; Veterans Benefits Improvement Act of 1994

References
Guzzardo, Joseph M., and Jennifer L. Monachino. "Gulf War Syndrome: Is Litigation the Answer? Learning Lessons from *In Re Agent Orange.*" *St. John's Journal of Legal Commentary* 10 (1995): 673–696.
Institute of Medicine. *Health Consequences of Service during the Persian Gulf War: Recommendations for Research and Information Services.* Washington, DC: National Academy Press, 1996.
Knight, Amy W., and Robert L. Worden. *The Veterans Benefits Administration: An Organizational History, 1776–1994.* Collingdale, PA: Diane Publishing, 1995.

Vietnam Syndrome

A term used to claim that the widespread American opposition to the Vietnam War (1965–1973) had resulted in pacifist and isolationist sentiments that restricted the ability of American leaders to engage U.S. forces in future military operations overseas. Following the successful conclusion of the 1991 Persian Gulf War, which was won quickly and with few casualties by coalition forces, many U.S. policy makers concluded that the Vietnam War Syndrome had been vanquished.

Opposition to the Vietnam War took several forms. Initially, it emerged among a small minority of pacifists who opposed virtually all wars and a minority who saw the Communist-led guerrilla movement as a legitimate national liberation struggle.

The antiwar movement later became widespread among college students. Opposition to the war later expanded to include many Americans who had initially supported the war but then turned against it following the widespread casualties, psychological damage to American troops, and the corrupt and ineffective nature of the regime in Saigon supported by the United States. By 1968, concerns mounted that the war—justified or not—was unlikely to result in a U.S. victory, and polls for the first time showed that a majority of Americans from across the political spectrum opposed the conflict. Popular frustration mounted as American combat operations continued for an additional five years.

Following the U.S. exit from Vietnam, subsequent polls revealed that while a solid majority of Americans still supported the use of military force if necessary to defend the national security interests of the United States, there was unprecedented skepticism regarding U.S. military operations in the developing world. In this instance, there were questions regarding the actual threat posed by the alleged enemy to U.S. national security, the ability of the United States to prevail in such a conflict, and the morality and legality of the intervention. This led Congress to pass new restrictions on presidential war-making authority, including the War Powers Act of 1973, the suspension of funding for U.S. military involvement in Angola's civil war in 1976, and strict limitations on direct military involvement in El Salvador's civil war during the 1980s.

Since the United States remained committed to "containing" the Soviet Union throughout the nearly half-century-long Cold War (1946–1991), restrictions on the use of force to pursue containment was problematic for Washington policy makers who tended to perceive the successes of any left-wing, Marxist or communist regime anywhere in the world—whether backed by the Soviet Union or not—as a direct challenge that must be met. Critics of congressional restrictions on the use of military force argued that all traditional elements of national power—economic, political, and military—should be available to the president. Yet, the wrenching experience of Vietnam left many in Congress—and the American public in general—loath to giving presidents a free hand in introducing U.S. troops into any situation that might draw the country into "another Vietnam."

An initial response to the Vietnam Syndrome came in the form of the Kissinger and Nixon doctrines. The Kissinger Doctrine, named for Henry Kissinger, national security adviser and secretary of state, is referred to in the Middle East as the Pillars Policy. The idea was to bolster strong allies in the Middle East, primarily Israel and Iran, and in a more secondary or indirect fashion, Saudi Arabia. They were to receive aid and military assistance. Some refer instead to the Nixon Doctrine, named for U.S. president Richard Nixon, by which the United States would help build up the military capabilities of developing world surrogates, such as Iran, to enable them to intervene in regional conflicts so as to minimize the potential for American involvement. Both of these policies underwent strain when the Shah of Iran's government fell and with Iran's 1979 Islamic Revolution. It was not clear if there was another "pillar" in the region to promote America's interests.

The Nixon and Kissinger doctrines were gradually replaced by a new one, known as the Weinberger Doctrine (later known as the Powell Doctrine, for its chief proponent General Colin L. Powell during his tenure as chairman of the Joint Chiefs of Staff [1989–1993]). The doctrine associated with President Ronald Reagan's secretary of defense from 1981 to 1987, Caspar Weinberger (whose military aide was Colin Powell), reemphasized direct U.S. military intervention, but with a number of caveats based on presumed "lessons learned" from Vietnam: commit U.S. troops only when American or allied vital national interests are at stake, and only when supported by the American public and Congress; establish in advance of troop commitments clear political and military objectives; commit troops wholeheartedly and with the clear intention of winning; use force appropriate to the threat, but generally apply overwhelming force to shorten the length of the conflict and minimize American casualties; and use force only as a last resort. Powell generally adopted all of the Weinberger Doctrine principles, although he added the development of an "exit strategy" to Weinberger's caveats.

The quick and decisive U.S. military victories in Grenada in 1983, Panama in 1989, and the 1991 Persian Gulf War against Iraq all followed, more or less, the prescriptions of the Weinberger/Powell Doctrine, and proved relatively popular with the American public. Indeed, in the wake of the Persian Gulf War, many claimed that the stunning application of U.S. military power had finally released America from the Vietnam Syndrome. Similarly, while the naval intervention in the Persian Gulf in 1987–1988 (Operation EARNEST WILL) and the air war against Serbia in 1999 were not without controversy, minimal American casualties allowed these military campaigns to move forward without much concern regarding public opinion.

By contrast, the 1982–1984 intervention in Lebanon and the 1992–1994 intervention in Somalia—which raised popular concerns about American casualties, the prospects of success, and the nature of the operation—appeared to have rekindled, albeit on a much smaller scale, public criticism over U.S. military intervention in the developing world. The William J. Clinton administration in particular was loath to put U.S. troops in harm's way in the wake of public outcry after the Mogadishu fiasco, in which U.S. troops were slain in the Somali capital. Restrictions placed on U.S. troops during Operation UPHOLD DEMOCRACY, the American intervention in Haiti during 1994–1995, witnessed U.S. troops being largely isolated from the Haitian population in so-called Kevlar Zones (named after the material used to make American helmets and flak jackets) lest American forces sustain any casualties at all.

Despite misgivings about waging a war against Afghan tribesmen who had previously defeated Soviet forces with American support, concerns about an overreliance on air power, and the failure to eliminate the Taliban and their Al Qaeda allies, the U.S.-led war in Afghanistan beginning in October 2001 (Operation

ENDURING FREEDOM) was widely supported as a strategic necessity and a morally and legally justifiable response to the September 11, 2001, terror attacks on the United States.

By contrast, the growing unpopularity of the war in Iraq, which began in March 2003 (Operation IRAQI FREEDOM), raised many of the same concerns that 30-plus years earlier had resulted in the Vietnam Syndrome. Indeed, the grim war toll in Iraq raised the specter of a possible "Iraq Syndrome" that would have a similar impact on U.S. policy in the decades to come. Whether an Iraq Syndrome will affect the exercise of national power by the new Barack Obama administration remains to be seen. President Obama's announcement in early 2009 that he intended to increase U.S. troop strength in Afghanistan by approximately 17,000 seemed to indicate that, at least in the case of Operation ENDURING FREEDOM, military force remained an option.

STEPHEN ZUNES

See also

Al Qaeda; Bush, George Herbert Walker; Bush, George Walker; Clinton, William Jefferson; DESERT STORM, Operation; ENDURING FREEDOM, Operation; IRAQI FREEDOM, Operation; Kissinger, Henry Alfred; Nixon Doctrine; Powell, Colin Luther; Powell Doctrine; Reagan Administration, Middle East Policy; September 11 Attacks; Taliban; Weinberger, Caspar Willard

References

DeYoung, Karen. *Soldier: The Life of Colin Powell.* New York: Knopf, 2006.

Hess, Gay R. *Presidential Decisions for War: Korea, Vietnam, and the Persian Gulf.* Baltimore: Johns Hopkins University Press, 2001.

Jeffords, Susan. *Seeing through the Media: The Persian Gulf War.* Camden, NJ: Rutgers University Press, 1994.

VIGILANT RESOLVE, **Operation**
See Fallujah, First Battle of

VIGILANT WARRIOR, **Operation**
Start Date: October 8, 1994
End Date: December 8, 1994

A U.S.-led military operation to deter potential Iraqi military action against Kuwait. Initiated on October 8, 1994, Operation VIGILANT WARRIOR ended on December 8. In the aftermath of the 1991 Persian Gulf War, coalition armed forces responded to a series of provocations by the Iraqi regime of President Saddam Hussein by increasing troop levels in the region as a deterrent to further aggression. Through 1993, however, U.S. forces in the region declined as the William J. Clinton administration sought to reduce military deployments and use United Nations (UN) sanctions and weapons inspections, along with enforcement of the northern and southern no-fly zones, to contain Hussein's regime.

In September 1994, Iraqi forces began to move toward the Kuwaiti border. By October 8, two armored Iraqi Republican Guard divisions were located south of the 32nd Parallel, where the southern no-fly zone began. This increased the number of Iraqi military forces near Kuwait from 50,000 to 71,000 men. One of the units, the elite Hammurabi Division, moved to within 12-and-one-half miles of the Kuwaiti border and deployed its artillery in that direction.

The Iraqi provocation was based on a variety of factors. First, Hussein had endeavored to rebuild his military in the aftermath of Iraq's defeat in the Persian Gulf War; the deployment of forces was a test of the capabilities of his forces. Second, Hussein sought to test the Clinton administration, which seemed to be increasingly preoccupied with the crisis in Bosnia and the potential for military action there. Third, the deployment was a warning to anti-Baathist elements in the southern areas of the country, especially among the predominately Shiite population of the region. It was also a warning to other opponents of the regime that the Iraqi military remained a potent force. Fourth, the deployment was an effort to test the will of the international community in maintaining economic sanctions.

Saddam Hussein had engaged in an unsuccessful diplomatic effort over the previous year to remove UN economic and military sanctions, which were crippling his nation. He had undertaken limited cooperation over the past year with the UN weapons inspections regime and gained some support from China, France, and Russia to end the sanctions. The Iraqi leader believed that a show of strength would prompt the international community to revise the sanctions regime rather than face the prospect of escalation and another war.

In response, the Clinton administration reacted quickly, both militarily and diplomatically. Operation VIGILANT WARRIOR was initiated on October 8, 1994. Army and marine units, including the I Marine Expeditionary Force (MEF), were put on alert, and air and naval units were ordered to the region. More than 1,800 additional U.S. troops were in Kuwait within five days of the Iraqi troop movement. In total, more than 156,000 U.S. troops were put on alert for possible deployment to Kuwait. Headquarters units, including that of U.S. Central Command (CENTCOM), were deployed to the Persian Gulf for the first time since 1991. Meanwhile, the United States worked to gain passage of a UN resolution calling for the withdrawal of Iraqi forces from the Kuwaiti border.

On October 15, 1994, the UN Security Council passed Resolution 949, which called on the Iraqi regime to withdraw its forces to their positions as of September 20, 1994, forbade any additional military buildup in the southern areas of the country, and condemned any aggressive or hostile acts toward Kuwait or other neighboring countries. It also called upon Iraq to expand its cooperation with ongoing UN weapons inspections. The Clinton administration was thus able to convince China, France, and Russia of the necessity of continued containment of Iraq.

Through October, the buildup of U.S. forces continued. An aircraft carrier battle group, centered on the *George Washington,*

Sergeant David Compton organizes 82-mm mortars during Operation VIGILANT WARRIOR in Oswesat, Iraq, February 19, 2006. The purpose of this air assault operation was to capture suspected terrorists and to capture or destroy their ordnance supplies to deter a planned raid on Abu Ghraib Prison in Baghdad. (U.S. Department of Defense)

steamed to the region, as did an amphibious ready group. In all, 20 additional U.S. naval vessels sailed to the Gulf. Two brigades of the army's 24th Mechanized Infantry Division were dispatched to Kuwait, as were elements of the 101st Airborne Division and special operations forces. Finally, the air force sent 275 additional aircraft to the area. In all, more than 28,000 additional personnel, including 2,000 marines, were deployed. The deployment of forces occurred rapidly, surprising the Iraqis, who were also preparing to move an additional division to the south.

Operation VIGILANT WARRIOR took advantage of lessons learned from the Persian Gulf War and from prepositioned equipment and facilities at Camp Doha, Kuwait. The air force airplanes flew more than 2,000 strategic lift sorties during the course of a single month, bringing in 21,000 troops and more than 9,000 tons of weapons and supplies. In addition to the 58 M-1 Abrams main battle tanks (MBTs) and 122 Bradley infantry fighting vehicles (IFVs) sent as part of the 24th Division, there were 116 Abrams and 122 Bradleys prepositioned in Kuwait, awaiting only crews and minor maintenance to make them combat ready. These and other weapons were left in Kuwait and maintained so that a brigade deployed to Kuwait would immediately be able to use the weapons and equipment. Although there were substantially fewer forces than in Operation DESERT STORM,

the coalition soldiers were in defensive positions and enjoyed both air and naval superiority. In addition, had combat commenced, the United States could have rapidly increased its forces.

As the troops came into Kuwait, the United States launched a series of military exercises that included both U.S. and select coalition forces. The missions included air, land, and sea activities. The training missions were designed to test the ability of incoming troops to be quickly acclimated and to be ready for combat operations. The exercises were also meant to deter the Iraqis by demonstrating the capabilities and resources of the allied forces. Finally, the training efforts provided the coalition forces opportunities to practice joint and combined operations. VIGILANT WARRIOR confirmed that the U.S. military had achieved significant improvements in strategic airlift and interservice communications.

One challenge that emerged from the operation was the strain that the deployment placed on available strategic lift. Because the reserves were not activated and only limited assets were brought in from outside of the theater, planners realized that current operational plans had a flaw: they were designed for a major deployment, similar to DESERT SHIELD and DESERT STORM. Pentagon plans had not envisioned a small or medium-sized deployment and had to be revised to address possible future contingencies.

During the operation, the United States had minor support from other coalition partners. The United Kingdom dispatched the destroyer *Cardiff* and frigate *Cornwall,* and it sent six additional fighter aircraft and an airborne refueling tanker to the region. The British also more than doubled their ground forces to 1,000 men with the deployment of an additional battalion along the Kuwaiti border. France dispatched the destroyer *Georges Leygues.* In addition to the American, British, and French troops, the United Arab Emirates provided one mechanized infantry battalion, and the allies had two Kuwaiti armored brigades, one mechanized infantry, and one motorized cavalry. Six members of the Gulf Cooperation Council, Bahrain, Kuwait, Oman, Qatar, Saudi Arabia, and the United Arab Emirates, granted the United States overflight permissions and offered the use of facilities in the event of war.

Even as U.S. and allied troops were being deployed, Hussein announced his intention to withdraw the additional forces he had put in place. However, there was little or no movement, and Clinton publicly repudiated the Iraqi assertions that they had begun to pull back. It was not until October 18 that the Republican Guard divisions began their withdrawal. On October 20, the United States and the United Kingdom issued separate but similar warnings to Iraq that they would enforce Resolution 949, including the use of military force if necessary. By the end of October, the Iraqi divisions had retreated north of the 32nd Parallel. U.S. redeployments began simultaneously. U.S. troops were taken off alert, and the bulk of forces that had been deployed were returned home by the end of November. Operation VIGILANT WARRIOR officially ended on December 8, 1994.

In an effort to deter future ploys by Iraq, the Clinton administration decided to increase its deployments in the region and maintain 5,000 ground troops and at least 120 aircraft in theater. As a result of VIGILANT WARRIOR, the U.S. military increased its predeployment resources in the area so that the army had equipment for eight battalions prepositioned in Kuwait. The United States also increased its exercises in the region so that there were at least two operations per year in Kuwait. Nonetheless, in August 1995, Hussein again moved forces toward Kuwait, leading to Operation VIGILANT SENTINEL, a much smaller-scale version of VIGILANT WARRIOR that ended with the same results. In response to the continued provocations, the southern no-fly zone was later extended northward to the 33rd Parallel.

TOM LANSFORD

See also

Clinton, William Jefferson; DESERT SHIELD, Operation; DESERT STORM, Operation; Hussein, Saddam; SOUTHERN WATCH, Operation; Special Republican Guards; United States

References

Davis, John, ed. *Presidential Policies and the Road to the Second Iraq War: From Forty One to Forty Three.* Aldershot, UK: Ashgate, 2006.

Knights, Michael. *Cradle of Conflict: Iraq and the Birth of Modern U.S. Military.* Annapolis, MD: Naval Institute Press, 2005.

Mahajan, Rahul. *Full Spectrum Dominance: U.S. Power in Iraq and Beyond.* New York: Seven Stories, 2003.

Woods, Kevin M. *The Mother of All Battles: Saddam Hussein's Strategic Plan for the Gulf War.* Annapolis, MD: Naval Institute Press, 2008.

VIKING HAMMER, **Operation**

Start Date: March 28, 2003
End Date: March 30, 2003

Part of the March 2003 Anglo-American–led invasion of Iraq (Operation IRAQI FREEDOM), Operation VIKING HAMMER was an offensive waged from March 28 to March 30, 2003, in northern Iraq by anti–Saddam Hussein Kurds with the assistance of coalition special operations forces, against the Islamic terrorist group Ansar al-Islam.

The original planning for Operation IRAQI FREEDOM had called for a northern front, but when the Turkish government denied the coalition the use of its territory, planners had to shift strategy. Instead, they hoped to utilize pro-American militias of the Kurdish Regional Government. The latter was dominated by two groups, the Patriotic Union of Kurdistan (PUK), led by Jalal Talabani; and the Kurdistan Democratic Party (KDP), led by Masoud Barzani. The PUK's Peshmerga militias were the largest and best trained of the Kurdish forces.

In the months prior to the invasion, the United States had inserted special operations forces to train and coordinate with the Kurds. Coalition planners believed that a Kurdish military campaign would keep Iraqi units tied down in the northern regions of the country and therefore render them unavailable to fight the two main prongs of the invading forces, which would advance from the south. To support the Kurds, the coalition planned to deploy additional special operations forces. Later, airborne units would be dropped in to fight alongside the Peshmerga and KDP fighters in attacks on Iraqi targets, including the important cities of Mosul and Kirkuk. The plan was a bold endeavor that asked a small number of special operations forces, airborne troops, and Kurdish fighters to accomplish the same goals as 60,000 U.S. ground troops, namely tying down 13 Iraqi divisions.

The Kurds were apprehensive that they would be vulnerable to attacks by Islamic terrorist groups, located along the border with Iran, if they deployed their forces to the south. VIKING HAMMER was designed essentially to neutralize the threat to the Kurdish heartland. VIKING HAMMER and subsequent offensives were also an effort by the United States to demonstrate the country's commitment to the Kurds and ensure support from the Kurdish Regional Government in a postwar Iraq. However, the United States was concurrently trying to avoid further straining relations with Turkey, which faced an ongoing Kurdish separatist insurgency. Consequently, the United States chose not to supply the Peshmerga with extensive weaponry for fear that some might be used against Turkish forces.

Before the Peshmerga could engage the Iraqi forces, they had to first secure their own territory and suppress Ansar al-Islam, a Kurdish Sunni Islamist group. Ansar al-Islam was originally formed in 2001 by Islamist Kurdish factions. The group was dominated by Kurds who had fought against the Soviets in Afghanistan. Led by Mullah Krekar, Ansar al-Islam sought to impose a strict version of Sharia (Islamic law) on towns near the border with Iran, including Halabja, Biyara, and Tawela. It also worked with other smaller Islamist groups against the Kurdish Regional Government and was blamed for a number of terrorist attacks against rival Kurdish groups. Ansar al-Islam had approximately 500–600 fighters and controlled more than 100 square miles of territory. Its allies in the other small Islamist groups provided an additional 100–300 fighters to Ansar al-Islam. U.S. defense officials were especially concerned about Ansar al-Islam because of intelligence that the group was harboring senior Al Qaeda figures, which was unfounded. The Peshmerga and KDP militias in VIKING HAMMER numbered approximately 7,000 troops of varying quality with an assortment of mainly Soviet-era weaponry, including mortars, some artillery, and a limited number of armored vehicles. Most were armed with AK-47s and had about 150–200 rounds apiece. Many lacked uniforms, boots, or helmets and instead wore tennis shoes and red scarves. However, the Kurds were highly motivated, and U.S. special operations forces provided the heavy firepower, including mortars, grenade launchers, and machine guns. They also had charge of communications between units. Most importantly, the U.S. personnel were able to coordinate ground support from coalition aircraft and cruise missiles.

There were approximately 600 U.S. soldiers from the 10th Special Forces Group with the PUK and KDP, organized into 12-member teams. U.S. colonel Charlie Cleveland was the operational commander of the covert U.S. troops. The special operations forces had previously staged in Romania and been given the code name Task Force Viking (which led, in turn, to the offensive's title, VIKING HAMMER). In VIKING HAMMER, the Kurdish offensive was led by 40 soldiers of the 3rd Battalion of the 10th Special Forces Group, commanded by Lieutenant Colonel Ken Tovo. Tovo divided his men into split teams; each 6-member group worked with a Kurdish unit of 150–800 troops.

Ansar al-Islam and its allies had constructed a series of complexes on mountains and hilltops overlooking the surrounding valleys, near Halabja, Iraq. The Kurds were apprehensive that any attack would leave them vulnerable to mortar and machine gun fire from the heights. U.S. personnel scouted the positions and pretargeted them for air strikes.

On March 21, 2003, 64 cruise missiles hit Ansar al-Islam bunkers in a three-hour period. The pro-U.S. Kurds were impressed by the precision and power of the attack. About 100 members of the radical Islamic Group of Kurdistan, an ally of Ansar al-Islam, were killed in the strikes, and the remainder of the group surrendered the following morning. Another small Islamic group also surrendered before the main offensive commenced.

On March 28, the U.S.-Kurdish force began its attack at 6:00 a.m. The allies were divided into four groups, each led by a special

forces team. The Ansar al-Islam fighters proved to be a tough and experienced foe, for they had the routes into the mountains covered with mortars and would fire a limited number of rounds and then move in an effort to avoid being targeted by U.S. spotters. Peshmerga artillery and mortars provided the opening salvos from the coalition forces. When the advance encountered its first organized resistance, air strikes were called in and two U.S. McDonnell Douglas/Boeing Navy F-18s dropped precision-guided 500-pound bombs on the Iraqi position. By 9:00 a.m., the Kurds had captured Gulp, the first significant village. Coalition forces found various weapons, including explosive suicide vests and bomb-making materials. The four teams had to assault and capture a series of bunkers and complexes under mortar fire and incoming rounds from Katyusha rockets. Slowly, they moved into the mountains, using the heavy weapons and sniper fire of the special operations forces to engage enemy positions. The mountainous terrain impeded the ability of the U.S. troops to radio for air strikes, and the coalition forces had to rely on their own weapons and capabilities. U.S. snipers proved especially effective because of their long-range capabilities. By the afternoon, the combined forces had taken the strategic town of Sagrat, which had served as the headquarters of the senior Ansar al-Islam leaders. Around 5:00 p.m., the U.S. forces were able to regain radio contact and arrange air strikes on enemy positions. Once again, 500-pound precision-guided bombs were used.

Over the next two days, the U.S.-Kurdish force continued its advance. Much of the fighting involved attacks on enemy cave complexes. The coalition forces endeavored unsuccessfully to use tear gas to force the fighters from the caves. When that tactic failed, the U.S. forces used grenades and antitank missiles to destroy the cave bunkers. The Peshmerga forces did not have equipment to engage in night fighting, which limited the ability of the coalition forces to pursue Ansar al-Islam fighters. After the first day of combat, an increasing number of the Islamic fighters had fled across the border into Iran. The Iranians reportedly disarmed the fighters but did not detain them. Some were forcibly returned across the border.

The U.S. forces were able to collect a considerable amount of intelligence on Ansar al-Islam and its links with Al Qaeda. In addition, the coalition forces found that almost half of the fighters killed or captured were foreign born and had come to Iraq to train for terrorist missions. On March 29, a U.S. team explored a suspected chemical weapons manufacturing and training facility in Sagrat. The team discovered instructions on the manufacture of chemical weapons; they also found chemical suits and traces of the highly toxic ricin.

Sporadic fighting continued until March 30, the day VIKING HAMMER officially ended. During the operation, 3 Peshmerga soldiers were killed and 23 were wounded. No U.S. personnel were killed or seriously wounded. Approximately 150–250 Ansar al-Islam fighters were killed, in addition to the 100 killed among the Islamic Group of Kurdistan. After VIKING HAMMER, the Kurdish forces moved south as part of the broader coalition northern offensive against the regular Iraqi Army. Ansar al-Islam reemerged after the fall of Saddam Hussein as one of the numerous groups in the anti-U.S. insurgency.

TOM LANSFORD

See also

Al Qaeda in Iraq; Ansar al-Islam; Cruise Missiles, Employment of, Persian Gulf and Iraq Wars; IRAQI FREEDOM, Operation; IRAQI FREEDOM, Operation, Coalition Ground Forces; Iraqi Insurgency; Kurdistan Democratic Party; Kurds; Patriotic Union of Kurdistan; Peshmerga; United States Army, Iraq War; United States Special Operations Command

References

Gunter, Michael M. *The Kurds Ascending: The Evolving Solution to the Kurdish Problem in Iraq and Turkey.* New York: Palgrave Macmillan, 2008.

McKiernan, Kevin. *The Kurds: A People in Search of Their Homeland.* New York: St. Martin's, 2006.

O'Leary, Brendan, John McGarry, and Khaled Salih, eds. *The Future of Kurdistan in Iraq.* Philadelphia: University of Pennsylvania Press, 2005.

Tucker, Mike. *Among Warriors in Iraq.* New York: Lyons, 2005.

Yildiz, Kerim, and Tom Blass. *The Kurds in Iraq: The Past, Present and Future.* London: Pluto, 2004.

Vines, John R.
Birth Date: 1950

U.S. Army general and commander of the Multi-National Corps–Iraq (part of the Multi-National Force–Iraq) during 2005–2006. Born in Birmingham, Alabama, in 1950, John R. Vines graduated from the University of Alabama with a BS degree in chemistry in 1971 and was commissioned a second lieutenant of infantry through the Reserve Officers' Training Corps (ROTC). Assigned to the 3rd Infantry Division, he served in Europe. After completing ranger training, Vines subsequently commanded a company of the 1st Ranger Battalion of the 75th Ranger Regiment and was a ranger instructor.

Vines held a number of command and staff assignments with the XVIII Airborne Corps, and during 1987–1989 he was assigned to the Joint Special Operations Command. He commanded the 4th Battalion, 325th Airborne Infantry Regiment during its parachute assault in the U.S. invasion of Panama (Operation JUST CAUSE) in 1989. He commanded the same unit when it was the first combat unit deployed on the ground during the buildup in Saudi Arabia (Operation DESERT SHIELD) prior to the 1991 Persian Gulf War (Operation DESERT STORM). His military education includes an MA degree in national security and strategy from the Naval War College.

Vines subsequently served with Task Force Ranger in Somalia during 1992–1994. He then commanded the 2nd Brigade of the

Commanding Generals of the Multi-National Corps–Iraq, 2004–Present

Name	Dates of Command
Thomas F. Metz	May 2004–January 2005
John R. Vines	January 2005–January 2006
Peter W. Chiarelli	January–December 2006
Raymond T. Odierno	December 2006–February 2008
Lloyd J. Austin III	February 2008–April 2009
Charles H. Jacoby Jr.	April 2009–present

101st Airborne Division at Fort Campbell, Kentucky. As a brigadier general, he was assistant divisional commander for operations of the 82nd Airborne Division, 1996–1997. He was then chief of staff of the XVIII Airborne Corps and Fort Bragg during 1997–1999. He next was chief of the Office of Military Cooperation, Cairo, Egypt. From August 2000 until August 2002, he commanded the 82nd Airborne Division.

Following the September 11, 2001, terror attacks on the United States and the U.S.-led invasion of Afghanistan (Operation ENDURING FREEDOM), Vines commanded the forward element of the 82nd Airborne Division deployed to Afghanistan and had charge of tactical missions as commander of Coalition Task Force 82 during September 2002–May 2003. On May 27, 2003, Vines succeeded Lieutenant General Dan K. McNeill as the commanding general of U.S. and coalition forces in Afghanistan (commander, Combined/Joint Task Force 180) at Bagram Air Force Base, Afghanistan, until October 2003.

Vines assumed command of the Multi-National Corps–Iraq in January 2005 and held that post until January 2006. The Multi-National Corps–Iraq was the tactical unit overseeing command and control functions for all Iraqi operations. Headquartered at Camp Victory in Baghdad, the corps was subdivided into five regional areas of responsibility: Baghdad; North; West; Center; Southeast; and Joint Base Balad. Vines concurrently served as commander of the XVIII Airborne Corps during August 2003–December 2006. He retired from active duty on February 1, 2007.

SPENCER C. TUCKER

See also

DESERT SHIELD, Operation; DESERT STORM, Operation; ENDURING FREEDOM, Operation; IRAQI FREEDOM, Operation; JUST CAUSE, Operation; McNeill, Dan K.; Multi-National Force–Iraq; Somalia, International Intervention in

References

Cockburn, Patrick. *The Occupation: War and Resistance in Iraq.* New York: Verso, 2007.

Keegan, John. *The Iraq War: The Military Offensive, from Victory in 21 Days to the Insurgent Aftermath.* New York: Vintage, 2005.

Murray, Williamson, and Robert H. Scales Jr. *The Iraq War: A Military History.* Cambridge, MA: Belknap, 2005.

W

Wadi al-Batin, Battle of
Event Date: February 26, 1991

Battle between U.S. VII Corps and the Tawakalnah Mechanized Division of the Iraqi Republican Guard on February 26, 1991, during Operation DESERT STORM. The engagement was essentially a tank battle. A desert gulch that originates near the town of Hafar al-Batin in Saudi Arabia and runs in a northeasterly direction for about 200 miles, the Wadi al-Batin also delineates most of Kuwait's western border with Iraq. It passes through the triborder area where the boundaries of Kuwait, Saudi Arabia, and Iraq intersect. The Wadi al-Batin provides a natural invasion route into Kuwait and played an important role in coalition planning for the liberation of Kuwait during the ground war phase of Operation DESERT STORM.

Coalition reconnaissance of Iraqi positions confirmed that the Iraqis had deployed their forces to fight off coalition attacks via the Wadi al-Batin, with additional attacks expected in southern Kuwait and from the sea off Kuwait. In fact, the main coalition attack would come to the west of the Wadi and take the form of a giant left hook around Iraqi positions in Kuwait. The Iraqis did not believe that coalition armored forces could navigate successfully through Iraq's featureless southwestern desert because Iraq's own armored forces experienced difficulty doing so. The Iraqis failed to understand that the introduction of Global Positioning System (GPS) technology in the American armed forces meant that topographical landmarks were not necessary in order to maneuver through the desert. The Iraqis also refused to believe that the Americans had sufficient logistical support necessary for a major armored advance through such difficult terrain. The main Iraqi defenses therefore did not extend much more than 100 miles to the west of Wadi al-Batin, leaving a major gap further to the west for coalition armies to exploit.

Coalition planners sought to divert the attention of Iraqi generals away from the western desert and keep them focused on Kuwait and the Wadi al-Batin. On February 16, 1991, U.S. 1st Cavalry Division artillery fired at Iraqi artillery positions in the Wadi. Attacks by Apache helicopters on Iraqi artillery followed. On February 19, units from the 1st Cavalry conducted a reconnaissance in force that ran into heavy resistance from the Iraqi 27th Division defending the Wadi. Both raids diverted Iraqi attention away from the buildup of the U.S. VII Corps, massing to the west for the main attack.

On February 24, the first day of the ground war, units of the 1st Cavalry launched a feint into the Wadi al-Batin. When the 1st Cavalry withdrew, the Iraqis concluded that they had repulsed the main coalition attack. Soon, however, the Iraqis realized the danger they faced from the coalition left hook and began redeploying Republican Guard divisions to meet that threat. The Tawakalnah Mechanized Division of the Republican Guard was deployed just west of the Wadi al-Batin to stop the American VII Corps and allow Iraqi troops to escape from Kuwait.

The U.S. VII Corps fought the Tawakalnah Division in the afternoon and evening of February 26 in the Battle of Wadi al-Batin. The Tawakalnah Division could muster only some 200 tanks to stop more than 1,000 American tanks that also enjoyed complete air supremacy. Although the Tawakalnah Division fought with great determination and tenacity, it also exercised poor tactical skill. Its older Iraqi T-72 tanks were completely outclassed by the American M1A1s. The American tanks could destroy the T-72s at a range of two-and-one-half miles, far beyond the effect range of the T-72s.

In the battle, the Tawakalnah Division lost 177 tanks and 107 armored personnel carriers and was destroyed as a fighting unit. Nevertheless, it succeeded in putting out of action four M1A1 tanks and a number of Bradley armored fighting vehicles, feats unmatched by any other Iraqi division in the war.

PAUL W. DOERR

See also

Antitank Weapons; Armored Warfare, Persian Gulf and Iraq Wars; DESERT STORM, Operation; DESERT STORM, Operation, Ground Operations; M1A1 and M1A2 Abrams Main Battle Tanks; Republican Guard; T-72 Main Battle Tank

References

Gordon, Michael R., and General Bernard E. Trainor. *The Generals' War: The Inside Story of the Conflict in the Gulf.* New York: Little, Brown, 1995.

Pollack, Kenneth M. *Arabs at War: Military Effectiveness, 1948–1991.* Lincoln: University of Nebraska Press, 2002.

Wahhabism

The Western term for the beliefs of the *muwahhidun,* the followers of Muhammad ibn Abd al-Wahhab (1702–1792). They constituted a political and religious movement that appeared in central Arabia in the 1740s. Wahhabism has its greatest influence in Saudi Arabia, where it is associated with the Saudi dynasty, and in the other Arab Gulf states.

Abd al-Wahhab's followers sought a return to the practices of the first three generations of Islamic history, and to cleanse Islamic practice of illicit innovations (*bida*). Abd al-Wahhab's followers also rejected Ottoman political as well as religious authority, accusing the Ottomans of corrupting Islam and Islamic society; indeed, they went further, choosing to regard the Ottomans as unbelievers and therefore legitimate targets for warfare. This process of labeling other Muslims as unbelievers is known as *takfir.* The Saudi government today, however, officially rejects *takfir* as employed by violent Islamic extremists.

The early Wahhabis attacked others who carried out practices they deemed innovative, syncretic, or polytheistic, such as visits to and veneration of Islamic holy figures' graves, including even the Prophet Muhammad's burial place. They also opposed and fought Shia groups and attacked their holy places in connection with their battles against the Ottomans. Because the followers of Abd al-Wahhab united with the expanding Saudi tribe, they are associated with all stages of the Saudi state's development.

Today in Saudi Arabia, the Hanbali *madhhab* (legal school) influenced by the followers of Abd al-Wahhab is the dominant—although not sole—doctrine in Islamic courts and education. The followers of Abd al-Wahhab do not believe in absolutely strict adherence to any legal school; however, because the Hanbali school was the first established, it is prevalent. When it comes to Saudi foreign policy, such as the Arab-Israeli conflict, Wahhabism is subordinate to government calculations of the national interest.

Sheikh Muhammad ibn Abd al-Wahhab was a religious scholar from a small town near the present-day Saudi capital of Riyadh. In 1740 he composed a theological essay condemning common Muslim religious practices. For example, many Muslims went to holy men to seek their blessings. Other Muslims visited the tombs of holy men to ask that they intercede with God on their behalf. Sheikh abd al-Wahhab considered such actions to be idolatry because they violated Islam's central belief in worshiping God alone without any intermediaries. Because abd al-Wahhab's followers branded other Muslims as unbelievers, their views were initially challenged.

Abd al-Wahhab was expelled from two Arabian towns before he formed an alliance with Muhammad ibn Saud in 1744. Sheikh Muhammad abd al-Wahhab gave religious legitimacy to Saudi military expeditions in the guise of Muslim holy war against unbelievers in return for Saudi political support.

By 1800, Saudi-Wahhabi forces had conquered much of Arabia. The major Muslim power of the time, the Ottoman Empire, responded to the Saudi conquest of the holy city of Mecca with a military campaign to crush the first Saudi state. That war lasted from 1811 to 1818 and ended in an Ottoman victory. However, the Saudis staged a comeback in the early 1820s to rule over a smaller Arabian realm. The second Saudi state refrained from aggression against Ottoman territories. Because the Saudis were unwilling to wage jihad, Wahhabi leaders urged their loyal followers to avoid all contact with outsiders, such as Egyptian or Iraqi Muslims, on the grounds that if these were truly unbelievers, their company would threaten the purity of true Muslims' belief. The second Saudi state fell to a rival Arabian power in 1891.

The present Kingdom of Saudi Arabia began to emerge when Saudi prince Abd al-Aziz ibn Saud, also known as Ibn Saud, seized Riyadh in 1902. Over the next 30 years, he conquered the territories that presently comprise the Kingdom of Saudi Arabia. A major element in those conquests was a new wave of the Wahhabi movement called Ikhwan (Brethren). The Ikhwan became fierce warriors for Ibn Saud and gained a fearsome reputation for their savage treatment of defeated enemies. They provided the shock troops for Ibn Saud's military campaigns, but he eventually had to restrain them from pursuing holy war against tribes in Iraq and Transjordan. At the time, those two countries were governed by British-appointed monarchs. Consequently, Ikhwan raids threatened to embroil Ibn Saud in a confrontation with Great Britain. When he ordered the Ikhwan to cease their raids, they rose up in rebellion, but he was able to crush them by 1930.

Three years later, Ibn Saud granted American oil companies the right to explore for petroleum. Wahhabi clerics were unhappy to see Americans permitted into the kingdom, but Ibn Saud and the oil companies minimized contact between Saudis and foreign workers by creating special self-contained residential compounds for non-Saudis. The first test of U.S.-Saudi relations came in 1947, when the United States supported the United Nations (UN) resolution for the partition of Palestine into Jewish and Arab states. Ibn Saud made clear his opposition to the creation of Israel to

The Amiriya Madrasah, a religious school built by Sultan Emir bin Abdul Wahhab in 1504, in Radaa City, some 168 miles southeast of the Yemeni capital of Sanaa, June 7, 2005. (Corbis)

the president of the United States, but American oil companies retained their interests in Saudi oil. Saudi anger over U.S. support for Israel disrupted U.S.-Saudi relations during the October 1973 Yom Kippur (Ramadan) War. Saudi Arabia's King Faisal responded to the U.S. emergency airlift of military supplies to Israel by imposing an embargo on oil sales and joining with other major oil producers to dramatically raise the price of oil.

Throughout the Cold War, Saudi Arabia joined forces with the United States to combat the spread of Nasserism and populism in the Muslim world and, like the United States, it opposed communism. Saudi efforts included their exporting of their own religious doctrine, which is firmly anticommunist. It is also firmly anti-Jewish because of its attachment to historical religious texts emphasizing early clashes between the Prophet Muhammad and Jewish clans in Arabia. When it comes to setting foreign policy, however, Saudi rulers take a practical approach and only consult Wahhabi leaders when seeking their approval for sensitive initiatives. Hence, Saudi Arabia supported the Madrid peace process of the 1990s and announced a peace initiative in March 2002 for a comprehensive settlement of the Arab-Israeli conflict, and King Abdullah has called for interfaith dialogue.

Before and during the 1991 Persian Gulf War, Saudi leaders had to walk a fine line when they allowed the buildup of hundreds of thousands of troops to occur on Saudi soil, lest they incur the wrath of Saudi religious leaders. Nevertheless, many Saudis did not like the presence of foreigners in their nation, and Saudi Arabia refused to garrison troops on its soil for the 2003 Iraq War.

Neo-Wahhabism has produced a current of opposition to the Saudi state, even though the vast majority of devout Wahhabis in Saudi Arabia support the government.

DAVID COMMINS

See also
Faisal, King of Saudi Arabia; Jihad; Saudi Arabia; Shia Islam; Sunni Islam

References
Bronson, Rachel. *Thicker Than Oil: America's Uneasy Partnership with Saudi Arabia.* New York: Oxford University Press, 2006.
Commins, David. *The Wahhabi Mission and Saudi Arabia.* London: I. B. Tauris, 2006.
Kostiner, Joseph. "Coping with Regional Challenges: A Case Study of Crown Prince Abdullah's Peace Initiative." In *Saudi Arabia in the Balance,* edited by Paul Aarts and Gerd Nonneman, 352–371. London: Hurst, 2005.
Piscatori, James. "Islamic Values and National Interest: The Foreign Policy of Saudi Arabia." In *Islam in Foreign Policy,* edited by Adeed Dawisha, 33–53. Cambridge: Cambridge University Press, 1983.

Wallace, William Scott
Birth Date: December 31, 1946

U.S. Army general. Born on December 31, 1946, in Chicago, Illinois, William Scott Wallace graduated in 1969 from the U.S. Military Academy, West Point. He also holds a master of science degree in operations research, and a master of arts degree in international relations and national security and strategic studies. On graduation, Wallace was commissioned in the armor branch.

Wallace has commanded troops at every level, from platoon to corps. He served a combat tour in Vietnam during 1972 as assistant district adviser and later operations adviser in the Bac Lieu Province. After Vietnam, he commanded a company in the 4th Battalion (Light) (Airborne), 68th Armored Regiment, 82nd Airborne Division at Fort Bragg, North Carolina. Wallace attended the Naval Postgraduate School, Monterey, California (1977), and in 1986 he became commander of the 3rd Squadron, 2nd Armored Cavalry Regiment in Germany.

As a colonel, Wallace returned to Germany in 1992 to take command of the 11th Armored Cavalry Regiment in Fulda. Following regimental command, Wallace was assigned to the National Training Center (NTC), Fort Irwin, California, and became NTC commander. As a major general, Wallace commanded the 4th Infantry Division at Fort Hood, Texas (1997–1999), after which he led the Joint Warfighting Center and was director of Joint Training, J-7, at the U.S. Joint Forces Command, Virginia, one of ten Department of Defense combatant commands.

Wallace is perhaps best known for his command of the U.S. V Corps during the March 2003 invasion of Iraq (Operation IRAQI FREEDOM). In July 2001, Wallace, now a lieutenant general, became V Corps commander. On March 20, 2003, V Corps became the vanguard of the American-led coalition that invaded Iraq. Wallace's V Corps spearheaded the drive to Baghdad, defeating the Iraqi Army in three weeks, and capturing Baghdad on April 9, 2003.

Despite Wallace's prominent role in the rapid and stunning defeat of Iraqi president Saddam Hussein's army, he became the center of some controversy concerning remarks he allegedly made to reporters while still in command of V Corps in Iraq. Wallace is reported to have said that "the enemy the U.S. was facing was different from the enemy the military had planned against." Because the alleged remarks came from a top military leader personally involved with combat actions, they were immediately seized upon by opponents of President George W. Bush's invasion of Iraq as representing strong criticism of Secretary of Defense Donald Rumsfeld and the administration's handling of the war.

In the book *Cobra II* (2006) by Michael R. Gordon and Bernard Trainor, the authors claim that Wallace's superior, General Tommy Franks, U.S. Central Command (CENTCOM) commander, threatened to fire Wallace over the remarks, a claim that Franks later disputed. Wallace weathered the controversy, however. He retained command of V Corps until June 2003, when he was reassigned after serving out a typical two-year corps command tour.

After handing over command of V Corps in Iraq to Lieutenant General Ricardo S. Sanchez, Wallace took over the U.S. Army Combined Arms Center (CAC) at Fort Leavenworth, Kansas. As CAC commander, Wallace was responsible for leader development and military and civilian education, including the U.S. Army Command and General Staff College, the Center for Army Lessons Learned, and the Battle Command Training Program. Known as the intellectual center of the army, CAC consists of 16 major schools and centers that prepare the army's future leadership for war.

In October 2005, Wallace was promoted to full general (four-star rank) and assigned as commander, U.S. Army Training and Doctrine Command (TRADOC). TRADOC is the army's "schoolhouse," the major command responsible for recruiting and training soldiers, developing and educating leaders, supporting training in units army-wide, and developing doctrine and standards. Wallace presided over a vast system of 33 schools and centers at 16 different army installations, conducting over 2,700 courses that train annually 500,000 soldiers, service members from other military services, civilians, and international soldiers from around the world. After a military career of more than 39 years, Wallace retired from the army on December 8, 2008.

JERRY D. MORELOCK

See also

Bush, George Walker; Franks, Tommy Ray; IRAQI FREEDOM, Operation; IRAQI FREEDOM, Operation, Ground Campaign; Rumsfeld, Donald Henry; Sanchez, Ricardo S.

References

Gordon, Michael R., and General Bernard E. Trainor. *Cobra II: The Inside Story of the Invasion and Occupation of Iraq.* New York: Pantheon Books, 2006.

Keegan, John. *The Iraq War: The Military Offensive, from Victory in 21 Days to the Insurgent Aftermath.* New York: Vintage, 2005.

Waller, Calvin Augustine Hoffman
Birth Date: December 17, 1936
Death Date: May 9, 1996

U.S. army officer and deputy commander in chief of the United States Central Command (CENTCOM) during the 1991 Persian Gulf War (Operation DESERT STORM). Born in Baton Rouge, Louisiana, on December 17, 1936, Calvin Augustine Hoffman Waller graduated from Prairie View A&M University in 1959. He entered the U.S. Army, and following the Infantry Officer Basic Course at Fort Benning, Georgia, embarked on a career path that found him serving in a wide range of infantry, chemical corps, armor command, and staff and school assignments in Korea, Germany, Vietnam, and the United States. He enjoyed steady promotion and ultimately achieved the rank of lieutenant general.

Waller attended the Command and General Staff College and the Army War College. In 1987 Waller assumed command of the

8th Infantry Division (Mechanized); two years later he took command of I Corps at Fort Lewis. In the autumn of 1990, while still serving as commander of I Corps, Waller was assigned as deputy CENTCOM commander to General H. Norman Schwarzkopf. In that role Waller made headlines by telling journalists in December 1990 that the ground forces would not be ready for a ground offensive until February, after the deadline of January 15, set by the United Nations (UN), for Iraq to withdraw from Kuwait. Many news outlets missed the seemingly obvious implication that an air offensive was possible (indeed, likely) before that date, and Operation DESERT STORM began on January 16, 1991.

As deputy commander, Waller handled many of the details of the American buildup in Saudi Arabia. Most accounts give Waller major credit for countering General Schwarzkopf's explosive, and often abusive, personality and maintaining the morale of the command's staff and commanders.

On February 14, 1991, Lieutenant General John J. Yeosock, commander of United States Third Army (and senior headquarters to the two United States army corps in the field), flew to Germany for an emergency gall bladder operation. Waller assumed interim command, expecting to be in that role for the upcoming ground campaign. Waller left the main command post in Riyadh near CENTCOM headquarters and directed operations from his mobile forward command post near the Iraqi border. From this location he energized the command process and began visiting commanders and making critical decisions, knowing that he had the confidence of the CENTCOM commander. However, in one of his more controversial moves, Schwarzkopf returned Yeosock to command on February 22, less than 48 hours before the beginning of the ground offensive. This last minute switch of senior commanders contributed to the friction in reporting and command, which became apparent during the latter phases of the operation. Certainly it was a blow to Waller, who returned to his original role as a buffer against Schwarzkopf's tirades and the de facto commander for Operation DESERT STORM's ground forces.

Following the war, Waller returned to the United States and retired from the service at the end of November 1991. As one of the senior African American officers in the service, his career spanned an important period of the U.S. civil rights movement, and his success served as a barometer of the great societal changes at the close of the 20th century. After retiring from the military, Waller moved to Denver, where he became president of RKK Limited, an environmental technology company. He subsequently became senior vice president for ICF Kaiser Environmental and Energy Group. His last position was as vice president of site operations for Kaiser-Hill, Inc. Waller died of a sudden heart attack while visiting Washington, D.C., on May 9, 1996.

STEPHEN A. BOURQUE

See also

DESERT STORM, Operation; Schwarzkopf, H. Norman, Jr.; United States Central Command; Yeosock, John J.

References

Atkinson, Rick. *Crusade: The Untold Story of the Persian Gulf War.* New York: Mariner Books, 1994.

Bourque, Stephen A. *Jayhawk! The VII Corps in the Persian Gulf War.* Washington, DC: Department of the Army, 2002.

Gordon, Michael R., and General Bernard E. Trainor. *The Generals' War: The Inside Story of the Conflict in the Gulf.* New York: Little, Brown, 1995.

Swain, Richard. *Lucky War: The Third Army in Desert Storm.* Fort Leavenworth, KS: U.S. Army Command and General Staff College Press, 1999.

War, Operational Art of

The operational art of war consists of the body of military activities that fall between tactics and strategy. The tactical and the strategic have long been recognized as distinct levels of warfare with their own peculiar requirements and dynamics. Recognition of the operational level of war only began to evolve slowly at the start of the 19th century and was not fully accepted by all militaries throughout the world until the final years of the 20th century. In the years following World War I, the Soviets fully embraced the concept of the operational art of war and for many years led the way in its theoretical development. The United States, in company with the rest of the North Atlantic Treaty Organization (NATO) countries, accepted the operational level of war only in the early 1980s, and that marked one of the key military turning points of the Cold War.

Simply stated, tactics is the art of winning battles, while strategy is the art of winning wars. The operational art focuses on winning campaigns, which are made up of battles and contribute to the winning of wars. In the late 1980s, the U.S. Army Command and General Staff College used the metaphor of a medieval military flail to illustrate the relationship among the three levels of war. The handle of the flail represented strategy, the overall directing force of the weapon. The spiked ball represented tactics, the part of the weapon that delivered the actual blow. The flexible chain that connected the handle to the spiked ball represented operational art, the vital link between strategy and tactics.

The flail metaphor was a simple and effective model for introducing the concept of the operational art, but it came apart if pushed too far. The difficulty in the relationships among the three levels of warfare is that success on one level does not automatically translate into success on another level. Major General Nathanael Greene's Southern Campaign of 1780–1781 during the War for American Independence is one example in which a general who lost the battles still won the campaign. Nor does winning all the battles and even all the campaigns necessarily guarantee winning the war. The Vietnam War demonstrated that, if nothing else.

The origins of the operational level of war can be traced to the mass armies of Napoleon and his practice of marching his corps in separate approach columns and then massing his forces at the

Painting of Napoleon surveying the battlefield at Wagram in July 1809. Napoleon is widely regarded as one of history's most brilliant military commanders. (William M. Sloane, *Life of Napoleon Bonaparte*, vol. 1, 1906)

decisive point just prior to battle. During the latter half of the 19th century, the German Army under Count Helmuth von Moltke recognized a body of activities it called *Operativ,* which involved all of the maneuvering and preparations prior to the initiation of a battle. The first forces to arrive fixed the enemy in position, while the follow-on forces maneuvered around the enemy's flank to gain decisive tactical advantage. The Germans did not, however, identify *Operativ* as a distinct level of war fighting. Throughout World War I, the Germans had the most advanced understanding of the operational art, although it was deeply flawed by contemporary standards. The flaws in their operational thinking would cost the German Army dearly in World War II.

In the late 19th and early 20th centuries some military writers, including J. F. C. Fuller, grouped operational-level activities under a concept they called Grand Tactics. But it was the Soviet military theorists who made the most significant contributions to advancing the concept of operational art as we know it today. As early as 1907, Russian military writers were debating a concept they called *Opertika.* Following the disastrous defeat of the Red Army in the 1920 Battle of Warsaw, two opposing schools of thought emerged in the Soviet military. Marshal Mikhail N. Tukhachevsky, the Red Army front commander at Warsaw, was the leader of the annihilation school of thought. Annihilation depended upon the ability to

conduct large-scale, immediate, decisive operations. It required a war industry and a large standing army. Tukhachevsky's 1924 paper "Maneuver and Artillery" had a strong influence on the Frunze Military Academy reforms of 1924–1925, and those ideas were later formalized in the Red Army's *Field Service Regulations* of 1927.

Soviet major general Aleksandr A. Svechin led the opposing school of thought. In his influential 1926 book *Strategy,* he advocated the doctrine of attrition, which relied more on Russia's traditional deep resources of space, time, and manpower. He also formally posited for the first time the concept that operations were distinct from strategy and tactics. He argued that tactics made up the steps from which operational leaps were assembled, "with strategy pointing out the path." Within a year of Svechin introducing the concept, the Soviets established a chair on the conduct of operations within the Department of Strategy at the Military Academy of the Red Army.

Svechin and Tukhachevsky were both eliminated in Stalin's purges of the 1930s, but their opposing theories were synthesized by Vladimir K. Triandafillov in his book *The Nature of the Operations of Modern Armies.* Published in 1929, the book is now regarded as one of the seminal works in Soviet military thought. Triandafillov was the first to introduce the planning norms that became one of the benchmarks of Soviet operational art. He also laid out the theory of successive operations and deep operations (*glubokaia operatsiia*), with the result that several successive operations were linked into a single continuous, deep operation. Thus, the point of Napoleon and line of Moltke gave way to the vector in depth, with its multiple effects—both sequentially and simultaneously—in three dimensions.

Although operational art emerged during the interwar years in the Soviet Union as a vibrant new field of military study, many of the operational concepts associated with it were stillborn or only partially developed. The Red Army learned this hard truth and suffered accordingly during the Winter War with Finland in 1939–1940 and in 1941 during the opening months of the war with Germany. Soviet operational art only reached its highest level of development through trial and error in the crucible of World War II. Yet for all its final sophistication, the Soviets never fully developed the air and naval components of operational art.

The widely held popular belief is that what the West called the German Blitzkrieg represented the most highly developed form of the operational art through the period of World War II. Many military analysts, however, have argued that Blitzkrieg was at best a deeply flawed expression of operational art. The keys to the operational level of war are depth and sequencing. Depth has both a temporal and a spatial component. Depth in terms of space meant that for the first time there was a recognition that the battle was not necessarily decided at the line of contact but could be carried deep into an enemy's rear area. Depth in time meant sequencing, which was the key to cumulative effects that built on the successes of one battle to the next. Unfortunately for the Germans, their military thinking from the time of Count Alfred von Schlieffen on was dominated by the concept of the battle of annihilation, what they called the *Vernichtungsschlacht.*

With its geographic position in Europe and relatively defenseless borders east and west, Germany's worst strategic nightmare was always the two-front war. To avoid this trap, German military thinking focused on conducting short wars that would be won by a single decisive battle. Thus, sequential effects and extended operations in time carried a low priority in German thinking. And since logistics is the critical enabler of any extended period of operations, the Germans never developed the robust logistics structure or the adequate logistics doctrine needed to carry them through a long war. But a long war on even more than two fronts is exactly what the Germans ended up fighting twice in a 30-year period.

Despite their rapid movements and deep armored thrusts, the German Blitzkrieg battles of World War II were not true operational campaigns but rather were tactical maneuvers on a grand scale. Blitzkrieg did feature the innovative use of combined arms tactics aimed at achieving rupture through the depth of an enemy's tactical deployment, and it did exhibit many of the features we now associate with the operational art. It also focused far too heavily on annihilation and rapid decision by a single bold stroke.

On the tactical level of war, the German Army was superior to the Red Army on almost every count, yet the Soviets still beat the

A German motorized detachment moves through the remains of a Polish town during the Blitzkrieg of September 1939 that began World War II. (Library of Congress)

Germans in the end. German tactics were innovative and flexible, and their leaders and soldiers were well trained and exhibited initiative down to the lowest levels. Soviet tactics were largely rigid, cookbook battle drills, with the soldiers and the lower-level leaders functioning as mere automatons. But the Soviets had developed a far superior concept of the operational art and especially the principles of depth and sequential effects. The Soviets became masters of striking deep into the German rear to disrupt command and control systems and the all-too-fragile German logistics system. In the end, Blitzkrieg was little more than the German Army's tactical response to German chancellor Adolf Hitler's totally incoherent strategy.

Despite the flaws in what eventually became Blitzkrieg, the post–World War I German Army did have a clear, albeit imperfect, understanding of a level of war between the tactical and the strategic. Writing in 1920, General Hugo Freiherr von Freytag-Loringhoven noted that among German General Staff officers, the term *Operativ* was increasingly replacing the term *Strategisch* to "define more simply and clearly the difference from everything tactical." The 1933 edition of *Truppenführung*, the primary German war-fighting manual of World War II, distinguished clearly between tactical and operational functions. *Truppenführung*'s principal author, General Ludwig Beck, considered *Operativ* a subdivision of strategy. Its sphere was the conduct of battle at the higher levels, in accordance with the tasks presented by strategic planning. Tellingly, when U.S. Army intelligence made a rough English translation of *Truppenführung* just prior to World War II, the term *Operativ* was translated throughout as "strategic."

Post–World War II American military doctrine focused almost exclusively on the tactical level. Although the U.S. Army and its British allies had planned and executed large and complex operational campaigns during the war, the mechanics of those efforts were largely forgotten by the early 1950s. Nuclear weapons cast a long retarding shadow over American ground combat doctrine, and the later appearance of battlefield nuclear weapons seemed to render irrelevant any serious consideration of maneuver by large-scale ground units. The Soviets, meanwhile, continued to study and write about operational art and the operational level of war. While the U.S. military intelligence community closely monitored and analyzed the trends in Soviet doctrine, American theorists ignored or completely rejected these concepts. Because of its dominant role in NATO, America's operational blinders were adopted for the most part by its coalition allies.

In the early to mid-1970s, American thinking began to change. The three major spurs to this transformation were the loss in Vietnam, the stunning new weapons effects demonstrated in the October 1973 Yom Kippur (Ramadan) War, and the need to fight and win against the superior numbers of the armed forces of the Warsaw Pact. The concept of the operational level of war entered the debate when the influential defense analyst Edward Luttwak published the article "The Operational Level of War" in the winter 1980–1981 issue of the journal *International Security.* About the same time, Colonel Harry Summers's book *On Strategy: The Vietnam War in Context* sparked a parallel renaissance in strategic thinking and the rediscovery of Clausewitz by the American military. The U.S. Army formally recognized the operational level of war with the publication of the 1982 edition of *FM 100-5, Operations,* which also introduced the concepts of AirLand Battle and Deep Battle.

The operational art was first defined in the 1986 edition of *FM 100-5,* along with the concept that commanders had to fight and synchronize three simultaneous battles: close, deep, and rear. The idea was that one's own deep battle would be the enemy's rear battle, and vice versa. The close battle would always be strictly tactical, but the deep and rear battles would have operational significance.

During the 1970s and 1980s the American military invested heavily in new weapons systems, force structure, and training to

A U.S. Air Force A-10 Thunderbolt II aircraft flies over Iraq on December 14, 2006. (U.S. Department of Defense)

complement its evolving doctrine. The U.S. Army acquired such advanced systems as the M-1 Abrams tank; the M-2 Bradley infantry fighting vehicle; the UH-60 Blackhawk airmobility helicopter; the AH-60 attack helicopter; and the M-270 multiple launch rocket system (MLRS). U.S. Air Force systems included the A-10 attack aircraft, specifically designed to kill tanks; the F-15 air superiority fighter; and the F-16 multirole fighter. The air force also developed a sophisticated array of precision-guided munitions for the various platforms. Most importantly, however, the United States committed extensive resources to developing its military manpower, producing officers, noncommissioned officers (NCOs) and enlisted men capable of operating the complex systems, exercising initiative, and making independent judgments and decisions in extremely stressful situations.

This superbly trained and equipped force with its new and sophisticated operational doctrine was never committed against the primary enemy it was designed to fight, the massed tank armies of the Soviet Union. That enemy largely disappeared with the collapse of communism and the Soviet Union. But as that was happening, Saddam Hussein of Iraq committed the strategic blunder of invading Kuwait. Believing he could bluff the Americans and their allies, Hussein then compounded his error by allowing his enemy the time to build up an overwhelming force in Saudi Arabia, prior to launching a counterattack through Kuwait and into Iraq itself.

The irony, then, is that even though the doctrine of AirLand Battle, heavily based on the concept of the operational art, was never tested against the Soviets, it did prove devastatingly effective against a Soviet surrogate, the Iraqi Army, armed with Soviet weapons and equipment and trained in Soviet doctrine. The lopsided victory of the ground phase, the so-called Hundred Hour War, was not, however, quite the same thing as defeating the Red Army. Although the American weapons vastly overmatched those of the Iraqis, Hussein's forces for the most part were not equipped with top-of-the-line Soviet systems. Also, the rigid and highly centralized command and control system, the officer corps conditioned to follow orders to the letter but not to exercise initiative, and the poorly trained individual soldiers that were all too typical of most Middle Eastern armies only compounded the Iraqi catastrophe.

Twelve years later, in 2003, Hussein's army had not been rebuilt to anywhere near the level it had been at in 1991, and this time the victory was even more lopsided, as the Iraqis were crushed by a significantly smaller American force. But rather than just defeating the Iraqi Army as they had done in 1991, the Americans this time sought to occupy the country and change its regime. The U.S. military had gone in with just enough forces to win the battle but not nearly enough forces to secure the peace. That, plus a series of key errors and poor decisions during the early phases of the occupation, resulted in an insurgency that killed many more American soldiers than the initial combat operations. Thus, although the Americans conducted the initial phase of the Iraq War with operational near-perfection, their overall strategy was significantly flawed by a failure to connect operational success with the overall strategic objectives. Ironically, this strategic incoherence was precisely the mistake the Americans had made in Vietnam.

DAVID T. ZABECKI

See also

Arab-Israeli Conflict, Overview; North Atlantic Treaty Organization; Starry, Donn Albert

References

McKercher, B. J. C., and Michael A. Hennessy, eds. *The Operational Art: Developments in the Theories of War.* Westport, CT: Praeger, 1996.

Naveh, Shimon. *In Pursuit of Military Excellence: The Evolution of Operational Theory.* London: Frank Cass, 1997.

Newell, Clayton, and Michael D. Krause, eds. *On Operational Art.* Washington, DC: U.S. Army Center of Military History, U.S. Government Printing Office, 1994.

Zabecki, David T. *The German 1918 Offensives: A Case Study in the Operational Level of War.* New York: Routledge, 2006.

Zabecki, David T., and Bruce Condell, eds. and trans. *Truppenführung: On the German Art of War.* Boulder, CO: Lynne Rienner, 2001.

War Correspondents

The history of news reporters covering combat operations dates back at least to the 1853–1856 Crimean War waged by Great Britain, France, and Turkey against Imperial Russia. William Howard Russell, who covered that war for *The Times,* is generally considered the world's first war correspondent. Since that time, correspondents have covered virtually every major conflict throughout the world. During the 20th century, war correspondents brought the realities of combat "up close and personal" to the readers and viewers in their respective countries in major wars, such as World War I, World War II, the Korean War, and the Vietnam War, and in countless lesser conflicts throughout the world. Yet, inevitably, the presence of civilian reporters on the battlefield creates an unavoidable tension between the correspondents, whose only job is to report the facts as they witness them, and the military officers and government officials whose principal duty is to win the war they are fighting. Increasingly, this tension centers on the degree of access to the wars' combat zones that governments grant to war correspondents. While reporters—driven by deadlines and the need to produce ratings-garnering headlines—consistently demand unrestricted free access, government officials and military officers seek to keep war correspondents' access limited to what they judge as "reasonable." The recent wars in the Middle East serve as prime examples of this issue.

In the modern Middle East, three recent or ongoing conflicts—the 1991 Persian Gulf War, the Afghanistan War (October 7, 2001–present), and the Iraq War (March 20, 2003–present)—have led to dramatic developments in the history of war correspondence. These include the growing prominence of media giants such as Cable News Network (CNN), MSNBC, and Fox News, news briefings by high-ranking military officers, news pools attached to military units, and journalists embedded with fighting forces. All of these developments have exposed news media to accusations of government and corporate control, however. An attempt to counter this alleged censorship has led to a proliferation of chiefly internet-based alternative news sites. Moreover, the rising casualty rates among journalists in Afghanistan and particularly Iraq have highlighted the inherent risks of war correspondence. No longer viewed as neutral observers, journalists are increasingly targeted for their alleged political or sectarian affiliations.

The roots of increasing governmental and military control over journalistic reporting go back to the Vietnam War, the Falklands War, and the U.S. invasions of Grenada (1983) and Panama (1989). U.S. supporters of the Vietnam War and many Vietnam War combat veterans alleged that negative journalistic reports were largely responsible for the erosion of American support for the war, in particular, coverage of the 1968 Tet Offensive. The general lack of the largely Saigon-based Vietnam War reporters' "up front" credibility and the perception of inaccurate reporting during Tet and the Vietnam War in general resulted in virtually an entire generation of military officers distrusting the media's accuracy and even their motives. This distrust of media methods, accuracy, and motives has had a profound impact on U.S. government attitudes and policies regarding reporters' access to combat operations when they are in progress. When many of the Vietnam-generation military officers assumed high command in the Persian Gulf War and the Afghanistan and Iraq conflicts, their perception of media bias in the past greatly influenced the U.S. government decision to forego a policy of unrestricted access for journalists in the later conflicts in the Middle East.

During the 1982 Falklands War, the British government sought to control press coverage. British governmental and military officials assigned no more than 29 correspondents and photographers to pools that accompanied the Falklands invasion force. Various reporters later complained of direct censorship. Following the British cue, American government and military officials largely excluded the media from Operation URGENT FURY, the 1983 invasion of Grenada. The 15 reporters finally allowed on Grenada found their movements severely curtailed. Similarly, Operation JUST CAUSE, the 1989 invasion of Panama to overthrow President Manuel Noriega, deployed a very select pool of journalists who complained that they were barely briefed and kept well away from military action.

Persian Gulf War

Although U.S. government and military officials aimed at creating more transparency during the Persian Gulf War, the inevitable accusations of censorship and disinformation abounded since the government did not permit reporters unrestricted access. Following governmental cues, the American media demonized Iraqi president Saddam Hussein, some echoing president George H. W. Bush's characterization of him as a "new Hitler," and representing the war as inevitable. Opposition to the war, which at any rate was slight and disorganized, was mainly ignored except for a few high-profile incidents. Although Iraqi forces committed sufficient outrages during their occupation of Kuwait to fill numerous news reports, charges of propaganda were raised when it was discovered that many of these were Kuwaiti public relations fabrications—such as reports of Iraqi soldiers throwing Kuwaiti babies out of incubators.

Seventeen members of the national media pool arrived in Saudi Arabia on August 13, well before Operation DESERT STORM was launched on January 17, 1991, and were closely monitored during Operation DESERT SHIELD. Headed by Michael Sherman, six government public affairs officers were to handle Persian Gulf media. These officials set up the main military briefing rooms and television studios in Dhahran and Riyadh, Saudi Arabia, and organized "media response teams," a pool system whose members were sometimes permitted to accompany select military units. An intense competition among journalists ensued, but reporters were largely denied access to actual combat. A number of disgruntled journalists affiliated with small media organizations filed a legal brief, claiming that the pool system violated their First Amendment right of free expression. The war ended, however, before courts ruled on the matter.

Those who tried to work outside the pool had little success. Some rented hotel rooms in Saudi Arabia and attended daily military briefings, where such well-prepared military spokespersons as coalition commander General H. Norman Schwarzkopf provided carefully selected information. Meanwhile, General Colin L. Powell, chairman of the Joint Chiefs of Staff, and other Defense Department officials provided daily briefings to reporters in the Pentagon. Pool members, however, largely failed to challenge the data they were given, before, during, and immediately after the conflict.

So-called unilaterals or freelancers also found their movements hampered. By mid-February 1991, some 20 had been detained or threatened with detention. Similarly, television correspondents Peter Arnett of CNN, John Simpson of the BBC, and Brent Sadler of Independent Television News (ITN) evoked criticism for reporting the first stage of the war from Baghdad. Their vivid film of initial air attacks garnered high viewer ratings and helped fuel the soaring popularity of major news networks. Nevertheless, U.S. government officials objected to the correspondents' presence in an enemy capital. In particular, reports of the bombing of a deep military command and control bunker in the Amariyah district of Baghdad—the upper levels of which were also being used as a civilian air raid shelter—which killed 408 civilians, deeply embarrassed coalition officials and provided the Saddam Hussein regime with useful propaganda.

Prompted by governmental and military spokespersons and backed by correspondents from major news media, a sanitized version of combat emerged from coverage of the Persian Gulf War. Critics cited the U.S. government's portrayals of the success of weapons systems such as smart bombs, Tomahawk cruise

The skies over Baghdad erupt with antiaircraft fire as U.S. warplanes strike targets in the Iraqi capital early on January 18, 1991. (AP/Wide World Photos)

missiles, and the Patriot antimissile system as grossly exaggerated, charges generally confirmed by postwar analysis. Criticism was far from limited to weapons systems, however. Charges abounded that unrestricted free press access had prevented reporters from independently verifying official information provided regarding the extent of U.S. friendly fire casualties, the true number of Iraqi military and civilian deaths resulting from coalition ground and air combat actions, and the amount of oil pollution caused by coalition bombing (versus that caused by Iraqi sabotage). Barry Zorthian's statement to the National Press Club on March 19, 1991, may well summarize the judgment of many war correspondents who felt shut out by Department of Defense press restrictions during the Persian Gulf War: "The Gulf War is over and the press lost."

Afghanistan War

As in the Persian Gulf War, war correspondents in the ongoing conflict in Afghanistan, which began as Operation ENDURING FREEDOM on October 7, 2001, have been targeted by appeals to patriotism and national security. For instance, shortly after the war began, major U.S. networks agreed to have any statements from Al Qaeda leader Osama bin Laden screened and edited by the government. The Arab-language television network Al Jazeera soon

was targeted for broadcasting a release from bin Laden on the eve of the first air strike on Afghanistan. On November 13, 2001, Al Jazeera's office in Kabul was struck by a U.S. missile, which officials claimed was intended to hit a well-known Al Qaeda facility. A second attack, again claimed to be mistaken, targeted Al Jazeera's Baghdad office on April 8, 2003, killing a reporter and wounding a cameraman.

From the outset of Operation ENDURING FREEDOM, U.S. defense secretary Donald Rumsfeld warned the media to expect little Pentagon cooperation. When the aerial bombardment began on October 7, 2001, no Western journalists were within the three-quarters of the country controlled by the Taliban, for reporters had gathered in Pakistan and territory held by the anti-Taliban Northern Alliance. By November 10, seven journalists had been killed as they spread out to areas abandoned by the Taliban, whose forces had earlier arrested *Sunday Express* reporter Yvonne Ridley on September 28. Several months later, the Pentagon unveiled plans to establish three Coalition Press Information Centers, in Mazar-e Sharif, Bagram, and Qandahar Airport. Staff members would be charged with helping journalists get photographs and interviews. Still, Assistant Secretary of Defense Victoria Clarke encouraged journalists to remain in Bahrain for best access to war coverage. These procedures led to questions about how much uncensored news was reaching Western readers or viewers. As early as 2002, for instance, *Daily Mirror* correspondent John Pilger claimed that about 5,000 civilian deaths had resulted from bombing raids in Afghanistan, almost double the toll of the September 11, 2001, terrorist attacks on New York.

Yet, the dangers of reporters' unrestricted access to war zones is clearly shown in Afghanistan. Faced with problems of access, an inhospitable terrain, language barriers, and the danger of ambush, journalists complain that they face a hidden war in Afghanistan. Particularly in the south of the country, correspondents have encountered difficulties in hiring local "fixers" willing to risk Taliban retribution. On March 4, 2007, for instance, Taliban forces abducted *La Republica* reporter Daniele Mastrogiacomo along with Afghan journalist Ajmal Nakshbandi and their driver, Sayed Agha, in Helmand Province. While Mastrogiacomo was later released in a prisoner exchange, both Afghans were beheaded. This incident followed the killing of two German *Deutsche Welle* journalists in October 2006.

New restrictions imposed in 2006, whereby media outlets have been told not to publish interviews and reports critical of Afghani president Hamid Karzai's foreign policy or the U.S.-led coalition forces, have led to further protests of curtailment of press freedom.

Iraq War

Operation IRAQI FREEDOM, an ongoing conflict that began with the invasion of Iraq on March 20, 2003, accomplished a new twist in the pool system that had been practiced in the Persian Gulf War and, to some extent, in Afghanistan. At the commencement of the campaign, such major news syndicates as CNN had announced huge budgets for war coverage, planning to devote 24 hours a day to the conflict. However, much to the disappointment of reporters demanding unrestricted free access to combat operations, the Department of Defense chose only to use reporters embedded with combat units. "Embeds" would receive basic training and accompany their assigned units through combat. Embeds were allowed to report what they wished so long as they revealed no information that the enemy could use.

While supporters saw the embed system as restoring "up front" credibility to reporters, whom they had perceived as being aloof and unsympathetic to the real problems faced by troops

NBC News correspondent David Bloom reports from Iraq in this undated television image. Bloom died during the Iraq War while serving as an embedded reporter. (AP/Wide World Photos)

engaged in waging war, critics of the embed system claimed that it resulted in a loss of objectivity among correspondents—who soon discovered that they identified with troops in their assigned units. A few correspondents, such as CNN's Christiane Amanpour (who became a media celebrity through her reporting of the Persian Gulf War and Bosnian conflict), objected to the restrictions, but she was warned that she had to abide by the rules.

More than in the 1991 Persian Gulf War, journalists found that dry, colorless government media briefings offered them little material to produce the dramatic headlines that garner top ratings in the highly competitive news business. Moreover, increasingly international television viewers have become the media giants' target audience, and correspondents often found their reports hampered by syndicate expectations. Yet, despite the claims that access was unduly restricted, war correspondents were instrumental in exposing such incidents as Abu Ghraib prisoner abuse, the overhyped Jessica Lynch "rescue" operation, and the extent of Iraqi civilian casualties due to coalition bombing, such as during the Second Battle of Fallujah, in November 2004.

In short, the war in Iraq suggests that correspondents, unlike during the Persian Gulf War, became more critical, a mood that reflects and even fuels the growing public opposition to the war. Statistics also suggest that Iraq is now the world's most dangerous location for journalists. The conservative estimates of the Committee to Protect Journalists indicate that violence in Iraq claimed the lives of 32 journalists in 2006, the highest number that the organization has recorded to date. Between 2003 and the end of 2008, the Committee to Protect Journalists reported that 136 journalists died in Iraq, while 56 additional media workers (nonjournalists) died. The conflicts in Kuwait, Afghanistan, and Iraq reveal that war correspondence is becoming an increasingly risky enterprise, whether "pooled," "embedded," or acting independently.

ANNA M. WITTMANN

See also

Abu Ghraib; Al Jazeera; Bin Laden, Osama; DESERT STORM, Operation; ENDURING FREEDOM, Operation; Hussein, Saddam; IRAQI FREEDOM, Operation; Karpinski, Janis; Lynch, Jessica; Missiles, Cruise; Patriot Missile System; Rumsfeld, Donald Henry; Schwarzkopf, H. Norman, Jr.; Taliban; Weapons of Mass Destruction

References

Allan, Stuart, and Barbie Zelizer, eds. *Reporting War: Journalism in Wartime.* New York: Routledge, 2004.

Allen, Tim, and Jean Seaton, eds. *The Media of Conflict: War Reporting and Representation of Ethnic Violence.* London: Zed Books, 1999.

Feinstein, Antony. *Dangerous Lives: War and the Men and Women Who Report It.* Toronto: Thomas Allen, 2003.

Fisk, Robert. *The Great War for Civilization: The Conquest of the Middle East.* New York: Vintage Books, 2007.

Knightley, Phillip. *The First Casualty: The War Correspondent as Hero and Myth-Maker from the Crimea to Iraq.* Baltimore: Johns Hopkins University Press, 2004.

McLaughlin, Greg. *The War Correspondent.* London: Pluto, 2002.

Tumber, Howard, and Frank Webster. *Journalists under Fire: Information War and Journalistic Practices.* London: Sage, 2006.

Ward, William E.
Birth Date: June 3, 1949

U.S. Army general and first commander of the U.S. Africa Command. William "Kip" Ward was born in Baltimore, Maryland, on June 3, 1949. He graduated from Morgan State University with a BA in political science in 1971 and received a commission as an infantry officer through the Reserve Officers' Training Corps (ROTC). He subsequently earned a master's degree in political science from Pennsylvania State University. His military education includes the U.S. Army Command and General Staff College and the U.S. Army War College. He was also an instructor at West Point.

Early service assignments included tours with the 82nd Airborne Division at Fort Bragg, North Carolina; the 2nd Infantry Division in Korea, a field artillery brigade in Germany, and command of a battalion of the 6th Infantry Division at Fort Wainwright, Alaska. In October 1993 Colonel Ward was commanding the 2nd Brigade of the 10th Mountain Division (Light) in Mogadishu, Somalia, as a part of Operation RESTORE HOPE, when two Blackhawk helicopters were shot down and 19 American soldiers died in the subsequent rescue operation.

Promoted to brigadier general in March 1996, from February 1998 to July 1999 Ward served as the chief of the Office of Military Cooperation, Egypt, working out of the U.S. embassy in Cairo. Promoted to major general in February 1999, he commanded the

U.S. Army brigadier general William E. Ward in 1995. (U.S. Department of Defense)

25th Infantry Division in Hawaii and then served as vice director for operations of the Joint Staff in Washington. Promoted to lieutenant general in October 2002, he was appointed to command the NATO Stabilization Force in Sarajevo, Bosnia-Herzegovina, holding that post until October 2003.

Ward was serving as the deputy commanding general of U.S. Army, Europe when, in February 2005, during a trip to the Middle East, Secretary of State Condoleezza Rice announced his appointment to the newly established position of United States security coordinator, Israel–Palestinian National Authority (PNA). The coordinator's job was to assist in U.S. efforts to encourage the Israeli government to stay on track with its promise to disengage from the Gaza Strip and the northern West Bank; and simultaneously to support new PNA president Mahmoud Abbas in his efforts to bring the various Palestinian militant organizations under control and to gain positive control over the disparate and fractured Palestinian security organizations.

It was that second task, where all Ward's predecessors had failed, that came close to being mission impossible. Under the long reign of Palestine Liberation Organization (PLO) head Yasser Arafat, the Palestinian military, police, and intelligence functions had evolved into a Byzantine network of overlapping feudal empires, as much in competition with each other as with the Israelis and the various militant groups. Compounding the problem, all too many of the members of the security forces were also members of militant groups. In May 2005 Ward announced the establishment of the Security Sector Working Group, composed of donors interested in supporting Palestinian security reform. The group was cochaired by Ward and Palestinian minister of the interior and national security, Nasser Yusif.

In December 2005 Major General Keith Dayton replaced Ward as the U.S. security coordinator. Ward returned to U.S. Army, Europe, headquarters in Heidelberg, Germany. Shortly thereafter he was appointed deputy commanding general of the U.S. European Command. He was promoted to general in May 2006. Ward is currently the senior ranking African American in the U.S. Army.

In October 1, 2007, Ward became the first commander of the U.S. Africa Command. One of six of the U.S. Defense Department's regional military commands, it has administrative responsibility for U.S. military assistance to support U.S. policy in Africa, including military-to-military relationships with 53 African nations. The command is headquartered in Stuttgart, Germany.

DAVID T. ZABECKI

See also

Abbas, Mahmoud; Arafat, Yasser; Rice, Condoleezza

References

Balaban, Oden, and Michael Graham Fry, eds. *Interpreting Conflict: Israeli-Palestinian Relations at Camp David II and Beyond.* New York: Peter Lang, 2005.

Leverett, Flynt, ed. *The Road Ahead: Middle East Policy in the Bush Administration's Second Term.* Washington, DC: Brookings Institution, 2005.

Warden, John Ashley, III
Birth Date: December 21, 1943

U.S. Air Force officer and one of the leading theorists on modern airpower whose ideas greatly influenced the Persian Gulf War air campaign. John Ashley Warden III was born in McKinney, Texas, on December 21, 1943. He graduated from the U.S. Air Force Academy in 1965 and was commissioned a second lieutenant in the air force. In 1975, he earned a master's degree from Texas Tech University.

Following pilot training, in 1969 Warden volunteered for duty in Vietnam, where he flew more than 250 missions as a forward air controller. He was often frustrated by the complicated rules of engagement during the Vietnam War, and later came to believe that the lack of a coherent strategic vision had led to America's failure in that conflict. Warden came to realize that several prerequisites had to be in place in order to successfully prosecute a war: a coherent, consistent overarching strategy; preponderant force; precise objectives; a clear and realistic exit strategy; and the full integration of military and political interests. Many of these ideas were also later advanced by General Colin L. Powell, in what came to be known as the Powell Doctrine, which was followed with much success during Operation DESERT STORM.

Warden held several positions before being assigned as a major to the Pentagon in August 1975 in the Directorate of Plans. Here he began to publicize his ideas on airpower. Warden then embarked on a series of operational assignments.

In 1988, Warden published his first book, *The Air Campaign: Planning for Combat.* In it, he laid out his own concepts of airpower. The book was well received, and many of its concepts were utilized in the air campaign against Iraq in 1991. From the book emerged an organizational structure known as the Prometheus Strategic Planning System. His prescriptions were not without critics, however. In the book, Warden had essentially challenged the prevailing AirLand Battle Doctrine, which suggested that airpower was not strategic in and of itself and that it must play a subservient role to ground forces.

Following a posting as wing commander in the 36th Tactical Fighter Group in Germany, in 1989 Warden returned to the Pentagon, where he continued to promote and fine-tune his theories on airpower and military grand strategy. Warden became the air force's preeminent strategist for the air campaign during the Persian Gulf War, traveling to Saudi Arabia to present his plans to U.S. Central Command commander General H. Norman Schwarzkopf in person. Warden grouped targets into five different categories, expressed as concentric rings. The center was the enemy leadership. Ranging out from it were system essentials, infrastructure, population, and fielded military forces. Warden stressed that it was important to attack as many of these as possible simultaneously, with special emphasis on the most important of enemy leadership, so as to bring about physical paralysis.

Promoted to colonel, Warden in mid-1991 became a special assistant to Vice President Dan Quayle, working on issues such as economic productivity and competitiveness. From 1992 to 1995, Warden was commandant of the Air Command and Staff College, where he undertook sweeping curriculum changes that focused on strategy rather than tactics and techniques. Warden retired as a colonel in June 1995 and began his own successful consulting business, which sought to wed his ideas on strategy to U.S. and international business concerns. He has written numerous books on strategy and business issues.

PAUL G. PIERPAOLI JR.

See also

AirLand Battle Doctrine; Powell Doctrine; United States Air Force, Iraq War; United States Air Force, Persian Gulf War

References

Atkinson, Rick. *The Generals' War: The Inside Story of the Conflict in the Gulf.* New York: Little, Brown, 1995.

Olsen, John Andreas. *John Warden and the Renaissance of American Air Power.* Dulles, VA: Potomac Books, 2007.

Schwarzkopf, H. Norman, with Peter Petre. *It Doesn't Take a Hero: General H. Norman Schwarzkopf, the Autobiography.* New York: Bantam Books, 1993.

Warden, John A., III. *The Air Campaign: Planning for Combat.* Washington, DC: National Defense University Press, 1988.

Warlords, Afghanistan

In Afghanistan, warlords traditionally have been military leaders who often served as the de facto government of provinces and cities, usually organized by ethnic or tribal affiliation, but sometimes by ideology, as with the mujahideen and Taliban. A warlord system has variously comprised the collection of taxes and customs duties, the maintenance of private armies and fiefdoms, and the exploitation of the criminal, or underground, economy.

Historically, Afghanistan has been the meeting point of the Indian subcontinent, Central Asia, and the Middle East. Over the course of numerous invasions it evolved into a nation comprising numerous ethnic groups. These include: Persian, Pashai, Baluch, Chahar, Tajik, Turkmen, Aimak, Pashtun, Uzbek, Arab, Nuristani, Kirghiz, and Hazara. Of these groups, the Pashtun emerged as the most dominant both numerically and politically. They represent about 50 percent of the total population; politically they have constituted the royal family and have often held power. The Tajiks are the second largest ethnic group, comprising some 25 percent of the population.

Afghan warlords emerged following the end of the British protectorate in 1919. In the aftermath of the Bolshevik Revolution in Russia in 1917 the king of Afghanistan, Amanullah, who ascended the throne in 1919, marked the country's independence by signing a treaty of aid and friendship with Russian revolutionary Vladimir Lenin and declaring war on Britain. In response, the British Royal Air Force bombed the Afghan capital of Kabul, and the British government conspired with conservative religious groups and land-owning communities who had grown contemptuous of Amanullah's attempts at secularization and reform. This gave birth to the warlords.

In 1929, Amanullah abdicated following an uprising and civil unrest, and the warlords then competed in earnest for power. The turn of events that led to the abdication of Amanullah marked the first, but not final, instance in which disgruntled religious and land-owning factions would collaborate with Western or Soviet powers to achieve change in Afghanistan.

Afghanistan's new king, Muhammad Nadir Shah, commenced an ill-fated reign that was cut short 4 years later with his assassination in 1933. Muhammad Zahir Shah succeeded to the throne. He ruled for 40 years before he was deposed by his cousin, Mohammad Daoud Khan, in 1973, whereupon Afghanistan was formerly declared a republic. In the meantime, warlords played a sizable role in Afghanistan, especially at the provincial and municipal levels.

From the early 20th century on, the significant role of the warlords in determining the political and religious orientation of Afghanistan indicates not only the deep-rooted nature of warlordism in the country, but also an enduring determination to vie for power both internally and with external intervening powers. Nevertheless, warlords of both the mujahideen beginning in the 1980s, and the Taliban in the 1990s, have demonstrated a willingness to court both Western and Soviet powers to serve national and personal interests. While the "Great Game" in the late 19th century had rendered Afghanistan a buffer between British and Russian interests, the end of the 20th century brought a proactive mobilization of the warlords.

The most recent contingent of warlords flourished during the ongoing civil war and Soviet occupation (1979–2001) and amidst the ensuing breakdown of central authority. As young military commanders usurped traditional governance structures and bodies of authority, such as the village *shura* or *jirga,* the warlords provided rudimentary public services while exhibiting predatory behavior toward local communities.

While the years 2001 and 2002 provided a period of uncertainty for Afghan warlords, especially after the beginning of Operation ENDURING FREEDOM began, the Bonn Agreement of 2001 consolidated the position of the warlords not only in their fiefdoms, but also within the newly restored power and authority of the state. Yet far from stabilizing the nascent government, led by President Hamid Karzai, the co-option of the warlords hindered state progress in the realms of reform and modernization. While nepotism has threatened the legitimacy of the government, the warlords have, in the eyes of the wider population, become synonymous with the destruction of the state, rather than its renewal. Notable warlords in Afghanistan include Abd al-Rashid Dostum, Gulbuddin Hekmatyar, Mullah Mohammed Omar, Pasha Khan Zadran, Abdul Malik, and the sole female warlord, Bibi Ayesha.

Men loyal to Afghan warlord Mullah Naqibullah ride in a pickup truck to their military base outside Kandahar, Afghanistan, March 1, 2002. (AP/Wide World Photos)

Despite the seemingly negative implications that have arisen from the assimilation of Taliban warlords into the Afghan state, their involvement has been endorsed by the international community, most notably the United States, which has favored the formation of alliances with regional commanders to preserve security and stability until the Afghan National Security Forces (ANSF) are trained and equipped.

Nevertheless, the strategy of placing warlords in government has so far lacked the degree of success that had been anticipated by both Afghanistan and international observers. A significant obstacle has been ongoing competition between the warlords. Between 2002 and 2003, the forces of Rashid Dostum, the leader of the predominantly Uzbek political group *Junbish-e Milli-ye-Islami*, and Ustad Atta Mohammed, a key figure in the Tajik-dominated *Jamaat-e-Islami*, clashed in northern Afghanistan, despite the fact that both Dostum and Mohammad were prominent allies of the government. While the hostilities between the two groups had been quelled through the intervention of the central government and international community, skirmishes continue to persist. In October 2006, fighting between two Pashtun clans in Herat killed 32 people and injured many more.

The integration of warlords into the Afghan government has also borne negative security implications. Just as warlords are able to stand in elections, they also find other avenues of political influence open to them. For example, the parliament's standing committees are being dominated by former jihadi commanders, often to the detriment of more qualified individuals. Moreover, the warlords have gained further protection since the passing of a motion on February 1, 2007, that guaranteed immunity to all Afghans who had fought in the civil war, thereby preventing further prosecution of commanders for their involvement in war crimes.

K. Luisa Gandolfo

See also

Afghanistan; Bonn Agreement; Dostum, Abd al-Rashid; Hekmetyar, Gulbuddin al-Hurra; Kakar, Mullah; Karzai, Hamid; Mujahideen, Soviet-Afghanistan War; Omar, Mohammed; Taliban; Taliban Insurgency, Afghanistan

References

Dorronsoro, Gilles. *Afghanistan: Revolution Unending, 1979–2002.* London: C. Hurst, 2003.

Hodes, Cyrus, and Mark Sedra. *The Search for Security in Post-Taliban Afghanistan.* Adelphi Paper 391. Abingdon, UK: Routledge for the International Institute for Strategic Studies, 2007.

Rashid, Ahmed. *Taliban: Militant Islam, Oil, and Fundamentalism in Central Asia.* New Haven, CT: Yale University Press, 2001.

Tanner, Stephen. *Afghanistan: A Military History from Alexander the Great to the Fall of the Taliban.* New York: Da Capo, 2003.

War on Terror

See Global War on Terror

War Powers Act

Joint resolution of the U.S. Congress, enacted on November 7, 1973. The War Powers Act limits the authority of the president to deploy U.S. troops and/or wage war without the express consent of Congress. It has influenced nearly every major American military deployment in the Middle East since its passing. The act became law over then president Richard M. Nixon's veto following the withdrawal of U.S. combat forces from the Republic of Vietnam (South Vietnam) during the Vietnam War. It was designed to assure that the president and Congress would share responsibility in making decisions that might lead the United States into a war. Its passage was prompted by the highly unpopular Vietnam War, during which both the Lyndon Johnson and Richard Nixon administrations enmeshed the United States in a major war while bypassing the constitutional provision that grants Congress the power to declare war (Article I, Section 8).

Under the War Powers Act, the president is required to notify and consult with Congress prior to deploying U.S. troops into hostile situations and to consult regularly with Congress once troops have been deployed. If within 60 days of introducing troops Congress has not declared war or approved of the military deployment, the president must withdraw the troops unless he certifies to Congress an "unavoidable military necessity" that requires an additional 30 days to remove the troops. Although every president, Democrat and Republican, has claimed the War Powers Act to be an unconstitutional violation of the president's authority as commander in chief, presidents have been careful nevertheless to notify Congress of their decision to deploy U.S. forces.

According to the Congressional Research Service, since the passage of the War Powers Resolution in 1973, U.S. presidents have submitted over 100 such reports to Congress. On April 24, 1980, following the failed attempt to rescue American hostages in Iran, President Jimmy Carter submitted a report to Congress. Some members of Congress objected to Carter's failure to consult with Congress before executing the operation. Carter, however, claimed that because the mission depended on complete secrecy, consultation was not possible; moreover, the White House argued that a rescue operation did not constitute an act of aggression or force.

On September 29, 1983, Congress invoked the resolution to authorize the deployment of U.S. Marines to Lebanon for 18 months as part of a United Nations (UN) peacekeeping mission there. Following several years of growing tensions with Libya and skirmishes between both countries, on April 14, 1986, President Ronald W. Reagan ordered air strikes on Libya for its involvement in a terrorist bombing in a West Berlin discotheque that killed two U.S. soldiers. Reagan informed Congress of the attack, but because the operation was short-lived the question of congressional approval was essentially moot.

In January 1991, President George H. W. Bush secured congressional authorization to use force to compel Iraq to withdraw from Kuwait per a UN mandate. After the end of the Persian Gulf War on February 28, 1991, the War Powers Act again became a potential issue regarding the situation in the Middle East. President William J. Clinton launched several air attacks against Iraqi targets in an effort to compel Iraqi dictator Saddam Hussein's compliance with UN resolutions. In 1998, Clinton also ordered cruise-missile attacks on targets in Afghanistan and Sudan in retaliation for two deadly bombings involving U.S. embassies, likely carried out by Al Qaeda. Clinton did not invoke the War Powers Act because of the brief and secretive nature of the operations, however.

Following the September 11, 2001, terrorist attacks on the United States, President George W. Bush secured congressional authorization a week later to use whatever force necessary against those responsible for the attacks. Based on this authorization, in October 2001 the U.S. attacked and invaded Afghanistan to overthrow the Taliban regime that had given Osama bin Laden and Al Qaeda sanctuary.

In 2002, the Bush administration sought another congressional approval to wage a potential war against Iraq to compel it to cooperate with the United Nations resolution that had called for the disarming of Iraq and the declaration of all weapons of mass destruction (WMD). On October 16, 2002, Bush signed into law the joint congressional resolution, which enjoyed wide bipartisan support, empowering him to wage war against the regime of Iraqi dictator Saddam Hussein. The October 2002 authorization of military force against Iraq obviated presidential compliance with the War Powers Act.

Although Congress authorized the use of force against Iraq, the March 2003 invasion of Iraq and subsequent war and insurgency there has called into question not only the effectiveness of the War Powers Act but also, and more importantly, Congress's role in foreign policy and decisions involving war. The failure to find any weapons of mass destruction, the principal reason cited by Bush for the invasion of Iraq, has led critics of the war to question not only the president's responsibility to both Congress and the public, but also the role of Congress in declaring war and, specifically, as the War Powers Act intended, checking or overseeing the president's war-making powers.

Regardless of which administration holds the White House, tension over the exercise of war powers undoubtedly will continue between the executive and legislative branches of government. Presidents, Democrat and Republican, will still seek to implement U.S. foreign policy through the unrestricted use of all elements of national power—economic, political, and military—while Congress, through its legislative powers, will continue to exercise its vital role of providing the necessary "checks and balances" to ensure that executive branch power does not become "unrestricted." Given the volatile situation in the Middle East, the region will likely continue to be the focal point for future confrontations between president and Congress over war powers.

Stefan M. Brooks

See also

Bush, George Herbert Walker; Bush, George Walker; Carter, James Earl, Jr.; Cheney, Richard Bruce; Reagan, Ronald Wilson

References

Bobbit, Phillip. "War Powers: An Essay on John Hart Ely's *War and Responsibility: Constitutional Lessons of Vietnam and Its Aftermath.*" *Michigan Law Quarterly* 92(6) (May 1994): 1364–1400.

Irons, Peter. *War Powers: How the Imperial Presidency Hijacked the Constitution.* New York: Metropolitan Books, 2005.

Yoo, John. *The Powers of War and Peace: The Constitution and Foreign Affairs after 9/11.* Chicago: University of Chicago Press, 2005.

Weapons Inspectors

See United Nations Weapons Inspectors

Weapons of Mass Destruction

Weapons of mass destruction (WMDs) refer to biological, chemical, and nuclear weapons capable of inflicting mass casualties. Use of these weapons is viewed as not only immoral but also contrary to international law and the laws of war because WMDs have the ability to kill indiscriminately large numbers of human beings and inflict extensive damage to man-made structures beyond combatants or military assets. During the Cold War, fears about nuclear weapons and their use was commonplace. Nevertheless, these weapons were under tight control, and neither side dared employ them for fear of the total destruction that a retaliatory strike would bring. With the end of the Cold War, however, nuclear proliferation has become a significant problem, and the likelihood of a rogue state or terrorist group attaining WMDs, including nuclear weapons, has increased substantially.

During the Iran-Iraq War (1980–1988), Iraq employed chemical weapons against Iranian troops, something Iraqi dictator Saddam Hussein publicly admitted to in December 2006 during his trial for war crimes. It remains in dispute whether Iran employed them as well. In 1988, as part of an operation to suppress a revolt by

Iraqi Kurds, the Hussein government unleashed a chemical attack on the northern Iraqi town of Halabja, killing at least 5,000 people in the first recorded event of such weapons being used against civilians after the Japanese use of chemical weapons against the Chinese during the Second Sino-Japanese War of 1937–1945.

Since the terror attacks of September 11, 2001, the fear of and danger posed by WMDs have increased significantly, owing to the desire of terrorist groups such as Al Qaeda and their affiliates to acquire and employ such weapons against the United States and other countries. The September 11 terrorist attacks on the United States and the 2004 Madrid and 2005 London bombings clearly demonstrated the ability and willingness of Al Qaeda to engage in terrorism to inflict mass casualties, leaving no doubt about their willingness to use WMDs in future terrorist attacks. Al Qaeda is believed to have been responsible for a series of terrorist attacks in March and April 2006 in Iraq, in which chlorine gas killed dozens and sickened hundreds.

Because of the instability and recurrence of war and conflict in the Middle East, the presence of WMDs has only heightened the arms race between Arab states and Israel and also among Arab states themselves. Egypt, Syria, Algeria, and Iran are all believed to have significant stockpiles of biological and chemical weapons. In 2003, seeking to normalize relations with the United States and Europe and end its international isolation and reputation as a sponsor of terrorism, Libya announced that it was abandoning its WMD programs. Observers have suggested that President George W. Bush's decision to invade Iraq in 2003, ostensibly to rid it of WMDs, and Libya's failure to end its isolation and convince the United Nations (UN) to lift its sanctions prompted this change of behavior.

Syria is believed to possess extensive chemical weapons stockpiles and delivery systems and to have been seeking to develop a similarly robust biological weapons program. Egypt was the first country in the Middle East to develop chemical weapons, which may have been prompted, at least in part, by Israel's construction of a nuclear reactor in 1958. The size of Egypt's chemical weapons arsenal is thought to be perhaps as extensive as Iraq's prior to the 1991 Persian Gulf War, although the end of hostilities between Egypt and Israel since the 1978 Camp David Accords may have obviated the need for maintaining the same quantities of such weapons.

In 1993, as part of the Arab campaign against Israel's nuclear weapons program, Egypt and Syria (along with Iraq) refused to sign the Chemical Weapons Convention (CWC), which bans the acquisition, development, stockpiling, transfer, retention, and use of chemical weapons. These states also refused to sign the Biological Weapons Convention (BWC) of 1975, which prohibits the development, production, acquisition, transfer, retention, stockpiling, and use of biological and toxin weapons. Iraq later signed the BWC, and it signed the CWC after Hussein's ouster. The extent of Egypt's biological weapons program is unknown, but it clearly has the ability to develop such weapons if it already does not have weaponized stockpiles.

2007 as punishment for its defiance of the UN. Since then, the West has pressed for more sanctions, but its efforts have met resistance from such nations as Russia and the People's Republic of China.

Of particular international concern in 2009 were Pakistan in southern Asia and the Democratic People's Republic of Korea (DPRK, North Korea) in East Asia. Pakistan had successfully conducted underground nuclear tests in May 1998 and is believed to possess a number of atomic bombs. Abdul Qadeer Kahn, widely regarded as the chief scientist in the development of Pakistan's atomic bomb, confessed in January 2004 to having been involved in a clandestine network of nuclear proliferation from Pakistan to Libya, Iran, and North Korea (which in October 2006 successfully conducted an underground nuclear test). Pakistani president General Pervez Musharraf then announced that he had pardoned Kahn, who is regarded by many Pakistanis as a national hero, despite the fact that the technology transfer is thought to have made possible North Korea's acquisition of the atomic bomb.

In the spring of 2009, however, major fighting erupted between Pakistani government forces and the Taliban, who controlled the Swat Valley in the northwestern part of the country. The stability of Pakistan and the security of its nuclear arsenal appeared in question.

STEFAN M. BROOKS

See also

Al Qaeda; Biological Weapons and Warfare; Chemical Weapons and Warfare; Egypt; Global War on Terror; International Atomic Energy Agency; Iran; Iran-Iraq War; Israel; Kurds; Kurds, Massacres of; Libya; Musharraf, Pervez; Nuclear Weapons, Iraq's Potential for Building; Pakistan; Syria; Terrorism

References

Hamel-Green, Michael. *Regional Initiatives on Nuclear- and WMD-Free Zones: Cooperative Approaches to Arms Control and Non-proliferation.* New York: United Nations Publication, 2006.

Katona, Peter, et al. *Countering Terrorism and WMD: Creating a Global Counter-Terrorism Network.* New York: Routledge, 2006.

Mauroni, Albert. *Where Are the WMDs? The Reality of Chem-Bio Threats on the Home Front and on the Battlefield.* Annapolis, MD: Naval Institute Press, 2006.

Schneider, Barry. *Avoiding the Abyss: Progress, Shortfalls, and the Way Ahead in Combating the WMD Threat.* Westport, CT: Praeger Publishing, 2006.

A United Nations (UN) team inspects areas of Iran to investigate the Iraqi use of chemical weapons during the Iran-Iraq War, March 14, 1984. (AP/Wide World Photos)

With respect to nuclear weapons, Israel is believed to possess as many as 100 nuclear warheads, although the Israeli government has never publicly confirmed possessing such weapons. On December 12, 2006, Israeli prime minister Ehud Olmert admitted in an interview that Israel possessed nuclear weapons, only to be contradicted the next day by a government spokesman, who denied that Olmert had made such an admission. In the meantime, Israel has refused to sign the Nuclear Non-Proliferation Treaty (NPT) and has not allowed UN International Atomic Energy Agency (IAEA) inspectors to inspect its suspected nuclear sites.

Israel has repeatedly shown its willingness to use force to maintain its suspected Middle East nuclear monopoly and deny any Arab state the ability to acquire or develop nuclear weapons. In 1981, the Israeli air force destroyed an Iraqi nuclear reactor site under construction at Osiraq, Iraq. In September 2007, Israeli warplanes carried out an attack against a suspected nuclear facility in Syria. Iran is currently enriching uranium for what it claims are peaceful purposes, but the United States and much of Western Europe have accused Iran of aspiring to build nuclear weapons. That state's refusal to cooperate with the IAEA led the United Nations to impose sanctions on Iran in December 2006 and March

Webb, James Henry, Jr.
Birth Date: February 9, 1946

Decorated Vietnam War veteran, attorney, author, filmmaker, assistant secretary of defense for reserve affairs (1984–1987), secretary of the navy (1987–1988), United States senator (2007–present), and strong opponent of the George W. Bush administration's prosecution of the Iraq War. James "Jim" Henry Webb Jr. was born on February 9, 1946, in Saint Joseph, Missouri, the son of a career air force officer. Following graduation from the United

States Naval Academy at Annapolis in 1968, Webb entered the U.S. Marine Corps and served in the Vietnam War as a platoon leader and company commander with the 5th Marine Regiment, earning the Navy Cross. Webb was subsequently an instructor in tactics and weapons at the Marine Corps Officer Candidate School and served on the military staff of the secretary of the navy before leaving the service in 1972.

Webb then attended Georgetown University law school, where he received his JD degree in 1975. During this time he wrote his first book, *Micronesia and U.S. Pacific Strategy* (1974). From 1977 to 1981, he served as counsel to the U.S. House Committee on Veterans Affairs. Webb also did pro bono legal work for veterans. In 1978, he came to public prominence as an author, in particular for his novel *Fields of Fire* (1978), a story of ground combat involving U.S. Marines in Vietnam.

During the Ronald Reagan administration, Webb was the assistant secretary of defense for reserve affairs (1984–1987) and then secretary of the navy from May 1, 1987, to February 23, 1988. A principal concern of the U.S. military resulting from the Vietnam War experience was the desire to achieve more effective integration of the reserves and National Guard with the regular military. Webb's posts, in particular the first, involved policy planning and implementation in this area, which was quite successful overall.

After leaving government service, Webb enjoyed a storied career as an author, a feature and documentary film producer, and a screenwriter. His published works include five novels and a book about the Scotch Irish experience in the United States. He produced the story line and was the executive producer of *Rules of Engagement* (2000), a popular legal-military-political drama starring Tommy Lee Jones and Samuel L. Jackson. Webb stayed active on the political scene, writing occasional columns and op-ed pieces, but was not wedded to one political party; indeed, in spite of his service during the Reagan years, he backed several Democratic candidates for office, and would run as a moderate Democrat in the 2006 senatorial election. In a March 2003 op-ed piece for the *New York Times,* written just days after the Anglo-American invasion of Iraq, Webb presciently warned that the United States could well become locked in a deadly guerrilla insurgency there.

In 2006, Webb secured Virginia's Democratic senatorial nomination and was elected by a razor-thin margin to the United States Senate, defeating incumbent Republican George Allen. In the campaign, Webb emphasized his moderate social positions, fiscal conservatism, and opposition to the U.S. invasion and occupation of Iraq. In November 2006, he publicly justified U.S. involvement in the Vietnam War, but was quick to add that the war strategy was badly flawed. Webb's victory as a Democrat in a conservative state drew considerable national attention and public discussion that he might be a candidate for higher office. His victory also helped solidify the Democratic Party's sweep of Congress, as it claimed control over both houses in the 2006 elections.

As a senator, Webb has been actively involved in sponsoring and supporting legislation for veterans' benefits and has been a continuing critic of the Bush administration's war and economic policies. In November 2006, shortly after his election, Webb had a notable contretemps with President George W. Bush, who asked about Webb's son, who was then serving as a marine in Iraq. Webb was reportedly furious over Bush's public inquiry, but the two men later reconciled when Bush invited Webb and his son to the Oval Office for a special meeting in March 2008.

ARTHUR I. CYR

See also

Antiwar Movements, Persian Gulf and Iraq Wars; United States Congress and the Iraq War

References

Webb, James. *Fields of Fire.* New York: Prentice Hall, 1978.
Woodward, Bob. *State of Denial: Bush at War, Part III.* New York: Simon and Schuster, 2006.

Webster, William Hedgcock
Birth Date: March 6, 1924

U.S. attorney, judge, director of the Federal Bureau of Investigation (FBI) from 1978 to 1987, and director of the Central Intelligence Agency (CIA) from 1987 to 1991. William Hedgcock Webster was born in St. Louis, Missouri, on March 6, 1924. During World War II, he served in the U.S. Navy. After the war and his return to the United States, Webster earned his undergraduate degree from Amherst (Massachusetts) College in 1947. Two years later, he received a law degree from Washington University in St. Louis.

From 1949 to 1959, Webster practiced law with a successful St. Louis law firm. In 1960, he began a long career in public service when he began serving as U.S. attorney for the Eastern District of Missouri, a post he held until 1961. Thereafter, he returned to private practice, and from 1964 to 1969 he sat on the Missouri Board of Law Examiners.

From 1970 to 1973, Webster served as U.S. federal judge for the Eastern District of Missouri. In 1973, he was appointed judge of the U.S. Court of Appeals for the Eighth Circuit, a post he retained until 1978. In 1978, President Jimmy Carter tapped him to become the sixth director of the FBI. His tenure with that agency was marked by efficient and effective leadership that helped stabilize it following the disruptive post-Watergate years and its transition from the long reign of director J. Edgar Hoover, which had ended with the latter's death in 1972.

In 1987, Webster left his post with the FBI to become the director of the CIA; he is the only individual to have held the directorship of both organizations. His appointment by the Ronald Reagan administration proved that he was able to function well under both Democratic and Republican administrations. Webster succeeded controversial CIA director William Casey, who died unexpectedly in May 1987 after a brief battle with brain cancer. Casey's death meant that he was never able to testify in the congressional hearings surrounding the Iran-Contra Affair, a scheme in which the CIA had been involved in selling weapons to Iran, the proceeds of which were illegally funneled to the anticommunist Contras in Nicaragua. Webster moved quickly to mitigate the damage to the agency caused by the Iran-Contra allegations and proved to be a far less visible and controversial director than Casey. Webster did continue Casey's policy of arming the mujahideen fighters in Afghanistan toward the tail end of the Soviet-Afghanistan War.

Webster retired from public service in September 1991 and was succeeded by Robert M. Gates as CIA director. He returned to private law practice, becoming a partner in the Washington, D.C., law firm of Milbank, Tweed, Hadley & McCloy. He has been the recipient of many prestigious honors and awards, including the Presidential Medal of Freedom in 1991. He retired from active practice in 2005 but still maintains a presence in the firm. He also served as vice chairman of the Homeland Security Advisory Council (HSAC) from 2002 to 2006, and in 2006, he became chairman of the HSAC.

Paul G. Pierpaoli Jr.

See also

Central Intelligence Agency; Gates, Robert Michael; Iran-Contra Affair; Mujahideen, Soviet-Afghanistan War; Soviet-Afghanistan War

References

Agress, Lynn F. *The Central Intelligence Agency*. Farmington Hills, MI: Greenhaven, 2002.

Theoharis, Athan, ed. *The Central Intelligence Agency: Security under Scrutiny*. Westport, CT: Greenwood, 2006.

Weinberger, Caspar Willard
Birth Date: August 18, 1917
Death Date: March 26, 2006

U.S. politician and secretary of defense (1981–1987). Born in San Francisco, California, on August 18, 1917, Caspar Willard Weinberger attended Harvard University, where he earned a bachelor of arts degree in 1938 and a law degree in 1941. He served in the U.S. Army during World War II, rising to captain.

After leaving the military in 1945, Weinberger clerked for a federal judge and then entered politics. Elected to the California State Assembly in 1952, he was chairman of the state Republican Party, then worked in Governor Ronald Reagan's cabinet in the late 1960s and early 1970s. Moving to Washington, Weinberger served as director of the Federal Trade Commission (FTC) in 1970; deputy director (1970–1972) and then director (1972–1973) of the Office of Management and Budget (OMB); and secretary of the Department of Health, Education and Welfare (HEW) during 1973–1975.

Weinberger served as an adviser to Reagan's 1980 presidential campaign, and Reagan appointed him secretary of defense in 1981. Many conservatives feared that Weinberger, known as "Cap the Knife" for his budget-cutting zeal, might oppose Reagan's plans to increase defense spending. Such worries proved

Caspar Weinberger was secretary of defense under President Ronald Reagan during 1981–1987. Weinberger directed an unprecedented peacetime buildup of U.S. military forces. (U.S. Department of Defense)

groundless, as Weinberger presided over the largest peacetime defense buildup in U.S. history. He was also an enthusiastic supporter of Reagan's Strategic Defense Initiative (SDI) to establish a laser-guided defense system in outer space that would be able to destroy ballistic missiles aimed at the United States.

In Middle Eastern affairs, Weinberger opposed the stationing of U.S. Marines in Lebanon in 1982, believing that the objective was not clearly defined. His fears over the vulnerability of this force were realized when 241 marines died in their Beirut barracks in a terrorist bombing in October 1983. U.S. forces there were subsequently withdrawn. Weinberger actively sought the prosecution of U.S. Navy intelligence analyst Jonathan Pollard, subsequently convicted of spying for Israel and sentenced to life imprisonment.

Weinberger opposed the secret transfer beginning in late 1985 of 500 U.S. TOW antitank missiles to Iran in exchange for the freeing of American hostages being held in the Middle East. The Reagan administration then illegally diverted some of the funds to the anticommunist Contra forces fighting the Sandinista government in Nicaragua. This activity became public in late 1986 and was known as the Iran-Contra Affair.

Weinberger also developed the Weinberger Doctrine, later known as the Powell Doctrine after General Colin L. Powell, the chairman of the Joint Chiefs of Staff, who had been Weinberger's senior military aide and adviser. The Weinberger Doctrine supported the intervention of U.S. military forces but with important caveats based on presumed "lessons learned" from Vietnam: commit U.S. troops only when U.S. or allied vital national interests are at stake, and only when supported by the American public and Congress; establish in advance of troop commitment clear political and military objectives; commit troops wholeheartedly and with the clear intention of winning; use force appropriate to the threat, but generally apply overwhelming force to shorten the length of the conflict and minimize American casualties; and use force only as a last resort. Powell generally adopted all of the Weinberger Doctrine principles, although he added the development of an "exit strategy" to Weinberger's caveats. The Weinberger/Powell Doctrine was applied with great success during the 1991 Persian Gulf War. Weinberger resigned his post in November 1987, citing his wife's poor health.

In the autumn of 1992 Special Counsel Lawrence Walsh indicted Weinberger on four felony counts of lying to a congressional committee and to the independent counsel's office and one count of obstruction of justice in conjunction with the Iran-Contra Affair. The case never went to trial, as defeated incumbent president George H. W. Bush pardoned Weinberger on December 24, 1992. Weinberger died in Bangor, Maine, on March 26, 2006.

FRANK J. SMITH

See also

Bush, George Herbert Walker; Iran-Contra Affair; Lebanon, U.S. Intervention in (1982–1984); Pollard, Jonathan; Powell, Colin Luther; Powell Doctrine; Reagan, Ronald Wilson

References

Cannon, Lou. *President Reagan: The Role of a Lifetime.* New York: Simon and Schuster, 1991.

Weinberger, Caspar W. *Fighting for Peace: Seven Critical Years in the Pentagon.* New York: Warner, 1990.

Weinberger, Caspar W., with Gretchen Roberts. *In the Arena: A Memoir of the 20th Century.* Washington, DC: Regnery, 1998.

Wilson, Charles Nesbitt
Birth Date: June 1, 1933
Death Date: February 10, 2010

U.S. Congressman from Texas who played a key role in orchestrating U.S. military assistance for the Afghan rebels fighting the Soviet occupation of their country. Charles Nesbitt Wilson was born in Trinity, Texas, on June 1, 1933. Wilson, known as "Charlie," briefly attended Sam Houston State University in Huntsville, Texas, before accepting an appointment in 1952 to the United States Naval Academy, Annapolis. Commissioned in the U.S. Navy upon graduation in 1956, Wilson spent several years as gunnery officer on a destroyer.

In 1960 while still on active duty in the U.S. Navy, Wilson felt drawn to public service after working as a volunteer on John F. Kennedy's presidential campaign. Taking leave from the navy, Wilson ran for and won election to the state legislature and served there for the next 12 years, establishing a reputation as a liberal Democrat who supported abortion rights, Medicaid, and the Equal Rights Amendment. In 1972 Wilson overcame a drunk driving arrest to win the election to the U.S. House of Representatives from the Second Election District. He managed to maintain his seat by balancing his liberal views on domestic policy with a hawkish foreign policy stance.

Wilson was an early strong supporter of Israel and visited the Jewish state during the Yom Kippur (Ramadan) War in October 1973. In the late 1970s he also took up the cause of the Anastasio Somoza Debayle Nicaraguan government, which was embroiled in a guerrilla war with the leftist National Liberation Front (FSLN, Sandinistas) for control of the country. Wilson pressured Congress into restoring the multimillion-dollar U.S. aid package to Somoza's government, which had been cut by President Jimmy Carter's administration because of the Nicaraguan dictator's poor human rights record.

In 1976 Wilson was appointed to the powerful Appropriations Committee, and he soon also secured a seat on its Foreign Operations Subcommittee. After being reelected for a fourth term in 1980 he gained a spot on the Defense Appropriations Subcommittee, which controls the purse strings of both the Central Intelligence Agency (CIA) and the Pentagon. Around that time he became involved in the plight of Afghanistan, which was experiencing a Soviet military occupation following an invasion of that country in late December 1979.

In October 1982 Wilson took a trip to Pakistan and visited Afghan camps outside Peshawar, the center of Afghan resistance. The camps, then filled with more than 2 million Afghans who were barely surviving with little food and no running water, inspired the congressman to do everything he could to support the mujahideen in their fight against the Soviet Union. On his return to the United States, Wilson, who had a much-deserved reputation as a hard-partying womanizer with the nickname "Good-Time Charlie," now used his longtime political connections to substantially increase U.S. financial aid to the Afghan rebels.

In a most unusual role for a congressman from eastern Texas, during the course of the next several years Wilson worked closely with CIA operative Gust Avrakotos to supply the mujahideen with some $5 billion in weapons to take down the vaunted Soviet war machine. Perhaps the most crucial of these weapons was the Stinger surface-to-air missile (SAM) that the CIA began shipping to the mujahideen in 1986. Up to that point, Soviet aerial supremacy in the form of jet fighters and helicopter gunships had devastated the Afghan rebels and provided vital logistical support to Soviet forces. The Stinger missiles forced Soviet aircraft to fly higher to avoid being shot down, greatly minimizing their effectiveness. That same year the Soviet Union began pulling troops out of Afghanistan, and by February 1989 all Soviet military forces had left the country.

The CIA recognized Wilson's key role in Afghanistan by bestowing on him its Honored Colleague award, marking the first time the award had been given to someone outside the agency. Wilson served in Congress for 12 terms until he retired in January 1997. For the next eight years he worked as a lobbyist on Capitol Hill, with Pakistan as his primary client. In 2003 George Crile published the book *Charlie Wilson's War,* chronicling the Texas congressman's involvement in the Soviet-Afghanistan War. The book was followed four years later by a movie of the same name that featured Tom Hanks in the title role.

In retirement, Wilson defended the U.S. government's support for the leftist rebels in Afghanistan and said that the real mistake was the U.S. decision to abandon Afghanistan and not help rebuild that country following the Soviet departure. Wilson believed that had the United States done so, Afghanistan would not have become a haven for the Al Qaeda terrorist organization. Wilson died of cardiopulmonary arrest at his home in Lufkin, Texas, on February 10, 2010, at the age of 76.

Spencer C. Tucker

See also

Al Qaeda; Missiles, Surface-to-Air; Soviet-Afghanistan War

References

Alexiev, Alex. *The United States and the War in Afghanistan.* Santa Monica, CA: RAND Corporation, 1988.

Crile, George. *Charlie Wilson's War.* New York: Grove, 2003.

Loyn, David. *In Afghanistan: Two Hundred Years of British, Russian and American Occupation.* New York: Palgrave Macmillan, 2009.

Russian General Staff. *The Soviet-Afghan War: How a Superpower Fought and Lost.* Lawrence: University of Kansas Press, 2002.

Wilson, Joseph Carter, IV
Birth Date: November 5, 1949

U.S. diplomat, career foreign service officer, and a central figure in the Valerie Plame Wilson incident, which dogged the George W. Bush administration for several years after the launching of the Iraq War. Joseph Carter Wilson IV was born in Bridgeport, Connecticut, on November 5, 1949, to a prosperous family and grew up in both Europe and California. He graduated from the University of California-Santa Barbara in 1971 with an undergraduate degree in history. After working for a time as a carpenter, he pursued graduate studies in public administration and entered the Foreign Service in 1976.

From 1976 to 1998, Wilson held a series of increasingly important diplomatic posts, both in Washington and abroad. Many of his postings were in Africa, where he earned a reputation as an earnest, well-informed diplomat who was easy to work with. During this time, Wilson, who hailed from a staunchly conservative Republican family, began to make connections with several influential Democratic legislators. Although he worked to distance himself from partisan politics as a diplomatic officer, during 1985–1986 he was a congressional fellow first for Democratic senator Al Gore and then for Democratic representative Tom Foley. This assignment gained him important connections within the Democratic Party hierarchy.

From 1988 to 1991, Wilson was stationed in Baghdad, Iraq, where he served as the deputy chief of mission to U.S. ambassador of Iraq April Glaspie. This placed him in the center of the crisis that resulted from the Iraqi invasion and occupation of Kuwait, which began on August 2, 1990. He was reportedly the last U.S. diplomat to have met with Iraqi president Saddam Hussein before the 1991 Persian Gulf War began in January 1991. Wilson told Hussein in no uncertain terms that he had to quit Kuwait immediately or face military consequences. Hussein scoffed at Wilson's demand, and subsequently sent him a letter in which he threatened to murder anyone harboring "foreigners" in Iraq. Wilson then publicly castigated Hussein for his threat, a rare move for a diplomat. As the war approached, Wilson provided refuge for more than 100 Americans at the U.S. embassy in Baghdad and was largely responsible for the orderly and safe evacuation of several thousand Americans from Iraq. President George H. W. Bush lauded Wilson's actions, calling him a "true American hero."

After holding several ambassadorial posts, Wilson served as the political adviser to the commander in chief of U.S. Forces, Europe (EUCOM), in Stuttgart, Germany, during 1995–1997. From 1997 to 1998, he served as special assistant to President Bill Clinton and senior director of African affairs for the National Security Council (NSC).

Wilson retired from government service in 1998 and began his own international consulting and management firm, JC Wilson International Ventures, Inc. He also began actively supporting numerous national Democratic lawmakers, including Senator Ted Kennedy, Representative Charles Rangel, and others.

Because of his lengthy diplomatic career, past dealings with Saddam Hussein, and expertise in African affairs, the Central Intelligence Agency sent Wilson on a clandestine mission to Niger in February 2002. His task was to ascertain the accuracy of reports that Saddam Hussein had attempted to purchase "yellowcake uranium" (enriched uranium) from Niger, which had become a key accusation of the George W. Bush administration as it built its case for war with Iraq. Wilson returned and concluded in a report to the Bush administration that it was "highly doubtful" that Iraq ever attempted to buy yellowcake uranium in Niger. Information showed that documents used to build this case were forged. However, in Bush's 2003 State of the Union Address, the president claimed that British reports (now presumed erroneous) indicated that Hussein had recently attempted to purchase "significant" quantities of uranium in Africa. This was a significant part of the American case for war against Iraq.

Outraged by the Bush administration's clear repudiation of his report and chagrined by the rush to war with Iraq, which had begun in March 2003, Wilson wrote a controversial op-ed piece for the *New York Times,* published on July 6, 2003. Titled "What I Didn't Find in Africa," Wilson's article clearly spelled out the case for faulty intelligence on Iraq and castigated the Bush White House for exaggerating the Iraqi threat. The article also spelled out the general outlines of his 2002 trip to Niger. The following week, conservative columnist Robert Novak, in an attempt to discredit Wilson's article, revealed that Wilson's wife, Valerie Plame Wilson, was a covert CIA officer.

Novak's revelation precipitated an avalanche of accusations and recriminations, including Wilson's claim that the outing of his wife—an ethics violation as well as illegal—was part of an elaborate White House plan to discredit him and take the focus off of the faulty intelligence that had led to war. The revelation led to a federal investigation by the Justice Department, which convened a grand jury. Several of Bush's top aides, including Karl Rove, came within the investigation's crosshairs, as did those of Vice President Dick Cheney. Ultimately, in March 2007, I. Lewis "Scooter" Libby, Cheney's chief of staff, was found guilty of numerous offenses, including lying under oath and obstruction of justice. Bush commuted Libby's sentence, but the entire affair sullied the White House and added more fodder to the antiwar lobby's fire. No one else was implicated in the leak scandal, although it is quite likely that others besides Libby were involved.

Wilson and his wife, Valerie, brought a civil suit against Cheney, Rove, Libby, and several others, but the case was dismissed on jurisdictional grounds. In 2004, Wilson published a popular if incendiary book titled *The Politics of Truth,* which expanded his side of the story in the Valerie Plame Wilson incident and excoriated the Bush administration for its conduct in the lead-up to, and during, the Iraq War. The book raised the stakes in the Washington blame game and only added to the increasingly shrill and bitter recriminations surrounding the war in Iraq. Wilson continues to speak out against the war and to criticize the Bush administration.

PAUL G. PIERPAOLI JR.

See also

Bush, George Walker; Central Intelligence Agency; Cheney, Richard Bruce; Glaspie, April; Hussein, Saddam; Libby, I. Lewis; Niger, Role in Origins of the Iraq War; Rove, Karl; Wilson, Valerie Plame

References

Ricks, Thomas E. *Fiasco: The American Military Adventure in Iraq.* New York: Penguin, 2006.

Wilson, Joseph. *The Politics of Truth: Inside the Lies That Led to War and Betrayed My Wife's CIA Identity.* New York: Carroll and Graf, 2004.

Wilson, Thomas Woodrow
Birth Date: December 28, 1856
Death Date: February 3, 1924

U.S. political leader and president of the United States, 1913–1921. Born on December 28, 1856, in Staunton, Virginia, Thomas Woodrow Wilson grew up in Augusta, Georgia, and in South Carolina. The son of a Presbyterian minister and seminary professor, he was raised in a strict religious and academic environment. Wilson studied history and politics at Princeton University, graduating in 1879. He then studied law at the University of Virginia for a year and passed the Georgia bar examination in 1882. Wilson practiced law for a time in Atlanta, but he abandoned it to earn a doctorate in constitutional and political history at Johns Hopkins University in Baltimore in 1886. By then he had joined the faculty at Bryn Mawr College. In 1890 Wilson returned to Princeton, first as professor of jurisprudence and political economy and then as president of the university in 1902. Wilson won national acclaim for his academic reforms.

Turning to politics, in November 1910 Wilson won election as governor of New Jersey. His success in bringing about progressive reform to the state led him to become the Democratic Party standard bearer in the 1912 presidential election. That year, the Republican Party split, and Wilson won the election of November, defeating incumbent William Howard Taft as well as Theodore Roosevelt and Socialist Eugene V. Debs.

As president, Wilson was preoccupied with domestic policy and his "New Freedom," the belief that government should encourage free, competitive markets by discouraging all monopolies and relying on markets to regulate themselves. Wilson pushed through the Underwood Tariff, which reduced import duties by about one-fourth and increased the number of duty-free items. To compensate for the loss of revenue, Wilson introduced the federal income tax. On his initiative, Congress also passed the Federal Reserve Act of 1913, which created 12 regional Federal Reserve banks, supervised by a central Federal Reserve Board. Its primary duty was to regulate the volume of money in circulation in order to ensure a healthy economy and adequate credit. Ironically, some of these reforms ran counter to his earlier New Freedom philosophy. Wilson also secured passage in 1914 of the Federal Trade Commission Act, which brought about a new regulatory agency, the Federal Trade Commission, to ensure free competition. That same year Wilson signed into law the Clayton Anti-Trust Act, which prevented interlocking directorates and declared illegal certain monopolistic business practices. This act also provided that labor unions were not necessarily subject to injunction.

Wilson was not as successful in his foreign policy, where he sought to implement diplomacy based on morality and American exceptionalism. Wilson pledged that the United States would forego territorial conquests, and he and his first secretary of state, William Jennings Bryan, worked to establish a new relationship between the United States and Latin America, whereby Western

Woodrow Wilson was president of the United States during 1913–1921. He sought to pursue a foreign policy based on morality and hoped to avoid U.S. involvement in World War I. The structure of the ensuing League of Nations was primarily his work. (Library of Congress)

Hemisphere states would guarantee each other's territorial integrity and political independence.

Despite Wilson's best intentions to avoid conflict with U.S. neighbors, his distaste for political upheaval in Mexico led him to send forces to occupy Veracruz in April 1914. Incidents along the border caused him two years later to mobilize the National Guard and dispatch a regular army force into northern Mexico under Brigadier General John Pershing in a vain attempt to capture Mexican revolutionary Pancho Villa. Although the operation was unsuccessful in its stated intent, it did provide useful training for the army.

Wilson proclaimed U.S. neutrality when World War I began in August 1914, calling on Americans to be neutral in thought as well as action. Germany's submarine warfare brought the nation to the brink of war, however. The sinking of the passenger liner *Lusitania* on May 7, 1915, which killed 128 American passengers, led Wilson to issue a series of threatening notes that compelled Germany to halt unrestricted submarine warfare. Yet, Wilson's stance was disingenuous, for the United States had for many months been actively aiding Great Britain and France with munitions deliveries and other trade that supported their war effort.

Although Wilson won reelection in 1916 primarily on the platform of having kept the United States out of the war, he had secured passage by Congress that year of the National Defense Act, which greatly enlarged the peacetime army and National Guard and provided for the establishment of reserve formations and the Reserve Officers' Training Corps (ROTC). German acts of sabotage against the United States and publication of the Zimmermann Telegram, in which the German government proposed an alliance with Mexico, alienated American opinion. When Germany resumed unrestricted submarine warfare on February 1, 1917, resulting in the sinking of U.S. merchant ships and the loss of American lives, Wilson addressed Congress on April 2, 1917, and requested a declaration of war, which Congress approved on April 6.

The old tradition of avoiding foreign entanglements was so strong that the United States never formally allied with the Allies. Wilson made it clear that the country was merely an "associated power," fighting the same enemy. Wilson also did not want to bind the United States to an annexationist peace settlement. With no military experience of his own, Wilson deferred to his military advisers. His directive to American Expeditionary Forces (AEF) commander Pershing (through his secretary of war, Newton Baker) was simply that Pershing was "vested with all necessary authority to carry on the war vigorously." Wilson instructed Pershing to cooperate with the forces of other countries fighting Germany, "but in doing so the underlying idea must be kept in view that the forces of the United States are a separate and distinct component of the combined forces, the identity of which must be preserved." Wilson supported Pershing in his refusal to have the Allies employ AEF units piecemeal, but when General Ferdinand Foch became supreme Allied commander in the crisis of the spring of 1918, Wilson made it clear that Pershing was subordinate to him.

Wilson's plan was to "make the world safe for democracy." He also unwisely referred to the conflict as "the war to end all wars." But Wilson was determined to keep the United States free of advance territorial commitments, and in January 1918 he announced his Fourteen Points as a basis of peace. These included "open covenants openly arrived at"; freedom of the seas; international disarmament; return of territory captured by the Central Powers, as well as the return to France of Alsace-Lorraine; an independent Poland with access to the sea; and a League of Nations. Although "self-determination of peoples," which Wilson believed would bring lasting peace to Europe, was not specifically one of the Fourteen Points, its basic principle was included in points 5, 6, 9, 10, 11, and 12 whose language used such phrases as "autonomous development," "interests of the populations concerned," "independent determination of political development and national policy," "recognizable lines of nationality," "freest opportunity to autonomous development," and "historically established lines of allegiance and nationality" in referring to the post–World War I disposition of Russia, Poland, Belgium, the Italian border, the former Austria-Hungarian Empire (including Czechoslovakia), the Balkan states, the Middle Eastern countries formerly part of the Ottoman Empire, and colonial claims of the Allied powers. Meanwhile, the United States tipped the balance of the scales on the battlefield in favor of the Allies, and Wilson played this to full advantage.

Following the armistice of November 11, 1918, Wilson unwisely decided to personally head the U.S. delegation to the 1919 Paris Peace Conference. By involving himself in the daily grind of negotiations, Wilson not only exhausted himself physically during the months of working out the treaty, but the specific agreements he made with the Allies immediately became presidentially approved U.S. policy, leaving little room for Wilson to work out any later compromises with Congress during treaty ratification. He traveled widely before the conference began and was lionized by the peoples of Europe. Wilson knew little of European affairs, and the very public adulation went to his head and convinced him that the peoples of Europe wanted him to be the arbiter of the peace and that they favored a settlement based on "right" rather than on narrow national self-interest. Although Secretary of State Robert Lansing accompanied Wilson to Paris, the president largely ignored him and other advisers. He also failed to include in the delegation key Republicans.

Although many countries participated in the Versailles Conference, the treaty process was largely controlled by the Big Three: Great Britain, France, and the United States. In Paris, Wilson developed a close working relationship with British prime minister David Lloyd George. The two men stood together on most key issues against French premier Georges Clemenceau, eager to ensure security for France, which had borne the brunt of wartime destruction and casualties. The League of Nations was based on an Anglo-American draft, and Wilson defeated French efforts to detach the Rhineland from Germany. The resulting Treaty of Versailles with Germany and general peace settlement was essentially Wilson's work.

Wilsonian internationalism also cast a long shadow over the Middle East, for its promises of a world free of spheres of influence and "self-determination" raised the hopes of many in the region that they would be able to control their own destinies. Such hopes were soon dashed. Indeed, the new states in the Middle East formed from the Ottoman Empire passed under British and French control as mandates, colonies in all but name. Wilson rejected any mandates for the United States and was loath to support colonialism; however, he compromised with Great Britain and France on the issue in order to achieve his greatest goal in the treaty, the League of Nations. Nonetheless, as a result of the peace settlement that he had helped craft, the Middle East became rife with pent-up nationalism and dissatisfaction with the Western powers. The result was decades of unrest, violence, and war.

By the time Wilson returned to the United States in July 1919, popular sentiment had moved toward isolationism. The Republicans, led by Senator Henry Cabot Lodge, insisted upon restricting the power of the League of Nations. Even some Democrats wanted amendments. Already physically exhausted by his work on the treaty, Wilson embarked upon a cross-country speaking tour in an effort to sway public opinion, but suffered a stroke on October 2, 1919, which left him virtually incapacitated for the remainder of his administration. When he insisted that Democrats in the U.S. Senate reject any compromises in the agreements, the Senate refused twice to either ratify the Treaty of Versailles or enter the League of Nations. Wilson died in Washington on February 3, 1924.

Sugita Yoneyuki and Spencer C. Tucker

See also
Article 22, League of Nations Covenant; World War I, Impact of

References
Ambrosius, Lloyd E. *Wilsonian Statecraft: Theory and Practice of Liberal Internationalism during World War I.* Wilmington, DE: Scholarly Resources, 1991.
———. *Woodrow Wilson and the American Diplomatic Tradition: The Treaty Fight in Perspective.* New York: Cambridge University Press, 1987.
Calhoun, Frederick S. *Power and Principle: Armed Intervention in Wilsonian Foreign Policy.* Kent, OH: Kent State University Press, 1986.
Cooper, John Milton, Jr. *Breaking the Heart of the World: Woodrow Wilson and the Fight for the League of Nations.* New York: Cambridge University Press, 2001.
Knock, Thomas J. *To End All Wars: Woodrow Wilson and the Quest for a New World Order.* New York: Oxford University Press, 1992.
MacMillan, Margaret. *Paris, 1919: Six Months That Changed the World.* New York: Random House, 2002.
Thompson, John A. *Woodrow Wilson.* London and New York: Longman, 2002.

Wilson, Valerie Plame
Birth Date: April 19, 1963

Central Intelligence Agency (CIA) covert officer whose identity was leaked to the press in 2003, precipitating the long and contentious Valerie Plame Wilson incident. Valerie Elise Plame was born on April 19, 1963, in Anchorage, Alaska, the daughter of a career U.S. Air Force officer. She graduated from Pennsylvania State University in 1985 and began her career with the CIA that same year as a new trainee. Because of the clandestine nature of the CIA and Plame's work, few details on her 20-year career with the agency are known. What is known is that she worked in various posts, usually with a dual role: a public position and a covert one in which she concentrated on weapons proliferation and counterproliferation activities. The CIA sponsored her graduate studies, which resulted in a master's degree from the London School of Economics in 1991 and another master's degree from the College of Europe (Belgium) that same year.

Plame met Ambassador Joseph C. Wilson IV at a party in Washington, D.C., in 1997. The following year they were married. At the time of their courtship, Wilson was working in the West Wing as special assistant to President Bill Clinton and senior director of African affairs for the National Security Council (NSC). Wilson retired from government service in 1998 and began his own international management and consulting company.

Former Central Intelligence Agency (CIA) operative Valerie Plame Wilson, shown here with her husband, former ambassador Joseph Wilson, on April 29, 2006, in Washington, D.C. Plame's identity and status as an undercover operative for the CIA were leaked to the media after her husband publicly criticized the George W. Bush administration's rationale for going to war with Iraq in 2003. (AP/Wide World Photos)

In February 2002 the George W. Bush administration and the CIA sent Wilson on a mission to Niger, where he was to ascertain the accuracy of reports that Iraq had attempted to purchase enriched (yellowcake) uranium from that nation. Wilson was well placed to do this given his extensive experience dealing with Saddam Hussein in the late 1980s and early 1990s. Upon Wilson's return, he stated in a report that there was no credible evidence that any Iraqi official tried to engage Niger in a scheme that would have resulted in the transfer of enriched uranium to Iraq. Nevertheless, the Bush administration continued to press this claim, and it was specifically mentioned in President Bush's 2003 State of the Union address. The Niger-Iraq connection was used as a major pretext for the war against Iraq, which commenced in March 2003.

Outraged by the Bush administration's continuing claims concerning the Niger-Iraq connection, Wilson wrote an op-ed piece that appeared in the *New York Times* on July 6, 2003. The article revealed his trip to Niger the year before and laid bare the administration's theory on the validity of the reports coming from Niger. He also asserted that the White House had knowingly exaggerated the Iraqi threat so as to legitimize its pretext for the Iraq War. Predictably, Wilson's article exercised the Bush administration and, if Wilson and Plame Wilson's allegations are true, triggered a deliberate attempt to discredit and sabotage them both, a plan that involved the West Wing and the staffs of both Bush and Vice President Dick Cheney.

On July 14, 2003, the syndicated conservative newspaper columnist Robert Novak wrote an article to counter Wilson's letter. In the *Washington Post,* Novak revealed that Wilson's wife was a CIA operative whose job was to work on issue of weapons proliferation and weapons of mass destruction (WMDs). That revelation, which presumably came from someone high up in the Bush administration, caused an instant sensation, as it is illegal for a government official to knowingly reveal the identity of a covert CIA officer. Besides sparking an acrimonious political atmosphere between Republicans and Democrats and between supporters of the war and antiwar activists, the revelation about Plame Wilson's identity triggered a federal investigation in the Department of Justice. The Wilsons immediately alleged that the leak was a purposeful attempt to retaliate against Ambassador Wilson for his op-ed piece.

After a tortuous investigation, a federal grand jury indicted Cheney's chief of staff, I. Lewis "Scooter" Libby, on several charges, including lying under oath and obstruction of justice. He was found guilty in March 2007, but Bush quickly commuted his sentence. No other Bush administrations officials were indicted or convicted in the Plame Wilson incident, but the investigation left a dark cloud over the White House during a time in which the Iraq War was going very badly. Interestingly, no one was actually indicted or convicted for having perpetrated the leak in the first place, although it has to be assumed that someone within the Bush administration, with top-secret clearance, did so. Some Bush supporters claim that Plame Wilson's clandestine activities were already known in Washington and that Wilson's op-ed piece was politically motivated and designed to discredit the president.

Wilson and Plame Wilson later brought a civil suit against those who were thought to be directly involved in the leak, including Cheney himself, but the case was denied on jurisdictional grounds. That case is now on appeal. Plame Wilson left the CIA in December 2005. She caused a stir in 2006 when it was reported that she was about to receive $2.5 million for her memoir. That figure, however, has never been verified by her or her publisher. Her detractors asserted that she was using the incident for personal gain. Others, however, argued that she had a right to tell her side of the story and that it might shed more light on the case. Plame Wilson encountered some difficulty with the CIA, which insisted that certain passages in her manuscript be rewritten before the book could be published. In October 2007 Plame Wilson's book was finally released, titled *Fair Game: My Life as a Spy, My Betrayal by the White House.* Despite the tantalizing title, the book did not shed any significant, new light on the Plame Wilson incident. Plame Wilson then embarked on a major speaking tour, promoting her book and relaying her side of the story.

PAUL G. PIERPAOLI JR.

See also

Bush, George Walker; Central Intelligence Agency; Cheney, Richard Bruce; Hussein, Saddam; Libby, I. Lewis; Niger, Role in Origins of the Iraq War; Wilson, Joseph Carter, IV

Plame Wilson, Valerie. *Fair Game: My Life as a Spy, My Betrayal by the White House.* New York: Simon and Schuster, 2007.

Ricks, Thomas E. *Fiasco: The American Military Adventure in Iraq.* New York: Penguin, 2006.

Wilson, Joseph. *The Politics of Truth: Inside the Lies That Led to War and Betrayed My Wife's CIA Identity.* New York: Carroll and Graf, 2004.

Wojdakowski, Walter
Birth Date: March 29, 1950

U.S. Army general. Walter Wojdakowski (his last name appears erroneously in numerous news accounts as Wodjakowski) was born in Illinois on March 29, 1950. He was commissioned in the infantry upon graduation from the United States Military Academy, West Point. He subsequently earned a master's degree in business administration from the University of Alaska and another master's degree in military arts ands sciences from the U.S. Army Command and General Staff College. His military education also included the Army School of Advanced Military Studies and the Army War College.

Beginning as a platoon leader, Wojdakowski held a variety of command and staff positions. Completing Ranger training, he was later a Ranger instructor. He was also an instructor in the Military Science Department of the University of Alaska, Fairbanks. Later he commanded a battalion of the 2nd Armored Division at Fort Hood and took part in DESERT SHIELD/DESERT STORM, after which he was an instructor at the National Training Center, Fort Irwin, California. After attending the Army War College, he commanded the 11th Infantry Regiment at Fort Benning, Georgia (1993–1995). Following service as the commander, Operations Group, Combat Maneuver Training Center of the Hohenfels Training Area in Germany, he was assistant commandant of the Infantry School at Fort Benning during 1997–1998. Wojdakowski's next assignment was as chief of the Office of Military Cooperation, Kuwait. In 2000 he became assistant division commander of the 24th Infantry Division, Mechanized, and deputy commanding general of the U.S. First Army.

In September 2002 Major General Wojdakowski became deputy commanding general of V Corps. He then held the same position in the Combined Joint Task Force 7, redesignated the Multi-National Force–Iraq. It was in this capacity as chief deputy to Lieutenant General Ricardo Sanchez that Wojdakowski became aware of policies in place in the administration of Abu Ghraib Prison, which was administered by the U.S. Army. Brigadier General Janis Karpinski, Abu Ghraib's commander, later placed him at a meeting in November 2003 in which there was discussion of a Red Cross report citing cases of abuse at the prison. After the Abu Ghraib scandal broke, a report of an investigation into the role of senior officers that was headed by former defense secretary James

Schlesinger faulted Wojdakowski as having "failed to initiate action to request additional military police for detention operations after it became clear that there were insufficient assets in Iraq." There is question as to whether Wojdakowski and Sanchez approved the use of dogs and other coercive measures to intimidate Iraqi prisoners prior to their interrogation.

In June 2005 Wojdakowski was named the commanding general of Fort Benning. He retired from the army in November 2008.

SPENCER C. TUCKER

See also

Abu Ghraib; Karpinski, Janis; Miller, Geoffrey D.; Sanchez, Ricardo S.

References

Danner, Mark. *Torture and Truth: America, Abu Ghraib, and the War on Terror.* New York: New York Review Books, 2004.

Greenberg, Karen J., and Joshua L. Dratel, eds. *The Torture Papers: The Road to Abu Ghraib.* Cambridge: Cambridge University Press, 2005.

Schmitt, Eric. "Army Advances Officers Linked to Abu Ghraib." *Washington Post,* May 26, 2004.

Strasser, Steven, ed. *The Abu Ghraib Investigations: The Official Independent Panel and Pentagon Reports on the Shocking Prisoner Abuse in Iraq.* New York: PublicAffairs, 2004.

Wojtyła, Karol Jósef
See John Paul II, Pope

Wolf, John Stern
Birth Date: September 12, 1948

U.S. diplomat, ambassador to Malaysia (1992–1995), special adviser to President William J. Clinton on Caspian energy diplomacy (1999–2000), and assistant secretary for nonproliferation under President George W. Bush (2001–2004). Born on September 12, 1948, in Philadelphia, Pennsylvania, John Stern Wolf graduated from Dartmouth College in 1970 and entered the U.S. State Department that same year. Concentrating on international economics, he was a midcareer fellow at the Woodrow Wilson School of Public and International Affairs at Princeton University during 1978–1979.

Wolf's early foreign service assignments included postings in Australia, Vietnam, Greece, Pakistan, and Washington, D.C. He was principal deputy assistant secretary of state for international organization affairs from 1989 to 1992. He assumed the ambassadorship to Malaysia in 1992 and was confirmed as ambassador for Asia Pacific economic cooperation in February 1997, a post he held until 1999 at which time he went to work for the Clinton administration for a year as adviser on Caspian oil diplomacy. Ironically, on September 11, 2001, the day that Al Qaeda attacked the United States, President George W. Bush nominated Wolf to serve as assistant secretary for the Bureau of Nonproliferation.

From June 2003 to January 2004 Wolf served as chief of the U.S. Coordination Monitoring Mission in Jerusalem, where his primary task was to monitor implementation of the first phase of the Road Map to Peace. Sponsored by the United States, the European Union (EU), the United Nations (UN), and Russia, the Road Map to Peace set a path to final settlement of the Israeli-Palestinian conflict by 2005. The plan was meant to accomplish three things: end violence, transition to a provisional independent state of Palestine, and reach agreement on a comprehensive peace between the two countries living within secure borders. A cease-fire was a prerequisite for success, and many obstacles lined the road to peace in a region where cultural and religious differences have existed since biblical times. Extremist religious groups, including Hamas and Palestinian Islamic Jihad, repeatedly used terror and violence to derail peace efforts.

Wolf followed several well-known U.S. envoys who had failed to negotiate a comprehensive peace between the two historical enemies. That Wolf came with almost no Middle East experience was viewed by many in Washington as an asset. He was not identified with previous initiatives and would be in a position to encourage forward progress. Under the Road Map to Peace, both sides had parallel commitments to reduce violence, dismantle the terrorist infrastructure, build civic institutions, improve the quality of life for Palestinians, remove illegal outposts, and stop the construction of illegal settlements. Wolf thus introduced a series of benchmarks to measure progress. When either side failed to meet deadlines, Wolf encouraged it to get back on track. Neither side progressed far, however, and Israel in particular held back, claiming that it would not and could not implement measures to which it committed in the absence of visible Palestinian efforts to reduce terrorism and violence. Although some progress was achieved, terrorist attacks in the autumn of 2003 all but ended the initiative.

Wolf retired from the State Department in 2004 after 34 years of service and assumed the presidency of Eisenhower Fellowships on August 16, 2004. He has been active as a speaker and lecturer and is a frequent guest on television news. He currently resides in Philadelphia and Washington, D.C.

RANDY TAYLOR

See also

Bush, George Walker; Hamas; Islamic Jihad, Palestinian; Terrorism

References

Abunimah, Ali. *One Country: A Bold Proposal to End the Israeli-Palestinian Impasse.* New York: Metropolitan Books, 2006.

Dajani, Souad R. *The Untold Story: The Cost of Israel's Occupation to the Palestinians in the West Bank and the Gaza Strip.* Washington, DC: Palestine Center, Jerusalem Fund for Education and Community Development, 2005.

Gordon, Neve. *Israel's Occupation.* Berkeley: University of California Press, 2008.

Miller, Aaron David. *The Much Too Promised Land: America's Elusive Search for Arab-Israeli Peace.* New York: Bantam Books, 2008.

Wolfowitz, Paul Dundes
Birth Date: December 22, 1943

Neoconservative academic, U.S. assistant secretary of state for East Asian and Pacific affairs (1982–1986), and deputy secretary of defense (2001–2005). Wolfowitz was the chief architect of the Bush Doctrine that advocated preemptive strikes against potential threats to U.S. interests. Wolfowitz first proposed preemptive strikes against Iraq during the Ronald Reagan administration (1981–1989) and strongly advocated the 2003 Iraq War. Paul Wolfowitz was born in Ithaca, New York, on December 22, 1943. He graduated from Cornell University in 1965. He earned a doctorate in political science from the University of Chicago in 1972. His dissertation focused on the potential for nuclear proliferation in the Middle East.

Wolfowitz taught political science at Yale University from 1970 to 1972 and became an aide in U.S. Democratic senator Henry "Scoop" M. Jackson's 1972 and 1976 presidential campaigns. Wolfowitz began working in the U.S. Arms Control and Disarmament Agency (ACDA) in 1972 and studied policies related to the SALT I strategic arms limitation talks and the Henry Kissinger/Richard Nixon policy of détente. George H. W. Bush, then director of the Central Intelligence Agency (CIA), formed a committee to which Wolfowitz, in his continuing capacity at the ACDA, was assigned as a member of a team that discredited both détente and SALT II. This work brought Wolfowitz's ideas to the attention of U.S. secretary of defense Donald Rumsfeld and Governor Ronald Reagan of California.

In 1977 Wolfowitz became deputy assistant secretary of defense for regional programs in the Jimmy Carter administration and continued to develop his theory that the best way to prevent nuclear war was to stop conventional war. It was also during this time that Wolfowitz became convinced that the highly petroleum-dependent West was extremely vulnerable to disruptions in Persian Gulf oil. In studying the issue, Wolfowitz envisioned the possibility that Iraq might some day threaten Kuwait and/or Saudi Arabia, a scenario that was realized when Iraqi president Saddam Hussein ordered the invasion and annexation of Kuwait in August 1990. Wolfowitz determined that the United States had to be able to quickly project force into the region. His studies formed the rationale for the creation of the U.S. Central Command (CENTCOM), responsible for the U.S. Rapid Deployment Forces that proved so important to the successful prosecution of the 1991 Persian Gulf War and the 2003 Iraq War.

Wolfowitz left the Defense Department in 1980 for a visiting professorship at the Paul H. Nitze School of Advanced International Studies (SAIS) at Johns Hopkins University. He reentered public service in 1981, becoming the director of policy planning for the State Department, tasked with conceptualizing President Reagan's long-term foreign policy. Wolfowitz's distrust of Hussein resurfaced when Wolfowitz disagreed with the administration's policy of covertly supporting Iraq in the Iran-Iraq War (1980–1988). He also disagreed with the administration's sale of Airborne Warning and Control System (AWACS) aircraft to Saudi Arabia and its incipient dialogue with the Palestine Liberation Organization (PLO).

U.S. secretary of state George P. Shultz appointed Wolfowitz assistant secretary for East Asian and Pacific affairs in 1982, and in that capacity Wolfowitz urged the Reagan administration to support democracy in the Philippines. Wolfowitz believed that a healthy democracy was the best defense against communism or totalitarianism, a view that would again be reflected as part of the rationale for the 2003 Iraq War. He then served as U.S. ambassador to the Republic of Indonesia (1986–1989).

President George H. W. Bush named Wolfowitz undersecretary of defense for policy (1989–1993). In this post, Wolfowitz was responsible for U.S. military strategy in the post–Cold War era and reported to Defense Secretary Richard (Dick) Cheney. Wolfowitz disagreed with the decision not to overthrow Hussein in the 1991 Persian Gulf War (Operation DESERT STORM). Wolfowitz saw the decision as poor strategy, believing that this task would then have to be undertaken in the future. He also saw it as a betrayal of the Iraqi Shiites and Kurds, whom the United States had encouraged to revolt and then largely abandoned.

Wolfowitz left public service during the William J. Clinton presidency, returning to Johns Hopkins as dean of the SAIS from 1993 to 2001. He did not forgo politics, however, and in 1997 became a charter member of the Project for a New American Century (PNAC), a neoconservative think tank. Fellow charter members included Donald Rumsfeld, Dick Cheney, and Richard Perle. In 1998 Wolfowitz signed an open PNAC letter to Clinton urging a policy shift away from containing Iraq to a preemptive attack against Iraq. Wolfowitz later joined a group that advised the 2000 Republican Party presidential candidate George W. Bush on foreign policy matters.

Wolfowitz became U.S. deputy secretary of defense in 2001 and served in that capacity until 2005. It was in this capacity that he urged Bush to mount a preemptive strike on Iraq following the September 11, 2001, terrorist attacks. This idea of preemptive strikes against potential threats, which Wolfowitz had first conceived during the Reagan era, came to be known as the Bush Doctrine. An American- and British-led military coalition invaded Iraq in March 2003, asserting in part that Iraq's alleged weapons of mass destruction (WMDs) were an imminent threat worthy of preemptive intervention. As the war dragged on and settled into a bloody stalemate and no WMDs were found in Iraq, Wolfowitz and his neoconservative cohorts were gradually shunted aside. Bush subsequently nominated Wolfowitz to be the 10th president of the World Bank Group, and he assumed the post on June 1, 2005.

Wolfowitz's tenure at the World Bank was almost immediately controversial, the result of several appointments he made that smacked of cronyism. His apparent romantic involvement with Shaha Riza, a Tunisian-born Middle East specialist employed as

a communications director by the World Bank, raised many eyebrows. The relationship clearly violated World Bank guidelines that forbade relationships between supervisors and subordinates. Later investigations found that Wolfowitz had sought and received pay increases for Riza that ran counter to World Bank guidelines. By the spring of 2007, the World Bank's board of executives had begun to pressure Wolfowitz to resign. After weeks of resisting such pressure, he finally agreed to step down on May 17, effective June 30. Wolfowitz is currently a visiting fellow at the American Enterprise Institute. He is also involved in a number of international organizations and continues to serve as a consultant for the State Department.

RICHARD M. EDWARDS

See also

Bush, George Herbert Walker; Bush, George Walker; Bush Doctrine; Cheney, Richard Bruce; DESERT SHIELD, Operation; DESERT STORM, Operation; Hussein, Saddam; Iran-Iraq War; IRAQI FREEDOM, Operation; Kurds; Kurds, Massacres of; Neoconservatism; Perle, Richard; Reagan Administration, Middle East Policy; Rice, Condoleezza; Rumsfeld, Donald Henry; Shia Islam; Shultz, George Pratt; United States Central Command; Weapons of Mass Destruction

References

Crane, Les, ed. *Wolfowitz on Point*. Philadelphia: Pavilion, 2003.
Mann, James. *Rise of the Vulcans: The History of Bush's War Cabinet*. New York: Viking, 2004.

Women, Role of in Afghanistan and Iraq Wars

Women's participation in military operations greatly expanded in scope and experience during Operations ENDURING FREEDOM (the coalition effort in Afghanistan) and IRAQI FREEDOM (the Iraq War). More women deployed, performed a greater variety of occupational specialties, and were dispersed more widely across active theaters of operations than ever before in U.S. military history. According to figures produced by the Defense Manpower Data System, as of September 2006, 112,832 women had deployed to these two operations, representing 11.1 percent of the active duty personnel. This figure is nearly double the just more than 6 percent female personnel who deployed to the Persian Gulf region earlier in Operation DESERT STORM (1991).

The U.S. Air Force deployed the largest number of women, roughly 15.8 percent, trailed closely by the U.S. Army and the U.S. Navy at 11 percent and 11.1 percent, respectively. The U.S. Marine Corps reported just 3.4 percent. Although the prohibition of women in direct ground combat remains in effect, many women found themselves under fire while in transportation convoys, returning fire in defensive combat roles and performing the majority of all available military duties. Military necessity dispersed women to geographically diverse positions throughout the theater of operations.

U.S. Marine Corps sergeant Angailque Skean provides security during a cordoned search in Helmand Province, Afghanistan, July 28, 2009. Skean was a member of one of the highly effective Female Engagement Teams working to reduce Taliban influence among the Afghan population. (U.S. Department of Defense)

While American women have always participated in military operations, few routinely deployed to active theaters of combat. This limitation reflected not only societal norms and expectations but also legislative and policy restrictions. In 1993 U.S. secretary of defense Les Aspin, following legislative action by the U.S. Congress, removed policy restrictions that barred women from training for combat aviation missions. Female aviators flew combat missions in 1998 for the first time over the no-fly zone in Iraq. Moreover, by 1994 the Department of Defense had abolished the risk rule, which prohibited women from serving in ground combat support groups. This action opened the bulk of all military occupational specialties to female personnel. More recently, policy makers reviewed the prohibition of women in units engaged in direct ground combat missions in response to the increased strain on forces brought about by the extended deployment in Iraq and Afghanistan.

Currently women routinely participate in a wide variety of missions, and there are no prohibitions on temporary excursions into active areas of combat. Indeed, women are essential to maintaining the volunteer military, and the armed forces continue to regard females as an important target audience for recruiting efforts.

Although it is too early to identify the effect that this level of participation will exert on American women, gender relations, societal norms, and the military, there are some indicators of the direction that legacy may take. Increased claims of sexual harassment and incidents of sexual assault suggest that the services and the country they serve have not yet resolved the intricacies involved in integrating and deploying a two-gender operational military force. Some psychology professionals claim that women may be more susceptible to stress-induced conditions such as post-traumatic stress disorder and that they may require longer and more intensive treatment to fully recover, possibly placing women at a disadvantage in certain positions.

The increased number of deployed women with children calls into question the advisability of an expanded role for mothers, especially single mothers, in extended military deployments. Although military personnel who are parents designate alternative caregivers should their unit be deployed, policy makers and society may consider the individual effect on the well-being of children, given these long parental separations and the daily stress inherent with the realization for a child that her or his mother may be in harm's way. Other military analysts wonder if the American public is willing to accept larger numbers of female casualties or women as prisoners of war. Relatively small numbers of each thus far have not brought Americans face to face with these possibilities.

Finally, many observers question whether or not the ground combat exclusion is a valid concept in the era of modern warfare in which battles occur in virtually 360 degrees, the front lines are nonexistent, and the enemy neglects to respect civilian noncombatant status, let alone gender, as a relative factor in pursuing hostilities. These and other issues will be the legacy of women's increasing participation in U.S. military operations. The experiences of female soldiers, sailors, air personnel, and marines, along with those of their male counterparts during Operations ENDURING FREEDOM and IRAQI FREEDOM, will undoubtedly guide policy makers and military leaders as they strive to provide effective forces, equal opportunities, and comparable responsibilities for all U.S. military personnel.

DEBORAH KIDWELL

See also

ENDURING FREEDOM, Operation; IRAQI FREEDOM, Operation

References

Biddle, Stephen. *Afghanistan and the Future of Warfare: Implications for Army and Defense Policy.* Carlisle, PA: Strategic Studies Institute, 2002.

Bowman, Steven R. *Iraq: U.S. Military Operations.* Washington, DC: Library of Congress, Congressional Research Service, 2006.

Brower, J. Michael. "PRO: Expanding Roles for Women Warriors." *Officer* 81(2) (March 2005): 38–42.

Women, Role of in Persian Gulf War

Women constituted more than 7 percent of all U.S. military personnel in the 1991 Persian Gulf War, including Operation DESERT SHIELD and Operation DESERT STORM. Indeed, some 41,000 of the approximately 500,000 U.S. troops deployed to Iraq and Kuwait were female marines, soldiers, sailors, and air personnel. Of those servicewomen deployed to the Persian Gulf region, approximately 70 percent were from the U.S. Army, 10 percent were from the U.S. Navy, 6 percent were from the U.S. Marine Corps, and 14 percent were from the U.S. Air Force. The U.S. military stationed these women throughout the deployed area, and many accompanied their units across the border into Iraq and Kuwait during the air and ground combat phases of the campaign.

Female officers commanded brigade-, battalion-, company-, and platoon-size units in the combat support and combat service support areas. Moreover, enlisted women and officers fulfilled a wide variety of professional and technical positions, including traditionally male roles such as military police and guards. Although some units (the 24th Infantry Division, for example) reported a significant increase in female soldier pregnancies after the units were placed on alert for deployment to the Middle East—making the women therefore ineligible for deployment—government studies after the war assessed women's job performance favorably

Female troops serving in Operation DESERT STORM. Approximately 41,000 women were deployed by coalition forces during the Persian Gulf War, although they were largely restricted to noncombat roles. (Corel)

Women in the U.S. Military Deployed to the Middle East during the Persian Gulf War

Branch	Number	Percentage
U.S. Air Force	5,740	8.1%
U.S. Army	28,700	10.6%
U.S. Marine Corps	2,460	2.6%
U.S. Navy	4,100	2.7%
Total, all branches	41,000	7.1%

and reported a low occurrence of the potential problems generally identified with gender-integrated units.

Under the so-called risk rule, the military did not assign women to units whose mission was direct combat, defined as "closing with the enemy by fire, maneuver, or shock effect to destroy or capture, or while repelling assault by fire, close combat, or counterattack." However, the intent of the rule was not to ensure that women avoided all hostilities. The Direct Combat Probability Coding System ranked each unit's probability of engaging in direct combat from highest to lowest based on the unit's mission, current tactical doctrine, and battlefield position.

Although women were not generally assigned forward of the brigade rear boundary, no limits existed on temporary excursions to deliver supplies or repair equipment or during defensive combat operations. Thus, female personnel saw combat. Five women were killed in action, and 3 others fell victim to nonbattle deaths. In addition, 21 women were wounded in action, 2 were held as prisoners of war (POWs), and 4 female marines were awarded the Combat Action Ribbon.

Operations DESERT SHIELD and DESERT STORM offered U.S. politicians and military leaders the first opportunity to assess the benefits and risks of gender-integrated military units during deployments that included thousands of women. The final report to Congress indicated that units with fully integrated female members performed vital roles under stressful battlefield conditions. The most profound legacy was the debate sparked over the appropriate role of women in military operations. Critics argued that females lacked physical strength, would negatively affect unit cohesion, would increase lost time and unit attrition due to pregnancy, and did not possess the ability to endure long deployments, hostile conditions, or POW status.

As a result of women's excellent service in the Persian Gulf War, the National Defense Authorization Act for Fiscal Years 1992 and 1993 repealed the statutory limitations on female military personnel, and the secretary of defense subsequently removed the remaining policy limitations that disqualified women from assignment to missions on combat aircraft and naval war vessels. By 1998 women were eligible for an estimated 80 percent of the services' positions.

Policy makers continue to question if the exclusion of women from combat remains relevant on a modern battlefield, where the front lines are difficult to identify and constantly changing.

Regardless, women are currently an important component of active duty and reserve forces and today serve in expanded roles inspired by their participation in Operations DESERT SHIELD and DESERT STORM.

DEBORAH KIDWELL

See also

DESERT SHIELD, Operation; DESERT STORM, Operation

References

Cornum, Rhonda, as told to Peter Copeland. *She Went To War: The Rhonda Cornum Story.* Novato, CA: Presidio, 1992.

Government Accounting Office/National Security and International Affairs Division 98-157. *Gender Issues in the U.S. Military.* Washington, DC: U.S. Government Printing Office, 1998.

Moore, Molly. *A Woman at War: Storming Kuwait with the U.S. Marines.* New York: Free Press, 1993.

Schubert, Frank N., and Theresa L. Kraus, eds. *The Whirlwind War: The United States Army in Operations Desert Shield and Desert Storm.* Washington, DC: U.S. Government Printing Office, 1995.

United States Department of Defense. *Conduct of the Persian Gulf War: Final Report to Congress.* Washington, DC: U.S. Government Printing Office, 1992.

United States General Accounting Office Studies, Government Accounting Office/National Security and International Affairs Division 93-93. *Women in the Military: Deployment in the Persian Gulf War.* Washington, DC: U.S. Government Printing Office, 1993.

Woodward, Robert Upshur
Birth Date: March 26, 1943

American journalist, acclaimed investigative reporter, and chronicler of the George W. Bush administration following the September 11, 2001, terror attacks on the United States. Robert (Bob) Upshur Woodward was born in Geneva, Illinois, on March 26, 1943, but spent his childhood in nearby Wheaton, Illinois. He graduated from Yale University in 1965 and was commissioned a lieutenant in the U.S. Navy. He left the navy in 1970.

Instead of attending law school as his father wished, Woodward went to work as a reporter for the *Montgomery Sentinel* before moving on to the much more prestigious *Washington Post* in 1971. The investigative work by Woodward and fellow *Washington Post* reporter Carl Bernstein on the June 1972 Watergate break-in ultimately led to revelations about President Richard M. Nixon's use of slush funds, obstruction of justice, and various dirty tricks that resulted in congressional investigations and the president's resignation in August 1974.

The Watergate Scandal made Woodward a household name and one of the most sought-after investigative reporters in the nation. He and Bernstein later wrote *All the President's Men,* which was later made into a movie starring Robert Redford and Dustin Hoffman, and *The Final Days,* covering their Watergate reporting. Woodward's work on the Watergate story garnered him a Pulitzer Prize. In 1979 the *Washington Post* promoted him to assistant

Robert Woodward, who, with fellow reporter Carl Bernstein, broke the story of the Watergate Scandal that forced President Richard Nixon from office. Woodward, shown here on May 7, 1973, has written a series of well-received books on the development of the George W. Bush administration's Iraq policy. (AP/Wide World Photos)

managing editor of the Metro section, and in 1982 he became assistant managing editor for investigative news. Woodward received a second Pulitzer Prize for his reporting on the attacks of September 11, 2001, and their aftermath.

Woodward's books are written in the voice of an omniscient narrator and are compiled from in-depth research, but they rely most heavily on extensive interviews with crucial principals. Most often, the subjects of these works have a natural interest in cooperating with Woodward. Without their input they are more likely to be portrayed poorly in the product. All of Woodward's books have received criticism from some commentators, who usually point to inconsistencies or contest the factuality of the interviews.

Woodward's *The Commanders* (1991) covered the George H. W. Bush administration's handling of the December 1989–January 1990 Panama invasion and the Persian Gulf War of 1991. In *The Agenda* (1994), Woodward examined the passing of President Bill Clinton's first budget. In *The Choice* (1996), Woodward covered the 1996 presidential election contest. In *Shadow* (1999), he examined how the legacy of Watergate has affected how five presidents have dealt with scandal since 1974. In 2000's *Maestro,* he analyzed the Federal Reserve Board; its chairman, Alan Greenspan; and the

American economy. In 2005 following the death of Marc Felt, the anonymous source "Deep Throat" from Watergate, Woodward and Bernstein wrote *Secret Man,* giving new revelations about their Watergate experience.

Woodward has also written four books on the George W. Bush administration following the terrorist attacks of September 11, 2001: *Bush at War* (2002), *Plan of Attack* (2004), *State of Denial* (2006), and *The War Within: A Secret White House History, 2006–2008* (2008). Woodward received criticism for being allegedly excessively friendly to Bush and his agenda after the publication of both *Bush at War* and *Plan of Attack.* The third and fourth books, however, were far more critical of the Bush administration and its failings in the Iraq War. All of the books illustrate well the divisions within the White House and the Pentagon and the manner in which decisions were made within the Bush administration.

Woodward's *Plan of Attack* chronicles the Bush administration's reaction to September 11, the opening salvos in the Global War on Terror, and the planning and implementation of Operation ENDURING FREEDOM, which saw U.S. and coalition forces topple the Taliban regime in Afghanistan. *Plan of Attack,* on the other hand, takes a more controversial slant by examining how, when, and why Bush decided to go to war against Iraq in 2003 and remove Saddam Hussein from power. Woodward's main contention is that the Bush administration had planned on regime change in Iraq just weeks after the September 11, 2001, attacks, even though there was no evidence linking Hussein to these. In *State of Denial,* the journalist chronicled the many missteps, mistakes, and gaffes that turned the 2003 war in Iraq into an embarrassing quagmire. The book also showed how many members of the administration were in denial about their role in the debacle and refused to see the seriousness of the situation. The book came out less than a month before the November 2006 congressional elections, which swept the Republicans from power in both houses and brought about the forced resignation of Secretary of Defense Donald Rumsfeld.

In 2008 Woodward published *The War Within,* his fourth book on the Bush presidency. Woodward's conclusions were damning, claiming that Bush was detached and divorced from reality vis-à-vis the Iraq War and that he had left management of the conflict to his generals. Bush's troop surge strategy was purportedly postponed until after the 2006 midterm elections because the president did not want to hamper the Republicans' chances at the voting booth.

Woodward is such a part of the Washington establishment that it is sometimes difficult to say to what extent his interpretations are affected by conventional wisdom, as he is one of the primary shapers of conventional wisdom. Certainly, his painstaking interviews and investigative research have fully established his credentials as one of today's most keen and insightful observers regarding presidential policy formation.

MICHAEL BEAUCHAMP AND PAUL G. PIERPAOLI JR.

See also

Bush, George Herbert Walker; Bush, George Walker; DESERT STORM, Operation; ENDURING FREEDOM, Operation; IRAQI FREEDOM, Operation; Neoconservatism; Rumsfeld, Donald Henry

References

Shephard, Alicia P. *Woodward and Bernstein: Life in the Shadow of Watergate.* Indianapolis: Wiley, 2006.
Woodward, Bob. *Bush at War.* New York: Simon and Schuster, 2002.
———. *Plan of Attack.* New York: Simon and Schuster, 2004.
———. *State of Denial: Bush at War, Part III.* New York: Simon and Schuster, 2006.
———. *The War Within: A Secret White House History, 2006–2008.* New York: Simon and Schuster, 2008.

World Trade Center Bombing
Event Date: February 26, 1993

The first attempt by Islamist terrorists to destroy the World Trade Center complex, which failed to seriously damage the structure. At 12:18 p.m. on Friday, February 26, 1993, Islamist terrorists exploded a bomb in the underground garage, level B-2, of One World Trade Center (North Tower). They employed a yellow Ford

Econoline Ryder rental truck filled with 1,500 pounds of explosives. The bomb was built using a mix of fuel oil and fertilizer with a nitroglycerin booster.

The conspirators were militant Islamists led by Ramzi Ahmed Yousef, who was of Kuwaiti and Pakistani descent with connections to the Al Qaeda terrorist organization. Yousef confessed to American authorities after his capture that they had selected the World Trade Center complex because it was "an overweening symbol of American arrogance." Other participants were Mohammed Salameh, Nidal Ayyad, Mahmud Abuhalima, and, to a lesser extent, the cleric Umar Abdul Rahman.

Beginning in January 1993, Yousef and his fellow conspirators began to locate and buy the ingredients for the bomb. They required everything, ranging from a safe place to work to storage lockers, tools, chemicals, plastic tubs, fertilizer, and lengths of rubber tubing. It took about $20,000 to build the bomb, although Yousef had wanted more money so that he could build an even bigger bomb. Most of the funds were raised in the United States, but some money came from abroad. Yousef's uncle, Khalid Sheikh Mohammed, had sent him $600 dollars for the bomb. It

Survivors of the car bomb that exploded in a garage under the World Trade Center in New York City on February 26, 1993. They are being assisted by rescue personnel outside the building. Although horrific, this bombing paled in comparison with the devastation of September 11, 2001, when commercial airplanes hijacked by extremist Muslim terrorists crashed into the buildings, killing thousands. (AP/Wide World Photos)

was Yousef's intention for the explosion to bring down the North Tower of the World Trade Center complex; its impact on the South Tower, he hoped, would bring it down also. This expectation was too high, however, as the North Tower shook in the explosion but withstood its force without major structural damage.

Despite the force of the explosion, casualties were relatively low. The bomb produced a crater 22 feet wide and five stories deep within the garage structure. The force of the explosion came close to breaching the so-called bathtub, a structure that prevented water from the Hudson River from pouring into the underground areas of the complex and into the subway system. If this breach had occurred, the resulting catastrophic loss of life would likely have eclipsed the losses from the subsequent attacks on September 11, 2001. Six people—John DiGiovanni, Bob Kirk-Patrick, Steve Knapp, Bill Backo, Wilfredo Mercado, and Monica Rodriguez-Smith—were killed in the attack, and more than 1,000 were injured.

The New York City Fire Department responded with 775 firefighters from 135 companies, but they arrived too late to do anything but tend to the wounded and carry away the dead. It took nearly 10 hours to get everyone out because the elevators shorted out in the explosion and power to the staircases failed. Evacuations took place in the dark and in the midst of heavy smoke. The tower was repaired at a cost of $510 million, and the complex reopened in less than one month. The bombing was significant in revealing how vulnerable the World Trade Center complex was to terrorist attacks.

At first investigators believed that a transformer had blown up, but once they began examining the site it became obvious that a large bomb had detonated. Within five hours the Federal Bureau of Investigation (FBI) and the New York City Police Department had confirmed that the explosion had been caused by a bomb. The next question was determining responsibility for the blast. There had been 20 calls to the police claiming responsibility, but this was not unusual. At first it was believed that the deed was the work of Balkan extremists upset with U.S. policy there, but the investigation was just beginning.

Within weeks the investigating team of 700 FBI agents had identified or arrested all of the World Trade Center bombers. What broke the case was the discovery of a unique vehicle identification number on the frame of the Ryder truck. From that number they learned that Salameh had rented the van because he had reported the van stolen and was trying to recover the $400 deposit. Salameh was arrested while trying to collect the deposit. Investigators then turned to identification of his fellow conspirators, and Yousef was finally determined to be the leader of the plot.

By the time authorities had identified Yousef as the leader and maker of the bomb, he was already in Pakistan planning other operations. Ultimately a Central Intelligence Agency (CIA) and FBI team captured him there, but not before he had initiated several other plots. Yousef had always been a freelancer, but there was evidence that he had connections with Al Qaeda operatives before and after the World Trade Center bombing.

Following a series of trials, the participants in the bomb plot were found guilty and received life sentences. Yousef was sentenced to 240 years in solitary confinement.

STEPHEN E. ATKINS

See also

Mohammed, Khalid Sheikh; September 11 Attacks; Yousef, Ramzi Ahmed

References

Bell, J. Bowyer. *Murders on the Nile: The World Trade Center and Global Terror.* San Francisco: Encounter Books, 2003.

Caram, Peter. *The 1993 World Trade Center Bombing: Foresight and Warning.* London: Janus, 2001.

Davis, Mike. *Duda's Wagon: A Brief History of the Car Bomb.* London: Verso, 2007.

Lance, Peter. *1000 Years for Revenge: International Terrorism and the FBI, the Untold Story.* New York: Regan Books, 2003.

Reeve, Simon. *The New Jackals: Ramzi Yousef, Osama bin Laden, and the Future of Terrorism.* Boston: Northeastern University Press, 1999.

World War I, Impact of

World War I (1914–1918) was perhaps the most important political event in the evolution of the modern Middle East. The issues that fuel the current Arab-Israeli dispute and the unsettled conditions in the Persian Gulf and North Africa originated during World War I and its immediate aftermath. The war had three notable effects on the development of what would become an ongoing war between Arabs and Zionists in Palestine. The first was the destruction of the Ottoman Empire and its division into a number of smaller political units that ultimately became independent states in the modern Middle East. The second was the assumption of direct administrative responsibility for the territories in and around Palestine by Britain and France, two of the victors in that war. The third was the British declaration of support for the central goal of the Zionist movement, a Jewish homeland in Palestine. This was accomplished with the 1917 Balfour Declaration.

World War I had larger consequences not only in Palestine but also in the region that stretched from the Dardanelles through North Africa as a whole. The war stimulated nationalism among the area's indigenous peoples through the Allied-supported revolt among the Bedouin tribes on the Arabian Peninsula, and through the many British military reversals at the hands of the Turks (at Gallipoli and Kut in 1915 and 1916, respectively), which demonstrated that the West was not invincible and boosted pride among the Turks. Nationalism was also stoked by Arab resentment at Allied intrigues to divide the region among themselves. Moreover, the declaration of jihad (holy war) by Turkish sultan Abdul Hamid on November 11, 1914, marked the first time that a Muslim leader had ever taken such a step against any of the Great Powers. The proclamation caused concern among the Allies, particularly the British, about the potential effects on the empire's Muslim subjects. Political and economic developments in Egypt and French

North Africa also stimulated Arab nationalism and resentment of Western rule.

The war accelerated political and social trends that had been eroding the strength of the Ottoman Empire for the preceding century and a half. Meanwhile, the Great Powers of Europe had been steadily expanding their influence in Turkish-controlled areas. Britain's worldwide influence and its strategic presence in the Middle East had grown considerably since the construction of the Suez Canal in 1869. Indeed, safeguarding the route to India was a cornerstone of British policy in the Middle East. As such, the British sought to dominate the territories near Suez and the Persian Gulf—Egypt, Palestine, and Iraq—in order to keep their passage to India and the Far East secure. France, for its part, sought to control Syria and Lebanon to safeguard the Maronite Christian population and give France a presence in the eastern Mediterranean. France also controlled French Morocco, Algeria, and Tunisia in Northwest Africa. Italy, having wrested Tripolitania from the Ottoman Empire during the Italian-Turkish War of 1911–1912, sought to consolidate and expand its control over the remainder of Libya. Czarist Russia sought an opening through the Dardanelles and the protection of Orthodox Christian sites in Jerusalem. Germany wanted to influence the region and tap its resources through the construction of the Berlin-to-Baghdad railway.

In addition to the growing encroachment of the European powers, the Ottoman Empire faced growing ethnic unrest among its minority populations. This was particularly the case among the Armenians, the growing Jewish population in Palestine (most of whom were fleeing persecution in Russia), and the Bedouin Arab tribes in the Arabian Peninsula.

The outbreak of war in August 1914 and the Turkish entry into the conflict on the German side in September along with wartime developments greatly accelerated the process of Ottoman disintegration. Wartime privations and Turkish repression (manifested in the Armenian massacres of 1915 and in intensified persecution of Jews in Palestine) triggered nationalist feelings and hatred of the Turks among these minorities. The British, hoping to take advantage of this, encouraged unrest among Arabs throughout the Ottoman Empire by promising them support for independence. At the same time, however, the British were negotiating postwar spheres of influence in the Middle East with the French. This was effected through the 1916 Sykes-Picot Agreement, which recognized France's sphere of influence in Syria and Lebanon and British predominance in Palestine, Jordan, and Iraq. Later, Italy and Russia would also become parties to these clandestine machinations.

The idea of instigating a revolt against the Turks among the Arabs originated with the British high commissioner in Egypt, Sir Henry MacMahon, in November 1914 and gained momentum with British military defeats at Gallipoli and Kut in 1915 and early 1916. With the Turks still threatening Suez and the British unable to make any headway in Sinai, the British command in Cairo needed to find some way to tie Turkish troops down. The British also hoped to undermine the sultan's proclamation of jihad.

In July 1915 Emir Abdullah Hussein, the sharif of Mecca, notified MacMahon of his willingness to initiate an Arab revolt if Britain would support an independent Arab state under Hussein after the war. MacMahon agreed, although he avoided any explicit promises about the exact borders of any such future state. Hussein hesitated to call for open revolt. The Turks' decision to reinforce their Medina garrison in June 1916 and the unrest that increase caused finally convinced Hussein to proceed.

Hussein and his oldest son, Emir Faisal, moved to attack the Hejaz Railway and isolate Medina. In October the British appointed as liaison to the Arabs Thomas Edward Lawrence (who would become immortalized as Lawrence of Arabia), an officer in the Arab Bureau in Cairo who spoke fluent Arabic and had a reputation for intense pro-Arab sympathies. Lawrence formed a close relationship with Faisal, whom Lawrence viewed as the most promising of the Arab leaders. The relationship eventually led to Faisal attending the 1919 Paris Peace Conference as spokesman for the Arab cause and Lawrence accompanying him as his adviser.

The importance of the Arab Revolt in British Middle East strategy grew after the failure of the drive to take Gaza in March 1917. The British provided arms and naval transport across the Red Sea to further the Arab uprising. Faisal and Lawrence provided leadership, with both men proving adept at guerrilla warfare. The Arabs cut rail lines, tied down thousands of Turkish troops in the Hejaz, and made a renewed British offensive across the Sinai and into Palestine possible. The most dramatic moment of the uprising occurred in August 1917 when Lawrence led a force of 2,000 Arabs across some of the worst desert in the Arabian Peninsula and seized the vital port of Aqaba by surprising the Turkish garrison with an attack from the landward side. Aqaba's capture secured the flank of the British forces in Palestine and opened the way for an offensive by the British and their Arab allies into Jordan and Syria.

Lawrence then made an equally dramatic journey across the Sinai to Cairo to report to the British command on the capture of Aqaba and the success of the Arab uprising. With Aqaba under Allied control, British forces, now commanded by General Edmund Allenby, launched a new offensive against the Turks in Gaza and Palestine that resulted in the capture of Jerusalem on December 11, 1917. The British were now in a position to attack into Jordan and Syria. At the same time, a renewed British drive in Mesopotamia succeeded in capturing Baghdad.

While in Cairo, Lawrence learned of the Sykes-Picot agreement, which threatened the prospects for Arab independence. On returning to the Hejaz, Lawrence urged Faisal—whose Arab forces were to support Allenby's upcoming attack into Jordan and Syria by protecting the British right flank—to push into Syria and Jordan, hoping that Britain and France would not be able to deny them Arab land that they already controlled. Just before the end of the war, in October 1918, the Arab army, with Faisal and Lawrence in the lead, captured Damascus, further muddying an already confused political situation.

Arab guerrillas led by Englishman T. E. Lawrence in the desert in July 1917. The Arab Revolt against the Ottoman Empire during World War I failed to achieve true independence for Arab states in the Middle East. (HultonArchive/Getty Images)

Anglo-French imperial ambitions had thus run head-on into growing Arab and Jewish nationalism. The fall of the Ottoman Empire destroyed the state that had united Turks, Arabs, Armenians, and Jews within a single political and social framework for more than four centuries. Its disappearance brought the emergence of a variety of competing nationalist movements that offered their citizens alternate approaches of constructing their political identities and their cultural communities. Many times, one movement's goals were diametrically opposed to those of another. British pledges to the Arabs and their support for uprisings on the Arabian Peninsula fueled Arab nationalism that was to translate into resentment of Allied duplicity and a sense of betrayal when Britain and France established League of Nations mandates in Iraq, Syria, Lebanon, and Palestine after the war.

Britain's postwar difficulties with Palestinian Arabs were greatly compounded by the Balfour Declaration. Of all the wartime promises made by the British, the Balfour Declaration would have the most far-reaching consequences. In July 1917 British foreign secretary Arthur Balfour placed a notice in the *Times of London* promising British support for a Jewish homeland in Palestine. Based on a draft written by Baron Edmund de Rothschild

(although Balfour modified it considerably before publication), it stated that the British government viewed favorably the establishment of a Jewish national home in Palestine. The declaration avoided any mention of a Jewish state and stated clearly that there was to be no impingement on the civil and religious rights of indigenous non-Jewish populations.

Why the British chose to support Zionist ambitions in 1917 has been the subject of considerable controversy among scholars and analysts of British wartime Middle Eastern policies. Clearly, a number of factors were involved. Some observers have emphasized the strategic benefits that the British government believed Britain would derive from Jewish settlement in Palestine. Many British policy makers believed that a Jewish national homeland in Palestine, surrounded by a large Arab population and dependent on Britain for support and security, would provide an ideal safeguard for the Suez Canal and the route to India. Others argue that the British had one eye on influential Jews in the United States, particularly prominent Zionists such as Louis D. Brandeis and Felix Frankfurter who were close to the Woodrow Wilson administration. In this view, the British government was influenced by a patrician form of anti-Semitism that overestimated Jewish influence in the United

States. Other viewpoints emphasize intense lobbying efforts by Zionist leaders, particularly Chaim Weizmann; fears that Germany might take over the Zionist movement; or efforts by Allied policy makers to reach out to the leaders of the Russian Revolution, many of whom were Jewish. No doubt all of these played a role.

Whatever the reasons behind Balfour's action and however careful the declaration's wording, the declaration ultimately poisoned Arab-Jewish relations in Palestine and undermined Britain's credibility in both communities. The leadership of the Zionist movement and the Jewish community in Palestine took the declaration as a British commitment to a Jewish state in the long run and as support for unlimited Jewish immigration to Palestine in the short run.

The Palestine, Mesopotamian, and Arabian campaigns of 1917–1918 were significant military victories for Britain. The many promises that British officials made to so many conflicting groups, however, put them in a precarious political position. Arabs, both in Palestine and in the wider Middle East, saw both the Balfour Declaration and the Sykes-Picot Agreement as a great betrayal and evidence of Britain's lack of good faith. Arab nationalism now took on an intensely anti-British and anti-Western bent that could not be contained by the fragmented postwar order of protectorates dominated by the British and the French. The administrators of the British Mandate for Palestine were plagued by intensifying communal violence between the growing number of Jewish settlers and the indigenous Arab population. Nationalistic feelings in both Arab and Jewish camps—intensified by the persecution and suffering during World War I and, in the case of the Jews, fueled by persecution in Europe—simply could not be reconciled. British and French wartime measures taken to aid the Allied war effort against the Ottoman Empire opened a Pandora's box that has not been closed.

The war also had long-term effects in North Africa west of Suez, although political unrest took differing forms and revolved around different issues. In the years before the war, Muslim leaders in French North Africa had pursued legal equality in assimilation into metropolitan French society. During the war years Muslim leaders stepped up their agitation for legal equality. This was true in North Africa as it was elsewhere; however, the French bitterly opposed nationalist agitation in Algeria, Morocco, and Tunisia (the so-called Maghreb) especially. Efforts by Germans agents to foster Bedouin uprisings in the Maghreb early in the war failed. There were scattered rebellions among Berber tribesmen throughout the war, often in reaction to recruiting for the military and labor in metropolitan France, but these outbreaks were too small and localized to cause much concern.

British troops march through the Jebel Hamrin Mountains during the Mesopotamian Campaign in 1917. World War I ended with Britain and France as the dominant foreign powers in the Middle East. (National Archives)

Wartime conditions in France generated extensive economic and social change in Northwest Africa. Before the war's outbreak, no French Third Republic government had given serious consideration to French North Africa's potential as an asset in a general European war. As the war continued, heavy casualties and the drain on manpower grew more desperate. Spurred by heavy recruiting campaigns by the French government, more than 130,000 people from Algeria, French Morocco, and Tunisia immigrated to France, mainly to take jobs in war factories. In addition, about 85,000 (mostly Algerian) men volunteered for the ground forces. The growing importance of French North Africans to the war effort raised hopes among their leaders that France would grant them full legal equality and French citizenship. Various Algerian organizations, such as the Mouvement de la Jeunesse Algérienne that had been active before the war intensified their demands, which fell on receptive ears in the government and parliament. In November 1915 future premier Georges Clemenceau proposed far-reaching reforms for Algeria that would have granted Algerians French citizenship without requiring them to renounce Islam.

These proposed reforms encountered fierce opposition from conservative colonialist elements and French colons in Algeria. They feared that concessions would lead to more demands for independence in North Africa and economic and social equality in France to the detriment of white Frenchmen. The Franco-Algerians also emphasized their sacrifices, claiming that Frenchmen did not die to open the way for what they feared would be Muslim dominance of France. Conservatives succeeded in limiting wartime reforms, and North Africans in the military and industry were subject to discrimination. Workers were kept in the most physically demanding and worst-paid jobs. The government also segregated them from other workers in order to minimize sexual contact with French women, a scenario completely alien to the colonialist value system. French resentment of the immigrants combined with fears—particularly among French soldiers—that Frenchmen were being socially and sexually marginalized led to frequent outbreaks of racial violence. Such incidents became more frequent in 1917 and 1918 as war weariness caused domestic morale to deteriorate.

In the post–World War I years the lines hardened between reformers and conservative French colonialists (supported by a growing fascist movement in France in the 1930s). Newer, more radical movements gained a wider following among younger Muslims who resented wartime racial discrimination that they had experienced during the war and among the Arab masses as a whole. This trend was most noticeable in Algeria but was also gaining momentum in Morocco and Tunisia. Although political unrest in Northwest Africa was minimal compared to that in the eastern Mediterranean, there were more ominous signs for the future. As with the British, the French were caught between conflicting promises. Another far larger and more disastrous war would bring these social divisions to a head and lead to the transformation of Muslim reform movements. By 1946 they would be heavily influenced by nationalism and would begin demanding full and unequivocal independence.

WALTER F. BELL

See also

Arab Nationalism; Balfour Declaration; Bedouin; Mandates; Sykes-Picot Agreement; World War II, Impact of

References

Albertini, Rudolf von. "The Impact of Two World Wars on the Decline of Colonialism." *Journal of Contemporary History* 4(1) (January 1969): 17–35.

Andrew, Christopher, and A. S. Kanya-Forster. "France, Africa, and the First World War." *Journal of African History* 19(1) (January 1978): 11–23.

Fromkin, David. *A Peace to End All Peace: The Fall of the Ottoman Empire and the Creation of the Modern Middle East.* New York: Henry Holt, 1989.

Gelvin, James L. *The Israel-Palestine Conflict: One Hundred Years of War.* Cambridge: Cambridge University Press, 2005.

Horne, John. "Immigrant Workers in France during World War I." *French Historical Studies* 14(1) (Spring 1985): 57–88.

Morris, Benny. *Righteous Victims: A History of the Zionist-Arab Conflict, 1881–2001.* New York: Vintage Books, 2001.

Morrow, John H., Jr. *The Great War: An Imperial History.* New York: Routledge, 2005.

Neiberg, Michael S. *Fighting the Great War: A Global History.* Cambridge: Harvard University Press, 2005.

Stovall, Tyler. "The Color Line behind the Lines: Racial Violence in France during the Great War." *American Historical Review* 103(3) (June 1998): 737–769.

World War II, Impact of

World War II directly affected the Middle East in the considerable fighting in the region but even more so indirectly in terms of decolonization, the spread of Arab nationalism, the growing importance of the region's oil resources, and the impact of Great Power rivalries that sprang from the war. For good or ill, the United States and the Soviet Union became the major players in the region. Nothing is more emblematic of the change in importance of the region than photographs of King Abdul Aziz bin Abdul Rahman Al Saud (Ibn Saud) of Saudi Arabia meeting as an equal with U.S. president Franklin D. Roosevelt aboard the U.S. Navy cruiser *Quincy* in Egypt's Great Bitter Lake on February 14, 1945.

North Africa was a major theater of war, particularly from 1940 to 1943, and combat there involved Egypt, Libya, Tunisia, Morocco, and Algeria. Fighting also occurred in the Horn of Africa, and there was limited combat in Syria and Iraq. The war brought decolonization, which most keenly affected Great Britain and France. Not only had much of each power's empire been cut off from the mother country during the conflict, but at least in the case of France portions of the empire had kept the war alive in its name. Clearly, the peoples of the French and British empires expected to be rewarded for their loyalty during the war. Charles de Gaulle recognized the necessity of a changed relationship between France and its empire during a meeting at Brazzaville in January 1944 that resulted in a declaration heralding the need for political, social, and economic reforms. Independence did not come all at once of course, nor did Britain and France intend it for all. Thus, France considered Algeria, with its large European population, to be an integral part of France as three French departments, even as the Muslim majority there did not enjoy equal rights.

Opposition to European rule brought some violence at the end of the war, as in Syria. There also was a bloody uprising in Sétif in May 1945 in Algeria that may have claimed as many as 10,000 lives, and in Madagascar a major uprising against French rule claimed between 11,000 and 80,000 lives. It was impossible not to recognize how the war had shattered myths of European military invincibility. The French had been forced to give in to Japanese demands in Indochina, and the British were humiliated in Malaya. The Japanese victory in the Battle of Singapore has been called one of the greatest military disasters in British history. After the war, the peoples of the British and French empires sensed their masters' weakness and were far less likely to be satisfied with slow evolutionary change. Of course, declarations of basic human rights by such organizations as the United Nations (UN) gave cachet to their aspirations.

Many in Britain and France were loath to give up their empires. This was most pronounced in France. It is said that it is hard for the weak to be generous, and France in 1945 was very weak indeed. It had suffered a humiliating defeat and occupation at the hands of Germany, and only with its empire could it still be counted as a major power after the war. This and the fact that Indochina was France's wealthiest colony help to explain the determination of the French to hold on to their Southeast Asian empire, even if it meant war. The same might be said of the British in Burma (today Myanmar). The British were also slow to yield some imperial privileges; thus, not until 1956 did they agree to cede their remaining bases in Egypt.

Of course, the most difficult problem in the Middle East became that of resolving the conflict between Arabs and Jews. In September 1939 the political situation in Palestine was at best troubled. British authorities had largely tamped down the Palestinian Arab Revolt of 1936–1939, but there was still considerable unrest. The British did try to win some Arab support by clamping down on Jewish immigration, and this brought acts of terrorism by Jewish extremists against British authorities. Indeed, a three-way struggle ensued as Jews and Arab fought the British occupier and each other. Toward the end of the war the British actually diverted warships to keep Jews out of Palestine, and yet pressures grew afterward—especially from the United States, which had the world's largest Jewish population—for the British to admit the survivors of the Holocaust. Some 6 million European Jews had died in the Nazi-inspired genocide, and there was worldwide support for resettling the few survivors in Palestine and also to permit establishment of some sort of Jewish state that might protect the interests of Jews in the future.

Arab nationalism remained relatively dormant during World War II, the British having made some concessions in Egypt and elsewhere. There was fighting between British forces and the Iraqi Army in Iraq and between British, British Empire, and Free French forces against Vichy France forces in Syria. Both of these conflicts were prompted largely by fears of spreading German influence in the region and the threat this might pose to the supply of oil.

The war left Britain and France financially and militarily exhausted. Prime Minister Clement Attlee in Britain, whose Labour Party came to power in Britain as a consequence of its stunning surprise victory in the July 1945 elections, was determined to reduce its imperial commitments, particularly those that seemed to be especially volatile. The haste to divest certain colonial holdings brought great bloodshed in both the Empire of India and in Palestine. In the case of the latter, when Britain was unable to arrange a partition agreement between Jewish and Arab leaders, it simply walked away from its guardianship responsibilities. The British government set a deadline of May 15, 1948, for the departure of its troops and the end of the mandate. Anticipated by all, on May 14 Jewish leaders in Palestine proclaimed the establishment of the new State of Israel, and the first Arab-Israeli war immediately began.

As a newcomer to the Middle East, the United States sought during the war to secure regional stability to ensure the flow of oil and war supplies to and through the region, including Lend-Lease assistance, to the Soviet Union. To help expedite Lend-Lease aid, during the war Soviet forces occupied northern Iran, while the British had moved into southern Iran. Little thought was given in Washington to the tensions that would surface at the end of the war. The focus was always on ending the war as quickly as possible and with as little cost in American lives as possible. Thus, Roosevelt assured Ibn Saud that the United States did not support the Zionist aspiration of a Jewish state in Palestine, and the Roosevelt administration acquiesced in British efforts to restrict immigration into Palestine, even with proof positive of the Holocaust. American public opinion helped force a change in policy after the war, prompted by the all-too-horrible revelations of Jewish wartime suffering. In 1948 the United States was the first nation to recognize the new State of Israel (closely followed, as it turned out, by the Soviet Union).

In time, American policy shifted from a hands-off approach to stalwart support of Israel while still claiming to be even-handed as far as the Arabs were concerned. U.S. support for the new Jewish state included arms shipments that made Israel by far the most powerful regional military power. The Soviet Union meanwhile largely reversed course to oppose Israel and to arm the Arab states against it. The theme was thus struck on which the Cold War in the Middle East would be played out, a theme that would make the region one of the most volatile in the world.

WALTER F. BELL AND SPENCER C. TUCKER

See also

Arab-Israeli Conflict, Overview; Arab Nationalism; France, Middle East Policy; Middle East, History of, 1918–1945; Middle East, History of, 1945–Present; Soviet Union, Middle East Policy; United Kingdom, Middle East Policy; United States, Middle East Policy, 1945–Present; World War I, Impact of

References

Albertini, Rudolf von. "The Impact of Two World Wars on the Decline of Colonialism." *Journal of Contemporary History* 4(1) (January 1969): 17–35.

Bauer, Yehuda. *From Diplomacy to Resistance: A History of Jewish Palestine, 1930–1945.* Translated by Alton M. Winters. Philadelphia: Jewish Publication Society of America, 1970.

Gelvin, James L. *The Israel-Palestine Conflict: One Hundred Years of War.* Cambridge: Cambridge University Press, 2005.

Hahn, Peter L. *Crisis and Cross-Fire: The United States in the Middle East.* Dulles, VA; Potomac Books, 2005.

Morris, Benny. *Righteous Victims: A History of the Zionist-Arab Conflict, 1881–2001.* New York: Vintage Books, 2001.

Oren, Michael B. *Power, Faith, and Fantasy: America in the Middle East, 1776 to the Present.* New York: Norton, 2007.

Segev, Tom. *The Seventh Million: The Israelis and the Holocaust.* Translated by Haim Watzman. New York: Hill and Wang, 1993.

Y

Yeltsin, Boris Nikolayevich
Birth Date: February 1, 1931
Death Date: April 23, 2007

Soviet reform politician during the last years of the Soviet Union and first elected president of Russia (1991–1999). Born on February 1, 1931, in Butka in the Sverdlovsk Oblast in the Ural Mountains, Boris Nikolayevich Yeltsin graduated from the Urals Polytechnical Institute in 1955 as a construction engineer. He joined the Communist Party of the Soviet Union (CPSU) in 1961 and worked on various construction projects in the Sverdlovsk area until 1968.

Yeltsin rose through the party ranks in the Sverdlovsk Oblast Party Committee. He was elected the region's industry secretary in 1975 and first secretary in 1976. During 1976–1985 he moved through the national ranks of the CPSU. He served as a deputy in the Council of the Union (1978–1989), a member of the Supreme Soviet Commission on Transport and Communication (1979–1984), a member of the Presidium of the Supreme Soviet (1984–1985), and chief of the Central Committee Department of Construction in 1985. The new CPSU general secretary, Mikhail Gorbachev, summoned Yeltsin to Moscow in April 1985 as part of a team of reform-minded party members.

Gorbachev asked Yeltsin to reform the Moscow City Committee. Yeltsin began to clear the city's Party Committee of corrupt officials, which endeared him to Muscovites. Eventually he became dissatisfied with the slow pace of the perestroika reforms and openly criticized the CPSU officials. This was directed at the power base of Yegor Ligachev, who endorsed a moderate party-led reform. In 1987 Yeltsin resigned to force Gorbachev to take sides. Gorbachev needed Yeltsin to counterbalance Ligachev's growing skepticism and rejected Yeltsin's resignation, asking him to curb his critiques.

Yeltsin ignored Gorbachev's plea. Thus, Gorbachev allowed Ligachev to continue the campaign against Yeltsin, which finally led to Yeltsin's dismissal as first secretary of the Moscow Party Committee. In 1988 Yeltsin was also expelled from the Politbuttee, but he remained in Moscow as the first deputy chair of the State Committee for Construction.

Yeltsin went on to win a landslide victory in the newly established Congress of People's Deputies of the Russian Soviet Federated Socialist Republic (RSFSR) in March 1989. In May 1990 he became chairman of the RSFSR. By June 12, 1990, the RSFSR, along with the other 14 Soviet republics, had declared its independence. Yeltsin was directly elected to the newly created office of president of the now-independent RSFSR on June 12, 1991. He then demanded Gorbachev's resignation. Gorbachev refused to step down but did agree to sign a new union treaty in late August 1991.

Hard-line conservative forces within the CPSU tried to prevent the signing of the treaty, which would lead to the dissolution of the Soviet Union. On August 19, 1991, the conservatives dispatched troops to key positions around Moscow and held Gorbachev under house arrest. Yeltsin climbed atop one of the tanks surrounding the parliament building, denounced the CPSU coup as illegal, and called for a general strike. The troops sent to quell the demonstrations refused to take action against the demonstrators, instead joining them. Yeltsin and his supporters remained in the parliament building as they rallied international support. For three days thousands of people demonstrated in front of parliament, holding off an expected attack on the building.

The failed putsch and massive street demonstrations quickly destroyed the credibility of Gorbachev's perestroika and glasnost reforms. On December 24, 1991, the RSFSR and then later Russia took the Soviet Union's seat in the United Nations (UN) Security

Council. The next day Gorbachev resigned, an act that officially dissolved the Soviet Union. Yeltsin, as president of Russia, immediately abolished the CPSU. In the meantime, he had negotiated with the leaders of Ukraine and Belarus to form the Commonwealth of Independent States (CIS) as a federation of most of the former Soviet republics.

With a stagnating economy and a hostile legislature and having survived an attempted coup (1993), Yeltsin was not expected to win reelection in 1996. However, he staged an amazing comeback. Under Yeltsin, Russia's foreign policy in the Middle East became something of a tightrope act. Throughout the 1990s Russia's Middle East primary focus was on Iran and Turkey. These nations were key to Russian economic growth (trade, oil issues, arms sales) and were crucial to the delicate balancing act that Moscow had to employ in Transcaucasia and Central Asia, where a Russian war in Chechnya and a civil war in Tajikistan worried Russian policy makers greatly. At the same time the Kremlin sought to maintain influence in the Persian Gulf without alienating the United States, Iraq, and other nations in the region. Yeltsin's policies saw the ongoing Arab-Israeli conflict as a distant third in its list of Middle East priorities, but by the end of the 1990s the Kremlin viewed Israel as one of its strongest partners in the region, and by then the two nations were engaged in significant trade exchanges. Yeltsin's Kremlin also sought to stop the takeover of Afghanistan by the Taliban, an endeavor in which Russia cooperated with Iran but to little effect.

Despite becoming increasingly unpopular and suffering from ill health due to years of alcoholism, Yeltsin continued as president of Russia until December 31, 1999, when he surprisingly named Vladimir Putin acting president. Yeltsin died in Moscow on April 23, 2007.

FRANK BEYERSDORF

See also
Gorbachev, Mikhail; Russia, Middle East Policy, 1991–Present

References
Braithwaite, Rodric. *Across the Moscow River: The World Turned Upside-Down.* New Haven, CT: Yale University Press, 2002.
Breslauer, George W. *Gorbachev and Yeltsin as Leaders.* Cambridge: Cambridge University Press, 2002.
Yeltsin, Boris. *Against the Grain.* New York: Summit, 1999.
———. *The Struggle for Russia.* New York: Random House, 1994.

Yemen

Middle Eastern nation located in the southern part of the Arabian Peninsula with an estimated 2000 population of 23.013 million people. Yemen's total area encompasses 203,846 square miles. Yemen borders Saudi Arabia to the north, Oman to the east, the Arabian Sea and the Gulf of Aden to the south, and the Red Sea to the west. Not far off the western and southern coasts of the country are the East African nations of Eritrea, Djibouti, and Somalia.

Since 1918, Yemen had been divided into North Yemen and South Yemen. In 1970, when South Yemen declared itself a Marxist state, many hundreds of thousands of Yemenis fled north. This precipitated a civil war between the two states that would endure for 20 years. Not until 1990 did the two states reconcile, forming a single state known as the Republic of Yemen. Since then, there have been several unsuccessful attempts by groups in southern Yemen to secede from the republic. The most serious secessionist move came in 1994.

Yemen's population is overwhelmingly Muslim and of Arab ethnicity, and Arabic is the official language. Of the nation's Muslims, about 52 percent are Sunni Muslims and 48 percent are Shia Zaydi Muslims. The Sunnis live principally in the southern and southeastern parts of the country. Yemen has one of the world's highest birthrates, and as a result its population as a whole is quite young. Indeed, some 47 percent of the population is 14 years old and under, while less than 3 percent of the population is older than 65. The median age is 16.

Yemen is a representative republic that has a popularly elected president and a prime minister appointed by the president. The executive branch shares power with the bicameral legislature. The legal system in Yemen is a mix of Islamic law, Ottoman Turkish law (a vestige of the Ottoman Empire), English common law, codes derivative from Anglo-Indian law, and local tribal law (known as *urf*). Ali Abdullah Salih has served as president of the Republic of Yemen since the 1990 unification. Before that, he had served as the president of North Yemen since 1978.

Recorded human habitation in the region of Yemen can be traced as far back as the ninth century BCE. Its strategic location on the Red Sea and the Gulf of Aden has made it an important crossroads for East-West trade as well as trade from Asia to Africa. Around the seventh century CE, Muslim caliphs began to exert their influence over the region. They gradually ceded authority to dynastic imams, who retained the caliph's theocratic government until the modern era. Over the centuries, Egyptian caliphs also held sway in Yemen. The Ottoman Empire controlled some or most of Yemen sporadically between the 1500s and 1918, when the empire crumbled as a result of World War I. Ottoman influence was most keen in northern Yemen. In southern Yemen, imams tended to control the local scene but were usually overseen to some extent by the central authorities in Constantinople (Istanbul).

In October 1918, with the collapse of the Ottoman Empire in World War I, Imam Yahya Muhammad declared northern Yemen to be independent. Rebels seized power in September 1962. They proclaimed a republic, which precipitated an eight-year-long civil war. The conflict pitted royalist supporters of the imamate against republicans. In southern Yemen until 1967 the British dominated, having established a protectorate in Aden in 1839. Soon, the British created a formal colony that incorporated Aden and southern Yemen. As such, the British had great command of the strategic waterways of the region. After World War II, however, Yemenis

A view of the skyline of Sanaa, the capital of Yemen. Sanaa is one of the oldest continuously inhabited sites in the world, and its ancient city walls still stand. (Zanskar/Dreamstime.com)

in the southern region came to greatly resent the British presence, and before long they had organized an anti-British insurgency with aid from the Egyptians.

Several attacks against British interests sponsored by Egypt's government under Gamal Abdel Nasser in addition to insurgents from northern Yemen essentially forced the British out in 1967. The former British colony of Aden now became South Yemen. In 1970 the South Yemen government declared a Marxist state and aligned itself with the Soviet Union. As a result, several hundred thousand Yemenis from the south fled to North Yemen, overwhelming that nation's resources. Southern Yemen did nothing to stop the mass exodus.

Before 1962 the ruling imams in North Yemen pursued an isolationist foreign policy. North Yemen did have commercial and cultural ties with Saudi Arabia, however. In the late 1950s the Chinese and Soviets attempted to lure North Yemen into their orbit with technological missions. By the early 1960s, North Yemen had become dependent upon Egypt for financial and technical support. Later still, the Saudis supplanted the Egyptians as the main conduit of support. During the civil war the Saudis backed the Imam and his tribal supporters, while Egypt and the Soviet Union aided the republicans. In the 1970s and 1980s, many Yemenis from the north found jobs in neighboring Saudi Arabia, boosting North Yemen's flagging economy. A large number of Yemeni men also immigrated to the United States for jobs.

After 1967 when South Yemen declared itself a Marxist state (with ties to the Soviet Union), it maintained tense—and sometimes hostile—relations with its conservative Arab neighbors. In addition to the ongoing conflict with northern Yemen, insurgents from South Yemen engaged the Saudis in military actions first in 1969 and again in 1973 and also openly aided the Dhofar Rebellion (1962–1975) in Oman.

After the 1990 unification, the Republic of Yemen has generally pursued a pragmatic foreign policy. It is a member of the Non-Aligned Movement and is a signatory to the Nuclear Non-Proliferation Treaty and attempted to stay impartial during the 1991 Persian Gulf War and subsequent wars in the Middle East. Its noncommittal stance in these areas, however, has not endeared it to the Persian Gulf states or Western nations.

Yemen is among the poorest nations in the Arab world. The long civil war of 1962–1970 wrought great havoc on an already struggling economy, and the agricultural sector has been hit by periodic droughts and male depopulation for work abroad. Coffee production, once a mainstay among northern Yemeni crops, has fallen off dramatically. The port of Aden in southern Yemen suffered dramatic curtailments in its cargo handling after the 1967

Six-Day War and the British exit that same year. Since 1991, the return of hundreds of thousands of Yemenis from other Persian Gulf states because of Yemen's refusal to aid the Western coalition in the Persian Gulf War brought with it staggering unemployment. Reduced aid from other nations at this time and a brief secessionist movement in 1994 conspired to keep Yemen's economy depressed. Yemen does have significant oil deposits, but they are not of the same quality as Persian Gulf oil and thus have not brought in a windfall profit. Yemen does have major natural gas reserves, but that industry remains underdeveloped.

As of 2009, the Yemeni government continues to struggle with high inflation, excessive spending, widespread corruption, and Islamist militants. Indeed, at least three different types of Islamic militants have waged a persistent low-level insurgency in Yemen, which the government has been unable to curtail. As a result, the kidnapping of foreigners in Yemen has remained an intractable problem. The October 12, 2000, terrorist attack on the U.S. Navy destroyer *Cole* at anchor in Aden's harbor, in which 17 U.S. sailors perished, strained U.S.-Yemeni relations for several years. Although the attack was reportedly planned by Al Qaeda, Washington was not entirely satisfied with the level of cooperation from the Yemeni government during the subsequent investigation. Washington has also disagreed with Yemen's decision to grant amnesties and its efforts to reeducate militants in jail.

In December 1992 Aden was the epicenter of another bombing, which some attribute to Al Qaeda, when bombs were detonated at two fashionable tourist-oriented hotels. The explosions killed two people. It is not clear whether these actions were by a cell affiliated with Al Qaeda or were the actions of a different militant group targeting Western and U.S. interests in Yemen because the United States had billeted troops there and replenished naval ships in Aden's port.

PAUL G. PIERPAOLI JR.

See also

Al Qaeda; *Cole*, USS, Attack on; Egypt; Houthi, Hussein Badr al-Din al-; Nasser, Gamal Abdel; Saudi Arabia; Yemen, Civil War in; Yemen Hotel Bombings

References

Dresch, Paul. *A History of Modern Yemen.* Cambridge: Cambridge University Press, 2008.

Jones, Clive. *Britain and the Yemen Civil War.* London: Sussex Academic, 2004.

Mackintosh-Smith, Martin. *Yemen: The Unknown Arabia.* Woodstock, NY: Overlook, 2001.

Yemen, Civil War in

Start Date: 1962
End Date: 1970

Civil conflict in northern Yemen (Yemen Arab Republic) that lasted from 1962 until 1970. Often known as the North Yemen Civil War, the conflict arose from a 20-year opposition movement in Yemen to the authority of the descendents of Imam Yahya, who had ruled Yemen since its independence from the Ottoman Empire. The most important office in Zaydi Islam is that of imam, and in Yemen it is a religious and political position that can only be held by one of the *sada* (sayyids), individuals descended from the Prophet Muhammad. In recent centuries, the imams came from only certain families of the *sada,* such as Bayt al-Qasim, Bayt Sharaf al-Din, Bayt al-Wazir, and Bayt Hamid al-Din (the family of Imam Yahya).

On October 30, 1918, following the collapse of the Ottoman Empire in World War I, Imam Yahya Muhammad declared Yemen to be independent. In 1926 he declared himself king of the Mutawakkilite Kingdom of Yemen. Among his goals was the imposition of Sharia (Islamic law) over all of Yemen, a difficult task because the tribes usually relied on *urf* (tribal law). To cement his authority, Yahya also sought to weaken the tribes politically and militarily so as to retain power. This would also serve to diminish the threat posed to the Hamid al-Dins from the other great families. Imam Yahya also wanted to secure for his kingdom parts of historic Yemen that had been taken by the British, such as Aden and Asir. There was considerable opposition to Yahya over his domestic policies, and the opposition factions to him united and assassinated him in 1948.

A usurper held power for several months, but Yahya's son, Ahmad bin Yahya, secured power. His reign saw growing repression as well as tension with Britain over the continued efforts to create a Greater Yemen by expansion to the south. In March 1955 Ahmad was briefly deposed in a coup led by army officers and two of his brothers, but it was soon reversed.

To bolster his position, Ahmad entered into a formal military pact with Egypt in 1956 that placed Yemeni military forces under a unified command structure. That same year, Ahmad also named his son, Sayf al-Islam Mohammed al-Badr (known as Muhammad al-Badr), as crown prince and heir apparent. Ahmad also established formal ties with the Soviet Union.

In 1960 Ahmad left northern Yemen to seek medical treatment. In his absence Crown Prince Badr began to implement several reform measures that his father had promised to implement but that had as yet gone unfulfilled. Outraged that his son made such moves without his knowledge or assent, Ahmad promptly reversed the measures when he returned home. This action did not, of course, endear him to his subjects, and several weeks of civil unrest ensued, which the government quashed with a heavy hand. The 1955 coup attempt and growing resentment toward Ahmad rendered the last years of his rule both paranoid and reactionary.

Ahmad died on September 19, 1962, and was followed by Crown Prince Badr as both imam and king. One of Badr's first official acts was to grant a blanket amnesty to all political prisoners who had been imprisoned during his father's reign. Badr did so in hopes of maintaining power and keeping the kingdom's detractors at bay. But his tactics did not stave off discord. Indeed, just a week later on September 27, Abdullah al-Sallal, commander of the royal

Yemeni royalist forces man a recoilless rifle on the crest of Algenat Alout in 1964 during the civil war. The North Yemen Civil War of 1962–1970 erupted after army officers successfully staged a coup against Yemeni leader Muhammad al-Badr in 1962. Egyptian leader Gamal Abdel Nasser eventually sent 75,000 troops to support the coup against the Saudi-sponsored royalists. (Hulton Archive/Getty Images)

guard who had just been appointed to that post by Badr, launched a coup in the capital city of Sanaa.

The rebels, supported by a half dozen tanks and several artillery pieces, proclaimed the establishment of the Free Yemen Republic. They seized key locations in Sanaa, including the radio station and armory. They also moved against Dar al-Bashair Palace in the capital of Sanaa. The Imamate Guard there rejected demands that they surrender, and fighting began, with the defenders surrendering the next day. This coup, however, brought on a full-blown civil war. Meanwhile, an insurgency continued against the British in southern Yemen.

Despite a radio announcement by the new government that he had been killed in the shelling by the rebels of the palace, Badr escaped to the northern reaches of Yemen, where he received the support of tribes allied to his family and loyal to him as imam. Badr was also supported by the conservative Kingdom of Saudi Arabia, which bordered Yemen on the north. At the same time, Sallal received military assistance from Egypt. Indeed, Egyptian General Ali abd al-Hamid arrived in Sanaa on September 29 to assess the needs of the new revolutionary government, and as early as October 5 an Egyptian battalion had arrived there to act as a personal guard for Colonel Sallal. Apparently, Egyptian president Gamal Abdel Nasser, reeling from the breakup of the United Arab Republic with Syria, hoped that Egyptian support for a republican victory in Yemen would recoup his prestige in the Arab world as well as deliver a rebuff to Egypt's rival Saudi Arabia.

Nasser soon discovered that many more troops would be required than initially thought. The number of Egyptian forces in Yemen steadily increased, to a maximum of some 55,000 men in late 1965. In so doing, Cairo ignored repeated warnings by Ahmed Abu-Zayd, Egyptian ambassador to royalist Yemen during 1957–1961, that the Yemenis lacked a sense of nationhood, that no Egyptian combat troops should be sent there, and that any aid should be limited to equipment and financial support. As well as underestimating the situation on the ground, Nasser failed to understand the depth of sentiment in Saudi Arabia regarding Egyptian intervention, which the Saudi royal family saw as a direct threat to its domination of Yemen and the other Persian Gulf states.

By the mid-1960s, the imamate's supporters had also secured the help of Iraq, Jordan, Pakistan, Iran, and Britain as well as covert assistance from Israel, while the Soviet Union and several other communist bloc nations supported the republican side. The conflict also became politicized along Cold War lines, with the United States, Great Britain, and many other Western powers siding with the royalists. On several occasions, the United Nations (UN) attempted to mediate an end to the bloodshed, but the regional and international dynamics of the struggle made this an almost impossible task.

Egyptian forces initially performed poorly in Yemen. The paucity of maps, an unfamiliarity with the terrain, and a lack of knowledge of local conditions all impeded their effectiveness. The Saudis did not have this problem, as they and the northern Yemeni tribes were closely related. In January 1964, royalist forces even laid siege to Sanaa.

Egyptian air strikes on Najran and Jizan within Saudi Arabia, staging areas for the Yemeni royalist forces, threatened a direct shooting war between Egypt and Saudi Arabia. U.S. president John F. Kennedy responded to appeals by supplying air defense systems to the Saudis. He also dispatched U.S. aircraft to the Dhahran air base in the kingdom, demonstrating an American commitment to defend Saudi Arabia against Egyptian attack.

Although Egyptian tactics gradually improved, to include the extensive use of airpower in a ground support role, the war settled into a protracted stalemate and was a huge drain on the Egyptian treasury and military. Indeed, the presence in Yemen of so many well-trained troops and much equipment was greatly felt in the June 1967 Six-Day War with Israel. Nasser desperately wanted a mutual withdrawal of Egyptian and Saudi forces, and his excuse came with Egypt's ignominious defeat in the Six-Day War.

The two Yemeni sides decided to strike a compromise, in part because they wished to rid themselves of their foreign supporters. By 1969, both sides had agreed that the first step to ending the war would be the withdrawal of all foreign troops. This formed the basis for a subsequent agreement on April 14, 1970. The agreement specified a republican form of government but one that would include some royalists. The Zaydi imam, Muhammad al-Badr, agreed to go into exile. (He lived in Britain until his death in 1996.) Discussion continued about creating a constitutional imamate.

As part of the peace settlement, Nasser was compelled to begin troop withdrawals from Yemen. That same year, the British withdrew from southern Yemen. This was an extremely significant time for Yemen that brought to the fore a number of intra-Yemeni conflicts, with south Yemen greatly impacted by socialist doctrine.

The North Yemen Civil War left deep scars on that country's society and politics that were a long time in healing. It is estimated that the eight years of war claimed the lives of 100,000–150,000 people. Border clashes continued between the two Yemen states, however. Finally, on May 22, 1990, following protracted and difficult negotiations, the two Yemen states united as the Republic of Yemen.

In the unification, the heavily socialist southern Yemen had to come to terms with the tribally dominated northern Yemen. Tensions continued as a result of past policies. For example, support from Saudi Arabia strengthened the tribes who supported salafism, and the Yemeni government employed these tribes against its other enemies, especially the Shia al-Houthi rebellion also supported by tribal elements. There is today in Yemen considerable support for the al-Qaida fi Jazirat al-Arabiyya (Al Qaeda on the Arabian Peninsula) movement. There have also been border clashes with Saudi Arabia, resulting in the construction of barriers between the two countries.

PAUL G. PIERPAOLI JR., SPENCER C. TUCKER,
AND SHERIFA ZUHUR

See also

Egypt; Egypt, Armed Forces; Houthi, Hussein Badr al-Din al-; Nasser, Gamal Abdel; Saudi Arabia; Saudi Arabia, Armed Forces; Shia Islam; Soviet Union, Middle East Policy; United Kingdom, Middle East Policy; United States, Middle East Policy, 1917–1945; United States, Middle East Policy, 1945–Present; Yemen

References

Dresch, Paul. *A History of Modern Yemen.* Cambridge: Cambridge University Press, 2008.

Jones, Clive. *Britain and the Yemen Civil War.* London: Sussex Academic, 2004.

Pridham, Brian. *Contemporary Yemen: Politics and Historical Background.* London: Palgrave Macmillan, 1984.

Wenner, Manfred W. *Yemen Arab Republic.* Boulder, CO: Westview, 1991.

Yemen Hotel Bombings
Event Date: December 29, 1992

The bombing of two hotels in Aden, Yemen, on December 29, 1992, attributed to the terrorist organization Al Qaeda in Yemen. Long before the events of September 11, 2001, the Al Qaeda group centered in Afghanistan and Pakistan was well known to intelligence experts. It carried out or was linked to a number of attacks on Western interests, including the bombings of the World Trade Center in February 1993, the U.S. embassies in East Africa in August 1998, and USS *Cole* in Yemen in October 2000. Al Qaeda in Yemen, a separate organization, has also been active within that country. One of its least-known and earliest plots unfolded in December 1992, aimed at Western hotels in Yemen.

The hotel bombings came at the end of a year that had witnessed considerable terrorist activity in the country. In April, the Yemeni justice minister was seriously wounded by a gunman while driving in the capital city, Sanaa. In June, the brother of Yemeni prime minister Haydar Abu Bakr al-Attas was assassinated in the city of Mukalla. In a separate incident the same month, an adviser to the minister of defense was killed by unknown assailants. Throughout the spring and summer of 1992, several top officers in the Yemeni military were also assassinated or mysteriously killed.

That August and September, bombs went off at homes and offices of leading Yemeni government officials.

Westerners were also targeted in the terror spree. In September and again in November 1992, small bombs detonated near the U.S. embassy, while another exploded just outside the German embassy in October. Yemeni officials released little information on the incidents to the world press, just as other countries such as Egypt and Saudi Arabia had not readily admitted opposition activity. Members of the Yemeni Islamic Jihad were eventually arrested for some of the attacks.

The larger attacks came on December 29, 1992, when bombs went off at two major hotels in the city of Aden. One exploded at the Gold Mohur Hotel, frequented by foreigners. A second bomb went off in the parking lot of the Aden Movenpick Hotel, adjacent to where U.S. military personnel were staying en route to assist with relief operations in Somalia. It is believed that the attacks were in protest of American soldiers being billeted in Yemen and the perceived Westernization of Aden, a major international port and the economic capital of the country.

Two people—an Austrian tourist and a Yemeni hotel worker—died in the first attack. Several dozen were wounded, including two suspected terrorists involved in the second attack. They turned out to be Yemenis trained in Afghanistan, where Al Qaeda had camps for an international network of operatives. There were no casualties from the second bombing. In response to the incidents, U.S. forces stationed in Aden were withdrawn by December 31.

Six men were eventually arrested in connection with the bombings, but all managed to escape from jail in July 1993. This development led to allegations that Yemeni government officials had connections to the terrorists and had aided in their escape. Two of the terrorist bombers involved in the hotel bombings later took part in other terrorist plots, including the attack on USS *Cole* that killed 17 U.S. sailors.

ARNE KISLENKO

See also

Al Qaeda; Bin Laden, Osama; *Cole*, USS, Attack on; Terrorism; Yemen

References

Rotberg, Robert I. *Battling Terrorism in the Horn of Africa.* Washington, DC: Brookings Institution Press, 2005.

Shai, Shaul. *The Red Sea Terror Triangle: Sudan, Somalia, Yemen, and Islamic Terror.* New Brunswick, NJ: Transaction Publishers, 2005.

West, Deborah L. *Combating Terrorism in the Horn of Africa and Yemen.* Cambridge, MA: World Peace Foundation, 2005.

Yeosock, John J.
Birth Date: March 18, 1937

U.S. Army general and commander during Operations DESERT SHIELD and DESERT STORM of the U.S. Third Army and simultaneously commander of Central Command Army Forces (ARCENT), which included British and French army forces. John J. Yeosock was born in Wilkes-Barre, Pennsylvania, on March 18, 1937. His poor eyesight prevented him from attending the U.S. Military Academy, West Point. After graduation from Pennsylvania State University in August 1959 with a degree in industrial engineering, he entered the U.S. Army through the Reserve Officers' Training Corps (ROTC).

Assigned to the armor branch, Yeosock first served in company-grade troop commands and staff positions in the 3rd Cavalry Regiment and 2nd Infantry Division in the United States and West Germany. From January 1966 to May 1967 he served as an adviser in Vietnam.

Yeosock was subsequently assigned as an operations research/systems analyst in the Management Information Systems Directorate of the Office of the Assistant Chief of Staff of the Army in Washington, D.C., and then as an analyst for Project Manager Reorganization in the Office of the Chief of Staff of the Army. In June 1973 Yeosock returned to the field as commander of the 3rd Squadron, 3rd Cavalry Regiment, stationed in Fort Bliss, Texas. From July 1976 through July 1978 he served as the chief of force development, Office of the Assistant Chief of Staff, J3, United Nations Command, United States Forces, Eighth U.S. Army, Korea.

Beginning in September 1978 Yeosock commanded the 194th Armored Brigade, Fort Knox, Kentucky. In February 1980 he became the chief of staff of the 1st Cavalry Division, Fort Hood, Texas.

Promoted to temporary brigadier general on June 1, 1981, Yeosock served as project manager for the Saudi Arabian National Guard Modernization Program. His rank became permanent on January 22, 1982. Thereafter he returned to the 1st Cavalry Division as the assistant division commander. Yeosock assumed duties as the deputy chief of staff, operations, U.S. Army Forces Command, Fort McPherson, Georgia, in January 1984. Promoted to major general on October 1, 1984, he again returned to Fort Hood and commanded the 1st Cavalry Division from June 1986 to May 1988.

In June 1988 Yeosock was assigned as assistant deputy chief of staff for operations and plans, Headquarters, Department of the Army. Promoted to lieutenant general on March 16, 1989, he assumed the positions of commanding general, U.S. Third Army, and deputy commanding general, Forces Command. Within the U.S. Army hierarchy of commands, assignment to Third Army was given to generals who were soon to retire. No one expected that it would soon become the premier combat assignment in the entire army.

Following the Iraqi invasion of Kuwait in August 1990, under Yeosock's command Third Army began deploying from its headquarters in East Point, Georgia, in August 1990 to Saudi Arabia to assume its role as the army component and senior Army headquarters within ARCENT. The first objective was to defend Saudi Arabia against a possible Iraqi invasion. Initially it was the XVIII Airborne Corps that received this defensive mission. In November 1990 massive reinforcements, including the tank-heavy VII Corps from Germany, gave the Third Army offensive capability. The buildup marked the largest U.S. deployment of armored forces since World War II. Before the war, Yeosock's major responsibilities involved managing the buildup, arranging logistical support, and resolving disputes among his subordinates. He handled these tasks well. However, many officers at CENTCOM and back in Washington doubted that he had the capacity to command two corps in combat.

In mid-February 1991 Yeosock had to fly to Germany for emergency gall bladder surgery. He insisted on returning to his command just before the ground offensive began on February 24. The Third Army attack was scheduled to commence after the marine offensive along the coast had pinned the Iraqis in position. On the eve of hostilities, Third Army comprised two corps. The XVIII Airborne Corps was an unusual formation with a mechanized infantry division, an air assault division, paratroop units, and one French light division. The VII Corps had four American divisions and one British division. Both corps also had an attached armored cavalry regiment. Planners intended for Third Army to serve as the major strike force for Operation DESERT STORM. Operating on the left flank, the army would sweep into southern Iraq on the morning of February 25, turn east, and defeat the elite Iraqi Republican Guard units. The original plan called for two days to breach the forward Iraqi defense and another six or so days to destroy the Republican Guard.

The rapid marine breakthrough and advance on Kuwait City upset this plan, however. CENTCOM commander General H. Norman Schwarzkopf asked Yeosock to advance one day ahead of schedule because it appeared that the Iraqis were already fleeing Kuwait. Yeosock complied, but he still expected fierce resistance. Consequently, the VII Corps attack proceeded cautiously. Third Army's slow pace of advance infuriated Schwarzkopf and contributed to the escape of substantial Iraqi forces from Kuwait. After the war, critics complained that Yeosock had been intimidated by Schwarzkopf and consequently had failed to assert his authority as commander of CENTCOM's ground forces. Yeosock retired in August 1992 at the rank of lieutenant general.

JAMES ARNOLD

See also

DESERT STORM, Operation; DESERT STORM, Operation, Ground Operations; Schwarzkopf, H. Norman, Jr.

References

Burton, James G. *The Pentagon Wars.* Annapolis, MD: Naval Institute Press, 1993.
Gordon, Michael R., and General Bernard E. Trainor. *The Generals' War: The Inside Story of the Conflict in the Gulf.* New York: Little, Brown, 1995.
Swain, Richard. *Lucky War: The Third Army in Desert Storm.* Fort Leavenworth, KS: U.S. Army Command and General Staff College Press, 1999.

Yousef, Ramzi Ahmed
Birth Date: April 27, 1968

Kuwaiti-born terrorist and mastermind of the World Trade Center bombing on February 26, 1993. Ramzi Ahmed Yousef was born Abd al-Basit Mahmud Abd al-Karim on April 27, 1968, in Fuhayil, Kuwait, the son of a middle-class engineer. Yousef was raised in a strict Wahhabist environment. His uncle was Khalid Sheikh Mohammed, a major figure in the September 11, 2001, terror attacks. In 1986 Yousef went to Great Britain to study English and engineering; from there he went to Afghanistan in 1988, ostensibly to help fight with the mujahideen against Soviet forces. Instead, he spent most of his time in Peshawar, the site of an Al Qaeda training camp. He attended a university in Afghanistan and became a member of a local Muslim Brotherhood cell. Yousef went to Kuwait, probably in late 1989, and took a job with the Kuwait government. But Iraq's invasion of Kuwait in August 1990 forced him to leave the country, and he subsequently settled in Quetta, Pakistan.

Sometime soon after he relocated to Pakistan, Yousef decided to focus his efforts on waging jihad against the West. Despite his father's strict Wahhabism, Yousef was not very religious. He was, however, upset over the plight of the Palestinians. In 1990–1991 Yousef attended another Al Qaeda training camp and began to plot terrorist acts against Israel.

Realizing that pulling a successful terrorist assault in Israel would be very difficult, Yousef instead turned his sights on the United States. His first target was to be the New York World Trade Center, which he hoped to destroy with a massive truck bomb.

In early 1992 Yousef traveled to the United States. Lacking a proper visa, he filed for religious asylum with the Immigration and Naturalization Service (INS). When he was denied the request, he was briefly arrested but then released on his own recognizance. His INS hearing was scheduled for December 1992, but he never appeared. Although he was then in the United States illegally, no efforts were made to track him down.

Within days, Yousef became associated with other extremist Muslims in New York's al-Kifah Refugee Center in Brooklyn. There, according to the Federal Bureau of Investigation (FBI), Yousef came under the influence of Sheikh Umar Abdel Rahman, who was preaching in Brooklyn and was alleged to have been planning terrorist attacks in the United States. While at the refugee center, Yousef recruited like-minded militants, including Mahmud Abu Halima, his chief coconspirator, to help him plan and execute the bombing of the World Trade Center, with the goal of destroying the complex and killing as many as 250,000 Americans.

Yousef was unable, however, to finance a bomb that would cause the damage he sought, so he settled on a 1,500-pound bomb hidden in a rented van, which would be driven into an underground parking garage and detonated. His accomplices were successful in getting the explosives-laden truck into the garage, and it detonated on the morning of February 26, 1993. The attack killed 4 people, wounded more than 1,000 others, and caused $30 million in damage.

When the bomb went off, Yousef had already fled the United States for Pakistan. Once there he began to plot more attacks, including flying bomb-laden planes into the Pentagon and other U.S. government buildings. Allegedly, his uncle Khalid Sheikh

Mohammed met with Al Qaeda leader Osama bin Laden in 1996 and detailed his nephew's plans to him. Meanwhile, Yousef helped carry out terror attacks in Pakistan, Iran, and Thailand. Sometime in 1994 he moved to the Philippines, where he hatched plots to assassinate Pope John Paul II and U.S. president Bill Clinton.

An ingenious bomb maker, Yousef tried—and almost succeeded—in blowing up several jetliners, including an American aircraft, in 1994 and 1995. When Philippine intelligence became suspicious of Yousef's activities in Manila, he fled the country and returned to Pakistan. In his hasty departure, he left behind a computer, which Philippine authorities used to link him to various terrorist attacks. That also led them to detain one of Yousef's lieutenants, who later detailed his chief's involvement in the 1993 World Trade Center bombing.

In February 1995 Yousef was arrested in a hotel in Islamabad. The Pakistani government immediately turned him over to U.S. authorities, who extradited him to the United States. Yousef was tried twice, once for his attempts to blow up American jetliners and once for his role in the World Trade Center bombing. In September 1996 he was found guilty in the jetliner conspiracy and was sentenced to life in prison without the possibility of parole. In February 1997 he was convicted on all counts for his involvement in the World Trade Center bombing. A judge sentenced him to 247 years in prison and a $4.5 million fine and also placed strict limits on his prison visits.

There has been much speculation about how much direct involvement Yousef had with Al Qaeda. The best guess is that he operated largely on his own, and although he had more than coincidental connections to Al Qaeda, it seems unlikely that he received funding from the organization.

PAUL G. PIERPAOLI JR.

See also

Al Qaeda; Bin Laden, Osama; Mohammed, Khalid Sheikh; Terrorism; World Trade Center Bombing

References

Bell, J. Bowyer. *Murders on the Nile: The World Trade Center and Global Terror.* San Francisco: Encounter Books, 2003.

Simon, Reeve. *The New Jackals: Ramzi Yousef, Osama bin Laden and the Future of Terrorism.* Boston: Northeastern University Press, 1999.

Yuhanna, Michael

See Aziz, Tariq

Z

Zahir Shah, Mohammad
Birth Date: October 16, 1914
Death Date: July 23, 2007

Last king of Afghanistan. Born in Kabul, Afghanistan, on October 16, 1914, Mohammed Zahir Shah was a member of one of the two Pashtun lines that had ruled Afghanistan for two centuries. Educated in France at the Pasteur Institute and the University of Montpellier, he became king (shah) on November 8, 1933, when his father, King Mohammad Nadir Shah, was killed in his presence during an awards ceremony in Kabul. For the next two decades, Zahir Shah reigned but did not rule, in effect ceding power to his paternal uncles.

Zahir Shah resumed direct rule in 1963. The next year he introduced a constitutional monarchy and broadened participation in government. Other changes included greater rights for women, including education. Such changes, particularly the latter, were not popular in his conservative Islamic country.

Zahir Shah ruled directly for a decade. Although the country was at peace, many faulted the king for the poor state of the economy, and a leftist political opposition movement gained momentum. Political unrest and a severe drought resulted in a military coup in 1973 while Zahir Shah was in Italy receiving medical treatment for an eye problem. The army placed in power his cousin, Sardar Mohammad Daoud Khan, whom the king had dismissed as prime minister a decade earlier. Rather than see his country swept up in civil war, Zahir Shah abdicated.

Zahir Shah remained in exile in Italy, and in 1991 he escaped an assassination attempt. He could only watch as his country was torn apart by political unrest, the Soviet invasion in 1979, and then a decade-long war. The radical Islamic student militia known as the Taliban took control of the country in 1996, remaining in power until 2001 when American-led coalition forces drove them out. On the return of democracy to Afghanistan, many called for a restoration of the monarchy, but by now the king was in his eighties and frail. He returned to Afghanistan in 2002 after three decades in exile, but rejected the idea of becoming king. He announced that he was willing to become head of state as president if that was asked of him. However, that did not occur, and he vowed not to challenge Hamid Karzai for that position. The new Afghan constitution granted Zahir Shah the title of "father of the nation," and many Afghans affectionately referred to him simply as "Baba" or "grandfather." He died in Kabul on July 23, 2007, following a prolonged illness.

SPENCER C. TUCKER

See also
Afghanistan; ENDURING FREEDOM, Operation; Karzai, Hamid; Soviet-Afghanistan War; Taliban

References
Dupree, Louis. *Afghanistan.* Princeton, NJ: Princeton University Press, 1980.
Hopkirk, Peter. *The Great Game: The Struggle for Empire in Central Asia.* New York: Kodansha, 1992.
Nyrop, Richard F., and Donald M. Seekins, eds. *Afghanistan: A Country Study/Foreign Area Studies.* Washington, DC: American University, 1986.

Zaidan, Muhammad
See Abbas, Abu

Zammar, Muhammad Haydar
Birth Date: 1961

An Al Qaeda operative who recruited the key leader of the September 11, 2001, terror attacks. Muhammad Haydar Zammar, who has extensive experience as a fighter for Islamist causes, was born in 1961 in Aleppo, Syria. When he was 10 years old his family moved to West Germany. After high school he attended a metal-working college; his goal was to work for Mercedes-Benz. He then traveled to Saudi Arabia, where he worked for a time as a translator. After returning to Germany, he found a job as a truck driver in Hamburg.

Zammar's strong religious views led him to abandon truck driving in 1991 and travel to Afghanistan, where he underwent Al Qaeda training. Upon returning to Germany he spent all of his time as a freelance mechanic and traveled around Europe and the Middle East. He volunteered to fight in Bosnia in 1995, and after leaving Bosnia in 1996 he visited Afghanistan, where Osama bin Laden invited him to join Al Qaeda.

On his return to Hamburg, Germany, Zammar became a full-time recruiter for Al Qaeda. He spent so much time as a recruiter for Al Qaeda that he had no time to work as a mechanic. Meanwhile Zammar, his wife, and six children lived on state welfare. He traveled around Germany making speeches praising bin Laden and other jihadist leaders. Zammar's association with the Tabligh organization, which is Islamist but not militant, afforded him some cover, but German police began watching him.

It was at the al-Quds Mosque in Hamburg that Zammar helped to form the Hamburg Cell. He first met and became friends with Muhammad Atta in 1998. Zammar persuaded Atta, Marwan al-Shehhi, Ramzi bin al-Shibh, and Ziyad Jarrah to train at Al Qaeda camps in Afghanistan for important missions. Zammar continued as the Al Qaeda contact person for the Hamburg Cell until its key leaders left for the United States.

Zammar continued to act as an Al Qaeda recruiter. Many other Muslims in Germany were willing recruits for Al Qaeda, and Zammar was Al Qaeda's principal contact in Germany. German authorities left him alone, but they watched his activities with interest. American intelligence was also displaying concern about Zammar's connections with Al Qaeda. In July 2001 he was briefly detained in Jordan but was released after a short interrogation. After the September 11 attacks German police questioned Zammar, but they released him because they believed that they had too little evidence to charge him with a crime.

On October 27, 2001, Zammar traveled to Morocco to divorce his second wife; while there he was arrested by Moroccan security forces. The Moroccans sent him to Syria, where he has undergone extensive interrogation at the notorious Far Falastin Detention Center in Damascus. Zammar remains in Syrian custody, but American officials have learned much about the September 11 plot from him in his answers to questions sent through the Syrians. There is evidence that Zammar has undergone torture at the hands of the Syrians, and this has led international organizations to protest. Regardless of how he is treated by the Syrians, Zammar knew the central players in the September 11 attack and had a general knowledge of the plot, so he has proven to be a valuable intelligence resource.

STEPHEN E. ATKINS

See also

Al Qaeda; Atta, Muhammad; Bin Laden, Osama; Hamburg Cell; Jarrah, Ziyad al-; September 11 Attacks; Shehhi, Marwan al-

References

Finn, Peter. "Al Qaeda Recruiter Reportedly Tortured." *Washington Post,* January 31, 2003, A14.

———. "German at Center of Sept. 11 Inquiry." *Washington Post,* June 12, 2002, A1.

McDermott, Terry. *Perfect Soldiers: The 9/11 Hijackers: Who They Were, Why They Did It.* New York: HarperCollins, 2005.

Strasser, Steven, ed. *The 9/11 Investigations: Staff Reports of the 9/11 Commission; Excerpts from the House-Senate Joint Inquiry Report on 9/11; Testimony from 14 Key Witnesses, Including Richard Clarke, George Tenet, and Condoleezza Rice.* New York: PublicAffairs, 2004.

Zardari, Asif Ali
Birth Date: ca. July 26, 1955

Wealthy and controversial businessman, husband of Benazir Bhutto (former two-time prime minister of Pakistan), and president of Pakistan (2008–). Asif Ali Zardari was born in Karachi, Pakistan, on July 26, 1955 (some sources claim July 21, 1956), to a well-to-do Sindhi family. He attended the Cadet College in Petaro; however, his completion of a graduate degree was questioned when he sought a parliament seat (a position that requires a college degree). His political party claimed that he had obtained a degree from the London School of Economics and Business.

Zardari engaged in a number of business ventures, some of dubious legality, and soon earned the reputation as a highly successful—if unscrupulous—businessman. By 2007 his personal fortune was estimated at $1.8 billion. Prior to his marriage to Benazir Bhutto in 1987, Zardari was a renowned playboy and was considered one of Pakistan's most eligible bachelors.

Zardari spent several years in jail in the early 1990s on corruption charges and was accused in 1990 of threatening to murder a business associate unless the latter immediately repaid a debt owed to him. These charges were never proven, and his imprisonment was based largely on political considerations. When Bhutto became prime minister for a second time in 1993, Zardari was immediately released and given a government ministry position. After Bhutto was swept out of office in 1996, Zardari was re-arrested and remained incarcerated until 2004. This time, he was also charged with the murder of Mir Murtaza Bhutto, Benazir's brother, a charge that was never proven. A court did find Zardari and his wife guilty of being involved in a kickback scheme with a

Swiss corporation, but Pakistan's Supreme Court later declared a mistrial, and the charges were dropped.

Zardari was not released from prison until 2004, the result of political machinations involving then-embattled Pakistani president Pervez Musharraf, who had begun to negotiate with his political enemies, including Benazir Bhutto, then in self-exile. Meanwhile, Bhutto continued to head the Pakistan People's Party (PPP) and by 2006 was vowing to return to Pakistan while she negotiated behind the scenes with Musharraf's government. She returned in October 2007, now free of corruption charges, to run in the 2008 national elections. Zardari fully supported his wife's ambitions, but the PPP kept him out of the public eye, viewing his past as a distinct liability.

On December 27, 2007, Bhutto was assassinated during a political rally in Rawalpindi, Pakistan. The circumstances surrounding her murder were suspicious, and many of Musharraf's detractors accused him of having engineered the killing. As Musharraf's rule now became more and more precarious, Zardari became a positive symbol for the PPP as the husband of its martyred leader. In a highly unlikely turn of events, by the end of December Zardari had become cochairman of the PPP along with his son, Bilawal Bhutto Zardari, who was then a college student in Great Britain. During much of 2008 Zardari, a shrewd politician as it turns out, worked with several rival political factions to unseat President Musharraf, whose government was nearly paralyzed. Zardari also worked to build a strong ruling coalition in parliament.

When Zardari and several other key political leaders moved to impeach Musharraf in the summer of 2008, the president finally relented and agreed to resign on August 18. Zardari immediately became the front-runner to replace Musharraf, with the endorsement even of chief PPP rival parties, particularly as his main rival, Nawaz Sharif, was supported by Saudi Arabia but opposed by the United States. A national election was held on September 6. Zardari won the election and was installed as president on September 9.

Zardari's job would be a daunting one. Pakistan had been badly weakened by Musharraf's dictatorial rule, the economy was in free-fall, and a growing insurgency threat by Taliban and Al Qaeda fighters in the western territories was spreading with alarming rapidity. Political instability was still a problem, and by the spring of 2009 Zardari's fragile alliance with his former political adversaries seemed on the verge of collapse.

At the same time that Zardari faced formidable challenges at home, he came under increased pressure to shore up his support abroad. His government protested when the Barack Obama administration stepped up U.S. drone air strikes against Islamic militants in northwestern Pakistan, but at the same time Zardari sought U.S. support to prevent the insurgency from spilling over into the rest of the country. Although his government brokered a truce with the Taliban that assured the latter control of the Swat Valley in northwestern Pakistan, when the Taliban broke the truce by extending its control beyond the Swat and threatening the capital of Islamabad, in later April 2009 Zardari, under

heavy pressure from Washington and from moderate elements in his own country, declared the truce with the Taliban to be at an end and ordered the Pakistani Army into the Swat Valley. Heavy fighting ensued, displacing an estimated 1.3 million Pakistanis. Some observers questioned whether Pakistan's army—trained essentially to fight a conventional war with India—could mount a successful counterinsurgency effort, but Zardari apparently had little choice. Many Western leaders expressed great concern that Pakistan might fall to Islamist extremists, who could gain control of its nuclear arsenal.

In May 2008 Zardari traveled to France, Great Britain, Libya, and the United States to shore up international support for his regime. During the trip he met with various national leaders, including Afghan president Hamid Karzai, in Washington. There Zardari pledged to cooperate with the Afghan leader in stamping out the Al Qaeda terrorist organization and Taliban in their two countries. Zardari also sought additional financial aid. His meeting with President Obama reportedly went well, but Obama again underscored the importance of stopping the insurgency before it spread any further. As a result of Zardari's junket, the U.S. House of Representatives approved a $1.9 billion aid package to Pakistan, while the British Parliament pledged £640 million of aid over four years. France offered considerable technical assistance.

PAUL G. PIERPAOLI JR.

See also

Al Qaeda; Bhutto, Benazir; Musharraf, Pervez; Pakistan; Taliban

References

Bhutto, Benazir. *Reconciliation: Islam, Democracy, and the West*. New York: HarperCollins, 2008.

Gall, Carlotta. "Musharraf-Bhutto Accord Sets Stage for Pakistan Vote." *New York Times*, October 5, 2007, A15.

Kras, Sara L. *Pervez Musharraf*. New York: Chelsea House, 2004.

Weaver, Mary Anne. *Pakistan: In the Shadow of Jihad and Afghanistan*. New York: Farrar, Straus and Giroux, 2003.

Zawahiri, Ayman al-
Birth Date: June 19, 1951

Former leader of the Egyptian organization Islamic Jihad, and second-in-command of the terrorist Al Qaeda organization. Born in Cairo, Egypt, on June 19, 1951, to a family of doctors and scholars (his father was a pharmacologist and chemistry professor), Ayman al-Zawahiri joined the Muslim Brotherhood at age 14. Soon he had become an Islamist militant. Following the execution by the Egyptian government of Islamist thinker Sayyid Qutb in 1966, Zawahiri established with several of his schoolmates an underground cell with the aim of overthrowing the Egyptian government. Zawahiri vowed "to put Qutb's vision into action." His cell eventually merged with others to form the Egyptian Islamic Jihad.

A good student, al-Zawahiri received an undergraduate degree in 1974 from Cairo University. He served as a surgeon in the

Egyptian Army for three years. He completed a master's degree in surgery in 1978 and set up a clinic. That same year he married.

In the late 1970s Islamic Jihad became active and came under attack by the Egyptian state security forces. After the arrest and torture of many of its members by the Egyptian security services, certain army members of the Islamic Jihad, including Lieutenant Khalid Islambouli, assassinated Anwar Sadat on October 8, 1981, and then carried out actions intended to bring down the government. This attempt failed in the face of security forces and army opposition. Zawahiri and hundreds of members of Islamic Jihad and the Gamaat Islamiya, an umbrella group, were jailed as coconspirators in the assassination of Sadat. After serving three years in prison, Zawahiri and many of his coconspirators were released in 1984.

Zawahiri subsequently went to Peshawar, Pakistan, and there joined the Maktab al-Khidmat (Jihad Service Bureau), under the leadership of Dr. Abdullah Azzam and supported by Saudi financier Osama bin Laden. By the time of the final Soviet withdrawal from Afghanistan in 1989, bin Laden had broken with his mentor Azzam over the nature of the jihad. The rift that developed between the two men was ideologically motivated. Bin Laden and Zawahiri wanted to export the jihad worldwide beyond Afghanistan and Palestine, and Azzam, who dissented from this plan, was killed.

In the early 1990s Zawahiri and bin Laden traveled first to Egypt and later to Sudan, where they established training camps at the behest of Sudanese leader and Islamist thinker Hassan al-Turabi. Zawahiri merged Islamic Jihad with bin Laden's Al Qaeda organization after issuing a joint fatwa on February 23, 1998. Zawahiri was subsequently instrumental in planning the bombing of the U.S. embassies in Nairobi and Dar es Salaam in 1998 as well as the planning for the attacks on September 11, 2001. Following the U.S. invasion of Afghanistan in October 2001 Zawahiri went into hiding, releasing videos and speeches periodically to incite others to engage in the jihad against the United States. He also published *Knights under the Prophet's Banner* (December 2001), which outlined Al Qaeda's ideology.

After the March 2003 Anglo-American–led invasion of Iraq, Zawahiri's speeches and writings have taken on an apocalyptic tone. In a July 2005 letter he framed the jihad in Afghanistan as a vanguard for the ultimate establishment of an Islamic state in the Levant, Egypt, Iraq, and neighboring states on the Arabian Peninsula; multiple public statements by Zawahiri have since repeated this point. In his video response to Pope Benedict XVI's remarks on Islam in September 2006, Zawahiri called Benedict a "charlatan" because of his remarks on Islam. However, the term used by Zawahiri to refer to the pope as a "charlatan and deceiver" was the theological term *al-Dajjal*. In Islamic theology and tradition, *al-Dajjal* refers to the Antichrist who will return just prior to the Day of Judgment. Zawahiri is known to have been influenced by the Saudi thinker Safar al-Hawali's book *The Day of Wrath*, which predicts that the world will end in 2012.

While the Terrorism Center at the United States Military Academy, West Point, is careful to note that the impact of Zawahiri's ideology is considered "totally insignificant," among most Islamist thinkers he still remains a potent figure in the Muslim World. Although his precise whereabouts are unknown, Zawahiri is believed to be living in the mountainous region along the Pakistan-Afghanistan border.

OJAN ARYANFARD

See also

Al Qaeda; Benedict XVI, Pope; Bin Laden, Osama; Dar es Salaam, Bombing of U.S. Embassy; Fatwa; Islamic Radicalism; Jihad; Mohammed, Khalid Sheikh; Muslim Brotherhood; Nairobi, Kenya, Bombing of U.S. Embassy; Sadat, Muhammad Anwar; September 11 Attacks; Terrorism; Yousef, Ramzi Ahmed

References

Gunaratna, Rohan. *Inside Al Qaeda: Global Network of Terror.* New York: Berkley Publishing Group, 2003.

Haddad, Yvonne, and Jane Smith. *The Islamic Understanding of Death and Resurrection.* Oxford: Oxford University Press, 2002.

Rabasa, Angel. *Beyond al-Qaeda: Part 1, The Global Jihadist Movement* and *Beyond al-Qaeda; Part 2, The Outer Rings of the Terrorist Universe.* Santa Monica, CA: RAND Corporation, 2006.

Zaydi, Muntadhar al-
Birth Date: December 14, 1979

Iraqi journalist best known for an incident on December 14, 2008 in which he threw his shoes at President George W. Bush during a joint news conference with Iraqi prime minister Nuri al-Maliki. Muntadhar al-Zaydi was born on November 12, 1979, in Sadr City (a Baghdad suburb). After graduating with a degree in communications from the University of Baghdad, he served as a print and broadcast reporter, joining al-Baghdadiyya TV in 2005. Since the 2003 Anglo-American–led invasion of Iraq, Zaydi had become well known to occupation authorities, and he was twice detained, but later released, by U.S. military police forces. The reasons for his detentions remain unclear.

In November 2007 Zaydi was kidnapped by unidentified armed gunmen in central Baghdad who beat him severely and questioned him repeatedly about his journalistic work. After three days of confinement he was released. Zaydi claims that his kidnappers were rogue gunmen not associated with an organized resistance group, but that assertion was never substantiated. In January 2008 U.S. forces conducted a search of his residence, but no reason was given for the intrusion. He reportedly later received an apology from occupation authorities. Reportedly he had lost members of his family in the Iraq War and was deeply concerned about the large number of civilian casualties from the ongoing violence.

Zaydi gained instant worldwide recognition on December 14, 2008, when he hurled both of his shoes at President Bush, who was standing at a podium next to Prime Minister Maliki. Bush and Maliki were appearing at a news conference to formally announce the recently negotiated U.S.-Iraqi Status of Forces Agreement. Upon throwing the first shoe Zaydi shouted, "This is a farewell kiss from the Iraqi people, you dog!" Immediately thereafter, he threw a second shoe, shouting, "This is for the widows and orphans and all those killed in Iraq!" Neither shoe hit its mark, as Bush deftly evaded the flying footwear. In Arab and Islamic cultures, the throwing of shoes at someone is considered a serious expression of disrespect.

Zaydi was quickly wrestled to the floor, subdued, and dragged away by Iraqi security guards. He was reportedly beaten repeatedly once he was in custody and being interrogated. Bush seemed unaffected by the event and made a joke about the shoe-throwing incident after Zaydi had been escorted out of the room. Some questioned how a person within a mere few yards from the president could have been allowed to perpetrate such an act, and still others wonder why Zaydi had not been stopped after throwing the first shoe. The incident was emblematic of the extreme unpopularity in the Middle East of Bush during his presidency.

The shoe-throwing incident engendered a great outpouring of support for Zaydi in both Iraq and the larger Arab world. The day after the press conference, thousands of Iraqis protested in Baghdad and Sadr City, Zaydi's birthplace, demanding his release. Similar protests took place in other Iraqi cities as well. On December 17 a group of Iraqi lawmakers demanded a full investigation of the incident, especially the reported beating of Zaydi after he went into custody. It was reported, but not substantiated, that Zaydi sent several letters of apology to Maliki in which Zaydi specifically stated that he would offer no apology to Bush. On December 23 the Speaker of the Iraqi parliament resigned his post in protest of the incident. Numerous high-level Iraqi politicians were sympathetic to Zaydi's predicament, but Maliki was forced to offer no such support, fearing that he might aggravate relations with the U.S. government. Large pro-Zaydi protests occurred in numerous Arab nations, including Syria, Lebanon, Egypt, Libya, and Egypt.

In late December an Iraqi court charged Zaydi with assault against a foreign head of state; he was denied bail, according to the court, "for the sake of the investigation and for his own security." Several days later Zaydi's attorney appealed the ruling, hoping to reduce the charge from assaulting a foreign dignitary to insulting a foreign dignitary. Meanwhile, Zaydi's family kept up a high-profile campaign to free the journalist, which garnered much attention in the Iraqi media. Their efforts were unsuccessful. On March 12, 2009, Zaydi was sentenced to three years in prison for assaulting a foreign head of state. On April 7 that sentence was reduced to one year.

PAUL G. PIERPAOLI JR.

See also

Bush, George Walker; Maliki, Nuri Muhammed Kamil Hasan al-; Status of Forces Agreement, U.S.-Iraqi

References

Meyers, Steven Lee, and Alissa J. Rubin. "Iraqi Journalist Hurls Shoes at Bush and Denounces Him as a 'Dog.'" *New York Times*, December 15, 2008, A6.

Williams, Timothy. "In Iraq's Shoe-Hurling Protest, Arabs Find a Hero." *New York Times*, December 16, 2008, A1.

Zinni, Anthony Charles
Birth Date: September 17, 1943

U.S. Marine Corps general, commander of U.S. Central Command (CENTCOM), and special envoy for the United States to Israel and the Palestinian National Authority (PNA). Anthony Charles Zinni was born to Italian immigrant parents in Philadelphia, Pennsylvania, on September 17, 1943. In 1965 he graduated from Villanova University with a degree in economics and was commissioned in the U.S. Marine Corps. In 1967 he served in Vietnam as an infantry battalion adviser to a South Vietnamese marine unit. In 1970 he returned to Vietnam as an infantry company commander. He was seriously wounded that November and was medically evacuated. Thereafter Zinni held a variety of command, administrative, and teaching positions, including at the Marine Corps Command and Staff College at Quantico, Virginia.

In 1991 as a brigadier general Zinni was the chief of staff and deputy commanding general of the Combined Joint Task Force (CJTF) for Operation PROVIDE COMFORT, the Kurdish relief effort in Turkey and Iraq. In 1992–1993 he was the director of operations for Operation RESTORE HOPE in Somalia. As a lieutenant general, he commanded the I Marine Expeditionary Force (I MEF) from 1994 to 1996. In September 1996, as a full general, he became deputy commanding general of the CENTCOM, the U.S. military combatant command responsible for most of the Middle East. He served as commanding general of CENTCOM from August 1997 until his retirement from the military in September 2000.

Upon leaving the military, Zinni participated in a number of different diplomatic initiatives. In late 2001, at the request of his old friend Colin L. Powell, then secretary of state, Zinni became the special envoy for the United States to Israel and the PNA.

Zinni arrived in Israel on November 25, 2001. He conducted several negotiating sessions with Prime Minister Ariel Sharon and PNA president Yasser Arafat individually but never with the two together. On December 12 the Palestinian suicide bombing of a bus near the settlement of Emmanuel effectively cut off all dialogue between the two sides. Zinni returned to the United States on December 17.

Zinni made his second short trip to the region during January 3–7, 2002. While he was conducting a meeting with Arafat, the Israelis intercepted and captured an illegal Palestinian arms ship in the Red Sea. The *Karine A* was carrying some 50 tons of weapons ordered by the PNA from Iran, a direct violation of the Oslo Accords.

Zinni returned to the region for the last time on March 12, 2002. While he believed that he was starting to make some headway, on March 27 a Palestinian suicide bomber struck a Passover Seder being held at an Israeli hotel. The Israelis launched a massive military retaliation against the Palestinians and severed all ties with Arafat. Zinni departed the region on April 15.

Although Zinni resigned his position as a special envoy, he continued to serve as an unofficial consultant. On August 5, 2003, he spent several hours in Washington, D.C., briefing Major General

Marine Corps general Anthony Zinni, commander of the U.S. Central Command (CENTCOOM) during 1997–2000, shown here briefing reporters at the Pentagon on December 21, 1998, on his assessment of Operation DESERT FOX, a four-day bombing campaign of Iraq. (U.S. Department of Defense)

David T. Zabecki, incoming senior security adviser of the newly established U.S. Coordinating and Monitoring Mission. In an address Zinni gave at Harvard's Kennedy School of Government on December 8, 2004, he stressed that resuming the peace process between Israel and the Palestinians was the single most important step the United States could take to restore its stature in the world. But interestingly enough, he noted that it would be a mistake to assign more high-profile special envoys to the mission. He favored the presence of professional negotiators.

Following his retirement from the military, Zinni held visiting appointments at several U.S. universities and in May 2005 became the president of international operations for M.C.I. Industries, Inc.

An initial supporter of the George W. Bush administration and its foreign policy, Zinni quickly became one of the highest-profile military critics of the war in Iraq after he retired from CENTCOM. Distinguishing Afghanistan from Iraq, Zinni continued to believe that the invasion of Afghanistan to oust the Taliban regime and deprive Al Qaeda of its operating base was the right thing to do. Iraq was a totally different case. Although Saddam Hussein was a regional nuisance, Zinni believed his regime was totally contained and was no real strategic threat. Zinni was also certain that the

case for weapons of mass destruction (WMDs) was vastly overstated, remembering well the intelligence picture he had monitored daily while at CENTCOM.

While Zinni was still at CENTCOM in early 1999 immediately following the air strikes of Operation DESERT FOX, intelligence indicators and diplomatic reporting painted a picture of Hussein's regime as badly shaken and destabilized. In anticipation of the possible requirement for CENTCOM to have to lead an occupation of Iraq should Hussein fall, Zinni ordered the preparation of a comprehensive operations plan (OPLAN). Code-named DESERT CROSSING, it called for a robust civilian occupation authority with offices in each of Iraq's 18 provinces. The DESERT CROSSING plan was a dramatic contrast to what eventually played out under the anemic Coalition Provisional Authority, which for almost the first year of its existence had very little presence outside Baghdad.

During the run-up to the invasion of Iraq, Zinni became increasingly concerned about the quality of the planning, especially the posthostilities phase. Queries to old contacts still at CENTCOM confirmed that OPLAN DESERT CROSSING had all but been forgotten. Zinni came to believe that the United States was being plunged headlong into an unnecessary war by political ideologues who had no understanding of the region. True to the promise he made to himself when he was wounded in Vietnam, Zinni became one of the first senior American figures to speak out against what he saw as "lack of planning, underestimating the task, and buying into a flawed strategy." Zinni soon found himself one of the most influential critics of the Bush administration's handling of the war in Iraq. In 2008 Zinni joined the teaching faculty at Duke University's Sanford Institute of Public Policy.

DAVID T. ZABECKI

See also

Arafat, Yasser; DESERT CROSSING, OPLAN; PROVIDE COMFORT, Operation; Sharon, Ariel; United States Central Command; United States Coordinating and Monitoring Mission

References

Clancy, Tom, with Anthony Zinni and Tony Kolz. *Battle Ready.* New York: Putnam, 2004.

Leverett, Flynt, ed. *The Road Ahead: Middle East Policy in the Bush Administration's Second Term.* Washington, DC: Brookings Institution, 2005.

Zinni, Anthony, and Tony Koltz. *The Battle for Peace: A Frontline Vision of America's Power and Purpose.* London: Palgrave Macmillan, 2006.

Zubaydah, Abu
Birth Date: March 12, 1971

Chief of Al Qaeda operations and number three in the terrorist organization's hierarchy until his capture in March 2002. His position placed him in charge of Al Qaeda training camps that selected the personnel for the September 11, 2001, terror attacks against the United States. Abu Zubaydah was born on March 12, 1971, in Saudi Arabia. His birth name was Zayn al-Abidin Mohamed Husayn, but he adopted the name Abu Zubaydah early in his career as a radical Islamist. Although born in Saudi Arabia, he moved to the West Bank as a teenager. Engaged in extremist Islamist activities from his youth, he took part in demonstrations against the Israeli occupation.

Zubaydah's first political association was with the radical Palestinian organization of Hamas. Ayman al-Zawahiri recruited him from Hamas to the Egyptian Islamic Jihad. When Zawahiri moved to Pakistan, Zubaydah went with him. As a teenager he fought with the Afghan Arabs in military operations against the Soviets. In one of these engagements in Afghanistan he lost an eye. His abilities allowed him to move up in the hierarchy of Al Qaeda until he became its chief of operations.

As chief of operations, Zubaydah played a role in all of Al Qaeda's military operations. Indeed, he selected Muhammad Atta for an important future martyr mission while Atta was in training at Khaldan camp in 1998. Zubaydah was also active in planning the failed Millennium plots in Jordan and the United States. After that he became field commander for the attack on the U.S. Navy destroyer *Cole* in Aden Harbor, Yemen, on October 12, 2000.

Khalid Sheikh Mohammed was the operational chief for the September 11 attacks, but Zubaydah was a participant in the final draft of the plan and was also active in post–September 11 plots. American authorities decided that Zubaydah was important enough to either capture or eliminate. What made him important in Al Qaeda was his role in keeping all members' files and in assigning individuals to specific tasks and operations.

A joint operation of Pakistani security, U.S. Special Forces, and Federal Bureau of Investigation (FBI) Special Weapons and Tactics (SWAT) units arrested Zubaydah in a suburb of Faisalabad, a town in western Pakistan, on March 28, 2002. From intercepted Al Qaeda communications, the National Security Agency learned that Zubaydah might be at a two-story house owned by a leader of the Pakistani militant extremist group Lashkar-e Tayyiba. In the subsequent assault 35 Pakistanis and 27 Muslims from other countries were arrested. Zubaydah was among them. He had been seriously wounded, with gunshots to the stomach, groin, and thigh. A medical unit determined that Zubaydah would survive, and he was taken into American custody.

Zubaydah has been held at an undisclosed American interrogation camp since his capture. The Americans decided to interrogate him, seeking to convince him that he was in Saudi Arabia. Instead of being put off by this, Zubaydah asked his phony "Saudi" interrogators to contact a senior member of the Saudi royal family, Prince Ahmed bin Salman bin Abdul-Aziz, who would save him from the Americans. This claim stunned the interrogators. They returned later to confront him for lying. Zubaydah instead gave more details about agreements among Al Qaeda, Pakistani, and Saudi high-level government leaders. He went so far as to indicate that certain Pakistani and Saudi leaders knew about the September 11 planning before the attack occurred. According to him, these officials did not have the details and did not want them, but they knew the general outlines of the plot. After Zubaydah learned that the "Saudi" interrogators were really Americans, he tried to commit suicide. This attempt failed, and Zubaydah no longer volunteered information and denied what he had said earlier.

When American investigators quizzed the Saudi government about Zubaydah's comments, government representatives called his information false and malicious. In a series of strange coincidences, three of the Saudi government officials named by Zubaydah died in a series of incidents in the months after the inquiries. Prince Ahmed died of a heart attack at age 41, Prince Sultan bin Faisal bin Turki al-Said died in an automobile accident, and Prince Fahd bin Turki bin Saud al-Kabir died of thirst while traveling in the Saudi summer at only age 25. The supposed Pakistani contact, Air Marshal Ali Mir, was killed in an airplane crash on February 20, 2003, with his wife and 15 senior officers.

Zubaydah remains in American custody, his eventual fate also unknown. Because American interrogators tricked him into talking, he has refused to provide further information about Al Qaeda or the September 11 plot. In September 2006 he was transferred to the Guantánamo Bay Detention Center.

In 2006 Ron Suskind published the book *One Percent Doctrine,* which claimed that Zubaydah was not nearly so important in al Qaeda as had been thought. Suskind claimed that Zubaydah was mentally ill and was only a minor figure in Al Qaeda. Suskind's assertions have been countered by numerous others, including former Al Qaeda operatives. Regardless of the controversy, Zubaydah appeared before a Combatant Status Review Tribunal in Guantánamo on March 27, 2007. There he downplayed his role in Al Qaeda but still claimed some authority. Zubaydah has also become part of another controversy because he was tortured by Central Intelligence Agency (CIA) operatives. A May 30, 2005, CIA memorandum states that Zubaydah was subjected to waterboarding 83 times.

Stephen E. Atkins

See also

Al Qaeda; Guantánamo Bay Detainment Camp; September 11 Attacks; Zawahiri, Ayman al-

References

Corbin, Jane. *Al-Qaeda: The Terror Network That Threatens the World.* New York: Thunder's Mouth, 2002.

Posner, Gerald. *Why America Slept: The Failure to Prevent 9/11.* New York: Ballantine Books, 2003.

Suskind, Ron. *One Percent Doctrine.* New York: Simon and Schuster, 2006.

Appendices

Appendix A

Military Ranks

All modern armies have two primary classes of soldiers in officers and enlisted men. This distinction originated in the armies of ancient times. In the medieval period the distinction was between knights and men at arms: nobility and commoners. Up through the beginning of the 20th century the distinction between military officers and enlisted soldiers reflected the social class distinctions of society as a whole. An officer was by definition a gentleman, while a common soldier was not. The breakdown in the old social orders that started during World War I was likewise reflected in the world's armies. By the end of World War II the distinction between officers and enlisted in most Western armies had become far more a professional one than a social one. In most Middle Eastern militaries, however, there remains even today a large class distinction between the commissioned and enlisted ranks.

Officers comprise 10–15 percent of most modern armies. Middle Eastern militaries with weak or nonexistent noncommissioned officer (NCO) corps generally have a much higher percentage of officers, as do all armies that were based on the Soviet model. Officers still comprise almost one-third of the post–Cold War Russian Army.

Officers are further divided into three basic groups. Company grade officers (lieutenants and captains) are responsible for the leadership of platoons and companies. Field grade officers (majors and colonels) lead battalions and regiments. General officers command the higher echelons and also coordinate the overall direction of an army and its military activities. It is the generals who answer directly to the political leadership of modern democracies. Navies also recognize three broad groups of officers, without necessarily using the army terms. In most militaries, generals and admirals are collectively called flag officers because each one has a personal flag bearing the insignia of his rank.

Although female flag officers are relatively common in the U.S. military today, there are very few in most other Western armies. With the exception of Israel, female officers are almost nonexistent in most Middle Eastern militaries, and even female soldiers are a rarity. American female officers and general officers in the Middle East routinely encounter stiff cultural resistance in societies with little tradition of women in positions of authority.

Enlisted soldiers, sailors, airmen, and marines are divided into two basic categories: enlisted men and NCOs. The term for an NCO varies from army to army—*Unteroffizier* in German, *sous officier* in French—but the meaning is universal. In all Western armies, NCOs are the backbone of the organization. They are the ones responsible for training individual soldiers and for training and leading fire teams and squads. They hold key leadership positions in platoons and companies. At the higher levels they assist staff officers in the planning and execution of operations.

In all armies the larger majority of the enlisted ranks denote the distinctions within the NCO corps. Most Middle Eastern armies have extremely weak NCO corps. Until the defeat of Iraq in 2003, the Iraqi Army did not even have NCOs, just officers and soldiers. Under American training and tutelage, the new Iraqi Army is building up its NCO corps, a process that requires years.

NCOs include corporals, sergeants, and, in some armies, warrant officers. In most navies the NCOs are called petty officers and in some cases warrant officers. It is this category of warrant officer that is the most difficult to classify, because the exact status varies from army to army. Many Western armies follow the British model in which warrant officers are the highest category of NCOs. In the American military, however, warrant officers are a distinct personnel class between officers and enlisted personnel. They are considered specialist officers, highly skilled in a certain functional area (such as pilots), receiving pay equivalent to company-grade officers but without the full range of command authority and responsibilities.

In the American military, warrant officers are much closer to commissioned officers. In the British military they are clearly the most senior of the NCOs. Contrary to widely held popular belief, for example, the rank of sergeant major does not exist in the British military. Rather, it is a position title—or an appointment, as the British call it—like squad leader or company commander. The rank of the NCO holding the sergeant major position is always a warrant officer, but he is addressed by his position title of sergeant major. The British do not have company first sergeants. The senior NCO in British companies is called the company sergeant major. Most British and Commonwealth militaries have two grades of warrant officer.

There is, then, no direct comparison between British and American warrant officers, which partially explains the difficulty in correlating exactly the military ranks of the world's armies. The confusion between American and British warrant officers causes problems to this day in many NATO headquarters. While most Western armies that have served recently in the Middle East have warrant officers on the British model, Italy, Denmark, Poland, and Japan have warrant officers on the American model.

The U.S. Army, U.S. Navy, and U.S. Marine Corps all have five grades of warrant officer. The U.S. Air Force does not have warrant officers. The new Iraqi Army has one grade of warrant officer on the American model, with the rank title of "Naib Arif."

Establishing rank equivalency among armies is an inexact science at best, as the confusion over warrant officers and sergeants major illustrates. Common sense would seem to dictate that two soldiers in different armies with the exact same rank titles would be essentially the same. This, however, is not necessarily always the case.

The problem of rank equivalency is further compounded by the fact that all armies do not have the same number of ranks, especially for enlisted personnel and NCOs. All four of the American military services have nine enlisted grades, but more than one rank may exist within a given pay grade. In the U.S. Army and U.S. Marine Corps, for example, the second-highest enlisted pay grade, E-8, includes the ranks of master sergeant and first sergeant. Both receive the same pay, but the duties of a first sergeant are more demanding, and therefore first sergeants always take precedence over master sergeants.

The lowest enlisted rank in the British Army has several different titles, depending on the branch to which the soldier is assigned. But privates, troopers, gunners, and sappers are all the same rank. The British Army also has three different pay grades for privates, troopers, gunners, and sappers, none of whom wear any rank insignia. Lance corporal is the first rank in the British Army that has a rank insignia. A lance corporal wears a single chevron and is an NCO. A U.S. Army soldier who wears a single chevron is only a private (E-2) and is two pay grades away from being an NCO.

The German Army has 11 enlisted ranks, Denmark has 6, the Italian Army has 10, the Italian Navy has 8, the Italian Air Force has 6, and the Carabinieri has only five. Norway has only 3 enlisted ranks, and its top NCO rank, *sersjant,* is only considered the equivalent of a U.S. Army sergeant, the second-lowest American NCO rank.

There is far more commonality among the officer ranks of the world's armies today. Most militaries have three levels each of company and field-grade officers and four levels of general officers. The initial general officer rank in most armies is brigadier general (one star), although the British Army and most of the Commonwealth armies use the rank title brigadier. In the British Royal Navy the first flag officer rank is commodore, and the next one up is rear admiral. In the U.S. Navy, however, those ranks are awkwardly designated rear admiral (lower half) and rear admiral (upper half), respectively.

Major generals (two stars) typically command divisions. Lieutenant generals (three stars) typically command corps. Generals (four stars) command field armies, theaters, and major commands and serve as national chiefs of staff.

Through the end of World War II most of the major armies had a five-star general rank. The rank has largely fallen into disuse in recent years, although it still remains as an official rank and is therefore listed in these tables. The last American promoted to general of the army was Omar Bradley in 1950 during the Korean War. The last French officer promoted to marshal of France was Marie Pierre Koenig, who died in 1970 but was promoted posthumously 14 years later. The last British officer promoted to field marshal was Sir Peter Inge in 1994 following the Persian Gulf War. The Russian Army suspended use of its various marshal ranks following the end of the Cold War. When the German Army was reconstituted in 1955, the rank of Generalfeldmarschall was not included in the Bunderwehr's rank structure.

All air forces grew from their respective armies, and since the end of World War II most have been separate services. Most air forces retained the rank structures and titles of the respective armies from which they originated. The British Royal Air Force has an officer rank structure parallel to the British Army but with completely different rank titles and insignia.

Officer candidates have their own separate rank structures in most armies. But the ranks of cadet, midshipman, aspirant, *Fahnrich,* etc., are essentially temporary training ranks. With the exception of Israel, officer candidates in most armies do not take part in combat operations until they receive their commissions.

The following table represents an attempt to equate the various enlisted and officer ranks of the various militaries of the Middle Eastern wars. In determining the level at which to place a given rank, the duties and responsibilities of the person holding that rank take precedence over the face value of the rank title or the insignia worn. The table does not include officer candidates or true warrant officers. Warrant officers as NCOs are included. Many armies also have special rank structures and designations for musicians, buglers, and pipers, which likewise are not included in the table.

David T. Zabecki and Konrad J. T. Zabecki

References

Davis, Brian L. *NATO Forces: An Illustrated Reference to Their Organization and Insignia.* London: Blandford, 1988.

Emerson, William K. *Chevrons: Illustrated History and Catalog of U.S. Army Insignia.* Washington, DC: Smithsonian Institution Press,

Army Ranks

	United States Army	United Kingdom Army	Federal Republic of Germany Army	France Army
Officers	General of the Army	Field Marshal		Maréchal de France
	General	General	General	Général d'Armée
	Lieutenant General	Lieutenant-General	Generalleutnant	Général de Corps d'Armée
	Major General	Major-General	Generalmajor	Général de Division
	Brigadier General	Brigadier	Brigadegeneral	Général de Brigade
	Colonel	Colonel	Oberst	Colonel
	Lieutenant Colonel	Lieutenant-Colonel	Oberstleutnant	Lieutenant-Colonel
	Major	Major	Major	Commandant
	Captain	Captain	Hauptmann	Capitaine
	First Lieutenant	Lieutenant	Oberleutnant	Lieutenant
	Second Lieutenant	Second Lieutenant	Leutnant	Sous-Lieutenant
Enlisted	Command Sergeant Major Sergeant Major	Warrant Officer Class 1	Oberstabsfeldwebel	Major
	First Sergeant Master Sergeant	Warrant Officer Class 2	Stabsfeldwebel	Adjudant-Chef
			Hauptfeldwebel	
	Sergeant First Class	Staff Sergeant Colour Sergeant	Oberfeldwebel	Adjudant
	Staff Sergeant	Sergeant	Feldwebel	Sergent-Chef Maréchal-des-Logis-Chef
	Sergeant	Corporal Bombardier	Stabsunteroffizier	Sergent Maréchal-des-Logis
	Corporal Specialist 4	Lance Corporal Lance Bombardier	Unteroffizier	Caporal-Chef Brigadier-Chef
	Private First Class	Private Class 1 Trooper Class 1 Gunner Class 1 Sapper Class 1	Hauptgefreiter	Caporal Brigadier
	Private (E-2)	Private Class 2 Trooper Class 2 Gunner Class 2 Sapper Class 2	Obergefreiter	Soldat de 1ère Classe
			Gefreiter	
	Private (E-1)	Private Class 3 Trooper Class 3 Gunner Class 3 Sapper Class 3	Soldat Grenadier Kannonier	Soldat de 2ème Classe

	Italy Army	Canada Army	Denmark Army	Norway Army
Officers				
	Generale di Corpo d'Armata con Incarichi Speciali	General	General	General
	Generale di Corpo d'Armata	Lieutenant-General	Generalløjtnant	Generalløytnant
	Generale di Divisione	Major-General	Generalmajor	Generalmajor
	Generale di Brigata	Brigadier-General	Brigadegeneral	Brigadier
	Colonnello	Colonel	Oberst	Oberst
	Tenente Colonnello	Lieutenant-Colonel	Oberstløjnant	Oberstløytnant
	Maggiore	Major	Major	Major
	Capitano	Captain	Kaptajn	Kaptein Rittmester
	Tenente	Lieutenant	Premierløjtnant	Løytnant
	Sottotenente	Second Lieutenant	Løjtnant	Fenrik
Enlisted	Sergente Maggiore	Command Warrant Officer Chief Warrant Officer		
	Sergente	Master Warrant Officer		
	Caporalmaggiore Capo Scelto	Warrant Officer		
	Caporalmaggiore Capo	Sergeant	Oversergent	
	Caporalmaggiore Scelto	Master Corporal	Sergent	Sersjant
	1° Caporalmaggiore	Corporal	Korporal	Korporal
	Caporalmaggiore	Trained Private	Overkonstabel af 1. Grad	Grenader
	Caporale Scelto	Basic Private	Overkonstabel af 2. Grad	
	Caporale			
	Soldato	Private Recruit	Konstabel	

Army Ranks

	Netherlands Army	Poland Army	Japan Ground Self Defense Force	Iraq Army	Saudi Arabia Army
Officers				Mushir	Masheer
	Generaal	General	Rikujō Bakuryōchō	Fariq Awwal	Fareeq Auwal
	Luitenant-Generaal	General Broni	Rikushō	Fariq	Fareeq
	Generaal-Majoor	General Dywizja	Rikushōho	Liwa	Lu-a'
	Brigade-Generaal	General Brygady		'Amid	Ameed
	Kolonel	Pulkownik	Ittō Rikusa	'Aqid	Aqeed
	Luitenant-Kolonel	Podpulkownik	Nitō Rikusa	Muqaddam	Muqudim
	Majoor	Major	Santō Rikusa	Raid	Raid
	Kapitein Ritmeester	Kapitian	Ittō Riku	Naqib	Naqeeb
	Eerste-Luitenant	Porucznik	Nitō Rikui	Mulazim Awwal	Mulazm Auwal
	Tweede-Luitenant	Podporucznik	Santō Rikui	Mulazim	Mulazim
Enlisted	Adjudant-Onderofficier	Starszy Sierżant	Rikusōchō		Raees Ruq-ba
	Sergeant-Majoor Opperwachtmeester	Sierżant	Ittō Rikusō		
	Sergeant der 1e Klasse Wachtmeester der 1e Klasse		Nitō Rikusō	Rais Urafa	Raqeeb Auwal
	Sergeant Wachtmeester	Plutonowy			Raqeeb
	Korporaal der 1e Klasse	Starszy Kapral	Santō Rikusō	Arif	Waqeel Raqeeb
	Korporaal	Kapral	Rikushichō	Naib Arif	Areef
	Soldaat der 1e Klasse Huzaar der 1e Klasse Kanonier der 1e Klasse	Starszy Szeregowiec	Ittō Rikushi	Jundi Awwal	Jundi Auwal
			Nitō Rikushi		
	Soldaat Huzaar Kanonier	Szeregowy	Santō Rikushi	Jundi	Jundi

Air Force Ranks

	United States Air Force	United Kingdom Royal Air Force	Federal Republic of Germany Air Force
Officers	General of the Air Force	Marshal of the RAF	
	General	Air Chief Marshal	General
	Lieutenant General	Air Marshal	Generalleutnant
	Major General	Air Vice Marshal	Generalmajor
	Brigadier General	Air Commodore	Brigadegeneral
	Colonel	Group Captain	Oberst
	Lieutenant Colonel	Wing Commander	Oberstleutnant
	Major	Squadron Leader	Major
	Captain	Flight Lieutenant	Hauptmann
	First Lieutenant	Flying Officer	Oberleutnant
	Second Lieutenant	Pilot Officer	Leutnant
Enlisted	Chief Master Sergeant	Warrant Officer	Oberstabsfeldwebel
	Senior Master Sergeant	Master Aircrew	Stabsfeldwebel
			Hauptfeldwebel
	Master Sergeant	Flight Sergeant Chief Technician	Oberfeldwebel
	Technical Sergeant	Sergeant	Feldwebel
	Staff Sergeant	Corporal	Stabsunteroffizier
	Sergeant Senior Airman	Junior Technician	Unteroffizier
	Airman First Class	Senior Aircraftsman	Hauptgefreiter
	Airman	Leading Aircraftsman	Obergefreiter
			Gefreiter
	Airman Basic	Aircraftsman	Flieger

Air Force Ranks

	France Army of the Air	Italy Air Force	Royal Canadian Air Force
Officers	Maréchal de France		
	Général d'Armée Aérienne	Generale di Squadra Aerea con Incarichi Speciali	General
	Général de Corps Aérienne	Generale di Squadra Aerea	Lieutenant-General
	Général de Division Aérienne	Generale di Divisione Aerea	Major-General
	Général de Brigade Aérienne	Generale di Brigata Aerea	Brigadier-General
	Colonel	Colonnello	Colonel
	Lieutenant-Colonel	Tenente Colonnello	Lieutenant-Colonel
	Commandant	Maggiore	Major
	Capitaine	Capitano	Captain
	Lieutenant	Tenente	Lieutenant
	Sous-Lieutenant	Sottotenente	Second Lieutenant
Enlisted			Command Warrant Officer Chief Warrant Officer
	Major	Sergente Maggiore	
	Adjudant-Chef	Sergente	Master Warrant Officer
	Adjudant		Warrant Officer
	Sergent-Chef		
		1ere Aviere Scelto	Sergeant
	Sergent	Aviere Capo	Master Corporal
	Caporal-Chef	Aviere Capo	Corporal
	Caporal	1ere Aviere	Trained Private
	Soldat de 1ère Classe	Aviere Scelto	Basic Private
	Soldat de 2ème Classe	Aviere	Private Recruit

Navy Ranks

	United States Navy	United Kingdom Royal Navy	Federal Republic of Germany Navy	France Navy
Officers	Fleet Admiral	Admiral of the Fleet		
	Admiral	Admiral	Admiral	Amiral
	Vice Admiral	Vice-Admiral	Vizeadmiral	Vice-Amiral d'Escadre
	Rear Admiral (Upper Half)	Rear-Admiral	Konteradmiral	Vice-Amiral
	Rear Admiral (Lower Half)	Commodore	Flotilenadmiral	Contre-Amiral
	Captain	Captain	Kapitän zur See	Capitaine de Vaisseau
	Commander	Commander	Fregattenkapitän	Capitaine de Frégate
	Lieutenant Commander	Lieutenant-Commander	Korvettenkapitän	Capitaine de Corvette
	Lieutenant	Lieutenant	Kapitänleutnant	Lieutenant de Vaisseau
	Lieutenant (Junior Grade)	Sublieutenant	Oberleutnant zur See	Enseigne de Vaisseau de 1ere Classe
	Ensign		Leutnant zur See	Enseigne de Vaisseau de 2eme Classe
Enlisted	Master Chief Petty Officer	Warrant Officer Class 1	Oberstabsbootsmann	Major
	Senior Chief Petty Officer	Warrant Officer Class 2	Stabsbootsmann	Maître-Principal
			Hauptbootsmann	
	Chief Petty Officer	Chief Petty Officer	Oberbootsmann	Premier-Maître
	Petty Officer First Class	Petty Officer	Bootsmann	Maître
	Petty Officer Second Class	Leading Rate	Obermaat	Second Maître
	Petty Officer Third Class		Maat	Quartier-Maître de 1ère Classe
	Seaman Airman Fireman	Able Seaman	Hauptgefreiter	Quartier-Maître de 2ème Classe
	Seaman Apprentice Airman Apprentice Fireman Apprentice	Able Seaman	Obergefreiter	Maître-Brevet
			Gefreiter	
	Seaman Recruit	Ordinary Seaman	Matrose	Matelot

Navy Ranks

	Italy Navy	Royal Canadian Navy	Denmark Navy
Officers			
	Ammiraglio di Squadra con Incarichi Speciali	Admiral	Admiral
	Ammiraglio di Squadra	Vice-Admiral	Viceadmiral
	Ammiraglio di Divisione	Rear Admiral	Kontreadmiral
	Contrammiraglio	Commodore	Flotilleadmiral
	Capitano di Vascello	Captain	Kommandør
	Capitano di Fregata	Commander	Kommandørkaptajn
	Captiano di Corvetta	Lieutenant-Commander	Orlogskaptajn
	Tenente di Vascello	Lieutenant	Kaptajnløjtnant
	Sottoenente di Vascello	Sub-Lieutenant	Premierløjtnant
	Guardiamarina	Acting Sub-Lieutenant	Løjtnant
Enlisted		Command Chief Petty Officer	
	Secondo Capo	Chief Petty Officer 1st Class	
	Sergente	Chief Petty Officer 2nd Class	
	Sottocapo di 1a Classe	Petty Officer 1st Class	
	Sottocapo di 2a Classe	Petty Officer 2nd Class	Oversergent
	Sottocapo di 3a Classe	Master Seaman	Sergent
	Sottocapo	Leading Seaman	Korporal
	Comune di 1a Classe	Able Seaman	Marinespecialist
	Comune di 2a Classe	Ordinary Seaman	Marineoverkonstabel
		Seaman	Marinekonstabel

Special Branch Ranks

	United States Marine Corps	United Kingdom Royal Marines	Italy Carabinieri
Officers			
	General	General	Generale di Corpo d'Armata con Incarichi Speciali
	Lieutenant General	Lieutenant-General	Generale di Corpo d'Armata
	Major General	Major General	Generale di Divisione
	Brigadier General	Brigadier	Generale di Brigata
	Colonel	Colonel	Colonnello
	Lieutenant Colonel	Lieutenant-Colonel	Tenente Colonnello
	Major	Major	Maggiore
	Captain	Captain	Capitano
	First Lieutenant	Lieutenant	Tenente
	Second Lieutenant	Second Lieutenant	Sottotenente
Enlisted	Sergeant Major Master Gunnery Sergeant	Warrant Officer Class 1	Brigadiere
	First Sergeant Master Sergeant	Warrant Officer Class 2	Vice Brigadiere
	Gunnery Sergeant	Colour Sergeant	
	Staff Sergeant	Sergeant	
	Sergeant	Corporal	
	Corporal	Lance Corporal	Appuntato Scelto
	Lance Corporal		
	Private First Class		Appuntato
	Private	Marine	Carabiniere

Appendix B

Military Medals, Decorations, and Awards

Military awards fall into three basic categories. Medals are widely awarded to recognize service in a war, a campaign, or a battle or for periods of long peacetime service. Decorations are selective individual awards presented for distinguished or meritorious service or for valor and gallantry in combat. Qualification badges, such as pilot's wings, are awarded to recognize proficiency with a particular weapon or piece of equipment, while skill badges, such as parachutist wings, indicate levels of proficiency in specific tactical techniques.

Medals and decorations consist of a metal badge suspended from a ribbon with a color scheme unique to that specific award. Some countries have special ways of draping the ribbon that are readily identifiable and unique to that country. The full award, the ribbon and the badge, is worn generally only on special occasions and on the dress uniform. During normal occasions the award is represented by a ribbon bar worn on the service uniform. During World War I and World War II soldiers in many armies wore their decorations and medals, at least in the form of the ribbon bar, on their combat field uniforms. Virtually no Western army today follows that practice, although some Middle Eastern armies still do.

The badge of the service medal generally, but not always, consists of a round bronze medallion. Decorations generally, but again not always, tend to have badges in some specific shape, with stars and crosses being the most common. The badges of the higher decorations are often made from silver or gold and sometimes have enameled or even jeweled portions.

The world's first true campaign medal awarded to soldiers of all ranks was probably the British Waterloo Medal, for the 1815 battle that brought about Napoleon's final defeat. In 1847 the British also established a Military General Service Medal, with bars to designate service in specific battles between 1793 and 1814.

During World War I and World War II most armies adopted the system of awarding campaign medals based on service in specific geographic theaters. In the American military, service in individual battles and campaigns within a given theater of operations is indicated by affixing a small Bronze Campaign Star Device to the campaign medal's ribbon or ribbon bar. One Silver Campaign Star Device represents five Bronze Campaign Star Devices.

In 1961 the American military established the Armed Forces Expeditionary Medal (AFEM) to recognize service in smaller combat actions for which no specific service medal is established. Operations in the Middle East for which the AFEM has been authorized includes Operation EL DORADO CANYON, Libya (April 12–17, 1986); Operation EARNEST WILL, Persian Gulf (July 24, 1987–August 1, 1990); Somalia (December 5, 1992–March 31, 1995); Operation SOUTHERN WATCH (December 1, 1995–March 18, 2003); Maritime Intercept Operation, Southwest Asia (December 1, 1995–March 18, 2003); Operation VIGILANT SENTINEL (December 1, 1995–February 15, 1997); Operation NORTHERN WATCH (January 1, 1997–March 18, 2003); Operation DESERT THUNDER (November 11–December 22, 1998); Operation DESERT FOX (December 16–22, 1998); and Operation DESERT SPRING (December 31, 1998–March 18, 2003).

During the Persian Gulf War the United States established the Southwest Asia Service Medal for direct service in Operations DESERT SHIELD and DESERT STORM, between August 2, 1990, and November 30, 1995.

On March 12, 2003, U.S. president George W. Bush established the Global War on Terrorism Service Medal and the Global War on Terrorism Expeditionary Medal for direct participation in or support of combat operations subsequent to September 11, 2001. The Global War on Terrorism Service Medal recognizes service in the United States, such as airport security, as well as direct support of forces deploying to Afghanistan or Iraq. The Global War on Terrorism Expeditionary Medal recognizes troops who actually deploy to foreign territory in support of post-9/11 operations.

As the size and duration of the deployments to Iraq and Afghanistan grew, however, pressure mounted for separate campaign medals to recognize service in those two theaters. The initiative was opposed initially by Secretary of Defense Donald Rumsfeld, but in May 2004 President Bush authorized the Iraq Campaign Medal for service subsequent to March 19, 2003. In November 2004 he authorized the Afghanistan Campaign Medal for service subsequent to March 19, 2003. The Global War on Terrorism Expeditionary Medal continues to be awarded for overseas service in at least 49 other countries. The military members of the U.S. Coordinating and Monitoring Mission in Israel in 2003, for example, received the Global War on Terrorism Expeditionary Medal.

The United Kingdom established the Gulf Medal for service in the Persian Gulf War between August 2, 1990, and March 7, 1991. The British Operational Service Medal for Afghanistan recognizes service in that country subsequent to September 11, 2001, and the Iraq Medal recognizes service in Iraq subsequent to January 20, 2003. Australia established its own Afghanistan Medal for service from October 11, 2001, and an Iraq Medal for service from March 18, 2003.

Both Kuwait and Saudi Arabia established identically named (but with different designs) Kuwait Liberation Medals to recognize service in the liberation of Kuwait in 1991. Both countries awarded these medals to their own militaries as well as to all other soldiers of the coalition. American troops are authorized to wear those medals on their uniforms. All British and Commonwealth troops, however, were authorized to accept both medals as a keepsake but were not allowed to wear them on their uniforms.

Modern military decorations evolved from the system of chivalric and noble orders that had been in existence in Europe for hundreds of years. In most of the Western armies and in Japan the system of military decorations at the higher end merged with the system of orders. Orders were always awarded only to officers. Some countries, such as Great Britain, developed a dual system of decorations: one for officers and one for enlisted men.

The United States, of course, had no system of chivalric or noble orders. The United States also was the first nation to confer military awards on common soldiers. In 1780 the Continental Congress authorized decorations for three New York militiamen for their roles in capturing British intelligence officer Major John Andre. The so-called Andre Medals were one-time creations. The first standing American military decoration was the Badge of Military Merit, established by General George Washington in 1782. The badge consisted of a purple cloth heart and was awarded only three times. After the American Revolution the award fell into disuse until it was reestablished in its modern form in 1932 as the Purple Heart, awarded for wounds (including mortal wounds) received in combat. The Purple Heart was made retroactive to service in World War I.

The U.S. Army established the Certificate of Merit in 1847, awarded to army privates and noncommissioned officers for acts of heroism. Originally the award consisted only of a certificate and an entry in the soldier's record. In 1905 a medal was authorized for all holders of the certificate. The Certificate of Merit became obsolete in 1918. Initially, all holders of the Certificate of Merit were authorized to convert their award to the newly established Distinguished Service Medal, which was later changed to the Distinguished Service Cross.

The Medal of Honor (often erroneously called the Congressional Medal of Honor) was established for the U.S. Navy on December 12, 1861, and for the U.S. Army on July 12, 1862. The highest American military decoration for battlefield heroism, it is awarded by the president in the name of Congress to those members of the U.S. armed forces who distinguish themselves by gallantry and intrepidity at the risk of their lives above and beyond the call of duty while engaged in combat against an armed enemy of the United States.

Originally authorized only for enlisted men, officers became eligible for the army Medal of Honor in 1863 and for the navy Medal of Honor in 1915. The army and navy Medals of Honor also differed in that the army Medal of Honor from the start could be awarded only for acts of combat valor. The navy Medal of Honor could, until 1942, be awarded for peacetime acts of heroism. Between 1917 and 1942 the navy actually had two different designs for the Medal of Honor, one for combat and one for noncombat. The suspension ribbon was the same for both. After the U.S. Air Force became a separate service in 1947, it adopted its own distinct design for the Medal of Honor but with the common suspension ribbon used by all the services. In almost all cases the U.S. Navy version of decorations, including the Medal of Honor, is used by the U.S. Marine Corps.

The Medal of Honor has been awarded eight times since the Vietnam War. U.S. Army Delta Force snipers Master Sergeant Gary Gordon and Sergeant First Class Randall D. Shugart received the Medal of Honor for the same action in Somalia on October 3, 1993. The Medal of Honor was not awarded during the relatively short Persian Gulf War. Four Medals of Honor have been awarded so far in the Iraq War: Sergeant First Class Paul Smith, U.S. Army (April 4, 2003); Corporal Jason Dunham, U.S. Marine Corps (April 22, 2004); Master-at-Arms 2nd Class (SEAL) Michael Monsoor, U.S. Navy (September 29, 2006); and Specialist Ross McGinnis, U.S. Army (December 4, 2006). Two Medals of Honor have been awarded to date for service in Afghanistan: Lieutenant (SEAL) Michael Murphy, U.S. Navy (June 28, 2005), and Sergeant First Class Jared C. Monti, U.S. Army (June 21, 2005).

From World War I through the Vietnam War the posthumous rate for the Medal of Honor has averaged somewhat less than 50 percent. All eight of the post–Vietnam War Medals of Honor, however, have been awarded posthumously, prompting many critics to charge that the bar for the decoration has been unofficially and unfairly raised.

The modern system of American military decorations came into being during World War I. Until that time the only American decorations were the Medal of Honor and the Certificate of Merit. With the establishment in 1918 of the Distinguished Service Cross, the Navy Cross, and the Distinguished Service Medal, Congress created the concept of the Pyramid of Honor. For the first time in American history, degrees of military service to the nation were established, each worthy of its own level of recognition. In the years following World War I, some dozen lower-level decorations for valor, distinguished service, or both have been added to the American Pyramid of Honor.

The Medal of Honor is at the apex of the Pyramid of Honor. Some levels of the Pyramid of Honor have more than one decoration because the army, the navy, and the air force each have their own unique award. At other levels all the services use the same award. At the second level below the Medal of Honor the decorations have slightly different names and completely different designs and ribbons, but the Distinguished Service Cross, the Navy Cross, and the Air Force Cross are equivalent as America's second-highest combat decorations. At the third level, the army, navy, and air force Distinguished Service Medals have the same name but completely different designs and ribbons. The Distinguished Service Medal is the highest American military award for extraordinary service at the highest levels in either peacetime or war.

On the fourth level of the American Pyramid of Honor, the Silver Star is awarded by all three services. America's third-highest decoration for combat valor was authorized in 1918 as the Citation Star, affixed to the ribbon of the World War I Allied Victory Medal to recognize soldiers who had distinguished themselves in combat. It was a mirror of the British Mentioned in Dispatches award. In 1932 the United States converted the Citation Star to a decoration in its own right. Sergeant Leigh Ann Hester was the first woman to receive the Silver Star since World War II. She earned the decoration for an action in Iraq in March 2005. Specialist Monica Lin Brown was the first female soldier to earn the Silver Star in Afghanistan; she earned the decoration for an action that occurred in April 2007.

The Legion of Merit (LOM) ranks directly after the Silver Star. The LOM is the only American decoration that is awarded in different classes: Legionnaire, Officer, Commander, and Chief Commander. Established in 1942, the LOM originally was intended to be a decoration to recognize foreign officers. By the end of World War II, however, it was being awarded to Americans as well but only in the Legionnaire class. That remains the practice to this day. Although the LOM can be awarded for combat bravery, it almost never is. It is generally the second-highest American award for distinguished service either in peacetime or war. The LOM is awarded by all four services.

Established in 1944, the Bronze Star Medal (BSM) is either the fourth-highest award for combat valor or the third-highest award for meritorious service, depending on the circumstances. As a valor decoration, the BSM is awarded with a bronze V Device attached to the suspension ribbon or to the ribbon bar. The "V" indicates valor. Without the V Device, the BSM is awarded for exceptionally meritorious service in wartime, although not necessarily in direct combat. The peacetime meritorious service equivalent of the BSM is the Meritorious Service Medal (MSM), established in 1969. All four services award both the BSM and the MSM.

In some countries soldiers wear multiple medals or ribbons for subsequent awards of the same decoration. Each subsequent award of a U.S. Army and U.S. Air Force decoration is indicated by a Bronze Oak Leaf Cluster device attached to the suspension ribbon or to the ribbon bar. A Silver Oak Leaf Cluster represents five subsequent awards. The U.S. Navy and U.S. Marine Corps use a Gold Star Device to represent subsequent awards and a Silver Star Device (not to be confused with the silver Citation Star of World War I) to indicate five subsequent awards.

Although technically not medals or decorations, a special category of American qualification badges carries a level of prestige equal to decorations. The various American services all have extensive systems of skill and qualification badges, ranging from pilot's and parachutist's wings to badges for missile operators, air traffic controllers, mechanics, and medics. Most of these badges are earned by taking a qualification test or by successfully completing a required course of instruction. A very small number of military badges are awarded only for direct combat service.

The U.S. Army's Combat Infantryman Badge (CIB) is the premier American combat badge. The distinctive blue badge with a silver wreath was established in 1943 to recognize service as an infantryman in ground combat in the rank of colonel and below. The eligibility period was retroactive to December 7, 1941. Additional service as a combat infantryman in a subsequent war is indicated by the addition of a star at the opening of the wreath. There have been five distinct periods for which award of the CIB has been authorized: World War II, the Korean War, the Vietnam War, the Persian Gulf War, and the current wars in Iraq and Afghanistan. Only about 250 American soldiers have ever received the CIB for service in three wars, all of them for World War II, the Korean War, and the Vietnam War. The CIB can only be awarded to soldiers who are trained as infantrymen and who are assigned to infantry units that engage in combat operations. Since the Vietnam War, Special Forces soldiers also have been eligible for the CIB.

The U.S. Army's Combat Medic Badge (CMB) was established in March 1945 and made retroactive to December 7, 1941, to recognize medics who serve with infantry units in combat. Service as a combat medic in subsequent wars is indicated by adding stars to the basic badge. The additional war periods are exactly the same as for the CIB. Only two American soldiers, Sergeant First Class Wayne Slagel and Master Sergeant Henry Jenkins, received the CMB for service in three wars. In 1991 the criteria for the CMB was expanded to include medics assigned to armored and armored cavalry units. During the Persian Gulf War the CMB was awarded to female medics for the first time. The CMB is considered equal in prestige to that of the CIB.

Parachute jumps in combat are among the most hazardous of all military operations. Since World War II soldiers in airborne units have been attaching a small bronze star device to their parachutist wings to designate each combat jump they made. The device is identical to the campaign service stars worn on the campaign medals. The practice was finally officially recognized and authorized by the U.S. Army in 1983 as the Combat Jump Device. Some 200 soldiers of the 75th Ranger Regiment received the Combat Jump Device for an assault near Kandahar, Afghanistan, on October 19, 2001. On March 26, 2003, 954 troopers of the 173rd Airborne Brigade earned the Combat Jump Device when they dropped into Basher in northern Iraq.

In the years following World War II there were many sporadic efforts to establish combat badges for the other combat arms branches of the U.S. Army. During the Korean War especially, many units produced and awarded various unofficial versions of a Combat Artillery Badge, Combat Armor Badge, and others. Despite widespread support from various quarters, such awards were never authorized or officially adopted. The pressure to establish some method of formal recognition for direct combat service other than infantryman, medics, and Special Forces soldiers never really abated. The issue again came to a head during the early days of the Iraq War. In May 2005 the army finally established the Combat Action Badge (CAB), with eligibility dating from September 18, 2001. The CIB and CMB still retain their positions as the army's most prestigious combat awards, but the CAB is awarded to all other soldiers who come under fire during ground combat operations. Unlike with the CIB and CMB, general officers are eligible for the CAB.

The U.S. Navy and U.S. Marine Corps established an award to recognize participation in ground or surface combat in February 1969, with eligibility for service in Vietnam retroactive to March 1961. Rather than a badge, the Combat Action Ribbon is a ribbon bar that ranks in order of precedence ahead of all campaign medals. In March 2007 the U.S. Air Force established its own award to recognize participation in either ground or aerial combat, with eligibility retroactive to September 11, 2001. Neither a badge nor solely a ribbon bar, the Air Force Combat Action Medal is a full decoration. In order of precedence, however, it is equal to the Department of the Navy's Combat Action Ribbon. General officers are not eligible for the air force award.

The United Kingdom has a long tradition and a broad system of orders to recognize distinguished military and civilian service. Originally established in 1399, the Order of the Bath (Military Division) was the most significant recognition for distinguished military service at the highest levels. In 1856 Queen Victoria established the Victoria Cross (VC) as the premier British decoration for combat heroism. From its inception up until the end of the Cold War period, the VC was the only British combat decoration for which officers and enlisted soldiers were both eligible. Significantly, the VC ranked in order of precedence ahead of all British orders, even the Order of the Garter, seldom awarded outside the royal family. The VC ribbon was dark crimson for the British Army and blue for the Royal Navy until 1920, when it was changed to crimson for all services. Most of the Commonwealth countries continued to use the British military decorations system until well after World War II. In 1991 Australia established the Victoria Cross for Australia, in 1993 Canada established the Victoria Cross of Canada, and in 1999 New Zealand established the Victoria Cross for New Zealand. All three decorations are almost identical to the original British VC, varying slightly in some minor design details of the badge.

Since the end of World War II the VC has been awarded only 15 times (including the Australian and New Zealand versions). Private Johnson Beharry of the Princess of Wales' Royal Regiment received the VC for a series of actions in Iraq between May 1 and June 11, 2004. Corporal Bryan Budd of the Parachute Regiment received the VC for a series of actions in Afghanistan between July 27 and August 20, 2006. Special Air Service corporal Bill Apiata, a native Maori, received the VC for New Zealand for an action in Afghanistan sometime during 2004. Special Air Service trooper Mark Donaldson received the VC for Australia for an action in Afghanistan on September 2, 2008. Apiata and Donaldson are the first two winners of the VC for New Zealand and the VC for Australia, respectively. Of the four VCs for Iraq and Afghanistan so far, only Corporal Budd's was awarded posthumously, which contrasts sharply with the thus-far 100 percent posthumous award for the American Medal of Honor.

Below the level of the VC, the original British awards system split into distinct groups for officers and enlisted men. Although technically decorations, the enlisted awards were called gallantry medals. In order of precedence, the lowest officer's decoration ranked above the highest enlisted gallantry medal. The British finally abandoned this dual system in 1993. The enlisted gallantry medals were eliminated, and all British soldiers for the first time became eligible for all decorations.

The highest British decoration for distinguished service is the Companion of the Most Honourable Order of the Bath (CB), which is roughly equivalent to the American Distinguished Service Medal. Next in precedence are the Commander of the Most Excellent Order of the British Empire (CBE) and the Distinguished Service Order (DSO). Until 1993 the DSO was awarded to officers for both distinguished service and for combat valor. As a valor decoration, it was second in precedence to the VC. Since 1993 it is awarded for distinguished service only. The gallantry component of the DSO was replaced by the newly established Conspicuous Gallantry Cross (CGC). Although the CGC is the rough equivalent to the American Distinguished Service Cross, it ranks much lower in overall precedence under the British awards system. While the American Distinguished Service Cross ranks immediately below the Medal of Honor and above the Distinguished Service Medal, the British CGC ranks below the CB, the CBE, and the DSO.

The third level of British gallantry awards are roughly equivalent to the American Silver Star, but each service has its own unique award: the Military Cross (MC), British Army; the Distinguished Service Cross (DSC), Royal Navy; and the Distinguished Flying Cross (DFC), Royal Air Force. The DFC is also awarded to British Army Air Corps and Royal Navy pilots for gallantry in aerial combat. Under the pre-1993 awards system the equivalent enlisted awards were the now-obsolete Military Medal (MM), Distinguished Service Medal (DSM), and Distinguished Flying Medal (DFM), respectively. The first female solder to win the MC was Private Michelle Norris for an action that took place in Iraq in June 2006. A combat medic who rescued a wounded British soldier under fire, Norris and her patient were evacuated from the battlefield by a helicopter flown by U.S. Marine Corps captain William Chesarek Jr., who was assigned to a British unit as an exchange officer. For his part in the action Chesarek

became the first American since World War II to be awarded the British DFC.

The primary level of recognition for acts of gallantry or distinguished conduct by British soldiers in combat operations is the Mention in Dispatches (MID). Soldiers so mentioned are authorized to wear a bronze oak leaf device on the ribbon of the appropriate campaign medal. As noted above, the American version of this practice in World War I later evolved into the Silver Star.

DAVID T. ZABECKI

References

Hall, Donald. *British Orders, Decorations, and Medals.* St. Ives, UK: Balfour, 1973.

Kerrigan, Evans. *American Medals and Decorations.* London: Apple, 1990.

Chronology

1777

Morocco recognizes the independence of the United States, the first nation to do so.

1783

The American War of Independence results in British recognition of the United States as a separate nation. The British Navy ceases to protect American shipping as part of the British Empire. This results in the seizure of American merchant vessels by North African pirates for ransom in the Mediterranean.

1785

First American diplomatic mission to the Middle East, headed by John Lamb.

June 1786

28   For a payment of $10,000 the sultan of Morocco agrees to end piracy off his coast.

1787

The inability of America under the Articles of Confederation to deal with the North African pirates is one of the factors leading to the Constitutional Convention in Philadelphia.

March 1794

27   Congress establishes the U.S. Navy with a bill authorizing the construction of six frigates to provide protection to American merchant shipping from the North African pirates.

1795–1797

Algiers, Tripoli, and Tunis sign treaties to cease piracy in their coastal waters.

1798–1801

Annual payment of tributes curtails piracy. Tribute reaches $2 million by 1801.

May 1801

10   U.S. president Thomas Jefferson dispatches a naval squadron of three frigates and a schooner under the command of Commodore Richard Dale.

14   The Bashaw of Tripoli, Yusuf Karamanli, formally declares war on the United States.

July 1801

24   The U.S. squadron under Commodore Richard Dale sent by President Thomas Jefferson to the Mediterranean arrives before Tripoli and initiates a loose blockade.

October 1803

31   The U.S. frigate *Philadelphia* runs aground near Tripoli while pursuing a Tripolitan ship and is captured with its crew by gunboats sent out from Tripoli. The Tripolitans begin work to convert the *Philadelphia* for their use as a warship.

February 1804

16   U.S. Navy lieutenant Stephen Decatur Jr. and a crew of volunteers sail into the port of Tripoli and burn the *Philadelphia* without the loss of a single man.

U.S. consul William Eaton concludes a convention with Hamet Karamanli, the former pasha of Tripoli, who had been deposed by his younger brother Yusuf and is in exile in Egypt. Eaton then takes command of an expeditionary force that departs Alexandria on March 6. Consisting of 10 Americans, 300 Arab horsemen, 70 Christian mercenaries, and 1,000 camels, this unlikely force advances 500 miles across the Libyan desert to Derna, where it assaults that place on April 27 with artillery support provided by three U.S. Navy brigs offshore under Captain Isaac Hull. Hamet and Eaton then take control of the town, and marine captain Presley O'Bannon raises the American flag for the first time ever over a conquered foreign city. On May 8 and June 10 Tripolitan forces fail in two attempts to retake the city.

June 1805

3   Bashaw Yusuf Karamanli of Tripoli agrees to a treaty with the United States. He accepts a $60,000 ransom for the release of the more than 300 American prisoners from the frigate *Philadelphia* but renounces future tribute from the United States.

July 1815

5   In the Barbary War of 1815 Captain Stephen Decatur Jr. sails to Algiers with a powerful squadron, captures two Algerine warships before that state learns of the U.S. Navy presence, and speedily concludes a peace treaty with Algiers. The dey releases his foreign prisoners, renounces tribute from the United States, and agrees not to attack American merchant vessels. Decatur continues on to Tunis and Tripoli, which reaffirm their peaceful intentions.

1817–1914

The Middle East evokes little American interest other than missionary activities and the continuation of trade. U.S. leadership generally considers the region a British-French sphere of influence.

1882

U.S. marines land in Alexandria, Egypt, after British ships shell the city.

1902

The term "Middle East" is first used by American naval strategist Alfred Thayer Mahan.

June 1914

28   Serbian nationalists assassinate Archduke Franz Ferdinand, heir to the Austro-Hungarian Empire, setting off a chain of events that leads to a declaration of war against Serbia by the Dual Monarchy on July 28. This sets into motion interlocking treaties of military support that plunges most of Europe into World War I, with the Central powers of Germany, Austro-Hungary, and the Ottoman Empire opposing the Allied (Entente) powers of Russia, France, Britain, and later Italy. The United States remains neutral until the German government resumes unrestricted submarine warfare on February 1, 1917. The United States enters the war as an Associated power with a declaration of war against Germany on April 6 but does not declare war on Austria-Hungary until December 7, 1917, and never does declare war on the Ottoman Empire. Its military effort is limited to Europe and does not include the Middle East.

January 1918

8   President Woodrow Wilson addresses Congress and presents his Fourteen Points, his vision for a peace settlement in World War I. These include this passage in Wilson's Point 12: "other nationalities [of the Ottoman Empire beyond the borders of Turkey] should be assured an undoubted security of life and an absolutely unmolested opportunity of autonomous development." This statement raises great expectations for autonomy or independence for the non-Turkish populations in the Ottoman Empire and fosters hopes among many that the United States will support self-determination and independence for ethnic, linguistic, and religious minorities in the Middle East and elsewhere in the world.

January 18, 1919–January 21, 1920

During the Paris Peace Conference negotiating the Treaty of Versailles, Wilson receives strong opposition to his Fourteen Points from British, French, and Italian allied leaders (who had not been consulted prior to Wilson's January 1918 announcement of the points). In order to get approval of his most cherished point, the League of Nations, Wilson is forced to compromise on the others. Only 4 of Wilson's original 14 points are fully implemented. Autonomy and independence of the non-Turkish former Ottoman Empire populations is not among them.

1919–1921

Extensive internal debate occurs in the United States over the Paris peace settlement ending World War I and the establishment of the League of Nations (largely crafted by U.S. president Woodrow Wilson and British prime minister David Lloyd George), ending with separate peace treaties with Germany, Austria, and Hungary on October 18, 1921. The U.S. Senate does not ratify the Treaty of Versailles, and America does not join the League of Nations. As an Associated power rather than an Allied power, the United States had not declared war on the Ottoman Empire and therefore could claim little voice in its dismemberment and in the subsequent establishment of the League of Nations mandates.

1922–1939

Although the United States continues to be engaged globally in commercial activities and trade, in general it follows a policy of isolationism regarding political involvement in world affairs. However, America gradually recognizes the threat posed by Germany and Japan.

1924

The United States recognizes the British mandate over Palestine.

1933

American oil companies receive the right to explore for oil in Saudi Arabia.

September 1939

1   German forces invade Poland. World War II in Europe formally begins on September 3 when Britain and France, acting in fulfillment of their treaty obligations with Poland, declare war on Germany. The United States continues its generally isolationist position.

June 1940

10   Italy declares war on France and Britain, spreading World War II to North Africa. Soon the Italian forces in Libya take the offensive against the British in Egypt.

March 1941

11   The U.S. Lend-Lease Act, passed by large majorities in both houses of Congress, provides American arms and equipment to nations resisting aggression.

June 1941

24   After Germany invades the Soviet Union on June 22, 1941, U.S. Lend-Lease is extended to the Soviet Union. The United States establishes a military mission in Iran to manage substantial quantities of aid channeled through the nation to the Soviets.

December 1941

7   The Japanese attack on Pearl Harbor in the Hawaiian Islands results in a U.S. declaration of war against Japan. Following Adolf Hitler's December 11 declaration of war on the United States, the United States finds itself at war with all of the Axis powers. The war will involve U.S. military action in the Middle East for the first time since the early 19th century.

August 1942

The military mission to Iran becomes the Persian Gulf Support Command and then in December 1943 the Persian Gulf Command. Some 30,000 U.S. troops deliver 4.5 million tons of military supplies to the Soviet Union via Iran (the route becomes known as the Persian Corridor).

November 1942

8   Operation TORCH, the U.S. and British invasion of French North Africa, begins. Overall Allied commander is General Dwight D. Eisenhower, who will later be the U.S. president during Middle East crises such as the 1956 Suez Crisis and the 1958 Lebanon intervention.

May 1943

13   The Allied campaign in North Africa comes to an end with the surrender of the remaining German and Italian forces in Tunis. This successful Allied North African campaign ends the Axis threat to the Suez Canal and a takeover of the Middle Eastern oil fields. It also renders impossible an Axis land linkage with the Japanese in eastern India. The focus of the U.S. effort now turns to Southern Europe.

February 1945

14   U.S. president Franklin D. Roosevelt meets with King Ibn Saud of Saudi Arabia aboard the U.S. Navy heavy cruiser *Quincy*. This meeting helps enhance the Saudi-American relationship, which had grown during World War II and resulted in the formation in 1944 of the Arab-American Oil Corporation (ARAMCO). The Saudi monarchy maintains close economic and strategic ties to the United States throughout the remainder of the century.

May 1945

8   World War II ends in Europe. The weakened condition of Britain and France portends a far greater U.S. role in the Middle East to counter the extension of Soviet power into the area.

1945–1949

Emergence of a bipolar Cold War pitting the United States and its allies against the Soviet Union and its allies. Meanwhile, there is growing dependence among Western nations on Middle Eastern oil. At the same time, however, anger among Arab states is created by strong Western support for the creation of a Jewish state in Palestine. The United States establishes military bases in Islamic countries, such as Incirlik in Turkey and Wheelus in Libya. Saudi Arabia hosts a small U.S. air base at Dhahran.

May 1946

4   The Soviet Union evacuates its troops from northern Iran under pressure from the United States and the new United Nations (UN).

March 1947

12   U.S. president Harry S. Truman announces what becomes known as the Truman Doctrine. It extends U.S. aid to support Greece and Turkey to stave off an internal communist threat and external pressure from the Soviet Union.

May 1948

14   Israel declares its independence and is immediately recognized by the United States and the Soviet Union. The declaration immediately brings invasions by neighboring Arab states, initiating the First Arab-Israeli War (1948–1949), also known as the Israeli War of Independence.

April 1949

4   Formation of the North Atlantic Treaty Organization (NATO), a pact that commits members to mutual support in the event of aggression. Turkey is among the first members. The Southeast Asia Treaty Organization (SEATO), established in 1954, and the 1955 Baghdad Pact, later called the Central Treaty Organization (CENTO), provides overlapping memberships in an effort to prevent Soviet expansion into these regions.

May 1950

25   Tripartite Declaration made by United States, Britain, and France opposing violation of the United Nations (UN) armistice ending the 1948–1949 Arab-Israeli war.

September 1950

30   U.S. president Harry Truman signs National Security Council Report 68 (NSC-68), formally committing the United States to a policy of containing communism wherever it might threaten throughout the world. The global commitment of the containment policy ensures that the Middle East will be drawn into the Cold War maneuvering between the superpowers as each side attempts to expand its influence in the region.

August 1953

16   Mohammad Reza Shah Pahlavi of Iran flees to Iraq as Iranian prime minister Mohammad Mossadegh consolidates power and moves toward nationalization of Iran's oil industry and limits on the power of the Iranian monarchy.

19   A coup supported by the U.S. Central Intelligence Agency (CIA) overthrows Prime Minister Mohammad Mossadegh of Iran, restoring Mohammad Reza Shah Pahlavi to power three days later.

September 1953

5   The U.S. government extends a $45 million aid package to Iran.

May 1955

14   The Warsaw Pact codifies previous commitments of the Soviet Union and East European communist states to support each other in possible armed conflicts with the West. This and the Truman Doctrine ensure that both sides of the Cold War will vigorously compete for influence and control throughout the world. The importance of Middle Eastern oil and the decline of British and French control in much of the Middle East lead to more active U.S. diplomatic, economic, and military efforts in the region.

July 1956

26   President Gamal Abdel Nasser of Egypt nationalizes the Suez Canal. This is in response to the removal of U.S. and British financial support for the building of the Aswan High Dam. President Dwight D. Eisenhower had withdrawn the U.S. pledge following the announcement of an arms deal whereby Egypt would trade cotton for modern arms, including jet fighters, from Warsaw Pact member Czechoslovakia. Nasser's step of nationalizing the canal initiates the Suez Crisis.

October 1956

29   Israeli forces invade the Sinai peninsula, beginning the 1956 Suez Crisis. This is in response to Egypt having announced that it is closing the Strait of Tiran. Israeli forces are operating in conjunction with a secret agreement with Britain and France. The two European powers then demand that all sides pull back from the Suez Canal. When, as expected, Egypt refuses, Britain and France launch long-planned military strikes on Egypt from Cyprus. This comes at the worst possible time for the West, however, providing a distraction for the brutal Soviet invasion and crushing of the Hungarian Revolution.

31   During October 31–November 5, 1956, the United States and the Soviet Union declare opposition to the use of force in the Middle East and threaten possible intervention. U.S. president Dwight D. Eisenhower is furious at the British and French action, which has been undertaken without American knowledge.

November 1956

6   Israel, France, and Britain withdraw forces from the Sinai and Suez under great U.S. pressure. A United Nations

Emergency Force (UNEF) takes over. This humiliation of France and Britain effectively ends any hopes that the two European nations had of remaining global powers and has significant implications for the United States. From that point on, America would replace France and Britain in protecting Western interests in the Middle East.

January 1957

5   U.S. president Dwight D. Eisenhower announces what becomes known as the Eisenhower Doctrine, promising assistance to any Middle Eastern nation requesting help in resisting communist aggression. Congress approves this policy on March 7.

July 1958

14   A coup in Iraq supported by Egypt and Syria overthrows the pro-Western Iraqi monarchy. Lebanon and Jordan fear the spread of the conflict and request protection from the United States and Great Britain.

15   President Dwight D. Eisenhower orders 5,000 U.S. marines to Lebanon. Britain airlifts troops to Jordan.

October 1958

25   U.S. forces complete their withdrawal from Lebanon.

June 1963

12   President John F. Kennedy authorizes Operation HARD SURFACE, the dispatch of a squadron of North American F-100 Super Sabre jet fighters to Saudi Arabia to deter Egypt from extending its involvement in the civil war in North Yemen (1962–1970) to Saudi Arabia. Participation of Jewish personnel in the mission delays deployment until July 2. The aircraft do not engage Egyptian forces, and President Lyndon B. Johnson (Kennedy's successor) allows the operation to end in January 1964.

November 1964

4   Ayatollah Ruhollah Khomeini, having actively opposed the rule of Mohammad Reza Shah Pahlavi and Iran's dependence on the United States since 1962, is expelled from Iran to Turkey. After exile in Iraq and France, Khomeini will return to Iran on February 1, 1979.

June 1967

5–10   Six-Day War between Israel, Egypt, Syria, and Jordan. The United States seeks an end to the conflict to prevent a wider war that might involve the superpowers.

September 1972

5   The Black September terrorist group massacres members of the Israeli Olympic team in Munich. Israel then launches a major manhunt for the assassins.

October 1973

6–26   Yom Kippur (Ramadan) War initiated by Egypt and Syria against Israel. President Anwar Sadat of Egypt initiates the war in consultation with Asad and its Arab neighbors. In a two-pronged attack, Egypt crosses the Suez Canal while Syria advances onto the Golan Heights. After early reversals, Israel is victorious and seizes large portions of Egyptian, Syrian, and Jordanian territory. The United States backs Israel but later demands that it end its offensive. The Soviets, who had threatened to intervene, back down after U.S. armed forces go to a higher stage of alert. U.S. secretary of state Henry Kissinger initiates shuttle diplomacy, traveling between the belligerents' capitals in an attempt to broker a peace agreement. His actions are later taken up by the Jimmy Carter administration.

April 1978

27   Communist coup d'état in Afghanistan.

September 1978

5–17   Tense negotiations at the U.S. presidential retreat at Camp David, Maryland, between Egyptian president Anwar Sadat and Israeli prime minister Menachem Begin, brokered by President Jimmy Carter, result in the Camp David Accords, signed on September 17. The accords will lead to a formal Egyptian-Israeli peace treaty in 1979.

December 1978

5   The new Afghan communist government signs a treaty with the Soviet Union that ensures military support from Moscow. A large number of Afghans, who believe that the new government threatens traditional Afghan practices, coalesce to begin resisting the rise of Soviet influence in Afghanistan.

January 1979

16   Mohammad Reza Shah Pahlavi of Iran, a staunch ally of the United States, bows to increased internal opposition to his pro-U.S. stance, uneven reforms, and considerable corruption and leaves Iran.

February 1979

1   Ayatollah Ruhollah Khomeini returns to Iran from France to support the revolution against the rule of Mohammad Reza Shah Pahlavi and to secure the establishment of a theocratic state governed by Islamic law.

March 1979

26   Egyptian-Israeli Peace Treaty signed in Washington, D.C.

October 1979

22   U.S. president Jimmy Carter allows Mohammad Reza Shah Pahlavi entry into the United States for treatment of cancer.

November 1979

4   Iranian students, with the support of Ayatollah Ruhollah Khomeini, seize the U.S. embassy in Teheran, taking the 52 Americans there hostage and holding them for 444 days. They are only released the day President Ronald Reagan takes office.

December 1979

24   Having provided major military support to several Afghan regimes but now seeing the communist regime there threatened and acting under the Brezhnev Doctrine (to defend communism wherever it is established in power), the Soviet Union invades Afghanistan and occupies it, employing as many as 115,000 troops and providing considerable military and economic aid to the Afghan regime. Osama bin Laden, from a prominent wealthy family in Saudi Arabia, travels to Afghanistan to assist the resistance to the Soviets, now known as the mujahideen. Extensive but classified U.S. assistance to the resistance also comes in the form of training and equipping Afghan rebels in Pakistan.

January 1980

23   President Jimmy Carter announces a boycott of the 1980 Moscow Summer Olympics because of the Soviet invasion and occupation of Afghanistan. The United States, the United Kingdom, Pakistan, Iran, and Saudi Arabia all provide financial and military aid to the Afghan resistance.

April 1980

24   President Jimmy Carter orders Operation EAGLE CLAW, an attempt to rescue the embassy hostages in Iran. The mission fails when 8 U.S. military personnel are killed and 4 are wounded when aircraft collide at the Desert One landing site. The crisis does not end until January 20, 1981, when President Ronald Reagan takes office.

September 1980

4   Ongoing tension between Iran and Iraq becomes open conflict upon Iran's artillery bombardment of Iraqi bases.

17   Iraq abrogates its treaty with Iran regarding shipments on the Shatt al-Arab waterway, essentially declaring the east bank to be the border rather than the thalweg (shipping lane) as the usual border of nations separated by rivers.

November 1980

10   Iraq occupies Khoramshahr and Abadan, beginning an eight-year war with Iran. Fearful of the influence of the Islamic Republic of Iran in the region, the United States backs Iraq and provides useful satellite intelligence to Baghdad.

January 1981

20   Following protracted negotiations, Iran frees the U.S. embassy hostages only minutes after Ronald Reagan is sworn in as U.S. president.

June 1981

7   Fearful that Iraq is developing an atomic bomb, the Israeli Air Force attacks and destroys the Iraqi nuclear facility known as Osiraq in Iraq.

February 1982

The U.S. government removes Iraq from its list of terrorist nations.

December 1982

A U.S. manufacturer ships 60 helicopters to Iraq, apparently not violating the Arms Export Control Act.

1982–1988

The U.S. Defense Intelligence Agency provides detailed information to the Iraqi government regarding Iranian military activities.

1983

Israel invades Lebanon to subdue terrorist attacks on northern Israel from Lebanon. President Ronald Reagan dispatches U.S. marines to Lebanon in an effort to stabilize the Israeli government. Iran and Syria are suspected of backing insurrection and attacks on Israel.

April 1983

18   A suicide bomber attacks the U.S. embassy in Beirut, killing 63 people, including 17 Americans.

October 1983

Ignoring the Arms Export Control Act, the U.S. government secretly encourages Arab nations to ship weapons to Iraq.

23   Suicide truck bomber attacks the poorly defended U.S. Marine Corps barracks at Beirut airport, killing 241 marines and wounding more than 100. President Ronald Reagan soon withdraws U.S. military forces from Lebanon.

November 1983

A National Security directive declares that the United States could prevent Iranian victory in the Iran-Iraq War if it provides $5 billion in loans to Iraq and allows shipments of industrial materials, including those necessary for development of nuclear, biological, and chemical weapons. Intelligence reports to the U.S. State Department note the Iraqi use of chemical weapons against Iran.

January 1984

14   The United States acknowledges shipping to Iraq dual-use exports (materials that can be used for routine industrial processes or for development of chemical, biological, or nuclear weapons).

September 1984

13   Secret U.S. shipment of 508 TOW missiles to Iran as part of the arms-for-hostages agreement.

20   A truck bomb explodes outside the U.S. embassy annex northeast of Beirut, Lebanon, killing 24 people, including 2 U.S. military personnel.

November 1984

The United States renews diplomatic ties with Iraq, severed in 1967.

March 1985

11   Mikhail Gorbachev becomes the general secretary of the Communist Party of the Soviet Union, the de facto ruler of the Soviet Union. He announces plans to reduce Soviet foreign military involvements. In Afghanistan, Gorbachev reduces the Soviet combat mission and refocuses it on training indigenous Afghan military and police forces.

1986

The United States supplies antiaircraft Stinger missiles to Afghan rebels.

January 1986

17   The Ronald Reagan administration authorizes shipment of 4,000 antiaircraft missiles to Iran, to be shipped through Israel. This is part of what becomes the Iran-Contra Affair, the sale of U.S. military equipment to Iran, the proceeds from which are then used to support the Contra insurgents fighting the communist Sandinista regime in Nicaragua.

April 1986

22   Indictment of 10 U.S. citizens for sales of missiles to Iran.

May 1986

The U.S. government licenses shipment of biological material to Iraq, including anthrax and botulin poisons.

November 1986

The Iran-Contra Affair becomes public knowledge through a Beirut, Lebanon, newspaper article.

January–March 1987

The United States reflags Kuwaiti tankers to protect them from Iranian attack in the Persian Gulf. In Operation EARNEST WILL, the United States also sends warships to the Persian Gulf to escort and protect commercial shipping.

March 1987

U.S. president Ronald Reagan admits illegal sales to Iran to finance Contra operations in Nicaragua.

May 1987

18   An Iraqi Exocet aircraft-launched missile strikes the U.S. Navy frigate *Stark* in the Persian Gulf, killing 37 sailors. The attack is declared accidental, a consequence of the continuing Iran-Iraq War.

April 1988

Shipment from the United States to Iraq of chemicals required for the manufacture of mustard gas.

14   The U.S. Navy guided missile frigate *Samuel B. Roberts* is severely damaged by a mine in the Persian Gulf. Other mines of Iranian manufacture are found in the area.

18   In retaliation for Iranian mining of the Persian Gulf, in Operation PRAYING MANTIS U.S. Navy warships attack two Iranian oil rigs in the Persian Gulf, sinking an Iranian frigate and damaging another.

July 1988

3   The U.S. Navy guided-missile cruiser *Vincennes* mistakenly downs an Iranian commercial jet believed to have been a military aircraft, killing all 290 people aboard. The U.S. government subsequently apologizes for the incident and pays reparations.

August 1988

20   Formal cease-fire declared in the eight-year-long Iran-Iraq War.

February 1989

15   The last Soviet forces depart Afghanistan. This frees the Islamic fundamentalist Taliban to begin a slow conquest of Afghanistan, aided by Osama bin Laden's Al Qaeda

terrorist organization. Al Qaeda thereby gains in Taliban-dominated Afghanistan a secure base for its operations.

August 1990

2   Iraq, having previously proclaimed Kuwait as a province, invades Kuwait to establish its sovereignty there. Following a 14 to 0 vote, the United Nations (UN) Security Council passes Resolution 660, calling for a cease-fire and Iraqi withdrawal from Kuwait. Kuwait requests military aid from the United States.

2–7   The United States Central Command (CENTCOM) at MacDill Air Force Base has responsibility for military operations in the Middle East and develops a plan to send 200,000 American troops to defend Saudi Arabia from an Iraqi attack should military aid be requested. General H. Norman Schwarzkopf, commander in chief of CENTCOM, begins work to implement the plan.

5   U.S. president George H. W. Bush announces that Iraq will not be allowed to absorb Kuwait.

6   Saudi Arabian king Fahd meets U.S. secretary of defense Richard Cheney to request military assistance. The United Nations (UN) Security Council passes UN Resolution 661 to prohibit the importation of all Iraqi and Kuwaiti goods, impose economic sanctions on Iraq, and prevent transfer of funds to Iraq and occupied Kuwait.

8   American fighter aircraft begin arriving in Saudi Arabia in Operation DESERT SHIELD. The Iraqi government formally declares Kuwait to be Iraq's 19th province.

9   The United Nations (UN) Security Council passes Resolution 662, declaring the annexation of Kuwait null and void.

12   Iraq seeks to tie its invasion of Kuwait to the Arab-Israeli dispute by declaring that it would withdraw from Kuwait if Israel withdraws from the occupied territories and Syria withdraws from Lebanon.

18   The United Nations (UN) Security Council unanimously passes Resolution 664, calling on Iraq to immediately withdraw from Kuwait. UN secretary-general Javier Perez de Cuellar plans to send envoys to Iraq to discuss the release of foreigners detained by the Iraqi government.

21   Syria joins Egypt in its commitment to defend Saudi Arabia in the event of an Iraqi invasion.

25   The United Nations (UN) Security Council approves Resolution 665 authorizing naval forces in the Persian Gulf to enforce the embargo against Iraq.

September 1990

5   Iraq calls for the removal of the leaders of Saudi Arabia and Egypt.

13   The United Nations (UN) Security Council approves Resolution 666, which imposes controls over humanitarian food aid to Iraq and directs its agencies to determine the necessity for aid and the means of distribution.

16   The United Nations (UN) Security Council unanimously approves Resolution 667, which condemns the Iraqi violation of diplomatic compounds in Kuwait and demands the immediate release of foreign nationals held in Kuwait.

24   The United Nations (UN) Security Council passes without dissent Resolution 669, which requires an examination of requests from people trapped in Iraq and Kuwait and recommendations to the Security Council on prospective actions.

25   The United Nations (UN) Security Council passes Resolution 670, which tightens sanctions against Iraq to include a prohibition on all air transportation to that country.

October 1990

29   The United Nations (UN) Security Council passes Resolution 674, again condemning Iraq for mistreatment of foreign nationals and demanding their immediate release.

November 1990

6   The George H. W. Bush administration declares its intention to double American forces in the Persian Gulf to 400,000.

19   Iraq augments its forces in Kuwait.

28   The United Nations (UN) Security Council passes without dissent Resolution 677, which condemns Iraq's occupation of Kuwait and destruction of Kuwaiti civil records.

29   The United Nations (UN) Security Council passes Resolution 678 to authorize "all means necessary," after January 15, 1991, to ensure the removal of Iraqi forces from Kuwait. This resolution essentially permits an international coalition to go to war with Iraq if it does not end its Kuwaiti occupation by that date.

December 1990

6   Under considerable international pressure, the Iraqi government decides to release foreign nationals held since August 2.

January 1991

9   In an effort to avoid armed conflict, U.S. secretary of state James Baker meets with Iraqi foreign minister Tariq Aziz. Baker presents a letter from President George H. W. Bush essentially demanding that Iraq leave Kuwait, but Aziz refuses to deliver it to Iraqi president Saddam Hussein.

12   The U.S. Congress formally authorizes the use of force against Iraq.

15   The United Nations (UN) calls for immediate withdrawal of Iraqi forces to comply with UN Resolution 678.

17   Multinational forces begin an air assault on Iraqi military, communications, and command and control positions in both Kuwait and Iraq, initiating Operation DESERT STORM (the Persian Gulf War). American general H. Norman Schwarzkopf commands the combined allied forces. Argentina, Australia, Bahrain, Belgium, Canada, Denmark, Egypt, France, Germany, Greece, Italy, Kuwait, the Netherlands, Norway, Oman, Poland, Portugal, Qatar, Saudi Arabia, Spain, Syria, the United Arab Emirates, and the United Kingdom all provide military forces. Other nations provide financial, medical, and logistical support.

18   Iraq responds to the allied air attacks by launching Scud surface-to-surface missiles against Israel, hoping to draw that nation into the war and fracture the Arab alliance arrayed against it. The missiles contain conventional warheads rather than chemical or biological agents, as previously feared. Bolstered by the commitment of the United States to rush antimissile Patriot missiles to Israel, Israel does not retaliate, and the Arab nations maintain their presence in the coalition to force the Iraqi Army from Kuwait.

17   From January 17 to February 24, 1991, the air offensive moves through four phases. The first phase is the destruction of Iraqi air defenses and offensive aircraft, along with communications, transportation, and nuclear, biological, and chemical production capacity. The second phase is to cut off those Iraqi forces not in the area of Kuwait from reinforcing there. The third phase is the destruction and demoralization of Iraqi forces in Kuwait. The final phase is preparation for the ground offensive.

February 1991

24   Beginning of the coalition ground assault on Iraq. The United States deploys some 530,000 military personnel and 2,000 tanks, supported by 1,376 aircraft and 108 warships (including 6 aircraft carriers and 2 battleships) deployed to the Persian Gulf. There are also 90,000 Saudis with 550 tanks, 40,000 Egyptians with 400 tanks, and 35,000 soldiers from the United Kingdom with 292 tanks. The allies add 444 additional combat aircraft as well as warships that include an aircraft carrier and 12 other ships from France and 11 destroyers and frigates from the United Kingdom. The Iraqis possess an army of some 1.1 million men, half of them in the Kuwaiti theater, with 4,300 tanks, 660 combat aircraft, and 87 naval vessels.

25   The U.S. Army 101st Airborne Division severs a key highway in the Euphrates Valley, isolating Iraq's reserves from supporting combat units in Kuwait and southern Iraq. An Iraqi counterattack fails to arrest the allied momentum. Meanwhile, in the most deadly such attack

of the war, an Iraqi Scud missile strikes a U.S. barracks in Saudi Arabia, killing 28 and wounding 98 others.

28   Almost exactly 100 hours after the ground war begins and with U.S. and allied forces poised to invade Iraq itself, U.S. president George H. W. Bush calls an end to the war. Iraq agrees to a cease-fire. Iraq's defeat is complete, with some 30,000–35,000 killed or wounded. Allied casualties are 240 killed and 775 wounded. President Bush's decision not to pursue Iraqi forces into Baghdad and topple President Saddam Hussein's regime is criticized by some, but the White House contends that getting rid of Hussein was not the coalition's stated purpose and that it would cause Arab nations to withdraw from the coalition and would likely lead to chaos in Iraq.

March 1991

1   After public encouragement from the United States and expecting American and coalition support, the Shia Arabs of southern Iraq begin a revolt against continued rule by Saddam Hussein and his Baath Party. The Shia revolt rapidly spreads.

2   The United Nations (UN) Security Council passes Resolution 686, which defines the terms of the Persian Gulf War cease-fire. These include Iraqi release of prisoners of war and those detained before the war, formal renunciation of annexation of Kuwait, restitution for damages caused by the invasion, and the prompt disclosure and mapping of minefields. UN forces would then be withdrawn from Iraq once all conditions had been met.

4   Iraqi Kurds rebel in northern Iraq, starting with the occupation of Rania near Sulaymaniyah. The Kurds take oil-rich Kirkuk on March 20.

April 1991

2   The United Nations (UN) Security Council passes Resolution 687, which demands the restoration of Kuwaiti sovereignty, validates all previous UN resolutions, demands Iraqi surrender of all weapons of mass destruction (WMDs) and missiles with a range of over 100 miles, and calls for the appointment of a UN commission to oversee the destruction of WMDs and long-range missiles. The U.S. military begins a search for WMDs and long-range missiles and also begins the destruction of Iraqi chemical weapons.

5   The provision in the cease-fire agreement ending the Persian Gulf War that allows Iraqi forces the use of helicopters for humanitarian purposes facilitates the brutal Iraqi suppression of the revolts of the Kurds and Shia by Iraqi forces. U.S. Central Command commander General H. Norman Schwarzkopf, who had agreed to the helicopter use, later admits to being taken in by the Iraqis. The United Nations (UN) Security Council passes Resolution

688, which condemns Saddam Hussein's regime for brutalizing its people, especially the Kurds and Shia. The resolution requires Iraq to allow international aid organizations to provide humanitarian assistance. Operation PROVIDE COMFORT begins on April 6. Although not mandated by Resolution 688, the U.S. and allied forces begin enforcing no-fly zones for Iraqi aircraft in both northern and southern Iraq. The resultant Operations NORTHERN WATCH and SOUTHERN WATCH are to prevent the Iraqi military from employing aircraft against the Kurds and Shia.

5   The Iraqi government announces the end of the Shia and Kurdish revolts. During its suppression of the revolts, Iraq had employed chemical weapons of mass destruction.

February 1993

26   Bombing of the World Trade Center in New York City by Muslim extremists with close ties to the Al Qaeda terrorist organization. The attack does little structural damage but results in 6 deaths and 1,042 wounded.

October 1994

8–10   Iraq deploys troops to the Kuwaiti border but withdraws in the face of United Nations (UN) Security Council protest and the movement of U.S., British, and French forces into the area.

April 1995

14   United Nations (UN) Security Council Resolution 986 establishes the Oil-for-Food Programme to provide relief for Iraqi citizens still suffering from disruptions caused by the Persian Gulf War. Loopholes in the program allow the Iraqi regime to use oil revenues for illicit rearmament, while President Saddam Hussein holds up the continued suffering of the Iraqi people as having been caused by the program. Corruption within the UN leads to widespread abuse of the program, while nations such as France and Germany make billions of dollars subverting the program.

August 1995

20   Iraq reveals documents that establish its attempt to develop a nuclear bomb.

May 1996

Osama bin Laden, leader of the Al Qaeda terrorist organization, returns to Afghanistan from Sudan. The Bill Clinton administration misses the opportunity to place bin Laden in custody.

June 1996

25   A truck bomb explodes outside Khobar Towers, home to half the U.S. force of 5,000 military personnel in Saudi Arabia. The blast kills 19 Americans and injures another 240. The U.S. government links the attack to Al Qaeda.

26   Failure of a coup backed by the U.S. Central Intelligence Agency (CIA) against Iraqi president Saddam Hussein.

August 1996

23   Osama bin Laden, leader of the Al Qaeda terrorist organization, issues a call for jihad against the United States for its continued military presence in Saudi Arabia.

31   Iraqi forces attempt to establish control of parts of Kurdish Iraq but fail and withdraw on September 2.

September 1996

3–4   The United States extends the Iraqi southern no-fly zone north into the suburbs of Baghdad.

December 1996

10   Funds finally flow into Iraq under Resolution 986 (passed in April 1995) that created the Oil-for-Food Programme. The Iraqi government diverts considerable sums from humanitarian assistance, however.

October 1997

29   The Iraqi government demands the removal of United Nations (UN) weapons inspectors who are seeking information on weapons of mass destruction; removal occurs on November 13, 1997, but under international pressure they soon return to their duties.

February 1998

23   Al Qaeda leader Osama bin Laden issues a fatwa against the enemies of Islam; topping his list is the United States, which he claims is the "root of all evil."

August 1998

7   Simultaneous bombings occur at the U.S. embassies in Kenya and Tanzania. Both actions are linked to the Al Qaeda terrorist organization.

20   The United States launches Operation INFINITE REACH, a series of cruise-missile attacks against targets in Afghanistan and Sudan, in retaliation for the August 7 bombings of the U.S. embassies in Kenya and Tanzania. Al Qaeda was reportedly culpable for the bombings.

26   The chief United Nations (UN) weapons inspector in Iraq, American Scott Ritter, resigns. He complains not only about the lax enforcement of post–Persian Gulf War resolutions concerning Iraq by the UN and the United States but also that Iraq did not have a weapons of mass destruction program that warranted inspection.

October 1998

26   The United Nations Special Commission (UNSCOM) established to investigate Iraqi chemical weapons reports that Iraq had VX nerve gas in spite of Iraqi claims to the contrary.

November 1998

1   Iraq declares that it will not cooperate with United Nations (UN) inspectors searching for weapons of mass destruction.

15   Under threat of force, Iraq pledges further cooperation with the United Nations (UN) on weapons inspections, leading to the cancellation of a planned punitive air strike by the United States.

December 1998

16–19   The decision by the Iraqi government to end cooperation with the United Nations (UN) on weapons inspection leads to Operation DESERT FOX, air strikes by U.S. and British aircraft against Iraqi air defense installations.

October 1999

15   The United Nations (UN) Security Council passes Resolution 1267, instituting economic sanctions against Afghanistan until the Taliban regime turns over Osama bin Laden, the leader of the Al Qaeda terrorist organization, to UN custody.

December 1999

17   The United Nations (UN) reorganizes its weapons inspection effort with passage of Security Council Resolution 1284. The resolution creates the United Nations Monitoring, Verification, and Inspection Commission (UNMOVIC). Iraq objects.

October 2000

12   The U.S. Navy Arleigh Burke–class destroyer *Cole,* anchored off the Yemeni port of Aden, comes under attack by a small boat laden with explosives. The suicide bombers, linked to the Al Qaeda terrorist organization, detonate the craft next to the ship. The explosion rips a large hole in the side of the ship and kills 17 sailors; 39 others are injured.

September 2001

11   Nineteen Al Qaeda suicide terrorists board four U.S. domestic aircraft flights in Boston, Newark, and Dulles Airport outside Washington, D.C. They hijack the planes in flight. One flight hits the North Tower of the World Trade Center in New York City at 8:46 a.m., another strikes the South Tower at 9:03 a.m., and the third slams into the Pentagon in northern Virginia at 10:03 a.m. The fourth plane, targeted for the White House or the U.S. Capitol building, crashes in western Pennsylvania after passengers overwhelm the hijackers but fail to control the aircraft. All 19 terrorists and 246 passengers and crew die, along with 2,603 in the collapse of the Twin Towers in New York and 125 at the Pentagon. Emergency personnel respond to the attacks, resulting in the deaths of 411 New York firefighters, police, and paramedics. Another 24 people thought to have been at the crash sites are missing, and there are serious injuries to rescue personnel and civilians near the attack areas. Both World Trade Center towers are completely destroyed, and seven nearby structures suffer complete destruction or severe damage. The Pentagon also sustains extensive structural damage.

14   U.S. deputy secretary of defense Paul Wolfowitz declares that the Global War on Terror must go beyond seeking out and destroying terrorist groups and must also punish nations that support terrorist activities.

20   Before a televised joint session of Congress, U.S. president George W. Bush introduces the term "Global War on Terror," blames the 9/11 attacks on the Al Qaeda terrorist organization based in Afghanistan, and demands that the Taliban government turn Al Qaeda leader Osama bin Laden over to the United States. Afghanistan refuses the demand. British and U.S. aircraft attack an Iraqi air defense installation in southern Iraq. Iraq denies any connection to September 11.

21   The George W. Bush administration claims a close connection between Saddam Hussein's Iraq and Al Qaeda, including training that supposedly took place on a model Boeing 707 aircraft at Salman Pak in Iraq.

23   Pakistan is the only country that continues to recognize the Taliban as the legitimate government in Afghanistan; Saudi Arabia and the United Arab Emirates had previously withdrawn recognition.

October 2001

7   The Taliban government of Afghanistan offers to try Osama bin Laden in an Islamic court. The U.S. rejects this and, along with the United Kingdom, begins bombing Afghanistan. This is the official opening of Operation ENDURING FREEDOM. Cruise missiles from American and British submarines and aircraft from two American aircraft carriers strike targets that include Kabul, Kandahar, and Jalalabad.

14   The Taliban government of Afghanistan offers to turn Al Qaeda leader Osama bin Laden over to a third nation for trial if the bombing ceases and the United States presents evidence of Al Qaeda involvement in the September 11 attack.

October–November 2001

Continuation of air attacks and Special Forces actions to destroy Afghan government communications, command, and control capabilities. Regional Afghan groups, such as the Northern Alliance, join the fight against Taliban forces. Meanwhile, thousands of Pashtun militia from Pakistan join the struggle on the side of the Taliban. Suspecting that Osama bin Laden and the Taliban leadership have moved into the Tora Bora mountains near the Afghan-Pakistani border, the United States employs Boeing B-52 Stratofortress bombers to strike suspected hiding places.

November 2001

9　A ground offensive in Afghanistan begins against Taliban and Al Qaeda forces in the Mazar-e Sharif area, a key concentration area for Taliban forces. Carpet bombing of the Chesmay Gorge at the entrance to Mazar-e Sharif allows forces of the Northern Alliance, supported by the United States, to sweep into the city.

10　The fall of Mazar-e Sharif permits forces of the Northern Alliance to take control of five northern provinces of Afghanistan.

12　The Taliban evacuates the Afghan capital of Kabul.

13　Al Qaeda and Taliban forces concentrate in the rugged Tora Bora region, utilizing the extensive cave complexes there.

15　A U.S. Hellfire missile targets Al Qaeda leaders near Gardez and kills several, including Muhammad Atef. Al Qaeda leader Osama bin Laden, however, remains elusive.

16　Continuation of bombardment of the Tora Bora mountain region and Special Forces operations. The United States undertakes the payment of Afghan militias to fight the Taliban and Al Qaeda. The siege of Kunduz begins.

25–26　The Afghan city of Kunduz falls to Northern Alliance forces after heavy bombardment by U.S. aircraft. Up to 5,000 Taliban and Al Qaeda fighters relocate across the border into northwestern Pakistan. U.S. and Afghan allies take hundreds of captives to Ala-i-Janghi near Mazar-e Sharif, where 300 rise up and attempt to take over the compound. The rebellion is quelled by allied ground forces and Lockheed AC-130 Spectre gunships. U.S. Central Intelligence Agency (CIA) officer Johnny Michael Spann, there to question prisoners, is killed, becoming the first American casualty of the Afghanistan War.

December 2001

5　Afghan leaders opposed to the Taliban agree in the course of a meeting in Bonn, Germany, to form an interim government after the defeat of the Taliban.

7　Taliban leader Mullah Mohammed Omar orders the evacuation of the city of Kandahar, the last major Taliban stronghold in Afghanistan. This follows intensive bombardment and ground attacks and includes several hundred U.S. marines, the first major American ground forces involved in the war. The Taliban also surrenders Spin Boldak on the Pakistani border.

12　The United Nations (UN) Security Council authorizes the International Security Assistance Force (ISAF) to help the interim Afghan government maintain order.

17　U.S., British, and allied Afghan forces overrun much of the Tora Bora mountain area. About 200 Taliban and Al Qaeda are killed in the fighting. Mullah Mohammed Omar and Osama bin Laden evade capture along with other Taliban and Al Qaeda leaders and an unknown number of fighters.

22　An interim Afghan government is established in Kabul, with Hamid Karzai as its chairman.

January 2002

9　Some 4,500 foreign peacekeepers under British leadership begin deployment in Afghanistan to support the interim government. The major focus will be security in the capital of Kabul.

29　During his State of the Union address, U.S. president George W. Bush declares Iraq part of the "Axis of Evil" that also includes Iran and North Korea, all of whom, he claims, are trying to develop weapons of mass destruction (WMDs).

March–May 2002

United Nations (UN) secretary-general Kofi Annan tries unsuccessfully to persuade Iraq to allow the return of weapons inspectors.

June 2002

13　The Afghan Loya Jirga (grand council) elects Hamid Karzai as head of state (interim president) until elections can be held in 2004.

July 2002

5–6　After the failure of his efforts in early 2002 to secure the renewal of United Nations (UN) weapons inspections, UN secretary-general Kofi Annan enters into personal talks with Iraqi foreign minister Naji Sabri. The negotiations fail.

25　The Iraqi government declares that arms inspections must be accompanied by the lifting of sanctions against Iraq and an end to the northern and southern no-fly zones.

September 2002

12   U.S. president George W. Bush addresses a special session of the United Nations (UN) and declares the need for a coordinated plan of action against Iraq. Iraq rejects this and states that it will not engage in discussions about weapons inspections unless the United States promises not to sponsor any more punitive resolutions against Iraq.

22   The British government releases information, later proved to be erroneous, indicating that Iraq has significant weapons of mass destruction (WMDs).

November 2002

8   United Nations (UN) Security Council Resolution 1441 demands that Iraq cooperate with its weapons inspectors and cease placing obstacles in their path. The resolution also demands that Iraq declare the destruction of all weapons of mass destruction (WMDs) by December 8, 2002. The United Nations Monitoring, Verification, and Inspection Commission (UNMOVIC) begins inspections.

December 2002

7   The Iraqi government presents documents detailing the destruction of all weapons of mass destruction (WMDs). U.S. experts declare that the documentation is neither complete nor convincing.

January 2003

27   United Nations Monitoring, Verification, and Inspection Commission (UNMOVIC) chief inspector Hans Blix and United Nations (UN) Atomic Energy Commission chief Mohammed ElBaradei present reports to the UN. Both acknowledge that Iraq has not convinced the international community that it has revealed all the details of its weapons of mass destruction (WMDs) programs.

February 2003

5   Armed with what is later revealed as a deeply flawed intelligence estimate, U.S. secretary of state Colin Powell addresses the United Nations (UN) Security Council plenary session charging that Iraq has or is developing weapons of mass destruction. Powell argues unsuccessfully in favor of UN-sanctioned international military action against Iraq.

March 2003

1   Iraq begins the destruction of some long-range missiles in response to demands during an Arab summit held in Sharm al-Sheikh, but that meeting does not call for regime change in Iraq, which is now a central demand of the United States and its allies.

7   United Nations Monitoring, Verification, and Inspection Commission (UNMOVIC) chief inspector Hans Blix reports to the United Nations (UN) Security Council regarding a U.S. and British resolution authorizing war with Iraq. Opposition to the resolution comes from France, Russia, Germany, and most of the Arab states.

18   The U.S. government unveils the so-called Coalition of the Willing, 30 nations agreeing to associate themselves with the United States in military action against Iraq; 15 more nations will provide support.

19   Operation IRAQI FREEDOM begins with a U.S. air attack on a conference of high-ranking Iraqi leaders where Saddam Hussein is expected to appear. Hussein escapes harm.

20   Beginning of a massive U.S. air assault on Iraq, described as shock-and-awe bombardment by the Pentagon. Coalition forces also commence a ground invasion of southern Iraq and initially meet little opposition. Allied troops later face more severe resistance at Basra and Um Qasr in the south and Nasiriyah on the road to Baghdad.

April 2003

9   U.S. forces take the city of Baghdad amid a highly symbolic and much-publicized toppling of a large statue of Saddam Hussein in Firdos Square.

24   The Quartet, consisting of the United States, Russia, the European Union (EU), and the United Nations (UN), supports a peace initiative between the Palestinians and Israelis known as the Road Map to Peace in the Middle East.

30   The United States releases the details of the Road Map to Peace initiative.

May 2003

1   Aboard the U.S. aircraft carrier *Abraham Lincoln* off the coast of San Diego, California, before a large "Mission Accomplished" banner, President George W. Bush declares an end to major combat operations in Iraq. Iraqi president Saddam Hussein is still at large, however. Iraqi forces also continue sporadic fighting against U.S. and coalition forces.

6   U.S. president George W. Bush appoints L. Paul Bremer to head the Coalition Provisional Authority (CPA) in Iraq. Bremer's controversial actions include removing all Baath Party officials from the Iraqi government (Iraq's only trained administrators) and releasing thousands of Iraqi Army prisoners of war (potential insurgent recruits).

June 2003

4   Israeli prime minister Ariel Sharon and Palestinian prime minister Mahmoud Abbas meet with President

George W. Bush at Aqaba and agree to abide by the terms of the Road Map to Peace. The United States Coordinating and Monitoring Mission (USCMM) is established by the Bush administration to advance the Road Map to Peace initiative.

July 2003

14   A U.S.-appointed Iraq Interim Council meets for the first time.

16   The U.S. military characterizes the resistance in Iraq as a "classic guerrilla-type campaign."

22   Suppression of resistance to allied occupation continues as former Iraqi dictator Saddam Hussein's two sons, Uday and Qusay, are killed in a shootout with U.S. forces.

August 2003

11   Forces of the North Atlantic Treaty Organization (NATO) assume responsibility for security in the Afghan capital of Kabul, simplifying a complex command structure for 5,500 troops assigned this duty.

19   Iraqi insurgents bomb the United Nations (UN) compound in Baghdad, leaving at least 20 people dead. Among those killed is the top UN envoy in Iraq, Brazilian native Sergio Vieira de Mello.

22   U.S. forces in Iraq capture Ali Majid, known as "Chemical Ali" for his role in the notorious poison gas attacks on the Kurds in northern Iraq.

29   Iraqi resistance to coalition forces continues, with Sunni insurgents targeting Shia, who were long persecuted under Sunni rule.

September 2003

24   Palestinian militants in Gaza fire on a United States Coordinating and Monitoring Mission (USCMM) convoy.

October 2003

15   Thinking they were attacking a United States Coordinating and Monitoring Mission (USCMM) convoy, Palestinian militants in Gaza mistakenly bomb an American diplomatic convoy that was on its way to interview candidates for Fulbright fellowships. Three security guards are killed, and a fourth is seriously wounded.

16   United Nations (UN) Security Council Resolution 1511 recognizes the U.S.-supported Iraqi government, authorizes UN aid supervised by the United States, and calls for a timetable for return to Iraqi self-governance.

November 2003

1   Members of the United States Coordinating and Monitoring Mission (USCMM) start leaving Israel/Palestine,

the mission all but dead following the October 15 attack in Gaza.

December 2003

13   U.S. forces capture deposed Iraqi dictator Saddam Hussein.

January 2004

4   The Afghan Loya Jirga (Grand Council) approves a constitution with provisions for a strong executive.

March 2004

1   As the insurgency against the U.S.-led coalition's occupation of the country continues, the Iraqi interim government agrees to an interim constitution approved by the United States.

11   Terrorists in Madrid, Spain, launch a series of coordinated bombings against the Cercanías (commuter train) system in the Spanish capital. Known as the Madrid Train Bombings, 3/11, and in Spanish as 11-M, the bombings kill 191 people and wound 1,800. The bombings occur three days before the Spanish general elections. An official Spanish investigation determines that the attacks were committed by a Spanish Al Qaeda terrorist cell.

31   Insurgents kill four security contractors employed by Blackwater, Inc., in Fallujah. They drag the bodies through the streets and then hang them on a bridge over the Euphrates River.

April 2004

4   An attack by the Mahdi militia organized by Muqtada al-Sadr on Najaf and Karbala signals the organized resistance of Iraqi Shias to the national government and the U.S. occupation.

18   The new Spanish government announces that it will recall immediately 1,300 Spanish troops serving in Iraq.

May 2004

4   U.S. Army major general Antonio Taguba announces results of an investigation ordered on January 24, 2004, confirming prisoner abuses at Abu Ghraib Prison by members of the 800th Military Police Brigade.

June 2004

7   United Nations (UN) Security Council Resolution 1546 recognizes the new Iraqi interim government and urges member states to support it.

28   President Iyad Alawi takes power in Iraq in a low-key ceremony; U.S. ambassador Paul Bremer leaves Iraq, and the North Atlantic Treaty Organization (NATO) pledges training assistance to Iraqi forces.

September 2004

30   Charles A. Duelfer, head of the Iraq Survey Group for the Central Intelligence Agency (CIA), returns to the United States and reports that there is no conclusive evidence of the presence in Iraq of weapons of mass destruction (WMDs), the George W. Bush administration's chief justification for the Iraq War.

October 2004

9   Hamid Karzai is elected president of Afghanistan with 55 percent of the popular vote.

November 2004

2   Incumbent president George W. Bush (Republican) wins reelection against challenger John Kerry (Democrat), signaling that U.S. policy in the Iraq and Afghanistan wars likely will remain unchanged.

7   Operation PHANTOM FURY, the Second Battle of Fallujah (November 7–December 23, 2004), focuses on Sunni rebels in the city, backed by forces claiming allegiance to Al Qaeda in Iraq and led by Abu-Musab al-Zarqawi. U.S. casualties are 95 killed and 560 wounded. Allied Iraqi casualties are 11 killed and 43 wounded. The insurgent death toll is approximately 1,350, while 1,500 are captured. President Iyad Alawi declares martial law to calm the situation pending the holding of parliamentary elections.

January 2005

30   Some 60 percent of eligible voters participate in Iraq's first free elections since Saddam Hussein came to power. Turnout for the parliamentary elections is heaviest among Shia Muslims and Kurds; Sunni participation is lower.

April 2005

6–7   Amid continued armed resistance to the national government, the Iraqi parliament chooses Jalal Talabani as president (April 6) and Ibrahim al-Jafari as prime minister (April 7).

May 2005

20   *The New York Times* reports abuse of prisoners by U.S. military forces at detention centers in Afghanistan.

September 2005

18   Afghans vote in parliamentary and provincial elections with about 50 percent turnout. The new assembly convenes on December 19, 2005. Significant disorder persists in the country outside of Kabul.

October 2005

15   Iraqi voters approve a constitution that declares Iraq to be an Islamic federal republic.

19   Former Iraqi dictator Saddam Hussein goes on trial before an Iraqi court in Baghdad. The particular charges relate to the killing of several hundred people in Dujail, Iraq, in 1982 during the Iran-Iraq War (1980–1988). The trial is televised throughout Iraq.

November 2005

19   U.S. marines kill up to 24 Iraqi civilians in Haditha. An investigation begins in January 2006, leading to charges on December 21, 2006, against eight of the marines.

December 2005

15   There is a heavy turnout among all Iraqis, including Sunnis, for elections to determine a permanent government. Iraqi Shia receive the most votes but not a decisive majority in the parliament.

April 2006

22   Following months of negotiations, Iraqi president Jalal Talabani appoints Nuri al-Maliki as prime minister to form a government.

May 2006

15   The North Atlantic Treaty Organization (NATO) announces an expansion of its role in Afghanistan, to include the entire country. NATO forces are to increase from 8,000 to 17,000 troops by October.

June 2006

7   A U.S. air strike near Baquba, Iraq, kills Abu Musab al-Zarqawi, leader of Al Qaeda in Iraq.

November 2006

5   An Iraqi court convicts former president Saddam Hussein of crimes against humanity and sentences him to death by hanging. Before his execution on December 30, Hussein tells U.S. Federal Bureau of Investigation (FBI) interrogators that he had misled the world to give the impression that Iraq had weapons of mass destruction (WMDs) in order to make Iraq appear stronger in the face of its enemy, Iran.

December 2006

6   The Iraq Study Group (ISG), a 10-member bipartisan U.S. study group, reports to President George W. Bush, recommending programs to rescue Iraq from a "grave and deteriorating" future. Recommendations include placing U.S. emphasis on training Iraqi Army and security forces.

30   Former president Saddam Hussein is executed by hanging in Baghdad.

January 2007

10   U.S. president George W. Bush announces a surge in American troops in Iraq to counter the growing insurgency. This will involve five additional combat brigades (as many as 30,000 troops), increasing the total of U.S. forces in Iraq to 160,000 over the next few months. By December 2007 Iraq's security environment reaches its best levels since early 2004, and that month's death toll of American troops is the second lowest of the entire war, while the Iraqi Interior Ministry announces similar results for civilian deaths. In July 2008 the death toll for U.S. forces drops to 13, the lowest monthly number since the 2003 invasion.

February 2007

10   U.S. Army general David Petraeus takes command of the Multi-National Force–Iraq.

March 2007

6   North Atlantic Treaty Organization (NATO) and Afghan forces begin Operation ACHILLES against the Taliban in southern Afghanistan. There is heavy fighting in Helmand.

27   The Iraqi parliament approves legislation allowing former members of Saddam Hussein's Baath Party to return to their posts, a major move toward achieving Sunni support for the fledgling Iraqi government.

April 2007

26   The Democratic Party–controlled U.S. Congress passes legislation calling for withdrawal of U.S. forces in Iraq. President George W. Bush vetoes the bill on May 1.

May 2007

13   United Nations (UN) and Afghan forces kill Mullah Dadullah, senior Taliban military commander in Afghanistan.

August 2007

26   The United Nations (UN) announces record opium production in Afghanistan, up 34 percent from 2006 levels. The Taliban uses proceeds from much of the drug production to purchase arms.

Spring 2008

    Intense presidential campaign begins in the United States leading to nomination of Senator John McCain as the Republican candidate and Senator Barack Obama as the Democratic candidate. McCain supports continued military efforts in Iraq, while Obama pledges withdrawal within 16 months of inauguration. Obama wins the presidency on November 4, 2008.

March 2008

11   Insurgent attacks in Iraq decline significantly. U.S. authorities announce that there were only 60 in January 2008 compared with 180 the preceding July.

April 2008

    The North Atlantic Treaty Organization (NATO) declares security its top priority in Afghanistan.

June 2008

15   Afghan president Hamid Karzai declares the intention of Afghan forces to attack Pakistani border areas if Pakistan does not subdue Taliban and Al Qaeda forces there.

July 2008

16   Beginning of a drawdown in U.S. forces in Iraq. There are now 150,000 troops in the country.

October 2008

16   The German Bundestag affirms Germany's commitment to provide military forces in Afghanistan but only in a noncombat role.

November 2008

27   The Iraqi parliament passes a Status of Forces Agreement with the United States, calling for a complete U.S. troop withdrawal from Iraq by December 31, 2010. However, language of the agreement suggests that either side could request reinsertion of U.S. combat forces if necessary.

February 2009

27   U.S. president Barack Obama announces his intention to increase American forces in Afghanistan by at least 17,000 personnel. Obama also announces his intention to withdraw U.S. combat troops from Iraq by August 31, 2010, leaving a residual of 35,000–50,000 support forces to train and provide support if needed to Iraqi forces.

March 2009

25   Britain announces its intention of keeping its 8,000 troops in Afghanistan for the foreseeable future.

April 2009

8   Showcasing a growing threat arising since the disintegration of the Somali national government in the 1990s, Somali pirates board the *Maersk Alabama*, a 30,000-ton

American-flagged cargo ship carrying relief supplies to Kenya. Hijackers take control of the ship 300 miles off the coast of Somalia with its crew of 20 Americans. USS *Bainbridge,* an American destroyer operating with other warships in the area to control piracy, intercepts the *Maersk Alabama* after its crew had retaken control, releasing it to continue its voyage. On April 12 Navy SEAL marksmen kill three pirates, capture one, and free the captain of the *Maersk Alabama,* who had been held hostage in the ship's lifeboat.

May 2009

11 Defense Secretary Robert Gates announces that General David McKiernan will be replaced as commander of International Security Assistance Force–Afghanistan by Lieutenant General Stanley McChrystal. The change of command reflects a new approach to the war in Afghanistan that will emphasize more special operations.

June 2009

2 The total of Americans killed in combat in Iraq reaches 3,453 (4,308 from all causes), with 3,345 of these since President George W. Bush's May 1, 2003, proclamation of the end of major combat operations.

July 2009

31 The multinational coalition comes to an end in Iraq, with the United States the last nation of the "coalition of the willing" having troops in the country. The Romanians and the Australians are the last two other nations to withdraw their forces. In all, 38 nations sent soldiers over a six-year period. Although the North Atlantic Treaty Organization (NATO) will retain a small troop training presence in the country, these units were never considered part of the international coalition. As of January 1, 2010, the Multi-National Force–Iraq will undergo an official name change, to the United States Forces–Iraq.

August 2009

19 In the deadliest day in Iraq since the U.S. handover of security in the cities to Iraqi authorities on July 30, six car bomb blasts rip Baghdad, killing 95 people and wounding several hundred others. The blasts show that the insurgents still have the ability to strike largely at will against major Iraqi installations.

21 Afghan citizens go the polls to elect a president. Sitting president Hamid Karzai is running for a second five-year term. Despite the presence of a legion of foreign observers and the deployment of troops at the polling places, turnout is generally light, especially in Taliban-controlled areas. Although the tabulation takes weeks, the election results are hotly disputed, with widespread irregularities reported. Karzai's principal opponent, Abdullah Abdullah, claims that Karzai has stolen the election, which was to have gone into a runoff in October because no candidate received a majority in the initial balloting. Abdullah refuses to stand in a runoff election, however, and Karzai is declared the winner of a second five-year term as president.

October 2009

17 Following a series of suicide bomb attacks mounted by the Taliban against both civilian and top security targets in Pakistan, the Pakistani Army begins a major offensive against the Al Qaeda terrorist organization and the Taliban in their stronghold of southern Waziristan.

25 In the deadliest bomb blasts since 2007, two massive synchronized truck bombs explode in Baghdad, killing at least 155 people and wounding more than 500. The blasts raise new questions about Iraqi government security efforts trumpeted by Prime Minister Nuri al-Maliki, who had recently ordered blast walls removed from dozens of streets in the capital and from in front of the very buildings targeted in the blasts.

December 2009

1 In a much-anticipated address to the nation at the United States Military Academy, West Point, U.S. president Barack Obama announces that he will send 30,000 additional U.S. forces to Afghanistan but that the United States will begin handing over security arrangements to the Afghan government by the middle of 2011 to allow the beginning of a drawdown in American forces.

4 North Atlantic Treaty Organization (NATO) officials announce that some two dozen member states will contribute an additional 7,000 men to the fighting in Afghanistan. This announcement follows U.S. president Barack Obama's decision to dispatch 30,000 additional U.S. forces to the war. The increase will be offset because some of the troops will be barred from fighting because of restrictions placed by their nations on participation in combat operations and because the Netherlands and Canada have already announced plans to withdraw nearly 5,000 troops over the course of the next two years.

6 Following months of haggling, members of the Iraqi parliament at last reach agreement on long-delayed legislation that is regarded as a key step toward national elections to be held in January 2010.

9 The government of Ukraine approves a $2.5 billion arms deal with the government of Iraq that will significantly

bolster the latter's forces before the U.S. pullout. The deal involves the production of 420 BTR-4 armored personnel carriers, 6 Antonov AN-32B twin-engine transport aircraft, and other military hardware.

25   Umar Farouk Abdulmutallab, a 22-year-old Nigerian, attempts to blow up Northwest Flight 253 from Amsterdam as it begins its descent into Detroit, Michigan.

The explosive device is PETN (pentaerythritol), which Abdulmutallab had hidden in his underpants and then removed and tried to ignite in his seat. This is the same explosive utilized by so-called shoe bomber Richard Reid in 2001 when he attempted to blow up another transatlantic flight with explosives hidden in his shoe.

DANIEL E. SPECTOR

Glossary

AAA   Antiaircraft artillery.

AAMs   Air-to-air missiles.

Abd   Arabic term meaning "slave" or "servant," often used in compound names.

ABM   Antiballistic missile.

ADC   Aide-de-camp (personal assistant to a flag officer).

AFV   Armored fighting vehicle.

ahl al-sunna wal-jamaa   Arabic for "people of the way" (or the Prophet), used to describe the community of Muslims. Often shortened to Sunni.

AK47   Russian-designed assault rifle, Automat Kalashnikov, manufactured throughout the communist bloc and considered to be one of the most successful infantry weapons of the 20th century.

al-futuhaat   Arabic name for the seventh-century battles that brought Islam to the region.

alim   A trained Muslim religious scholar. The plural form is "ulama."

Allah   Arabic for "God."

al-Quds   Arabic for "sacred" or "holy," only used in reference to the City of Jerusalem.

amphibious x   Military activity that involves landing from ships, either directly or by means of landing craft or helicopters.

annex   The action of one nation in which it takes control of another territory and makes it a part of itself.

anti-Semitism   Hostility against those of the Jewish faith.

armistice   An agreement between opposing sides in a conflict to suspend military actions for a period of time.

ASM   Air-to-surface missile.

autonomy   Self-government.

AWACS   The Airborne Warning and Control System is a mobile long-range radar surveillance and control center for air defense.

awlama   Arabic word for "globalization."

ayatollah   Arabic for "sign of God" and a title used for high-ranking Shiite clerics in Iran.

ballistics   The science of projectiles, divided into interior and exterior ballistics. Its aim is to improve the design of shells and projectiles so that increased accuracy and predictability are the result. Ballistics also deals with rockets and missiles.

bombing raid   A military tactic in which airplanes and seaplanes drop a successive number of bombs on specified targets within a short period of time.

breastworks   A barricade usually about breast high that shields defenders from enemy fire.

buffer zone A piece of territory between two opposing groups.

caliph From the Arabic word *khalifa*, or "successor," a title given to Muslim leaders who followed the Prophet Muhammad as leader of the community after his death.

cease-fire A cease-fire, which occurs during times of war, may involve a partial or temporary cessation of hostilities. A cease-fire can also involve a general armistice or a total cessation of all hostilities.

coastal defense The defense of a nation's coast from an enemy sea invasion or blockade, accomplished with heavy artillery, mines, small warships, and nets.

Cold War The period of economic and military competition between the communist nations, led by the Soviet Union, and the capitalist nations, led by the United States, from the late 1940s to the early 1990s.

Crusades A number of military pilgrimages blessed by the pope in Rome and determined to retake the holy sites of the Middle East for Christian Europe. The first Crusades initially set up European dominance in the region, but subsequent actions returned many sites to the hands of the Muslim leaders.

death squads Clandestine and usually irregular organizations, often paramilitary in nature, that carry out extrajudicial executions and other violent acts against clearly defined individuals or groups of people.

defense perimeter A defense without an exposed flank, consisting of forces deployed along the perimeter of a defended area.

deforestation The removal of the forest cover from an area.

demilitarized zone A piece of territory between two opposing zone groups in which military forces cannot be stationed.

desertification The process of desiccation or drying of climate in areas that historically experience a deficiency of precipitation. Desertification may be caused by climatic change, but the process may be exacerbated by removal of vegetation on desert margins.

dislocation The displacement of populations of people from one geographic location to another, most often caused by sudden and extreme situations of a political, military, or economic nature.

Druze A religious group based mainly in Lebanon and Syria.

echelon attack A refused advance on an enemy position, meaning that the advance occurred in sequence from right to left or vice versa in parallel but nonaligned formations. Ideally, an echelon attack would compel the reinforcement of those parts of the enemy line first assailed thereby weakening the latter parts and increasing the chances of breaching them, but more frequently such an attack becomes disorganized and falters in confusion.

economic warfare Compelling an enemy to submit either directly by action against its economic basis or indirectly through blockade or boycott.

electronic warfare The use of the electromagnetic spectrum to gain knowledge of the presence and movement of an opposing force and also to deny any opposing force the use of that spectrum.

emir Arabic title meaning "commander" or "prince."

enfilade To fire upon the length rather than the face of an enemy position. Enfilading an enemy allows a varying range of fire to find targets while minimizing the amount of fire the enemy can return.

envelopment To pour fire along the enemy's line. A double envelopment means to attack both flanks of an enemy, but this is a risky venture. A strategic envelopment is not directed against the flanks but rather is a turning movement designed at a point in the rear whereupon the enemy had to vacate his position to defend it.

espionage The practice of spying to learn the secrets of other nations or organizations. Espionage has always been an important component of any military operation.

ethics of war Rules, principles, or virtues applied to warfare.

ethnic cleansing A policy by which government, military, or guerrilla forces remove from their homes members of different ethnic communities considered to be enemies of the country.

Euphrates One of the two great rivers of Mesopotamia. The Euphrates is located to the west of the Tigris River.

fatwa
A judicial opinion made by a qualified Islamic scholar or mufti based on Sharia (Islamic law). Traditionally, fatawa were used to settle legal disputes and to establish precedence. In modern times, fatawa have been used to proclaim judgments against non-Muslims and to support political agendas.

firefight
A brief and violent exchange of small-arms fire between two opposing units rather than combat action between two larger forces during an assault.

fossil fuels
Materials rich in carbon and hydrogen, these compounds (primarily coal, petroleum oil, and natural gas) are produced by decayed living matter. They have served as the major fuels for the last 200 years.

friendly fire
Friendly fire describes the incidence of casualties incurred by military forces in active combat operations as a result of being fired upon by their own or allied forces.

Global Positioning System (GPS)
A series of satellites that broadcast navigational signals by ultraprecise atomic clocks, providing accurate positioning.

guerrilla
A type of warfare involving small groups, not part of the official government forces. A type of military action involving hit-and-run tactics against more powerful forces.

hafiz
Arabic for "guardian." A person who has memorized the entire text of the Qur'an in Arabic.

hajj
The annual pilgrimage to Mecca (in present-day Saudi Arabia) during the month of Dhul-Hijja in the Islamic lunar calendar. The hajj brings Muslims from all around the world to worship together. It is the fifth of the Five Pillars of Islam.

hegemony
The dominance of one nation over other nations, based on the dominant nation's transfer of core values and basic societal institutions rather than through military conquest.

hijab
Arabic for "cover." In many modern Muslim societies, *hijab* is used to refer to the head coverings or veils of women in public view.

Ikhwan al-Muslimin
Often translated in English as the Muslim Brotherhood (or Society of Muslim Brothers), founded by Hassan al-Banna.

imam
Arabic for "leader." Sunni Muslims use the term for the leader of the Islamic prayers. Shiite Muslims believe that the imam is the divinely chosen leader of the people.

indemnity
An amount of money paid by a nation defeated in war to the victor as compensation for damages it inflicted.

intelligence community
The intelligence community comprises the government agencies charged with gathering information (intelligence) about other countries' military abilities and general intentions in order to secure a country's foreign policy goals.

international waters
All waters apart from nations' territorial waters.

Islamic lunar calendar
The traditional dating system of most Muslim societies, also referred to as the *hijri* calendar. It takes as its starting point the *hijra* and is a purely lunar system; that is, each month is determined by the actual cycle of the moon. Because this calendar does not use any system of intercalating days, it is shorter than the solar calendar by an average of 11 days a year.

Islamist
Term used to refer to the movement of political Islam.

Ithnaashari Shiites
The largest subsect of Shiism, also referred to as the Twelvers or Imami Shiites. They follow the teachings of the Twelve Imams descended from Ali and Fatima and believe that the Twelfth Imam has been in a state of mystical occultation since the 10th century.

jet engine
An internal combustion engine in which hot exhaust gases generated by burning fuel combine with air, causing a rearward thrust of jet fluid to propel an aircraft.

Jordan River
A river that flows 198.4 miles (320 kilometers) from northern Israel, with tributaries in Syria, to the Sea of Galilee and thence through the nation of Jordan and the West Bank to the Dead Sea. The Jordan River's waters are a matter of importance and controversy to the nations of the area.

Kaaba
Structure at the center of the mosque in Mecca housing a mystical black stone. Muslims all over the world pray in the direction of the Kaaba, where Islamic tradition says that God's presence is most felt on Earth.

Kurds
A numerous people inhabiting Kurdistan, a region that is the combined areas of southeastern Turkey, northern Iraq, and western Iran. The Kurds speak an Indo-European language distantly related to Farsi, the language of Iran.

Lake Nasser
The reservoir impounded on the Nile River by the Aswan High Dam. The lake extends upstream into Sudan, where it is called Lake Nubia.

Levant
The geographical area comprising Israel, the Palestinian territories, Jordan, Syria, and Lebanon.

madrasah
Arabic for "school." In common usage the word is used for religious schools. Originally, madrasahs were institutions developed for the instruction of Islamic law. Madrasah courses have been expanded for the instruction of Muslim children in the ways of their community.

mandate
Official command from authority organization.

martial law
Martial law is the temporary military governance of a civilian population when the civil government has become unable to sustain order.

melee
Hand-to-hand combat resulting from an advance that has brought a body of troops into close quarters with an enemy.

mercenaries
Hired professional soldiers who fight for a state or entity without regard to political interests or issues.

Mesopotamia
Greek for "land between the rivers," the Arabic word is "Ma Bayn Nahrain." Both refer to the region known in the west as the Cradle of Civilization. Watered by the Tigris and Euphrates rivers, this area saw the rise of the Sumerian, Akkadian-Babylonian, and Assyrian civilizations. It is now a part of the nations of Iraq and Kuwait and includes parts of Iran, Turkey, and Syria.

militant
A supporter of a particular cause who utilizes aggressive, often violent action to make his or her point.

militarism
The view that military power and efficiency are the supreme ideals of the state.

mufti
A Muslim religious scholar charged with issuing religious opinions, or fatawa.

mujahideen
A term, meaning "those who engage in jihad," used to refer collectively to disparate groups of Islamic militants who fought against the Soviet occupation of Afghanistan in the 1980s.

Mutual Assured Destruction (MAD)
A Cold War term stressing nuclear deterrence between the United States and the Soviet Union to prevent a full-scale nuclear exchange. The doctrine was based on the premise that both superpowers had sufficient nuclear weapons to destroy each other many times over. Thus, if one superpower launched a nuclear first strike, the other would reply with a massive counterstrike, resulting in the total devastation of both nations.

Nasserism
A term coined from the name of Egyptian president Gamal Adbel Nasser. A particular form of Islamic nationalism grown from the policies and actions of Nasser.

nationalism
The understanding that a people organized into a nation are superior to another nation.

Nile River
The longest river in the world at more than 4,000 miles long, it is the primary water source for Egypt. The origins of the river are found in East Africa.

Nobel Prize
The Nobel Foundation was established in 1900 and awarded its first annual prize in 1901.

Non-Aligned Movement
The Non-Aligned Movement was initiated by many Third World nations during the 1950s and 1960s in an attempt to steer a course of neutrality between the United States and the Soviet Union in the atmosphere of the Cold War. These countries felt that they had nothing to gain from entering direct alliances with either of the two superpowers, although they frequently courted both sides in attempts to gain greater amounts of economic and military assistance. The Non-Aligned Movement first met at the Bandung Conference in Indonesia in 1955. International meetings were held periodically over the next two decades, but the neutral nations were never able to formulate any cohesive policies because of the wide variety of member countries. With the end of the Cold War, the Non-Aligned Movement lost any importance that it once held in international affairs.

nonproliferation
A collective term used to describe efforts to prevent the spread of weapons of mass destruction (WMDs) short of military means.

paramilitary Something paramilitary is organized after a military fashion.

paramilitary organizations Unofficial groups organized along military lines yet lacking the traditional role or legitimization of conventional or genuine military organizations.

pastoralism A way of life in which people care for, subsist upon, and control the movements of herds of large herbivorous animals, using their products such as meat, milk, skins, and wool. In the Mediterranean area the animals involved in pastoralism are most notably sheep, goats, cattle, horses, and camels.

peaceful coexistence An expression that describes the act of living together without hostility, peaceful coexistence is often a foreign policy goal of nations that wish to avoid war.

political machine A party organization staffed by city workers who were hired by the party into patronage jobs as a reward for their loyalty or service.

propellants Compounds used to move a projectile from the firing device to the target.

Prophet Refers to Muhammad. Islam theorizes that God's final revelation, completing the message of the prophets of Christians and Jews, came through his final prophet, Muhammad.

Ramadan A month of the Islamic lunar calendar when Muslims fast from dawn to dusk.

rationing Often implemented during a war, famine, or national emergency or in times of scarcity, rationing is a government policy consisting of the planned and restrictive allocation of scarce resources and consumer goods.

rearmament The process that a nation undertakes to rebuild its arsenal of weapons that were exhausted during a time of war or other military action.

refugee An individual who moves or is moved to another location.

renewable resource A resource that is constantly replenished so that it can be used sustainably. Examples are forests, fish, and other animal and plant populations.

retrograde An orderly retreat usually designed to move away from an enemy.

salat The five daily prayers conducted at dawn, midday, midafternoon, sunset, and evening. It is the second of the Five Pillars of Islam.

salient A military position that extends into the position of the enemy.

salvo The simultaneous firing of a number of guns.

SAM Surface-to-air missile.

sanctions Activities taken against a nation by other nations to pressure them into a change of policy. There are political, economic, and military sanctions.

satellite state A country that is under the domination or influence of another. The term was used to describe the status of the East European states during the Cold War.

sawm Arabic term for "fasting," the fourth pillar of Islam.

Scud missile Name given to a type of tactical ballistic missile developed by the Soviet Union during the years of the Cold War.

Semitic A family of languages including modern Arabic and Hebrew, based on ancient languages of the region of the Middle East.

shahada The first of the Five Pillars of Islam, it is the profession of faith for all Muslims. The profession translates into English as "There is no god but God, and Muhammad is his messenger."

Sharia General term connoting the whole of Islamic law.

Shatt al-Arab A tidewater estuary found at the mouths of the combined Tigris and Euphrates rivers and stretching to the Persian Gulf. A portion of the estuary forms part of the boundary between Iraq and Iran.

sheikh Term of respect for older men (fem., sheikha) referring to people of wisdom or religious knowledge.

Shiites Arabic expression for "partisans," referring to the partisans of Ali ibn Abi Talib, the cousin and son-in-law of the Prophet Muhammad. The Shiites, who now constitute about 10 percent of Muslims worldwide, support the claim that Ali and his family are the legitimate religious and political successors to the Prophet.

sortie One flight by one aircraft.

standing army Used since the Middle Ages, a standing army is a permanent military unit of paid soldiers.

Sunnis Arabic expression for "people of the way [of the Prophet] and the community" that refers to the majority Muslim community. After the death of the Prophet, the earliest Sunnis were those who supported determining Muhammad's successor through community consensus rather than through blood lineage.

takfir Arabic term used to declare that a Muslim group has strayed from the precepts of Islam. Often used by radical militant groups to justify violent actions against other Muslims. Al Qaeda is an extension of these radical Islamic fundamentalist groups, although Al Qaeda does not declare ordinary Arabs to be infidels.

Tigris One of the two great rivers of Mesopotamia. The Tigris is located to the east of the Euphrates. The major sources of the Tigris are in the eastern part of modern Turkey and in the Zagros Mountains of Iran, and with the Euphrates the Tigris flows into the head of the Persian Gulf.

traverse Sandbags or other obstacles placed along a trench to prevent enfilading fire.

UHF Ultrahigh frequency.

ulama Arabic term for "scholars" that refers to the body of knowledgeable scholars in Muslim society. Ulama often refers to the experts who study Sharia.

umma Arabic term for "people" that refers to the community of Muslims around the world.

urbanization The origin and growth of cities as areas of human habitation that include transportation, markets, government and religious buildings, and other infrastructure.

VHF Very high frequency.

VLF Very low frequency.

VSTOL Vertical and/or short takeoff and landing.

VTOL Vertical takeoff and landing.

Wahhabism A movement of scripturalist reformism initiated in the Arabian Peninsula by Muhammad ibn Abd al-Wahhab (d. 1792).

waqf Endowments of land revenue established for the financial support of religious institutions such as mosques, schools, and charitable facilities.

war crimes Violations of the laws and customs of war entailing individual criminal responsibility directly under international law.

war reparations Restitution usually imposed by the victorious party as part of the peace negotiations at the end of a war.

Zagros A mountain range in Iran that separates the Mesopotamian lowlands from the Iranian plateau. The Zagros marks the eastern margin of Mesopotamia.

zakat Arabic term for "almsgiving," the third pillar of Islam.

Selected Bibliography

Aarts, Paul, and Gerd Nonneman. *Saudi Arabia in the Balance: Political Economy, Society, Foreign Affairs.* New York: New York University Press, 2006.

Abbas, Mahmud. *Through Secret Channels: The Road to Oslo: Senior PLO Leader Abu Mazen's Revealing Story of the Negotiations with Israel.* Reading, UK: Garnet, 1997.

Abdo, Geneive, and Jonathan Lyons. *Answering Only to God: Faith and Freedom in Twenty-first Century Iran.* New York: Henry Holt, 2003.

Abrahamian, Ervand. *A History of Modern Iran.* New York: Cambridge University Press, 2008.

———. *Tortured Confessions: Prisons and Public Recantations in Modern Iran.* Berkeley: University of California Press, 1999.

Abrams, Dennis. *Hamid Karzai.* Langhorne, PA: Chelsea House, 2007.

Aburish, Said K. *Arafat: From Defender to Dictator.* New York: Bloomsbury, 1998.

Adnan, Abu-Odeh. *Jordanians, Palestinians, and the Hashemite Kingdom in the Middle East Peace Process.* Washington, DC: United States Institute of Peace Press, 1999.

Agha, Hussein, Shai Feldman, Ahmad Khalidi, and Zeev Schiff. *Track-II Diplomacy: Lessons from the Middle East.* Cambridge, MA: MIT Press, 2004.

Agresto, John. *Mugged by Reality: The Liberation of Iraq and the Failure of Good Intentions.* New York: Encounter Books, 2007.

Ajami, Fouad. *The Arab Predicament.* New York: Cambridge University Press, 1981.

———. *The Foreigner's Gift: The Americans, the Arabs, and the Iraqis in Iraq.* New York: Free Press, 2008.

Alfonsi, Christian. *Circle in the Sand: Why We Went Back to Iraq.* New York: Doubleday, 2006.

Algosaibi, Ghazi A. *The Gulf Crisis: An Attempt to Understand.* London: Kegan Paul International, 1993.

Ali, Jaffer. *Palestine and the Middle East: A Chronicle of Passion and Politics.* Tempe, AZ: Dandelion Books, 2003.

Alimi, Eitan. *The First Palestinian Intifada and Israeli Society: Political Opportunities, Framing Processes, and Contentious Politics.* London: Routledge, 2006.

Allawi, Ali A. *The Occupation of Iraq: Winning the War, Losing the Peace.* New Haven, CT: Yale University Press, 2007.

Amirahmadi, Hooshang, ed. *The United States and the Middle East: A Search for New Perspectives.* Albany: State University of New York Press, 1993.

Amos, Deborah. *Lines in the Sand: Desert Storm and the Remaking of the Arab World.* New York: Simon and Schuster, 1992.

Anderson, Irvine H. *Biblical Interpretation and Middle East Policy: The Promised Land, America, and Israel, 1917–2002.* Gainesville: University Press of Florida, 2005.

Anderson, Jon Lee. *The Fall of Baghdad.* New York: Penguin, 2004.

An-Na'im, Abdullahi Ahmed. *Islam and the Secular State: Negotiating the Future of Shari'a.* Cambridge, MA: Harvard University Press, 2008.

Ansari, Ali. *A History of Modern Iran since 1921: The Pahlavis and After.* Boston, MA: Longman, 2003.

Arkin, William M., Damian Durrant, and Marianne Cherni. *On Impact: Modern Warfare and the Environment; A Case Study of the Persian Gulf War.* Washington, DC: Greenpeace, 1991.

Arkin, William M., Joshua Handler, and Damian Durrant. *US Nuclear Weapons and the Persian Gulf Crisis.* Washington, DC: Greenpeace, 1991.

Asmar, Marwan. *Intifada II: Media & Politics.* Amman: Ad Dustour Commercial Presses, 2001.

Association of the United States Army. *Crusade: The Untold Story of the Persian Gulf War.* New York: Mariner Books, 1994.

———. *Operation Desert Shield and Desert Storm: The Logistics Perspective.* Arlington, VA: Institute of Land Warfare, 1991.

———. *The US Army in Operation Desert Shield: An Overview.* Arlington, VA: Institute of Land Warfare, 1991.

Atkinson, Rick. *In the Company of Soldiers: A Chronicle of Combat.* New York: Henry Holt, 2005.

Azza, Henry T. *The Arab World: Facing the Challenge of the New Millennium.* London: I. B. Tauris, 2002.

Baer, Robert. *The Devil We Know: Dealing with the New Iranian Superpower.* New York: Random House, 2007.

Bahmanyar, Mir. *Shadow Warriors: A History of the US Army Rangers.* Oxford, UK: Osprey, 2006.

Bahrampour, Tara. *To See and See Again: A Life in Iran and America.* New York: Farrar, Straus and Giroux, 1999.

Bailey, Sydney Dawson. *Four Arab-Israeli Wars and the Peace Process.* Basingstoke, UK: Macmillan, 1990.

Ball, George W., and Douglas B. Ball. *The Passionate Attachment: America's Involvement with Israel.* New York: Norton, 1992.

Baram, Amatzia. *Building toward Crisis: Strategy for Survival.* Washington, DC: Washington Institute for Near East Policy, 1998.

Barari, Hassan A. *Israel and the Decline of the Peace Process, 1996–2003.* Abu Dhabi: Emirates Center for Strategic Studies and Research, 2003.

Barkey, Henri J., and Graham E. Fuller. *Turkey's Kurdish Question.* Lanham, MD: Rowman and Littlefield, 1998.

Barnea, Amalia, and A. Barnea. *Mine Enemy.* London: Halban, 1989.

Barnett, Michael N. *Dialogues in Arab Politics: Negotiations in Regional Order.* New York: Columbia University Press, 1999.

Baroud, Ramzy, et al. *The Second Palestinian Intifada: A Chronicle of a People's Struggle.* London: Pluto, 2006.

Barthop, Michael. *Afghan Wars and the Northwest Frontier, 1839–1947.* New York: Cassell, 2002.

Bashiriyeh, Hossein. *The State and Revolution in Iran.* New York: St. Martin's, 1984.

Batatu, Hanna. *Syria's Peasantry, the Descendants of Its Lesser Rural Notables, and Their Politics.* Princeton, NJ: Princeton University Press, 1999.

Beinin, Joel, and Rebecca L. Stein. *The Struggle for Sovereignty: Palestine and Israel, 1993–2005.* Stanford, CA: Stanford University Press, 2006.

Bennis, Phyllis, and Michel Moushabek, eds. *Beyond the Storm: A Gulf Crisis Reader.* New York: Olive Branch Press, 1991.

Benvenisti, Meron. *Intimate Enemies: Jews and Arabs in a Shared Land.* Berkeley: University of California Press, 1995.

Berberoglu, Berch. *Power and Stability in the Middle East.* London: Zed Books, 1989.

———. *Turmoil in the Middle East.* Albany, NY: SUNY Press, 1999.

Bergen, Peter L. *The Osama bin Laden I Know: An Oral History of Al Qaeda's Leader.* New York: Free Press, 2006.

Berry, Mike, and Greg Philo. *Israel and Palestine: Competing Histories.* London: Pluto, 2006.

Bethlehem, D. L., ed. *The Kuwait Crisis: Sanctions and Their Economic Consequences.* Cambridge, UK: Grotius, 1991.

Bhatia, Michael, and Mark Sedra. *Afghanistan, Arms and Conflict: Armed Groups, Disarmament and Security in a Post-War Society.* New York: Routledge, 2008.

Biddle, Stephen. *Afghanistan and the Future of Warfare: Implications for Army and Defense Policy.* Carlisle, PA: Strategic Studies Institute, 2002.

Bin, Alberto, Richard Hill, and Archer Jones. *Desert Storm: A Forgotten War.* Westport, CT: Praeger, 1998.

Binachi, Robert R. *Guests of God: Pilgrimage and Politics in the Islamic World.* New York: Oxford University Press, 2004.

Blackwell, James. *Thunder in the Desert: The Strategy and Tactics of the Persian Gulf War.* New York: Bantam Books, 1991.

Blincoe, Nicholas. *Peace under Fire: Israel/Palestine and the International Solidarity Movement.* London: Verso, 2004.

Bloxham, Donald. *The Great Game of Genocide: Imperialism, Nationalism, and the Destruction of the Ottoman Armenians.* New York: Oxford University Press, 2005.

Boaz, John, ed. *The U.S. Attack on Afghanistan.* Detroit: Thompson/Gale, 2005.

Bodansky, Yossef. *The Secret History of the Iraq War.* New York: Regan Books, 2004.

Bonin, John A. *U.S. Army Forces Central Command in Afghanistan and the Arabian Gulf during Operation Enduring Freedom: 11 September 2001–11 March 2003.* Carlisle, PA: Army Heritage Center Foundation, 2003.

Bourque, Stephen A. *Jayhawk! The VII Corps in the Persian Gulf War.* Washington, DC: Department of the Army, 2002.

Bowden, Mark. *Guests of the Ayatollah: The First Battle in America's War with Militant Islam.* New York: Atlantic Monthly, 2007.

Bowen, Jeremy. *Six Days: How the 1967 War Shaped the Middle East.* New York: Thomas Dunne Books, 2005.

Bowman, Steven R. *Iraq: U.S. Military Operations* [Electronic Resource]. Washington, DC: Library of Congress, Congressional Research Service, 2006.

Boyne, Walter J. *Beyond the Wild Blue: A History of the U.S. Air Force, 1947–2007.* 2nd ed. New York: Thomas Dunne Books, 2007.

———. *Operation Iraqi Freedom: What Went Right, What Went Wrong and Why.* New York: Forge Books, 2003.

Bragg, Rick. *I Am a Soldier, Too: The Jessica Lynch Story.* New York: Vintage, 2005.

Bremer, L. Paul, with Malcolm McConnell. *My Year in Iraq: The Struggle to Build a Future of Hope.* New York: Simon and Schuster, 2006.

Briscoe, Charles H., Richard L. Kiper, James A. Schroder, and Kalev I. Sepp. *Weapon of Choice: U.S. Army Special Operations Forces in Afghanistan.* Fort Leavenworth, KS: Combat Studies Institute Press, 2003.

Brockwell, Lord Butler of. *The Review of Intelligence on Weapons of Mass Destruction.* London: Stationery Office, 2004.

Brown, Ben, and David Shukman. *All Necessary Means: Inside the Gulf War.* London: BBC, 1991.

Brown, Nathan J. *Palestinian Politics after the Oslo Accords: Resuming Arab Palestine.* Berkeley: University of California Press, 2003.

Bulliet, Richard W. *Islam: The View from the Edge.* New York: Columbia University Press, 1994.

Bulloch, John, and Adel Darwish. *Water Wars: Coming Conflict in the Middle East.* London: Weidenfeld and Nicolson, 1995.

Bulloch, John, and Harvey Morris. *Saddam's War: The Origins of the Kuwait Conflict and the International Response.* London: Faber and Faber, 1991.

Bush, George, and Brent Scowcroft. *A World Transformed.* New York: Knopf, 1998.

Carothers, Thomas, and Marina Ottaway, eds. *Uncharted Journey: Promoting Democracy in the Middle East.* Washington, DC: Carnegie Endowment for International Peace, 2005.

Carter, Jimmy. *Palestine: Peace Not Apartheid.* New York: Simon and Schuster, 2007.

Cassidy, Robert. *Counterinsurgency and the Global War on Terror: Military Culture and Irregular War.* Palo Alto, CA: Stanford University Press, 2008.

Cavaleri, David. *Easier Said Than Done: Making the Transition between Combat Operations and Stability Operations.* Fort Leavenworth, KS: Combat Studies Institute Press, 2005.

Chubin, Shahram. *Iran's National Security Policy: Capabilities, Intentions and Impact.* Washington, DC: Carnegie Endowment for International Peace, 1994.

Catherwood, Christopher. *Churchill's Folly: How Winston Churchill Created Modern Iraq.* New York: Carroll and Graf, 2004.

Chandrasekaran, Rajiv. *Imperial Life in the Emerald City: Inside Iraq's Green Zone.* New York: Viking Books, 2007.

Chehab, Zaki. *Iraq Ablaze: Inside the Insurgency.* New York: I. B. Tauris, 2006.

Claire, Rodger William. *Raid on the Sun: Inside Israel's Secret Campaign That Denied Saddam the Bomb.* New York: Broadway Books, 2004.

Clark, Bruce. *Twice a Stranger: The Mass Expulsions That Forged Modern Greece and Turkey.* Cambridge, MA: Harvard University Press, 2006.

Clements, Frank A. *Conflict in Afghanistan: A Historical Encyclopedia.* Santa Barbara, CA: ABC-CLIO, 2003.

Cleveland, William L. *A History of the Modern Middle East.* 3rd ed. Boulder, CO: Westview, 2004.

Cobban, Helena. *The Israeli-Syrian Peace Talks: 1991–96 and Beyond.* Washington, DC: U.S. Institute of Peace Press, 2000.

Cockburn, Andrew, and Patrick Cockburn. *Out of the Ashes: The Resurrection of Saddam Hussein.* New York: HarperCollins, 2000.

Cockburn, Patrick. *Muqtada: Muqtada al-Sadr, the Shia Revival, and the Struggle for Iraq.* New York: Scribner, 2008.

———. *The Occupation: War and Resistance in Iraq.* New York: Verso, 2007.

Cohen, Roger, and Claudio Gatti. *In the Eye of the Storm: The Life of General H. Norman Schwarzkopf.* New York: Farrar, Straus and Giroux, 1992.

Collins, John. *Desert Shield and Desert Storm: Implications for Future US Force Requirements.* Washington, DC: Congressional Research Service, 1991.

Combat Studies Institute, Contemporary Operations Study Group. *A Different Kind of War: The United States Army Operation Enduring Freedom (OEF), September 2001–September 2005.* Fort Leavenworth, KS: Combat Studies Institute Press, 2009.

Connelly, Matthew. *A Diplomatic Revolution: Algeria's Fight for Independence and the Origins of the Post–Cold War Era.* New York: Oxford University Press, 2002.

Cook, David. *Understanding Jihad.* Berkeley: University of California Press, 2005.

Cook, Steven A. *Ruling but Not Governing: The Military and Political Development in Egypt, Algeria, and Turkey.* Baltimore: Johns Hopkins University Press, 2007.

Cooley, John K. *Payback: America's Long War in the Middle East.* Washington, DC: Brassey's, 1991.

Coopersmith, Nechemia, and Shraga Simmons. *Israel: Life in the Shadow of Terror: Personal Accounts and Perspectives from the Heart of the Jewish People.* Southfield, MI: Targum, 2003.

Cordesman, Anthony. *Arab-Israeli Military Forces in an Era of Asymmetric Wars.* Westport: Praeger, 2006.

———. *Iran's Military Forces in Transition: Conventional Threats and Weapons of Mass Destruction.* Westpoint, CT: Praeger, 1999.

———. *Iraqi Security Forces: A Strategy for Success.* Westport, CT: Praeger Security International, 2005.

———. *The Iraq War: Strategy, Tactics, and Military Lessons.* Westport, CT: Praeger, 2003.

Cordesman, Anthony H., and Abraham R. Wagner. *The Lessons of Modern War,* Vol. 4, *The Gulf War.* Boulder, CO: Westview, 1996.

Cornelius, Peter K. *The Arab World Competitiveness Report, 2002–2003.* New York: World Economic Forum, 2003.

Cornum, Rhonda, as told to Peter Copeland. *She Went To War: The Rhonda Cornum Story.* Novato, CA: Presidio, 1992.

Coughlin, Con. *Saddam: King of Terror.* New York: Gale, 2003.

Crews, Robert D., and Amin Tarzi, eds. *The Taliban and the Crisis of Afghanistan.* Cambridge, MA: Harvard University Press, 2008.

Crystal, Jill. *Kuwait: The Transformation of an Oil State.* Boulder, CO: Westview, 1992.

Curtis, Michael, ed. *Religion and Politics in the Middle East.* Boulder, CO: Westview, 1981.

Daalder, Ivo H., Nicole Gnesotto, and Philip H. Gordon. *Crescent of Crisis: U.S.-European Strategy for the Greater Middle East.* Washington, DC: Brookings, 2006.

Dale, Catherine. *War in Afghanistan: Strategy, Military Operations, and Issues for Congress.* Washington, DC: Congressional Research Service, Library of Congress, 2009.

Dannreuther, Rolan. *The Gulf Conflict: A Political and Strategic Analysis.* Aldelphi Paper No. 264. London: IISS, 1991–1992.

Darius, Robert G., John W. Amos II, and Ralph H. Magnus, eds. *Gulf Security in the 1980s.* Stanford: Hoover Press, 1984.

Darraj, Susan Muaddi. *Bashar Al-Assad.* New York: Chelsea House, 2005.

———. *Hosni Mubarak.* New York: Chelsea House, 2007.

Davis, Joyce M. *Martyrs: Innocence, Vengeance, and Despair in the Middle East.* New York: Palgrave Macmillan, 2003.

DeLong, Michael, with Noah Lukeman. *Inside CENTCOM: The Unvarnished Truth about the Wars in Afghanistan and Iraq.* Washington, DC: Regnery, 2004.

Department of the Air Force. *Reaching Globally, Reaching Powerfully: The United States Air Force in the Gulf War.* Washington, DC: U.S. Government Printing Office, 1991.

Department of Defense. *Conduct of the Persian Gulf Conflict: An Interim Report to Congress.* Washington, DC: U.S. Government Printing Office, 1991.

———. *Conduct of the Persian Gulf War: Final Report to Congress.* Washington, DC: U.S. Government Printing Office, 1992.

Department of State. *Patterns of Global Terrorism, 1991.* Washington, DC: U.S. Government Printing Office, 1992.

DeYoung, Karen. *Soldier: The Life of Colin Powell.* New York: Knopf, 2006.

Diamond, Larry. *Squandered Victory: The American Occupation and the Bungled Effort to Bring Democracy to Iraq.* New York: Times Books, 2005.

Dickinson, William. *Defense for a New Era: Lessons of the Gulf War.* Washington, DC: Brassey's, 1992.

Diehl, Paul F. *A Road Map to War: Territorial Dimensions of International Conflict.* Nashville: Vanderbilt University Press, 1999.

Dietl, Wilhelm. *Holy War.* New York: Macmillan, 1985.

DiMarco, Louis A. *Traditions, Changes and Challenges: Military Operations and the Middle Eastern City.* Fort Leavenworth, KS: Combat Studies Institute Press, 2004.

Docherty, Bonnie L. *United States/Afghanistan: Fatally Flawed: Cluster Bombs and Their Use by the United States in Afghanistan.* New York: Human Rights Watch, 2002.

Donnelly, Thomas. *Operation Iraqi Freedom: A Strategic Assessment.* Washington, DC: AEI Press, 2004.

Dorronsoro, Gilles. *Afghanistan: Revolution Unending, 1979–2002.* London: C. Hurst, 2003.

Dreyfus, Robert. *Devil's Game: How the United States Helped Unleash Fundamentalist Islam.* New York: Metropolitan Books, 2005.

Drogin, Bob. *Curveball: Spies, Lies, and the Con Man Who Caused a War.* New York: Random House, 2007.

Dudley, William, ed. *The Attack on America, September 11, 2001.* San Diego: Greenhaven, 2002.

Dunnigan, James F., and Austin Bay. *From Shield to Storm: High-Tech Weapons, Military Strategy, and Coalition Warfare in the Persian Gulf.* New York: William Morrow, 1992.

———. *A Quick and Dirty Guide to War: Briefings on Present and Potential Wars.* 3rd ed. New York: Morrow, 1996.

Eban, Abba. *Diplomacy for the Next Century.* New Haven, CT: Yale University Press, 1999.

Eickelman, Dale F., and James Piscatori. *Muslim Politics.* Princeton, NJ: Princeton University Press, 1996.

Eland, Ivan. *Partitioning for Peace: An Exit Strategy for Iraq.* Oakland, CA: Independent Institute, 2008.

Elon, Amos. *A Blood-Dimmed Tide: Dispatches from the Middle East.* London: Penguin, 2001.

Engbrecht, Shawn. *America's Covert Warriors: Inside the World of Private Military Contractors.* Dulles, VA: Potomac Books, 2010.

Enderlin, Charles. *The Lost Years: Radical Islam, Intifada, and Wars in the Middle East, 2001–2006.* New York: Handsel Books, 2007.

Engel, Richard. *War Journal: My Five Years in Iraq.* New York: Simon and Schuster, 2008.

Epstein, Joshua M. *War with Iraq: What Price Victory?* Washington, DC: Brookings Institution, 1991.

Esposito, John L. *The Islamic Threat: Myth or Reality?* New York: Oxford University Press, 1992.

Fandy, Mamoun. *Saudi Arabia and the Politics of Dissent.* New York: St. Martin's, 1999.

Fawn, Rick, and Raymond A. Hinnebusch, eds. *The Iraq War: Causes and Consequence.* Boulder, CO: Lynne Rienner, 2006.

Feickert, Andrew. *U.S. and Coalition Military Operations in Afghanistan: Issues for Congress.* Washington, DC: Congressional Research Service, 2006.

Feldman, Noah. *The Fall and Rise of the Islamic State.* Princeton, NJ: Princeton University Press, 2008.

Feldman, Shai. *The Raid on Osiraq: A Preliminary Assessment.* Tel Aviv: Center for Strategic Studies, Tel Aviv University, 1981.

Fialka, John J. *The Hotel Warriors: Covering the Gulf.* Washington, DC: Woodrow Wilson Center, 1991.

Fiscus, James W. *America's War in Afghanistan.* New York: Rosen, 2004.

Fisk, Robert. *The Great War for Civilization: The Conquest of the Middle East.* New York: Vintage Books, 2007.

Fontenot, Gregory, et al. *On Point: The United States Army in Iraqi Freedom*. Annapolis, MD: Naval Institute Press, 2005.

Forbes, Archibald. *The Afghan Wars*. Whitefish, MT: Kessinger, 2004.

Ford, Peter S. *Israel's Attack on Osiraq: A Model for Future Preventive Strikes?* Colorado Springs, CO: USAF Institute for National Security Studies, United States Air Force Academy, 2005.

Francona, Rick. *Ally to Adversary: An Eyewitness Account of Iraq's Fall from Grace*. Annapolis, MD: Naval Institute Press, 1999.

Franks, Tommy, with Malcolm McConnell. *American Soldier*. New York: Regan Books, 2004.

Freedman, Lawrence, and Efraim Karsh. *The Gulf Conflict, 1990–1991: Diplomacy and War in the New World Order*. Princeton, NJ: Princeton University Press, 1993.

Freedman, Robert Owen. *The Intifada: Its Impact on Israel, the Arab World, and the Superpowers*. Miami: International University Press, 1991.

———, ed. *The Middle East after Iraq's Invasion of Kuwait*. Gainesville: University Press of Florida, 1993.

———, ed. *The Middle East and the Peace Process: The Impact of the Oslo Accords*. Gainesville: University Press of Florida, 1998.

Friedman, Norman. *Desert Victory: The War for Kuwait*. Annapolis, MD: Naval Institute Press, 1991.

Friedman, Thomas. *From Beirut to Jerusalem*. New York: Anchor Books, 1995.

Friedrich, Otto, ed. *Desert Storm: The War in the Persian Gulf*. Boston: Time Books, 1991.

Fuller, Graham E. *The New Turkish Republic: Turkey as a Pivotal State in the Muslim World*. Washington, DC: U.S. Institute of Peace, 2007.

Fuller, Graham E., and Rend Rahim Francke. *The Arab Shi'a: The Forgotten Muslims*. Hampshire, UK: Palgrave Macmillan, 2001.

Furnish, Timothy R. *Holiest Wars: Islamic Mahdis, Their Jihads, and Osama Bin Laden*. Westport, CT: Greenwood, 2006.

Gaddis, John Lewis. *Surprise, Security and the American Experience*. Cambridge, MA: Harvard University Press, 2005.

Galbraith, Peter. *The End of Iraq: How American Incompetence Created a War without End*. New York: Simon and Schuster, 2006.

Gause, F. Gregory. *Oil Monarchies: Domestic and Security Challenges in the Arab Gulf States*. New York: Council on Foreign Relations Press, 1994.

Gerges, Fawaz A. *America and Political Islam: Clash of Cultures or Clash of Interests?* New York: Cambridge University Press, 1999.

———. *The Far Enemy: Why Jihad Went Global*. New York: Cambridge University Press, 2005.

Gerrard, Howard. *U.S. Army Soldier: Baghdad 2003–04 (Warrior)*. Oxford, UK: Osprey, 2007.

Gheissari, Ali, and Vali Nasr. *Democracy in Iran: History and the Quest for Liberty*. New York: Oxford University Press, 2006.

Gittings, John, ed. *Beyond the Gulf War: The Middle East and the New World Order*. London: Catholic Institute for International Relations, 1991.

Gnesotto, Nicole, and John Roper, eds. *Western Europe and the Gulf*. Paris: Institute for Security Studies of WEU, 1992.

Goodson, Larry P. *Afghanistan's Endless War: State Failure, Regional Politics, and the Rise of the Taliban*. Seattle: University of Washington Press, 2001.

Gordon, Matthew. *Hafez Al-Assad*. New York: Chelsea House, 1989.

Gordon, Michael R., and General Bernard E. Trainor. *Cobra II: The Inside Story of the Invasion and Occupation of Iraq*. New York: Pantheon Books, 2006.

———. *The Generals' War: The Inside Story of the Conflict in the Gulf*. New York: Little, Brown, 1995.

Gordon, Philip, and Jeremy Shapiro. *Allies at War: America, Europe, and the Crisis over Iraq*. New York: McGraw-Hill, 2004.

Graham, Bradley. *By His Own Rules: The Ambitions, Successes, and Ultimate Failures of Donald Rumsfeld*. New York: PublicAffairs, 2009.

Graham-Brown, Sarah. *Sanctioning Saddam: The Politics of Intervention in Iraq*. London: I. B. Tauris, 1999.

Grau, Lester W., ed. *The Bear Went over the Mountain: Soviet Combat Tactics in Afghanistan*. London: Frank Cass, 1998.

Graveline, Christopher, and Michael Clemens. *The Secrets of Abu Ghraib Revealed*. Dulles, VA: Potomac Books, 2010.

Greenberg, Bradley S., and Walter Gantz, eds. *Desert Storm and the Mass Media*. Cresskill, NJ: Hampton Press, 1993.

Greffenius, Steven. *The Logic of Conflict: Making War and Peace in the Middle East*. Armonk, NY: M. E. Sharpe, 1993.

Guazzone, Laura, ed. *The Islamist Dilemma: The Political Role of Islamist Movements in the Contemporary Arab World*. Reading, UK: Garnet, 1996.

Guistozzi, Antonio. *Koran, Kalashnikov and Laptop: The Neo-Taliban Insurgency in Afghanistan*. New York: Columbia University Press, 2008.

Gunaratna, Rohan. *Inside Al Qaeda: Global Network of Terror*. New York: Berkley Publishing Group, 2003.

Gunning, Jeroen. *Hamas in Politics: Democracy, Religion, and Violence*. New York: Columbia University Press, 2008.

Haass, Richard. *The Opportunity: America's Moment to Alter History's Course*. New York: PublicAffairs, 2006.

———. *War of Necessity, War of Choice: A Memoir of Two Iraq Wars*. New York: Simon and Schuster, 2009.

Haass, Richard, and Martin S. Indyk, eds. *Restoring the Balance: A Middle East Strategy for the Next President*. Washington, DC: Brookings, 2008.

Hadar, Leon T. *Quagmire: America in the Middle East*. Washington, DC: Cato Institute, 1992.

———. *Sandstorm: Policy Failure in the Middle East*. New York: Palgrave Macmillan, 2005.

Hadawi, Sami. *The Middle East Reality: Between War and Peace*. Dallas, TX: American-Arab Society, 1974.

———. *The Realities of Terrorism & Retaliation*. Toronto: The Arab Palestine Association, 1987.

Hafez, Mohammed. *Suicide Bombers in Iraq: The Strategy and Ideology of Martyrdom.* Washington, DC: United States Institute of Peace Press, 2007.

Hajjar, Sami G. *Hezbollah: Terrorism, National Liberation, or Menace?* Carlise Barracks, PA: Strategic Studies Institute, U.S. Army War College, 2002.

Hall, John G. *Palestinian Authority: Creation of the Modern Middle East.* Langhorne, PA: Chelsea House, 2002.

Halliday, Fred. *Soviet Policy in the Arc of Crisis.* Washington, DC: Institute for Policy Studies, 1981.

Hallion, Richard P. *Storm over Iraq: Air Power and the Gulf War.* Washington, DC: Smithsonian Institution Press, 1997.

Hamdi, Mohamed Elhachmi. *The Politicization of Islam: A Case Study of Tunisia.* Boulder, CO: Westview, 1998.

Hamzeh, Nizar. *In the Path of Hizbullah.* Syracuse, NY: Syracuse University Press, 2004.

Hanson, Victor Davis. *Between War and Peace: Lessons from Afghanistan to Iraq.* New York: Random House, 2004.

Harik, Judith Palmer. *Hezbollah: The Changing Face of Terrorism.* London: I. B. Tauris, 2004.

Harms, Gregory, and Todd Ferry. *The Palestine-Israel Conflict: A Basic Introduction.* London: Pluto, 2005.

Hart, Alan. *Arafat: A Political Biography.* London: Sidgwick and Jackson, 1994.

Hashim, Ammed S. *Insurgency and Counter-insurgency in Iraq.* Ithaca, NY: Cornell University Press, 2006.

Hatina, Meir. *Islam and Salvation in Palestine: The Islamic Jihad Movement.* Syracuse, NY: Syracuse University Press, 2001.

Heikal, Mohammed Hasanyn. *Illusions of Triumph: An Arab View of the Gulf War.* London: HarperCollins, 1992.

Herb, Michael. *All in the Family: Absolutism, Revolution, and Democratic Prospects in the Middle Eastern Monarchies.* Albany: State University of New York Press, 1999.

Herring, Eric, and Glen Rangwala. *Iraq in Fragments: The Occupation and Its Legacy.* Ithaca, NY: Cornell University Press, 2006.

Hiro, Dilip. *Desert Shield to Desert Storm: The Second Gulf War.* Lincoln, NE: IUniverse, 2003.

Hodes, Cyrus, and Mark Sedra. *The Search for Security in Post-Taliban Afghanistan.* Adelphi Paper 391. Abingdon, UK: Routledge for the International Institute for Strategic Studies, 2007.

Holmes, Tony. *US Navy Hornet Units in Operation Iraqi Freedom.* 2 vols. Oxford, UK: Osprey, 2004–2005.

Hroub, Khaled. *Hamas: A Beginner's Guide.* London: Pluto, 2006.

———. *Hamas: Political Thought and Practice.* Washington, DC: Institute for Palestine Studies, 2000.

Hudson, Michael C. *Middle East Dilemmas: The Politics and Economics of Arab Integration.* New York: Columbia University Press, 1999.

Humphreys, Stephen. *Between Memory and Desire: The Middle East in a Troubled Age.* Berkeley: University of California Press, 1999.

Hunter, Shireen T. *The Future of Islam and the West: Clash of Civilizations or Peaceful Coexistence?* Westport, CT: Praeger, 1998.

Hunter, Shireen T., and Huma Malik. *Modernization, Democracy, and Islam.* Westport, CT: Praeger, 2005.

Huntington, Samuel. *The Clash of Civilizations and the Remaking of World Order.* New York: Simon and Schuster, 1998.

Hussain, Mehmood. *The Revolutionary Arabs: The Unfinished Agenda.* Delhi: Independent Publishing, 2003.

Hussain, Zahid. *Frontline Pakistan: The Struggle with Militant Islam.* New York: Columbia University Press, 2007.

Isikoff, Michael, and David Corn. *Hubris: The Inside Story of Spin, Scandal, and the Selling of the Iraq War.* New York: Three Rivers/Random House, 2007.

Jaber, Hala. *Hezbollah: Born with a Vengeance.* New York: Columbia University Press, 1997.

Jamal, Amaney A. *Barriers to Democracy: The Other Side of Social Capital in Palestine and the Arab World.* Princeton, NJ: Princeton University Press, 2007.

Jones, Seth G. *Counterinsurgency in Afghanistan: RAND Counterinsurgency Study No. 4.* Santa Monica, CA: RAND Corporation, 2008.

———. *In the Graveyard of Empires: America's War in Afghanistan.* New York: Norton, 2009.

Kagan, Frederick. *Finding the Target: The Transformation of American Military Policy.* New York: Encounter, 2006.

Karetzky, Stephen, and Norman Frankel. *The Media's Coverage of the Arab-Israeli Conflict.* New York: Shapolsky, 1989.

Karsh, Efraim. *Saddam Hussein: A Political Biography.* New York: Grove/Atlantic, 2002.

Karsh, Efraim, and Inari Karsh. *Empires of the Sand: The Struggle for Mastery of the Middle East, 1789–1923.* Cambridge, MA: Harvard University Press, 1999.

Katzman, Kenneth. *Afghanistan: Post-War Governance, Security, and U.S. Policy.* Washington, DC: Congressional Research Service, September 2008.

Keddie, Nikki R. *Modern Iran: Roots and Results of Revolution.* New Haven, CT: Yale University Press, 2003.

Keegan, John. *The Iraq War: The Military Offensive, from Victory in 21 Days to the Insurgent Aftermath.* New York: Vintage, 2005.

Kellerman, Barbara, and Jeffrey Z. Rubin. *Leadership and Negotiation in the Middle East.* New York: Praeger, 1988.

Kelsay, John. *Arguing the Just War in Islam.* Cambridge, MA: Harvard University Press, 2007.

Kemp, Geoffrey. *Forever Enemies? American Policy and the Islamic Republic of Iran.* Washington, DC: Carnegie Endowment for International Peace, 1994.

Kepel, Gilles. *Beyond Terror and Martyrdom: The Future of the Middle East.* Cambridge, MA: Harvard University Press, 2008.

Khadduri, Majid. *The Islamic Concept of Justice.* Baltimore: Johns Hopkins University Press, 1984.

Khalid bin Sultan, Prince, with Patrick Seale. *Desert Warrior: A Personal View of the Gulf War by the Joint Forces Commander.* New York: HarperCollins, 1995.

Khalidi, Rashid. *Resurrecting Empire: Western Footprints and America's Perilous Path in the Middle East.* Boston: Beacon, 2004.

Kilcullen, David. *The Accidental Guerrilla: Fighting Small Wars in the Midst of a Big One.* New York: Oxford University Press, 2009.

Kinzer, Stephen. *All the Shah's Men: An American Coup and the Roots of the Middle Eastern Terror.* Hoboken, NJ: Wiley, 2003.

Klieman, Aharon. *Constructive Ambiguity in Middle East Peace-Making.* Tel Aviv: Tami Steinmetz Center for Peace Research, 1999.

Knights, Michael. *Cradle of Conflict: Iraq and the Birth of Modern U.S. Military.* Annapolis, MD: Naval Institute Press, 2005.

Kostiner, Joseph. *The Making of Saudi Arabia, 1916–1936.* New York: Oxford University Press, 1993.

Kuran, Timur. *Islam and Mammon: The Economic Predicaments of Islamism.* Princeton, NJ: Princeton University Press, 2004.

Lambeth, Benjamin S. *American Carrier Air Power at the Dawn of a New Century.* Santa Monica, CA: RAND Corporation, 2005.

Larrabee, Stephen, and Ian O. Lesser. *Turkish Foreign Policy in an Age of Uncertainty.* Santa Monica, CA: RAND Corporation, 2002.

Laqueur, Walter, and Yonah Alexander, eds. *The Terrorism Reader: The Essential Source Book on Political Violence Both Past and Present.* New York: Signet, 1987.

Lauterpacht, E., C. J. Greenwood, Marc Weller, and David Bethlehem, eds. *The Kuwait Crisis: Basic Documents,* Vols. 1–3. Cambridge International Documents Series. Cambridge, UK: Grotius, 1991.

Lawrence, Bruce B. *Shattering the Myth: Islam beyond Violence.* Princeton, NJ: Princeton University Press, 1998.

Lenczowski, George. *American Presidents and the Middle East.* Durham, NC: Duke University Press, 1990.

———. *The Middle East in World Affairs.* 4th ed. Ithaca, NY: Cornell University Press, 1980.

Lesch, David W. *The Middle East and the United States: A Historical and Political Reassessment.* New York: Perseus Books, 2006.

———. *The New Lion of Damascus: Bashar al-Asad and Modern Syria.* New Haven, CT: Yale University Press, 2005.

Lesser Ian O. *Oil, the Persian Gulf, and Grand Strategy: Contemporary Issues in Historical Perspective.* Santa Monica, CA: RAND Corporation, 1991.

Leverett, Flynt. *Inheriting Syria: Bashar's Trial by Fire.* Washington, DC: Brookings Institution Press, 2005.

Levite, Ariel, Bruce W. Jentleson, and Larry Berman. *Foreign Military Intervention: The Dynamics of Protracted Conflict.* New York: Columbia University Press, 1992.

Lewis, Bernard. *The Crisis of Islam: Holy War and Unholy Terror.* New York: Random House, 2003.

———. *From Babel to Dragomans: Interpreting the Middle East.* New York: Oxford University Press, 2004.

———. *A Middle East Mosaic: Fragments of Life, Letters and History.* New York: Random House, 2000.

———. *The Multiple Identities of the Middle East.* New York: Schocken, 1999.

———. *What Went Wrong? The Clash between Islam and Modernity in the Middle East.* New York: Oxford University Press, 2002.

Lieblich, Amia. *Seasons of Captivity: The Inner World of POWs.* New York: New York University Press, 1994.

Little, Douglas. *American Orientalism: The United States and the Middle East since 1945.* Chapel Hill: University of North Carolina Press, 2002.

Livingston, Gary. *An Nasiriyah: The Fight for the Bridges.* North Topsail Island, NC: Caisson, 2004.

Lockman, Zachary. *Contending Visions of the Middle East: The History and Politics of Orientalism.* New York: Cambridge University Press, 2004.

Lowry, Richard, with Howard Gerrard. *US Marines in Iraq: Operation Iraqi Freedom, 2003.* Oxford, UK: Osprey, 2006.

Lunt, James D. *Hussein of Jordan: Searching for a Just and Lasting Peace.* New York: Morrow, 1989.

MacArthur, Brian, ed. *Dispatches from the Gulf War.* London: Bloomsbury, 1991.

MacArthur, John R. *Second Front: Censorship and Propaganda in the 1991 Gulf War.* Berkeley: University of California, 2004.

MacGregor, Douglas. *Warrior's Rage: The Great Tank Battle of 73 Easting.* Annapolis, MD: Naval Institute Press, 2009.

Mackey, Sandra. *The Reckoning: Iraq and the Legacy of Saddam Hussein.* New York: Norton, 2002.

Maddy-Weitzman, Bruce, and Shimon Shamir. *The Camp David Summit—What Went Wrong? Americans, Israelis, and Palestinians Analyze the Failure of the Boldest Attempt Ever to Resolve the Palestinian-Israeli Conflict.* Sussex, UK: Sussex Academic Press, 2005.

Maley, William. *The Afghanistan Wars.* New York: Palgrave Macmillan, 2002.

Maloney, Sean M. *Enduring the Freedom: A Rogue Historian in Afghanistan.* Washington, DC: Potomac Books, 2007.

Mango, Andrew. *Atatürk: The Founder of Modern Turkey.* Woodstock: Overlook, 2000.

———. *The Turks Today.* New York: Overlook, 2004.

Marolda, Edward, and Robert Schneller. *Shield and Sword: The United States Navy and the Persian Gulf War.* Annapolis, MD: U.S. Naval Institute Press, 2001.

Martin, Lenore G. *The Unstable Gulf: Threats from Within.* Lexington: Lexington Books, 1984.

Martinez, Luis. *The Algerian Civil War, 1990–1998.* New York: Columbia University Press, 2000.

Matthews, James K., and Cora J. Holt. *So Many, So Much, So Far, So Fast: United States Transportation Command and Strategic*

Deployment for Operation Desert Shield/Desert Storm. Washington, DC: Joint History Office, Office of the Chairman of the Joint Chiefs of Staff and Research Center, United States Transportation Command, 1996.

Matusky, Gregory, and John P. Hayes. *King Hussein.* New York: Chelsea House, 1987.

McFarland, Stephen L. *A Concise History of the United States Air Force.* Washington, DC: Air Force History and Museum Program, 1997.

Meisler, Stanley. *United Nations: The First Fifty Years.* New York: Atlantic Monthly Press, 1997.

Menarchik, Douglas. *Powerlift-Getting to Desert Storm: Strategic Transportation and Strategy in the New World Order.* Westport, CT: Praeger, 1993.

Metz, Steven. *Learning from Iraq: Counterinsurgency in American Strategy.* Carlisle, PA: Strategic Studies Institute, 2007.

Meyer, Karl E., and Shareen Blair Brysac. *Kingmakers: The Invention of the Middle East.* New York: Norton, 2008.

———. *Tournament of Shadows: The Great Game and the Race for Empire in Central Asia.* Washington, DC: Counterpoint, 1999.

Middleton, Drew. *Crossroads of Modern Warfare.* Garden City, NY: Doubleday, 1983.

Miller, Judith, and Laurie Mylroie. *Saddam Hussein and the Crisis in the Gulf.* New York: Times Books, 1990.

Miller, Raymond H. *The War on Terrorism: The War in Afghanistan.* Chicago: Lucent Books, 2003.

Miller, Richard F. *A Carrier at War: On Board the USS Kitty Hawk in the Iraq War.* Washington, DC: Potomac Books, 2003.

Millett, Allan R., and Peter Maslowski. *For the Common Defense: A Military History of the United States of America.* New York: Free Press, 1994.

Mills, Greg. *From Africa to Afghanistan: With Richards and NATO to Kabul.* Johannesburg: Wits University Press, 2007.

Mingst, Karen A., and Margaret P. Karns. *United Nations in the Twenty-First Century.* 3rd ed. Boulder, CO: Westview, 2006.

Mir-Hosseini, Ziba. *Islam and Gender: The Religious Debate in Contemporary Iran.* Princeton, NJ: Princeton University Press, 1999.

Mohammed Reza Pahlavi, Shah of Iran. *Answer to History.* New York: Stein and Day, 1980.

Moin, Baqer. *Khomeini: Life of the Ayatollah.* New York: St. Martin's, 2000.

Moore, Molly. *A Woman at War: Storming Kuwait with the U.S. Marines.* New York: Free Press, 1993.

Moore, Rebecca R. *NATO's New Mission: Projecting Stability in a Post–Cold War Era.* Westport, CT: Praeger Security International, 2007.

Mowlana, Hamid, George Gerbner, and Herbert I. Schiller, eds. *Triumph of the Image: The Media's War in the Persian Gulf—A Global Perspective.* Boulder, CO: Westview, 1992.

Muasher, Marwan. *The Arab Center: The Promise of Moderation.* New Haven, CT: Yale University Press, 2008.

Mufti, Malik. *Sovereign Creations: Pan-Arabism and Political Order in Syria and Iraq.* Ithaca, NY: Cornell University Press, 1996.

Munthe, Turi, ed. *The Saddam Hussein Reader.* New York: Thunder's Mouth, 2002.

Murray, Williamson, and Robert H. Scales Jr. *The Iraq War: A Military History.* Cambridge, MA: Belknap, 2005.

Musharraf, Pervez. *In the Line of Fire: A Memoir.* New York: Simon and Schuster, 2006.

Myers, Richard B., and Malcolm McConnell. *Eyes on the Horizon: Serving on the Front Lines of National Security.* Riverside, NJ: Threshold Editions, 2009.

Mylorie, Laurie. *Bush vs. The Beltway: How the CIA and the State Department Tried to Stop the War on Terror.* New York: Regan Books, 2003.

Naipaul, V. S. *Beyond Belief: Islamic Excursions among the Converted Peoples.* New York: Random House, 1998.

Nair, V. K. *War in the Gulf: Lessons for the Third World.* New Delhi: Lancer International, 1991.

Naji, Kasra. *Ahmadinejad: The Secret History of Iran's Radical Leader.* Berkeley: University of California Press, 2008.

Nakash, Yitzhak. *Reaching for Power: The Shi'a in the Modern Arab World.* Princeton, NJ: Princeton University Press, 2006.

Nakdimon, Shlomo. *First Strike: The Exclusive Story of How Israel Foiled Iraq's Attempt to Get the Bomb.* New York: Summit Books, 1987.

Nasr, Vali. *The Shia Revival: How Conflicts within Islam Will Shape the Future.* New York: Norton, 2006.

Navias, Martin. *The Spread of Nuclear, Chemical and Ballistic Missile Weaponry in the Middle East.* London: Brassey's, 1991.

———. *Tanker Wars: The Assault on Merchant Shipping during the Iran-Iraq Conflict, 1980–1988.* London: I. B. Tauris, 1996.

Naylor, Sean. *Not a Good Day to Die: The Untold Story of Operation Anaconda.* New York: Berkley Trade, 2006.

Neville, Leigh. *Special Operations Forces in Afghanistan: Afghanistan, 2001–2007.* Oxford, UK: Osprey, 2008.

———. *Special Operations Forces in Iraq (Elite).* Oxford, UK: Osprey, 2008.

Newsom, David D., ed. *The Diplomatic Record, 1990–91.* Boulder, CO: Westview, 1992.

Nolan, Janne E. *Hezbollah: A Short History.* Princeton, NJ: Princeton University Press, 2007.

———. *Trappings of Power: Ballistic Missiles in the Third World.* Washington, DC: Brookings Institution, 1991.

Nusse, Andrea. *Muslim Palestine: The Ideology of Hamas.* London: Routledge, 1999.

Nye, Joseph S., Jr., and Roger K. Smith, eds. *After the Storm: Lessons from the Gulf War.* Lanham, MD: Madison Books, 1992.

Obaid, Nawaf E. *The Oil Kingdom at 100: Petroleum Policymaking in Saudi Arabia.* Washington, DC: Washington Institute for Near East Policy, 2000.

O'Ballance, Edgar. *Afghan Wars: 1839 to the Present Day.* London: Brassey's, 2003.

O'Leary, Brendan, John McGarry, and Khaled Salih. *The Future of Kurdistan in Iraq.* Philadelphia: University of Pennsylvania Press, 2005.

Oren, Michael B. *Power, Faith, and Fantasy: America in the Middle East, 1776 to the Present.* New York: Norton, 2007.

Packer, George. *The Assassins' Gate: America in Iraq.* New York: Farrar, Straus and Giroux, 2005.

Pagonis, William G., and Jeffrey Cruikshank. *Moving Mountains: Lessons in Leadership and Logistics from the Gulf War.* Cambridge, MA: Harvard Business School Press, 1992.

Palmer, Michael A. *On Course to Desert Storm: The United States Navy and the Persian Gulf War.* Washington, DC: Naval Historical Division, 1992.

Parker, Richard Bordeaux. *The Politics of Miscalculation in the Middle East.* Bloomington: Indiana University Press, 1993.

———. *Uncle Sam in Barbary: A Diplomatic History.* Gainesville: University Press of Florida, 2004.

Parrish, Robert D., and N. A. Andreacchio. *Schwarzkopf: An Insider's View of the Commander and His Victory.* New York: Bantam Books, 1991.

Parsons, Nigel Craig. *The Politics of the Palestinian Authority: From Oslo to Al-Aqsa.* London: Routledge, 2003.

Pelletiere, Stephen. *Losing Iraq: Insurgency and Politics.* Westport, CT: Praeger Security International, 2007.

Perlmutter, Amos, Michael I. Handel, and Uri Bar-Joseph. *Two Minutes over Baghdad.* London: Corgi, 1982.

Person, J. E. *The Politics of Middle Eastern Oil.* Washington, DC: Middle East Institute, 1983.

Peters, Rudolph. *Islam and Colonialism: The Doctrine of Jihad in Modern History.* The Hague: Brill, 1979.

Phillips, David L. *Losing Iraq: Inside the Postwar Reconstruction Fiasco.* Boulder, CO: Westview, 2005.

Pintak, Lawrence. *Reflections in a Bloodshot Lens: America, Islam, and the War of Ideas.* Ann Arbor: University of Michigan Press, 2006.

Pipes, Daniel. *The Hidden Hand: Middle East Fears of Conspiracy.* New York: St. Martin's, 1996.

Plame Wilson, Valerie. *Fair Game: My Life as a Spy, My Betrayal by the White House.* New York: Simon and Schuster, 2007.

Pokrant, Marvin. *Desert Storm at Sea: What the Navy Really Did.* Westport, CT: Greenwood, 1999.

Polk, William R. *Understanding Iraq: The Whole Sweep of Iraqi History, from Genghis Khan's Mongols to the Ottoman Turks to the British Mandate to the American Occupation.* New York: Harper Perennial, 2006.

Pollack, Kenneth M. *Arabs at War: Military Effectiveness, 1948–1991.* Lincoln: University of Nebraska Press, 2002.

———. *A Path out of the Desert: A Grand Strategy for America in the Middle East.* New York: Random House, 2008.

———. *The Threatening Storm: The Case for Invading Iraq.* New York: Random House, 2002.

Pope, Hugh, and Nicole Pope. *Turkey Unveiled: A History of Modern Turkey.* New York: Overlook, 1999.

Potter, Lawrence G., and Gary G. Sick, eds. *Iran, Iraq, and the Legacies of War.* New York: Palgrave Macmillan, 2004.

Powell, Colin, and Joseph E. Persico. *My American Journey.* New York: Ballantine, 2003.

Purdum, Todd S., and the Staff of *The New York Times. A Time of Our Choosing: America's War in Iraq.* New York: Times Books/ Henry Holt, 2003.

Quandt, William B. *Between Ballots and Bullets: Algeria's Transition from Authoritarianism.* Washington, DC: Brookings, 1998.

———. *Saudi Arabia in the 1980s: Foreign Policy, Security, and Oil.* Washington, DC: Brookings, 1981.

———. *The United States and Egypt.* Washington, DC: Brookings, 1990.

Quilter, Charles J., II. *U.S. Marines in the Persian Gulf, 1990–1991: With the I Marine Expeditionary Force in Desert Shield and Desert Storm.* Washington, DC: U.S. Government Printing Office, 1993.

Raas, Whitney, and Austin Long. *Osirak Redux? Assessing Israeli Capabilities to Destroy Iranian Nuclear Facilities.* Cambridge: Security Studies Program, Massachusetts Institute of Technology, 2006.

Rabil, Robert G. *Embattled Neighbors: Syria, Israel and Lebanon.* Boulder, CO: Lynne Rienner, 2003.

Rajaee, Farhang. *The Iran-Iraq War: The Politics of Aggression.* Gainesville: University Press of Florida, 1993.

Ramadan, Tariq. *Western Muslims and the Future of Islam.* New York: Oxford University Press, 2004.

Randal, Jonathan. *Osama: The Making of a Terrorist.* New York: Knopf, 2004.

Rasanayagam, Angelo. *Afghanistan: A Modern History.* London: I. B. Tauris, 2005.

Rashid, Ahmed. *Descent into Chaos: The United States and the Failure of Nation-building in Pakistan, Afghanistan, and Central Asia.* New York: Viking, 2008.

———. *Jihad: The Rise of Militant Islam in Central Asia.* New York: Penguin, 2002.

———. *Taliban: Militant Islam, Oil, and Fundamentalism in Central Asia.* New Haven, CT: Yale University Press, 2001.

Raz, Eyal, and Yael Stein. *Operation Defensive Shield: Soldier's Testimonies, Palestinian Testimonies.* Jerusalem: B'Tselem, the Israeli Information Center for Human Rights in the Occupied Territories, 2002.

Record, Jeffrey. *Hollow Victory.* Washington, DC: Brassey's, 1993.

———. *Wanting War: Why the Bush Administration Invaded Iraq.* Dulles, VA: Potomac Books, 2009.

Reinhart, Tanya. *The Road Map to Nowhere: Israel/Palestine since 2003.* London: Verso, 2006.

Renshon, Stanley A., ed. *The Political Psychology of the Gulf War.* Pittsburgh: University of Pittsburgh Press, 1992.

Reuter, Christoph. *My Life Is a Weapon: A Modern History of Suicide Bombing.* Princeton, NJ: Princeton University Press, 2004.

Ricks, Thomas E. *Fiasco: The American Military Adventure in Iraq.* New York: Penguin, 2006.

———. *The Gamble: General David Petraeus and the American Military Adventure in Iraq, 2006–2008.* New York: Penguin, 2009.

Robins, Philip. *Suits and Uniforms: Turkish Foreign Policy since the Cold War.* Seattle: University of Washington Press, 2003.

Robinson, Linda. *Tell Me How This Ends: General David Petraeus and the Search for a Way Out of Iraq.* New York: PublicAffairs, 2007.

Rohr, Janelle. *The Middle East: Opposing Viewpoints.* St. Paul, MN: Greenhaven, 1988.

Romjue. John L. *American Army Doctrine for the Post–Cold War.* Washington, DC: Military History Office and U.S. Army Training and Doctrine Command, 1997.

Rose, Lisle. *Power at Sea: A Violent Peace, 1946–2006.* Columbia: University of Missouri Press, 2007.

Ross, Dennis. *The Missing Peace: The Inside Story of the Fight for Middle East Peace.* New York: Farrar, Straus and Giroux, 2004.

Roth, S. J. *The Impact of the Six-Day War: A Twenty-Year Assessment.* Basingstoke, UK: Macmillan in Association with the Institute of Jewish Affairs, 1988.

Rougier, Bernard. *Everyday Jihad: The Rise of Militant Islam among Palestinians in Lebanon.* Cambridge, MA: Harvard University Press, 2007.

Roy, Oliver. *The Politics of Chaos in the Middle East.* New York: Columbia University Press, 2008.

Rubin, Barry. *Islamic Fundamentalism in Egyptian Politics.* New York: St. Martin's, 1990.

———. *Paved with Good Intentions: The American Experience and Iran.* New York: Oxford University Press, 1980.

———. *Revolution until Victory? The Politics and History of the PLO.* Cambridge, MA: Harvard University Press, 1996.

———. *The Tragedy of the Middle East.* Cambridge: Cambridge University Press, 2003.

Rubin, Barry, and Thomas A. Keaney, eds. *Armed Forces in the Middle East: Politics and Strategy.* Portland, OR: Frank Cass, 2002.

Rubin, Barry, and Judith Colp Rubin, eds. *Anti-American Terrorism and the Middle East.* New York: Oxford University Press, 2002.

Ryan, Mike. *Battlefield Afghanistan.* London: Spellmount, 2007.

Said, Edward. *The End of the Peace Process: Oslo and After.* New York: Vintage Books, 2001.

Sanchez, Ricardo S., and Donald T. Phillips. *Wiser in Battle: A Soldier's Story.* New York: Harper, 2008.

Satloff, Robert B. *Islam in the Palestinian Uprising.* Washington, DC: Washington Institute for Near East Policy, 1988.

———, ed. *War on Terror: The Middle East Dimension.* Washington, DC: Washington Institute for Near East Policy, 2002.

Savir, Uri. *The Process: 1,100 Days That Changed the Middle East.* New York: Random House, 1998.

Scales, Robert H. *Certain Victory: The U.S. Army in the Gulf War.* Washington, DC: Brassey's, 1994.

Schubert, Frank N., and Theresa L. Kraus, eds. *The Whirlwind War: The United States Army in Operations Desert Shield and Desert Storm.* Washington, DC: U.S. Government Printing Office, 1995.

Sciolino, Elaine. *The Outlaw State: Saddam Hussein's Quest for Power and the Gulf Crisis.* New York: Wiley, 1991.

Schroen, Gary. *First In: An Insider Account of How the CIA Spearheaded the War on Terror in Afghanistan.* Novato, CA: Presidio, 2005.

Schwarzkopf, H. Norman, with Peter Petre. *It Doesn't Take a Hero: General H. Norman Schwarzkopf, the Autobiography.* New York: Bantam Books, 1993.

Segev, Tom. *1967: Israel, the War, and the Year That Transformed the Middle East.* New York: Metropolitan Books, 2007.

Shadid, Anthony. *Night Draws Near: Iraq's People in the Shadow of America's War.* New York: Henry Holt, 2004.

Shaffer, Brenda. *The Limits of Culture: Islam and Foreign Policy.* Cambridge, MA: MIT Press, 2006.

Shlaim, Avi. *War and Peace in the Middle East: A Critique of American Policy.* New York: Whittle Books, 1994.

Sifry, Michah, and Christopher Cerf, eds. *The Gulf Reader: History, Documents, Opinions.* New York: Random House, 1991.

Silver, Eric. *Begin: The Haunted Prophet.* New York: Random House, 1984.

Simon, Reeva Spector, and Eleanor H. Tejirian, eds. *The Creation of Iraq, 1914–1921.* New York: Columbia University Press, 2004.

Simpson, John. *From the House of War: John Simpson in the Gulf.* London: Arrow Books, 1991.

———. *The Wars against Saddam: Taking the Hard Road to Baghdad.* New York: Macmillan, 2003.

Sinno, Abdulkader. *Organizations at War in Afghanistan and Beyond.* Ithaca, NY: Cornell University Press, 2008.

Smith, Hedrick, ed. *The Media and the Gulf War: The Press and Democracy in Wartime.* Washington, DC: Seven Locks, 1992.

Smith, Jean Edward. *George Bush's War.* New York: Henry Holt, 1992.

Snow, Peter John. *Hussein: A Biography.* Washington: R. B. Luce, 1972.

Solecki, John. *Hosni Mubarak.* New York: Chelsea House, 1991.

Souryal, Sam. *Islam, Islamic Law, and the Turn to Violence.* Huntsville, TX: Sam Houston State University, 2004.

St. John, Robert Bruce. *Libya and the United States: Two Centuries of Strife.* Philadelphia: University of Pennsylvania Press, 2002.

Stewart, Richard W. *Operation Enduring Freedom: The United States Army in Afghanistan, October 2001–March 2002.* Washington, DC: U.S. Army Center of Military History, 2003.

Summers, Harry G., Jr. *On Strategy II: A Critical Analysis of the Persian Gulf War.* New York: Dell, 1992.

Sundquist, Leah R. *NATO in Afghanistan: A Progress Report.* Carlisle Barracks, PA: U.S. Army War College, 2008.

Swisher, Clayton E. *The Truth about Camp David: The Untold Story about the Collapse of the Middle East Peace Process.* New York: Thunder's Mouth, Nation Books, 2004.

Tanner, Stephen. *Afghanistan: A Military History from Alexander the Great to the Fall of the Taliban.* New York: Da Capo, 2003.

Taylor, Philip M. *War and the Media: Propaganda and Persuasion in the Gulf War.* Manchester, UK: Manchester University Press, 1992.

Telhami, Shibley. *The Stakes: America and the Middle East.* Boulder, CO: Westview, 2002.

Terrill, W. Andrew. *Kuwaiti National Security and the U.S.-Kuwaiti Strategic Relationship after Saddam.* Carlisle, PA: Strategic Studies Institute, 2007.

Thaler, David E., Theodore W. Karasik, Dalia Dassa Kaye, Jennifer D. P. Moroney, Frederic Wehrey, Obaid Younossi, Farhana Ali, and Robert A. Guffey. *Future U.S. Security Relationships with Iraq and Afghanistan: U.S. Air Force Roles.* Santa Monica, CA: RAND Corporation, 2008.

Tibi, Bassam. *The Challenge of Fundamentalism: Political Islam and the New World Disorder.* Berkeley: University of California Press, 1998.

Toffolo, Chris E., and Peggy Kahn. *The Arab League.* London: Chelsea House, 2008.

Towle, Philip. *Pundits and Patriots: Lessons from the Gulf War.* London: Institute for European Defence and Strategic Studies, 1991.

Tucker, Robert, and David Hendrickson. *The Imperial Temptation: The New World Order and America's Purpose.* New York: Council on Foreign Relations, 1992.

U.S. News and World Report Staff. *Triumph without Victory: The Unreported History of the Persian Gulf War.* New York: Time Books, 1992.

Vandewalle, Dirk. *A History of Modern Libya.* New York: Cambridge University Press, 2006.

Villiers, Gérard de Bernard Touchais, and Annick de Villiers. *The Imperial Shah: An Informal Biography.* Boston: Little, Brown, 1976.

Viorst, Milton. *In the Shadow of the Prophet: The Struggle for the Soul of Islam.* New York: Anchor Books, 1998.

———. *Storm from the East: The Struggle between the Arab World and the Christian West.* New York: Modern Library, 2006.

Warden, John A., III. *The Air Campaign: Planning for Combat.* Washington, DC: National Defense University Press, 1988.

Warschawski, Michel. *On the Border.* Cambridge, MA: South End, 2005.

Watson, Bruce W., ed. *Military Lessons of the Gulf War.* London: Greenhill Books, 1991.

Weiner, Myron, and Ali Banuazizi. *The Politics of Social Transformation in Afghanistan, Iran, and Pakistan.* Syracuse, NY: Syracuse University Press, 1994.

West, Bing. *The Strongest Tribe: War, Politics, and the Endgame in Iraq.* New York: Random House, 2008.

West, Bing, and Ray L. Smith. *The March Up: Taking Baghdad with the 1st Marine Division.* New York: Bantam, 2003.

Westwood, J. N. *The History of the Middle East Wars.* London: Bison Books, 1991.

Willet, Edward C. *The Iran-Iraq War.* New York: Rosen, 2004.

Williams, Garland H. *Engineering Peace: The Military Role in Postconflict Reconstruction.* Washington, DC: United States Institute of Peace, 2005.

Williams, M. J. *NATO, Security and Risk Management, from Kosovo to Kandahar.* Milton Park, UK: Routledge, 2008.

Williams, Richard, Joanne Heckman, and Jon Shreeberger. *Environmental Consequences of the Persian Gulf War, 1990–1.* Washington, DC: National Geographic Society, 1991.

Wilson, Joseph. *The Politics of Truth: Inside the Lies That Led to War and Betrayed My Wife's CIA Identity.* New York: Carroll and Graf, 2004.

Wingate, Brian. *Saddam Hussein: The Rise and Fall of a Dictator.* New York: Rosen, 2004.

Woodward, Bob. *Bush at War.* New York: Simon and Schuster, 2002.

———. *The Commanders.* New York: Simon and Schuster, 1991.

———. *Plan of Attack.* New York: Simon and Schuster, 2004.

———. *State of Denial: Bush at War, Part III.* New York: Simon and Schuster, 2006.

———. *The War Within: A Secret White House History, 2006–2008.* New York: Simon and Schuster, 2008.

Wright, Donald P., and Timothy R. Reese. *On Point II: Transition to the New Campaign; The United States Army in Operation IRAQI FREEDOM, May 2003–January 2005.* Fort Leavenworth, KS: Combat Studies Institute Press, 2008.

Wright, Lawrence. *The Looming Tower: Al-Qaeda and the Road to 9/11.* New York: Vintage Books, 2007.

Wright, Robin. *Dreams and Shadows: The Future of the Middle East.* New York: Penguin, 2008.

———. *The Last Great Revolution: Turmoil and Transformation in Iran.* New York: Knopf, 2000.

Yaqub, Salim. *Containing Arab Nationalism: The Eisenhower Doctrine and the Middle East.* Chapel Hill: University of North Carolina Press, 2004.

Yetiv, Steve A., *The Persian Gulf Crisis.* Westport, CT: Greenwood, 1997.

Zabecki, David T. "Torture: Lessons From Vietnam and Wars Past." *Vietnam* Magazine, October 2008, 32–35.

Zinsmeister, Karl. *Boots on the Ground: A Month with the 82nd Airborne in the Battle for Iraq.* New York: St. Martin's, 2004.

———. *Dawn over Baghdad: How the U.S. Military Is Using Bullets and Ballots to Remake Iraq.* New York: Encounter Books, 2004.

DAVID M. KEITHLY

List of Editors and Contributors

Volume Editor

Dr. Spencer C. Tucker
Senior Fellow
Military History, ABC-CLIO, Inc.

Editor, Documents Volume

Dr. Priscilla Roberts
Associate Professor of History,
School of Humanities
Honorary Director,
Centre of American Studies
University of Hong Kong

Associate Editor

Dr. Paul G. Pierpaoli Jr.
Fellow
Military History, ABC-CLIO, Inc.

Assistant Editors

Dr. Jerry D. Morelock
Colonel
U.S. Army, Retired
Editor in Chief, *Armchair General*
    Magazine

Dr. David Zabecki
Major General
Army of the United States, Retired

Dr. Sherifa Zuhur
Visiting Professor of National Security
    Affairs
Regional Strategy and Planning Department
Strategic Studies Institute
U.S. Army War College

Contributors

Dr. Rebecca Adelman
Assistant Professor
University of Maryland, Baltimore County

Kristian P. Alexander
Associate Instructor
University of Utah

Dr. Alan Allport
Lecturer
University of Pennsylvania

Christopher Paul Anzalone
Independent Scholar

James Arnold
Independent Scholar

Ojan Aryanfard
Independent Scholar

Stephen E. Atkins
Adjunct Professor of History
Texas A&M University

Dr. Gayle Avant
Associate Professor
Baylor University

Ralph Martin Baker
Independent Scholar

Lacie A. Ballinger
Independent Scholar

Matthew Basler
Assistant Professor
U.S. Air Force Academy

Dr. Jeffrey D. Bass
Assistant Professor of History
Quinnipiac University

Dr. Robert F. Baumann
Professor of History
U.S. Army Command & General Staff College

Michael K. Beauchamp
Texas A&M University

Walter F. Bell
Information Services Librarian
Aurora University

Berch Berberoglu
Professor
University of Nevada, Reno

Robert Berschinski
Independent Scholar

Claude G. Berube
U.S. Naval Academy

Frank Beyersdorf
University of Heidelberg
Germany

Amy Hackney Blackwell
Independent Scholar

Scott Blanchette
Independent Scholar

Dr. John Bonin
U.S. Army War College

Dr. Stephen A. Bourque
Professor
U.S. Army Command and General Staff
    College

Walter Boyne
Independent Scholar

James C. Bradford
Professor of History
Texas A&M University

Ron Briley
Assistant Headmaster
Sandia Preparatory School

Jessica Britt
Independent Scholar

Dr. Stefan Brooks
Assistant Professor of Political Science
Lindsey Wilson College

Robert M. Brown
Assistant Professor
U.S. Army Command & General Staff
    College

Dean Brumley
Independent Scholar

Dino E. Buenviaje
University of California, Riverside

Dr. James F. Carroll
Associate Professor
Iona College

Dr. Jeffery A. Charlston
Associate Professor
University of Maryland University College

Elliot Paul Chodoff
University of Haifa
Israel

Robert Clemm
Ohio State University

Dr. David Coffey
Associate Professor and Chair
Department of History and Philosophy
University of Tennessee at Martin

Dr. Justin P. Coffey
Assistant Professor of History
Quincy University

David Commins
Dickinson College

Justin Corfield
Geelong Grammar School
Australia

Dr. Arthur I. Cyr
Director, Clausen Center
Carthage College

Dr. Dylan A. Cyr
Department of History
University of Western Ontario

John R. Dabrowski
Independent Scholar

Benedict Edward Dedominicis
Associate Professor of Political Science
American University in Bulgaria

Dr. Bruce J. DeHart
Associate Professor of History
University of North Carolina at Pembroke

Marcel A. Derosier
Independent Scholar

Christopher Dietrich
University of Texas at Austin

Scott R. DiMarco
Director of Library and Information
    Resources
Mansfield University of Pennsylvania

Dr. Paul William Doerr
Associate Professor
Acadia University
Canada

Michael Doidge
Independent Scholar

Dr. Michael E. Donoghue
Assistant Professor
Marquette University

Joe P. Dunn
Independent Scholar

Colonel Donald Redmond Dunne
U.S. Army

Dr. Richard M. Edwards
Senior Lecturer
University of Wisconsin Colleges

Chuck Fahrer
Assistant Professor of Geography
Georgia College & State University

Shawn Fisher
University of Memphis

Major Benjamin D. Forest
Air Command and Staff College

William E. Fork
Independent Scholar

Elun A. Gabriel
St. Lawrence University

Dr. K. Luisa Gandolfo
University of Exeter
United Kingdom

Brent Geary
Independent Scholar

Jason Godin
Independent Scholar

Dr. Benjamin John Grob-Fitzgibbon
Assistant Professor of History
University of Arkansas

Dr. Michael R. Hall
Associate Professor of History
Armstrong Atlantic State University

Neil Hamilton
Independent Scholar

Magarditsch Hatschikjan
Department of East European History
University of Cologne
Germany

Dr. William P. Head
Historian/Chief, WR-ALC Office of History
U.S. Air Force

Glenn E. Helm
Director
Navy Department Library

Gordon E. Hogg
Director, Special Collections Library
University of Kentucky

Dr. Arthur M. Holst
MPA Program Faculty
Widener University

Dr. Charles Francis Howlett
Associate Professor
Molloy College

Dr. Timothy D. Hoyt
Professor of Strategy and Policy
U.S. Naval War College

Dr. Harry Raymond Hueston II
Independent Scholar

Dr. Donna R. Jackson
Wolfson College, Cambridge

Dr. Robert B. Kane
Adjunct Professor of History
Troy University

David M. Keithly
Independent Scholar

Dr. Gary Lee Kerley
North Hall High School

Chen Kertcher
School of History
Tel Aviv University

Burcak Keskin-Kozat
University of Michigan, Ann Arbor

Dr. Deborah Kidwell
U.S. Army Command and General Staff
    College

Robert Kiely
Independent Scholar

Dr. Arne Kislenko
Ryerson University
Canada

Matthew Krogman
Independent Scholar

Dr. John T. Kuehn
Associate Professor
U.S. Army Command and General Staff
    College

Daniel W. Kuthy
Georgia State University

Jeremy Kuzmarow
Independent Scholar

Dr. Martin Laberge
Professor
Université du Québec en Outaouais

Jeffrey Lamonica
Assistant Professor of History
Delaware County Community College

Dr. Tom Lansford
Dean, Gulf Coast
University Southern Mississippi

Alison Lawlor
Independent Scholar

Mark F. Leep
Independent Scholar

Keith A. Leitich
Independent Scholar

Shawn Livingston
Public Service Librarian
University of Kentucky

Clare M. Lopez
Vice President
Intelligence Summit

Adam B. Lowther
Independent Scholar

Shamiran Mako
Independent Scholar

Robert W. Malick
Adjunct Professor of History
Harrisburg Area Community College

Steven Fred Marin
Associate Professor
Victor Valley College

Dr. Jerome V. Martin
Command Historian
U.S. Strategic Command

Dr. James Matray
Professor and Chair of History
Department of History
California State University, Chico

Dr. Terry Mays
Associate Professor
The Citadel

Mitchell McNaylor
Independent Scholar

Dr. Julius A. Menzoff
Savannah State University

Herbert F. Merrick
Independent Scholar

Patit Mishra
Professor
Sambalpur University
India

Josip Mocnik
Bowling Green State University

Kirsty Anne Montgomery
Independent Scholar

Dr. Jerry D. Morelock
Colonel
U.S. Army, Retired
Editor in Chief, *Armchair General* Magazine

Gregory Wayne Morgan
Independent Scholar

Dr. Lisa Marie Mundey
Assistant Professor
University of St. Thomas

Dr. Keith Murphy
Associate Dean
Fort Valley State University

Dr. Michael S. Neiberg
Professor of History
University of Southern Mississippi

Benjamin P. Nickels
Independent Scholar

Charlene T. Overturf
Adjunct Faculty
Armstrong Atlantic State University

Major Jason Palmer
United States Army

Brian Parkinson
Independent Scholar

Dr. James D. Perry
Independent Scholar

Allene S. Phy-Olsen
Austin Peay State University

Dr. Paul G. Pierpaoli Jr.
Fellow
Military History, ABC-CLIO, Inc.

Robert G. Price
Historian
Maritime Research Associates LLC

Dr. Peter J. Rainow
Independent Scholar

Carolyn Ramzy
University of Toronto

Dr. John David Rausch Jr.
Associate Professor
West Texas A&M University

Dr. Priscilla Roberts
Associate Professor of History,
School of Humanities
Honorary Director,
Centre of American Studies
University of Hong Kong

Russ Rodgers
Staff Historian
U.S. Army

Karl Lee Rubis
University of Kansas

Mark M. Sanders
Head of Reference
Joyner Library, East Carolina

Captain Carl Schuster (retired)
U.S. Navy
Hawaii Pacific University

Dr. Jeff R. Schutts
Instructor
Douglas College

Larry Schweikart
Independent Scholar

Jeff Seiken
Independent Scholar

Robert Shafer
California State University Northridge

James E. Shircliffe Jr.
Principal Research Analyst
CENTRA Technology, Inc.

Rear Admiral John Sigler (retired)
U.S. Navy

Dr. Rami Y. Siklawi
University of Exeter
United Kingdom

Dr. George L. Simpson Jr.
Professor of History
High Point University

Tara Simpson
Independent Scholar

Dr. Ranjit Singh
Assistant Professor of Political Science and
    International Affairs
University of Mary Washington

Frank J. Smith
Covenant Reformed Presbyterian Church

Dr. Yushau Sodiq
Associate Professor
Texas Christian University

Jason M. Sokiera
University of Southern Mississippi

Dr. Lewis Sorley
Independent Scholar

John Southard
Texas Tech University

Dr. Daniel E. Spector
Independent Scholar

Phoebe Spinrad
Independent Scholar

Dr. Paul Joseph Springer
Assistant Professor
United States Military Academy

Robert Stacy
Independent Scholar

Melissa Stallings
Independent Scholar

Dr. Stephen K. Stein
Independent Scholar

Luc Stenger
Independent Scholar

Dr. Nancy L. Stockdale
Assistant Professor, Middle Eastern History
University of North Texas

Yoneyuki Sugita
Independent Scholar

Kenneth Szmed
Independent Scholar

Dr. David Tal
Emroy University

Dr. Jason Robert Tatlock
Assistant Professor of History
Armstrong Atlantic State University

Randy Jack Taylor
Librarian
Howard Payne University

Moshe Terdiman
Independent Scholar

Dr. W. Andrew Terrill
General Douglas MacArthur Research Pro-
    fessor of National Security Affairs
U.S. Army War College

William H. Thiesen
Independent Scholar

Dr. Haruo Tohmatsu
Associate Professor
Tamagawa University
Japan

Hannibal Travis
Associate Professor of Law
Florida International University College of
    Law

Dr. Stephanie Lynn Trombley
Assistant Professor of History
Embry-Riddle Aeronautical
    University–Prescott

Dr. Spencer C. Tucker
Senior Fellow
Military History, ABC-CLIO, Inc.

Dallace W. Unger Jr.
Independent Scholar

Dr. Richard B. Verrone
Texas Tech University

Dr. William E. Watson
Associate Professor of History
Immaculata University

Tim J. Watts
Subject Librarian
Kansas State University

Thomas J. Weiler
Universities of Bonn, Erfurt, Trier
Germany

Dr. Wyndham E. Whynot
Assistant Professor of History
Livingstone College

Dr. James H. Willbanks
Director, Department of Military History
U.S. Army Command and General Staff
    College
Fort Leavenworth

Adam P. Wilson
The University of Mississippi

Harold Lee Wise
Adjunct Professor
College of the Albermarle

Dr. Anna M. Wittmann
University of Alberta

Laura Matysek Wood
Independent Scholar

Dr. David T. Zabecki
Major General
Army of the United States, Retired

Dr. Sherifa Zuhur
Visiting Professor of National Security
    Affairs
Regional Strategy and Planning
    Department
Strategic Studies Institute
U.S. Army War College

John S. Zunes
Professor of Politics
University of San Francisco

Categorical Index

Individuals

Events

Groups, Organizations, and Programs

Places

Ideas, Movements, and Policies

Objects, Artifacts, and Weapons

Treaties, Acts, and Other Written Material

Miscellaneous

Index